Theory and Design in Counseling and Psychotherapy

Theory and Design in Counseling and Psychotherapy

Susan X Day
Iowa State University
University of Houston

Lahaska Press
Houghton Mifflin Company
BOSTON   NEW YORK

In memory of Dawn Lewis,
an active listener.

Publisher, Lahaska Press: Barry Fetterolf
Senior Project Editor: Carol Newman
Editorial Assistant: Marlowe Shaeffer
Production/Design Assistant: Bethany Schlegel
Senior Manufacturing Coordinator: Priscilla Bailey

Cover image: *Out of My Mind* © 1999 Jerry Grossman (20th c./American), Watercolor/SuperStock.

Text credits begin on p. 501

Lahaska Press, a unique collaboration between the Houghton Mifflin College Division and Lawrence Erlbaum Associates, is dedicated to publishing books and offering services for the academic and professional counseling communities. Houghton Mifflin and Lawrence Erlbaum will focus on becoming the major conduit for educational and academic materials in the psychological and educational counseling fields. The partnership of Lahaska Press was formed in late 1999. The name "Lahaska" is a Native American Lenape word meaning "source of much writing." It is also a small town in eastern Pennsylvania, named by the Lenape.

Printed in the U.S.A.

Library of Congress Catalog Number: 2002109429

ISBN: 0-618-19142-9

1 2 3 4 5 6 7 8 9—MV—07 06 05 04 03

CONTENTS

4 **Psychoanalytical and Psychodynamic Approaches   68**

5 **Adlerian Psychology   114**

6 **Humanistic Approaches and Their Existentialist Roots   146**

7   Gestalt Therapy   193

8   Behavioral Therapies   234

9 **Cognitive-Behavioral Therapies**   **287**

10 **Systemic Approaches: Family Therapy**   **337**

11 **Systemic Approaches: Culture and Gender Bases**   **389**

PREFACE

"The only books that influence us are those for which we are ready, and which have gone a little farther down our particular path than we have yet got ourselves."—E. M. Forster

Theory and Design in Counseling and Psychotherapy introduces students to the practice of psychotherapy as informed by the major theories in use today. The word *design* in the book's title is meant to reflect the brew of intentionality, art, science, and constructivist thinking that animates good counseling. Graduate students and advanced undergraduates in counseling, psychology, social work, human relations, and other helping professions are the intended audience, having already gone some way down this particular path. This text provides an organized inventory of the major current theories of counseling and psychotherapy. Therefore, I aimed to include content covered in licensure, certification, and comprehensive examinations. *Theory and Design* also invites students to compare systems and choose which to integrate into their practice. This process involves not only content learning, but also some self-examination, so throughout the book *Reflection* exercises encourage readers to consider the material in relation to their own experience, often involving personality and cultural variety. These reflections can be collected in a private journal, with or without instructor monitoring. They can later be helpful when students write statements of their theoretical orientations, or when they interview at internship and job sites.

In the first three chapters, I cover fundamental issues in the practice of helping, discussing topics that apply to all approaches, such as why common factors bolster specific techniques, how theory necessarily underpins good case analysis, and what to do in facing ethical dilemmas. The other ten chapters take up major systems of counseling and psychotherapy: psychodynamic, Adlerian, existential/humanistic, gestalt, behavioral, cognitive-behavioral, family systems, gender- and culture-based, transpersonal, and integrative.

A common organization gives form to the theory chapters. All the chapters include

- An opening selection from a significant primary source, capturing the tone and style of original works in the area. Sigmund Freud, Carl Rogers, B. F. Skinner, and Aaron Beck, for example, write in characteristic manners that are lost in even the most artful summaries of their thoughts.
- Essential concepts, introducing the basic philosophy and mode of case conceptualization.
- A summary of how therapy is expected to progress across time.

- Customary techniques and research findings on the effectiveness of these techniques.

- Common uses for the approach, inviting students to think about how therapies match client problems.

- An example of a case conceptualization from a practitioner who uses the approach. This way, the choice of approach clearly corresponds with client characteristics.

- Critiques, giving an overview of the main objections to each approach, with counter-arguments if there are any.

- Media, Internet, and library activities to help students go beyond the textbook in developing a knowledge base. These are designed so that students can become active, competent academic researchers who know important sources in each chapter's area.

- A brief biography of a key contributor to the practice of the theory under study.

Interspersed among all these features are plentiful classroom discussion topics, class and small group activities, and reflection topics. These are designed to assist the instructor by supplying classroom variety, to tie theoretical approaches to practice situations, to clarify difficult concepts and readings, and to maintain readers' attention through self-referential exploration. Matters of gender, culture, and class are interwoven into the chapters, as recommended by the American Psychological Association's task force on diversity. Important research findings are integrated into essential concepts, uses, and critiques sections. I present key terms for each chapter with exercises in which students create and discuss the definitions.

In writing this book, I followed the suggestion of many instructors and students, and gave prominence to its readability and classroom-friendliness.

Supplements to This Text

Instructors using *Theory and Design in Counseling and Psychotherapy* will receive pedagogical advice and an examination item bank in an accompanying **Instructors' Manual**.

In a separate volume, *Applying Clinical Judgment*, Patricia Andersen and I provide activities to augment the main textbook. For each text chapter, we present a summary, key terms and definitions, and a quiz to assist students in studying the course content. Other distinctive features apply critical thinking to

- professional development (finding a balance between personal style and professional performance),

- case conceptualization and treatment planning (*case applications*—three to five cases for each theory, including some core cases that are used in several different chapters), and

- reading in the field (*research articles*—reprints of a published articles exemplifying research related to theory).

The *research article* is a unique addition to this type of manual and focuses on developing students' abilities to participate in the profession as intelligent consumers of research. Many students reach advanced schooling without being carefully educated in how to read research articles, and we mean to mend this frailty.

A series of ten **Counseling Demonstration Videos** will be available for instructors and departments using *Theory and Design*. These 40-minute tapes show experienced counselors using identifiable theories in sessions, with presession and debriefing interviews that tie theory to technique. Clients and therapists reflect our society's diversity. In devising these videos, Lahaska Press surveyed classroom instructors and followed their advice about what will be most useful.

Acknowledgments

I owe thanks to many people for their contributions, confidence in me, and good nature. Barry Fetterolf, publisher of Lahaska Press, invited me to write this book and saw the project through with *sprezzatura*. The support of Charles Ridley, Indiana University, has been inspirational. Mary Falcon, development editor, assisted constructively in shaping the book's scheme, and in early stages, Sylvia Shepherd offered valued editorial guidance. Christine Arden, copyeditor, improved the manuscript with impressive rhetorical skill, and Carol Newman, project editor, deftly orchestrated the production of the text to its final flourish. Bess Wareing researched and wrote the brief biographies, while furnishing great companionship and mirth. My friend Ann C. Lewis, a therapist at Family Services in Madison, Wisconsin, consistently provided the viewpoint of a gifted daily practitioner. There's nothing like an old graduate school buddy, and Jana Reddin Long was always willing to help me remember what we once both knew. My husband, Brian Carter, cheerfully tolerated having his dreams and motivations analyzed from ten perspectives and what's more, was willing to discuss. I can't imagine a better partner.

Many reviewers improved the manuscript through their detailed comments, and their suggestions are gratefully incorporated in the book you are holding:

Linda Barclay, Walsh University
Lakota Lynn Brown, Northern Arizona University
Lynn Calhoun Howell, Queens College, City University of New York
Laurie A. Carlson, Colorado State University
Lynne Carroll, University of Northern Florida
Dibya Choudhuri, Eastern Michigan University
Y. Barry Chung, Georgia State University
Jelane Kennedy, College of Saint Rose

Kathryn Ness, Troy State University
Quinn M. Pearson, University of North Alabama
Jack Presbury, James Madison University
John L. Romano, University of Minnesota
Peggy Smith, San Francisco State University
Beverly Snyder, University of Colorado, Colorado Springs
Sarah Toman, Cleveland State University
Richard E. Watts, Baylor University

Most of all, my art and reason in this pursuit flow from the thousands of college students who have graced my fortunate path and lit the way.

Susan X Day
Iowa State University
University of Houston

Theory and Design in Counseling and Psychotherapy

CHAPTER 1

Effective Ingredients of Counseling and Psychotherapy

"I'm too intense, or too sensitive, or something. . . . I don't know what. I just left my fourth good teaching position. With the first couple positions, I thought I had the bad luck of landing in places where I wasn't appreciated, but after this last time, I'm beginning to think it may be something about *me* that makes me keep losing good jobs."

This is your client, Brad, on his first appointment with you. From your intake interview you have basic information on him that is largely unremarkable—no abuse in his past, no addictive behaviors, no suicidal impulses, no trouble with the law. Brad tells you that he has a great résumé (except that now it shows a lot of job-hopping) and that he is a talented and dedicated teacher. Yet every department he joins seems to disappoint him in some way—his colleagues turn against him, he has personality conflicts with his superiors, he doesn't get the promotions he expects, he is overburdened—and he finally leaves in a huff, sure that he would be invited to leave otherwise. He has usually gone on to a better job, hoping that this next one will work out. But it doesn't.

What Do You Bring to Therapy?

As Brad's new therapist, what are you thinking? If you had to stop right now and conceptualize the case of Brad (that is, fit it into a coherent framework), how would you look at it? The following Reflection exercise will help you understand the personal profile and scientific viewpoint that you bring into a therapy session. I will expand on these topics after you complete the exercise.

R e f l e c t i o n

No matter where you are in your psychological studies, start a counseling journal to record your thoughts and feelings as you proceed. (Your professor may make this journal part of your coursework, if time permits.) I will frequently give you questions to reflect upon; these are intended to help you discover your theoretical orientation, preferences, and talents. So, even if you feel totally inadequate for the task, take on Brad as a client and answer a few questions (there is no right and wrong here).

1. Let's say that all clients appear for therapy because they have some conflict. These conflicts can be within the client, between the client and other people, and between the client and society as a group. What's your first inclination concerning the source of Brad's conflict?

   Is it intrapersonal—that is, within himself? Does he sabotage his work life because he's not really sure that's what he wants? Does he believe he

is not really worth a good position in the world? Is he too anxious to
act normal at work? Is every part of his life stained by his negativity?
Is the conflict interpersonal, having to do with how Brad deals with other
people? *Is* he too sensitive? Does he react to perceived slights from
colleagues too angrily? Does every boss remind him of his overcritical,
demanding father, and does he often react childishly when asked to
do something?
Or, is the conflict between Brad and society? Is there something wrong
with the institutions he works in that makes him feel belittled and
alienated after a while? Do the schools he works in pressure him to
behave in a manner that rubs him the wrong way? If he is visibly different from the majority of people in the setting (in a wheelchair, from
a minority race, effeminate), does this difference lead others to treat
him as a lesser being?

As you read through your choices, you probably thought that you
couldn't choose just one. Now give weights to the three choices—intrapersonal, interpersonal, and societal conflict—according to how you look
at their contributions to Brad's problem. Make the weights percentage
points so that they add up to 100 percent. Jot down notes that will remind
you why you assigned the weights the way you did.

2. Let's say, furthermore, that successful therapy involves some kind of
   change in the client. At first contact, where do you believe successful
   change will lie for Brad?

Thinking: Brad needs to change the way he looks at his job, his colleagues,
and his bosses. He may have excessively high expectations for how
fulfilling and perfect his career should be, for example. After four tries,
he may go in with a pessimistic point of view that poisons the well.
Emotion: The main problem is Brad's distress when he finds the job disappointing. He needs to learn to not take things so hard. Maybe he *is*
too intense!
Behavior: Brad is probably acting in some way that puts other people off.
He may be bragging about his expertise, or spending all his time
preparing his courses while ignoring friendly overtures. He may insult
other teachers, or invade their personal space, or spit when he talks,
or never make the coffee.

Again, after thinking about your choices, give weights to the three types
of change according to the way you are understanding Brad right now (use
points adding to 100 if you wish). Note down why you distributed points
the way you did.

3. One more question to ponder: What will your role be in this therapy? If you can agree that there are two extremes, nondirective and active, where do you think your best course stands? The very nondirective therapist encourages or insists that the client do all the talking and explore the situation and its solutions for himself or herself. The nondirective therapist believes that most people can come up with their own solutions if a counselor pays close attention and makes the right, minimal responses. The active therapist also listens closely but believes in offering interpretations of the client's talk and behavior, providing education about the client's problem areas, assigning homework, and confronting the client about his or her hang-ups. Here is a graphic representing the continuum. Make a mark where you would probably place yourself as Brad's therapist.

Very nondirective_____Very active

Your Inner Therapist

Though you probably feel glad that you don't have to figure out Brad's case with so little information and guidance, you were nonetheless able to come up with answers to the three questions above. I hope you had time to discuss them with classmates or the class as a whole, so that you could see the different ways people approached the situation. Look at what operated in how you answered the questions.

Knowing that you are taking a college course in theories of counseling, I can guess that you have some personality characteristics that led you to this spot in your career. You are armed with intelligence, perseverance, insight, empathy, and an interest in people's behavior. There's a good chance that you like people and always have, and that you have been able to help others with their problems on an informal basis. Most individuals develop interests based on their successes—so if you'd never had any luck giving advice to the lovelorn, you'd be unlikely to choose the helping vocations. And you are probably an optimist, because you think that people can change for the better.

In your approach to Brad, your own particular personality profile showed. Extroverts often choose a more active role in therapy than introverts. In fact, extroverts have to learn to restrain their tendency to talk when they learn to do therapy. This was a hard lesson for me to learn, and I still have to remind myself that silence is golden. Introverts have to learn lessons, too, in that they may passively let a client wander self-protectively off a touchy topic or complain at length without getting anywhere. Both types of people can exploit their natural leanings in a good way, of course. An extroverted therapist sets a tone of energy and expressiveness. My best friend Ann, who is also a psychotherapist, uses her introversion to good effect by taking a low-key, Columbo-style, "I don't quite understand—tell me more" approach.

That calls to mind another element you bring to the therapy table: your strengths as a person. Take a minute to list a few of your best qualities. I have no doubt that they all come to the foreground when you are in a helping role. You may be blessed with a large portion of patience, for example. This is a sterling quality in a therapist, because you must often make do with very slow change in very small steps. I possess the quality of being basically unflappable, and my clients frequently mention the comfort they feel in being able to say *anything* without fear of shocking me. When you ponder theories of psychotherapy in terms of your own practice, as you will throughout this book, remember to take into account whether the approach makes full use of your existing strengths.

Your training and experience came into play when you considered the case of Brad. As a vocational psychologist, I had to wonder whether Brad had chosen the best career path, since it seems that he is having what we call "person-environment fit" problems. My experience also affected my response because Brad reminds me of a friend who has similar problems, and so I built some conjectures about Brad based on my ideas about my friend. A person with experience in mood disorders would want to evaluate Brad further for depression, because his pattern of trying the same failed solution over and over is characteristic of depressed people. A psychodynamically minded person would first consider Brad's relationship with his father and mother. And a health enthusiast would want to know about his diet and exercise habits!

R e f l e c t i o n

Write down a list of your good qualities. Next to each entry in the list, speculate about how this quality will be important to you as a counselor.

Your Internalized Culture

When you answered the reflection questions about Brad, your values and philosophy of life were operating. Just think about one piece of evidence: While reading about Brad at the beginning of the chapter, how did you feel about him? Did you feel sorry for him because he couldn't find his right place in the world? Did you identify with him as a person who has trouble fitting in within bureaucracies? Were you impatient with an educated, privileged man being so whiny? Did you immediately sympathize with his beleaguered wife and family, if they exist? Whatever you felt reflected something about your orientation to the world, your *world view*. Sometimes your orientation will match the situation well, and sometimes you will have to force yourself to put a lid on it. Sometimes, you will find your orientation changing as you put yourself in various clients' shoes.

Your values and philosophy of life are part of your *internalized culture*, which is the way your social history operates within you. Your race, ethnicity, sex, age, geographical roots, religion, and economic class compose your internalized culture in different strengths, depending on how much they help form your habitual world view and ways of reacting to other people. To some people, religion is psychologically a driving force, while for others it is not. I have known people whose world view was pervaded with a sense of rich versus poor, and they evaluated every situation with this in mind. When you talk about a short story or novel with others, you become aware of internalized cultures, because some people will see the story's conflict as a tale of male versus female, others will see it as a struggle between the economically powerful and the powerless, still others will see it as a character's crisis of faith, and so on.

You and your client each have an internalized culture unique to your individual psyches, which is why Ho (1995) asserts that all interpersonal encounters are cross-cultural in nature. As a therapist, then, you are challenged to transcend your internalized culture and to feel the world from other hearts. Ho suggests that our foundation must be overcoming egocentrism, our foolhardy assumptions that other people think and feel the same way we do. (Life would indeed be boring if they did.) Throughout this book, I emphasize tuning up your world view so that you can make a mutually credible connection with the different and ever-surprising people who cross your path.

Your Systematic Viewpoint

As you saw in the last section, you already have a collection of therapeutic viewpoints. You make up hypotheses about Brad's situation, and you mentally plan out what information you need to collect next in order to support or rule out your hypotheses. In fact, you probably thought to yourself that you needed more information to conceptualize Brad well. You are already working from a theory of people that you started developing as a small child. It's important that you come to realize what your underlying theory of people is, and I will encourage you to do so as you read this book. Your theory can be enriched, organized, and informed through studying the major established theories that practitioners work from today.

SMALL GROUP EXERCISE

You have another appointment with Brad tomorrow. Write down the ten most important questions you want to ask him. Then pass your questions around among a group of three or four classmates. Discuss the similarities and differences you see, and as a group come up with an explanation for why these similarities and differences exist. Remember to consider personality, strengths, values, philosophy of life, and theory of people when you work on your explanation.

_____

Common Factors in Psychotherapy and Counseling

The good news is that psychotherapy does work: The average client who gets counseling is better off than 79 percent of similar people who do not receive counseling (Wampold, 2001). This figure is based on a statistical technique that allows researchers to pull together the results of many studies that compare treatment with no treatment. The technique is called meta-analysis, and before it became popular (that is, before 1977), there was some doubt about whether treatment worked at all, in comparison to the ordinary effects of time passing or of other life events. Beginning with the meta-analysis by Smith and Glass in 1977, therapy has been found effective even by researchers who really wanted to prove otherwise (Wampold, 2001). Furthermore, the gains people make in therapy are maintained over time (Nicholas & Berman, 1983).

Exactly *why* therapy is effective is a source of controversy, which we will discuss at the end of this chapter. For now, you can think of therapy as having two components: common factors and specific factors. The common factors, which we are about to consider, are part of psychotherapy no matter which theory you espouse. Paying attention to the client, for example, happens in all therapies. The specific factors are parts of psychotherapy that are tied to a theory and don't exist in all therapies. For example, dream analysis is a part of Freudian, Jungian, and psychodynamic therapy because these are based on a theory of the unconscious, which is glimpsed in dreams. You generally won't find dream analysis in many other therapies because they are based on theories that downplay or reject the idea of the unconscious. So, dream analysis is specifically tied to a single theoretical approach.

An analogy might help here. Good parents all provide emotional warmth, support, and appropriate monitoring. These are common factors. Yet children also benefit from other parental legacies, such as a musical atmosphere, a great sense of humor, world travel, psychological mindedness, or a love of nature. These are specific factors that may contribute to optimal development, but the common factors must support them, as a good foundation can support many kinds of building.

When a person's mental health improves during a course of psychotherapy, it's possible that both common and specific factors are working, and a third element also comes in. This element includes things that happen outside of therapy—for example, help from a friend, improved living conditions, a distracting crisis, or the healing power of time passing. A good outcome for a client, then, can be diagrammed as shown in Figure 1.1.

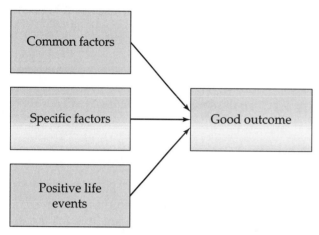

FIGURE 1.1   **Contributions to a Good Outcome
from Counseling and Psychotherapy**

Three Shared Components

There are several ways to look at the commonalities among therapies. I will draw from a conceptualization by Frank and Frank (1991, pp. 39–44) because it covers the ground thoroughly in a short list. Think of these commonalities as the basic ingredients in a recipe. Just as any traditional cookie recipe will include flour, fat, sweetener, and a rising agent, psychotherapy includes basic ingredients. You can think of the specific factors as the ingredients that make cookies different from one another: the addition of chocolate chips, for example. Frank and Frank have managed to corral the common factors of counseling into conceptual groups:

1. An emotionally charged, confiding relationship with a helping person.
2. A healing setting, in which the client communicates with a professional. The client believes this professional can provide help and trusts him or her to work on the client's behalf.
3. A rationale, conceptual scheme, or myth that provides a plausible explanation for the client's symptoms and prescribes a ritual or procedure for resolving them; the client and therapist both must accept the rationale, scheme, or myth.

   Let's take a closer look at each of these shared components.

The Therapeutic Alliance

The first component, the relationship between client and therapist, is often called the therapeutic alliance, the working alliance, or the helping alliance (Stiles, Shapiro, & Elliot, 1986). It can be thought of as the quality of the personal relationship between therapist and client that allows them to function as a team with goals, and as the positive affective aspect of the same relationship that allows the client to feel valued and liked. This alliance is often considered the main predictor of outcome: Researchers found scientific support for alliance-outcome relationships no matter how outcome was measured, who measured it, or what psychotherapeutic school of thought was represented (Henry, Strupp, Schacht, & Gaston, 1994). A meta-analysis of seventy-nine studies between 1977 and 1997 (Martin, Garske, & Davis, 2000) confirmed the relationship. An earlier meta-analysis (Horvath & Symonds, 1991) revealed that the client's judgment of the alliance predicts outcome better than the therapist's. That is, the client's perception of a warm, accepting relationship is more important than the counselor's.

Taking into account all the elements that contribute to client improvement, about 30 percent of the improvement can be attributed to the relationship between client and therapist (Lambert, 1992).

R e f l e c t i o n

Think of your own experience as a counseling client, or, if you have not been a client, imagine yourself in therapy. Why do you think the emotional relationship between the client and therapist is so important? What did (or could) the therapist do to develop a personal relationship with you in early sessions? Try to consider what would appeal to you in particular, considering your personality and what attracts you to others. What would (or did) dampen your positive feelings toward your counselor?

DISCUSSION IDEAS

Reread Brad's presenting complaint (that is, the reason the client originally gives for coming in to counseling). Even though you haven't got much to go on there, what little clues can you pick up that might help you build a positive relationship with Brad? For example, what can you make of the fact that he is a teacher? Also, what clues can you glean that would help you avoid a negative relationship with Brad at this point? Since the therapeutic alliance is established early (Martin et al., 2000; Sexton, Hembre, & Kvarme, 1996), you need to consider these hints now. Discuss your ideas with the class.

The Healing Setting

The client must believe that the therapist is trustworthy and competent. Imagine spilling out your private thoughts and feelings to someone you greet with suspicion! In such circumstances, you would do a careful editing job on everything you said—and this would not advance your therapeutic goals at all. People rarely get a chance to tell the unvarnished truth, and will do so only under conditions of trust.

Besides trustworthy, you need to appear competent: Clients need to feel that you know what you're doing (even though there are many moments when *you* don't feel that way). Otherwise, why would they accept your guidance, do the homework you suggest, or seriously consider your interpretations? Think of what implies trustworthiness and expertise in other professions, and you'll see that the same standards apply to psychotherapists—for example, straightforwardness in business arrangements, keeping a timely schedule, remembering what your client said earlier, and carrying on where you last left off (Seligman, 2001). A thorough knowledge of your subject comes through in the way you do therapy, too, and this is one reason to be acquainted with theories of counseling.

Furthermore, the healing setting is limited. The relationship between counselor and client is well defined, happening only in planned places and times. The counselor helps the client only in certain ways; for example, you don't help a client find a used car or a good salsa recipe. Bear in mind, too, that in this setting you do not ordinarily bring up your own tales and woes as matters for discussion. The focus remains on the client (Tyler, 1969). These are some characteristics of the setting that make it different from talking over a problem with a helpful friend.

The healing setting can expand far outside the walls of a counselor's office in a clinic. We might grab a few minutes with clients at their place of work, between classes, at their bedside, during physical therapy or rehab periods, before or after worship, or in the exercise yard. Even when physical settings are not ideal, we can project trustworthiness, competence, and focus on the client in the way we approach the encounter. For example, we can ensure that no one overhears what we say and that we make the most of the time we do have together through having an idea of what the encounter is supposed to accomplish. Sometimes this goal is a moment of psychological contact, empathy, or encouragement.

DISCUSSION IDEAS

What if a client entering your office could see other clients' folders on your desk labeled by name? What if three times in a row you arrived for the session at the same time as the client, frazzled from battling traffic? List some other ways in which you might undermine your client's trust in you and belief in your competence. How do you think professionals convey their expertise without bragging?

Coherent Rationale and Procedure

Bordin (1979) conceptualized the therapeutic alliance as including the emotional bond between client and therapist, the quality of client and therapist involvement in the tasks of therapy, and the amount of concordance on goals between therapist and client. This idea of the alliance overlaps with Frank and

Frank's (1991) third component (as well as with their first and second ones): By *rationale, conceptual scheme, or myth* these authors mean that you and your client agree on what has gone wrong, and on what life would look like if the problem were set right. This vision of the improved life makes up the therapeutic goals. By *ritual or procedure*, they mean that you and your client agree on what needs to be done to set things right. These are the tasks. Different theories vary on whether the goals and tasks come mostly from the client or mostly from the therapist, but in any case both of you must have some faith in them. Your clients will undergo some distress or at least inconvenience in the therapeutic process, and they must believe that it will be worthwhile in the long run.

You might be wondering why the words *myth* and *ritual* are included in the third component listed by Frank and Frank (1991), considering that they sound so unscientific. But they may be helpful, if practitioner and client both believe in them. Consider how many people are emotionally soothed by religious rituals such as performing the penance given by a priest at confession or undergoing healing ceremonies in Native American cultures. Myth sometimes serves a purpose: I know someone who has achieved self-acceptance through her belief that she is now encountering the repercussions of things she did in a previous life.

In Chapter 2, I will encourage you to consider why knowing psychological theories helps you achieve a rationale and procedure that you and your clients can have faith in.

R e f l e c t i o n

The American Heritage Dictionary provides this definition of *coherent:* "Marked by an orderly, logical, and aesthetically consistent relation of parts." Why do you think that coherence is important in the rationale, conceptual scheme, or myth that operates in psychotherapy?

Contributions to a Good Outcome

As you may have noticed in looking at the ingredients of effective therapy, the personal characteristics and motivations of the therapist and client are always active. Though the persons and the activity are difficult to separate (Who can tell the dancer from the dance? as Yeats put it), let's explore the contributions of the participants as individuals.

The Client's Contribution

"It is the client who is the primary change agent, who takes what is offered (a therapist, a self-help book, a computer program), invests it with life, and makes it work" (Tallman & Bohart, 1999, p. 97). Though we may like to think of ourselves as the heroes of the story when counseling turns out well, really it is the client who used what we offered in effective ways, and kindly overlooked our errors or transformed them into something useful. Tallman and Bohart bring up a good analogy: You join a gym that provides exercise options, equipment, and tips on building fitness, but your own efforts determine the outcome, and you make the choices about how (and whether) to use what is provided. Similarly, each client makes use of the therapist's offerings in his or her own way.

What characteristics of clients predict that they will make good use of therapy? In a summary of publications about common factors, Grencavage and Norcross (1990) noted three top client contributions. First, the client has positive expectations for therapy, feelings of hope and faith that it will do good. Second, a distressed client is more likely to experience positive change from counseling than a complacent client. Third, the client actively seeks help. All of these qualities, obviously, suggest a high level of motivation to participate. Clients like this are likely to communicate freely, be involved emotionally, and collaborate in the therapeutic process (Bachelor & Horvath, 1999). On the other hand, clients whose basic style is hostile are less likely to collaborate fully. These clients often include people who are forced into counseling by courts or by other people in their lives, such as spouses, bosses, and parents.

SMALL GROUP EXERCISE

1. In a first or second session with a client, how can you discover whether the client has characteristics that predict a good outcome? Discuss with three or four classmates how to make this assessment.

2. If you do have a mandated client (assigned by the court) or a coerced client (therapy was someone else's idea), what are some measures you can take to improve the odds of therapeutic success? Brainstorm with classmates about hostile or unmotivated clients. Think about what your own stance would be if you went to counseling at someone else's insistence. What would help you benefit from the situation?

The Counselor's Contribution

Carl Rogers (1951) and his followers established a short and enduring list of therapist qualities that enhance the enterprise: accurate empathy, nonpossessive warmth, and genuineness. As you will see in Chapter 6, these theorists believed such qualities were not only necessary, but also sufficient, for therapeutic change. Even though others didn't agree that these are *all* you need to be successful, almost all experts now concur that they are inherent components of effective counseling (Beutler, Machado, & Allstetter Neufeldt, 1994). They are often included in lists of general, or common, factors in the counseling process.

DISCUSSION IDEAS

1. As a class, analyze the qualifiers in the Rogerian list above. Note that it says not only empathy but *accurate* empathy, and not only warmth but *nonpossessive* warmth. Why are these qualifiers important? Take the client's point of view in thinking about this.

2. What is genuineness? Look up the dictionary definition of *genuine. The American Heritage Dictionary* includes these: "Actually possessing the alleged or apparent attribute or character," and "Honestly felt or experienced." When you feel that a person you're dealing with is being genuine, what evidence are you are looking at? Some class members may be able to provide counterexamples (that is, instances in which another person did *not* seem genuine) to help clarify the concept.

It may seem that "training" should be added to the list of "empathy, warmth, and genuineness" to describe optimal therapist attributes. But, in fact, more professional training and experience do not guarantee a more effective therapist. Several studies have compared trained professionals to new graduate students, to less experienced therapists, and to nice college professors, and have found no big differences in client improvement (for examples, see Tallman & Bohart, 1999). A meta-analysis by Stein and Lambert (1995) discovered that well trained, experienced therapists had a small edge over novices. However, as Tallman and Bohart point out, you should see a *big* difference—like the one you'd see in trained versus untrained plumbers or computer technicians—if training and practice were critical matters. Don't take these findings wrong—there are certainly some people who are better therapists than others. And you individually can certainly improve as a therapist through education, training, and practice. After all, the studies finding little difference compare two existing groups of helpers, not the same people early and later in their careers.

DISCUSSION IDEAS

What would be the advantages of going to a less experienced therapist versus an old hand, in your opinion? If you were looking for a counselor, what type of training background would you desire? Would a certain type of training—for example, a certificate from a workshop rather than a degree from a college—be a warning to you? What questions might your clients ask about your training? If they didn't ask any, would you say anything about it?

Other than personal qualities like warmth and processes like education, you can look at what therapists do and you will find common elements. Six were identified by Frank and Frank (1991, pp. 44–50). The therapist

- develops and maintains a relationship with the client;
- links hope to the process of counseling;
- offers new learning experiences;
- arouses the client's emotions;
- enhances the client's sense of self-efficacy and confidence;
- and provides opportunities for practicing new ways of responding and behaving.

Although Frank and Frank list these as therapist activities, if you look closely you will see that the client is at least an equal partner in all six.

Underlying many of the common factors for therapists are the abilities to observe well and listen well. These abilities stem from personal qualities and are developed through practice; they guide the counselor's approach to the six activities listed above. According to Carkhuff (2000), counselors observe body movements, facial expressions, grooming, body build, and posture; and they listen by suspending personal judgment, focusing on the client, resisting distractions, recalling the client's expressions accurately, and noticing common themes in the client's talk.

R e f l e c t i o n

Think about yourself in terms of Rogerian qualities. Can you describe instances from everyday life during the past week in which you displayed accurate empathy, nonpossessive warmth, and genuineness? Can you think of times when these qualities were called for and you didn't come through with them? What causes you to falter sometimes in delivering empathy, warmth, and genuineness?

SMALL GROUP EXERCISE

In a small group of classmates, discuss several ways in which you could begin right now to develop better observing and listening skills.

The Common Factors Versus Empirically Supported Therapies Debate

In this chapter we have focused on features common to all kinds of counseling approaches. These are the substance on one side of a huge controversy in the psychological community: the common factors versus empirically supported therapies debate. Empirically supported therapies are often referred to as ESTs, and you will also see references to EVTs, meaning empirically validated therapies. (The shift from the EVT to the EST term just means that *validated* had too final and certain a ring to it, so the more accurate term *supported* came to be preferred.) *Empirical* means derived from scientific experimentation. So, ESTs are treatments that have been studied by researchers in controlled experiments and found to be efficacious, in comparison with no treatment or with some other treatment.

An analogy might help: Let's say you've gone on three different types of weight-loss diet and have an idea about which diet works best. That diet is not an EST. What you would need to do is find a large group of similar overweight people and assign them at random to three treatments, such as Weight Watchers, Slimfast, and a low-fat diet, making sure that they all stuck to their assigned plans. Then, after a predetermined period, you would weigh all the people and see whether one diet is more successful than the others. That particular diet would have empirical support, because it has won out in a scientific experiment. If you were using American Psychological Association (APA) guidelines, though, the diet would have to win out in *two* well-designed group experiments or in a large series of case studies before it would gain status as an EST.

The EST movement uses medical experimentation and treatment as a model. When you seek the help of a physician, you hope that the treatment prescribed has been tested scientifically and found effective in cases like yours. You especially want assurance that it is more effective than going home and doing nothing at all! And you wish for a doctor who keeps up on the latest reports of treatments that work. Translating this line of reasoning to psychotherapy is straightforward: If psychological research supports a certain treatment for a disorder, you want to give that treatment to your clients who have the disorder. Peter Nathan and Jack Gorman (1998), in *A Guide to Treatments That Work*, put the matter this way:

> Today . . . we are closer than ever to being able to specify which psychotherapy delivered by which psychotherapist is most effective for which person in which treatment setting. (p. 12)

To extend the diet analogy, this is to say that research can specify what diet would be most effective for you, considering your personality and lifestyle, your particular type of weight problem, and the skills of your diet counselor (if you had one). And in fact, the twenty-eight chapters in *A Guide to Treatments That Work* do match treatment, client type, and psychological problem. Proponents of the EST movement assert that common factors research finds no difference among types of psychotherapy because different types of clients and problems are all mixed in together, and differences between treatments are washed out. By analogy, we might have found that Weight Watchers, Slimfast, and the low-fat diet all bring about the same weight loss in our experiment, but we have not disallowed that a certain type of overweight person might benefit more from Weight Watchers than from Slimfast. This situation would be easy to imagine: Just think how highly social Weight Watchers is and how likely it is that sociable people would stick to cheery meetings rather than drink a lonely Slimfast twice a day. So, says the EST side, psychotherapists have a responsibility to learn what treatment, person, and problem matches are supported by research and to deliver the most efficacious one—or refer the client to someone who can. (For example, a physician would be needed to prescribe psychopharmacological treatments like lithium, the EST for bipolar disorder; or you may not have the expertise to deliver a particular EST yourself and thus need to refer your client elsewhere.)

A significant contribution from the field of medicine is evident in the EST literature. This boon is the efficacy of pharmacological treatments (drug therapies) for defined psychological problems such as schizophrenia, major depressive disorder, and attention deficits. You should familiarize yourself with this body of knowledge, because you will no doubt be seeing clients who can benefit from drug therapy. In "A Summary of Treatments That Work" (Nathan & Gorman, 1998, pp. xix-xxx), of the 27 disorders listed, 20 have pharmacological ESTs. In 19 of those 20, psychosocial ESTs are also indicated. As a rule, EST and common factors supporters don't knock heads over the proof of drug efficacy: Rather, the two sides part company on whether the medical model of proof can be extended to psychosocial treatments (that is, specific techniques used in various types of nondrug therapy).

The common factors advocates point to the fact that when you look at the sum total of therapy outcome research, specific techniques (emphasized in ESTs) account for only 15 percent of a client's improvement, while client expectancies and the therapeutic alliance account for 45 percent (Lambert, 1992). (The other 40 percent consists of the strengths the client already has and life events that occur outside of therapy.) These estimates derive from a review of the research: Wampold, for example (2001), estimated the effect of specific techniques at only 8 percent. Therefore, why focus on the smallest piece of the pie? Common factors proponents also point out that EST experiments are not like therapy as it is really practiced. As just one example, consider that patients are accepted in controlled experiments if they have only the disorder under study and no others, so that the researchers can be sure they are targeting what they claim to target. But of course it is rare in everyday clinical life to see a client who has a tidy diagnosis: Troubled people are usually troubled from various directions at once. So, common factors enthusiasts question whether EST results apply to counseling practice.

Furthermore, studies that focused on comparing specific treatment strategies, when the researchers also collected data on common factors, have found that common factors predict outcome better than strategies, and that the strategies come out about equal in terms of how well they predict outcome (e.g., Krupnick, Simmens, Moyer, Elkin, Watkins, & Pilkonis, 1996; Miller, Taylor, & West, 1980). (The idea that all treatments are equally successful is often jokingly called the Dodo Bird verdict, a term originally coined in 1936 by Saul Rosenzweig, who was referring to an episode in *Alice in Wonderland*. In this episode, after a race the Dodo Bird declares that everyone has won and all deserve prizes.) Studies that do show differences in effectiveness between treatments are often suspect because the research investigators already had an allegiance to the winning treatment (Wampold, 2001). This doesn't mean that the investigators cheated, but that their hopes and preferences somehow affected the outcome, in a subtle form of researcher bias.

Of course, money and power are involved in this controversy. For some kinds of reimbursement (in managed care plans, for instance), you must agree to use APA's EST for the client's presenting problem—and this may mean that your judgments about the complexities of the client's situation fall on deaf ears. Another money question is whether a client could sue you for not delivering the official EST, just as you could sue an obstetrician for not performing a Caesarean section when it was medically indicated. Many counseling practitioners abhor the thought of giving up their clinical intuition about what treatment is best, for fear of being sued. Among scholars, the two sides must battle for research money in academic departments and from other funding sources, so each must justify its superior value. And then there is the whole question of how future therapists should be trained: Should the emphasis lie on rigorously following well-defined ESTs or on strengthening basic counseling skills? The answer influences decisions about who is hired to do the training—that is, who obtains desirable academic positions. Predictably, too, each side stereotypes the other, with common factors people portrayed as unscientific, touchy-feely types, and EST people portrayed as overcontrolling, out-of-touch medical minions.

What does all this mean to you? The controversy is certainly one that will come up during your training as a helping professional. In the next chapter, I will explain why theory is important to counseling. One main reason goes back to Frank and Frank's (1991) assertion that the therapist and client must have faith in a coherent explanation of the problem and a rationale for curative tasks consistent with the explanation. Theory provides such coherence. It also implies a systematic approach to what we do in counseling, which is to apply specific techniques. Ideally, we tailor our interventions to the client's personality, abilities, perspective on the world, and private theory about his or her own problem. Chwalisz (2001) called for a compromise: "technique selection based on research support, within the context of a relationship driven by the common factors" (p. 264). To me, this seems the best course to steer.

DISCUSSION IDEAS

Take a vote in class: If you were forced to choose one approach or the other, would you be a proponent of ESTs or of common factors? Discuss your reasoning, as well as what aspects of your background, experience, education, and personality affected the way you voted.

REFERENCES

Bachelor, A., & Horvath, A. (1999). The therapeutic relationship. In M. A. Hubble, B. L. Duncan, & S. D. Miller (Eds.), *The heart and soul of change: What works in therapy* (pp. 133–178). Washington, DC: APA.

Beutler, L. E., Machado, P. P. M., & Allstetter Neufeldt, S. A. (1994). Therapist variables. In S. L. Garfield & A. E. Bergin (Eds.), *Handbook of psychotherapy and behavior change* (4th ed.) (pp. 229–269). New York: Wiley.

Bordin, E. S. (1979). The generalizability of the psychoanalytic concept of working alliance. *Psychotherapy: Theory, Research, and Practice, 16,* 252–260.

Carkhuff, R. R. (2000). *The art of helping in the 21st century* (8th ed.). Amherst, MA: Human Resource Development Press.

Chwalisz, K. (2001). A common factors revolution: Let's not "cut off our discipline's nose to spite its face." *Journal of Counseling Psychology, 48,* 262–267.

Frank, J. D., & Frank, J. B. (1991). *Persuasion and healing: A comparative study of psychotherapy* (3rd ed.). Baltimore: Johns Hopkins University Press.

Grencavage, L. M., & Norcross, J. C. (1990). Where are the commonalities among the therapeutic common factors? *Professional Psychology: Research and Practice, 21,* 372–378.

Henry, W. P., Strupp, H. H., Schacht, T. E., & Gaston, L. (1994). Psychodynamic approaches. In S. L. Garfield & A. E. Bergin (Eds.), *Handbook of psychotherapy and behavior change* (4th ed.) (pp. 467–508). New York: Wiley.

Ho, D. Y. F. (1995). Internalized culture, culturocentrism, and transcendence. *The Counseling Psychologist, 23,* 4–24.

Horvath, A. O., & Symonds, B. D. (1991). Relation between working alliance and outcome in psychotherapy: A meta-analysis. *Journal of Counseling Psychology, 38,* 139–149.

Krupnick, J. L., Simmens, S., Moyer, J., Elkin, I., Watkins, J. T., & Pilkonis, P. A. (1996). The role of the therapeutic alliance in psychotherapy and pharmacotherapy outcome: Findings in the National Institute of Mental Health treatment of depression collaborative research program. *Journal of Consulting and Clinical Psychology, 64,* 532–539.

Lambert, M. J. (1992). Implications of outcome research for psychotherapy integration. In J. C. Norcross & M. R. Goldstein (Eds.), *Handbook of psychotherapy integration* (pp. 94–129). New York: Basic Books.

Martin, D. J., Garske, J. P., & Davis, M. K. (2000). Relation of the therapeutic alliance with outcome and other variables: A meta-analytic review. *Journal of Consulting and Clinical Psychology, 66,* 832–837.

Miller, W. R., Taylor, C. A., & West, J. C. (1980). Focused versus broad-spectrum behavior therapy for problem drinkers. *Journal of Consulting and Clinical Psychology, 48,* 590–601.

Nathan, P. E., & Gorman, J. M. (Eds.). (1998). *A guide to treatments that work.* New York: Oxford University Press.

Nicholson, R. A., & Berman, J. S. (1983). Is follow-up necessary in evaluating psychotherapy? *Psychological Bulletin, 93,* 261–278.

Rogers, C. (1951). *Client-centered therapy: Its current practice, implications and theory.* Boston: Houghton Mifflin.

Rosenzweig, S. (1936). Some implicit common factors in diverse methods of psychotherapy: "At last the Dodo said, 'Everyone has won and all must have prizes.'" *American Journal of Orthopsychiatry, 6,* 412–415.

Seligman, L. (2001). *Systems, strategies, and skills of counseling and psychotherapy.* Upper Saddle River, NJ: Prentice-Hall.

Sexton, H. C., Hembre, K., & Kvarme, G. (1996). The interaction of the alliance and therapy microprocess: A sequential analysis. *Journal of Consulting and Clinical Psychology, 64,* 471–480.

Smith, M. L., & Glass, G. V. (1977). Meta-analysis of psychotherapy outcome studies. *American Psychologist, 32,* 752–760.

Stein, D. M., & Lambert, M. J. (1995). Graduate training in psychotherapy: Are therapy outcomes enhanced? *Journal of Consulting and Clinical Psychology, 63,* 182–196.

Stiles, W. B., Shapiro, D. A., & Elliot, R. (1986). "Are all psychotherapies equivalent?" *American Psychologist, 41,* 165–180.

Tallman, K., & Bohart, A. C. (1999). The client as a common factor: Clients as self-healers. In M. A. Hubble, B. L. Duncan, & S. D. Miller (Eds.), *The heart and soul of change: What works in therapy* (pp. 91–131). Washington, DC: APA.

Tyler, L. E. (1969). *The work of the counselor* (3rd ed.). New York: Appleton-Century-Crofts.

Wampold, B. E. (2001). *The great psychotherapy debate: Models, methods, and findings.* Mahwah, NJ: Lawrence Erlbaum Associates.

CHAPTER **2**

Theory and Case Analysis

If you are reluctant to study theories of counseling and psychotherapy, you are not alone. I remember having intelligent, enthusiastic classmates who dreaded the idea of reading and discussing dry, boring, abstract ideas. These students would rather be doing hands-on work, building up expertise through experience. Many people fancy that there is a brick wall between theorists and practitioners, and that they are on one side or the other. I hope in this chapter to persuade you that this is not true. Good practice is built on theory, and theory is built on observations from practice and everyday life. Ideally, theory gives form to your case analysis—that is, your case conceptualization and what you do with a diagnosis.

You have several theories of your own. Let's take an illustration. If you have children, you have a theory of each of them. By this I mean that if I presented you with a new situation—for example, their first ride on a Ferris wheel—you could tell me how you think each child would react to the experience. Then you could take the kids to the fair and see whether your predictions were right. If they weren't, you'd take your theories back to the drawing board, maybe adding some new twists to cover the way each child behaved at the fair.

Your thoughts on your children pass several of the tests of whether an idea qualifies as a theory. A theory organizes, integrates, and articulates principles, using both objective facts and knowledge from experience. It explains how things fit together in a systematic way, not just as a junk drawer of unrelated observations and facts. From a theory, you can make predictions, such as the ones about how your children would react to the Ferris wheel, and you can test whether your predictions are right by designing experiments that will support them, or prove them wrong or incomplete. A theory is different from a fact in that it encompasses more elements, and it can never be proven, though it can be disproven. Even if your children do behave as you expected at the Ferris wheel, there may be another experiment that would not pan out the way you thought. Your theories, or parts of them, need to be tested over and over in various situations. When you revise the theories based on the evidence you find, you have to test the new versions.

Many theories are well supported, so well supported that we consider them proven (though they are not). The theories of gravity, of relativity, and of evolution are accepted by most people. These are based on empirical scientific experimentation and investigation. Theories about people, especially about people in general, are much more slippery because a person is more complex than a falling rock, and people vary so much individually. Just think of the many theories about the differences between men and women, theories that constantly stumble over compelling examples that contradict them.

Theories of psychotherapy are built on theories of human behavior patterns, which try to explain the system of paths that make us what we are individually—extroverts or introverts, well balanced or neurotic, adventurous or staid, and so on—as well as why we sometimes deviate from our usual character. Imagine what a task this is, to come up with one theory that covers the diversity of human beings. This is why there are so many theories of counseling—over

400, according to a 1995 count (Corsini & Wedding, 1995). Once when I had surgery, I asked the doctor what was the best way of operating on a certain problem. He said that there were four or five ways surgeons do it, and the very fact that there were four or five ways meant that no one had come up with the perfect way, or else it would be the way everyone chose by now. The same goes for psychological theories. If anyone had come up with one that tested out right every time, including the test of acceptance by practitioners, you would not be studying ten or twelve prevailing, and often competing, theories (except in a history of psychology course).

I am using the word *theory* in a loose sense here, believe it or not. There are several other qualities that an idea needs to possess in order to be called a *theory* in the strictest, most philosophical sense. In this textbook, however, we will employ the word in its everyday sense. Specifically, a *theory* is a set of related principles that

- explains a group of phenomena or facts,
- can be used to make predictions about future or coexisting phenomena,
- can be tested by checking the accuracy of these predictions, and
- helps comprehension of the phenomena it explains and guides action in relevant situations.

R e f l e c t i o n

To practice illuminating your own theories, describe a situation in which you did not act like yourself, as in the statements "I was not quite myself" or "I surprised myself." What did you do, think, say, or feel that made you label it "not me"? What general principle of *you* was violated? What explanation do you have for your deviation from your regular self?

Beyond Trial and Error

Hands-on clinical experience seeing clients helps you build your own theories of what makes people tick, and what might help when they're in trouble. All of us call to mind other clients when thinking about the one in front of us at the moment, comparing and contrasting and choosing techniques. This is good, professional style. However, as Roth and Fonagy (1996) point out in their critical review of psychotherapy research, this alone should not guide clinical practice: "No single clinician can accumulate experience sufficient in quantity to ensure generalizability" (pp. 33–34). That is, you don't have a big enough client sample to develop your theories and test and revise and retest them. But you do have a big jump-start if you are knowledgeable about the theories of human behavior that other people have already developed and tested, and that experts have challenged with their own testing and theorizing. In a study comparing experienced and novice counselors' case analyses, researchers found that "experienced counselors possessed a parsimonious, underlying set of deep principles for structuring client information that allowed them to easily 'contextualize' and situate the client" (Mayfield, Kardash, & Kivlighan, 1999, p. 512). The novice counselors tended to note irrelevant superficial details, while the experienced counselors looked at deeper, essential patterns. Such patterns are the substance of theory.

I will give you two analogies to consider when you think about guiding your practice by well-known theories. First, if you go to the doctor with an ailment and she proposes a treatment, you want to know that this treatment has been used before for your ailment, by this doctor and by other ones. You want to know how probable a recovery is if you get this treatment. You would most likely *not* return to this doctor if she told you she treated ailments based on her own intuition rather than on the facts she learned in medical school and from current research. Remember from Chapter 1, Frank and Frank's (1991) common factors, which include "A rationale, conceptual scheme, or myth that provides a plausible explanation for the client's symptoms and prescribes a ritual or procedure for resolving them; the client and therapist both must accept the rationale, scheme, or myth." As a patient, it would be hard for you to accept the rationale of a stranger's intuition to explain and prescribe for you. Thus, as a counselor, you will be able to explain and treat psychological problems more effectively if you have the theoretical foundation built by our forebears, through their research and experience. Your plan will be more coherent and organized, and your client is more likely to believe in it—and in you.

The second analogy comes from the experience of learning mathematics. With the introduction of a new math concept, most of us have gone through the stage of merely learning what operations we need to perform to get the right answer—commonly called the "plug and chug" technique. Otherwise, many people wouldn't make it through the first statistics class! But we know there's a difference between knowing the formula and knowing the idea behind the formula. I hope you have felt the pleasant, dizzying moment of insight that occurs when you realize what principle underlies the math operation—*why* the operation you blindly used actually worked. Clearly, students who only "plug and chug" never reach the heights of mathematical prowess, though luckily they can survive basic courses. Similarly, as a counselor you can be taught to treat a client successfully using a step-by-step manual, but that spark of understanding *why* you are doing this makes a lot of difference. That difference is the illuminating power of theory. If you are following preset steps, and one of the steps goes awry, knowing the theory will help you set the process right by choosing alternative techniques that remain consistent and believable. If you don't know the theory, this would be impossible.

DISCUSSION IDEAS

1. Discuss the math analogy—that being able to do something mechanically is qualitatively different from being able to understand the theory behind it. Think of other arenas where this principle holds true—cooking, teaching, child-raising, and coaching a team are some of them. Give examples of the difference between "plug and chug" and insight from several arenas you know.

2. Divide the class into halves. One half will play devil's advocate and defend the idea that it isn't necessary to know theories of psychotherapy in order to be a stellar counselor. The other half will present the case for knowing theory. Remember that no one is necessarily representing his or her own opinion on this matter—just the opinion assigned to that half of the room.

How Theory Connects with Case Conceptualization

For everyone you help professionally, you need to develop a *case conceptualization*. This is basically a theory of the person—a theory that draws together information you have and organizes it in a way that helps explain current, past, and future behavior. So, it's not just a list of facts and ideas you have about the person, but an integrated system that bears some insight into how these facts and ideas are connected. The way you gather information, and what you consider important, and, finally, what kind of treatment you plan are driven by general psychological theory and the theories of psychotherapy that derive from them. For example, a psychodynamic theory would call for detailed investigation of an adult client's childhood, while a cognitive theory would demand close introspection about thinking habits, and a behavioral theory would require observations of a person's actions. In this book, I am encouraging you to think about two levels of theory—on one level, what makes people in general tick (your psychological theory) and, on another level, what makes a certain client tick (your case conceptualization or *theory of this person*). The two levels ultimately need to harmonize.

You will work on your case conceptualization continually, finding evidence and counterevidence and revising your theory as you go along. However, the more quickly and efficiently you can devise a sturdy conceptualization, the more effective your help will be. Without a meaningful conceptual framework, novice therapists can get bogged down and lose their sense of direction.

A case conceptualization is not the same as a diagnosis, which will be covered later in this chapter. It differs in that it integrates and explains the client's healthy, adaptive behavior as well as his or her distress. No matter what theory you employ, you begin your case conceptualization with your first contact with the client—even if it's over the phone. You know what a depressed person sounds like—flat, slow, sad—as well as how a manic person speaks—fast, energetic, rambling. In person, you can look at how the client dresses, stands, sits, and gestures, and try to fit your inferences together. You will depend a great deal, though, on the client's verbal content during your first session together. Many interviewing textbooks and articles provide helpful lists of questions and informative discussions; you may want to consult these before or during your first interview (or first few) (e.g., Ivey, 2002; Morrison, 1994; Seligman, 2001; Stevens & Morris, 1995). Stevens and Morris list six basic content areas that most formats include:

- descriptive data, like age, sex, notable features;
- presenting problem (why the person is seeking help);
- relevant history (events in the past that the client associates with the presenting problem);
- interpersonal style, such as whether the client is passive or active, pleasant or abrupt;
- environmental factors, such as poverty or fame, and
- personality dynamics (what seems to motivate the client's actions).

In the next section, you will find a much more detailed approach.

SMALL GROUP EXERCISE

Divide the six content areas from Stevens and Morris among two or more small groups (in other words, each of three groups could take two areas, each of two groups could take three areas, and so forth). For the content areas assigned to your group, brainstorm a list of questions and observations that would gather information to help you in case conceptualization. Returning to a united class session, each group can then report its results to the other groups.

Kelly's Theory of Personal Constructs

In a classic theories of counseling book, C. H. Patterson (1980) supplies focused areas of investigation for the counselor, based on George Kelly's (1955) theory of personal constructs. Think of a *construct* as what comes from *constructing* the world around you, psychologically. Connect it with the analogy of a building, which has a foundation, an edifice with various interdependent parts, a use in the world, and a flow of energy systems (such as electricity and plumbing). For instance, some people build a hostile world full of enemies, while others build a friendly world full of helpful people, and both can point to evidence for their personal constructs (neither of which are exact representations of reality). To me, Kelly's personal constructs seem to get to the heart of case conceptualization. Some of his constructs refer to information your client will reveal directly, and some require you to reflect on the client and the client's world and come up with your own interpretation. Furthermore, depending on what theory you choose to inform your work with this client, you can choose areas that reflect the theory and investigate them in more depth in later sessions. For example, a psychodynamically oriented counselor would specifically probe past relationships and their reflections in current relationships. Kelly's personal constructs cover fourteen areas, which I organize by categories (adapted from Patterson, 1980, pp. 364–365):

Social Setting and Network of Relationships

1. *Figure Matrix.*   What kinds of people has the client known intimately? For example, a student brought up in an intellectual family and sent to high-powered private schools throughout life probably has a restricted view of humanity. A student brought up in a poverty-stricken family in a dangerous neighborhood also has a restricted view of humanity. Restrictions like these may affect the client's value system and may be important in understanding his or her current problem.

2. *Cooperative Relationships.*   What socially constructive activities does the client participate in? A teacher or preacher may have no trouble at all with this question, while an avant-garde artist, a burglar, or a philosopher may need to think it through for a while. Those clients who engage in no cooperative relationships, or who don't care to do so, can also give you provocative clues about their emotional life.

3. *Thematic Repertory.*   What are the habits and patterns in the social world that the client belongs to? In my own world, the prevailing pattern of socializing is chat. In someone else's, the major focus of socializing may be a common hobby such as falconry or weight-lifting, or a common site such as a place of worship, a school, or a tavern.

4. *Climate of Opinion Out of Which Complaints Arise.*   In the client's social setting, what kinds of complaints are conventional or acceptable? Within our little worlds, some things are all right to talk about, while other things are not. In many groups, it is okay to complain about most physical health problems, but not at all okay to say you cry all the time, or purposely throw up everything you eat, or never want to have sex.

5. *Supportive Status.*   In what way is the client seen as necessary to other people? This question helps you understand how the client sees his or her roles in life. If the first thing a client mentions is that she is necessary as a mother, you know that this role dominates her self-concept, for better or worse. If a client first mentions that she is the linchpin of her whole work crew's functioning, you know something else.

External Views of the Client

6. *Characterizations of the Client.*   How do other people—with whom the client lives, socializes, and works—describe the client? If you ask the client this question, you will of course get only his point of view, which may be skewed. But it is certainly diagnostically helpful to know how the client *thinks* others view him. With children, you might ask questions like "What would your teacher in school say about you? What would your martial arts instructor say about you?" With adolescents, the important query is probably "What would your friends say about you?"

7. *Externally Imposed Group Identifications.*   What stereotypes and generalizations do other people make based on the groups the client is a member of (male or female, student or worker, gay or straight, Black or White, for example)? The stereotypes may be right or wrong, and the client will definitely have opinions on this question. External stereotypes frequently contribute to an individual's psychological problems, as we see in cases of racial prejudice. Even finding out what groups the client perceives herself as belonging to is significant. For instance, a person who chooses to describe herself as Democrat, Republican, or Independent has a world view different from that of a person who would never dream of describing herself with a political-party label.

8. *Areas in Which the Client Is Incorporated or Alienated.*   Which people see the client as like themselves, and which ones are unwilling to do this? One example comes from married couples. Does the wife see the husband as "from Mars," as a totally different life form than herself? Or vice versa? Or do they see themselves as a matched pair?

9. *External Patterns of Conflict and Solution.*   What political and social issues and conflicts touch the client's life? An extreme case involves young people in the army reserves or active service who may at any moment be called to a distant country or a dangerous situation, or both. Such a possible disruption of ordinary life surely affects day-to-day psychological status. For people with ties to other countries, strife abroad strikes close to home psychologically.

Patterns of Activity, Speech, and Thought

10. *Symbolic System.*   What kind of language background forms the client's speech? What speech habits are perceptible—for example, frequent use of sports metaphors or money metaphors, or a huge vocabulary, or a tendency to leave sentences unfinished? If the main language of the country is the client's second language, what effect does this have on him or her emotionally?

11. *Versatility.*   What is the range or variety of the client's activities and thinking? Is he or she open to experience? You can discover whether your client prefers the regular and familiar over the exotic and exciting. Clients at either extreme have defined problems that you will want to investigate.

Physical Resources

12. *Physical Means.*   How much income, savings, and property does the client have? Also, what are the resources of the community he or she lives in? As a therapist, I have often invited a social worker into cases where relief from the burdens of poverty or joblessness seemed to be the most pressing problem confronting the client and, thus, was one that had to be addressed concurrently with psychological counseling. On the other hand, a very well-to-do client can afford to consider suggestions like taking a break from work or retreating to ponder a problem in a lovely setting.

13. *Dependencies.*   Are there resources upon which the client has become so dependent that their loss would interrupt his or her whole pattern of life? For instance, a person may absolutely refuse to take a lower-paying job, even if you think this job would do wonders for her mental health. In that case, higher pay is a dependency you must take into account in your conceptualization. Another common example is the client who would find it impossible to separate from her family of origin, even though they drive her crazy. She comes with a "package deal," psychologically.

Important Incidents and Events

14. *Biographical Turning Points.*   What points of change have occurred in the client's life? How did the client manage these changes? The first transition to parenthood, for example, is one that many couples face with shock and chagrin. Among children themselves, how their first entry into the school system is managed tells a good deal about their inner life. And for families with adolescents, the growing independence of the teens is a problematical turning point for all members.

I emphasize this particular list because it includes so much material about the client's surroundings as well as about his or her internal states. Also, I think that if you carefully collected information in each of these areas, you would get a valid picture of the client's culture and thereby avoid stereotyping by appearance, nationality, color, class status, and so on.

R e f l e c t i o n

Take some time to consider the fourteen categories above in terms of your own self. As you do so, note down your own reactions to the task. Which items require more thought? Do any of them make you anxious? Do you think your responses give a good all-around picture of you? If not, what other information is needed?

DISCUSSION IDEAS

Counselors usually avoid question-and-answer interviews, which may make clients feel interrogated. The descriptive questions in each of the above categories are rarely in the form you would phrase them to a client. Which items need to be softened and made more indirect? How can you gain the information you seek without alienating your client?

Seven Practical Aids for Case Conceptualization

You develop theories of your partner, your relatives, and your friends from years of close contact in varying situations. But you don't have that chance with most clients, so you need to be more purposeful about developing your case conceptualization and testing it out. Here are seven suggestions to help you do this.

1. *Predict.*   Keep predictions about your clients in your personal notes (not in the formal records). What do you think they will do (and not do) between this session and the next one? If your predictions are mostly correct, you are developing a good case conceptualization (Patterson, 1980).

2. *Map.*   On unlined paper, draw a cognitive map of the client's presenting problems, other problems, and, then, any behaviors, thoughts, history, and external situations that are related to the problems. Draw arrows that show what influences what, including double-headed arrows to show influences that work both ways (for example, being shy makes a person avoid parties, but avoiding parties also keeps a person shy). You may even consider showing your map to your client and asking for feedback. I once showed a client the map I had made for her case, and she was unexpectedly thrilled with it, even though it was pretty grim. In this case, it meant to her that I cared enough to give her situation a lot of thought and effort outside of sessions. This reaction in itself provided me more information for conceptualizing her. Figure 2.1 shows an example of a cognitive map I once made.

3. *Challenge.*   Take your case conceptualization and challenge it. Brainstorm for completely different points of view that could be explanatory and predictive. Consult in private with your supervisor and other counselors (keeping confidentiality in mind), and encourage them to challenge your conceptualization.

4. *Describe.*   Generate a metaphor for your relationship with the client (Stevens & Morris, 1995). Can you describe it in terms of other types of relationship—mentor, teacher, doctor, parent, pal? At the student counseling center, I often found that I felt like a big sister to my clients. The way you interact with your clients gives you information about how other people probably interact with them, for better or worse. In this way, you can get a sense of their interpersonal style.

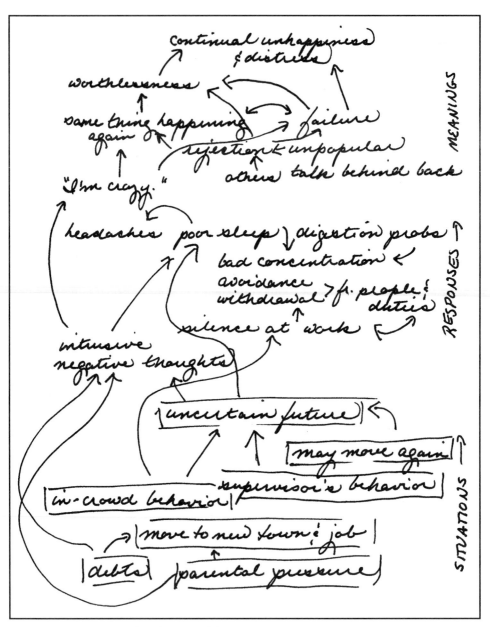

FIGURE 2.1 Example of a Cognitive Map

5. *Collect.* Make use of established psychological tests if they are available, if the client is willing to take them, and if you or another expert can interpret the results competently. Personality, vocational, and behavior inventories can cover a much broader range of material than an interview can, and the results can suggest areas you should investigate that might otherwise take forever to

come up in sessions. At that point, you should analyze how these results agree or disagree with other information you have collected from the clients, such as artwork, photos, journal writings, recordings, and self-monitoring worksheets. One of my clients brought in letters from her mother that I found extremely helpful in my understanding of their problematic relationship.

6. *Contemplate.*   Let your mind run free sometimes. When I encounter lines at the grocery store and long waits at the bus stop, I choose one client and just ponder him or her. Unstructured thought, like daydreaming, can bring forth surprising revelations. Although you need mental and emotional time off from counseling, you may find it enjoyable to muse on clients at times when you are not under pressure to come to any conclusions. When I read for pleasure, I often find that a novel or story leads me to relevant ideas about my clients and students.

7. *Compare and contrast.*   Think about your own similarities to and differences from your client early and often. This will help you perceive areas where you might have misconstrued what your client says and does. A conflict in values can hinder your progress together; conversely, it can become a source of illuminating discussion for both of you. For example, women vary individually and culturally in terms of how much self-worth they draw from being good wives and mothers. With clients who value this virtue highly, a counselor who pushes independence will not be as successful as a counselor who can see traditional feminine virtues as strengths. Indeed, clients will seek and accept courses of action that are consistent with their own values, not yours. Similarities between you and your client can also mislead you. For example, you both may be the parents of average-intelligence boys in third grade, which seems to give you a lot in common. However, your client may be deeply disappointed that his child is not super-intelligent academically, while the same situation never loses you a minute of sleep. You could mistakenly overlook the intensity of the client's feelings since you don't share them.

Many of these steps involve writing and drawing and note-taking. Be sure that you protect your clients' privacy, as well as your own, by not placing your personal speculations into records that could become public. Be careful to keep your papers where no one else can see them, and your computer or PDA files securely locked with passwords. To be most cautious, it is best not to tell anyone that you have personal notes.

R e f l e c t i o n

Practice drawing a cognitive map, using one of your own problems. Follow the directions in the second suggestion above. After you are finished, consider whether this activity has provided any insight into your problem.

Diagnosis, the DSM-IV-TR, and Theory

As I noted earlier, case conceptualization should not be equated with *diagnosis*, which involves giving a name to the client's problem. Diagnosis is part of case conceptualization, just as recognizing the Big Dipper is part of astronomy. The accuracy of diagnosis varies in importance from theory to theory, but it may be critical in your work setting no matter what your theory.

Many of you will be (or have already been) required to evaluate clients using the *Diagnostic and Statistical Manual of Mental Disorders*—usually called the DSM, followed by the edition abbreviation. This book is published by the American Psychiatric Association (2000) and is the world's most used reference book for classifying psychological problems. The DSM is closely coordinated with the *International Statistical Classification of Diseases and Related Health Problems* (ICD-10; World Health Organization, 1992), the world's official medical coding system. Experts in all fields of mental health contribute to the construction of the DSM, and it is based on scientific studies of patients and clients whose symptoms and characteristics have much in common. The classification helps clinicians and researchers communicate clearly to one another, because the terms are shared and defined. When a physician reads your notation that a client is depressed, he or she knows just what you mean. The book is descriptive, not prescriptive—that is, it describes a group of signs that characterize a certain problem, and includes an essay about how the problem might develop and who is likely to have it, but it does not give advice about how to fix it.

The DSM-IV-TR is also considered *atheoretical*. That is, you cannot discern a consistent theory behind the symptom lists or the descriptive essays. It's desirable to become an expert DSM diagnostician, partly because the book contains the common language of our field. But a diagnosis does not lead directly to a theory of the person and thence to a treatment plan. Your own theoretical expertise is the critical factor in following up a diagnosis with appropriate, effective action. Once a person receives an accurate diagnosis of anxiety, for instance, different theories suggest different therapies—a behaviorist might start with relaxation training, while a psychodynamic therapist would start by investigating family relationships.

The Five DSM Axes

Reporting a DSM diagnosis involves five axes—maybe you can think of them as five different categories related to the client's status. You will give a code or a score on three axes, and a description in words on two axes.

Axis I. Clinical Disorders and Other Conditions That May Be a Focus of Clinical Attention   On Axis I, all mental diagnoses except personality disorders and mental retardation are coded according to the sections of the DSM, along with the severity of the problem. On this axis, you are likely to record the client's presenting problems. The principal diagnosis or reason for the visit comes first, but you can list several diagnoses after that. Most people you see in community practice have Axis I diagnoses.

Axis II. Personality Disorders and Mental Retardation On Axis II are the more lasting and intractable problems of mental retardation and personality disorders, which also have sections in the DSM. There is a code for the absence of these problems, too. The reason for a separate axis for these problems is that they may consistently underlie many Axis I difficulties, and the diagnosis should indicate that you think there is this underlying personality pattern or retardation. On Axis II, you also note maladaptive personality elements that are not quite prominent enough to be called personality disorders—for example, "Axis II. Avoidant Personality Disorder; frequent use of intellectualization."

Axis III. General Medical Conditions Axis III reports on physical conditions and disorders, which, as we know, affect a client's psychological state (and vice versa). You want to communicate medical status in the diagnosis because it may be directly relevant to the development or worsening of the client's mental state. For example, being hypoglycemic can cause a person to experience mood swings, while having a chronically painful condition such as arthritis certainly affects one's view of life's possibilities.

Axis IV. Psychosocial and Environmental Problems Problems the client has in the outside world, such as poverty, housing difficulties, loss of work, jail time, and so forth, are described in words on Axis IV. You also note on this axis the interpersonal stressors influencing the client, such as divorce or friendlessness. Generally, you put down only the problems that have occurred within the last year. However, if a more distant event is still contributing to a mental disorder, you should note that on Axis IV as well. One therapist told me of a client whose ten-year-old divorce is still a focus of treatment.

Axis V. Global Assessment of Functioning Axis V comprises the Global Assessment of Functioning (called the GAF for short), where you give a score from 1 to 100 on an overall judgment of how poorly or well clients are managing their life, and how severe their psychological symptoms are. You should consider psychological, social, and occupational functioning here. The DSM has a description of each ten-point interval on the scale. For example, 1 to 10 is "Persistent danger of severely hurting self or others (e.g., recurrent violence) or persistent inability to maintain minimal personal hygiene or serious suicidal act with clear expectation of death," and 90 to 100 is "Superior functioning in a wide range of activities, life's problems never seem to get out of hand, is sought by others because of his or her many positive qualities. No symptoms." If a client's functioning and symptomatology are at odds, give the GAF that reflects the worse of the two. For example, a person might maintain good hygiene and perform well at work but still have a suicide plan that he considers every day.

The GAF should be below 20. The series of GAF ratings you give someone are particularly helpful for professionals looking at a client's progress over time.

A DSM diagnosis might look like this:

Axis I 300.23	Social phobia
Axis II V71.09	No diagnosis
Axis III	Asthma, skin hives
Axis IV	Career requires frequent transfers from state to state, which are stressful
Axis V	GAF = 59

Sometimes you will see an Axis V expanded, offering a comparison between current status and highest status within the last year:

Axis V	GAF = 59 (current) 78 (in last year)

The cryptic numbers on Axes I and II come from the largest part of the DSM, the classification and criteria for various mental disorders. For each disorder you will find a brief essay describing the disorder, followed by a list of criteria. It is frequently the case that, in order to qualify for a particular diagnosis, the client has to display a certain number of symptoms from a checklist and the problem has to have persisted for a required length of time. To give you a feel for this process, I present below an example of a case from *DSM-IV Case Book* (Spitzer, Gibbon, Skodol, Williams, & First, 1994) followed by a list of diagnostic criteria from DSM-IV-TR.

CASE STUDY: GENERALIZED ANXIETY DISORDER

A 27-year-old married electrician complains of dizziness, sweating palms, heart palpitations, and ringing of the ears of more than 18 months' duration. He has also experienced dry mouth and throat, periods of extreme muscle tension, and a constant "edgy" and watchful feeling that has often interfered with his ability to concentrate. These feelings have been present most of the time over the previous 2 years; they have not been limited to discrete periods. Although these symptoms sometimes make him feel "discouraged," he denies feeling depressed and continues to enjoy activities with his family.

Because of these symptoms the patient had seen a family practitioner, a neurologist, a neurosurgeon, a chiropractor, and an ear-nose-throat specialist. He had been placed on a hypoglycemic diet, received physiotherapy for a pinched nerve, and told he might have "an inner ear problem."

He also has many worries. He constantly worries about the health of his parents. His father, in fact, had a myocardial infarction 2 years previously, but is now feeling well. He also worries about whether he is "a good father," whether his wife will ever leave him (there is no indication that she is dissatisfied with the marriage), and whether he is liked by co-workers on the job. Although he recognizes that his worries are often unfounded, he can't stop worrying.

For the past 2 years the patient has had few social contacts because of his nervous symptoms. Although he has sometimes had to leave work when the symptoms became intolerable, he continues to work for the same company he joined for his apprenticeship following high school graduation. He tends to hide his symptoms from his wife and children, to whom he wants to appear "perfect," and reports few problems with them as a result of his nervousness. (Spitzer et al., 1994, pp. 298–299)

Diagnostic Criteria for Generalized Anxiety Disorder, from DSM-IV-TR

A. Excessive anxiety and worry (apprehensive expectation), occurring more days than not for at least 6 months, about a number of events or activities (such as work or school performance).

B. The person finds it difficult to control the worry.

C. The anxiety and worry are associated with three (or more) of the following six symptoms (with at least some symptoms present for more days than not for the past 6 months). Note: Only one item is required in children.

(1) restlessness or feeling keyed up or on edge

(2) being easily fatigued

(3) difficulty concentrating or mind going blank

(4) irritability

(5) muscle tension

(6) sleep disturbance (difficulty falling or staying asleep, or restless unsatisfying sleep).

D. The focus of the anxiety and worry is not confined to features of an Axis I disorder, e.g., the anxiety or worry is not about having a Panic Attack (as in Panic Disorder), being embarrassed in public (as in Social Phobia), being contaminated (as in Obsessive-Compulsive Disorder), being away from home or close relatives (as in Separation Anxiety Disorder), gaining weight (as in Anorexia Nervosa), having multiple physical complaints (as in Somatization Disorder), or having a serious illness (as in Hypochondriasis), and the anxiety and worry do not occur exclusively during Posttraumatic Stress Disorder.

E. The anxiety, worry, or physical symptoms cause clinically significant distress or impairment in social, occupational, or other important areas of functioning.

F. The disturbance is not due to the direct physiological effects of a substance (e.g., a drug of abuse, a medication) or a general medical condition (e.g., hyperthyroidism) and does not occur exclusively during a Mood Disorder, a Psychotic Disorder, or a Pervasive Developmental Disorder. (American Psychiatric Association, p. 476)

Take note that the third item requires you to count at least three of the symptoms, not all of them (for adults), and also that these symptoms have to have been present half the time over the last six months. ■ ■

DISCUSSION IDEAS

Does the electrician meet the criteria for Generalized Anxiety Disorder? Carefully work through the diagnostic criteria as they apply or do not apply to this client. Be sure you can justify your decision with exact reference to the criteria.

To become proficient in using the DSM, you will need to study it in other coursework or read a supplementary book like *DSM-IV Made Easy: The Clinician's Guide to Diagnosis* (Morrison, 1995). The DSM is not written for the layperson, and without training you could do some harm by diagnosing unwisely.

Criticisms of the DSM

The DSM has been an object of controversy. Some clinicians believe that it encourages pigeonholing people into categories and treating them in terms of their diagnoses rather than as individuals. Keep in mind that people with the same diagnosis vary widely in many other ways, including what treatment will work best. Also, the DSM is not comprehensive. People have problems that are simply not classified by the experts who put together the DSM. And since the DSM is largely based on research done in the United States and Canada, some psychologists fear that it does not apply to cultures that are not well represented here. However, it has been used world-wide with great success (Morrison, 1995). Moreover, the DSM-IV-TR reflects efforts to embrace cultural diversity and describe specific cultural syndromes (APA, 2000, pp. 897–903).

A large problem in the managed care environment, and for the client who returns to treatment periodically, is trailing paperwork indicating diagnoses that may not be precise. I have had clients in a rural mental health center whose paper trail includes fourteen or fifteen Axis I and II diagnoses from various therapists and clinics. You need to be cautious in your diagnosis, making sure that the DSM criteria are really met. You don't want to send a person out into the world with a personality disorder diagnosis (a most serious and difficult problem, which can cause prejudice and suspicion) when you are not absolutely sure. And, you need to be cautious in accepting a previous diagnosis. See for yourself whether you agree.

What I have found is that the DSM helps you ask the right questions. Once you know the DSM well, when you see a set of symptoms that fit a diagnostic profile, you can look up the diagnosis and pursue the question of whether the client fits the diagnosis in other ways. For example, a client who complains of being restless, tired, and irritable needs to be asked whether she worries often. If she replies "I worry all the time!" you need to systematically investigate the other criteria for Generalized Anxiety Disorder. Furthermore, the DSM guides you to diagnoses that are more accurate than a client's vocabulary may encompass. For example, I have noticed that many people report that they are depressed when, in reality, they are anxious. This is a critical distinction for treatment planning. Recall, too, that the DSM provides a common vocabulary for counselors and other helping professionals to use among ourselves.

Observation and Inference in Case Analysis

We all leap to conclusions, all the time. You see a middle-aged person with dirty, ragged clothes shuffling down the street, obviously tired and beat, and you assume that the person is down and out, maybe homeless. But—could it be a college professor who has put on old clothes for the purpose of moving from one house to another, and he is weary from hauling boxes? You meet a client whose parent has just died, and you assume that she is grieving. But—could this be a case in which the client is feeling relief after a long period of caretaking? I remember after moving to the South from the Midwest that, at first, I was often a little surprised when I heard people speaking quite intelligently in deep Southern accents. Embarrassingly, I had associated a strong Southern accent with an ignorant mind, even though intellectually I knew better.

Clear observations and well-examined inferences help us part the clouds of our own internalized cultures.

Making Good Observations

We make the most accurate decisions about personality under four conditions (Funder, 2001):

1. When we are *good judges*—that is, practiced experts in observing behavior. Socially experienced and well-adjusted observers tend to be more accurate since they are used to interacting with others, and their own neuroses don't cloud their perceptions.

2. When we have *good targets*—that is, when clients themselves are not too disorganized cognitively or too interpersonally impaired. Expressiveness on the clients' part helps here, too.

3. When we have *good traits*—that is, visible and obvious behaviors to observe. Traits that are heavily socially desirable, such as loving one's children, are difficult to judge because everyone is motivated to imitate them no matter what.

4. When we have *good information*—that is, information based on observation. More observation is better than less, and ideally we would be making observations across many situations.

In a typical counseling setting, we can't always meet these perfect conditions. We usually observe our clients in only one setting: conversation with us. If our clients express themselves freely, we are lucky; but even if they do not, they are still our clients. What's important to remember is that we do have control over developing our expertise at observation and trying to let go of our own problems and prejudices during the session.

One way we can get good information, even without outside observations, is by using a thorough, structured interview such as one based on Kelly's personal constructs. Having a protocol that covers many areas of the client's life keeps us from zooming in on one that we have particular interest in for our own reasons. We should also have a protocol for making observations about the nonverbal behavior of our client, so that we don't miss anything there. In this connection, remember Carkhuff's (2000) list:

- observing body movements, facial expressions, grooming, body build, and posture;
- suspending personal judgment;
- focusing on the client;
- resisting distractions;
- recalling the client's expressions accurately; and
- noticing common themes in the client's talk.

Two activities can help you expand your skills in observation. First, write detailed notes after each session. My clinical supervisor insisted on notes that separated observations from inferences, a useful exercise that you will try later in this chapter. Writing out your observations makes you process them more thoroughly, helps you be aware of links and contradictions, and lets you know whether there are holes in your surveillance. Second, if you have equipment and client consent to video- or audiotape, it is extremely instructive to let another clinician go over the session and present his or her observations to you. Another person's point of view can surprise you by exposing the lenses you see things through.

Avoiding Inferential Errors

Separating observation from inference is a crucial skill for everyone, but especially for those of us in the helping professions. We need to see clearly the line between facts and inferences—that is, between what we see and hear and how we interpret it. Otherwise, we are prey to inferential errors (Stevens & Morris, 1995) that cloud our judgment and mar our performance. Some of the most common inferential errors are these:

1. *Single-cause etiologies:*   We get hung up on one hypothesis about the root of the client's problem, and can't see other explanations. One of my friends went to a counselor who discovered on intake that, many years ago, she had had an abortion. Even though my friend had made her own peace with her choice, the counselor could not let go of the idea that the abortion was the

cause of her current marital difficulties. My friend finally left the counselor in frustration, feeling unheard.

2. *Availability heuristic:*   We read a compelling piece, listen to a persuasive talk, have a powerful personal experience, or take a fascinating course that keeps a certain point of view foremost in our mind, and then we interpret our clients' problems from that point of view, whether it is appropriate or not. It is highly available in our minds. If you ever take a course in endocrinology, you will see what I mean. Every problem starts looking like an endocrine imbalance!

3. *Confirmatory bias:*   A tendency to notice things that support our hypotheses and to ignore things that disprove our hypotheses is common among us. It is tempting to mentally emphasize clients' remarks that agree with our previous diagnosis, even when they are making an equal number of remarks that call that diagnosis into question.

4. *Fundamental attribution error:*   If *I* walk away from a store counter knowing I got too much change back, I explain it by the situation—I was in a hurry, the item cost way too much in the first place, I got short-changed last time, and so on. If *you* walk away knowing you got too much change, I think you are a little sleazy. This is the fundamental attribution error: We explain our own behavior situationally, and we explain other people's behavior by attributing it to their personality traits and other inherent characteristics. This is unfair. Automatically attributing an instance of behavior to someone's race, sex, religion, color, sexuality, or educational level is similarly unfair. A male artist I know told me that his wife is always getting complimented on the great décor of their apartment, even though he did it all, and she can't tell mauve from taupe!

5. *Illusory correlations:*   Simply by chance, we sometimes see two things occur together often enough that we think they are actually associated. There was a time when psychologists thought that men with two Y chromosomes rather than one were prone to criminality, because they are overrepresented in prison populations. As it turns out, however, such men tend to be larger and dumber than others, so when they commit crimes they are caught more easily. So the association did not mean that double-Y men committed more crimes than other men, just that more of them went to jail when they did.

The popularity of these mental mistakes doesn't mean that you should avoid making inferences. In fact, your job is to infer underlying patterns from the data you gather and to create treatment plans based on your inferences. The point here is that a strong background in psychological theory can help you make good inferences instead of faulty ones. You will have available several coherent ways of looking at a problem, ways that have stood the test of time, and these will help you organize your thoughts free from the prejudices and hasty conclusions rampant in everyday life.

DISCUSSION IDEAS

Discuss your own examples of the inferential errors listed on the previous page. Can you think of any faulty inferences that are not on the list? How does knowledge of inferential errors fit in with psychologists' efforts to be multiculturally aware?

R e f l e c t i o n

Here's an exercise in separating observation and inference. Go to a public place where you can people-watch without being obvious about it. Or, observe people from the back, as you sit behind them in a class or a movie theater. Take detailed notes on one or two of the people you observe. Then, when you get home, write a three-part journal entry in which you first describe your observations and, second, reveal the inferences you made as you watched. In the third part, argue with your own inferences, thinking of others that might be just as good. Finally, going back to the first part, weed out any inferential wording or statements: You will find it is harder than you think.

LIBRARY, MEDIA, AND INTERNET ACTIVITIES

Using the key words *theory* and *psychology* in your library's database, find another textbook on theories of counseling and psychotherapy. As an alternative, your counseling and psychology professors may let you use other such textbooks in their offices, since publishers send them samples. Find the section of the textbook that discusses why theory is important—it is most likely near the beginning of the text—and read another author's perspective on the subject.

REFERENCES

American Psychiatric Association. (2000). *Diagnostic and statistical manual of mental disorders* (4th ed., text revision.). Washington, DC: Author.

Carkhuff, R. R. (2000). *The art of helping in the 21st century* (8th ed.). Amherst, MA: Human Resource Development Press.

Corsini, R. J., & Wedding, D. (1995). *Current psychotherapies* (5th ed.). Itasca, IL: Peacock.

Frank, J. D., & Frank, J. B. (1991). *Persuasion and healing: A comparative study of psychotherapy* (3rd ed.). Baltimore: Johns Hopkins University Press.

Funder, D. C. (2001). Accuracy in personality judgment: Research and theory concerning an obvious question. In B. W. Roberts & R. Hogan (Eds.), *Personality psychology in the workplace* (pp. 121–140). Washington, DC: APA.

Ivey, A. E. (2002). *Intentional interviewing and counseling.* New York: Wadsworth.

Kelly, G. A. (1955). *The psychology of personal constructs* (Vol. 2). New York: W. W. Norton.

Mayfield, W. A., Kardash, C. M., & Kivlighan, D. M. (1999). Differences in experienced and novice counselors' knowledge structures about clients: Implications for case conceptualization. *Journal of Counseling Psychology, 46,* 504–514.

Morrison, J. (1994). *The first interview.* New York: Guilford Press.

Morrison, J. (1995). *DSM-IV made easy: The clinician's guide to diagnosis.* New York: Guilford Press.

Patterson, C. H. (1980). *Theories of counseling and psychotherapy.* New York: Harper & Row.

Roth, A., & Fonagy, P. (1996). *What works for whom: A critical review of psychotherapy research.* New York: Guilford Press.

Seligman, L. (2001). *Systems, strategies, and skills of counseling and psychotherapy.* Upper Saddle River, NJ: Prentice-Hall.

Spitzer, R. L., Gibbon, M., Skodol, A. E., Williams, J. B. W., & First, M. B. (1994). *DSM-IV Case Book* (4th ed.). Washington, DC: American Psychiatric Press.

Stevens, M. J., & Morris, S. J. (1995). A format for case conceptualization. *Counselor Education and Supervision, 35,* 82–94.

World Health Organization. (1992). *International classification of diseases and related mental health problems* (10th ed.). Geneva, Switzerland: Author.

CHAPTER **3**

Ethics in Psychotherapy, Counseling, and Research

The first three chapters of this book focus on topics that are relevant no matter which theory of psychotherapy you eventually adopt. Ethical behavior in your role as a helping professional matters a great deal, and I emphasize it early because it serves as a background for much of your decision making. I include in this third chapter a brief overview of the common principles of ethics. In your curriculum, you probably will have a whole course or a large part of a course that focuses on ethics. If not, you will need to read a book devoted to ethical issues, such as Pope and Vasquez's (1998) *Ethics in Psychotherapy and Counseling*, Kenyon's (1999) *What Would You Do? An Ethical Case Workbook for Human Service Professionals*, or Remley and Herlihy's (2001) *Ethical, Legal, and Professional Issues in Counseling*.

Codes of Ethics

Codes of ethics are published for most helping professions, and they are updated every few years to reflect changes in philosophy and in the world. You must read and understand your code of ethics, as it provides a general framework for making decisions when you encounter an ethical dilemma. When you document your decision process in your notes, you should refer to the code and section upon which you base your thinking. Websites for most codes of ethics are listed at the end of this chapter.

Since you have chosen a helping profession, you are most likely a decent person with humanitarian values. But these qualities don't always define exactly what you should do in every situation, do they? The same is true of the ethics you apply in counseling and psychotherapy. You must combine the written ethical code of your profession with your own interpretation and judgment. Later in the chapter, I will summarize main points that the ethical codes share and refer you to the codes in print. But for now, as an interesting introduction to this subject, let me suggest some typical situations to ponder. You can discuss these with classmates, friends, and family from a common-sense point of view. What are the pros and cons of the various courses of action you might take?

1. Your client, an electrician, offers to help you put up a new ceiling fan in your waiting room. You have been intending to install it but have procrastinated because you're not sure you can do it. Should you let your client help you?

2. One of your track teammates casually remarks, "Oh, my friend Sue is seeing you for counseling! She says you are really helping her." What do you say?

3. You saw Sharon as a client for seven months, helping her get back on her feet after an abrupt and ugly romantic break-up. Six months after she leaves therapy, she sends you a joyous invitation to her wedding. Will you go?

4. You are running a research study comparing two treatments for depression, both of which are considered effective. Your friend has a 30-year-old daughter who suffers from depression, and she begs you to let her daughter into your

study, where she can receive treatment free of charge. Do you accept the daughter as a research participant?

5. After seeing a client for about six months, making great progress, you realize that you are preoccupied with him outside of session, and you find yourself thinking about him sexually. What do you do?

6. You occasionally counsel a student in the middle school where you work in guidance. The student's mother interviews for the position of secretary in the guidance department. Do you need to take any action?

7. You are seeing a couple for marriage counseling. They freely admit that the husband often slaps the wife. Both agree that in their culture, this behavior is common and considered okay, in order to keep the wife in her place. What do you do?

8. You gave your 10-year-old client an IQ test and reported the results to your client and his father. The father wants you to hand over the test so he can see exactly which items his child missed. Do you give it to him?

9. Your agency performs psychological assessments for the school system. You assess a truant high school student and report that he has no diagnosable mental disorder. However, your agency reminds you that unless you give him a diagnosis of mental disorder, the school system will not pay for the assessment and his parents will be billed. Do you change your report?

How Professionals Know Their Ethical Responsibilities

The American Counseling Association Code of Ethics (2002) and the American Psychological Association Ethical Principles of Psychologists and Code of Conduct (2002) serve as good examples of most ethics codes in the helping professions. Membership in the ACA or APA commits you to following these codes, and this commitment holds in other helping professions, too. By violating the ethics code, you may or may not be violating the law. The Ethics Committee of each professional organization acts separately from the law and justice system; nevertheless, it can take a range of actions, from reprimand to expulsion from your professional organization, and can also refer your violation to other bodies, including the long arm of the law. Like most ethics codes, the ACA's version provides general principles as well as more specific standards of practice.

Five General Principles for Ethical Practice

The APA's ethics code begins with a statement of purpose: "to provide specific standards to cover most situations encountered by psychologists." Its General Principles provide overall points of view that psychologists should adopt, and its Ethical Standards apply the principles to more specific situations, such as whether you can barter with a client rather than deal in cash, how to keep records of your therapy, and when you must break confidentiality. The decision rules themselves are often very general and open to interpretation, so you may still not be out of the woods even if your problem is addressed there. For example, if a court wants you to produce something that your ethics code says you should not reveal due to confidentiality, here is the decision rule: "If psychologists' ethical responsibilities conflict with law, regulations, or other governing legal authority, psychologists make known their commitment to this Ethics Code and take steps to resolve the conflict in a responsible manner." In a situation like this, one tactic is to return to the General Principles and think about how they apply to your problem. Below are the APA's General Principles (which, again, are very similar to the ACA and other organizations' principles, including the American College of Physicians Ethics Manual [1998]). As you read them, refer back to the dilemmas at the beginning of the chapter. Underline or highlight sentences that apply to one or more of the dilemmas.

Principle A: Beneficence and Nonmaleficence

Psychologists strive to benefit those with whom they work and take care to do no harm. In their professional actions, psychologists seek to safeguard the welfare and rights of those with whom they interact professionally and other affected persons, and the welfare of animal subjects of research. When conflicts occur among psychologists' obligations or concerns, they attempt to resolve these conflicts in a responsible fashion that avoids or minimizes harm. Because psychologists' scientific and professional judgments and actions may affect the lives of others, they are alert to and guard against personal, financial, social, organizational, or political factors that might lead to misuse of their influence. Psychologists strive to be aware of the possible effects of their own physical and mental health on their ability to help those with whom they work.

Principle B: Fidelity and Responsibility

Psychologists establish relationships of trust with those with whom they work. They are aware of their professional and scientific responsibilities to society and to the specific communities in which they work. Psychologists uphold professional standards of conduct, clarify their professional roles and obligations, accept appropriate responsibility for their behavior, and seek to manage conflicts of interest that could lead to exploitation or harm. Psychologists consult with, refer to, or cooperate with other professionals and institutions to the extent needed to serve the best interests of those with whom they work. They are concerned about the ethical compliance of their colleagues' scientific and professional conduct. Psychologists strive to contribute a portion of their professional time for little or no compensation or personal advantage.

Principle C: Integrity

Psychologists seek to promote accuracy, honesty, and truthfulness in the science, teaching, and practice of psychology. In these activities psychologists do not steal, cheat, or engage in fraud, subterfuge, or intentional misrepresentation of fact. Psychologists strive to keep their promises and to avoid unwise or unclear commitments. In situations in which deception may be ethically justifiable to maximize benefits and minimize harm, psychologists have a serious obligation to consider the need for, the possible consequences of, and their responsibility to correct any resulting mistrust or other harmful effects that arise from the use of such techniques.

Principle D: Justice

Psychologists recognize that fairness and justice entitle all persons to access to and benefit from the contributions of psychology and to equal quality in the processes, procedures, and services being conducted by psychologists. Psychologists exercise reasonable judgment and take precautions to ensure that their potential biases, the boundaries of their competence, and the limitations of their expertise do not lead to or condone unjust practices.

Principle E: Respect for People's Rights and Dignity

Psychologists respect the dignity and worth of all people, and the rights of individuals to privacy, confidentiality, and self-determination. Psychologists are aware that special safeguards may be necessary to protect the rights and welfare of persons or communities whose vulnerabilities impair autonomous decision making. Psychologists are aware of and respect cultural, individual, and role differences, including those based on age, gender, gender identity, race, ethnicity, culture, national origin, religion, sexual orientation, disability, language, and socioeconomic status and consider these factors when working with members of such groups. Psychologists try to eliminate the effect on their work of biases based on those factors, and they do not knowingly participate in or condone activities of others based upon such prejudices.

SMALL GROUP EXERCISE

Divide the dilemmas from the opening of this chapter among several small groups in your class. Looking at both the ACA's code of ethics and the APA's General Principles, discuss the options the counselor has in each of your group's assigned dilemmas. Can you agree on a course of action? What principles did you use in accepting or ruling out various options? Who could you consult to help you make decisions?

Profile of an Ethicist

KEN POPE

Ken Pope's career in psychology has been marked by his commitment to making psychological services available to underserved and neglected populations. Through practice, research, and writing, Ken has consistently sought ways to apply findings in the field to those who are least likely to seek help for themselves—namely, those who have faced severe adversity or oppression. This interest has naturally coincided with his care for fairness and client protection, reflected in *Ethics in Psychotherapy and Counseling* (1998), which he co-authored with Melba Vasquez (see Chapter 11).

Ken was raised in the small West Texas town of Breckenridge, and spent time in Austin, Dallas, and Houston as well. While attending Southern Methodist University in Dallas, he was inspired by Saul Alinsky's work on community organization. After graduating with a B.A. in English, Ken moved to Chicago to work directly with the Alinsky organization. He then relocated to Florida, where he worked in an impoverished inner-city community during the 1960s and 1970s. Through his work, Ken witnessed firsthand the injustices of poverty, racism, and sexism. He began to challenge the social, institutional, and psychological forces that maintained the status quo and hindered advancement for marginalized populations.

Following his time in Florida, Ken returned to graduate school at Harvard, where he received an M.A. in English and then began studying psychology. Harvard did not offer a doctorate in clinical psychology at the time, so Ken transferred to Yale to complete his Ph.D. After graduating, he worked as the psychology director in a hospital and community health center, where he continued to develop and promote programs targeted at those with limited resources.

Throughout his studies and professional career, Ken has built a reputation for confronting aspects of psychology that are messy or complex, and encouraging other mental health professionals to do so as well. For example, he has conducted research and written numerous articles and books on topics such as psychologists' negative feelings toward their clients, processes of ethical decision making, and the impact of client-therapist sex. He has received numerous awards and citations for his commitment to public service and his continued efforts to advance the field of psychology. On multiple occasions, Ken has acknowledged the importance—to his own career as well as to the profession—of remaining open to new ways of thinking, altering, and applying one's knowledge of psychological functioning. A leader in the field, Ken Pope, throughout a career spanning more than three decades, has overtly blended the experience of the individual with larger social and contextual influences.

Ethics in Daily Practice

Let me expand on a few of the ways that ethical principles—including competence, integrity, scientific and professional responsibility, respect for people's rights and dignity, concern for others' welfare, and social responsibility—will directly affect your practice from day one.

The Client's Best Interests

In their classic text, *The Skills of Helping*, Carkhuff and Anthony (1979) wrote, "One of the most documented principles of helping is that all helping is for better or worse" (p. 3). This is a blunt statement coming from some pretty cautious guys, so it bears weight. No client is left unchanged by your efforts: Some clients improve their functioning and emotional state, some confirm their idea that change is hopeless, and some end up worse than before. Your behavior affects which path is taken. This is why I exhort you to think about the ethical meanings of what you do. The codes you follow are designed to help you make decisions that will enhance your clients' conditions. We will go into five topics that are sure to come up as you work in the helping field.

Avoid Exploitation   When you read Principle A of the ACA's code of ethics and the APA's General Principles, you saw that the client's needs are considered paramount. You should always ask yourself if your course of action might harm your client, directly or indirectly. The people you help should feel that they are respected and valued by you, and that in your professional relationship they are the focus of your attention.

Such statements may seem obvious to you, but the situation is trickier than it seems. For example, following the "avoid exploitation" principle involves looking into your own heart and asking whether you are meeting your own needs more than the client's when you are counseling. We all have needs for respect, power, and friendship, and many of us get these needs fulfilled in our professions. We also need to work out our aggressive impulses and our conflicts. But the therapy session should not be dominated by these forces. You will see what I mean if you think about a friendship you have or had, in which you have suspected that the relationship serves the other person more than it does you—the other person takes more than he or she gives, and you feel a bit used. You would *really* feel used if you were asking for help and paying for this relationship!

When we are counseling, often we carry the ball in determining the direction of the conversation: We ask the questions, we interpret, we focus on certain elements and not on others. Our own experiences should not take over this process. When I was in training, my supervisor once said, "Do you think it's a *coincidence* that every woman client you see has trouble with her mother?" Of course it was not a coincidence. My own problematic relationship caused me to indicate a lot of interest when a woman brought up difficulties with her mom. I had to learn not to pursue a topic of my own within my clients' array of stories.

One subtle way that counselors may exploit clients is by keeping them in therapy when no progress is expected. A counselor may enjoy the client's personality even after problems are resolved, or avoid the thought that the therapy is not working, or wish to keep collecting fees, and therefore not close the relationship or refer the client to someone else. Similarly, you may be fulfilling your needs to have someone dependent on you for his or her well-being, and thus may encourage a state of neediness in your client. In some cases, you may relish being the object of a client's romantic crush, and prolong it. One check on whether you are putting your client first is to evaluate frankly whether you have treatment plans and goals that are attainable, and whether you keep these plans and goals updated and discuss them with the client. This way, you both know why you are there.

SMALL GROUP EXERCISE

Discuss how your own inner conflicts might affect your counseling. Are there certain problems or types of people likely to push your buttons? Why? How do you think you can best handle such a situation? If some of your conflicts are too personal to discuss, write about them in your journal and think about how you will deal with them as a helping professional.

Practice Informed Consent   Respecting and valuing the client includes letting him or her in on what will happen in therapy. Some clients don't know what to expect. Others may want to go to a different counselor once they know what techniques you are likely to use or what theory you espouse. Therapists usually print up a document about goals, techniques, theory, fees, expectations, and such matters. After giving this document to clients, they discuss each point to be sure the clients understand what they're getting into. Clients then sign the document, showing agreement to undergo treatment, which is called *informed consent*. You will have such a form provided if you work in an organization like a clinic or university mental health center, and you can add whatever else you wish your clients to know in advance. When you write your own document, remember that you must use wording that a nonexpert can grasp quickly. You don't want to drown your clients in theoretical or technical seas. Some topics are better discussed in the ongoing process of counseling, while others need to be clear at the outset.

Clients who are young (under 18 in some states and under 16 in others) may need a parent or guardian to sign for informed consent. Find out what your own state laws require. In several states, young clients can seek help for certain problems without parental knowledge or consent—problems such as pregnancy, sexually transmitted diseases, and drug abuse, for which the state places help for the troubled youth above parental rights. Even when a parent gives the informed consent, you need to provide the youngster with as much information about counseling and your intentions as possible. You might have the child sign an information sheet geared to his or her age.

Respect Confidentiality   By this time in your education, you know that your clients expect what goes on between you to be confidential; that is, you will tell no one. Otherwise, how can they trust you with their secrets, deepest thoughts, and most naked emotions? We build an atmosphere of trust and freedom by guaranteeing that the client's privacy is protected, and we must stick to that. When we consult with colleagues about a case, as we often do, we must try not to divulge anything that would identify the person individually, and we should not discuss anything other than the relevant details, no matter how interesting we find the tale. As a trainee, you will be speaking openly with your supervisor about your cases, and your supervisor is bound by confidentiality to protect both you and your clients. You will also give case presentations in your classes; in these, you should make sure that the client's identity is disguised. Leave out demographic facts that are not important to your conceptualization (for example, whether someone is from Chicago or Milwaukee). Check any paperwork you bring or pass out to make sure that the client's name, social security number, or clinical case number is blacked out, and collect all of the paperwork when you are finished. Be sure to tell your clients from the beginning that you will be speaking with your supervisor about them, and that you may consult with other professionals, emphasizing that these other professionals are also obliged to maintain confidentiality. Even when you are asked, you should not acknowledge that you are seeing someone: Part of confidentiality involves protecting clients from public knowledge that they are receiving therapy at all.

In some circumstances, confidentiality is properly broken. In 1976, the California Supreme Court ruled in a famous case, *Tarasoff v. Board of Regents of the University of California*. A counselee at the university mental health center told his therapist that he intended to kill his girlfriend. Though the therapist alerted the police, he did not alert the girlfriend. Two months later, the client did kill her. The court decided that the failure to warn the victim was irresponsible, and, since then, psychologists have considered themselves bound to warn an intended victim against harm in such cases. You'll hear this called "the Tarasoff rule" or "the Tarasoff decision." Exactly how it is put into action is a matter of lively debate. Generally, your client needs to make a threat that you *believe* against an *identifiable* victim before you must take action to protect the victim. You have to use your judgment about what statements in sessions are likely to be acted upon; for example, an irate student saying that he felt like killing a professor who flunked him, in the absence of other clues that he is violent, is most likely expressing a strong feeling rather than a plan to murder. If you work in an organization, your workplace will have a set of guidelines for dealing with potentially violent clients, and you should make sure to follow these. If you must make the decision privately, you need to have your own set of guidelines to follow. Read current writings on the Tarasoff decision, which will have up-to-date positions on handling the situation.

Other situations in which you must break confidentiality include the following:

- when child abuse is revealed within therapy,
- when your client is suicidal and you must involve outsiders to protect his or her life,
- when the court subpoenas records, and
- when clients request the release of records.

You break confidentiality in a limited way when you submit bills to an insurance company or managed care firm, inasmuch as you are giving out clients' names and usually diagnoses; some insurers also want treatment plans.

Psychotherapists disagree about whether to list all of these exceptions when a client first appears. A client with a career decision problem may be bewildered to hear cautions concerning murder, suicide, and child abuse in her initial session. On the other hand, clients do need to know, before the fact, when they cannot expect privacy. Many therapists put these cautions onto a printed form and give it out to all clients as a standard procedure, along with the informed consent material. By doing so you can help the client understand that you are not predicting violence in his or her specific case.

Overall, remember that you must not only promise confidentiality but show your commitment to it. If you talk about clients in the elevator, even without using names, someone in that elevator may notice that you are loose-lipped, or they may even know who you are talking about and pass it on. Tossing case folders into the back seat of your car, labeled with names or initials, gives the appearance of carelessness about privacy. Leaving paperwork out on your desk or on a table at home also suggests a thoughtless attitude.

Maintaining confidentiality often involves being clear on just who is your client. When you counsel patients in a hospital, are you working for the hospital or the patients? If you are expected to report on a patient to the doctors and nurses, you need to be sure that the patient understands this. In the same manner, when a court asks you to evaluate a person, you are working for the court and must report to its agents. The person you evaluate needs to know that you are not *his or her* psychologist.

When children have the legal capacity to give informed consent (this age differs state by state between 12 and 18, and sometimes by situation such as drug treatment), their confidentiality is protected even from their parents, in most cases (DeKraai & Sales, 1991). When the children are minors and a parent or other adult substitute has given informed consent, parents' requests for access to therapy information are dealt with on a case-by-case basis. The best course is to get the parents to sign an agreement that the children's treatment will remain confidential, ahead of time. When the children have been promised confidentiality, the counselor believes that confidentiality is in their best interests, and the children themselves do not want the material disclosed, the parents should be denied access. They can then seek it legally, and the court will determine whether the therapist must break confidentiality. When an agency such as a school or court requests that a child be seen in therapy and expects a report, the child should know from the outset that the contact is not confidential, and that there are advantages and disadvantages of cooperating in counseling (Reisman & Ribordy, 1993).

Reflection

Read more about the Tarasoff implications by visiting these helpful websites: *http://mercury.sfsu.edu/~swpersp/tarasoff.htm* and *http://mentalhealth.about.com/cs/legalissuessw.* Type "Tarasoff" into your web browser, such as Yahoo! or Lycos, and you will find further readings to inform your thinking about this important decision. Write up your own guidelines to follow in situations where a client makes a violent statement.

Friends and Acquaintances My friends and acquaintances often say, "Hey, you're a psychologist. Maybe you can help me with this problem I have." I always reply, "I can help you as a friend, but not as a psychologist. I'll give you my opinion, my advice, and my personal experiences, which I rarely do in my professional work, so I love to do it in my private life!" As someone who understands psychology, you will find yourself in a similar position, and maybe you already have. There's no reason not to use your knowledge to help out a friend, if you can, but you shouldn't take on friends as clients. The same goes for family members, students, and colleagues.

Avoid Dual Relationships Dual relationships, or multiple relationships, occur when you play more than one role in a client's life, and vice versa. Most counselors agree that dual relationships should be avoided whenever possible. You can refuse to be your uncle's therapist but still bend his ear with your advice. And though you can enjoy a train ride interpreting the dreams of your fellow passengers, you would never dream of charging them for it! Problems occur when you take a *professional* role along with other roles. This can happen when you accept people you already know into therapy with you, or when you enter into other roles with clients you already have.

SMALL GROUP EXERCISE

As a whole group, predict what problems might arise if you took on the following multiple roles:

1. Taking on your child's teacher as a paying client for psychotherapy
2. Accepting help on your taxes from a client who is an accountant

3. Going to a party given by a client
4. Taking on your best friend as a paying client for career assessment
5. Being on a church committee with a paying client
6. Trading counseling sessions for handyperson work on your house
7. Inviting a client to your wedding
8. Taking on a client's husband as a paying client

The examples in this group exercise show a range of difficulty in management. This range usually reflects how intimate each relationship is, and how much power imbalance is inherent in each one. An intimacy like friendship often rules out a professional therapeutic relationship: You are not objective about your friends, because you love them. In a counseling arrangement, the therapist is almost always seen as more powerful than the client (whether you like it or not), so you enter a business, barter, or committee relationship with a client in an unequal position. And what if you find fault with your new faucets, after bartering with a client for them? What if the client thinks that she worked too hard for a so-so therapy session? Things get touchy.

I have worked in two very small towns. In these settings, I was bound to have some level of dual relationship with clients. The checkout clerk in the little grocery store was a client, and so was the mail carrier's brother. If I wanted to hire a short-haul delivery truck, the only person to hire it from was a client. And I often ended up with two clients who were each other's friend or enemy, in kind of a dual-role once-removed. When multiple roles coexist naturally, you should (1) keep the secondary role as nonintimate as feasible and (2) make decisions with the client about how to manage the situation. For example, some clients prefer that you *not* greet them on the street, since they might be hard-pressed to explain to a companion how you know each other. Others would feel slighted if you passed them by. So you want to clarify rules of behavior. Many counselors who work in small communities prefer to live in another town nearby and commute to work, thus avoiding everyday role proliferation.

After you are out of the formal therapeutic relationship, can you become friends with your clients? Should an ex-client become your accountant? These are interesting questions, and a single answer is not forthcoming. Some experts believe that becoming friends with ex-clients is common and harmless, while others believe that it should be avoided completely. On the friendship side is the argument that most of the time, two people come to know and like each other through some more formal association like work or school or church, and it is natural to follow through informally if both parties want to. Why shouldn't two people who meet on the formal basis of counseling follow through in a similar way? On the avoidance side is the argument that once you are someone's therapist, you will always carry that role with you into another relationship, including the power imbalance between therapist and client.

My own argument on the avoidance side is that your client carries an *idea* of you away from therapy, an image of your support, wisdom, warmth, and even your confrontation. Frequently, you hear people say that they consult an image of their former therapist in their mind at various times. "What would Dr. Lewis say?" In becoming a friend, however, you become a real person with your own flaws and habits and crazy spots, and that helpful image of *you as therapist* fades. Furthermore, if your ex-client ever wanted to return to therapy, he or she would have to go to someone else, since your shift back to therapist would be implausible. This return is something to think about, because one possibility for the future of psychotherapy is to model itself after the family doctor system, in which people come in and out of therapy with the same counselor whenever needed, over a lifetime (Cummings, 1987).

In situations involving dual relationships, three considerations can guide your decisions (Smith, 2003):

- *Power differences.* If one person has power over the other, or if the power relationship is complicated, a dual-role situation can become sticky. For example, a co-therapist in a group may offer to do childcare for you in a pinch. This is fine unless you are supervising or evaluating your co-therapist, in which case you can never be sure whether you are exploiting your power when you accept favors.

- *Length of contact.* When the dual relationship exists only briefly and at one time, fewer problems are foreseen than in situations where it is lengthy or repeated. For example, few of us would balk at a short, structured friendly relationship with clients such as going to their wedding or their parent's funeral, when invited. On the other hand, volunteering to be on a standing church committee with a client is a lengthy commitment to a dual role.

- *Termination.* When you are tempted to become friendly or to take on some other relationship with a former client, be sure that both of you agree that your client-counselor relationship is over. Your ex-client should concur that he or she will find a different counselor in the future if the need arises.

Sexual Relationships

Sexual relationships with current clients not only violate dual-role guidelines but also break the rule of putting the clients' welfare first. Here, the power imbalance is unavoidable, and the therapist can take advantage of a confused, troubled person. Therapists who do this are putting their own needs first—needs not only for sexual gratification but for power and control, too. All ethics codes in the helping professions decree that sexual intimacies with current clients are beyond the pale. The harmfulness of sexual intimacies with clients has been supported by research (Pope, 1994). Feeling exploited, clients can report you to your professional ethics board and sue you for malpractice (not to mention vandalizing your truck or shooting at you as you mow the lawn). In several states, sexual exploitation of clients is a crime for which you can be jailed. In academia, psychology professors should apply the same brakes regarding sexual contact with students, and the same goes for supervisors with counselors-in-training.

Like the friendship question, the matter of sex after therapy is over does not meet such unified rejection. ACA Code A.7.b. places a minimum of two years between professional and sexual contact and requires the counselor to examine the potentials for exploitive relationships. Similarly, the APA's code of ethics hesitates to ban sexual intimacies with former clients, although it restricts the practice heavily:

> Psychologists do not engage in sexual intimacies with former therapy patients and clients even after a two-year interval except in the most unusual circumstances. The psychologist who engages in such activity after the two years following cessa-tion or termination of treatment bears the burden of demonstrating that there has been no exploitation, in light of all relevant factors, including (1) the amount of time that has passed since therapy terminated, (2) the nature and duration of the therapy, (3) the circumstances of termination, (4) the patient's or client's personal history, (5) the patient's or client's current mental status, (6) the likelihood of ad-verse impact on the patient or client and others, and (7) any statements or actions made by the therapist during the course of therapy suggesting or inviting the possibility of a post-termination sexual or romantic relationship with the patient or client. (1995, Section 4.07)

Such restrictions make it quite unlikely that a sexual relationship even after two years could be justified ethically. Furthermore, having sexual relationships with former clients, even if ethical in the literal sense, fuels a negative stereo-type of our profession among the community. There are more than enough news flashes, TV shows, and films that portray us as sex-obsessed phonies, and we need to avoid even the appearance of bad behavior in this realm.

In therapy, as in the rest of your life, knowing that you should not have sex with someone doesn't automatically mean you don't want to. Having sexual feel-ings toward clients is very common among therapists. We are engaged in an intimate, deep process with our clients, and we do learn to like almost all of them. These are conditions that lead to physical intimacy in private life, so it's no sur-prise that they sometimes operate in the wrong places, too. When you are sex-ually attracted to a client, you need to analyze your feelings and where they come from. What needs are being pulled upon? How could they be addressed in your private life, instead of in your professional life? Consulting with a supervisor or another psychotherapist about the problem is usually helpful. Realize that you may need to refer the client to a different therapist if your feelings persist and interfere with the counseling process. When a client appears to be sexually at-tracted to you, you need to address the matter with similar straightforwardness.

SMALL GROUP EXERCISE

In a small group, discuss the problem of clients who develop romantic feel-ings for you. What signs do you think you would see as the feelings develop? At what point, if any, do you need to bring the problem into the open with the client? Can the therapeutic process ever benefit from this situation, or should you always consider referring the client elsewhere? Report on your discussion to the class as a whole.

Using Standardized Tests Responsibly

Just as diagnosis is a topic of debate, so is testing, and for the same reasons. In Chapter 2, you read about how some psychologists believe that diagnosis, using the DSM system, tends to label or pigeonhole people. It may encourage us to think of the client as a member of a diagnostic category rather than as a whole human being. Using standardized tests in counseling falls under the same cloud. A person is much more than a profile of numbers to be compared against the average profile of numbers. However, just as I defend DSM diagnosis as a useful tool, I defend using standardized psychological tests as an adjunct to therapy. Sometimes the tests themselves are therapeutic; for example, you see couples who understand their relationship better after they each take a test of values or needs.

I once gave the Edwards Personal Preference Schedule (EPPS; Edwards, 1959) to a couple who were unsatisfied with their domestic life. Both women had demanding jobs that they enjoyed, but their home life was disappointing. The EPPS profile provides a list of needs in order of their importance to the individual. When my clients compared their profiles, they saw that each partner had a very high need for *succorance* (the need to be cared for, comforted, and protected), while both of them had a very low need for *nurturance* (the need to care for, comfort, and protect). In other words, both of them wanted to be nurtured, and neither of them wanted to do the nurturing! This was an important insight and helped direct what to do next in therapy. Remember, the test didn't say what to *do* about the situation; it just clarified what the situation was.

The Value of Assessments   In this kind of way, many tests of personality, interests, values, needs, cognitive status, and psychopathology can be valuable. But you need to be sure that you know why you are giving the test—that is, what you want to learn from it. A scatter-shot approach, in which you give the client lots of inventories and tests, may swamp you and fatigue the client needlessly. Pinpoint exactly what you need to know, and use a test that will give you that information. Furthermore, use a test that has been widely used, with a manual that provides information about the reliability and validity of the test (whether it measures accurately, and whether it measures what it claims to measure), and about how to interpret the scores. In general, don't use a test unless you've studied its administration under supervision or in a class. Many psychological tests would be difficult to learn on your own, including both how to give them and how to interpret the results. Your workplace may employ a psychometrician, a person trained in giving several different tests, who will administer and score the ones you choose; however, you still need to learn how to interpret the scores meaningfully. One reason for seeking supervision or consultation when interpreting scores is that you want to be careful about biased judgments—that is, paying attention to certain scores because they fit in with preconceptions about the client based on sex, color, religion, ethnicity, and so forth.

Include your client in the process of testing. Discuss why you are interested in giving the test, and let the client decide whether he or she wants to take it. Let clients know what they will find out from the results. Presenting results well is a genuine skill: You don't want your clients to feel reduced to numbers and codes, and you need to avoid undermining their hopes with bad news. Hanson, Claiborn, and Kerr (1997) studied two styles of giving test feedback. In the first style, the counselor pointed out notable scores and gave the client interpretations and examples of the concepts represented by the scores. In the second style, the counselor asked the client to point out high and low scores, then described what the scores meant, and, finally, had the client provide examples, if possible, and draw conclusions about him- or herself. The second, more interactive style allowed the clients to see the counselors as more expert, trustworthy, and attractive. Overall, clients who participate in the whole testing process are more likely to benefit from its discoveries.

SMALL GROUP EXERCISE

Take three minutes or so to jot down your memories of a testing situation you recall, from any time in your life. Examples could come from achievement testing, college entrance tests, job application tests, career interest inventories, classroom exams, medical tests, and so on. Try to remember how the test was administered, your thoughts and feelings, and the results and how you received them. Discuss in class some of the positive and negative experiences students have had with testing. What made the positive experiences good? What could have been done to improve the bad experiences?

Test Security   Psychological tests of quality are extremely difficult to construct, to check for reliability, and to norm (that is, to set the standards for what constitutes a high and a low score on a scale, in comparison with other people's scores). If test items and tasks become public, the work that's gone into creating the test is compromised. To clarify, consider an easy example. The typing test you take for a job is a fairly good measure of how well you can type. However, if you got hold of the exact passage used in the test, in advance, you could achieve results much higher than your abilities. This is why even your testing and measurement textbooks don't give real test items as examples when explaining a test: They give items that are similar but not exact duplicates. Also, most test publishers require proof of your educational background before letting you order tests to use. You are obliged by ethical standards to help protect the security of test content. Don't send standard psychological tests to clients through the mail, and don't allow clients to take tests home. As a trainee, when you share printed matter and results, be sure that test materials are not left lying around or in an open-ended mailbox.

Test results also need to be treated the same way as other client information. Your client should be assured that the results will not be seen by anyone who has no right to them. Raw test results are rarely shared due to the weird interpretations that nonexperts could make. A written summary of test outcomes is more exact and informative, although release of such a document would still require your client's consent. You should insist on sharing a summary report rather than raw scores or test materials even when the materials are required in court.

Using the Belmont Principles to Guide Research

In this textbook, I will frequently refer to the research that has been done to support or critique various theories of psychotherapy. Researchers design controlled studies on various features of therapy: One example is the study I summarized above, in which clients were given one of two kinds of test feedback. After the feedback, both groups completed inventories asking them to rate their counselors, and the two groups' ratings were compared, finding that the interactive kind of feedback produced better impressions of the counselor. Other research is done on how the course of therapy unfolds, and whether the client gets better: These are called *process and outcome studies*. Many psychotherapy studies focus on one or a small number of clients to explore how (and whether) counseling works. If you decide to enter this fascinating pursuit, there are ethical guidelines to make sure that you protect the participants while gathering trustworthy information. You should also use these rules when evaluating the research that you read in books and journals.

Psychologists' research efforts are guided by the Belmont Principles, which came from a 1978 meeting of the National Commission for the Protection of Human Subjects in Biomedical and Behavioral Research. These are three general ethical principles, upon which specific rules and decisions should be based.

Respect for persons: This principle comprises two points of view on how people should be treated: autonomy and protection. Individuals should be treated as free, self-determining agents unless they are incapacitated due to illness, mental disability, or other restrictions on judgment, such as immaturity in children. Even for those in the incapacitated group, degrees of autonomy should be observed. How much they are protected depends on the risk of harm and the degree of benefit from any course of action. The principle of respect for persons means that individuals should knowingly consent to participate in experiments—and be aware of the risks and benefits involved—to the fullest extent of their capability. If they cannot be fully aware, it is your duty to protect them.

Beneficence: You are not only bound to respect people's decisions and protect them from harm; you are also obliged to maximize the benefits and minimize the harm. You must decide whether it is justifiable to take some risks in order to gain knowledge that will benefit humanity as a whole. For example, some studies experimentally lower participants' self-esteem by giving them negative feedback, and then explore how the lowered self-esteem makes them behave (e.g., will they judge others more harshly?). But is creating a bad feeling in these participants worth the trade-off of finding out about the effects of low self-esteem?

Justice: This principle encourages you to think about the fairness of the research you do. Who receives the most benefits, and who bears the burden? Research done on institutionalized mental patients and jailed criminals in the past has not benefited them, but has instead helped the free and intact population. An example is the 1940s Tuskegee syphilis study, in which poor, rural Black men were deprived of treatment for syphilis in order to study the course of the disease. This was clearly unfair and exploitive. A more veiled instance occurs when public funds are used for research on costly treatments that will benefit only those who can afford them.

The principles of respect, beneficence, and justice are good cornerstones not only for making decisions in research but for dealing with clients and colleagues in general.

SMALL GROUP EXERCISE

In your small group, follow up on the dilemmas you discussed in an earlier exercise. Would you change any of your decisions? Why? Did you find support in the chapter for any of your decisions?

Ethical Dilemmas: Safeguarding Your Decisions Step by Step

When you are faced with an ethical dilemma, safeguards should immediately kick in. It's best to decide ahead of time on a sequence of steps that will guide your decision, and these will most likely include conceptualizing the problem, referring to ethical codes and guidelines, and consulting with other helping professionals. Keep a written record of the episode as it unfolds:

1. In your clinical notes, you need to document your decision-making process and what actions you take. Include descriptions of events that spurred you to define the situation as an ethical dilemma, and keep an ongoing record as the situation develops. Date each entry.

2. Include in your documentation the ethical principles that are behind your decision. Note down the sections and numbers of the principles and standards you consider relevant. If you ever need to prove that you have exercised care in your actions, this documentation will be valuable.

3. Discussing the situation with other helping professionals can help you make tough decisions. Your supervisor, training director, or a more experienced colleague may have a point of view that clarifies your problem skillfully. These experts may also offer emotional support for you, and they may be able to point out how your own personality, world view, or conflicts are affecting the problem.

4. Besides giving assistance, consultation with another professional proves that you attempted to do the right thing. Be sure to document the consultation.

Culturally Sensitive Counseling

The Belmont Principles of respect for persons, beneficence, and fairness, as well as helping-profession ethics of beneficence and nonmaleficence, integrity, and respect for people's rights and dignity, clearly require us to deliver services unbiased by our clients' age, sex, ethnicity, nationality, physical ability, or any other identifiable group marker. Historically, counseling and psychotherapy have been practiced by White people from the middle and upper classes (Sue & Sue, 1999). And the values, qualities, and lifestyles considered optimal were often defined by White, middle- and upper-class standards. These standards blurred counselors' vision when they tried to analyze the distress of people who were not from the same background. Mainstream counselors found that even the goals of therapy, the very definition of mental health, might change with the group membership of the client. In 1990, the American Psychological Association approved *Guidelines for Providers of Psychological Services to Ethnic, Linguistic, and Culturally Diverse Populations*.

Socioeconomic and Religious Issues

Two illustrations will make the idea clear. Therapists used to learn that breaking away from parental rule was a natural and desirable task of adolescence and early adulthood; however, among some socioeconomic, ethnic, and religious groups even grown children are expected to follow their parents' wishes as long as the parents are alive, and, for them, *this* seems natural and right. These clients would reject a therapist's pep talk on standing up against parental authority, and client and counselor would be mystified by each other's stance. Similarly, therapists used to learn that a client's spiritual life was not their business; yet now it is clear that, for many people, spiritual life is intertwined with their psychological well-being.

Issues Concerning Sexual Orientation

Another example comes from the treatment of gay and lesbian clients. Once, psychologists assumed that the most positive goal would be conversion to heterosexuality. Now this approach is considered unethical (Perez, 2001), due in part to its violation of the principle of autonomy. Over the last twenty-five years, a major focus of training has been the issue of how group differences affect the process and goals of therapy. A group that experiences ongoing discrimination may be expected to be more depressed, anxious, and stressed out than a mainstream group (DeAngelis, 2002), whereas gay men or lesbians who manage to live in a setting where their own orientation is the norm might have few or no mental health risks due to discrimination. On the other hand, many bisexual and transgendered people feel that they fit into no group at all, intensifying existential questions of loneliness and meaning.

The APA has devised *Guidelines for Psychotherapy with Lesbian, Gay, and Bisexual Clients.*. Even if you believe that you are a well-informed person in this area, I encourage you to read this material, as it will highlight several areas of concern that you might not have considered before.

Multicultural Issues

As a result of multicultural efforts, you will often come across, in your training materials, statements like "Hispanics are family centered," "Religion plays an important role in African American life," "Asian clients value restraint of feelings," and "Men need a period of quiet isolation when they get home from work"—statements intended to help you become more competent in understanding your clients from these groups. However, even when stereotypes are positive, they are still stereotypes, and people within the group range far afield from the stereotype. While visiting Austria, I asked my Viennese companions what the stereotypes of Americans were over there, and after some embarrassed giggling, their reply was "Americans are poorly educated and dress very badly." How do you like *that*?

Sue and Zane (1987) acknowledged that not knowing anything about someone's cultural background is a problem, but cautioned that teaching counselors group-specific cultural values and behavior may increase stereotyping of minority clients.

SMALL GROUP EXERCISE

Make a list of the groups to which you belong. If you have trouble doing this, think about your age, sex, ethnicity, nationality, social class, level of education, job, career aspirations, geographical background, and institutional or organizational membership. Be sure to consider what groups are suggested by your physical appearance. (For example, are you a blond? Are you over six feet tall? Are you overweight?)

Now, pass your list to another group member. Next to each group-membership entry on the list that is passed to you, write down some stereotypes of the group. Then get your own paper back, and make notes on how well the stereotypes fit you. Would the stereotypes help or hinder a counselor in understanding you? Discuss the stereotypes with your group.

How does knowledge of a client's culture, and how he or she fits into it, help us as therapists? Remember Frank and Frank's (1991) common components of successful counseling, especially that the client and therapist must both accept a rationale that explains the symptoms and suggests a procedure for resolving them. To achieve this acceptance, you need to conceptualize the client in a fashion consistent with his or her belief system (Sue & Zane, 1987). You have a head start if you understand something about the client's culture. I was at a disadvantage when I took my first Korean client, an international student who had been here in the United States for several years. In the second session, I stumbled into asking the right question: "Well, just how Korean *are* you?" My client replied, "I don't know," but then launched into a lengthy and extremely informative discourse about ways that she was and was not Korean and how she felt about Korean expectations of her.

Later, I got to know classmates and students from Korean backgrounds, and I was able to use generalizations I learned from them when I talked to Korean clients, saying things like "I had a Korean friend whose parents thought that majoring in psychology was like majoring in Ping-Pong or something totally frivolous. Is that how your family looks at your choice of a humanities major?" and "I've heard that in the Korean family, the dad is always the last to know what's going on. Is that right?" Whether or not my clients said the generalizations applied to them, they did recognize the gist, and their replies were always enlightening.

Our goal as counselors should be to learn as much as we can about cultures and subcultures, and then to find out where our clients stand in that environment. This goal is labeled by Atkinson and Lowe (1995) as *culturally sensitive counseling*, meaning that the counselor is aware of, shows recognition of, demonstrates some knowledge of, and expresses an interest in the client's ethnic identity and cultural background. In empirical research on counseling ethnic minorities, Atkinson and colleagues discovered that counselors who openly attended to racial aspects of students' concerns were perceived more favorably than counselors who did not bring these matters up (Atkinson, Casas, & Abreu, 1992; Gim, Atkinson, & Kim, 1991; Thompson, Worthington, & Atkinson, 1994). The culturally sensitive counselor actively attempts to discover how the client's distress may or may not be related to ethnic background or other group identification. Thus, a Filipina's decision to disobey her parents in a choice of college major may be more earthshaking than an American student's decision of the same type . . . or not! Either the Filipino family or the American one might operate outside the predicted system. Sue and Zane (1987) suggest that, instead of using a cookbook approach to work with ethnic minorities ("This client is Hispanic, so I should be directive"), we practice good therapeutic tactics for, first, gaining credibility and, second, providing direct benefits of treatment, such as normalization, reassurance, and anxiety reduction.

In many ways, I believe that every encounter is a multicultural encounter. Someone who appears completely different from you can turn out to be a soulmate, while your next-door neighbors of your own sex, class, and race can shock you with their strange beliefs and assumptions. My friend Verna, who grew up in a Navy family, says that she has much more in common with other military brats (of any color or sex) than with other African American women. My nephews, Black children, were both adopted before the age of six months by a White, upper-class couple, a doctor and a nurse. Will they share more cultural heritage with other African Americans? Or with other Midwestern doctors' children? Finally, consider the number of international adoptions nowadays. A person with an Asian appearance can easily come from a thoroughly mainstream North American background. I think that with the melting-pot effect, the homogenization of mass culture, and the increasing number of mixed families, we are no longer able to guess someone's background from his or her appearance—a trend I find positive and invigorating.

If we don't go by appearance, we need other information about the cultural background of our clients. I suggest a culture-sensitive interview, including the following topics. In a counseling relationship, you will probably not fire off all these questions in a row, during a single session. You will collect the knowledge incrementally over a few sessions, and you may choose indirect questioning to get the answers. But no matter how you collect the data, you should be able to consider all the topics in creating your case conceptualization.

Topics for a Culture-Sensitive Interview

1. *Language:*   Is English your first language? Is there a second or third? What language was (or is) used in the family home? Do you feel that your language is standard English or nonstandard?

2. *Family roles:*   What are the expectations of the children in your family? How do these expectations change from childhood, to adolescence, to adulthood? Are adult children responsible for their parents' welfare? How much power do parents have over adolescent and adult children's decisions? Were your parents strict or permissive, and do you endorse the same parenting style? What role do elderly family members, if any, play in your culture?

3. *Sex roles and sex differences:*   What are the beliefs of your culture about the sexes? How different are the sexes? What beliefs are acted out in your family? Which ones do you endorse and follow yourself?

4. *Sexual orientation:*   How closely are you affected by your own and others' sexual orientations (gay, lesbian, bisexual, transgendered, straight, confused)?

What did you learn about minority sexual orientations in your family, if anything? Have your ideas about sexual orientation been challenged?

5. *Independence:* Is freedom from others' influence important to you? Is interdependence in a family or community more important? Whose opinion other than your own is very important to your decisions?

6. *Spirituality:* How often are religious and spiritual matters brought up in your family or social group? Is organized religion a part of your weekly routine? Do your religious and spiritual beliefs influence your behavior on a daily basis? What beliefs and rituals are followed when there is a death in the family?

7. *Success:* How is success defined in your culture? How is it defined in your particular family? In your culture, how does a person gain status and power? Do you agree with your family's and culture's definitions?

8. *Conflict:* What is the most common way of dealing with conflict in your culture? In your family? Are indirect or direct methods more approved? Is violence sometimes condoned? Would you like to deal with conflict differently?

9. *History:* How much does the history of your people influence you today? How much does your family history influence you today? Does history influence what your family wants (and doesn't want) for you? Is your culture or family historically prejudiced against some other group, and do you hold this prejudice today?

10. *Money:* What economic class or classes do you identify as your own? Has your family shifted upward or downward in the class system? What are your financial goals? How important is wealth in your culture and your family? Do you follow your culture's and family's points of view on money, or do you rebel against them? Who are you expected to support financially, and for how long? What beliefs about spending and saving influence the way you deal with money?

11. *Acculturation:* How much does your family identify themselves with the nation in which you live? Would they be more likely to describe themselves as "Jewish," "Italian," "working-class," or "American," for instance? In everyday life, does your family follow customs and choose friends from an identifiable subculture based on ethnic background, social class, profession, or religion? Do you intend to follow the same patterns in your life?

SMALL GROUP EXERCISE

Divide the class into two groups. This exercise begins outside of class with interviews of non-class-members: All members of one group will interview someone with a background different from their own or having clearly different group identifications. Members of the other classroom group will interview someone who seems similar to them in most ways, but whom they don't know well. Use the topics in the list above. Take notes on your

American Association for Marriage and Family Therapy
    http://www.aamft.org/about/revisedcodeethics.htm
International Association of Marriage and Family Counselors
    http://www.iamfc.org/ethicalcodes.html
Association for Specialists in Group Work (a division of the ACA)
    http://asgw.educ.kent.edu/best.htm
American Nursing Association
    http://www.nursingworld.org/ethics/ecode.htm
Commission on Rehabilitation Counselor Certification
    http://www.crccertification.com/html/code_of_professional_ethics.html
National Board for Certified Counselors, Inc.
    http://www.nbcc.org/ethics
    (This site includes guidelines for the practice of Internet counseling.)
National Association of Student Personnel Administrators
    http://www.naspa.org
American College Personnel Association
    http://www.acpa.org
The ethical codes of many other professions can be found through
    http://www.ethics.ubc.ca/resources/professional/codes.html

Choose two of the specialized sites above and note three similarities as well as three differences between them. Why do different organizations need their own ethical codes, instead of sharing a common one?

3. To become a competent multicultural counselor, you will need to explore various cultures in more detail. Here are some resources that will get you off to a good start:

Sue and Sue's (1999) book, listed in the References below, is a standard text in multicultural counseling courses.
The APA's Division 45 (Society for the Psychological Study of Ethnic Minority Issues) web address is *www.apa.org/divisions/div45.*
The International Association for Cross-Cultural Psychology web address is *www.fit.edu/CampusLife/clubs-org.iaccp.*
The Institute on Aging's web address is *http://aging.ufl.edu.*
Perez, R. M., DeBord, K. A., & Bieschke, K. J. (Eds.). (2000). *Handbook of counseling and psychotherapy with lesbian, gay, and bisexual clients.* Washington, DC: American Psychological Association. Available online at *http://www.apa.org.*
Pedersen, P. (2000). *A handbook for developing multicultural awareness* (3rd ed.). Alexandria, VA: American Counseling Association. Available online at *http://www.counseling.org.*

REFERENCES

American College of Physicians. (1998). Ethics manual. *Annals of Internal Medicine, 128,* 576–594.
American Counseling Association. (2002). *ACA code of ethics and standards of practice.* Alexandria, VA: Author.

interview and share them with a partner from your class, being sure to guise the identity of your interviewee. Reflect on what you learned ab someone else's culture. What similarities and differences from your c stood out? Were there any surprises in store? What elements of the inter wee's culture would you consider crucial, as a counselor, in creating a conceptualization? What would affect your choice of techniques in thera Compare the experiences of the "different" group and the "similar" gr in a class discussion.

LIBRARY, MEDIA, AND INTERNET ACTIVITIES

1. Watching films is an enjoyable and accessible way of exploring wo and world views that may not embellish your everyday life, helping you come a more culturally sensitive person. Following is a list of movies tha you glimpse different cultures, subcultures, and lifestyles. Using your Inte search engine, such as Google or Yahoo!, you can find reviews and summa of the films.

All About My Mother (1999)
Boys Don't Cry (1999)
Breaking the Waves (1995)
Do the Right Thing (1989)
East Is East (2000)
El Norte (1988)
Guantanamera (1995)
La Bamba (1987)
Like Water for Chocolate (1993)
Ma Vie en Rose (1997)
Mi Familia (1995)
Mississippi Marsala (1992)
My Beautiful Laundrette (1985)
Paris Is Burning (1991)

Passion Fish (1998)
Secrets and Lies (1995)
Selena (1996)
Shall We Dance (1997)
Smoke Signals (1998)
Strangers in Good Company (1991)
Strawberry and Chocolate (1993)
The Color of Paradise (1999)
The Shower (1999)
The Teena Brandon Story (1998)
The Trip to Bountiful (1985)
The Wedding Banquet (1993)
Waterdance (1992)

2. Most organizations make their up-to-date codes of ethics available the Internet. Here are the websites for several of them:

American Counseling Association
http://www.counseling.org/resources
American Psychological Association
http://www.apa.org/ethics/code.html
American School Counselor Association
http://www.schoolcounselor.org
National Association of Social Workers
http://www.naswdc.org/pubs/code

American Psychological Association. (2002). *Ethical principles of psychologists and code of conduct.* Washington, DC: Author.

Atkinson, D. R., Casas, A., & Abreu, J. (1992). Mexican-American acculturation, counselor ethnicity and cultural sensitivity, and perceived counselor competence. *Journal of Counseling Psychology, 39,* 515–520.

Atkinson, D. R., & Lowe, S. M. (1995). The role of ethnicity, cultural knowledge, and conventional techniques in counseling and psychotherapy. In J. G. Ponterotto, J. M. Casas, L. A. Suzuki, & C. M. Alexander (Eds.), *Handbook of multicultural counseling* (pp. 387–413). Thousand Oaks, CA: Sage.

Carkhuff, R. R., & Anthony, W. A. (1979). *The skills of helping.* Amherst, MA: Human Resource Development Press.

Cummings, N. A. (1987). The future of psychotherapy: One psychologist's perspective. *American Journal of Psychotherapy, 41,* 349–360.

DeAngelis, T. (2002). New data on lesbian, gay and bisexual mental health. *Monitor on Psychology, 33*(2), 46–47.

DeKraai, M. B., & Sales, B. (1991). Legal issues in the conduct of child therapy. In T. R. Kratochwill & R. J. Morris (Eds.), *The practice of child therapy* (2nd ed., pp. 441–458). New York: Pergamon.

Edwards, A. L. (1959). *Edwards personal preference schedule.* San Antonio, TX: The Psychological Corporation.

Frank, J. D., & Frank, J. B. (1991). *Persuasion and healing: A comparative study of psychotherapy* (3rd ed.). Baltimore: Johns Hopkins University Press.

Gim, R. H., Atkinson, D. R., & Kim, S. J. (1991). Asian-American acculturation, counselor ethnicity and cultural sensitivity, and ratings of counselors. *Journal of Counseling Psychology, 38,* 57–62.

Hanson, W. E., Claiborn, C. D., & Kerr, B. (1997). Differential effects of two test-interpretation styles in counseling: A field study. *Journal of Counseling Psychology, 44,* 400–405.

Kenyon, P. (1999). *What would you do? An ethical case workbook for human service professionals.* Pacific Grove, CA: Brooks/Cole.

Perez, R. M. (2001). Issues in counseling and psychotherapy with lesbian, gay, and bisexual clients. *Clinician's Research Digest, 25 (supplemental bulletin),* 1–2.

Pope, K. S. (1994). *Sexual involvement with therapists: Patient assessment, subsequent therapy, forensics.* Washington, DC: American Psychological Association.

Pope, K. S., & Vasquez, M. (1998). *Ethics in psychotherapy and counseling* (2nd ed.). Hoboken, NJ: Jossey-Bass.

Reisman, J. M., & Ribordy, S. (1993). *Principles of psychotherapy with children* (2nd ed.). New York: Macmillan.

Remley, T. P., & Herlihy, B. (2001). *Ethical, legal, and professional issues in counseling.* Upper Saddle River, NJ: Prentice-Hall.

Smith, D. (2003). Ten ways practitioners can avoid frequent ethical pitfalls. *Monitor on Psychology, 34,* 50–55.

Sue, D. W., & Sue, D. (1999). *Counseling the culturally different* (3rd ed.). New York: Wiley.

Sue, S., & Zane, N. (1993). The role of culture and cultural techniques in psychotherapy: A critique and reformulation. *American Psychologist, 42,* 37–45.

Thompson, C. E., Worthington, R., & Atkinson, D. R. (1994). Counselor content orientation, counselor race, and Black women's cultural mistrust and self-disclosures. *Journal of Counseling Psychology, 41,* 155–161.

CHAPTER 4

Psychoanalytical and Psychodynamic Approaches

❧ A Selection from
The Interpretation of Dreams, 1900
Sigmund Freud

I once had an opportunity of making a detailed study of a young woman who passed through a variety of psychical conditions. Her illness began with a state of confusional excitement during which she displayed a quite special aversion to her mother, hitting and abusing her whenever she came near her bed, while at the same period she was docile and affectionate towards a sister who was many years her senior. This was followed by a state in which she was lucid but some-what apathetic and suffered from badly disturbed sleep. It was during this phase that I began treating her and analysing her dreams. An immense number of these dreams were concerned, with a greater or less degree of disguise, with the death of her mother: at one time she would be attending an old woman's funeral, at another she and her sister would be sitting at table dressed in mourning. There could be no question as to the meaning of these dreams. As her condition im-proved still further, hysterical phobias developed. The most tormenting of these was a fear that something might have happened to her mother. She was obliged to hurry home, wherever she might be, to convince herself that her mother was still alive. This case, taken in conjunction with what I had learnt from other sources, was highly instructive: it exhibited, translated as it were into different languages, the various ways in which the psychical apparatus reacted to one and the same exciting idea. In the confusional state, in which, as I believe, the second psychical agency was overwhelmed by the normally suppressed first one, her unconscious hostility to her mother found a powerful motor expression. When the calmer condition set in, when the rebellion was suppressed and the domination of the censorship re-established, the only region left open in which her hostility could realize the wish for her mother's death was that of dreaming. When a nor-mal state was still more firmly established, it led to the production of her exag-gerated worry about her mother as a hysterical counter-reaction and defensive phenomenon. In view of this it is no longer hard to understand why hysterical girls are so often attached to their mothers with such exaggerated affection.

On another occasion I had an opportunity of obtaining a deep insight into the unconscious mind of a young man whose life was made almost impossible by an obsessional neurosis. He was unable to go out into the street because he was tor-tured by the fear that he would kill everyone he met. He spent his days in preparing his alibi in case he might be charged with one of the murders committed in the town. It is unnecessary to add that he was a man of equally high morals and education. The analysis (which, incidentally, led to his recovery) showed that the basis of this distressing obsession was an impulse to murder his over-severe father. This impulse, to his astonishment, had been consciously expressed when he was seven years old, but it had, of course, originated much earlier in his childhood. After his father's painful illness and death, the patient's obsessional self-reproaches appeared—he was in his thirty-first year at the time—taking the shape of a phobia transferred on to strangers. A person, he felt, who was capable of wanting to push his own father over a precipice from the top of a mountain was not to be trusted to respect the lives of those less closely related to him; he was quite right to shut himself up in his room.

In my experience, which is already extensive, the chief part in the mental lives of all children who later become neurotics is played by their parents. Being in love with the one parent and hating the other are among the essential constituents of the stock of psychical impulses which is formed at that time and which is of such importance in determining the symptoms of the later neurosis. It is not my belief, however, that psychoneurotics differ sharply in this respect from other human beings who remain normal—that they are able, that is, to create something absolutely new and peculiar to themselves. It is far more probable—and this is confirmed by occasional observations on normal children— that they are only distinguished by exhibiting on a magnified scale feelings of love and hatred to their parents which occur less obviously and less intensely in the minds of most children. (1900/1965, pp. 292–294) ■ ■

DISCUSSION IDEAS

1. What did Freud do in his treatment of the young woman? What idea or feeling did he decide was driving the young woman's behavior?

2. Freud describes three stages of the young woman's "psychical conditions," all of which he thinks stemmed from the same source. What are the stages? How does he explain the stages of the disorder?

3. In the case of the obsessional young man, what did Freud believe was the basis of his obsession? In other words, what had happened that made the obsessions appear?

4. In both cases, what was the role of the unconscious in the clients' disorders? That is, what motivations were outside of the clients' awareness?

5. In Freud's view as he expressed it in this passage, what causes children to grow up neurotic? Is there a distinct difference in the past experiences of neurotic versus normal adults?

6. From reading this selection, what impression do you get of Freud as a person? How might you describe him, from this limited evidence? What clues did you use to describe him?

An Introduction to Psychodynamic Thought

The passage you just considered, from Freud's most famous book *The Interpretation of Dreams* (1900), represents many typical concepts from the psychoanalytic and psychodynamic schools of thought. The term **psychoanalytic** usually refers to a system that is strictly Freudian or extremely close to Freudian. It involves certain premises and techniques that were later given up, even by therapists who still worked from a Freudian basis. The systems of these later therapists are called **psychodynamic** (and sometimes *neo-Freudian*). The reason that psychoanalytic and psychodynamic systems are often presented together is that they have many of the same features, which I will describe in this section, because they flow from the same wellspring, Freudian thought. Purely psychoanalytic practice is now relatively rare, while psychodynamic practices are extremely common.

In a summary of surveys of American psychotherapists, Prochaska and Norcross (1999) report that 18 percent of clinical psychologists, 12 percent of counseling psychologists, 35 percent of psychiatrists, 33 percent of social workers, and 11 percent of counselors identified their orientations as psychoanalytic/psychodynamic. These percentages are exceeded only by identifications with the orientation of "eclectic/integrative"—and that orientation usually includes psychodynamic thought, too, as it pulls together many theories. You could say that almost any working therapist includes some psychodynamic elements in his or her conceptualizations of clients, and as I describe these elements you will see why.

In this chapter I will give you some Freudian background and then discuss three of its progeny that are widely in practice today: **ego, object relations,** and **self theories.** Carl Jung, whose theory is a cousin to psychodynamic thought, will be considered also, though briefly: Jungian therapy is much rarer than the three psychodynamic practices I will focus upon, and it has some striking essential differences. Ego, object relations, and self theories are all based to some extent on Freudian thought, and the originators of these theories were often students and colleagues of Freud's. For example, the originator of ego psychology is usually considered to be Anna Freud, Sigmund Freud's daughter, who collaborated with him throughout his life.

The commonalities among psychoanalytic, ego, object relations, and self psychology are strong and basic. All of these approaches seek to understand universal principles of our inner life (Hansen, 2000). In each approach, that is, individuals are studied closely, but with the goal of understanding how people in general function psychologically. So there is an underlying belief that there *are* common principles that apply to all humans, in all different settings and all around the globe. (Not everyone believes this.) One of the most important universal hallmarks is the **unconscious**—an area of mental life that is outside of awareness and perception, yet still affects the way we think, feel, and behave. You probably use the term *unconscious* in exactly this way in everyday conversation, saying things like "I must have unconsciously wanted to get fired from that job, because I had some reason for being late every day," or "I had an unconscious resentment of having to do all the housework even though I was good at it," or "He unconsciously chooses girlfriends who are just like his mother."

DISCUSSION IDEAS

Can you remember the last time you or a friend described something as *unconscious*? Recently, a friend of mine said that his wife *unconsciously* picks up conversation topics from what people at other tables in restaurants are talking about: His wife swears that she has not heard what they were saying and is not aware of what prompted her to bring up these topics. See whether members of your class can think of other examples. Do you think that the unconscious is a nonexistent, weak, medium, or strong influence on your behavior? You might take a class tally to see where most people stand on the issue right now.

Other Common Themes in Psychoanalytical and Psychodynamic Theories

Concepts of life as a dependable sequence of stages, and of psychological energy as having physical properties, also drive psychoanalytical thought and its successors.

Life as a Series of Stages

All the theories discussed in this chapter solidly share the idea that the past continues in the present. The experiences of our childhood, in particular, resonate in our personalities as adults. Psychoanalytic, ego, object relations, and self psychologists all investigate clients' childhoods as an integral part of understanding their problems (as well as their strengths). The emphasis on childhood is part of another shared concept as well: These psychologists all see social and personal development as occurring in identifiable stages as we go through time. At each stage, we adapt to other people and the environment in predictable patterns, and psychological problems develop when we fail to adapt as expected for some reason.

For example, Erik Erikson (1950), an ego psychologist, identifies the stage of life from six years old until puberty as the School Age, and maintains that the adaptation we make in this stage is "industry"—that is, learning to work and acquire skills, resulting in a basic feeling of competence that will probably last a lifetime. If during this stage we encounter continual frustration and failure, we fail to develop the feeling of competence and instead establish a feeling of inferiority that also will last a lifetime unless some corrective experiences help us out. Psychotherapy might be such a corrective experience. Erikson's School Age is just an example of how a stage theory works: Various theorists have divided up life into stages in different ways and see the tasks of each stage differently (see Table 4.1). The main point is that all the psychodynamic and psychoanalytic frameworks see our lifelines in a sequence of developmental eras. Getting stuck at one stage or failing to complete the adaptive task of one stage results in psychological distress. This stuckness is called a *fixation* in psychoanalytic terms.

TABLE 4.1
Freud's and Erikson's Stages of Life

Freud's model is arranged according to sources of pleasure, and Erikson's is arranged according to social forces.

Stage (Freud)	Psychosexual process	Age Erikson	Psychosocial process
Oral (0 to 18 months)	Exploration focused on mouth. Fixation: too much talk, eating, dependency	First year	Trust versus mistrust. Expectation that needs will be met, or not.
Anal (18–36 mos.)	Pleasure focused on defecation, in conflict with social demands. Fixation: stinginess and orderliness, or impulsivity and sloppiness.	Second year	Autonomy versus shame and doubt. Choice and self-control, or uncertainty about abilities.
Phallic (3–6 years)	Pleasure focused on genital area, resolved by identification with same-sex parent. Fixation: rebelliousness, sexual identity problems.	3–5 years	Initiative versus guilt. Self-direction, purpose, and personal goals, or guilt over making these efforts.
Latency (6 years to puberty)	Pleasure focused away from sexual, toward play, school, friendship.	6 years to puberty	Industry versus inferiority. Pleasure in feeling competent, or incompetence and lack of engagement.
Genital (puberty onward)	Pleasure again focused on genitals, for the rest of life. Mature sexual relationships and desire to reproduce, if other stages are successfully resolved.	Adolescence	Identity versus role confusion. Coherent sense of self, or undefined or oppositional identity.
		Early adulthood	Intimacy versus isolation. Ability to form and enjoy close relationships, or sense of aloneness.
		Middle age	Generativity versus stagnation. Sense of contributing to the world and the future, or inactivity and lack of purpose.
		Old age	Integrity versus despair. Reflection on life as meaningful and satisfying, or not.

Structures Sharing Energy

Another similarity involves the concept of mental operations as separable into component parts; thus, all these systems are analytical. Usually, the metaphor of structure is used. For example, Freud saw mental life as divided into the ego, the id, and the superego, while object relations theorists see mental life as divided into representations of the self and representations of others. These structures will be explained soon; for now, however, simply note that all the systems in this chapter endorse the idea that the psyche is divisible into parts. These parts interact and share an energy source, and energy expended in one structure can't also be used in another. Therefore, an economic view of psychological energy prevails, in which effort spent in one place is unavailable to be spent somewhere else. It is also a hydraulic view, in that energy blocked in one place must go somewhere else, like dammed water: It doesn't just disappear. So, for example, if you are spending a lot of psychological energy dealing with anxiety about a test, you don't have much left for effectively studying the material. And, if you are *not* expressing something like anxiety in one way, it'll come out in another way. As a behavioral example, consider that if you are trying not to bite your fingernails, you might end up smoking more cigarettes than usual. The anxiety you previously expressed in one bad habit is just transferred to another bad habit.

The excerpt from Freud at the beginning of this chapter shows these ideas at work. You can see that he conceives of both clients according to a hydraulic model. When their hatred of their parents could not be directly expressed or even acknowledged, it came out in different ways. In the case of the young woman, her unconscious feelings came out in three ways in sequence. When one way was blocked, the feelings took another form of expression, "translated as it were into different languages" (1900/1965, p. 293).

Reflection

What do you think about the economic and hydraulic metaphors for psychological energy? Can you remember a time in your own life when your psychological state fit these metaphors? In other words, was your psychological energy depleted or spent all in one place, or dammed up in one spot and overflowing into others?

Some people don't believe these metaphors are good ones. For example, it could be that using psychological energy creates *more* psychological energy, in a muscle-building metaphor (Baumeister, 2001). Can you think of examples of this competing metaphor?

Because there are strong commonalities among the approaches in this chapter, you will see that they share many essential concepts as well. The main divergence is that over time, the psychodynamic schools have prevailed and have demonstrated a general movement toward **humanism**—that is, an awareness of the values, capacities, and worth of people—and away from the strictly Freudian view of people as creatures motivated by sex and aggression and shaped by their attempts to fend off anxiety (Gelso & Fassinger, 1992). The next major section of the chapter summarizes what forms this movement has taken.

Profile of a Theorist

SIGMUND FREUD (1856–1939)

Sigmund Freud was born on either March or May 6 of 1856 in Freiburg, Moravia. Confusion over his birth records is likely just a technicality, but over the years it has given rise to speculation that his 20-year-old mother was pregnant at the time of her marriage to his 40-year-old father—a fact that some believe influenced Freud's early views and eventually his theories of psychology.

There is no argument, however, that Freud was his mother's favorite and benefited from her early belief that he was destined for greatness. Though seven siblings followed, Freud was never close to any of his brothers and sisters and often enjoyed preferential treatment in service of his intellectual gifts. When he was 4 years old, his family moved to Vienna where he spent his entire life until the rise of Nazism in Austria prompted his move to London the year before his death at the age of 82.

Though he had a gift for languages and was intensely interested in literature, Freud's choices for a prestigious career were limited to law and medicine, the only professions available to Jews in Vienna at the time. Influenced by exposure to the works of Goethe and Darwin, Freud developed an interest in science and entered medical school at the University of Vienna in the fall of 1873. While he wanted to pursue a career in research, the desire for financial independence necessitated that he develop his skills for clinical practice. He was further motivated after meeting and falling in love with Martha Bernay. The two became engaged in 1882 but postponed their marriage until Freud could establish himself in private practice.

During this time, Freud made the unfortunate mistake of believing in and promoting the therapeutic properties of cocaine. Though he recognized his error and eventually renounced the drug, the episode hurt his reputation as a clinician and cast a shadow over the formative years of his medical career.

Through his association with physician Josef Breuer, Freud developed an interest in Breuer's patients suffering from *hysteria*, a condition involving complex physical symptoms for which there appeared to be no identifiable medical cause. Breuer's early success with a technique he dubbed the "talking cure" intrigued Freud. This cure involved encouraging the patient to talk freely about any thoughts or feelings, regardless of a direct connection to the patient's distress. During this unstructured exploration, with guidance from

Freud, many patients appeared to achieve some insight that freed them from their symptoms of hysteria. While the alleviation usually proved temporary, Freud's practice grew from Breuer's referrals and he elaborated on the technique until it included many elements recognized today as components of psychoanalysis, such as free association and the interpretation of dreams.

Along the way to eventual acceptance of his theories by the psychological community, Freud experienced a number of setbacks that, again, threatened his reputation. In 1896, he published a paper on seduction theory and was shunned by many as a result. Seduction theory posited that many of the neuroses seen in adulthood had roots in childhood experiences of sexual molestation, most frequently perpetrated by fathers. Freud's initial claims that children were sexual beings was difficult enough for the tight-laced Victorians to swallow, to say nothing of his assertion that deviant behavior by adults was rampant. Freud later revised his theory, suggesting that the many recollections of sexual abuse in neurotic patients could be explained by the patients' own conflicted sexual desires; but the damage left its mark and discouraged many in the field from embracing his theories. In the modern era, many psychologists believe his initial theory was closer to the truth.

Also in 1896, Freud's father died and his friendship with Breuer disintegrated, due in part to Breuer's reluctance to support Freud's unconventional theories. Freud suffered from constant worries over his financial situation, fear of heart disease, and a disabling preoccupation with thoughts of his own death. In 1897, he began what was to be a grueling three-year process, performing psychoanalysis on himself. His efforts were helpful, alleviating him of his most troubling symptoms and helping to crystallize his theory of psychoanalysis in the process. By 1900, Freud emerged a healthier individual, ready to accept the attention and fame his work was about to receive. *The Interpretation of Dreams*, his most famous work, was published the same year.

The following years saw the creation of the Wednesday Psychological Society, a group of prominent scientists interested in furthering the development of the analytic school of psychology. They were led by Freud and included Alfred Adler and Otto Rank, among others. The group grew in number and evolved into the Vienna Psychoanalytic Society, but Freud's lifelong tendency to alienate those who challenged his ideas surfaced again, and eventually the group splintered. Ironically, while his fame grew, Freud's personal life suffered as he lost the support of his closest colleagues. He spent much of his late career working in relative solitude.

Diagnosed with cancer of the upper jaw in 1923 due to his habit of smoking twenty cigars a day, Freud's physical health failed rapidly during his final years. Nonetheless, he continued to work productively and produced many important writings before reluctantly fleeing Austria for London in 1938. When more than thirty operations failed to remedy his suffering, Freud enlisted the help of his physician and died of a lethal dose of morphine in September 1939 at the age of 82.

Essential Concepts of Psychoanalytical and Psychodynamic Theories

Some essential concepts, such as the ideas of the unconscious and of stages of life, run throughout all the psychoanalytical and psychodynamic theories. Others are specialized, or revised versions of older concepts. The four theories we focus upon here can be briefly explained in terms of their hypotheses about the sources of human distress and the goals of psychological treatment.

Freudian Psychoanalysis

The psychoanalytic viewpoint is **deterministic.** It maintains that your personality and behavior were fixed by the time you were about 6 years old. You do not have free will (Hansen, 2000). Much of this determinism has to do with the fact of basic, innate **drives,** which are sex and aggression (in other terms, love and death) (Freud, 1920). The rest has to do with how you and your parents negotiated infancy and childhood stages, particularly one stage. This crucial period is called the **Oedipal stage,** sometimes in girls called the **Electra complex.** Basically, between ages 3 and 6, children want the opposite-sex parent all to themselves and hate the same-sex parent for monopolizing their love object. So, boys want their mothers for themselves and wish their fathers would disappear from the face of the earth, or die. Girls want their fathers and wish their mothers would disappear or die.

This situation causes so much anxiety (because the children fear that the same-sex parent will find out about their wishes and punish them severely) that the children cannot stand the state of affairs, and in adjustment they turn to identifying with the same-sex parent. At least, with this identification, they can vicariously possess the opposite-sex parent and experience less fear. This identification is what creates sex typing. And in Freud's view, sex typing is the proper resolution of the stage: Boys identify with father, and girls with mother. Sex roles are firmly established, and in puberty people are attracted to the opposite sex and are able to form relationships with them that will eventually lead to choosing a mate and reproduction. Failure to resolve the Oedipal and Electra complexes in this direction creates lifelong problems with sexual matters, according to Freud. (Obviously, many people fervently disagree. D. J. Bem [1996] offers evidence against the Freudian stance and a far different developmental point of view.)

Drives are biological and inborn. Sexual and aggressive urges are unavoidable, but their free expression is in conflict with society (Pine, 1998). Civilized society insists that we control our basic urges, and we learn this as children, from our parents. (One of the first examples we encounter is that we have to be toilet-trained!) We *internalize* this message of controlling ourselves when external prompting by parents is replaced by internal prompting from within our own psyches.

Freud (1923) believed that three psychological structures perform a juggling act to achieve healthy functioning in society. The **id** represents the drives in their raw, uncontrolled state. When the id is in charge, we eat too much, drink too much, have sex promiscuously, beat each other up when angry, seek oblivion in reckless drug use, and basically act like we are constantly on spring break. The **superego** is the internalized civilization message from our parents—we often call it the conscience. When the superego is in charge, we are perfectionistic and uptight and demand too much of ourselves. Obviously these two structures are at war. The peacemaker is the **ego,** which represents the mediator between the superego and the id. It works according to the **reality principle** (while the id works according to the **pleasure principle**). The reality principle says, "You can't act out your id urges, but you can't live up to your superego in the real world either." The ego manages by setting up defense systems and adaptations that aim to satisfy or at least appease both the id and the superego. If you've ever felt like you had an angel on one shoulder and a devil on the other, both urging you to follow their demands, you've got an image of what the ego has to manage.

Many conflicts the ego must manage create **anxiety,** a central concept in Freudian and other psychodynamic theories (Freud, 1923). This type of anxiety is not the kind that naturally occurs in the face of an actual threat, such as a growling dog in your path, but it is the kind that occurs when id instincts threaten to overpower the ego, or when you unconsciously fear that id instincts are going to take over, and so you expend a lot of psychic energy keeping them tamed. Freud distinguished realistic anxiety from *neurotic anxiety*, the fear that you will not be successful in taming the id, and *moral anxiety*, the fear that you are offending the standards of the superego (Sharf, 2000). The feeling of anxiety is a signal that the war among psychological structures is escalating and something must be done.

What must be done? Usually, the ego marshals your favorite **defense mechanisms** (A. Freud, 1936). Since the ego is the structure that is in touch with reality, it can redefine reality to make it less threatening. All of this happens unconsciously. There are many defense mechanisms, including both fairly adaptive and severely damaging ones. For example, transforming id drives into acceptable social behavior such as work, humor, and creative arts is usually healthy. This is called *sublimation.* On the other hand, *repression* and *denial,* which seek to remove pain by excluding it from awareness, and *regression,* which seeks to avoid a threatening situation by returning to an earlier stage of development, are usually considered dangerous to mental health.

- Freud believed, and many psychologists still agree, that repressed memories of traumatic experiences are converted to overt pathological symptoms like depression and even paralysis, which seem mysterious until the memory is retrieved.

- Denial is problematic because it prevents a person from taking relevant action (Kernberg, 1968). In my own experience, my elderly father exhausted himself caring for my declining mother long after she should have had outside help, all the time insisting that things weren't as bad as they really were. His expert use of denial hastened his death.

- Regression can take a mild form, such as when a person "turns into a big baby" during a minor illness, or a more serious form, such as when a middle-aged man suddenly dyes his hair, buys a sports car he can't afford, and cheats on his wife.

More on defense mechanisms will follow under the topic of ego psychology, since defense mechanisms are the territory of the ego.

DISCUSSION IDEAS

In what circumstances do you think *sublimation* (for example, transfer of id energy into work, humor, and art) might be unhealthy? Do you think *repression, denial,* or *regression* are ever adaptive and normal? Can you think of any instances in which you or other people you know used these defense mechanisms when under stress?

Another common defense mechanism is *fantasy*, including daydreaming. In your opinion, what are the pros and cons of using this mechanism?

In the mid-1980s, I taught writing on computers to students who mostly had never used word processors before, and the clunky computer systems of the time had even more quirks and glitches than computers today do. Many times, desperately frustrated students would need assistance from me—and they would cry out, "Mom! Help!" Absorbed in their feelings and not thinking clearly, they would accidentally call me "Mom." This is an example not only of regression but of an important Freudian concept: transference. **Transference** is the current repetition of old patterns of relationships that are firmly rooted in the personality (Pine, 1998). In this example, a woman of my age who could rescue a kid in distress received the transferred identity of a mother, which makes perfect sense. Usually, transference is not as obvious as this. Interpersonal experiences from the past determine how we view others in the present and strongly influence the nature of our interactions with others (Oremland, 1991). As another illustration, consider the fact that some people seem naturally to trust new acquaintances while others have an automatic suspicion of new acquaintances. You probably know both types of people. The difference may be explained by each type's early experiences—whether the important people in their lives were trustworthy or crooked.

Other instances of transference include always seeing one's strict father in authority figures, or always judging a person of the other sex as out to exploit you, or thinking that you are going to get yelled at for every little misstep. Some people have trouble keeping jobs because they perceive every boss as a mean old daddy and, consequently, act like resentful teenagers themselves. Psychoanalytic and psychodynamic therapists are always sensitive to what kind of transference is occurring between the client and therapist. This provides important clues about how the client relates to everyone else, and to what might have happened in his or her early life. Let me give you another example from my computer lab. Sometimes there would be a student obviously in trouble with the word processor, who yet would *never* ask me for help, and would only warily accept it when I offered. Looking at this situation from a transference angle, I would say that in the student's past, asking for help was either punished or ignored by important adults, and so the student unconsciously cast me in the same unhelpful mold, even though to most people I am clearly a helpful type. The student *transferred* an idea of the unhelpful adult onto me.

A significant related concept is **countertransference**—that is, how I respond to the transference that was laid on me. When a student would accidentally call me "Mom," I thought it was funny—probably as a humor defense mechanism, since the idea of being a mother makes me very anxious. When students were afraid to ask for help, what this brought out in me was a protective streak that made me want to keep an eye on them and spring to their aid at the slightest sign of trouble. These reactions say something about me. Countertransference reactions also say something about the other party, since the way one person responds to someone else is very likely the way other people do, too. So, for instance, if a client irritates me with her continual whining, I can guess that other people probably find her irritating as well, and she walks around in a world where everyone is trying to avoid her. This is not the same world most people inhabit, and it has to affect her mental state.

Goals of Freudian Analysis   The goal of psychoanalysis is to bring the unconscious into the conscious. For Freudian analysts, this goal constitutes **insight,** bringing into awareness conflicts and feelings that previously were inaccessible. Insight engenders structural change in the basic relations among id, ego, and superego, so that the juggling act runs smoothly, with the ego successfully managing id and superego demands. According to Freud, insight is enough. Once an accurate analysis is performed and the client has become aware of what had previously been festering in his or her unconscious, the client will do whatever is necessary behaviorally, on his or her own (Pine, 1998).

Ego Psychology

Sigmund Freud placed the ego in a central role, but a role derived from the mandates of the id and superego. His daughter, Anna Freud, developed the concept of the ego further, and she is the person who elaborated on the idea of defense mechanisms in *The Ego and the Mechanisms of Defense* (1936). (Several defense mechanisms are listed in Table 4.2.) In ego psychology, these became normalized, and their adaptive functions were considered along with their distorting functions. Anna Freud was also one of the earliest psychologists to study children's development through direct observation of both the normal and disturbed. She began to see the ego not merely as a mediator of urges, but as having its own energy and normal purposes. This line of thinking was followed by Heinz Hartmann (1958), who saw the ego as having its own healthy

TABLE 4.2
Commonly Used Defense Mechanisms

Rationalization. You create a logical reason to explain a painful experience and thus remove it from the sphere of feelings. For example, you might say that you failed a test because it was unfair in some way, rather than facing the fact that you didn't study hard enough and are disappointed.

Reaction formation. You act and speak in opposition to impulses you wish you didn't have. In the Freud excerpt you read in this chapter, the young woman was especially solicitous of a mother she hated, at one stage. Some people think that homophobia is a reaction formation against a person's own same-sex attractions.

Projection. You attribute to others your own characteristic ways of being. For example, an insanely jealous person might see everyone else as driven by jealousy. This defense mechanism could either normalize your own state or entail denying your own characteristic while accusing others of it excessively. (People also project *positive* aspects of themselves onto others, which can be dangerous in situations like interviewing someone for a job.)

Fantasy. You escape a real world that is aversive or boring by dreaming of a better situation. A law student slaving away at her books might stop and daydream about the good, exciting life that will come after she has her degree.

Repression. You forget painful experiences and situations. Trauma victims, in the past decade, have been subjects of investigation about repression of traumas such as wartime horrors and child sexual abuse. Repression is an unconscious process, whereas **suppression** is a conscious effort to forget about something. Some theorists think that an experience repeatedly suppressed can become repressed.

Emotional insulation. You mask your pain by believing that you do not really care. People who lack a romantic relationship for long periods may do this. Again, emotional insulation is the unconscious version, in contrast with the conscious version of pretending you don't really care and *knowing* that you are pretending.

Displacement. For various reasons, you cannot act out your hostility to the person you are really angry at, so you take it out on someone less threatening. The classic story is the worker who gets yelled at by his boss and comes home to yell at his family and kick the dog.

Denial. You simply do not see the bad things that are going on. Parents of a child who is bullied at school may be blind to the signs of a severe social problem for their child. They are protected from having to confront an ugly reality.

Sublimation. You transform sexual and aggressive drives into a socially acceptable form. For example, teaching school and coaching sports are both exercises of power and can satisfy aggressive urges. Other types of work and creative expression may also absorb id energy.

Regression. You behave as though you are at an earlier stage of development. Children with new baby siblings often revert to thumb-sucking, bed-wetting, clinging, and other habits they have outgrown. Adults who return to their parents' home for a visit sometimes return to less mature behavior than they display elsewhere.

Identification. You get satisfaction and overcome inferiority feelings by allying yourself psychologically with a powerful, successful entity. Being a fan of a winning team is a mild example. Becoming a Nazi is a serious one.

functions outside of defensive ones, and by Erik Erikson (1950), who developed a stage theory that encompassed the whole span of life rather than ending with puberty, as Freud's did. Erikson's theory defined the phenomenon of the School Age, discussed earlier in this chapter, during which ego functioning blossoms in terms of relating to demands from the outside world, whereas Freud labeled the same age as *latency* and saw nothing much going on at the time, psychologically. The ego psychologists began to place emphasis on psychosocial development, in contrast with Freud's focus on psychosexual development, so the question of how people function in the social world became as important as how they control their biological drives.

The ego is concerned not just with impulse control but with a larger sense of control such as mastery of language, competence and persistence in chosen tasks, independence, judgment, and moral reasoning (Prochaska & Norcross, 1999). While Freud saw the ego as serving the demands of the id and superego, ego psychologists and their successors saw the ego as striving for relationship with the outside world, including other people. Basically, it takes on a life of its own in this theory, which was considered not a break away from psychoanalytic theory but an addition to it.

Goals of Psychotherapy in Ego Psychology   A focus on the ego changes the goals of psychoanalysis somewhat. Improved reality testing and judgment are emphasized in therapy based on **ego psychology,** so one important goal is seeing the outside world as it is, without too much distortion from inner distress and transference. Analysis of defense mechanisms also takes a major place in this form of therapy. Neurotic adults are trapped in a rigid pattern of defenses that needs to be loosened, with a bigger repertoire of appropriate responses developed. For instance, I have an acquaintance who is characteristically angry about everything, and using the defense mechanism of *projection,* she assumes that everyone else is angry all the time. I was surprised once when she sympathized with how horribly I had been treated on the job, when I was actually quite satisfied with how I'd been treated. Being locked into this pattern, she has lost opportunities by misinterpreting others' statements and responding defensively as though *they* were angry. This is the sort of problem that ego psychologists address. They also attempt to build **ego strength,** the capacity of the ego to pursue its healthy goals in spite of threat and stress (or perceived threat and stress).

R e f l e c t i o n

We all have our favorite defense mechanisms, even if we are not rigidly stuck using one or two. You probably recognized yourself in some of the descriptions in Table 4.2. I am a fantasy, sublimation, and denial expert, myself, and I saw the sublimation and denial tactics in both of my parents, from whom I probably learned them. Think about what your characteristic defense mechanisms are, and consider examples. Do you see these in your parents?

If it is difficult to perceive your own defenses (after all, they are unconscious), you may be able to see how your best friend or a sibling defends against painful realities.

Object Relations

While id and ego psychology use Freud's structural scheme to explain how the mind works, object relations psychology views the relationship between self and objects as the organizing principle of the psyche (Prochaska & Norcross, 1999). **Objects** are mental representations of other people. It may seem strange to call people objects. The term originally came from Freudian theorists who wanted to emphasize that at a certain point for infants, other people are merely objects for gratifying needs. In object relations language, objects are mental representations of the self and other people, and these mental representations of others are not to be confused with the actual person, who may not be accurately represented.

Most of the way we mentally represent others comes from our first relationships, those with our parents—especially the mother, since she is usually the main caretaker. This is a change from the Freudian emphasis on the paternal side; Freud focused on the Oedipal complex, the boy's process of identifying with the father, and only added the Electra complex later when required to explain girls' development. Even then, his conception of girls' development remained sketchy, and mothers functioned mainly as early love objects for boys. Object relations theory changed that point of view, regarding the mother's behavior as critical to the development of both boys and girls. Also, the pre-Oedipal period, from birth to 3 years of age, took center stage for the object relations theorists. Finally, while Freud saw sex and aggression as the pre-eminent inborn drives, the object relations and self theorists added the need to relate to others as a biological given. John Bowlby (1958) and other researchers who directly observed babies, youngsters, and mothers believed that offspring had an innate need for contact with the mother.

The stage theory of object relations has to do with the process of becoming an independent individual and seeing other people as stable, complex, and real. The theory places most importance on the first three years of life, during which a child moves from fusion with the mother (no psychological awareness of separateness), to total dependence, to limited self-directed exploration, and then to individuation. Fairbairn (1941) expresses the process as moving from "taking" to "giving" in interacting with other people. Fairbairn didn't mean that we become altruistic by the age of 3 but, rather, that toddlers realize that they are in give-and-take interactions with other people, not demand-and-take relationships. What they put into an interaction helps determine what comes out of it, and the other person has her own needs and personality.

The responsiveness of the mother to each stage is critical. For example, when the child is totally dependent, the mother must be "good enough" (Winnicott, 1965), in that she dependably meets the child's needs for physical contact, food, and comfort. However, she should not be "perfect" in these tasks, because the infant needs to feel frustration and learn to trust that help will arrive eventually. When the child is between 18 and 36 months old, the mother must perform a balancing act between physically serving the child's needs and merely being available as the child becomes more independent. By the age of 3 if all goes well, the child learns that she and the mother are separate individuals yet closely related and reliably loving. The child also learns that both she and the mother have good and bad sides, and can synthesize these sides as belonging to a whole person (Kernberg, 1980/1994). The images of self and others are introjected; that is, the child mentally and emotionally accepts them to the point of incorporating them as her own (Winnicott, 1965). The images become psychological structures that have both feelings and thoughts associated with them, exist both consciously and unconsciously, and serve as the center of subjective experience throughout life (Hansen, 2000). Remember that they are not accurate images of the actual people: "Parental introjects must by definition be personalized, idiosyncratic, and distorted" because they are created from the point of view of children under the age of 3 (Bornstein, 1993, p. 7).

These images stick with us: "A great deal of our life is involved in the concealed repetition of early object relationships in one form or another" (Sandler & Sandler, 1978, p. 287). The outcome of having a responsive mother, who has supported the natural process of individuation, is an adult who has a stable image of self and sees other people realistically. A person with normal object relations views self and others as having identities continuous through time, with both positive and negative aspects coexisting (Kernberg, 1980/1994).

Disruptions or failures in early relationships, on the other hand, produce adults with various psychopathologies. If early frustrations have been too severe and unrelieved, the adult will view others as hostile and threatening. If the mother has been unpredictable, unstable, anxiety ridden, hostile, or unconfident, the child acquires a representation of others as discontinuous and untrustworthy (Mahler, 1968). Kernberg (1968) called this kind of representation of others a "nonmetabolized internal object," because it is not integrated into the self. Some mothers stop providing availability when a child is around 2 because they perceive the child as exploring on his own and figure that they are not needed so much, or because they have a new baby, or because they are depressed. Some children lose their mothers through death and divorce at this time. When such children become adults, they expect other people to abandon them. They may also be self-centered, having not developed a well-rounded representation of others since they were left on their own so early. Thus, they may have trouble understanding other people's responses and motivations. Alternatively, some mothers are too helpful and intrusive during the second and third years of a child's life, and the resulting adults expect to depend on others to meet their needs. These are examples of how early relationships serve as blueprints for adult relationships (Bornstein, 1993).

DISCUSSION IDEAS

Some psychologists believe that a girl's relationship with her father determines her relationships with men throughout her life, and the same with a boy and his mother. In your experience, have you observed this phenomenon? Discuss examples and counterexamples.

A particularly important failure of self and object representations involves the inability to synthesize good and bad—in infancy, the giving mother and the frustrating mother, and in early childhood, the loving child and the angry child. This inability could stem from fear of punishment if anger and frustration were expressed to powerful parents, so the bad parts are "split off"—that is, not integrated into the self or object as a whole. In short, when a mature view of positive and negative qualities does not gel, **splitting** occurs. The splitter views self and others as all good or all bad. Such people lack **object constancy**—the ability to keep an image of the good object even when frustrated by it (Kernberg, 1980/1994). They also feel split and unstable within themselves and fail to achieve a secure identity (Prochaska & Norcross, 1999). Consequently, relationships with others are stormy, confusing, and often short, as any disappointment can cast the other person from being an angel into being a devil. Obviously, the splitter does not see others as real, stable, complex individuals and often has a cartoon-like conception of other people. In the same vein, the sense of his or her own identity is fragile and easily shaken up, and at times the sufferer has the feeling of falling apart psychologically (Prochaska & Norcross, 1999). In its extreme form, splitting is rare and may result in the DSM diagnosis of *borderline personality*.

Research supports the continuity of quality of interpersonal relationships from age 3 to adulthood. That is, people stay the same in relationships throughout life. A large longitudinal study, done in New Zealand (Caspi, 2000), comprehensively assessed personality and behavioral variables in 1,037 individuals at ages 3, 5, 7, 9, 11, 13, 15, 18, and 21. This impressive study found coherence in relationship quality and psychiatric disorders within each participant's life: Temperament at age 3 could predict problems or successes at age 21.

Freud focused on psychological conflicts, while psychodynamic thinkers also focus on defects and deficits (Pine, 1998). People grow up to experience relationships that are vexed by their imposition of inappropriate prototypes upon other people. These inappropriate prototypes were formed due to defects in their upbringing, not due to intrapsychic conflicts among id, ego, and superego (Hansen, 2000).

Goals of Psychotherapy in Object Relations Approaches   The goal of therapy based on **object relations psychology** is to revise impaired object representations. Kernberg (1968), who maintained Freudian structural theory within object relations, identified the purpose of counseling as "a gradual broadening of the conflict-free ego sphere," meaning that the ego is freed up to pursue its healthy functions. He further specified goals that address particular problems of disturbed object relations (Kernberg, 1980/1994): distinguishing the self from the nonself; making a distinction between perceptions and stimuli that come from outside and those that come from inside; and being able to evaluate whether one's feelings, behaviors, and thoughts are in keeping with social norms. (Often a person with impaired object relations will surprise others by inappropriately judging an interpersonal situation—for example, describing an intimate traumatic experience to a group of strangers at a party.) Object relations counseling shares with the other psychodynamic approaches the mission of enhancing ego strength—that is, the ability to withstand frustration and nurture one's self. This mission is even more strongly reflected in the next theory, self psychology.

Self Psychology

Self psychology can be thought of as part of object relations theory, since our inner world has both self and object representations (Buckley, 1986). While object relations theory emphasizes interpersonal relationships, self psychology emphasizes the inner representation of the self. In both theories, very early, pre-Oedipal relationships with parents, especially the mother, determine the course of mental health or distress. In both, the parents must respond appropriately to the stages of the child's development, or else inner structures become defective. The self is the structure of interest to self psychologists, obviously.

Self is difficult to define, though we use the word daily. Pine (1998) gives a three-part description:

> An ongoing inner subjective state in each of us serves as a filter through which we experience the world—our personal tinted glasses, as it were. Typically these subjective states are organized around worth, continuity, wholeness, and well-being, on one side; around boundaries, realness, agency, and individuality, on another; and around comfort or basic anxiety and disease, on yet another. (p. 42)

To reframe the three parts Pine mentions, you might say that the self includes the part of you that generally is optimistic or pessimistic, the part of you that has a clear sense of individuality or a vague sense of identity, and the part of you that is relaxed or worried. The self is defined by your usual or baseline levels of these qualities, not by the way you might temporarily feel during the normal ups and downs of life.

Like object representations, a sense of self develops in the first three years of life. Infants and toddlers have two psychological needs (Kohut, 1977). The first is the need to be *mirrored*—that is, to have their activities and efforts accurately noticed by the parents and admired lavishly or lamented empathetically. The term **mirroring** thus refers to the accurate reflection of what the child is doing or feeling. Mirroring builds one component of the self, the **grandiose self,** which conveys to the child that he or she is perfect and the center of attention. The second psychological need is for **idealization.** The child needs to see the parents as all-powerful and flawless. Idealization builds a second component of the self, the inner representation of the *idealized parent.* This component, since the child is not individuated yet, says, "You are perfect, but I am a part of you" (St. Clair, 1996).

These are both immature needs. Between the ages of 1½ to 2½ or so, the child begins to develop a cohesive self that will fulfill versions of these needs from within him- or herself instead of strictly from the parents. Because parents cannot always accurately mirror nor serve the child perfectly, the child starts to build inner structures that take on the services once performed by the parents. These inner structures become the self. The grandiose self is damped down and modified, yet remains a source of ambition, energy, and self-esteem (Kohut, 1971). The idealized parent is incorporated as the superego—including the conscience as well as the **ego ideal,** or the idea of what one would be like if perfection were attainable. Thus, adults with cohesive selves have both a self-enhancing side that gives them hope and vitality, and a self-limiting side that keeps them within society's guidelines, makes them take other people's feelings into account (empathy), and reminds them that they are not, after all, perfect. These elements operate within the individual and do not constantly depend on others' behavior. Yet the cohesive self does not quickly pop up in a toddler: The seeds are planted. Acquisition of self is a lifelong process (Pine, 1998).

If parents are chronically unable to provide mirroring and to present idealized images, the process just described is damaged. St. Clair (1996) asserts that this chronic failure is most likely due to the parents' own psychological problems. For example, a depressed mother may not be able to notice her child's behavior well enough to adequately mirror. An emotionally cold father would not provide rich material for idealization. And deprivation of a parent or both parents could interrupt the process. In these cases, the immature needs for mirroring and idealization continue into adult life. The cohesive self, with transformed versions of these needs, does not develop, and there are deficits in the sense of self (Pine, 1999). The adult is not able to rely on inner sources of identity and regulation and may feel empty and depressed.

Relationships with others, in such cases, are distorted because the adult continually seeks an object to idealize and become one with, in order to achieve a feeling of well-being and self-esteem. People with missing aspects of the self do not have independent feelings of self-worth: They need to find powerful and idealized objects and to be affirmed by them. The deficient self seeks someone to provide the mirroring that was not forthcoming in childhood. Other people are dealt with as objects that might perform functions to bolster the self, not empathetically as real individuals. The playboy who goes through girlfriend after girlfriend (all beautiful, of course), and the dependent woman who feels she is nothing without her man, both suffer from defective self structures. For such people, not having an idealized object at hand disturbs self-esteem, and they feel "lethargic, powerless, and worthless" (Kohut, 1971, p. 92). Unfortunately, the object can lose its ideal status easily, especially upon negative judgment by a third party (Reich, 1953). Other people's opinions are over-influential upon those who lack trust in their own inner judgments.

Kohut (1971) saw the roots of narcissistic disorders in the defective self. Narcissists characteristically use other people to fulfill their needs and behave ruthlessly in attempts to get the admiration they cannot provide themselves from within. Because of a defective conscience, they seem to be strangers to shame. In a class I taught recently, every student had a story about someone they know with a narcissistic streak that produced shockingly unempathetic behavior. And, in my own case, I once had to call a narcissistic friend and cancel a movie date because my mother had a medical emergency, and I had to drive to her town and take care of her for the weekend. My friend responded, "Oh, that's okay, I have someone else coming over for the movie, anyway."

Goals of Psychotherapy in Self Psychology   Therapy based on self psychology seeks to strengthen the structure of the self (Hansen, 2000). The client should develop an appreciation of shadings of negative and positive in other people, establishing "a greater acceptance of reality, an ability to stand tension, to wait for gratification, to judge and think without being overwhelmed by desires and emotion" (Reich, 1953, p. 42). Kohut (1977) and other self psychologists believe that the cohesive self can be built or restored even in adulthood.

For future comparisons with other theories, notice that all four of these psychodynamic psychologies (Freudian, ego, object relations, and self) are grounded in painful affect, and their goals involve attempts to deal with that affect. They also aim to avoid harmful patterns that repeat ineffective childhood solutions to problems, and to usher in a future where the client has a better chance to fulfill his or her potential (Oremland, 1991).

Jungian Psychology

Jungian psychology, though not an offspring of Freudian psychoanalysis, is closely related in its emphasis on the unconscious and to psychoanalysis's historical time. Jung was already a psychiatrist when he read Freud's *The Interpretation of Dreams* (1900) and thought it was brilliant. The two men began to correspond in 1906, met for the first time in 1907 and reputedly talked for thirteen hours, and traveled to the United States to give lectures in 1909. By 1912, Jung's ideas had strayed far enough from Freud's that their friendship was severed (a common episode for the dogmatic Freud), and in 1914 Jung resigned as president of the International Psychoanalytic Association. The two men remained at odds, despite several productive years of exuberant collaboration.

Jung disagreed with Freud on the definition of *libido*, which Freud viewed as sexual energy. Jung believed that libido was a general life energy that found outlets in sex and in other ways, such as enjoyment of nature, creativity, and movement. Overall, Jung veered away from strictly sexual explanations, and he rejected the Oedipal complex. He simply did not believe that every boy wanted to possess his mother. Historians Schultz and Schultz (1999) speculate that these differences lay in biography: Freud had sexual inhibitions and prohibitions, while Jung did not. Freud had a beautiful, adoring mother, while Jung did not.

In his system of **analytical psychology,** Jung added another level of the unconscious. The personal unconscious consisted of memories and feelings that could be accessible to awareness. Beneath that was the *collective unconscious,* which holds the experience of our species throughout history, all the way back to animal precursors. This collective unconscious motivates us in certain directions and explains cross-cultural and ancient phenomena such as the universal appeal of certain types of stories, including the heroic-journey story and the stranger-comes-to-town-and-nothing-is-ever-the-same story, both of which are clearly still alive in films like *Lord of the Rings* and *E.T.*

From our ancestors we receive unconscious images of **archetypes,** which are universal characters that make up part of our personalities. These characters appear in religions, mystical systems, and artistic creations of our own and earlier civilizations. They also appear in our dreams. We each carry an archetypal **persona,** the mask we wear for the world to see, and the **shadow,** our unacceptable urges and desires or darker self that is usually hidden from others. We each also incorporate an archetype of the opposite sex: The **anima** represents the feminine side of a man, and the **animus** represents the male side of a woman. The **self,** which unifies all the others in a whole, healthy psyche, is the most important archetype. Other archetypal characters appear in dreams and fiction and appeal to us automatically: the savior, the wise old man, the earth mother, and the clever trickster, for example.

Jung had a positive view of human nature, in contrast to Freud's grim determinism. Jung was a religious Christian and a mystic and believed that we strive for higher goals than damping down the id. In particular, he thought we had a drive toward self-actualization, which was ripe at the ages of 35 to 40 (in the early 1900s, this was middle age!). **Self-actualization** means living up to our full potential as individuals and as members of society, and it is a concept that continues in the thinking of humanist psychologists. Jung's stage theory was quite a departure from Freud's, which emphasized the period from age 3 to 6 as the most important.

In *The Practice of Psychotherapy* (1954), a collection of essays Jung wrote between 1930 and 1954, he describes how his theory translates into action (although the essays devote much more space to theory than to practice). The process of psychotherapy involves four stages. The first involves a narrative of personal history, labeled a **confession** because it should involve revealing conscious and unconscious secrets: "A secret shared with several persons is as beneficial as a merely private secret is destructive" (p. 56), he wrote, later adding that "[t]o cherish secrets and hold back emotion is a psychic misdemeanor for which nature finally visits us with sickness" (p. 58). The next stage is **elucidation,** which uses something like the Freudian processes of interpreting transference and countertransference, and achieving insight. The third stage is **education,** in which the therapist helps translate the insights into responsible action in everyday life. The last stage, which is not reached by all clients, is **transformation,** in which self-actualization is pursued and the therapist and client become equals in the pursuit. In fact, Jung thought that the therapist often had to change himself in order to move forward at this stage.

Dream analysis is frequently used in all four stages. Jung saw dreams as revealing more than concealing meaning. Not only can they reflect wishes and fears; they also might suggest solutions to a client's current dilemma, or enact in archetypal characters and stories the client's psychological state. Following a series of dreams and watching the changes in them thus serve as measures of the client's progress in therapy.

Partly because of its mystical and abstract content, and partly because of a vague and tangential writing style, Jung is difficult for most people to read and is usually studied in secondary sources. Jungian analysts can be found in most large cities in the United States, and all kinds of people go to them for help, for all kinds of problems. Jungians are uniquely prepared to help with difficulties concerning religious and mystical matters, dilemmas having to do with the meaning of life, and concerns of the elderly and dying.

SMALL GROUP EXERCISE

Make up a chart that reflects the distinctions among Freudian psychoanalysis, ego psychology, object relations psychology, and self psychology. Next to each theory, list a few key terms that will help you remember the characteristic focuses and goals of each approach.

The Therapeutic Process

The four approaches in this chapter entail differing therapeutic processes, determined by the focus of the intervention: for Freudians, *drives*; for ego psychologists, *ego*; for object relations, *relationships*; and for self psychologists, *identity*. They also, however, share certain elements.

The Three Phases of the Therapeutic Process

I will first give an overview—derived from Oremland (1991), Winnicott (1965), and Horner (1991)—of three phases that the approaches usually have in common. Then I will survey how each approach is specially tailored to its focus.

The Initial Stage   In the initial stage, the psychotherapist makes use of transference and countertransference. These are identified and interpreted in various contexts, mainly or exclusively in terms of the relationship between the counselor and client. **Interpretation** consists of drawing inferences from what the client is saying, feeling, and enacting. For example, I had a client who always arrived for her sessions about one minute late, and then proceeded to gushingly apologize and lengthily explain her lateness. I inferred, first, that she had some need to elicit forgiveness that might have some roots in childhood experience; second, that she wanted to be sure that I knew I was not in complete control of her actions, suggesting a conflict with authority; and, third, that she avoided the more painful content of our sessions for a while by her long explanations, and that this might be the way she avoided other pain—through distraction with minor details. This inference process may sound like jumping to conclusions, but it shows the analytic frame of mind involved in therapy. As it turned out in this case, all the inferences were correct. But I had to collect more evidence in various contexts to make sure.

Whether and when such inferences are shared with the client is a matter of expert clinical judgment. Winnicott (1965) limited himself to one or two verbal interpretations per session. In this first stage of the therapeutic process, flooding the client with interpretations will backfire. Interpretations can easily be seen as criticism, rebuffs, or instructions (Oremland, 1991), until the client gets used to the safety of the therapeutic relationship. Limiting interpretations to what the client might accept or at least ponder at each point of the process is an art. Interpretations are usually made when the counselor feels that the idea is close to the client's conscious mind already, that the client is closing in on the same conclusion. An interpretation that is not very close to the client's own consciousness is a *confrontation*—as when a therapist points out a significant omission in a story, an omission of which the client is totally unaware. For example, one client attended four sessions in which she talked about her adult daughters extensively, and in the fifth mentioned her son as part of a tale about a daughter. The therapist exclaimed, "For all this time, it was not evident that you even *had* a son!" Confrontations are risky but sometimes powerful due to their unexpectedness.

My client's slight but constant lateness and explanations could be seen as an instance of **resistance.** No matter how distressing, the territory we know is less threatening than the territory we haven't explored. Clients will display some clinging to the status quo by being late, missing sessions, denying interpretations' accuracy, refusing to speak, creating distractions from touchy subjects, and so on. Counselors interpret the client's resistances. For example, when a client is stubbornly silent, the therapist might say, "You are afraid to let me know you." It's important to realize, however, that every behavior that *could* be resistant might not be. Over-labeling of resistance denies the client's legitimate reasons for being late, missing a session, and, especially, denying an interpretation. The therapist really could come up with a mistaken interpretation. When a client vehemently denies an interpretation, it is either really wrong or exactly right, and the therapist has to back off and wait for more evidence, or for more readiness on the client's part.

During the initial stage or even before therapy begins, transference begins, and a major task is to analyze the transference (Arlow, 2000). What feelings and actions toward the therapist are unconscious re-enactments of forgotten childhood experiences and repressed fantasies? Understanding the transference assists the client in evaluating how he or she might be relating to others unrealistically, through distorted lenses. Concurrently, understanding countertransference helps therapists see how others may be responding to the client in the outside world and assists them in separating their personal preferences and opinions from their analytic stance.

In all psychoanalytic and psychodynamic initial stages, an investigation of the client's childhood experiences is desirable. Since the past continues in the present, the client's view of his or her past (whether factual or not) is critical to accurate interpretations.

The Middle Stage: Working Through   The middle stage begins as the client becomes confident in the analytic process and in interpretations. Clients become more free in their thought and speech, less restricted by the rules of conversation they follow outside therapy. They have insight into how some of their conflicts and object relations are played out in their present life. At this stage, relationships with others are clarified and interpreted, and clients experiment with new ways of dealing with people, including the therapist. Shifts in perspective on relationships are expected. Themes from the past and themes from the present are interwoven. For example, my client realized that her strict, criticizing father, long dead, was still in action, affecting her difficulty in deciding on a dissertation adviser. She feared that when she made this commitment, she would face years of being negatively evaluated by a powerful man (all the choices were males). Characteristically, she avoided the risk by making up detailed arguments for and against each possible adviser and continuing undecided. At the time she came for counseling, she was in danger of being dropped from her program due to this delay.

Material from the initial stage is gone over again at this more conducive, evolving stage, in a **working-through process.** Clients may acknowledge interpretations they resisted before. They may also provide more evidence willingly. Ideally, the middle stage includes some resolution, redirection of strivings, or restructuring of the psyche that potentiates the future. My client was able to list her adviser choices from most liked to least liked and begin approaching them in that order.

Pine (1998) points out that, in his experience, problems that had existed over a long term responded to psychotherapeutic interpretations with insight but no change, while problems that were shorter term lent themselves to a sudden shift through insight. So, while my client was able to resolve the adviser problem (short term), I would never expect her problems with authority or her tendency to avoid through distraction (long term) to be erased!

The Final Stage: Termination   In ideal cases, **termination** of sessions with a client denotes a process of ending or completing, not quitting or stopping (Oremland, 1991). Nevertheless, it may seem similar to the process of loss and mourning. It should be planned in advance, never an abrupt closure. During this last stage, the therapist is usually seen more realistically and less idealistically than before. Material that has been worked through in the middle stage is revisited in terms of the present relationship, which is ending. Because both parties feel the loss, both may defend against it. The presenting problem of the client may recur, or the client may bring up new problems. The therapist may have concerns that the work is not really completed.

Both client and therapist benefit from discussing the gains made over the course of their relationship. They reminisce about incidents from early sessions. Clients maintain successes better when therapists are able to help them realize and verbalize the gains they have made.

Differences Among the Approaches

I will describe some of the features that distinguish the four psychodynamic approaches to counseling.

Freudian Psychoanalysis   Freudian psychoanalysis is relatively rare. It typically takes five to seven years, two to five sessions a week. The average termination phase is nine months. In consequence, it is very expensive, especially since most insurance plans and managed care organizations will not pay for such lengthy treatment. People who *can* afford psychoanalysis often are the same people who do not want to commit so many hours per week to it. Finally, psychoanalysis has a reputation for possessing no proof of effectiveness, being almost impossible to study empirically (that is, using controlled research designs) (Arlow, 2000).

The setting of Freudian psychoanalysis is familiar to most people from cartoons making fun of it. The client reclines on a couch with the analyst sitting in a chair behind it, unseen. The purpose is to relax the client for talking freely, and to prevent the client from being influenced by the facial expressions, body language, and appearance of the therapist. Since transference is so important, the analyst wants to allow the client to project any characteristics at all onto him or her, and this is more likely if the analyst remains unseen in reality. In addition, the analyst speaks very little and attempts to balance (a) being a blank slate for the client to inscribe meaning upon and (b) giving verbal interpretations according to the stage of the process. The client always starts the discourse; psychoanalysts do not wish to direct the client's flow of talk, especially in the first stage as they develop and check interpretations.

Psychoanalysts endorse a code of neutrality, abstinence, and relative anonymity. **Neutrality** means that their interpretations are based not on personal opinion but on analytical thought. **Abstinence** means that they do not participate in clients' fantasies or desires, to protect against fulfilling the analysts' own needs instead of the clients'. For example, if a client describes a daydream of running away and living on a Caribbean island, the analyst does not chime in, remarking how sometimes she would like to do that too. **Anonymity** means that the analysts' personal selves and lives are not topics for discussion. If a client asks a personal question, it is turned around: "Why is it important to you whether I have any children or not?" "What difference does it make to you whether I am heterosexual?" This is often frustrating for the client at first, but it precludes the analyst from self-centered talk, and allows a freer transference.

People often think that the psychoanalysts' code means that they are cool, aloof, and unsupportive. However, this is not necessarily true. In the analytic relationship, the analyst shows great support of the client by being reliable, being attentive, taking a nonjudgmental stance, and refraining from interpretation according to expert judgment about the client's ability to tolerate it (Pine, 1998). Ideally, analysts provide a context of safety and confidentiality, as well as an unadulterated focus on the client (as much as this is possible among human beings).

Freudian analysis has been transformed into briefer approaches that alter the process somewhat and are much more commonly employed. *Psychoanalytical psychotherapy* and *psychoanalytic counseling*, which are terms used interchangeably most of the time, usually take place once or twice a week and make use of face-to-face interaction instead of the couch. The therapist also adheres less strictly to neutrality and anonymity, and speaks more. While Freudian analysts assume that insight will lead to change and relief on its own, psychoanalytical psychotherapists do not; rather, they assist the client in implementing change. In addition, psychotherapists often focus on narrower targets of change, rather than on restructuring the psyche. Yet their basis for conceptualization of problems remains Freudian—that is, based on intrapsychic conflict.

Ego Psychology   While Freudian analysis focuses on the transference, ego psychology focuses on the defenses and whether they are rigid or flexible, few or many, readily available or not, effective or not, and adaptive or not. Remember that defense mechanisms serve to defuse anxiety over drive impulses. Some defenses are considered primitive, such as regression and displacement, and some are mature, such as a reasonable amount of sublimation in work, humor, sports, and art. Ego-oriented therapy follows the stages of Freudian therapy, with the substitution of interpretation and clarification of defenses in place of transference. The working alliance between client and counselor is more significant because part of the process involves breaking through negative defenses so that the client is free to feel and talk about threatening fears, self-esteem problems, and longings (Mishne, 1993). These have been buried under habitual defenses like denial, projection of blame, and emotional insulation. The counselor assists the client in loosening rigid defense patterns and employing a broader and more appropriate range. When energy is not consumed by defensive operations, it can be deployed in other, healthy ego functions such as tolerating frustration, planning toward goals, and exploring identity.

Object Relations   An object relations approach to treatment escalates the role of the therapist far beyond the "blank slate" of the psychoanalyst. In this approach, the therapist provides a "good object" to be internalized by the client in hopes of repairing past and present disturbed relationships (Buckley, 1986).

As the counselor and client move through the process of investigating childhood experiences and interpretation of distortions in perceiving other people, there is no doubt that at some points the client will become angry at and frustrated by the counselor. Through absorbing and processing the negative feelings without retaliation or abandonment, the counselor models a relationship that can survive them. The client learns that "aggression need not destroy, seduction need not seduce, that a steady relationship can continue despite such assault and threats" (Pine, 1998, p. 210). Through the relationship with the therapist, the client renounces the "all good" or "all bad" judgment of others and self, realizing that variation can exist within one person. This realization should transfer to how the client views people outside therapy as well.

Self Psychology The distinctive feature of self psychology treatment is Kohut's methodology of empathic immersion in the client's inner life (St. Clair, 1996). The counselor, instead of taking the stance of an outside expert, attempts to listen to the clients from their own perspectives (Bacal & Newman, 1990). You will see this feature again in existential and humanistic approaches. Clients grow from the experience of having someone truly try to understand how the world looks to them, something that may never have happened before. Having someone in tune with their needs and wishes, as evidently their parents were not, is a healing process. Often, the parents themselves were not able to give and receive affirmation and understanding (Mishne, 1993). The shift from outside observer to empathic identification requires the counselor to identify the core feelings of pain and chaos beneath belligerence, selfishness, abuse, and rage.

Therapist **empathy** and client **introspection** are the cornerstones of self psychology treatment. The fact that the counselor is nonjudgmentally trying to enter the client's world encourages the client to describe feelings that he otherwise hides from self and others, and to identify the ways in which he hides them (frequently, rage and withdrawal). The therapist, realizing the client's need for mirroring, is generous with praise and admiration for any signs of self-esteem, frustration tolerance, self-control, and acceptance of minor hurts. Meanwhile, she models "the essence of the perfect parent who provided insight, calmness, strength, and power" (Mishne, 1993), appealing to the need for idealization. Thus, the self psychologist attempts to provide a corrective emotional experience that heals the fragmented identity.

Self psychology predates contemporary theory in another way: It identifies psychotherapy as a two-person pursuit (or, if a family of three is being seen, a four-person pursuit, and so on). The therapist's contribution *as a person* to the relationship is considered. The self psychologists' point of view is that the dynamics and episodes of a relationship are affected by personalities and defenses on both sides, even in counseling. This is a huge step away from traditional analytic neutrality, abstinence, and anonymity. As Renik (1995) put it, "If an analyst places primary emphasis on the importance of healing interactions within the treatment relationship, as opposed to the pursuit of insight, there is no reason for the analyst to strive for a posture of anonymity" (p. 475).

SMALL GROUP EXERCISE

Now that you have read about these four theories and the treatments that flow from them, think about problem-treatment-therapist matching. In a small group, brainstorm a list of problems for which people seek treatment. Discuss which of the psychodynamic approaches would be most appropriate for each problem. If you were adept at all of the treatment approaches, how would you choose which one to emphasize when a client entered therapy? If you could be adept at only one of these approaches, which one do you think would best suit your personality and philosophy? Compare your responses with other group members' responses.

Customary Techniques

Several of the customary techniques of psychoanalysis and psychodynamic therapy have come up already in my discussion of theories and processes. Now let's look at the techniques as a group of interventions.

Interpretation

Interpretation is key to Freudian analysis, ego psychology, and object relations psychology. In *The Interpretation of Dreams* (1900), Freud called interpretation *decoding*, and this is an accurate metaphor. The client presents seemingly disorganized material that the therapist attempts to translate into coherent, meaningful language. Earlier I wrote about interpreting transference, countertransference, and resistance, all of which are codes for the client's habitual, unconscious responses to people, situations, and therapy. Other sources of material for interpretation also exist. For example, Freud thought that slips of the tongue were never merely accidents. A colleague gave me a funny example from a student who had missed an exam. The student came to class the next week and blurted, "Professor R., I would've been here for the test, except my grandma lied." Forgetting, too, is never just an accident in Freudian terms. Most of us would agree that forgetting a wedding anniversary, for instance, carries symbolic meaning about the marriage. Losing things is a similar example. I once took a course that I intensely disliked, and I continually lost my textbook, leaving it behind in other people's offices or putting it in strange places I couldn't remember. Freudians also interpret the symbolic content of physical symptoms. In *The Interpretation of Dreams* (1900), Freud told the story of a young woman who was plagued by fits of vomiting. In Freud's interpretation, this was the fulfillment of a fantasy she had had since puberty: the wish to be continuously pregnant. Many people do encode their psychological problems physically, more in some cultures than in others. People from Asian cultures, for example, tend to complain of physical ailments when they are not at ease emotionally (Uba, 1994). However, there is evidence that Freud overdid the interpretation sometimes and mistook a medical illness for a wish fulfillment. Freud is famous for interpreting dreams, of course—a topic I will take up separately.

Oremland (1991) provides an example of an exchange involving several interpretations. In this scene, the client has asked the psychotherapist a question, and the psychotherapist has not responded. The client then speaks:

> "You are trying to get me to think of it [the answer] myself?" The psychotherapist interprets, "You're justifying me to protect me from your anger." Perhaps the patient then falls silent, and the psychotherapist continues, "You withhold from me the way you felt I withheld from you—a kind of anger." The patient responds, "If I get angry, you won't talk to me." The psychotherapist responds, "You see me as easily frightened by your feelings and clamming up to punish you." (pp. 47–48)

Free Association

The client's major input into the interpretive pursuit is **free association.** She lies on the couch and is asked to say everything she is thinking and feeling, no matter what it is or whether it makes any sense or coherence. This free flow of talk provides the analyst with material for interpretation. The client's unconscious, in such an unusual discourse, emerges encoded as choice of topic, slips of the tongue, descriptions of dreams, memories, thoughts, preoccupations, and even silences and omissions. How one subject leads to another is more grist for the mill. Disruptions and blockages in the flow of talk can also be interpreted, usually denoting some anxiety about a topic. Clients get better at free association as they become used to it. As the client talks, the analyst is conceiving of interpretations, looking for evidence or counterevidence of them, and deciding which, if any, of the acceptable interpretations should be verbalized to the client at the time.

Reflection

To get a feel for free association, place a tape recorder next to your sofa or recliner and lie down. Set a timer for ten minutes. Follow the directions for free associating: Say whatever comes into your mind for ten minutes, letting your thoughts roam anywhere. If you get stuck, describe everything you are aware of at the moment and the associations you make to those things.

Next, think about what the experience was like. Did you enjoy it? Was it difficult or easy? Would you be embarrassed if you were in a psychoanalyst's office? Would you be embarrassed if a friend heard your tape? Do you think you would get better at this with practice?

Now, listen to the tape. Try to think of it as a psychoanalytic therapist would. Can you see your deepest wishes, needs, and fears reflected? Can you see basic themes and preoccupations? Are there blocks and shifts after material that causes you anxiety?

If your class wants to, you can have a whole-group discussion about the experience of free associating.

Dream Interpretation

Freud wrote that dreams were "the royal road to a knowledge of the unconscious activities of the mind" (1900). He was certain that the underlying meanings of dreams represent forbidden instinctual wishes. A person's needs, fears, and characteristic ways of being are reflected in the dream. Freud did believe in some universal images that symbolized the same things for all dreamers: Long objects are penises, going up and down stairs represents sexual activity, flying represents power or grandiosity, and many other such codes. The psychoanalyst also asks the client, after describing the dream in detail, to free-associate to various elements within it, so the client does get his or her personal symbolism into the interpretation.

A dream has *manifest content*, which is the surface action and emotion of the dream, and *latent content*, the symbolic meaning (Shapiro, 1995). Manifest content is often derived from events in recent real life, and we can often identify these easily. I might dream about catching a bus when I have thought during the day about taking a trip, for example. The manifest dream has processed unconscious meanings in several ways—in effect, disguising the latent content. Symbolism is one example. Another is condensation, a process in which many ideas are represented with a single visual image. I will give you an illustration.

One time I was writing a book and came to a chapter that I had difficulty composing; I had a case of writer's block, you might say. During this time, I dreamed that I was in a parking garage and couldn't find my truck, unable to remember where I parked it. I was with some people who were disgusted with me for forgetting where I'd parked, and I was panicky because I needed to be at an appointment soon and needed to drive my truck there. I looked down at my fingers and noticed that they were damaged, becoming shorter, with pieces falling off.

On the manifest level, in reality, I had been in an unfamiliar parking garage two days earlier and remembered memorizing my level number so that I would be able to find my truck later. Also, within the past six months I had moved to a building with a parking garage, which none of my other homes ever had. My hands are in my visual field all day long because I sit in front of a computer and write. Where the manifest material came from was not a mystery.

The latent content had to do with my distress about my writer's block. I wasn't able to get anywhere on my chapter, symbolized by losing my truck and not being able to get anywhere. I had also been worried about editors waiting for my manuscript (the disgusted people in the dream) and fearful about missing a deadline (the appointment in the dream). My damaged fingers, I think, were an example of condensation: First, I was having trouble "getting a grip" on the material I was writing; and, second, I make my living using my hands on the computer keyboard, and the damage meant that I was unable to do my work, which, at that time, I was. A Freudian analyst would probably find even deeper symbolic meanings, such as my fingers being symbols of the phallus and their damage representing my loss of power (my writer's block).

Ego psychologists think about manifest content as a clue to personality organization. The surface material suggests whether the personality is obsessional, chaotic, or organized, for example (Shapiro, 1995). The sleeping mind's choice of which manifest content to use is also suggestive, especially when the therapist is looking at several dreams from the same person. Are all the dreams full of people? Or are they devoid of anyone but the dreamer? Are they outdoors or indoors? Is the emotional tone usually positive, negative, neutral, or shifting from one to the other? Next to the dreamer, who appears most often? If there is conflict, is it resolved, and how? And so on. Self psychologists look at these types of questions to explore with clients how the dream preserves identity through themes. From this point of view, analyzing the dreams brings the state of self to conscious awareness.

R e f l e c t i o n

Place a pen and notepad beside your bed and record your dreams. To help you do this, remind yourself before you go to sleep each night that you want to remember your dreams. Oddly enough, this works. If you can, note down after the dream description any ideas you have about the source of the manifest content. After you have collected a few dreams, read them all in sequence. Can you see your wishes, needs, and fears reflected? If a stranger read them, could they make any educated guesses about your usual ways of thinking, feeling, and relating to others? Are there themes that recur?

Corrective Emotional Experiences

In object relations and self psychotherapy, the therapist functions as a person in a close relationship in order to provide a **corrective emotional experience** for the client. In object relations work, the therapist attempts to establish a relationship that can weather the client's frustrations and outbursts without punishment or abandonment. The goal is for the client to realize that the therapist is neither hateful nor perfect but, rather, a whole person who can withstand emotions and remain intact. The client's outside relationships are re-evaluated in the light of that new understanding.

In self psychology, the therapist does what some writers call "reparenting" or "remothering." She (or he) provides corrective experiences by catching the client's cues about feelings and needs, when the real mother was unable or un-available to catch these cues in the client's infancy. She also accurately mirrors the client and bolsters his self-esteem, by admiring and praising his successes and progress. Meanwhile, she displays the wisdom and strength of a perfect parent, serving as an object for idealization. In these approaches, the therapist foregoes traditional anonymity.

Uses of Psychodynamic Approaches

Psychodynamic and psychoanalytic approaches have been used for all kinds of problems, from writer's block to criminal impulses. A few common problem types prevail in today's practice.

Anxiety-Based Disorders in Individuals and Families

Freudian analysis, because it focuses on the anxiety produced by intrapsychic conflict and our attempts to deal with this anxiety, lends itself to distress that is clearly linked to the feeling. This distress can take several forms, including neurosis in general (that is, a characteristically negative response to self, others, and the world), depression, obsessive-compulsive behavior, phobias, sexual difficulties, eating disorders, hypochondria, aggressive behavior, nonorganic health problems (including paralysis) (Freud, 1895), and, of course, anxiety. All of these disorders, psychoanalysts say, improve or disappear when insight into the underlying source (usually aggressive or sexual) is achieved in analysis. Mishne (1993) argued that Freudian psychoanalysis was appropriate only for "intact individuals with circumscribed intrapsychic conflicts" (p. 78). By *intact* Mishne meant that the client needs to be able to establish the transference, which cannot be done by people whose psychological structures are too disorganized to distinguish self from other, past from present, frustration from rage, and so on. Thus, Freudian analysis is not recommended for actively psychotic disorders.

Children, too, are usually unable to establish a transference in traditional couch therapy, though they also suffer from the disorders listed above. Anna Freud applied psychoanalytic theory to children by observing them in play therapy and in their natural settings, and involved the parents directly. Winnicott (1965) applied psychoanalytic principles to child therapy in an object relations framework, which involves "controlled regression"—that is, a return to an early, dependent stage at which there was a failure in the environment to adapt to the child's needs. When controlled regression is achieved, the therapist provides a successful experience to replace the early failure. Winnicott used creative, playful techniques such as the "squiggle game," in which he and the child would alternate in drawing random squiggles, which the partner had to make into recognizable objects by completing the drawing. This is like a child's version of free association and serves the same purposes.

Scharff and Scharff (1991, 1997) describe techniques for applying psychoanalytic principles to couples and families suffering from group disarray with contributions from each member's anxiety management patterns (such as defense mechanisms). They apply "psychoanalytic techniques of listening and following associations, making the unconscious conscious through interpretation of resistance and defense, developing insight, and working through toward change" (p. 14). However, the structural aspect of the theory is dispensed with as it applies to individual psyches, meanwhile focusing on similar structures as they work in a dynamic system within the couple or family.

Narcissistic Personality Disorder

As categorized in DSM-IV-TR, **narcissistic personality disorder** is a pattern of grandiosity, need for admiration, and lack of empathy that occurs across contexts (American Psychiatric Association, 2000). Narcissists overestimate themselves and underestimate others, feel that they should be famous or privileged, need positive attention constantly, and are unaware that other people have feelings and needs that should be considered. Underlying these features is a pervasive lack of self-esteem. I brought up this disorder earlier, and self psychology is acclaimed for providing the best conceptualization of how it develops and can be treated (Kohut, 1971; Reich, 1953).

When parents are perceived by a child to have withdrawn from, lost interest in, or abandoned him or her as a toddler, the child fails to develop positive feelings about the self. Absent or impoverished mirroring (feeding the child's grandiosity need) and availability for idealization (the second major need) leave the child without the resources for transforming these needs into their mature forms in the cohesive self. Mirroring should transform into self-esteem and energy, and idealization should transform into conscience and high standards. Both should be integrated and exist in a balance in the mature adult. However, without the immature versions of grandiosity and idealization, the child is left on his own and becomes the major object of his psychological universe. The lack of affirmation from outside continues to drive adult behavior in the narcissist. Therapy, as I mentioned before, involves re-parenting the client with appropriate mirroring and becoming an idealized object so that the client moves from self-centeredness to interest in the therapist and then, later, to attention to others.

Borderline Personality Disorder

Otto Kernberg (1968) developed an "expressive psychoanalytic approach" (p. 616) to **borderline personality disorder.** Like narcissism, borderline disorders are considered extremely difficult to change. As categorized in DSM-IV-TR, borderline personality disorder is marked by instability of interpersonal relationships (friends and romantic partners are never kept long but are very intense while they exist), unstable sense of self (lots of changes in opinions and plans), impulsivity (especially self-destructive actions), and drastic mood swings (American Psychiatric Association, 2000).

Kernberg (1968) believes that the disorder grows from continuous frustration without attentive relief before the age of 4. The frustrated child feels anger and hatred for the negligent parents and concludes that they are also angry and hateful toward her (in a process of projection). The object relation result is that others are seen as dangerous rather than nurturing. The therapist is seen this way, too, and the borderline client makes efforts to keep the therapist's imagined anger under control. Meanwhile, she cannot help expressing her outrage at the therapists' imagined aggressive, hostile actions. The therapist refuses to be drawn into a fight.

Traditional analysis is modified for the borderline client (Kernberg, 1968). Instead of encouraging the negative transference, which is described above, the therapist deflects it by examining not feelings about the therapist but relationships with other people. (In contrast, during the first stage of other clients' analysis, the transference to the therapist is emphasized.) The therapist actively tries to block the borderline client's pattern of acting out negative transferences by structuring the sessions and even the client's environment (using hospitalization or day treatment to prevent self-destructive opportunities). Positive transference—perceiving the therapist as a good object—is encouraged, and therefore confrontations are rare since they will automatically be seen as angry threats. Kernberg assumes that borderline clients possess a longing for a good relationship with a powerful man or woman, and the therapist tries to provide this corrective emotional experience while protecting the client from self-destruction.

Schizoid Disorders

Fairbairn (1941), an object relations theorist, applied psychoanalytic thinking to a group usually not included in that arena: psychotic individuals. Fairbairn concluded that the schizoid group included more people than usually considered to be the case. Today's DSM-IV-R (American Psychiatric Association, 2000) describes the main features of **schizoid personality disorder** as lack of desire for human intimacy, and constricted expression and experience of emotions. Fairbairn's theory included schizophrenic, schizoid, and "a high percentage of anxiety states and of paranoid, phobic, hysterical and obsessional symptoms" (p. 250) in the schizoid category. He believed the basis for all these was a "disintegration of the ego" (p. 251), involving a failure to integrate opposites like loving and hating, active and passive, into a coherent self. This malfunction stems from a failure of the environment (parents) to adapt to the child's needs, blocking the normal growth process that leads to a feeling of continuity of self, harmony with one's body, and capacity for relating to others.

Fairbairn (1941) wrote that "[f]rustration of his desire to be loved and to have his love accepted is the greatest trauma that a child can experience; and indeed this is the only trauma that really matters from a developmental standpoint" (p. 261). Adults who have not been able to depend on giving and receiving love as infants are never able to renounce infantile dependence, which fills them with anxiety because they have no evidence that love is forthcoming. Similarly to other object relations and self approaches, therapy involves providing a corrective emotional experience that can be generalized to outside relationships.

✎ Case Conceptualization: An Example

Here is a case description and conceptualization published by D. W. Winnicott, a major figure in object relations theory. As you read, think about object relations psychology and identify elements of the theory in Winnicott's conceptualization.

STRING: A TECHNIQUE OF COMMUNICATION
D. W. Winnicott (1965)

A boy aged seven years was brought to the Psychology Department of the Paddington Green Children's Hospital by his mother and father in March 1955. The other two members of the family also came: an M.D. [mentally deficient] girl aged ten, attending an E.S.N. school, and a rather normal small girl aged four. The case was referred by the family doctor because of a series of symptoms indicating a character disorder in the boy. For the purposes of this description all details that are not immediately relevant to the main theme of this paper are omitted. An intelligence test gave this boy an I.Q. of 108.

I first saw the parents in a long interview in which they gave a clear picture of the boy's development and of the distortions in his development. They left out one important detail, however, which emerged in the interview with the boy.

It was not difficult to see that the mother was a depressive person, and she reported that she had been hospitalized on account of depression. From the parents' account I was able to note that the mother cared for the boy until the sister was born when he was 2 years 3 months. This was the first separation of importance, the next being at 3 years 3 months when the mother had an operation. When the boy was 4 years 9 months the mother went into a mental hospital for two months, and during this time he was well cared for by his mother's sister. By this time everyone looking after this boy agreed that he was difficult, although showing very good features. He was liable to change suddenly and to frighten people by saying, for instance, that he would cut his mother's sister into little pieces. He developed many curious symptoms such as a compulsion to lick things and people; he made compulsive throat noises; often he refused to pass a motion [use the toilet] and then made a mess. He was obviously anxious about his elder sister's mental defect, but the distortion of his development appears to have started before this factor became significant.

After this interview with the parents I saw the boy in a personal interview. There were present two psychiatric social workers and two visitors. The boy did not immediately give an abnormal impression and he quickly entered into a squiggle game with me. (In this squiggle game I make some kind of an impulsive line drawing and invite the child whom I am interviewing to turn it into something, and then he makes a squiggle for me to turn into something in my turn.)

The squiggle game in this particular case led to a curious result. The boy's laziness immediately became evident, and also nearly everything I did was translated by him into something associated with string. Among his ten drawings there appeared the following: lasso, whip, crop, a yo-yo string, a string in a knot, another crop, another whip. After this interview with the boy I had a second one with the parents, and asked them about the boy's preoccupation with string. They said they were glad that I had brought up this subject, but they had not mentioned it because they were unaware of its significance. They said that the boy had become obsessed with everything to do with string, and in fact whenever they went into a room they were liable to find that he had joined together chairs and tables; and they might find a cushion, for instance, with a string joining it to the fireplace. They said that the boy's preoccupation with string was gradually developing a new feature, one which had worried them instead of causing them ordinary concern. He had recently tied a string round his sister's neck (the sister whose birth provided the first separation from his mother).

In this particular kind of interview I knew I had limited opportunity for action: it would not be possible to see these parents or the boy more frequently than once in six months, as the family lived in the country. I therefore took action in the following way. I explained to the mother that this boy was dealing with a fear of separation, attempting to deny separation by his use of string, as one would deny separation from a friend by using the telephone. She was sceptical, but I told her that should she come round to finding some sense in what I was saying I would like her to open up the matter with the boy at some convenient time, letting him know what I had said, and then developing the theme of separation according to the boy's response.

I heard no more from these people until they came to see me about six months later. The mother did not report to me what she had done, but I asked her and she was able to tell me what had taken place soon after the visit to me.

She had felt that what I had said was silly, but one evening she had opened the subject with the boy and found him to be eager to talk about his relation to her and his fear of a lack of contact with her. She went over all the separations she could think of with him with his help, and she soon became convinced that what I had said was right, because of his responses. Moreover, from the moment that she had this conversation with him the string play ceased. There was no more joining of objects in the old way. She had many other conversations with the boy about his feeling of separateness from her, and she made the very important comment that she felt the most important separation to have been his loss of her when she was seriously depressed: it was not just her going away, she said, but her lack of contact with him because of her complete preoccupation with other matters.

At a later interview the mother told me that a year after she had her first talk with the boy there was a return to playing with string and to joining together objects in the house. She was in fact due to go into hospital for an operation, and she said to him: "I can see from your playing with string that you are worried about my going away, but this time I shall only be away a few days, and I am having an operation which is not serious." After this conversation the new phase of playing with string ceased.

I have kept in touch with this family and have helped with various details in the boy's schooling and other matters. Now, four years after the original interview, the father reports a phase of string preoccupation, associated with a fresh depression in the mother. This phase lasted two months, and cleared up when the whole family went on holiday, and when at the same time there was an improvement in the home situation (the father having found work after a period of unemployment). Associated with this was an improvement in the mother's state. The father gave one further interesting detail relevant to the subject under discussion. During this recent phase the boy acted out something with rope which the father felt to be significant, because it showed how intimately all these things were connected with the mother's morbid anxiety. He came home one day and found the boy hanging upside down on a rope. He was quite limp and acting very well as if dead. The father realized he must take no notice, and he hung around the garden doing odd jobs for half an hour, after which the boy got bored and stopped the game. This was a big test of the father's lack of anxiety. On the following day, however, the boy did the same thing from a tree which could easily be seen from the kitchen window. The mother rushed out severely shocked and certain that he had hanged himself.

The following additional detail might be of value in the understanding of the case. Although this boy, who is now eleven, is developing along "toughguy" lines, he is very self-conscious and easily goes red in the neck. He has a number of teddy bears which to him are children. No one dares say that they are toys. He is loyal to them, expends a great deal of affection, and makes trousers for them which involves careful sewing. His father says that he seems to get a sense of security from his family, which he mothers in this way. If visitors come, he puts them all into his sister's bed, because no one outside the family must know that he has this family. Along with this is a reluctance to defaecate, or a tendency to save up his faeces. It is not difficult to guess, therefore, that he has a maternal identification based on his own insecurity in relation to his mother, and that this could develop into homosexuality. In the same way the preoccupation with string could develop into a perversion.

Comment

The following comment seems to be appropriate.

(1) String can be looked upon as an extension of all other techniques of communication. String joins just as it helps in the wrapping up of objects and in the holding of unintegrated material. In this respect string has a symbolic meaning for everyone; an exaggeration of the use of string can easily belong to the beginnings of a sense of insecurity or the idea of a lack of communication. In this particular case it is possible to detect abnormality creeping into the boy's use of string, and it is important to find a way of stating the change which might lead to its use becoming perverted.

It would seem possible to arrive at such a statement if one takes into consideration the fact that the function of the string is changing from a joining into a *denial of separation*. As a denial of separation string becomes a thing in itself, something which has dangerous properties and has to be mastered. In this case the mother seems to have been able to deal with the boy's use of string just before it was too late, when the use of it still contained hope. When hope is absent and string represents a denial of separation, then a much more complex state of affairs has arisen—one which becomes difficult to cure, because of the secondary gains which arise out of the skill that develops whenever an object has to be handled in order to be mastered.

This case therefore presents special interest if it makes possible the observation of the development of a perversion.

(2) It is also possible to see from this material the use that can be made of parents. When parents can be used they can work with great economy, especially if the fact is kept in mind that there will never be enough psychotherapists to treat all those who are in need of treatment. Here was a good family that had been through a difficult time because of the father's unemployment; that had been able to take full responsibility for a backward girl in spite of the tremendous drawbacks, socially and within the family, that this entails; and that had survived the bad phases in the mother's depressive illness, including one phase of hospitalization. There must be a great deal of strength in such a family, and it was on the basis of this assumption that the decision was made to invite these parents to undertake the therapy of their own child. In doing this they learned a great deal themselves, but they did need to be informed about what they were doing. They also needed their success to be appreciated and for the whole process to be verbalized. The fact that they have seen their boy through an illness has given the parents

confidence with regard to their ability to manage the other difficulties which arise from time to time.

Summary

A case has been briefly described in order to illustrate a boy's compulsion to use string, at first in an attempt to communicate symbolically with his mother in spite of her withdrawal during depressive phases, and then as a denial of the separation. As a symbol of the denial of separation, string became a thing that was frightening and that had to be mastered, and its use then became perverted. In this case the mother herself did the psychotherapy, her task being explained to her by the psychiatrist. ■ ■

DISCUSSION IDEAS

1. What elements of object relations psychology did you see in Winnicott's case?

2. Did you also see elements of basic Freudian concepts? Which ones?

3. What were the symbolic meanings of string?

4. What was the treatment that Winnicott suggested to the mother? Did it work?

5. Are there features of the case study that strike you as out of date? What are they?

6. In the summary, Winnicott writes as though a cure was effected. Do you agree? Why or why not? If the boy were your client, what would you do next?

Critiques of Psychodynamic Approaches

Freudian psychoanalytic theory has come under fire for being "tautological, sexist, refractory to operational definitions, largely untested, and accepted by its adherents as gospel truth" (Masling & Bornstein, 1993). Freud is the subject of myriad jokes both among psychologists and laypeople, partly because of the theory's application to any behavior at all: "In Freudian therapy sessions, if you arrive early, you're anxious; if you arrive on time, you're compulsive; and if you're late, you're resistant." There's a Freudian explanation for every word and behavior if you reach for it. Reflecting what most people think of Freud, a hit situation comedy on television frequently ridicules Niles and Frasier Crane, both Freudian psychiatrists who continually misunderstand people in everyday life, while their father, an ex-cop, is usually right on the mark.

Attitudes Toward Women

Sexism is a major, serious, and prevalent critique of Freud's theory. In various works, Freud presented women as "masochistic, passive, narcissistic, envious, deficient in superego, and moreover inferior in relation to men (due at the core to anatomy and biology)" (Gelso & Fassinger, 1992). Karen Horney, who took orthodox psychoanalytic training, came to question several of Freud's tenets including the idea of **penis envy.** According to Freud, a driving force in girls' and women's psychology is their disappointment that they do not have penises, first discovered when they notice their brothers', fathers', or schoolmates' appendages. Horney (1945) ridiculed this thought and suggested that instead men suffered from womb envy since they cannot bear children, and they subsequently make efforts to keep women subservient because of this envy. Horney argued that if women felt envy of men, it was due to the obvious privileges men enjoyed in terms of power and freedom, not merely due to their possession of penises. Today, prominent psychologists such as Nancy Chodorow (1978) have revised Freudian theory to propose that men and women have different lines of development that are mixtures of environment and biology, each with its advantages and disadvantages.

In Freudian, ego, object relations, and self psychology, mothers are to blame for a great deal of psychopathology. Mothers fail at mirroring, for example, if they are unpredictable, unstable, anxiety-ridden, hostile, unavailable, or unconfident (Mahler, 1968). They even fail when they don't fail enough, not allowing the infant or child enough self-development. This thinking puts mothers in a no-win situation, especially in an era when most women must work outside the home, or want to do so.

Like many men of the Victorian era (and today's), Freud held contradictory views of women personally. Though he believed that the female sex was naturally subordinate and flawed, he welcomed discourse with many of the most cultivated and intelligent women of Europe and respected their opinions deeply. He credited women patients with their contributions to his techniques (free association in particular), and developed his theories through exploration of women and men from many social classes as well as intense scrutiny of history, anthropology, biography, and literature (Gay, 1988).

Heterosexual Ennoblement

Freud's stage theory closes with the ability to establish mature heterosexual relationships, leading to reproduction. Homosexuality reflects a fixation at the Oedipal stage and is considered a psychological disorder in conventional Freudian theory. Today's psychologists and psychiatrists do not agree, however, as evidenced by the removal of homosexuality as a disorder from the DSM in 1972. Most psychodynamic counselors, while endorsing many of Freud's theories, reject the idea that the only mature sexuality is between men and women. And most would renounce the idea that reproduction is the only healthy outcome of sexual and romantic relationships.

Limitations of Culture

Comas-Diaz and Minrath (1985), in an article on ethnic minority borderline clients and psychoanalysis, mention several cautions and special considerations due to cultural elements. They point out that identity problems are complicated when a client feels unstable not only within herself but also within mainstream society, wondering, "Where do I belong?" This is particularly true of mixed-race clients. Furthermore, the counselor's countertransference is likely to be complicated by unconscious or conscious racial and ethnic stereotypes. The working alliance between minority and majority members may be more difficult to establish due to mistrust and suspicion on either or both sides, based on social phenomena outside of the therapeutic situation.

Therapeutic Inefficiency

One of the foremost criticisms of psychoanalysis is its lack of proven effectiveness. Freud supports his theories with examples from his experience as a psychoanalyst, presented as case studies, and other psychoanalysis success stories are also case studies from people who already endorse the system. This type of support is not accepted by the scientific community as proof. People have a tendency to distort, omit, and invent when they report (or do not report) on their own cases. There have been a few controlled studies of therapeutic effectiveness that include psychodynamic approaches. Surveying three large outcome studies and five meta-analyses (which combine results from several studies) and reviews of research, Prochaska and Norcross (1999) summarized the consistent findings: "Measurable outcomes of psychoanalytic psychotherapy and short-term psychodynamic psychotherapy are superior to no-treatment and slightly to considerably inferior to alternative psychotherapies" (p. 60) such as behavioral, cognitive, and supportive treatments. (Notice that strictly conventional Freudian analysis was not included in these controlled studies, probably due to its length and rarity; instead, its modern successors were included.)

On the other hand, from the 1970s on, there have been many well-designed empirical studies testing and extending psychoanalytical *concepts* (Masling & Bornstein, 1993). Cognitive psychological experiments have supported the fact that we are often influenced and motivated by perceptions and memories outside of awareness. Moreover, we hold mental schemas that we impose on our experiences, as predicted by object and self theories. The fact that a theory was generated from case observations and introspection does not automatically make it untrue. As Masling and Bornstein assert, "Relatively few truly creative ideas have originated in laboratory studies of personality" (p. xxii), but instead have been inspired by therapist-client interactions and case studies.

Negativity

Finally, many people find Freud's outlook on human nature distasteful and dreary. The idea that we go through life basically motivated by our struggles against id urges and efforts to control anxiety flies in the face of our preferences for free will, self-fulfillment, altruism, and the natural goodness of the human being. Several theorists after Freud developed their work at least partly in reaction to Freud's deterministic view of human strivings.

KEY TERMS

abstinence
analytical psychology
anima
animus
anonymity
anxiety
archetypes
borderline personality
    disorder
confession
corrective emotional
    experience
countertransference
defense mechanisms
denial
deterministic
displacement
dream analysis
drives
education
ego
ego ideal
ego psychology
ego strength
ego theory
Electra complex

elucidation
emotional insulation
empathy
fantasy
free association
grandiose self
humanism
id
idealization
identification
insight
interpretation
introspection
mirroring
narcissistic personality
    disorder
neutrality
object constancy
object relations theory
object relations
    psychology
objects
Oedipal stage
penis envy
persona
pleasure principle

projection
psychoanalytic
psychodynamic
rationalization
reaction formation
reality principle
regression
repression
resistance
schizoid personality
    disorder
self
self-actualization
self theory
shadow
splitting
sublimation
superego
suppression
transformation
termination
transference
unconscious
working-through
    process

Exploring Key Terms

Divide the above list of key terms evenly among your small groups. Within your small group, divide your part of the list evenly among members. Outside of class, work on definitions in the following way:

Each member needs to use this textbook, as well as another theories of psychology textbook, a history of psychology textbook, or a general psychology textbook (available from the library, your own shelves, or your professors' collections). Using these textbooks (look in the index and table of contents for help), each member should write one to three sentences defining the key terms assigned to him or her. Feel free to add refinements based on books outside this one.

Back in class, pass definitions around in your small group for editing: Make sure they are correct and complete. Compile them and make copies of the revised definitions for the whole class, or send electronic copies to all class members. This way, everyone will have a list of definitions to study.

LIBRARY, MEDIA, AND INTERNET ACTIVITIES

1. The American Psychological Association, between 1998 and 2002, published a series of five collections of research study reports on psychoanalytic theories. Each one focuses on a different area of theory. Go to the organization's website at *http://www.apa.org/books* and read about these books. The series as a whole is called *Empirical Studies in Psychoanalytic Theories*.

Decide which book best fits your own interests and take it out of your library or order it from interlibrary loan. Read at least one of the chapters and prepare a summary to present to your small group or class. Set a date a few weeks ahead for this purpose.

2. The major psychoanalytic and psychodynamic journals are *American Journal of Psychoanalysis, Bulletin of the Menninger Clinic, Dynamic Psychotherapy, Issues in Ego Psychology, Journal of Analytic Social Work, Journal of Psychoanalytic Psychology, Psychoanalytic Abstracts,* and *Journal of the American Psychoanalytic Association.* Find out which of these your library carries and write down their call numbers and locations.

3. The APA's Division 39 (*www.apa.org/about/div39.html*) is focused on psychoanalytic psychology. Another website of interest is the American Psychoanalytic Association's (*www.apsa-co.org*), which includes key concept definitions in "About Psychoanalysis" and a spot where you can read the archives of "Ask a Psychoanalyst." The Brill Library, home of many important Freud documents, can be found at *www.psychoanalysis.org*, and I have had my questions about Freud answered by experts through this site. At *www.selfpsychology.org* and *www.objectrelations.org*, you find information and links about psychodynamic approaches.

Review two of these sites and jot down what type of material is available from each. Also, use a general search engine like Google to see whether there are other sites relevant to Freudian, ego, object relations, and self psychology. Use both the names of the approaches and the names of major figures in this search.

REFERENCES

American Psychiatric Association. (2000). *Diagnostic and statistical manual of mental disorders* (4th ed., text revision). Washington, DC: Author.

Arlow, J. A. (2000). Psychoanalysis. In R. J. Corsini & D. Wedding (Eds.), *Current psychotherapies* (6th ed.) (pp. 16–53).

Bacal, H., & Newman, K. M. (1990). *Theories of object relations: Bridges to self psychology.* New York: Columbia University Press/Itasca, IL: Peacock Publishers.

Baumeister, R. F. (2001). Ego depletion, the executive function, and self-control: An energy model of the self in personality. In B. W. Roberts & R. Hogan (Eds.), *Personality psychology in the workplace* (pp. 299–316). Washington, DC: American Psychological Association.

Bem, D. J. (1996). Exotic becomes erotic: A developmental theory of sexual orientation. *Psychological Review, 103,* 320–335.

Bornstein, R. F. (1993). *The dependent personality.* New York: Guilford Press.

Bowlby, J. (1958). The nature of the child's ties to the mother. *International Journal of Psychoanalysis, 39,* 350–373.

Buckley, P. Introduction. In P. Buckley(Ed.), *Essential papers on object relations* (pp. ix–xxv). New York: New York University Press.

Caspi, A. (2000). The child is father of the man: Personality continuities from childhood to adulthood. *Journal of Personality and Social Psychology, 78,* 158–172.

Chodorow, N. (1978). *The reproduction of mothering.* Berkeley: University of California Press.

Comas-Diaz, L., & Minrath, M. (1985). Psychotherapy with ethnic minority borderline clients. *Psychotherapy, 22,* 418–426.

Erikson, E. H. (1950). *Childhood and society.* New York: Norton.

Fairbairn, W. R. D. (1941). A revised psychopathology of the psychoses and psychoneuroses. *International Journal of Psychoanalysis, 22,* 250–279.

Freud, A. (1936). *The ego and mechanisms of defense.* New York: International Universities Press.

Freud, S. (1895). *Studies on hysteria.* (Standard Edition, Vol. 2). London: Hogarth Press.

Freud, S. (1920). *Beyond the pleasure principle.* (Standard Edition, Vol. 18). London: Hogarth Press.

Freud, S. (1923). *The ego and the id.* (Standard Edition, Vol. 19). London: Hogarth Press.

Freud, S. (1965). *The interpretation of dreams.* New York: Discus. (Original work published 1900)

Gay, P. (1988). *Freud: A life for our time.* New York: Doubleday.

Gelso, C. J., & Fassinger, R. E. (1992). Personality, development, and counseling psychology: Depth, ambivalence, and actualization. *Journal of Counseling Psychology, 39,* 275–298.

Hansen, J. T. (2000). Psychoanalysis and humanism: A review and critical examination of integrationist efforts with some proposed resolutions. *Journal of Counseling and Development, 78,* pp. 21–28.

Hartmann, H. (1958). *Ego psychology and the problem of adaptation.* New York: International Universities Press.

Horner, A. J. (1991). *Psychoanalytic object relations therapy.* Northvale, NJ: Jason Aronson.

Horney, K. (1945). *Our inner conflicts.* New York: Norton.

Jung, C. G. (1954). *The practice of psychotherapy.* New York: Pantheon.

Kernberg, O. (1968). The therapy of patients with borderline personality organization. *International Journal of Psychoanalysis, 49,* 600–619.

Kernberg, O. F. (1994). *Internal world and external reality.* Northvale, NJ: Jason Aronson. (Original work published 1980)

Kohut, H. (1971). *The analysis of the self.* New York: International Universities Press.

Kohut, H. (1977). *The restoration of the self.* New York: International Universities Press.

Mahler, M. S. (1968). On human symbiosis and the vicissitudes of individuation. *Journal of the American Psychoanalytic Association,* 740–763.

Masling, J. M., & Bornstein, R. F. (1993). Introduction: On the empirical testing of psychoanalytic concepts. In J. M. Masling & R. F. Bornstein (Eds.), *Psychoanalytic perspectives on psychopathology* (pp. xxii–xxix). Washington, DC: American Psychological Association.

Mishne, J. M. (1993). *The evolution and application of clinical theory.* New York: Free Press.

Oremland, J. D. (1991). *Interpretation and interaction: Psychoanalysis or psychotherapy?* Hillsdale, NJ: Analytic Press.

Pine, F. (1998). *Diversity and direction in psychoanalytic technique.* New Haven: Yale University Press.

Prochaska, J. O., & Norcross, J. C. (1999). *Systems of psychotherapy: A transtheoretical analysis* (4th ed.). Pacific Grove, CA: Brooks/Cole.

Reich, A. (1953). Narcissistic object choice in women. *Journal of the American Psychoanalytic Association, 1,* 22–44.

Renik, O. (1995). The ideal of the anonymous analyst and the problem of self-disclosure. *Psychoanalytic Quarterly, 64,* 466–495.

Sandler, J., & Sandler, A. (1978). On the development of object relationships and affects. *International Journal of Psycho-Analysis, 59,* 285–296.

Scharff, D. E., & Scharff, J. S. (1991). *Object relations family therapy.* Northvale, NJ: Jason Aronson.

Scharff, J. S., & Scharff, D. E. (1997). Object relations couple therapy. *American Journal of Psychotherapy, 51,* 141–173.

Schultz, D. P., & Schultz, S. E. (1999). *A history of modern psychology* (7th ed.). Belmont, CA: Wadsworth.

Shapiro, S. (1995). *Talking with patients: A self psychological view of creative intuition and analytic discipline.* Northvale, NJ: Jason Aronson.

Sharf, R. S. (2000). *Theories of psychotherapy and counseling* (2nd ed.). Pacific Grove, CA: Brooks/Cole.

St. Clair, M. (1996). *Object relations and self psychology.* Pacific Grove, CA: Brooks/Cole.

Uba, L. (1994). *Asian Americans: Personality patterns, identity, and mental health.* New York: Guilford Press.

Winnicott, D. W. (1965). *The maturational processes and the facilitating environment.* New York: International Universities Press.

CHAPTER **5**

Adlerian Psychology

𝕏 A Selection from
Understanding Human Nature, 1927
Alfred Adler

It is better to remain careful and mindful of the fact that we must have a complete whole in view before we can draw any conclusions about its parts. Such conclusions, furthermore, should be published only when we are quite certain that they are to someone's advantage. One can accomplish a great deal of mischief by asserting in a bad way, or at an improper moment, a correct conclusion concerning character.

We must now, before going on with our considerations, meet a certain objection which has already suggested itself to many readers. The foregoing assertion, that the style of life of the individual remains unchanged, will be incomprehensible to many, because an individual has so many experiences in life which change his attitude toward it. We must remember that any experience may have many interpretations. We will find that there are no two people who will draw the same conclusion from a similar experience. This accounts for the fact that our experiences do not always make us any cleverer. One learns to avoid some difficulties, it is true, and acquires a philosophical attitude towards others, but the pattern along which one acts does not change as a result of this.

We will see in the course of our further considerations that a human being always employs his experiences to the same end. Closer examination reveals that all his experiences must fit into his style of life, into the mosaic of his life's pattern. It is proverbial that we fashion our own experiences. Everyone determines how and what he will experience. In our daily life we observe people drawing whatever conclusions they desire from their experiences. There is the man who constantly makes a certain mistake. If you succeed in convincing him of his mistake, his reactions will be varied. He may conclude that, as a matter of fact, it was high time to avoid this mistake. That is a very rare conclusion.

More probably he will object that he has been making this mistake so long that he is now no longer able to rid himself of the habit. Or he will blame his parents, or his education, for his mistake; he may complain that he has never had anyone who ever cared for him, or that he was very much petted, or that he was brutally treated, and excuse his error with an alibi. Whatever excuse he makes, he betrays one thing, and that is that he wishes to be excused of further responsibility. In this manner he has an apparent justification and avoids all criticism of himself. He himself is never to blame. The reason he has never accomplished what he desired to do is always someone else's fault. What such individuals overlook is the fact that they themselves have made very few efforts to obviate their mistakes. They are far more anxious to remain in error, blaming their bad education, with a certain fervor, for their faults. This is an effective alibi so long as they wish to have it so. The many possible interpretations of an experience and the possibility of drawing various conclusions from any single one enable us to understand why a person does not change his behavior pattern, but turns and twists and distorts his experiences until they fit it. The hardest thing for human beings to do is to know themselves and to change themselves.

Anyone who is not a master in the theory and technique of the science of human nature would experience great difficulty in attempting to educate human beings to be better men. He would be operating entirely on the surface, and would be drawn into the error of believing that because the external aspect of things had changed, he had accomplished something significant. Practical cases show us how little such technique will change an individual, and how all the seeming changes are only apparent changes, valueless so long as the behavior pattern itself has not been modified.

The business of transforming a human being is not a simple process. It demands a certain optimism and patience, and above all the exclusion of all personal vanity, since the individual to be transformed is not in duty bound to be an object of another's vanity. The process of transformation, moreover, must be conducted in such a way that it seems justified for the one changed. We can easily understand that someone will refuse a dish which would otherwise be very tasty to him if it is not prepared and offered to him in an appropriate manner. (1927/1957, pp. 19–21) ■ ■

DISCUSSION IDEAS

1. What does it mean to avoid some difficulties and to acquire a philosophical attitude toward others (paragraph 2)? Give examples of difficulties you have learned to avoid and difficulties you have learned to take a philosophical attitude toward.

2. Do you think that we "fashion our own experiences" (paragraph 3)? Let's say that when you get to class one day, your professor inexplicably never shows up. What are some different ways that students might "fashion" this experience?

3. Reread paragraph 4. From Adler's point of view, who is ultimately responsible for people's behavior?

4. Look at the final metaphor in the passage: "Some one will refuse a dish which would otherwise be very tasty to him if it is not prepared and offered to him in an appropriate manner." How does this metaphor apply to the practice of counseling?

5. In this passage, is Adler writing only about men? How can you explain the use of *he* and *him* throughout?

Profile of a Theorist

ALFRED ADLER (1870–1937)

Alfred Adler was born in a suburb of Vienna, Austria, in 1870. His early childhood was marked by illness and feelings of intense jealousy toward his older brother. Adler considered himself small, physically weak, and painfully unattractive. In addition, he was a poor student and was told by teachers he would never succeed academically. Determined to defy negative predictions, Adler worked diligently to overcome his multiple deficiencies, eventually gaining both social acceptance and academic acclaim. He received a medical degree from the University of Vienna in 1895 and quickly attained a respected position in the medical community as an accomplished physician, specializing in ophthalmology.

Adler's interests, like those of others who eventually found their way to psychology and psychoanalysis, were initially rooted in the symptomology of physical disorders. His particular interest was in the role that environmental and psychological factors played in the development of disease and illness. His studies led him to explore the world of psychiatry, and in 1902, Sigmund Freud invited Adler to join his small band of clinicians furthering the cause of psychoanalysis at the turn of the twentieth century.

Biographers generally agree that Adler's theory of psychology differed significantly from Freud's from its early inception, though he is often portrayed as a loyal Freud follower who later broke rank and struck out on his own. Nevertheless, he accepted Freud's offer to serve as president of the Vienna Psychoanalytical Society in 1910, but by 1911, bitter disagreements and fundamental theoretical differences with Freud prompted his resignation. He and several other members formed their own organization called the Society for Free Psychoanalytic Research.

Adler's theory of Individual Psychology, as he came to call it, was based on the premise that human beings are driven to create meaning in their lives through connections to others and their environment. This social orientation, together with the belief that people possess free will and are capable of making choices that help shape their lives, represents Adler's departure from traditional psychoanalytic thinking. He was adamantly opposed to Freud's emphasis on sexuality and the belief that innate drives determine one's personality to the exclusion of external social influences.

While his theories of the importance of birth order are familiar to many, Adler's perspective on development went beyond the family to incorporate multiple forms of social influence, including educational and community settings. Unlike the psychoanalytic purists, Adler was not content to focus solely on the internal psychological world of the individual. He initiated programs that became precursors of community-outreach programs and child guidance centers throughout Austria. Adler's form of psychotherapy was particularly well received in the United States and remnants of his education-based programs remain popular today, though their Adlerian roots are seldom credited. In fact, Adler's far-reaching influence in a wide variety of psychological applications consistently goes unrecognized. Today, therapists, educators, and social scientists routinely consider family constellations and an individual's social milieu when conceptualizing human problems. The concepts of meaning-making and choice emerged as central to existential psychotherapies some years after Adler had written about their centrality to living successfully versus developing neuroses. Indeed, it is difficult to explore any popular aspect of psychology without detecting some overlap with Adlerian principles, though he remains one of the lesser-known personalities from the psychoanalytic era.

Essential Concepts in Adlerian Approaches

Adler was forward-looking philosophically, and you will see many of the following concepts surface again and again as you study theories of counseling.

Holistic and Existentialist Core

The short passage reprinted here from Alfred Adler's *Understanding Human Nature* (1927/1957) reflects many of the basic concepts of Individual Psychology, which, as noted, is the label Adler gave to his theory. The emphasis was on the word *individual*, a mark of breaking away from Freud's point of view. Adler thought that Freud lumped everyone together unreasonably, given his belief that we are all motivated in the same way, spending our lives fending off anxiety (successfully or not, mostly in ways we are not aware of), and that we all have the same sources of anxiety determined by id impulses and superego demands. Adler, in naming his theory, wanted to stress that people can be better understood as integrated *individuals*. Each individual has a social history that fashions his or her personality in a unique way, and personality is a "complete whole." Thus, his theory is a **holistic** one, a theory that takes each person as unified rather than as a collection of symptoms or a battlefield where psychic structures struggle with each other.

Adler felt that the unity of personality was ignored in case conceptualization: Too often, one symptom or manifestation was singled out for scrutiny. He used a musical metaphor to explain:

> Sometimes such a manifestation is called a complex, and the assumption is that it is possible to separate it from the rest of an individual's activity. But such a procedure is comparable to singling out one note from an entire melody and attempting to understand the significance of this one note apart from the string of notes which make up the melody. (1930a, p. 24)

Freud's psychoanalytic theory assumes that gratification is our central need, while Adler assumed that there are countless motivating factors besides gratification. Needs for power, security, self-esteem, achievement, and social welfare may also be central motivators in people's lives. And, though we may not be in control of our needs, we can choose how to express them. For example, a need for power could express itself in being either a dominating bully or an inspirational teacher. A need for security could be expressed by a ridiculous degree of caution, or it could manifest itself in the development of a close, stable family.

Therefore, personal choice plays an important role in Adlerian psychology. While this is a hopeful stance because it offers the possibility of behavior change, it also often lends a harsh tone to Adler's writing, as you can see in paragraph 4 of the reprinted passage. Freedom of choice includes responsibility for our own actions, and we aren't always happy to take on such responsibility. This idea explains why Adlerian psychology is called **existential**, because it deals with dilemmas of existence such as freedom, choice, responsibility, and the meaning of life. Many widely endorsed psychotherapies today have at least some existentialist underpinning, as you will see in Chapter 6. In fact, you will perceive the spirit of Adler hovering near most of the therapies in this book from now on (Watts & Pietrzak, 2000; Watts, 2000).

SMALL GROUP EXERCISE

You just read some examples of how needs for power and for security could be expressed in both negative and positive behaviors. In your small group, discuss these and some other motivations and think up at least four different ways each one could manifest itself behaviorally. If you can, include examples from history, from literature, from films, or from your own life. Here are some motivations that can be considered from an Adlerian point of view:

1. achievement
2. control
3. security
4. power
5. self-esteem
6. social welfare
7. comfort
8. pleasing others
9. attention
10. affiliation

Style of Life

In the passage reprinted above, Adler mentions **style of life,** the mosaic of life's pattern. This is an essential concept of his theory. In computer parlance, you might think of style of life as the default settings of your character. According to Adler, these defaults were set by the time you were about 6 years old, and they remain fairly constant throughout life. They are the internal sources of your values, beliefs, goals, and interests. Most important, your style of life determines how you perceive your own experiences: Another common metaphor compares it to the eyeglasses through which you see the world. Like your computer defaults, your style of life and its expression can be changed, but only through very purposeful efforts. Adler believed that changing one's style of life was much more difficult than making changes *within* one's style of life. A change within the style of life might involve, for example, expressing your need for attention through becoming an actress rather than through being sick all the time. Style of life is very similar to personality, in that it persists over various situations and through time.

Adler placed less influence at the door of genetics than Freud did. Instead, Adler believed that the main influence on your style of life is your social world as a child, mostly your **family constellation.** As a small child, you were aware of your limitations and weaknesses in comparison to parents and siblings—an awareness that Adler labeled a **sense of inferiority.** And in response to these feelings, you developed physical and psychological ways to overcome them: in Adler's terms, your **strivings for superiority.** So, even though in everyday speech we use phrases like *superiority complex* or *acting superior* in a negative way, meaning snobby or pretentious, that is not the way Adler meant them. Strivings for superiority can be negative or positive or anywhere in between, or mixed. Adler believed that his own nearly fatal illnesses and accidents in early childhood provided the basis for his goal of becoming a doctor and foiling death. Discouraging reports from his school teachers propelled him to study harder and prove his potential for the medical profession. We all strive to make up for the inferiority we felt in childhood, though not all as successfully as Adler. As adults, we respond to problems and unfamiliar situations by using psychological patterns we learned in childhood.

Birth Order

The psychological make-up of the family as a whole affects the style of life established by each child. My own development demonstrates this idea. In my parents' basement were two boxes full of memorabilia, one for me and one for my older brother. When I was sorting through these boxes as an adult, I was amused by the sharp contrast in the contents: My brother's box contained certificates of academic achievement dating back to his junior high years, letters from state and local officials about his involvement in civic affairs during high school, admissions to advanced study programs, news clippings about his awards, and that sort of thing. In my box were dozens of photos from parties, dances, proms, and all kinds of social events, as well as autograph books, letters, dried flowers, postcards, poems, and stories. It's easy to look at the situation from an Adlerian point of view. My brother, the first-born, pretty much cornered the market intellectually in our family; and I chose to put my human capital into sociability and creativity. The division was consistent not only with our birth order but with the sex roles of the time. Instead of trying to equal or surpass my brother, which would have been impossible in our context, I chose a different arena, including more stereotypically feminine activities. Throughout our lives, my brother sought intellectual achievement, while I strenuously directed my powers toward having fun!

Adler formulated **birth order analysis,** a typological system that assigns personality characteristics according to chronological place in the family. This typology is prominent in popular psychology. Research studies support the idea that the first-born is often dominant, most responsible, most conservative, and achievement-oriented. The last child tends to be more dependent, less responsible, and socially apprehensive. As in my own case, the second child is more carefree than the first. This is probably because most parents are more relaxed in caring for their second infant than for their first, whose addition to the household brought out their self-doubts alarmingly.

Naturally, to explain a person's character wholly in terms of birth order is inadequate. What about a last child who is born after older children have left home? Will she be like a last child who shares a home with four older siblings? What about the situation of a second child among three versus a second child among seven? Or a second child who got most of his care from a devoted grandmother? Though some popular books take a simplistic view of birth order typology, Adler did not. He emphasized the importance of *psychological* birth order, or position in the *family constellation.* Like a constellation of stars, the family as a whole takes on a form, with each member anchoring a definite spot. Often the roles we play within the family are complementary or compensatory—for example, a fun-loving child balances out a studious sibling, or a rebellious adolescent serves as a cautionary model for a conformist younger family member. Like me, many people try to take on roles that aren't already mastered by some other family member, or else they face a lifetime of competition. Adler's thoughts on family constellation still inform family therapy systems of all sorts today.

R e f l e c t i o n

Consider your own family in terms of your style of life. Can you see how your sense of inferiority and strivings for superiority made you who you are today? Did you compete with your siblings? Or did you choose a different focus, as I did? Do you think you compensated for your family members' weaknesses more than you imitated their strengths, or vice versa? If your considerations are not too personal, explain your psychological response to your family constellation in a class discussion.

Phenomenology

Adler wrote that "any experience may have many interpretations. We will find that there are no two people who will draw the same conclusion from a similar experience." The idea that reality is not objective but subjective, not public but personal, is a **constructivist** attitude (Watts & Pietrzak, 2000). The world is the way that you see it and interpret it, according to your style of life. Your experience may not be shared by others. When I signed a book contract, I crowed to my friend Jenny: "I get to sit at my desk and read and write about psychology all day!" Jenny replied, "It sounds like pure hell to me. It sounds like being sentenced to graduate school forever!" What for me is a dream job, for Jenny is a prison term. A constructivist attitude, therefore, requires a **phenomenological** method of exploring reality—that is, it uses human experience as raw material (rather than, say, statistical norms, moral touchstones, or general categories of diagnosis).

We each have a cognitive map of the world and its inhabitants, and we place events on this map. What we pay attention to and what we ignore are determined by whether they fit the geography of our map. This is clear in the circumstances of a depressed person, who walks down the street noticing the trash in the gutter rather than the brilliant sunrise. You have probably had the phenomenological experience of seeing a film or reading a book in a different way than your friends and classmates do.

The way that we perceive and interpret the world determines how we behave. If you see the world as hostile and yourself as never quite adequate, your main goal is to protect yourself from blows to your self-esteem. This stance, according to Adler, makes you avoid risk-taking, because you might look like a fool and will probably fail anyway. Since the pursuit of a meaningful, happy life always involves risk-taking, avoiding risks completely is a no-win strategy. Consider your own situation: Every time you sign up for a class, you risk failure or disappointment; yet obviously you consider your goals to be worth the risk, and you expect that you are capable of passing. Adlerians define mentally healthy people as those who see the world as friendly and themselves as competent. They see opportunity where others see risk. Theoretically, this stance leads naturally to goals such as improving society and helping fellow humans.

Adler enthusiastically embraced the ideas of philosopher Hans Vaihinger, whose book *The Philosophy of "As If"* (1911/1925) came out the same year that Adler left Freud's inner circle of psychoanalytic theorists. Adler found Vaihinger's term *fictions* a good way to describe people's cognitive maps, since they are not reality but constructed out of inner experience, like fictional writing. So Adler saw each of us as having a **fictional self** to whom we conform our behavior (to clarify Vaihinger's title, we behave "as if" we were that self), and we choose goals that also conform to the fictional self, in what he called **fictional finalism**. We have a **private logic** that determines our interpretations of experience, and a **life script** that is like a play in which we direct our own character. Adler provides a good series of examples in *What Life Should Mean to You* (1931):

> Unhappy experiences in childhood may be given quite opposite meanings. One man with unhappy experiences behind him will not dwell on them except as they show him something which can be remedied for the future. He will feel, "We must work to remove such unfortunate situations and make sure that our children are better placed." Another man will feel, "Life is unfair. Other people always have the best of it. If the world treated me like that, why should I treat the world any better?" It is in this way that some parents say of their children, "I had to suffer just as

much when I was a child, and I came through it. Why shouldn't they?" A third man will feel, "Everything should be forgiven me because of my unhappy childhood." In the actions of all three men, their interpretations will be evident. They will never change their actions unless they change their interpretations. (pp. 13–14)

Each of the three men deals with his experience according to his "private logic." Adler clearly thinks that the first man's "fiction" is best. All three "private logic" premises are untrue: (1) "We can remove our children from all harm," (2) "Unfairness dominates the world," and (3) "Bad experiences excuse bad behavior." However, the first one leads to goals of social welfare, while the others do not, and social feeling is a major element in Adler's ideal style of life.

It may be hard to realize that many of our well-loved assumptions are fictions, despite plenty of evidence disproving them. But remember that they may still be socially and personally beneficial. "All humans are created equal," "It takes all kinds to make a world," "Good deeds are rewarded": These are fictions that promote civilized society.

SMALL GROUP EXERCISE

For each of the numbered situations below, discuss what thoughts, feelings, and actions would result if your private logic said either "The world is friendly, and I am competent" or "The world is hostile, and I am inadequate."

1. Your child receives a bad grade report in school.
2. You consider changing careers in mid-life.
3. You win the lottery.
4. Your friend makes an unusual travel suggestion.
5. Your spouse leaves you.

Social Interest

Adler believed in the purposeful nature of behavior. Obviously, the style of life has a purpose: to compensate or overcome a sense of inferiority and to meet one's needs. As he wrote in *Understanding Human Nature* (1927/1957), "a human being always employs his experiences to the same end." The assertion that we are goal-driven sets Adler apart again from the Freudians, who saw us driven by the past, not the future. For Adler, goals, plans, ideals, and self-determination were very real forces in human behavior, while Freud would have said that these concepts are rationalizations for behavior that is actually propelled by unconscious conflicts. If you are an Adlerian, you have a more positive view of human nature than a strict Freudian would. An Adlerian allows that a great artist may be motivated by a desire to touch or amuse an audience, while a Freudian would insist that the artist is motivated by sexual repressions (Adler, 1929).

Even though Adler saw no inherent meaning in life, he strongly believed that the psychologically healthy "fiction" lay in **social interest.** This concept covers cooperation with other people, concern for their welfare, contribution to society, and value placed on humanity. Social interest is an innate aptitude that develops with life experience, if everything goes well. As adults, we have three arenas for expressing social interest: community, work, and love (sometimes labeled society, work, and sex). We interweave our lives with other people's by living cooperatively among others, pursuing a useful occupation, and being part of a loving couple. The three areas overlap, and an improvement in one area is likely to result in an improvement in the others. People with underdeveloped social interest may exploit others through crime, bullying, political clout, physical strength, or economic power; or they may be loners, avoiding involvement with other people in all three arenas. Adler placed such a value on social interest that he equated it with psychological well-being. He even wrote, "A man of genius is primarily a man of supreme usefulness" (Adler, 1929, p. 35), and he placed social interest above intelligence: "In our over-intellectualised civilisation especially, practically everyone is wonderfully adept in the use of his own individual tricks: The really important differences of conduct are not those of individual cleverness but of usefulness or uselessness" (p. 78).

DISCUSSION IDEAS

1. Discuss examples of characters in film and literature from an Adlerian point of view. For example, can you see how Hamlet falls short in all three arenas of social interest? Where on the spectrum of social interest would James Bond lie? How about Harry Potter, or Bilbo Baggins?

2. Do you think we have an overintellectualized civilization? In other words, does our society place more value on intelligence than on usefulness? Considering that we are a pluralistic society, do some subcultures place more value on intellectuality than others? Think of examples and anecdotes to support your answers.

Courage, Discouragement, and Encouragement

Adler clearly believed that change was difficult for us—in fact, "The hardest thing for human beings to do is to know themselves and to change themselves" (1927, p. 21). Think for a moment about the hard things you have had to do. Did they entail knowing yourself and changing yourself? I once went to a psychotherapist for a case of what I then called "workaholism." In the first session, I listed all the different activities and responsibilities that were overwhelming me. After my lengthy discourse, my therapist said, "Well, what are you willing to give up?" I was shocked. I wanted him to produce some formula that would let me continue *all* my occupations and yet not be stressed out. I didn't want to look inside myself and figure out my priorities and actually change my behavior! Since then, in conceptualizing my own clients, I often wonder what current idea, emotion, or habit they are willing to give up in exchange for mental health. That is an Adlerian question.

We cling to the mental, emotional, and behavioral habits that we developed in childhood, even when they are clearly not working toward the best outcome in adult life. Adler wrote that people insist that they cannot change these habits because they are too long-standing. Indeed, certain habits of thought provide us with excuses or alibis for not changing. Because we interpret experience however it suits our style, we can come up with plenty of evidence for ideas like "Nothing ever works out for me" or "I never get the love and support I need." (Remember that the very same background of experience could provide evidence for a person who thinks, "Things usually work out for the best" and "I can get love and support when I need it.") For Adler, psychopathology equals a feeling of **discouragement,** a feeling that oneself and the world are not going to change, and why try? Therefore, a major goal of therapy is to encourage the client. He or she must feel that change is possible and worth the effort. Making the effort is what takes courage.

R e f l e c t i o n

Think of an idea, habit, or emotion that you would be happier without. Let me give you a mild example of each: 1. The idea that your kitchen counters must be spotless or people will think you are a slob. 2. The habit of biting your nails while you read. 3. The emotion of feeling jealous when a classmate does better on an exam than you do.

Describe your idea, habit, or emotion and give an example or two. What would it take to change? Why haven't you changed yet? What would you have to be willing to give up? Would the change take courage?

The Therapeutic Process

Although Adler was a physician, he never conceived of psychological distress using the medical model. This model assumes that the client has the disease of mental illness, and the therapist attempts a cure as a medical doctor would. In several respects, the medical model was a bad fit for Adler's way of thinking. For one thing, he thought of psychological problems not as an illness but as a failure of courage to deal with life's demands. The client, then, needs to become inspired with courage. The medical model suggests that you could get rid of the disease and leave the person as he or she was before, while Adler would say that the whole person needs treatment. The problem is not separate from the person. Adler would have been loathe to say that there is a clear line between the sick and the well: He would have insisted that almost all of us could improve our social interest and feel better. In fact, Adler and his followers were interested in promotion of mental health among the general public, not just therapy clients. Finally, the doctor-patient relationship usually endorses the doctor as the powerful and knowledgeable party and the patient as the compliant and ignorant party. The doctor rarely consults the patient about how he or she should best be treated. An Adlerian counselor and client relationship is collaborative, respectful, and shared. The counselor's case conceptualization and what form of treatment might help are discussed with the client as a co-worker in the venture. In short, Adler's principles compose a **growth model** rather than a medical model.

Basic Mistakes

Adlerian therapy doesn't progress through a series of distinct stages, though it does move toward an overall goal that might be expressed as "becoming a decent human being." According to Adler, many of us embrace **basic mistakes** as we develop our style of life in childhood. Since we are so naïve as children, we make up reasons and principles behind what we see, and these reasons and principles are purely or partly fictional. These errors continue into adulthood as firm convictions about ourselves, others, and the world, and they lie behind how we interpret experience and how we choose to behave. An example you have no doubt seen occurs when a child's parents divorce, and the child wrongly decides that if he or she had behaved better, the marriage would have stayed intact. One (among many) mistaken convictions carried into adulthood from this experience might be "I need to please everyone to maintain harmony in my world." What a stressful belief this is! You can see how the person holding it would suffer. An Adlerian therapist would seek to substitute a different conviction for this damaging one: "You can never please everyone, and trying makes you look like a phony." Though most of our lifestyle convictions are fictions, some promote well-being in community, work, and love, while others toss up wall after insurmountable wall around us.

SMALL GROUP EXERCISE

Here is a list of basic mistakes compiled by a modern Adlerian, H. H. Mosak (2000). Mosak provides examples of each. In a small group, make up two or three more examples for each of the five categories.

1. *Overgeneralizations:* "People are hostile." "Life is dangerous."
2. *False or impossible goals of "security":* "One false step and you're dead." "I have to please everybody."

3. *Misperceptions of life and life's demands:* Typical convictions might be "Life never gives me any breaks" and "Life is so hard."

4. *Minimization or denial of one's worth:* "I'm stupid" and "I'm undeserving" or "I'm just a housewife."

5. *Faulty values:* "Be first even if you have to climb over others."

After your group comes up with examples, discuss how each one could make someone miserable in the arena of community, work, or love.

Features of Adlerian Therapy

In an Adlerian encounter, therapy doesn't proceed in tidy stages. But it's convenient to divide the Adlerian therapeutic process into four elements, all of which are ongoing throughout. These elements are (1) a collaborative therapeutic relationship, (2) case conceptualization, (3) interpretation and insight, and (4) reorientation. I will expand on each of them.

Collaborative Therapeutic Relationship

As I mentioned earlier, the client-therapist relationship is established as existing between two complete human beings, not merely an authority and a supplicant. However, Adlerian alliances do often take on a teacher-student flavor, because psychoeducation is part of the process. For example, Adlerians doing family therapy teach the family about how its constellation gives each member distinct roles to play. An Adlerian with an alcoholic client would explain the principle of self-distraction from life's tasks. Unlike most theories of psychotherapy, Adler's condones advice-giving in certain circumstances, just as equals give each other advice when they can.

The counselor also serves as a role model of social interest and vigor. The client may never have observed such a model closely before. The therapist clearly cares about people and acts on the feeling through his or her choice of occupation. Most important, the counselor admits to being fallible and flawed, and models a healthy response to failings—for example, being able to laugh at oneself, or to shrug off minor mistakes as an expected part of living. Thus, the counselor is not a blank slate upon which the client inscribes transference. In Adlerian therapy, transference and countertransference are considered evidence of the client's typical interpersonal patterns, because the same dynamics will operate in session as well as outside. For instance, a client whose basic mistake is "I have to please everybody" will try to figure out what the therapist wants, and then to provide it, while the therapist will feel courted rather than trusted. The therapist then uses this feeling to guess that other people in this client's life also wonder whether his congeniality is a mask.

Case Conceptualizations

The Adlerian therapist seeks to understand the client's style of life, including how it originally developed in the family and other social settings, what basic convictions are operating, and how the style of life is hampering the client's participation in community, work, and love. This search for understanding is called a *lifestyle investigation* or *lifestyle assessment,* and it typically includes both free-form and structured exercises. An Adlerian will often simply ask a new client to tell his or her life story. Since we can never capture our whole life story, the events and people we dwell on in our summary are those that we are now considering important. A listener can also discern themes in the life story, such as abandonment or achievement, and can label the overall emotional tone of the story. These are the themes and tone of the person's style of life.

Adler himself used a structured interview in order to assess clients thoroughly. This way, he did not miss things they left out of their life story (on purpose or not). In *Social Interest: A Challenge to Mankind* (1933, pp. 408–409), he provided the following outline for the interview:

1. What are your complaints?

2. What was your situation when you first noticed your symptoms?

3. What is your situation now?

4. What is your occupation?

5. Describe your parents as to their character, and their health. If not alive, what illness caused their death? What was their relation to yourself?

6. How many brothers and sisters have you? What is your position in the birth order? What is their attitude toward you? How do they get along in life? Do they also have any illness?

7. Who was your father's or your mother's favorite? What kind of up-bringing did you have?

8. Inquire for signs of pampering in childhood (timidity, shyness, difficulties in forming friendships, disorderliness).

9. What illnesses did you have in childhood and what was your attitude to them?

10. What are your earliest childhood recollections?

11. What do you fear, or what did you fear the most?

12. What is your attitude toward the opposite sex? What was it in childhood and later years?

13. What occupation would have interested you the most, and if you did not adopt it, why not?

14. Is the patient ambitious, sensitive, inclined to outbursts of temper, pedantic, domineering, shy, or impatient?

15. What sort of persons are around you at present? Are they impatient, bad-tempered, or affectionate?

16. How do you sleep?

17. What dreams do you have? (Of falling, flying, recurrent dreams, prophetic, about examinations, missing a train.)

18. What illnesses are there in your family background?

Notice that the interview investigates the *family constellation*, the particular social arrangement of the individual's family (like an arrangement of stars in a constellation). In the interview questions, you no doubt saw reflections of many Adlerian concepts. Two of these questions invite further discussion, because they constitute key assessment techniques in this methodology.

Early Childhood Recollections   An Adlerian will usually ask the client to describe in detail his or her earliest childhood recollection. These are specific scenes, not general memories, often called up from age 4 or 5. It makes little difference whether the client remembers correctly, or whether the client could come up with a different recollection given enough time. The memory recounted will reveal the client's current style of life. Let me give you an example from my professional training.

Like army buddies, students who go through graduate school together usually form a close-knit group and know each other well. When we studied Adler in graduate school, we first were asked to write down our earliest childhood recollection. One student, Joe, volunteered to read his to the class. It went something like this:

> I was at a kid's birthday party at about the age of 4, outdoors in the summer. I had on a new sailor outfit with white pants and a sailor top, an outfit I really liked, and I was having a lot of fun. At one point we were rounded up to sit on the ground for a story, and I was worried about sitting on the grass and getting my new pants dirty. Before I decided what to do, my mother came over with a blanket for me to sit on, and I was very relieved and happy. I felt very loved and understood.

By the time we heard the ending, we were all laughing out loud. Joe didn't realize at the moment how much his **early childhood recollection** reflected him as we knew him, as an adult. We all knew he was a snappy, fashionable dresser, standing out in our school where most people dress down. He also cared for his clothes well—he even ironed his T-shirts. We knew Joe as a sociable guy who enjoyed parties, too. These characteristics evidently had already existed at age 4. On top of that, Joe had recently become engaged to a woman he obviously adored, who was quite a few years older than he, and we had noticed how she fussed over him protectively! Joe was not the only student whose recollection bore his unique stamp. All of us could see, in our own early childhood recollections, the seeds of our current selves. I have used this exercise in college classes since then, and students have been surprised at the verbal snapshots of their adult selves taken at the age of 4 or 5.

The early childhood recollection, like the life story, exposes the style, themes, core conflicts, and tone of the personality. Adlerians look at polarities that reflect one's habitual way of organizing the world. Is the situation dangerous or safe?

Social or solitary? Active or subdued? Is the child helpless or competent? Trusting or mistrusting? Participant or observer?

Dream Analysis   Adler wrote, "Freud has claimed from the first that dreams are fulfillments of infantile sexual wishes. On the basis of actual experience this appears to assign to dreams a too limited scope" (1929/1956, p. 358). Adler assessed clients' dreams in much the same way as their early childhood recollections: as a source of speculation about their style of life. He did not assign fixed meanings to objects and events in dreams, as Freudians tend to do. The meaning of each dream element is specific to the dreamer. The interpretation should be reconcilable with other evidence, such as early recollections, current problems, and usual tendencies. In dreams, we experiment with possible actions that we might never consider in waking life. According to Adler, a forgotten dream means that we reject or postpone the action it suggested, while a nightmare discourages us from a contemplated action (Mosak, 2000). We will see in the next section how dream analysis is used as a therapeutic technique as well as an assessment technique.

SMALL GROUP EXERCISE

It's hard to write and analyze your own early childhood recollections after you've read about how they are interpreted. Instead, outside of class each student in your small group should transcribe a recollection from a friend *not* in your class, without explaining how it will be analyzed until the friend is through with his or her description. Then, as I did with Joe's story above, each group member should interpret the friend's recollection and whether or how it reflects the person's current style of life. Like an Adlerian, you should ask your friend to collaborate on the interpretation by asking questions like "Can you see any seeds of your current self in this memory?" Being sure to hide your friend's identity, bring the results of your investigation back to discuss in your group.

Interpretation and Insight

You will study other theories of psychotherapy in which the therapist withholds his or her own interpretations from the client; however, in an Adlerian encounter the counselor and client build interpretations together from the evidence gathered in the course of assessment. While part of lifestyle investigation involves pondering childhood roots, more attention is paid to the client's current and future patterns of thought, emotion, and behavior.

For a worthwhile interpretation, the client needs to answer the questions "What life task is my symptom allowing me to avoid?" and "What price am I paying for this?" Adler was sure that each symptom had an underlying purpose, serving as an excuse to retreat from life's demands. Look at Brad, the client in Chapter 1 who had left four good teaching positions because he felt disappointed in each one. Even without further details, we can guess that one thing he's avoiding is formal evaluation, which occurs in the third to sixth year of an academic's job. Since he leaves before evaluation, Brad never has to face it. He avoids rejection, embarrassment, and stress. And the price? Brad sacrifices job security, as well as self-confidence (remember, he comes to therapy because "I'm beginning to think it may be something about *me* that makes me keep losing good jobs"). If he continues job-hopping, he may sabotage his entire professional career.

Nira Kefir (1981), who devised a system of therapy based on Adlerian principles, interprets clients' style of life in terms of four *personal priorities:*

1. *Control.* This person attempts to control every situation in order to avoid being ridiculed or embarrassed.

2. *Superiority.* This person seeks achievement, fame, and advancement in order to avoid insignificance and meaninglessness.

3. *Pleasing.* This person looks for affection and approval in order to avoid rejection.

4. *Comfort.* This person refuses to take risks and make commitments in order to avoid any kind of stress.

We all share these priorities to some extent: You probably recognized your own favorite right away. Problems arise when the price of the avoidance is too high. An Adlerian insight might be just that—a realization that the effort to avoid something produces worse results than the bad thing itself would. Most of us who have been college students know that *putting off* writing a paper is often much more painful than finally writing it!

Insight may concurrently involve an analysis of one's basic mistakes and how they are affecting one's life. However, for Adler insight was never enough. While Freud believed that bringing unconscious motivations into consciousness was curative in itself, Adler thought that such insight was superficial if it did not lead to a change in motivation and, from there, to a change in behavior.

Reorientation

The client needs to gain (or regain) the courage to face life's demands. This probably involves giving up long-held convictions that produce avoidant behavior and pursuit of impossible goals. Another way to look at Brad's problem is that he holds a damaging conviction: "The perfect job exists." He would be much better off if he could substitute "No job is perfect." Reorientation turns insight into action. Clients discover that taking the risks they once avoided is not as bad as they'd expected.

A focus on assets is another reorientation task. Many clients have come to dwell on their problems so deeply that they forget to develop their strong points.

Accepting a weakness may be necessary, but a compensating strength should be cultivated. For example, if it turns out that Brad thrives on having a series of jobs rather than one stable job, he could look at his mobility and flexibility as his assets. He could decide to take advantage of the huge market for temporary workers in academia and look forward to a life of change and variety. I once had a client with a shockingly bad life history (for instance, her fiancé got killed on the way to the wedding), which she recounted with vividness and detail. When she realized that she was well prepared to become a novelist, it was a turning point in her life. Learning to look at her experiences as material ripe for her verbal skills was one reorientation that renewed her courage.

Customary Techniques

Adlerian counselors are free to choose any ethical techniques that work toward encouraging and revitalizing their clients. Therapists are encouraged to be creative, so you will see Adler's followers prescribing outdoor adventures or asking clients to stay awake and worry all night. Techniques can be divided into three categories: reframing, behavior experiments, and resource development.

Reframing

As discussed earlier, clients need to change their cognitive map of the world and self. This requires alteration of old, habitual ways of thinking and the substitution of new ways, which is labeled *reframing*. (You have probably noticed how the same picture looks quite different when you put it into a new frame.)

The Question   Adler (1929) advised asking the client **The Question,** which goes something like this: "If I could magically eliminate your symptom immediately and completely, what would be different in your life?" The client's answer may lead directly to an understanding of what he or she fears most, or what is being avoided. An agoraphobic client might answer, "I'd be able to do my own grocery shopping." This might indicate that the client fears the burden of self-sufficiency.

The Push-Button   Adler asked clients to imagine pushing a button and then picturing a pleasant experience they'd had, in as much detail and vividness as possible. He exhorted them to notice how the memory made them feel good in the present moment as they imagined it. Then he would have them do the same with the memory of an unpleasant event, and notice how it made them feel bad in the present. He repeated this technique, asking clients to switch back and forth, to get them to realize that they have inner control of how they feel at the moment, through control over what they think about.

Role Playing   The client acts out a distressing encounter but must take the character of a different person. For example, a teenager might act out a scene of his father picking on him, taking the role of the father. The counselor would act out the teen's role, with advice from the client to make it realistic. In role plays, the client is able to reframe the situation from a different point of view, and perhaps break the mold of his habitual ways of construing it. This technique is used in family, couples, and group therapy as well.

Brainstorming   After identifying some basic mistakes in thinking, counselor and client brainstorm alternative convictions that could be substituted and discuss the implications of adopting those instead. For "I never get what I need," try out "I usually get what I need." Evidence can be found on both sides, but one conviction promotes healthy behavior.

Humor   Clients are encouraged to see the funny side of human frailty. The counselor models laughing at oneself and at absurd situations. I once had a 30-year-old client whose mother repeatedly tried to control and monitor her, treating her like a child. We worked on the client's ability to resist without feeling guilty. I knew that she was improving when we met after her Christmas family visit. She was laughing heartily when she pulled out a photo she said she'd taken just to share with me, showing her presents from her mom: a high-necked, flowered flannel nightgown and a stuffed bear. She said she had to chuckle every time she thought of those symbolic gifts. Her mother's attempts to infantilize her had become amusing instead of depressing.

Behavior Experiments

Because Adlerian counseling is action oriented, cognitive reframing alone is not enough. Adlerians suggest active experiments outside the counseling session. Kefir (1981) noted that clients often come equipped with a narrow repertoire of behaviors and therefore have limited choices when faced with unfamiliar or threatening situations. Broadening this repertoire is a goal of therapy. In these experiments, the stress is not upon a perfect outcome, but on the effort and process. Adlerians frequently use contracts to solidify the agreements between counselor and client about what the client will do in the real world between sessions. A contract makes it more likely that the client will not avoid or forget the homework.

Behaving "As If"   The client tries out behaving **"as if"** he or she were psychologically better. You have probably done this exercise yourself—for example, forcing yourself to go to a social gathering even though you feel sluggish, knowing that you will feel lively once you are there. I have a friend who was usually tongue-tied on the phone and avoided making calls even when they were necessary. She has improved since she decided on an "as-if" technique herself: When she has to make a call, she imitates our pal Pam, who is great on the telephone. "I just pretend I'm Pam and act like she does!"

Task Setting   An Adlerian counselor might have given a homework task to my friend with the phone problem—asking her, for example, to force herself to make one phone call a day, no matter what. The counselor might then have helped her make a list of some easy tasks to start with, such as calling the bookstore to find out its hours of operation. Threatening situations become less and less scary with more exposure, usually. Otherwise, people would never drive cars in Los Angeles!

A graduate student in education came to see me for her dissertation writer's block. One distressing aspect of the block was that she was avoiding her adviser for fear he would ask about the project and then proceed to scold her for being behind. He had turned into quite a monster in her mind. I gave her the task of calling him and making a standing appointment with him, just for fifteen minutes each week. Of course, he was not a monster, and gave her some advice and encouragement right away. The weekly meetings helped her, since she wanted to show a bit of progress every week. And the nagging dread of running into her adviser disappeared, of course.

Because social interest is so critical in Adlerian philosophy, clients are often assigned to do community service homework, like volunteering in a soup kitchen or literacy brigade. This type of useful work reorients clients away from the self-centeredness that usually comes along with psychological distress, especially depression. It also spurs activity rather than passivity.

Catching Yourself   Since your habitual ways of thinking and acting have become so automatic, if you want to change them you need to become more aware of when they kick in. Counselors who help people quit smoking or overeating usually ask them to keep records of their cigarettes or food. The very act of writing down each instance increases their awareness of the behavior and helps them see what spurs them to overindulge. In the same way, you can "catch yourself" about to respond to a situation in an old maladaptive way, and choose to respond otherwise. In my own life, I sometimes have to write a section of a book that bores me, usually through overfamiliarity or simply lack of inspiration. I've noticed that, at these times, I suddenly remember that the dishwasher isn't unloaded, I haven't checked my e-mail lately, and the cat really needs to be played with. In other words, I distract myself from the job I'm supposed to be doing. Over the years, I've come to "catch myself" when my attention turns to things like refolding all my sweaters, and I know that I need to sit down and write instead.

Adlerians help their clients identify other habits and short-circuit them, even emotional habits. For example, a husband who doesn't make much money feels that he is being criticized whenever his wife admires a beautiful, expensive item. The wife, on her part, has no such intention at all. She is just sharing her enjoyment of window-shopping. Both partners could benefit from "catching themselves." The husband could remind himself that his wife is more artistic than acquisitive. He could catch himself feeling belittled and choose instead to look for the item's beauty. And the wife could catch herself before remarking on how adorable this year's Jaguars are!

Countersuggestions   Asking clients to increase or intensify a pattern they wish to get rid of may seem strange, but this Adlerian technique survives in several more modern therapies; an example is the use of *paradoxical intention* in family therapy. If a habit that produces painful feelings is repeated ceaselessly, it will become aversive in itself. Some quit-smoking programs use this phenomenon and begin treatment with a session in which the client smokes one cigarette after another as fast as possible, until sick.

In Adlerian therapy, countersuggestion may take the form of asking an insomniac to stay awake all night, or telling a worrier to try to worry about everything continually and avoid any nonworrying thoughts. If a client's basic mistake was a conviction that life was unfair, Adler might have asked him or her to whine about every grievance, no matter how small. The mechanisms that make countersuggestions work are complex. Probably, many habits become boring, painful, ridiculous, or humorous when intensified. There may be relief in giving up the fight and finding that the result is not so bad after all, or not so satisfying. The result may even be self-limiting (as in the insomniac's efforts to stay awake).

Adler (1929) also used countersuggestion in task setting with some clients. For example, he once suggested that a mother apologize at length to her 9-year-old daughter for putting a crippling degree of academic pressure on her. He explained how apologizing would improve the child's behavior, but also told the mother, "I don't really think you can bring yourself to do this, but it's what I would do in your situation." The woman immediately made the apology, with the expected good results.

Resource Development

In times of psychological distress, people often let the positive side of their lives wither on the vine. A physically fit person who becomes depressed is likely to stop working out, even though the exercise would surely be a boon. An anxious person who enjoys reading novels may forget to pick one up at the library. Adler encouraged clients to develop the neglected healthy aspects of life.

Compensation   In many areas, we accept our weaknesses rather than try to cure them. We compensate by making the most of our strengths. But when discouragement prevails, assets are neglected as well. An Adlerian therapist asks a client to inventory his or her strong points and skills, and the pair investigates what can be done with those. Let's say that Brad, the job-hopping academic, is a very good teacher but realizes in therapy that many conditions of work in a college setting are distasteful to him. His therapist would encourage him to think about other ways in which he could use his talents—for example, organizing and giving workshops for business firms or doing industrial training. A job has much more to it than one activity, and people with the right skill frequently find that they are mismatched with the job in most other ways. This mismatch is a source of deep unhappiness; yet if a person is too discouraged to take risks, he or she feels stuck.

In another type of compensation, Adler would ask how a depressed client could use his or her strengths in a socially useful way to balance an unsatisfactory personal life. One of my friends in school, Serafita, got abruptly and brutally jilted by her fiancé. She felt hopeless about romance, and had bad periods of loneliness and sadness in the evening hours. At the time, students in the class behind ours were preparing for their comprehensive examinations, a two-day written test on which Serafita had done very well the year before. She began offering help sessions for the exam in her apartment, which filled her evenings with interesting work and good company. She says that this activity was what got her through a really rough time, and reminded her that love and marriage were not the only things that could make her happy.

Dreams   Dreams, according to Adler, rehearse possible actions. These may be actions that our style of life excludes from waking thoughts. Dreams can be used for solving problems we are having at the time. My housemate Liz recounted the following dream. As you read it, try to interpret it in Adlerian terms.

> Liz's dream: She suddenly found herself assigned to play the role of Lady Macbeth in a performance that same day. She felt very panicky because she is not an actress and didn't know the part. After a period of being anxious, she looked around at the troupe and thought, "Well, I don't know what I'm doing, but maybe I'm the best person around to play the part. At least I've read the play." She decided she'd just carry the book with her, read the lines, and do her best. This made her feel better, even upon awakening.

You will immediately see the significance of Liz's dream when you know the situation in which she told it to me. Liz was finishing her graduate degree in economics, and she was in the process of interviewing for a job with the Illinois Commerce Commission. The job was specialized and challenging, and Liz was not sure that her academic background in economics gave her the knowledge she would need to do well. She had been worried about this lately. Obviously, her dream provided her with a way to look at the circumstance in a positive way. Her plan for playing Lady Macbeth was, in reality, a good plan for making the transition from academia to the world of work in general. (Lady Macbeth, if you remember, seeks power in a man's world. Do you think that Liz's position as a female economist in the 1980s had anything to do with her dream's choice of character?)

DISCUSSION IDEAS

In keeping with Adler's common-sense view of human behavior, his customary techniques—reframing, behavior experiments, and resource development—are often used without a therapist, as several of my examples show. Look back over the descriptions of these techniques and see whether you can think of a time when you or someone you know used one of them. Discuss the anecdotes that emerge and the results people found from using the techniques.

Uses of Adlerian Therapy

Adler was ahead of his time, as a psychologist, in seeing the individual embedded in a broad social context. Because of his vision of each of us functioning in a network of other people and institutions, some beneficent and some hostile, many of his ideas are identical to those of today's theorists. He contributed to the systemic approaches of counseling to the establishment of group therapy, and to the vision of social constructions of reality, all of which are integral in modern theory.

Social Disparities

Adler would be happy to see that students of psychology are now exhorted to investigate the social group identity of each client, and to determine whether the client embraces or rejects this group identity. As I have said earlier, this is not a matter of making generalizations based on visible differences like skin color. Instead, it is an exploration of the values, world view, and practices dominant in the life of each client. Adler would say that these are *always* relevant to the client's problems. Adlerian therapy in this way is tailored for working with clients who belong to minority groups.

How your group is viewed by the world is just as relevant as how you view the world, since your fictional self is formed in a social setting. Adler was aware that many of women's problems, and many marital problems as well, stemmed from women's inferior status in society. He felt that they suffered not from some primal penis envy, but from envy of the real power and privilege that men hold. Men, on the other hand, found it too easy to translate their strivings for superiority into towering above women. Marital discord, he felt, was not merely a private matter but a symptom of social inequality between the sexes, often exacerbated by the tendency of insecure men to marry women whom they considered their inferiors. Adler's thoughts were a precursor of feminist theory in many ways. He would have been pleased with the proclamation,

"The personal is political." Problems between ethnic and racial groups, too, can be considered in the light of struggles to gain power or maintain privilege.

Child and School Problems

Because of Adler's positive view of humanity and the ability to change, he and his followers practiced among the general population, giving lectures and parenting workshops and consulting with schools. Their focus was upon designing social settings in which neurosis would *not* develop. Adler believed that children's behavior, like adults', is purposive, and can be understood by its function in the family or classroom constellation. Children's problems stemmed from "inability to cooperate with society, feeling inferior, and lack of a life goal" (Utay & Utay, 1996), the same sources of adult problems. Therefore, his work with schools and parents emphasized orienting or reorienting the children toward successful and satisfying group activity. If the children had developed lonely, discouraged, and isolated styles, they could gain encouragement through participation in teams that made use of their skills in ways that were challenging but within reach. Adler's student Rudolf Dreikurs made Adlerian educational principles popular in the United States. These principles included democratic rules, individual responsibility, encouragement, social awareness, and natural consequences rather than punishment (Pryor & Tollerud, 1999). Modern school-based interventions for attention deficit-hyperactivity disorder (Edwards & Gfroerer, 2001), raising self-esteem through adventure therapy (Wick, Wick, & Peterson, 1997), counseling for ridiculed children (Utay & Utay, 1996), and motivating defiant children (Pryor & Tollerud, 1999) are firmly based in Adlerian thought. The same principles inform Adlerian practices in child-raising, evidenced in popular books like *Discipline Without Tears* (Dreikurs & Cassel, 1972) and in the choice theory of William Glasser (Chapter 9).

Alienation: Adventure-Based Therapy

Adlerian techniques do not all require high levels of verbal or cognitive skill, so they are applicable to a broader population than many talk therapies. Adventure therapy, for example, often involves cooperative tasks like building a bridge with a limited set of materials, blindfolded trust walks, and mountain climbing (Wick, Wick, & Peterson, 1997). Like Adler's ideas for school reform, such challenges are realizable yet require cooperation. These activities build legitimate self-esteem through problem-solving and actions that benefit each participant and the group they belong to. Errors have natural consequences that the whole group must deal with; for example, breaking a piece of the bridge material means that the group has to come up with a plan to fix it or build without it. This demonstrates the difference between punishment and natural consequences.

People who are not strong in verbal expression or academics may find themselves leaders in adventure therapy groups. The charm of an unfamiliar task, like those designed in adventure therapy, is that the participants cannot fall back on "private logic" habits, and they often discover unexplored parts of themselves. Adler and his followers see the group as a natural basis for individual change since it is a social setting that can re-enact the family constellation with a better outcome. The 1985 film *The Breakfast Club*, which was wildly popular among teenagers, exemplified Adlerian adventure therapy principles (the adventure was enduring a day-long school detention!). You might enjoy renting the film and looking at it as an Adlerian.

Perfectionism

Though we often look at perfectionism as a *symptom* of a disorder, like obsessive-compulsive disorder or body dysmorphic disorder, Adler saw psychopathology as a *response* to perfectionism (Lombardi, Florentino, & Lombardi, 1998). Perfectionism is striving for superiority gone amuck. Generalized anxiety disorder, eating disorders, somatoform disorders, alcoholism, and drug addiction are some of the problems addressed through the basic mistake, "I must be perfect." Less severe but nonetheless self-destructive habits also stem from perfectionism: wanting to excel no matter what the price, concealing and denying one's emotions, doing nothing if it can't be done flawlessly. Adler encouraged such clients to give up ideal perfection and strive for "normal perfection," which includes striving for improvement through taking risks and making mistakes—the "courage to be imperfect."

Case Conceptualization: An Example

The following selection demonstrates how counselors today apply Adlerian psychology. The client benefits from the therapist's exploration of how cultural expectations affect the individual.

THE CASE OF JIN

J. M. Carlson and J. D. Carlson (2000)

Jin was a 15-year-old Asian-American of Japanese ancestry who lived in a western U.S. city. He was referred for treatment by the counselor at the private (elite) high school that he attended. Jin's academic performance and grades had been declining while behavior problems (e.g., truancy, failure to complete assignments, insubordination with teachers) had been increasing. The school suspended Jin and indicated that if he underwent counseling the school would consider accepting him back for the next academic year.

Both of Jin's parents brought him to treatment, and each appeared to be a combination of angry and embarrassed. Both parents were exceptionally polite, and they expressed a willingness to do whatever it would take to get Jin help.

They had become increasingly frustrated with his behavior and attitude at home and now with the school's decision. Dad appeared reserved and rigid while Mom did most of the talking. Each statement she made was supported by his nonverbal agreement in the form of a slight nod. The therapist carefully listened to their story and agreed to see Jin. The therapist took charge and suggested that a lifestyle assessment be conducted to focus on how Jin defined himself in the current culture with an understanding that Jin was a product of his family history and ancestry. This suggestion was well received. The White male therapist expressed having some knowledge of the Japanese culture through participation in local Japanese cultural events and having made a personal visit to Japan. He did, however, ask this family to explain how their Japanese heritage has affected who they are today and to educate the therapist about their cultural world view.

Family Constellation

Jin was an older child with one 13-year-old sister. His immediate family lived with the maternal grandparents, who emigrated from Japan after World War II. The paternal grandparents were second-generation Japanese immigrants who had been born in the United States. The paternal grandparents' family had been interned in the United States during World War II and had some fears of government and outsiders. Japanese traditions of patriarchy, restrained communication, and the importance of hierarchy and generational differences were present.

Jin found his place within the family through alienation, self-centered behavior, and risk-taking and by being very competitive. He saw himself as having the most intelligence and being the most daring, assertive, mischievous, and rebellious. He reported being punished the most but also getting away with the most. He had the most friends, sought excitement, and had a chip on his shoulder. His sister appeared to find her place through dependency, optimism, cooperation, and passivity. She received good grades and was helpful, industrious, methodical, patient, obedient, and responsible. Considerate and shy, she had high standards of right and wrong and tried to please others. Jin expressed wanting to "fit in" to the American Way and wanting to be his own boss. He did not want to be Japanese but American. He felt his parents were forcing him to do what they wanted—earn high grades in school, spend a great deal of time at home, dress conventionally, and ask permission often.

Early Recollections

Age 5: "Dad asked me to wash my hands and I wouldn't do it. He beat me with a wooden spoon but I still wouldn't wash my hands. I fell asleep in the bathtub. I never did wash my hands. Most vivid: I didn't give in" (satisfied).

Age 6: "I went to school all by myself. I walked out into the street and met my friend. I turned and waved good-bye to my mom and sister. It was thrilling. Most vivid: I felt so grown up."

Jin felt important, special and unique. He felt entitled to have his own way. Life was exciting, but it made too many demands. Therefore he could do what ever he wanted and not submit to others' demands.

Treatment

The therapist encouraged Jin's wanting to acculturate and acknowledged the courage he showed by "breaking the mold." A supportive accepting method allowed Jin to feel comfortable with the individuation he sought. Circular questions were used to ask Jin what his grandparents, parents, and sister believed about him. Jin's responses revealed awareness of their care, concern, and worry for him. He began to see that for him to individuate did not necessitate harming them. [Ways that] Jin could be himself and use his abilities while staying connected were explored. He decided to go to the local public school where he signed up for honors, college-prep classes. He agreed to work at a local flower shop rather than for his father's hardware store. His parents were asked to attend an exit session where changes were examined and Jin's role in the family was negotiated. Although the parents hoped for more involvement in Jin's life, the parents willingly accepted that less involvement could still be positive, and they showed respect and commitment for Jin's choices. It was agreed that the family would return for follow-up visits every three months to gauge and discuss how the family was adapting to the changes in the family roles. (pp. 221–223) ■ ■

DISCUSSION IDEAS

1. In their introduction to the case of Jin, Carlson and Carlson (2000) wrote, "Although Adlerian theory is referred to as Individual Psychology, its focus is on the person in his or her social and cultural context. Adlerian psychotherapists look for clients to define themselves within their social environments; they do not try to fit clients into preconceived models. Adlerian psychotherapists allow broad concepts of age, ethnicity, lifestyle, and gender differences to emerge in therapy and then attend to a client's individual meaning of culture" (p. 218). What did the therapist in the case study do to attend to Jin's individual meaning of culture?

2. Consider the family constellation of Jin, including the grandparents. How does the family's history affect Jin? What do you think about Jin's sister's style of life? What effect do you think her choices have on Jin's behavior, and vice versa?

3. What Adlerian techniques and ideas were applied in the case of Jin, and with what results? What did the therapist find out about Jin's style of life? Summarize what one of Jin's *basic mistakes* might be.

4. Why do you think that changes in school and job were important for Jin? Think of several ways these concrete changes might make a psychological

difference. Have you ever seen a case in which changing schools or jobs made a difference for a teenager? What was the effect of the change?

5. If you were Jin's counselor, what areas of his life (inner and outer) would you like to investigate further, and why?

_____

Critiques of Adlerian Psychology

In many ways, Adler was ahead of his time; in other ways, he was limited by his historical moment. His rejection of heredity as a source of psychopathology, for example, is brought into question by today's genetic research, which suggests genetic contributions to such conditions as obsessive-compulsive disorder, schizophrenia, depression, and anxiety. However, heredity always interacts with environment, so Adlerian investigation of the social setting of pathology is still crucial.

Judgments About Sexuality

Adler believed that he was thoroughly convinced of the equality between the sexes, and stood for the unpopular position that there was no innate difference between men and women. However, he expressed a conviction that women have an innate desire to be mothers, and that the absence of this desire is pathological. In *Problems of Neurosis* (1927), he wrote, "Self-absorbed women generally show their lack of human and social interest by an unwillingness to have children" and "If a woman is re-adjusted socially, I am sure she will wish to have a baby without suggestion or pressure from anyone" (pp. 60–61). No parallel judgments are made about the natural occupations of men. In this area, Adler's sympathy for women's condition falters; his social constructionism flickers out.

Like Freud, Adler held the belief that heterosexuality was the normal and healthy outcome of a good childhood. Homosexuality was a disorder to be treated as other neuroses were. "The great difficulty of changing a homosexual lies not only in his lack of social adjustment, but in the invariable absence of the right training, which ought to begin in early childhood" (1927, p. 115). Homosexuality was removed as a category of illness from the *Diagnostic and Statistical Manual of Mental Disorders* in the 1970s, based on research proving that homosexuality in itself is not a clinical problem (though clinical problems may be rooted in the experience of prejudice, as is true for any minority group).

Essentialism

While Adler rejected most inborn sources of human behavior, he often referred to the ideals of social interest and striving for perfection in terms that make them sound innate. "The origin of humanity and the ever-repeated beginning of infant life impresses with every psychological act: 'Achieve! Arise! Conquer!'" (Adler, 1930b). While this point of view informs Adler's optimism about human nature, it has not yet found empirical proof.

Case Study Basis

Adler's theories were developed through his experience with many clients, and he explains his principles through case examples. His conclusions are completely drawn from this case method of research, which is not persuasive to the scientific community. The case method is eminently susceptible to the researcher's biased interpretations. Since Adler's writings, though, some of his principles have been tested out in empirical studies, such as Wick, Wick, and Peterson's (1997) measurement of self-esteem before and after Adlerian adventure therapy for fifth graders. The survival and rediscovery of Adlerian principles in later, empirically supported therapies such as cognitive-behavioral treatment lend support to his astuteness.

Harshness

Finally, as I mentioned early in this chapter, to read Adler's original text is to encounter a tone harsher than we see in modern psychology. To call clients' explanations for their behavior "alibis" and "excuses" and to refer to troubled people as "failures," as Adler did, implies a bluntness that may sound judgmental to us, because we are used to euphemistic language.

KEY TERMS

"as if"	family constellation	sense of inferiority
basic mistakes	fictional finalism	social interest
birth order analysis	fictional self	strivings for
constructivist	growth model	superiority
discouragement	holistic	style of life
early childhood	life script	The Question
recollection	phenomenological	
existential	private logic	

Exploring Key Terms

In your small group, create a paragraph of no more than 125 words that makes sensible use of at least five of the terms in the list above. Your paragraph should explain some aspect of Adlerian theory or practice, and it should follow from a single topic sentence. When the whole class reconvenes, read each group's paragraph aloud and critique the usage of the terms. Mark off which terms were never used by any group, and discuss why they might have been left out. Create definitions of these leftover terms.

LIBRARY, MEDIA, AND INTERNET ACTIVITIES

1. In the United States, case studies and empirical research based on Adler's theory appear in the *Journal of Individual Psychology* (formerly called *Individual Psychology: Journal of Adlerian Theory, Research, and Practice*). In fact, if you come across a source from this journal, you can be sure that it is Adlerian in nature.

Find the *Journal of Individual Psychology* in your library. By surveying the tables of contents, you will be able to identify articles in your particular area of interest in psychology. Create a bibliography of at least five such articles.

Because of Adler's interest in schools, many of the references to his work are published in education journals rather than in psychology journals. Look in your education database and see whether "Adler" appears as a keyword in articles published in the last two years.

2. Online, at *http://www.ourworld.compuserve.com/homepages/hstein*, you will find a wealth of Adlerian information. This site has video clips of Adler and Adlerians (including a newsreel of Adler in Vienna in 1929), a question-and-answer page, quotations, concept maps, and references. At *http://www.alfredadler.org*, the North American Society of Adlerian Psychology displays its webpage with news about the national organization's meetings and links to Adlerian schools and other organizations. And *http://www.cmitpress.com* is the site for a publisher of Adlerian materials, including works by Don Dinkmeyer, a modern Adlerian, and the Kern personality scale, based on Individual Psychology.

REFERENCES

Adler, A. (1929). *Problems of neurosis*. London: Kegan Paul.

Adler, A. (1930a). *The education of children* (E. Jensen & F. Jensen, Trans.). South Bend, IN: Gateway.

Adler, A. (1930b). Individual Psychology. In Murchison, C. E. (Ed.), *Psychologies of 1930* (pp. 395–405). Worcester, MA: Clark University Press.

Adler, A. (1931). Extract from *What life should mean to you*. In H. L. Ansbacher & R. R. Ansbacher (Eds.), *The Individual Psychology of Alfred Adler: A systematic presentation in selections from his writings* (p. 209). (Reprinted from *What life should mean to you*, Boston: Little, Brown, 1931.) New York: Harper Torchbooks.

Adler, A. (1933). Extract from *Social interest: A challenge to mankind*. In H. L. Ansbacher & R. R. Ansbacher (Eds.), *The Individual Psychology of Alfred Adler: A systematic presentation in selections from his writings* (pp. 408–409). (Reprinted from *Social interest: A challenge to mankind*, London: Faber & Faber, trans. 1938.) New York: Harper Torchbooks.

Adler, A. (1956). Extracts from *The science of living*. In H. L. Ansbacher & R. R. Ansbacher (Eds.), *The Individual Psychology of Alfred Adler: A systematic presentation in selections from his writings* (pp. 357–358). New York: Harper Torchbooks. (Reprinted from *The science of living*, New York: Greenburg, 1929.)

Adler, A. (1957). *Understanding human nature* (W. Beran Wolfe, Trans.). New York: Fawcett. (Original work published 1927)

Carich, P. A. (2001). Use of Adlerian concepts in healing severe physical and sexual abuse. *Journal of Individual Psychology, 57,* 116–120.

Carlson, J. M., & Carlson, J. D. (2000). The application of Adlerian psychotherapy with Asian-American clients. *Journal of Individual Psychology, 56,* 214–225.

Dreikurs, R., & Cassell, P. (1972). *Discipline without tears.* New York: Penguin.

Edwards, D. L., & Gfroerer, K. P. (2001). Adlerian school-based interventions for children with attention-deficit/hyperactivity disorder. *Journal of Individual Psychology, 57,* 210–223.

Kefir, N. (1981). Impasse/priority therapy. In R. J. Corsini (Ed.), *Handbook of innovative psychotherapies* (pp. 401–415). New York: Wiley.

Lombardi, D. N., Florentino, M., & Lombardi, A. J. (1998). Perfectionism and abnormal behavior. *Journal of Individual Psychology, 54,* 61–71.

Mosak, H. H. (2000). Adlerian psychotherapy. In R. J. Corsini & D. Wedding (Eds.), *Current psychotherapies* (6th ed.) (pp. 54–98). Itasca, IL: Peacock.

Pryor, D. B, & Tollerud, T. R. (1999). Applications of Adlerian principles in school settings. *Professional School Counseling, 2,* 299–304.

Utay, J., & Utay, C. (1996). Applications of Adler's theory in counseling and education. *Journal of Instructional Psychology, 23,* 251–256.

Vaihinger, H. (1925). *The philosophy of "as if": A system of the theoretical, practical, and religious fictions of mankind.* New York: Harcourt, Brace. (Original work published 1911)

Watts, R. E. (2000). Adlerian counseling: A viable approach for contemporary practice. *TCA Journal, 28,* 11–23.

Watts, R. E., & Pietrzak, D. (2000). Adlerian "encouragement" and the therapeutic process of solution-focused brief therapy. *Journal of Counseling and Development, 78,* 442–447.

Wick, D. T., Wick, J. K., & Peterson, N. (1997). Improving self-esteem with Adlerian adventure therapy. *Professional School Counseling, 1,* 53–56.

CHAPTER 6

Humanistic Approaches and Their Existentialist Roots

 # A Selection from

On Becoming a Person, 1961

Carl R. Rogers

Let me try to explain what I mean when I say that it appears that the goal the individual most wishes to achieve, the end which he knowingly and unknowingly pursues, is to become himself. When a person comes to me, troubled by his unique combination of difficulties, I have found it most worthwhile to try to create a relationship with him in which he is safe and free. It is my purpose to understand the way he feels in his own inner world, to accept him as he is, to create an atmosphere of freedom in which he can move in his thinking and feeling and being, in any direction he desires. How does he use this freedom?

It is my experience that he uses it to become more and more himself. He begins to drop the false fronts, or the masks, or the roles, with which he has faced life. He appears to be trying to discover something more basic, something more truly himself. At first he lays aside masks which he is to some degree aware of using. One young woman student describes in a counseling interview one of the masks she has been using, and how uncertain she is whether underneath this appeasing, ingratiating front there is any real self with convictions.

I was thinking about this business of standards. I somehow developed a sort of knack, I guess, of—well—habit—of trying to make people feel at ease around me, or to make things go along smoothly. There always had to be some appeaser around, being sorta the oil that soothed the waters. At a small meeting, or a little party, or something—I could help things go along nicely and appear to be having a good time. And sometimes I'd surprise myself by arguing against what I really thought when I saw that the person in charge would be quite unhappy about it if I didn't. In other words I just wasn't ever—I mean, I didn't find myself ever being set and definite about things. Now the reason why I did it probably was I'd been doing it around home so much. I just didn't stand up for my own convictions, until I don't know whether I have any convictions to stand up for. I haven't been really honestly being myself, or actually knowing what my real self is, and I've been just playing a sort of false role.

You can, in this excerpt, see her examining the mask she has been using, recognizing her dissatisfaction with it, and wondering how to get to the real self underneath, if such a self exists.

In this attempt to discover his own self, the client typically uses the relationship to explore, to examine the various aspects of his own experience, to recognize and face up to the deep contradictions which he often discovers. He learns how much of his behavior, even how much of the feeling he experiences, is not real, is not something which flows from the genuine reactions of his organism, but is a facade, a front, behind which he has been hiding. He discovers how much of his life is guided by what he thinks he should be, not by what he is. Often he discovers that he exists only in response to the demands of others, that he seems

147

to have no self of his own, that he is only trying to think, and feel, and behave in the way that others believe he ought to think, and feel, and behave. In this connection I have been astonished to find how accurately the Danish philosopher, Soren Kierkegaard, pictured the dilemma of the individual more than a century ago, with keen psychological insight. He points out that the most common despair is to be in despair at not choosing, or willing, to be oneself; but that the deepest form of despair is to choose "to be another than himself." On the other hand "to will to be that self which one truly is, is indeed the opposite of despair," and this choice is the deepest responsibility of man. As I read some of his writings I almost feel that he must have listened in on the statements made by our clients as they search and explore for the reality of self—often a painful and troubling search. . . .

Let us pursue a bit further this question of what it means to become one's self. It is a most perplexing question and again I will try to take from a statement by a client, written between interviews, a suggestion of an answer. She tells how the various facades by which she has been living have somehow crumpled and collapsed, bringing a feeling of confusion, but also a feeling of relief. She continues:

You know, it seems as if all the energy that went into holding the arbitrary pattern together was quite unnecessary—a waste. You think you have to make the pattern yourself; but there are so many pieces, and it's so hard to see where they fit. Sometimes you put them in the wrong place, and the more pieces mis-fitted, the more effort it takes to hold them in place, until at last you are so tired that even that awful confusion is better than holding on any longer. Then you discover that left to themselves the jumbled pieces fall quite naturally into their own places, and a living pattern emerges without any effort at all on your part. Your job is just to discover it, and in the course of that, you will find yourself and your own place. You must even let your own experience tell you its own meaning; the minute you tell it what it means, you are at war with yourself.

Let me see if I can take her poetic expression and translate it into the meaning it has for me. I believe she is saying that to be herself means to find the pattern, the underlying order, which exists in the ceaselessly changing flow of her experience. Rather than to try to hold her experience into the form of a mask, or to make it be a form or structure that it is not, being herself means to discover the unity and harmony which exists in her own actual feelings and reactions. It means that the real self is something which is comfortably discovered in one's experiences, not something imposed upon it.

Through giving excerpts from the statements of these clients, I have been trying to suggest what happens in the warmth and understanding of a facilitating relationship with a therapist. It seems that gradually, painfully, the individual explores what is behind the masks he presents to the world, and even behind the masks with which he has been deceiving himself. Deeply and often vividly he experiences the various elements of himself which have been hidden within. Thus to an increasing degree he becomes himself—not a facade of conformity to others, not a cynical denial of all feeling, nor a front of intellectual rationality, but a living, breathing, feeling, fluctuating process—in short, he becomes a person. (pp. 108–114) ■ ■

DISCUSSION IDEAS

1. Rogers writes of the client *using* the atmosphere of freedom in the therapeutic relationship. How is this *use* different from the client's role in psychoanalytic or psychodynamic therapy? How is the role similar? Why do you think the therapeutic relationship is emphasized?

2. Do you know anyone like the young woman described in paragraph 4? What sort of problems might this pattern of behavior cause, in your opinion? Is the pattern ever a positive characteristic?

3. Rogers suggests that there are two levels of false faces—first, a conscious facade based on social expectations, and, second, a facade that people are themselves not even aware of—"the false faces which they had not known were false faces." Do you agree that the second level exists? In other words, can we fool ourselves about who we really are?

4. What are some of the masks that middle school, high school, and college students usually feel compelled to wear? What about children: Do you think they are genuine, without masks? What masks do other roles in life seem to require—of mothers, fathers, nurses, teachers, counselors, social workers, managers, secretaries?

5. Does this passage help you understand the title of Rogers's most famous book, *On Becoming a Person?* What do you think the title means?

6. If the goal of therapy is becoming one's self, without facades or denial, what view of human nature is implied?

7. What do you think of Rogers's writing style? Was the passage easy or difficult to read? Why do you think he chose to use the word *I* instead of following the conventions of scientific writing at the time, which did not use the first-person point of view?

Profile of a Theorist

CARL ROGERS (1902–1987)

Carl Rogers was born in January 1902, the fourth of six children of devoutly religious parents living in Oak Park, Illinois. As a boy, he was characterized as shy and not particularly social and was often teased for being sensitive. Just before high school, the Rogers family moved to a farm twenty-five miles outside of Chicago, where his parents hoped to provide a more wholesome and religious environment for their children. It was there that Carl developed an interest in the natural world that led him to pursue a degree in agriculture at the University of Wisconsin.

After two years at university, Rogers's growing fascination with religious issues prompted him to abandon agriculture and explore a career in ministry. In 1924, at the age of 22, he met and married Helen Elliott and moved to New York City to attend the Union Theological Seminary. While in seminary, his interests evolved once again, this time away from the doctrines of religion and toward psychology and education. He transferred to Teacher's College, where he obtained his master's and doctoral degrees in education and clinical psychology.

Rogers's early professional positions revolved around treating children and incorporated new ideas and trends emerging from the traditional psychoanalytic approaches. His emphasis on understanding the therapeutic relationship as a mechanism for change and the importance of the client's phenomenological experience took root during his years in New York. Rogers operated from the assumption that people are generally oriented toward growth and fulfillment and promoted the role of therapist as a facilitator in that process. In a dramatic departure from previous beliefs that the therapist (or doctor) should be passive and emotionally detached from clients, Rogers suggested that the therapist can and must engage in an interpersonal relationship with the client. Furthermore, he posited that the relationship should be one in which the client receives unconditional positive regard from the therapist and consequently feels free to explore new feelings and behaviors.

Following a move to Ohio State where he assumed a full professorship in 1940, Rogers further developed his growing conceptualization of psychotherapy with the publication of *Counseling and Psychotherapy*. Rogers's deliberate move away from a focus on pathology coupled with his radical notion that clients possess the key to their *own* improvement proved controversial, as did his relative lack of attention to a tightly woven theory of personality. Nonetheless, the support for his client-centered approach grew, and in 1945 he accepted the directorship of the Counseling Center at the University of Chicago.

The years at Chicago were highly productive for Rogers. Not only did the publication of his book, *Client-Centered Therapy*, serve to articulate his theory of personality and refine his methodology for psychotherapy, but it was also during this time that he pioneered research on process and outcome in a therapeutic setting. Taking advantage of new personal audiotape recorders, Rogers recommended observing therapy sessions directly in an effort to demystify the process, subject it to scientific scrutiny, and optimize the potential for positive change by analyzing the process of therapy itself.

In 1957, Rogers moved to the University of Wisconsin, where he assumed a joint professorship in psychology and psychiatry in an effort to apply his theories and techniques to the more severely disordered. He left the world of academia to pursue independent projects through the Western Behavioral Sciences Institute in California and eventually founded the Center for the Study of the Person in La Jolla, where he worked until his death in 1987. His later contributions encouraged the use of the successful principles of client-centered therapy in a variety of settings, such as group therapy, family relationships, and teaching and learning environments.

The Humanistic Approach

Humanism is "a system of thought that centers on humans and their values, capacities, and worth" and is concerned with "the interests, needs, and welfare of humans" (*American Heritage Dictionary*, 2000). The dictionary definition might seem self-evident, but notice the emphasis on the positive and constructive side of human life rather than on the troubled, psychopathological side. Sharing many beliefs, existential and humanistic psychology are frequently lumped together (as they are in this text). However, a major difference is that most existentialist philosophers saw human nature as a blank, or neutral, until the human makes choices. Humanist psychologists see human nature as good, with an inborn **actualizing tendency** that drives us toward our highest potential and an **organismic valuing process** that leads us to prize choices that are good for us and for the peace and harmony of humanity. A humanist would hold the opinion that if we act as *authentic* beings, we will act for the best. (Look at the opening passage from Carl Rogers to see his explication of **authenticity,** or genuineness.)

Freud thought that humans were born with ruinous drives that had to be suppressed or redirected in civilized society; humanists believe that constructive inborn drives should be expressed and celebrated. Abraham Maslow (1968) augmented Freud's conception of the superego: We have not only the internalized conscience coming from our parents but also an "intrinsic conscience . . . based upon the unconscious and preconscious perception of our own nature, of our own destiny, or our own capacities, of our own 'call' in life" (p. 7). Rogers made an analogy between the actualizing tendency and infants' learning to walk: In spite of painful episodes of falling down, the child naturally persists in moving forward toward behavior that signifies maturity and freedom. Obviously, humanism entails an optimistic view of human nature.

An Introduction to Existentialist Thought

As you gathered from the passage at the beginning of the chapter, Rogers believed that you are better off as a genuine person than as a collection of facades or masks. The idea of genuineness or authenticity runs throughout the philosophy described in this chapter (existentialism) as well as throughout therapy approaches that derive from that philosophy (most commonly, Rogers's person-centered approach). These therapy approaches depend upon an authentic encounter between the client and counselor. The client-counselor relationship is the center of attention in therapeutic process.

Recently, a friend saw the book I was reading, *Person-Centred Therapy Today* (Mearns & Thorne, 2000), and asked me, "What does this title mean? Isn't all counseling person-centered?" I had to think a minute about that one. I believe that Rogers and others call their process **person-centered** because it focuses on knowing the person or people who are clients, and formulating case conceptualizations based on that knowledge, rather than knowing a theory or theories, and using those theories to understand the clients. *Person-centered* emphasizes a contrast with *theory-centered*. Of course, the existential and humanistic stance is itself a theory. The contrast lies in the source of case conceptualization: Is it the client's felt experience, or a theoretical template applied to the client's situation?

People experience the world in four dimensions simultaneously:

- the self, including *awareness* of feelings, thoughts, body, and individuality, continuous in time and space;
- the natural world and the environment;
- relationships with other people; and
- spiritual dynamics (this fourth dimension was a 1990s addition [Vontress, 1996]; original existential thought, which crested from the mid-'40s to the late '60s, included only the first three dimensions).

Think of preparing to take an exam, for instance. There are private processes within the self, such as memorizing, thinking, getting motivated, feeling pressured or anxious or confident, and hoping. You also live according to natural laws at the time: You need food and sleep, and you feel the consequences if you neglect them. You may study with classmates, talk with friends about your studies, or think about the effects of your test performance on other people (such as your family), adding a social dimension to the experience. Finally, you may call on a higher power for help, or you may use meditation or yoga to get spiritually ready for the exam. All four worlds of experience are operating in this example, though different ones take center stage at different times.

These are the elements of our existence, and the word *existence* is the root of the label **existentialism.** Existential psychologists believe that beneath specific problems and personality defects are always problems inherent to all human existence. Clemmont Vontress, considered by many to be one of the founders of cross-cultural counseling theory, believes that these universals make the existential model suitable for clients of any cultural background: "Since I began reading African, Asian, and Arab writers, I have learned that people all over the world try to make sense of life" (1996, p. 161). Yalom (1980) outlined the four basic problems we all confront in one way or another: meaninglessness, freedom, isolation, and death. They are all part of the package deal we get with being born. In the following sections, I will explain each basic problem of existentialism more fully and then tie it together with the therapy born from it, the humanistic approach.

R e f l e c t i o n

Think about a stressful incident in the recent past. Consider how you experienced the incident from four points of view: the worlds of self, others, nature and environment, and spirituality. Which world or worlds were in the forefront at the time? When you look back on it, do you see different phenomenological worlds involved than you saw during the incident itself?

Meaninglessness

At some point, we all wonder why we were ever born, or what our purpose on earth might be. We ponder the meaning of life. According to existential thought, the universe is not designed, purposeful, or coherent. There is no preset and stable meaning in life. But people need a sense of meaning, or they fall prey to hopelessness, discouragement, and emptiness—the essence of depression. We must create meaning for ourselves. Subjective well-being demands that we are able to balance the immediate situation against something bigger than ourselves. We want to see a pattern in what happens to us and our loved ones, but existentialists say that we must weave that pattern ourselves.

Look at the storylines that we find satisfying in fiction and film: We like to see conflict, adversity, and suffering that lead to a discovery of meaning (often, meaningful relationships with others). In the film *Regarding Henry* (1991), a heartless businessman incurs a severe brain injury that sends him into a state of amnesia. In recovery, he regresses to an old self that is open to experience, rekindling his love for his wife and for life in general. In fairy tales and myths, the hero or heroine must go through dangerous trials to earn spiritual rewards in the end, often including a revelation of *why* they had to go through the trials. Our love for survival-and-transformation stories reflects our desire to see meaning in the hardships life hands us. We must make up our own life stories.

Though there are no universal values, a constructed meaning in life implies a system of values. Rollo May and Irvin Yalom, two modern existential psychologists, wrote, "Values provide us with a blueprint for life conduct: values tell us not only *why* we live but *how* to live" (2000, p. 286). That is, once we have our life's purpose in mind, we are able to make choices. Many values are individual. For example, some people would have to be too poor or sick to feed their dogs or cats before giving them up, while others see pets as unnecessary luxuries. A fairly common instance of value-driven choice occurs when someone changes jobs for less pay, in order to make time for pursuits they see as more meaningful than a high salary: art, writing, teaching, political activism, child-raising, and so forth.

People's values usually derive from the particular cultural pattern they grew up with. For example, people from traditional Japan may be expected to value paying attention to people in authority, while people from an Israeli kibbutz may be expected to value paying attention to peers within their group (Triandis & Bhawuk, 1997). Culture operates within the family unit to form values: You and your friends probably vary in terms of how much value you place on making your grandparents proud of you, for example. In my family, ancestors were vague background forms, best left unmentioned, while in my neighbor's family, tales and pictures of ancestors were prominent in daily life. These contrasting styles definitely provided different senses of family identity and responsibility. To a counselor, it's important to understand variations in value systems, because people will be most comfortable and likely to persist in changes that are consistent with their values.

Reflection

Do you make a list of to-do items for the day or week? If you do, mark what items are related to your long-term goals in life. How much of the list concerns day-to-day details, and how much promotes your values or meaning in life? Write your thoughts on looking at the list this way.

If you don't make a list, how do you decide on priorities for action on a day-by-day basis? Think about what principles you use in deciding what must be done, what can be put off, and what can fall by the wayside if necessary. What values are reflected in your decisions?

SMALL GROUP EXERCISE

Below is a list of values—activities and qualities that people consider mean-ingful. Check off all the values that are important to you. Then check off the three that are most important. Discuss your decision-making process with your group. (This exercise is adapted from Seligman, 2001.) When you interact with a client, can you see how your values might come into play?

1. achievement
2. beauty
3. career success
4. child-rearing
5. creativity
6. fame
7. friendship
8. health and fitness
9. helping others
10. independence
11. learning and knowledge
12. love and romance
13. nature/outdoors activities
14. order
15. possessions
16. power
17. prestige and admiration
18. security
19. variety
20. wealth

Profile of a Theorist

ROLLO MAY (1909–1994)

Rollo May was born in Ohio on April 21, 1909. One of six children, he grew up in an intellectually poor environment. When his older sister suffered a psychotic breakdown during May's adolescence, his father blamed it on too much education. His mother and father fought frequently and eventually separated. Seeking relief from family tension, May spent much of his time away from home, developing interests in art and literature and taking refuge in reading.

May attended college at Michigan State but was asked to leave due to his involvement with a radical student publication. He transferred to Oberlin College, graduated in 1930, and then traveled in Europe for several years, living as an artist and financing his journeys as a tutor in English. While in Europe, he attended summer seminars by Alfred Adler at a resort in Vienna, and his enthusiasm for studying human nature grew.

Fascinated with the role of meaning, May enrolled in seminary when he returned to the United States, just as Carl Rogers had done ten years earlier. During his studies, he met and befriended Paul Tillich, the renowned existential theologian, and the cornerstone of his theory was set. After a brief stint as a minister, May left parish work to pursue his growing interest in psychology. He studied psychoanalysis and was strongly influenced by Harry Stack Sullivan, co-founder of the institute where May studied. He was particularly drawn to Sullivan's views of the therapist-client relationship as interactive.

Another of the most profound influences on the development of May's theory of therapy was his own bout with a life-threatening illness during his 30s. He contracted tuberculosis and struggled to survive and recover over a three-year period in a sanitarium in upstate New York. By his own account, he wrestled with feelings of helplessness, depression, acute awareness of mortality, and meaninglessness. Witnessing the recovery or demise of fellow patients, May formulated ideas about the importance of personal responsibility and free will in healing and life in general. He also read and wrote extensively about anxiety as a natural by-product of consciousness and the desire to avoid *non-being*. After leaving the sanitarium, May submitted his work on anxiety as a dissertation study and was awarded the first Ph.D. in psychology granted by Columbia University in 1949, at the age of 40.

Though the existential movement had been under way for some time in the United States, May's work in the 1950s and 1960s contributed to the rising popularity of applying existential concepts to psychotherapy. His books *Existence: A New Dimension in Psychiatry and Psychology*, published in 1958, and *Love and Will*, published ten years later, mirror the emergence and evolution of existential therapy in this country. May was a popular speaker and visiting professor at many universities and, as an authority on existentialism, paved the way for those who followed, including his friend and colleague Irvin Yalom. Though the do-what-you-feel therapy of the 1960s and 1970s was sometimes associated with existential principles, May was critical of quick fixes that lacked components of consciousness and personal responsibility. He continued to write about the human condition until his death in 1994 at the age of 85.

Freedom

It may seem odd to view **freedom** as a problem. In the existential sense, we have some extent of freedom even in the most restrictive circumstances. Viktor Frankl's (1946/1984) account of his four years in Nazi concentration camps serves as a touchstone text for learning about mental and spiritual freedom within terrible physical enslavement. He observed that prisoners who found something to live for survived longer than those who gave up. Frankl applied his revelations to human psychology in general, saying that though we may not choose what happens to us, we choose our attitudes toward it and what we make of it. Through his best-seller *Man's Search for Meaning*, other writings, and lectures across the world, he used his insights from being a prisoner to construct a philosophy of life that has helped thousands of people find a way to make meaning out of suffering. He wrote,

> We who have lived in concentration camps can remember the men who walked through the huts comforting others, giving away their last piece of bread. They may have been few in number, but they offer sufficient proof that everything can be taken from a man but one thing: the last of the human freedoms—to choose one's attitude in any given set of circumstances, to choose one's own way. . . .
> Even though conditions such as lack of sleep, insufficient food and various mental stresses may suggest that the inmates were bound to react in certain ways, in the final analysis it becomes clear that the sort of person the prisoner became was the result of an inner decision, and not the result of camp influences alone. Fundamentally, therefore, any man can, even under such circumstances, decide what shall become of him—mentally and spiritually. . . . The prisoner who had lost faith in the future—his future—was doomed. With his loss of belief in the future, he also lost his spiritual hold; he let himself decline and became subject to mental and physical decay. (1946/1984, pp. 86–87, 95)

Existentialists see freedom as a great responsibility, since having freedom of choice means taking personal responsibility for choices. People blame parents, spouses, bosses, or society's injustices, but in existential terms responsibility includes not blaming others for one's own inner state. Thus, people who explain their bad behavior, failures, or interpersonal problems by pointing to abuse in childhood (or other past trauma) are dodging the freedom to change and to make something positive out of the negative. This positive transformation often involves caring for other people and striving for their happiness or their relief from pain. This idea is similar to Adler's endorsement of *social interest*, which you read about in the previous chapter.

Rollo May (1969) relates freedom to our chance to construct meaning. He uses the word **wishing** to describe a pull toward our life purpose, and **willing** to describe the movement from wish into action. He sees depression as a deficit in wishing. Impulsive and compulsive behaviors are seen as denials of *willing* in that we give no thought to what we really want, and follow our first urges. Buying things we can't afford, using drugs to distract ourselves from tasks, and performing repetitive rituals to stave off threats are examples. May and Yalom (2000) echo Adler in perceiving that some people evade responsibility by entering "a temporary irrational state in which they are not responsible even to themselves for their behavior" (p. 285). Remember that Adler always pondered what life task the client was *avoiding* through mental illness. In this way, even insanity can be viewed as a rejection of freedom and the coexisting burden of choice.

DISCUSSION IDEAS

In your study of human behavior, you have run into concepts of how we attribute success and failure: externalizing (attributing to others or to the situation) and internalizing (attributing to yourself) (Rotter, 1966). You may say that you ran a red light because the green was too short, the sun was in your eyes, or the car behind you was tailgating (externalizing), or instead because you were in a hurry, not paying attention, or a bad driver (internalizing). Give some other examples. What are the benefits and pitfalls of externalizing? What are the benefits and pitfalls of internalizing?

R e f l e c t i o n

Sometimes you make a decision by *not* making a decision—you waver back and forth till the decision time has passed, or you conveniently forget to take decisive action. Can you think of an example from your own or someone else's life? Write about deciding by not deciding. In your example, was it an evasion of freedom?

Isolation

We are ultimately alone. This fact strikes us most forcefully in times of crisis or profound change. Because we have a sense of self and individuality, we also have a sense of aloneness: I am the only I there is. When people are dying, they are keenly aware of their isolation, and many terminally ill patients turn away from others in the last part of their lives. We are alone in the final decision about *how* we should live as well. As the Christian hymn goes, "You have to walk this lonesome valley by yourself—nobody else can walk it for you."

Loving relationships relieve our **isolation,** and for most of us the pursuit and maintenance of such relationships constitute a primary value. How many people in your small group chose "friendship" and "love and romance" from the list in the earlier exercise? Seeing your friend or loved one as a whole being, not as an object to relieve your isolation or serve your other needs, is the ideal. This type of relationship was described in Martin Buber's (1970) book *I and Thou,* and you will see it referred to as an I/Thou relationship. In an **I/Thou relationship,** "one must truly listen to the other: relinquish stereotypes and anticipations of the other, and allow oneself to be shaped by the other's response. . . . [O]ne must lose or transcend oneself" (Yalom, 1980, p. 365). However, existential isolation persists in the face of intimacy, and we live the human paradox of being related to, yet separate from, other people.

The problem of isolation creates some destructive interpersonal solutions, too. Some people are unable to tolerate being alone and use others to avoid the pain. One way is through **fusion,** in which a person lets ego boundaries loosen and attempts to become one with an idealized other person (therefore, not an I/Thou situation). Such a relationship used to be common among women who identified heavily with their husband's achievements and preferences, to the detriment of their own individuality and freedom. Fusion also may occur in people with borderline personality disorders, as self psychologists such as Kernberg have conceptualized them (see Chapter 4). The related defense mechanism, in psychodynamic terms, is *identification.* Compulsive sexuality is yet another frail defense against loneliness. Paranoia and schizophrenia exemplify the most extreme cases of isolation: In such cases, the sufferer is incapable of perceiving other people as whole beings and has no one with whom he or she can double-check reality.

May and Yalom (2000) see an important part of existential psychotherapy as learning what you *cannot* get from others—what you must create from within. This is a hard lesson, as you probably know. Our romantic films and songs would lead us to believe that the perfect love partner meets every need. Notice, however, that the films and songs are almost always about the *beginning* of love, not the middle or the end, where existential aloneness reigns.

R e f l e c t i o n

Choose one or more of the three topics below to consider privately or to write about.

1. How comfortable are you with isolation? Think of the last time you were alone for more than a few minutes without a structured task to do. What did you do, how did you feel, and why?
2. What do you do while alone? How many of these activities are distractions from loneliness, and how many are expressions of your wishes and will?
3. Do you ever seek companionship just because you are lonely? Have you ever been lonely even when you are among other people?

Death

Our lives are finite: We and our loved ones will die. Psychologically, we struggle with this reality by defending ourselves against it, starting early in childhood. Yalom (1980) reports a study of ninety-eight children aged 5 to 10 who were asked to complete open-ended stories. When given story beginnings that did not refer to death, 50 percent of the children referred in their completions to death, funerals, killings, or ghosts. When the story beginnings were potentially tipped toward the theme ("She lost one of her children . . ."), over 60 percent of the children referred to death. As children, we defend against the threat by a belief in specialness (for various reasons, death will not happen to *us*) and a belief in the ultimate rescuer, a wondrous parental figure who will save us from harm. As adults, we defend against death in the same irrational ways, perhaps in bigger words.

We also lessen our anxieties about death by leading meaningful lives (by our own definitions, of course). "A sense of fulfillment, a feeling that life has been well lived, mitigates against the terror of death" (Yalom, 1980, p. 208). I come from a family of teachers, and our belief that we have altered many students' lives for the better has given us a sense that we leave a legacy behind when we die. Creative artists, counselors, architects, medical workers, builders, ecologists, scientists, and sometimes parents feel similar comfort in how their contributions to humanity and nature will survive beyond their life spans.

Too great a fear of death leads to "a life dedicated more to safety, survival, and relief from pain than to growth and fulfillment" (Yalom, 1980, p. 208). Since pursuit of a meaningful goal usually involves taking risks, both great and small, a person motivated by **death anxiety** will avoid the pursuit and choose the course of security. I know a woman who appreciated great art but refused to visit Chicago's Art Institute for fear of being attacked in the big city—not a totally irrational fear, but one that kept her from enjoying life to its fullest. In contrast, acceptance of the limits of a lifetime motivates us to use the time we have to create a meaningful existence: to live *authentically*, on our own terms. In a paradoxical way, an awareness of death impels us to live with zest and creativity.

DISCUSSION IDEAS

What have you heard children say about death? Yalom saw one of the child's main developmental tasks as dealing with the fear of death. How do children in your life, or children you see portrayed fictionally, conceptualize death? Do you remember your first encounters with death during your childhood? What do you think children should be taught about death, and at what age? As you think about your classmates' contributions to this discussion, inquire into whether cultural variations among yourselves affect your opinions.

The twentieth-century existential psychologists' thoughts on meaninglessness, freedom, isolation, and death were influenced by nineteenth-century existentialist philosophers, especially Kierkegaard (1813–1855) and Nietzsche (1844–1900). Common themes were "an emphasis on human emotions; the importance of subjective experience; a deep respect for individuality; a belief in free will; . . . [and] the importance of the individual attempting to make sense out of his or her life and freely acting upon his or her interpretations of life's meaning" (Hergenhahn, 2001, p. 198). These are themes that also bloomed in humanistic psychology.

Essential Concepts in Existentialist and Humanist Psychology

Carl Rogers believed that the best counseling relationship resembled an existential encounter more than a meeting between the expert and the needy (Bachelor & Horvath, 1999). Meaninglessness, freedom, isolation, and death are crucial issues in existential philosophy. When they focus on bettering the human situation, they are also humanist philosophical issues. We will look at how these philosophies relate to the theory and practice of psychology. The interrelationships encompass ten topics, areas where philosophy and action interact in counseling: phenomenology, anxiety, guilt, self-actualization, peak experiences, core conditions of therapy, congruence, locus of evaluation, the fully functioning person, and the role of traditional diagnosis. Each of these topics will now be explored.

The Phenomenological Stance

One feature that unifies existential, humanistic, individual (Adler), and self (Kohut) psychology is the **phenomenological stance.** This stance contrasts with the structural stance of most psychoanalytically oriented therapies. As you may remember, a structural approach embraces the idea that our psyches can be divided into parts and that different parts need fixing in cases of psychological distress. There is an idea that a person's problem can be corralled off and separated from him or her as a person. The phenomenological point of view rejects this parts-in-need-of-repair model. (Rollo May [1961] wrote that Freud *knew about* anxiety, while Kierkegaard *knew* anxiety.) Existentialists understand people's problems as characteristics of their whole response to existence as they see it. "What looks like a minor fault may be a necessary concomitant of one of the person's most valuable traits. What looks like a sterling virtue may be a defense against anxiety destined to change its shape as anxiety diminishes" (Tyler, 1969, p. 35). For example, my friend Jana's tendency to worry (a minor fault) is part of her deep caring about other people's welfare (a virtue). And a person who is consistently five minutes early for all appointments (no matter how relaxed the event) may be neurotically defending against losing control of the situation.

From a phenomenological stance, the same occurrence is different when perceived by different people. We attach subjective interpretations to experience, interpretations that are quite individual. I was once talking with a friend before I flew out of town, and I mentioned that I didn't mind getting to the airport early because airports always seemed so exciting, with all those people going off on vacations and adventures, or else happy to be heading home. My friend could hardly believe her ears. She thought that everyone at the airport looked like they were going off to a funeral or a stressful family scene. And we were talking about the same airport! The existential therapist attempts to immerse herself in the client's private world of experience. "The therapist moves back and forth between noticing patterns in what a client finds happening in his world and supposing there to be some point which that pattern creatively fulfills" (Russell, 1978, p. 264). Unlike other approaches, the counselor does not purposefully acquire a life history from each client. Early on, Rogers (1940) realized that "[o]ur most profound emotional patterns are as evident in our daily experience as in our past history, as plain in the immediate counseling relationship as in our childhood reactions" (p. 162).

R. D. Laing, a physician famous for his work with schizoid and schizophrenic people, took a phenomenological approach to even the most out-of-touch patients: "The therapist must have the plasticity to transpose himself into another strange and even alien view of the world. In this act, he draws on his own psychotic possibilities, without forgoing his sanity. Only thus can he arrive at an understanding of the patient's *existential position*" (Laing, 1969, p. 35). Notice the parallels in this useful definition provided by Rollo May (1961):

> Phenomenology is the endeavor to take the phenomena as given. It is the disciplined effort to clear one's mind of the presuppositions that so often cause us to see in the patient only our own theories or the dogmas of our own systems, the effort to experience instead the phenomena in their full reality as they present themselves. (p. 26)

DISCUSSION IDEAS

Tyler (1969) wrote that sometimes a minor fault can be characteristic of a major virtue, and a virtue may be a defense against anxiety. Can you think of other examples? Think of the things you admire about your friends, and the things that irritate you. Is there a way you can see the faults relating to your friends' virtues, or the good points relating to their anxieties?

Anxiety as a Perception of Threat

The discussion of phenomenology above included several references to *anxiety*. Freud saw anxiety as a signal that the ego was faltering in its efforts to control the id's and superego's urges. However, existentialists view anxiety more holistically (as a whole), as a response to perceived threats to existence or to values we find fundamental to existence (May, 1977). For example, you probably know someone who becomes anxious if his household is not orderly, in circumstances where another person wouldn't mind a bit of a mess. From an existential point of view, the hyper-orderly person is attempting to ward off chaos, a disorder that threatens his position in the world. We each have a natural need to survive, to preserve our being, and to assert our being, and in the face of death this need causes an unavoidable anxiety. How we deal with this anxiety varies. Yalom insisted, "The study of psychopathology . . . is the study of failed death transcendence" (1980, p. 109).

May (1961) gave an example of a woman who went to a counselor for difficulty in speaking, a hoarseness that had no organic cause. Her first therapist told her that she was "too proper, too controlled," and she became upset and left treatment. May commented:

> Now, technically he [the counselor] was entirely correct; existentially he was entirely wrong. What he did not see, in my judgment, was this very properness, this overcontrol, far from being things that Mrs. Hutchens wanted to get over, were part of her desperate attempt to preserve what precarious center she had. As though she were saying, "If I opened up, if I communicated, I would lose what little space in life I have." We see here, incidentally, how inadequate is the definition of neurosis as a failure of adjustment. *An adjustment is exactly what neurosis is; and that is just its trouble.* It is a necessary adjustment by which centeredness can be preserved; a way of accepting *non-being* . . . in order that some little *being* may be preserved. (pp. 76–77)

Existential anxiety, like Freud's neurotic anxiety, calls forth defenses like Mrs. Hutchens's inability to speak up. Existential anxiety, however, does not come from a battle of id, ego, and superego, but from "a deep feeling of unease that arises from our awareness of the givens: our existence is finite, we are mortal, and there is no purpose but the one we create for ourselves" (Bauman & Walso, 1998, p. 19). We must then choose to live with dread or with courage. The courageous response is to accept the facts of existence and say, "This is the way it is. Now I will live my life" (p. 20).

In this manner, you can understand the sullenness, secretiveness, and withdrawal that some parents complain of in teenagers. The adolescents are preserving and asserting their beings, as Mrs. Hutchens did, when their phenomenological experience is that they fit nowhere (existing as they do between child and adult) and that their beings are threatened by adults' attempts to control them. This may be why teens who have some commitment to goals that transcend their individual dilemmas—sports team members, thespians, intellectuals, activists—tend to be tolerable at home (when they are there). In cultures and families that basically skip teenagehood, by propelling grown children directly into adult responsibilities and roles, adolescent angst is rare. (There may, of course, be other attendant problems in that system.)

Guilt as a Message

Existential anxiety is unavoidable, and an offshoot of it is **existential guilt.** This is guilt *not* for sins of commission (actions) but for sins of omission (not taking action). A failure to live up to our potentialities, a dreadful feeling that we have created a self-restricted life due to fear of the unknown, is the source of existential guilt. We are denying the one inborn human impulse that we possess—the "character of self-affirmation," as May (1961) labeled it, the power of wishing, willing, decisions, and choice. Existential guilt, like Freudian anxiety, acts as a signal that all is not well. It is welcomed by therapists because it acts as a guide to action, frequently being the feeling that brings people into therapy, "a message from the deeper part of oneself that is seeking to take charge of one's life" (Bauman & Walso, 1998, p. 19).

R e f l e c t i o n

Can you think of ways that you restrict your life in the service of security rather than growth? Of the known rather than the unknown? Let me give you examples to get you started: Many people stay in stagnant relationships because they fear isolation. Others choose career paths for reasons of marketability, salary, convenience, or gender, when in their hearts they would prefer a riskier course. We all have smaller pockets of self-restriction, like not trying new foods, sticking to precise daily routines, refusing to try a new computer program, or dressing the same way year after year.

Innate Striving for Self-Actualization

Self-actualization is the opposite of the self-restriction that comes from existential anxiety and guilt. It is the reverse of shame, defeat, anxiety, and perception of life as meaningless. The term is associated with Abraham Maslow and is the pinnacle of his pyramid-shaped hierarchy of human needs: physiological needs, safety, belongingness and love, respect, self-esteem, and self-actualization. Maslow (1968) wrote that self-actualization can be defined

> as ongoing actualization of potentials, capacities and talents, as fulfillment of mission (or call, fate, destiny, or vocation), as a fuller knowledge of, and acceptance of, the person's own intrinsic nature, as an unceasing trend toward unity, integration or synergy within the person. (p. 25)

Notice that Maslow and Rogers both viewed self-actualization as an innate impulse, while a strict Freudian or a strict behaviorist (whom you will study in Chapter 8) would reject this view. The humanist approach is based on an active, affirmative, growth-oriented idea of human nature. Our distinctive potentials struggle for expression:

> The muscular person likes to use his muscles, indeed, *has* to use them in order to self-actualize, and to achieve the subjective feeling of harmonious, uninhibited, satisfying functioning which is so important an aspect of psychological health. People with intelligence must use their intelligence, people with eyes must use their eyes, people with the capacity to love have the *impulse* to love and the *need*

to love in order to feel healthy. Capacities clamor to be used, and cease their clamor only when they *are* used sufficiently. (Maslow, 1968, p. 152).

Unless our situation is so bad that we seek safety instead of growth, we naturally move toward self-actualization, though usually the movement is a continuous process and never utterly completed (that is, an act of becoming). Self-actualization is not the same thing as selfishness: It may come in many forms, including self-sacrifice for the betterment of a group or for a spiritual goal, as well as the heights of individual achievement.

The development of neurosis, according to Maslow, is a result of a thwarted need for self-actualization: "If this essential core of the person is denied or suppressed, he gets sick sometimes in obvious ways, sometimes in subtle ways, sometimes immediately, sometimes later" (1968, p. 4).

SMALL GROUP EXERCISE

Give each member of your group a few minutes to think of the most self-actualized person they know and some reasons behind their choice. Discuss the people you have identified and what aspects of self-actualization stand out in them.

In this context, some of Maslow's own life events are interesting: He attended law school at his father's urging, but one night walked out of class, leaving his books behind, and transferred to a different college where he began his study of psychology. He was later a member of Alfred Adler's Friday-night seminars.

DISCUSSION IDEAS

Reread the last quotation from Maslow, above. What do you think about this conceptualization of how neuroses come about? Can you apply this theory of the thwarted "essential core" to any of your counselees, to people you know, or to characters in literature and film?

Peak Experiences

Maslow took the then-unusual route of studying healthy personality rather than doing animal experiments or focusing only on psychologically disturbed individuals. He noticed that individuals on the road to self-actualization reported periodic episodes he called **peak experiences,** in which they felt wonder and awe, lost track of time and place, and were convinced that something valuable had happened. "The B-love [nonpossessive, unselfish, I-Thou love] experience, the parental experience, the mystic, or oceanic, or nature experience, the aesthetic perception, the creative moment, the therapeutic or intellectual insight, the orgasmic experience, certain forms of athletic fulfillment, etc. These and other moments of highest happiness and fulfillment I shall call the peak-experiences" (Maslow, 1968, p. 73). These experiences give us a sense of what existential *being* is like, and Maslow thought of them as rewards for *becoming*.

Today, Mihalyi Csikszentmihalyi (1990), in his studies of happiness and well-being, describes many of the same features as the experience of **flow,** a pleasant to ecstatic state of un-self-conscious absorption during a mental or physical activity. Csikszentmihalyi identifies the state of flow as occurring at times when one is sufficiently challenged to stay engaged and yet sufficiently competent to be self-confident. Your ideal tennis partner might fulfill these qualities, or a crossword puzzle that is just the right level for your skills (not too easy but not discouraging either).

Study of the healthy personality, which has long been the province of counseling psychology, is today more widespread in the field, with a strong, well-funded **positive psychology** movement (Seligman & Csikszentmihalyi, 2000). This movement investigates subjective well-being, optimism, the experience of flow, peak experiences, and similar subjects.

Core Conditions: Necessary and Sufficient Conditions of Therapy

Rogers's most famous and controversial assertion was that certain conditions are not only *necessary* for successful therapy but also *sufficient*. By *necessary*, he meant that constructive change cannot happen unless these conditions are present. Most counselors agree with this idea in some form, especially those who take the *common factors* point of view summarized in Chapter 1. By *sufficient*, Rogers meant that no other theoretical backing or technical skills need to be applied to a case. Improvement will come about naturally if his six conditions are met. (These are listed below.) The sufficiency assertion is much more controversial. Rogers was able to specify the conditions not only from his memory, notes, and observations, but also from analysis of audiotaped sessions: It was not until the 1940s that this technology was used as a research tool, and Rogers was a pioneer. Imagine how different psychological theory might be if we were able to hear Freud's sessions on tape!

I will quote directly from Rogers's (1957) article in which he listed the six conditions:

> For constructive personality change to occur, it is necessary that these conditions exist and continue over a period of time:
>
> 1. Two persons are in psychological contact.
> 2. The first, whom we shall term the client, is in a state of incongruence, being vulnerable or anxious.

3. The second person, whom we shall term the therapist, is congruent or integrated in the relationship.

4. The therapist experiences unconditional positive regard for the client.

5. The therapist experiences an empathic understanding of the client's internal frame of reference and endeavors to communicate this experience to the client.

6. The communication to the client of the therapist's empathic understanding and unconditional positive regard is to a minimal degree achieved.

No other conditions are necessary. If these six conditions exist, and continue over a period of time, this is *sufficient.* The process of constructive personality change will follow. (p. 96, italics mine)

Items 3, 4, and 5 describe qualities of the therapist. You will often see references to Rogers's *three* facilitative conditions, and these are congruence (also called genuineness or authenticity), unconditional positive regard (nonpossessive warmth), and accurate empathy (understanding). These are sometimes labeled with shorthand terms: *the core conditions,* or even just *the conditions.* (Items 1, 5, and 6 are contextual variables and are less often debated.)

Therapist Congruence   Congruence is "the opposite of presenting a facade, either knowingly or unknowingly" (Rogers, 1957, p. 97). The therapist must present him- or herself as a person (in contrast with presenting as a blank slate). The counselor's feelings, thoughts, and actions are not at odds, though not all thoughts and feelings are expressed (like in any human relationship). For example, the thought might cross your mind that you like your client's new haircut, but you would probably decide not to say so. Your decision is not a breach in congruence, since the thought is not *at odds with* your behavior; it is just not important at the time. A process of selection constantly operates during your session. Therapist incongruence would be exemplified by your saying, "I think you are a good daughter," when you really think that the client is not. A Rogerian would maintain genuineness by saying something like "You may not always be a good daughter. Tell me, how would you define 'a good daughter'?" Another Rogerian might choose an honest personal response, such as "It seems to me that this label *good daughter* is something you beat yourself up with."

In child therapy, the counselor's congruence is often tested since children may act impulsively in session and bring forth negative reactions (Ellinwood & Raskin, 1993). Ellinwood and Raskin provide an example:

Sometimes the therapist's feelings, revealed by facial expression, tone of voice, or body movements, may be communicated to the child before the therapist is fully aware of the feelings. For example, in one session, a 6-year-old boy was emptying everything on the playroom shelves (toys, crayons, books, dolls, small figures, cards, chips from board games, dominoes, etc.) onto the floor in the middle of the room. He had done this in a previous session, with great delight, delight which the therapist shared with him, sensing the particular meaning the experience had for him at a time when his freedom was being severely restricted at home and at school. This time, however, he stopped suddenly, looked searchingly at the therapist and said, "You don't like it today." Only then did the therapist realize that she was concerned because she knew that she had another client coming immediately after his hour and that last time it took her an hour to get things back on the shelves in some semblance of order. She agreed with him that she didn't like it today (thereby confirming his accurate awareness of her feelings) and explained why. He then said, "I knew it because you didn't say anything and frowned and last time you laughed and said it was fun." (pp. 266–267)

Singh and Tudor (1997) offer a multicultural point of view on therapist congruence, emphasizing that to many clients therapist congruence is judged not only within a session but also in terms of how the therapist behaves as a member of the community, in everyday transactions and social responsibility. "This perspective is not unusual in African, Asian and Oriental societies in which the therapist/healer/shaman/wise woman/man is both a part of and separate from their society: an accepted and respected outsider" (p. 40).

Unconditional Positive Regard   **Unconditional positive regard** entails "a warm acceptance of each aspect of the client's experience as being a part of that client . . . no *conditions* of acceptance, no feeling of 'I like you only *if* you are thus and so'" (Rogers, 1957, p. 97). Such an acceptance is especially curative when clients are used to *conditional* acceptance: "You are a good daughter if you follow in my footsteps"; "I will love you if you bear my children"; "Sons of mine should make the football team"; "I will leave you if you continue to be anxious." Furthermore, positive regard is shown by respect for the client: "The client-centered therapist respects the client's self-directing abilities and consistently evidences respect for these abilities in practice. This philosophy holds, in unabated and perhaps more dramatic forms, when children are the clients, because children are commonly regarded and treated as immature, not responsible, not knowing enough, requiring guidance and supervision, and needing to be molded" (Ellinwood & Raskin, 1993, p. 259). The same could be said for adolescents and even college students, and for clients who have been *infantilized*—that is, treated as though they were children. These people have learned not to trust themselves; the counselor's trust in them may be a new experience and, one hopes, a contagious one (Seligman, 2001).

DISCUSSION IDEAS

Leona Tyler (1969) wrote that unconditional positive regard is "a fundamental aspect of the counselor's total personality, one that finds expression in many situations other than counseling" (p. 33). Do you agree? If Tyler is right, what are the implications for counselor selection and training?

Within a therapy session, positive regard is often shown by a sympathetic rewording of what the client has said and by background verbalizations of "uh-huh" and "mmm-hmm." Through analyzing tape recordings of a long-term treatment, Truax (1966) found that Rogers selectively applied these positive reinforcements, giving them when the client expressed insights, focused on the problem, discriminated between herself and her feelings, expressed herself with clarity, and spoke in a style similar to Rogers's. True to learning theory, the client over time did more of these things, having learned what Rogers liked to hear. This research effort tells us that we do control our clients' behavior even in nondirective therapy, by reinforcing certain types of talk. It's unavoidable, since randomly responding to the client would be quite unhelpful. However, it's a good idea to listen to your own tapes and be aware of just how your patterns reinforce your client. For example, if you take a typically Western, individualistic point of view, you may be subtly reinforcing these values when your clients speak in a self-centered way, and *not* responding when your clients talk about responsibilities to their families or community. This would be a subtle imposition of your own values on your client, outside of your awareness.

Empathy   To have **empathy** is "to sense the client's anger, fear, or confusion as if it were your own, yet without your own anger, fear, or confusions getting bound up in it" (Rogers, 1957, p. 99). Empathy involves the existential psychologist's goal of seeing the world from the client's existential position, or entering his or her phenomenological world. When a client feels this understanding coming from the counselor, she feels "really free to explore all the hidden nooks and frightening crannies" of her experience (Rogers, 1961, p. 34). Thus, freedom is an outgrowth of receiving accurate empathy. Empathy is achieved through ardent, responsive attention to the client's thoughts and feelings.

The redemptive view of human worth exemplified by qualities like empathy and warmth might seem questionable in the light of real-world problems like crime, but Rogerian conditions have research support for application to tough problems. In one experiment (Truax, Wargo, & Silber, 1966), lower-class teenaged girls who had misbehaved severely enough to end up in an institution were divided into two groups: One group received therapy from a counselor high in accurate empathy and nonpossessive warmth, while the other, a control group, received the usual treatments the institution offered. The girls who were offered accurate empathy and nonpossessive warmth spent significantly less time outside an institution in the year after treatment, received significantly reduced scores on delinquency-related personality tests, and showed increased congruence between self-concept and ideal self.

SMALL GROUP EXERCISE

Ask a member of your small group to volunteer to talk freely about a decision or problem he or she is currently struggling with, or one well remembered from the recent past, for three minutes. Other members should strive to pay complete attention to the speaker and avoid attending to anything else. After the three minutes are up, discuss the experience. Was it difficult to focus completely on the speaker? What other thoughts intruded on your attention? What kind of training would help you learn to maintain complete attention?

Differences from Other Positive Relationships   When you were reading about genuineness, unconditional positive regard, and accurate empathy, you may have thought that your loving relationships fulfill the facilitative conditions. Certainly, best friends and spouses frequently display these qualities, and indeed people often say, "Why do I need counseling? Why can't I just talk to my best friends about my problems?" Rogers (1957) provided an answer to such questions: "For brief moments, at least, many good friendships fulfill the six conditions. Usually this is only momentary, however, and then empathy falters, the positive regard becomes conditional, or the congruence of the 'therapist' friend becomes overlaid by some degree of facade or defensiveness. Thus the therapeutic relationship is seen as a heightening of the constructive qualities which often exist in part in other relationships, and an extension through time of qualities which in other relationships tend at best to be momentary" (Rogers, 1957, p. 101). From this viewpoint, friends usually have some stake or personal advantage or disadvantage in what you think, feel, and do, while therapists do not have their own well-being in mind. Friends also rightly expect the relationship to be reciprocal, in that you help them with *their* problems, and they can bring up their own stories parallel to yours, unlike the clear focus on *you* that you would find in therapy.

Client Congruence and Incongruence

In the soap opera I watch, the characters sometimes say one thing, while a voiceover heard only by the viewer says something else, reflecting their inner commentary. Austin gushes to his fiancée (Sami) about his desire to have a houseful of children. Sami replies, "Of course!" But, "Don't bet on it," she thinks to herself. A Midwestern high school senior tells his girlfriend that he plans to attend Pepperdine University in California. She smiles sweetly, while we hear her think: "We'll *see* about *that!*"

The voiceovers represent the characters' glaring incongruence, which the existentialists usually labeled *inauthenticity*. **Incongruence** is "a discrepancy between the actual experience of the organism and the self picture of the individual insofar as it represents that experience" (Rogers, 1957, p. 96). The congruence of the *therapist* is one of the facilitative conditions discussed in the previous section. Congruence and incongruence also apply to clients and people in general. As a beginning therapist, I was taken aback by a client who fiercely insisted that she loved her 3-year-old ("with all my heart," she said), yet had given up on toilet-training as "too hard," and usually slept later in the morning than her son did, leaving the child to his own devices for hours.

The soap opera characters are obviously aware of their incongruence, but in real life this is not always the case. Sometimes people unknowingly suffer tensions, defenses, and inadequate functioning that accompany a lack of wholeness. They have tried to disown aspects of themselves. They may be rigid in their thinking, because to let alternative perspectives in would threaten exposure of some blocked-off part of themselves. For example, it would be very painful for a mother like my client to face the evidence that she did not consistently love her child. Yet her incongruence was creating depression, as well as endangering the toddler.

We all behave incongruently in some situations, out of politeness or convenience. But long-standing, cross-situational incongruence, whether conscious or not, is considered damaging to mental health by existential/humanist psychologists.

Locus of Evaluation

Locus refers to a place, and **locus of evaluation** means the place you value in terms of judging your actions and motivations, successes and failures. An external locus of evaluation is dominated by public opinion, family appraisal, and custom. Due to these influences, for example, most couples in lasting relationships get married, even when one or both of them are not fond of inviting the state into their private lives. Another example: You are using an external locus when you are embarrassed at your college's lack of prestige, even when you know that you got an excellent education there. You are letting outside judgment overcome your own inner judgment. On the other hand, "[a] creative response is one that comes from within rather than being based on externally imposed values" (Bauman & Walso, 1998, p. 20). I have graduate degrees from both an unprestigious state college and a renowned university, and I see both their good and bad points as balancing out. I'm proud of what I learned at both.

With an internal locus of evaluation, you don't reject others' opinions or the influence of your culture. You consider the values and beliefs of others respectfully without making them your own automatically. As a counselor, you need to investigate how strongly each client has internalized the dictates of his or her culture. For example, one Korean client may find it right and natural to let her parents choose her college major, while another might firmly reject this cultural obligation.

The Fully Functioning Person

The goal of humanistic counseling is to produce a **fully functioning person,** someone who possesses an openness to experience, a trust in one's own experience, an internal locus of evaluation, and a willingness to be in process. In short, this person is clearly on a path toward self-actualization, a path that might never end but will be fulfilling in itself because it follows the organismic valuing process in making choices. Fully functioning people have a sense of meaning or purpose in life, and not one merely accepted from an outside authority. Moreover, they accept and trust others rather than regarding them suspiciously.

Downplay of Diagnosis and Assessment

Diagnosis, using conventional categories as you saw in the DSM system described in Chapter 2, is usually dismissed by existential and humanist psychologists. Rogers called diagnosis "for the most part, a colossal waste of time" (1957, p. 102). Rogers (1961) was trained in a conventional model that involved diagnosis, analysis of the problem, careful interpretation and explanation provided to the client, and re-education directed by the clinician. However, he wrote, "Gradually I observed that I was more effective if I could create a psychological climate in which the client could undertake these functions himself—exploring, analyzing, understanding, and trying new solutions to his problems" (p. 87). Existentialists diagnose by considering the client's phenomenological experience of life's inherent problems (meaninglessness, freedom, isolation, and death) and the arenas in which this experience is played out (self, others, nature, spirit). Since the existential stance involves looking at the person as a whole, not as a person who has a disorder to be detached or repaired, existential psychologists resist classifying clients into diagnostic categories.

Assessment is used mainly for research purposes, not as a therapeutic guide. Some of the tests designed to measure existential conditions are the Purpose in Life inventory (PIL; available from *alanleak@cs.com*), the Seeking of Noetic Goals test (SONG; Crumbaugh, 1977), and the Existential Vacuum Scale of the Minnesota Multiphasic Personality Inventory (EVS, a set of items from the MMPI; Hutzell & Peterson, 1985). These are described in Guttmann's (1996) *Logotherapy for the Helping Professional: Meaningful Social Work*, chapters 9 and 10.

Rogers and other humanist researchers use the Q-sort technique, which was developed by Stephenson (1953). In this technique, test items are written on separate cards, and the respondent is asked to sort the cards into piles according to a stated principle. For example, the cards might all have self-descriptors such as "I usually like people" and "I don't trust my emotions," and a client would sort them into groups according to "This is like me" and "This is not like me." Rogers and colleagues collected Q-sorts before, during, and after therapy to see how people's self-descriptors changed. He found that clients' ideal and real selves became closer during client-centered therapy. Other types of Q-sort card sets and principles exist as well.

Remember that diagnosis and assessment are not considered essential to counseling: This is a major difference from other theories.

The Therapeutic Process

Like Alfred Adler's psychology, humanistic therapy endorses a growth model rather than a medical model. The client experiences development from within.

Existential Process

The goals of existential psychotherapy are embedded in its philosophy: The client should deal more effectively with fears and anxieties about the inescapable problems of life (meaninglessness, freedom, isolation, and death). Successful clients make better use of their potentials, whether their talents lie in running a household smoothly or in creating timeless art. Basically, a good outcome is a person who is not trapped by past events, past decisions, and past patterns of behavior, and is not trapped by concern for the future, either. This person is able to live in the moment while staying purposeful and finding meaning in existence. Viktor Frankl (1946/1984) designed a system of existential psychotherapy called *logotherapy*, which has the goals just described but places emphasis on transferring growth from therapy into life in the outside world, using both listening and persuasion. We will return to this topic shortly.

Generally, existential therapy does not progress in clear stages with identifiable transitions between them. Yalom (1980) describes the beginning, middle, and end of therapy without including how long each period lasts, since one stage flows into the next, and reversion to earlier stages can happen. In the beginning of the process, the aim is to understand the client's existential position—her four worlds of self, other, nature, and spirit. That is, the counselor enters the phenomenological world of the client. This process makes an existential (and humanistic) approach appropriate for people from varied ethnic, cultural, socioeconomic, and gendered backgrounds (Vontress, Johnson, & Epp, 1999).

Yalom (1980) described joining the client's world this way: "The therapist will, implicitly and explicitly, wonder about the patient's belief systems, inquire deeply into the loving of another, ask about long-range hopes and goals, explore creative interests and pursuits. I have, for example, found it singularly rewarding to take an in-depth history of the patient's efforts to express himself or herself creatively" (p. 471).

SMALL GROUP EXERCISE

Have each member of your small group take a minute to jot down "efforts to express himself or herself creatively." Use a broad definition of *creative*—include the arts and other activities as well. Then take turns talking about your creative efforts. Other members should ask questions, as an existential counselor would, to get at the meaning of the activity and the significance of the effort's outcome.

In the middle part of existential therapy, the counselor helps the client make use of material from within herself to identify meanings, purposes, and values. The client may restructure attitudes about herself, others, her environment, and her spiritual life, and she may have insights into the glue of meaning that holds her behavior in a pattern. For example, a 19-year-old client came to therapy representing herself as worried about her unstable romantic relationships with men. It seemed that her friends had all settled down with steady boyfriends, while she had a series of boyfriends whom she dated for a month or so and then moved on from. In therapy, she realized that she was worried about loneliness in the future, not at the moment. She was able to reassure herself that not finding a life-mate at age 19 didn't mean that she would be a lonely old lady. She also changed her attitude toward her dating, thinking of herself as very selective and brave, not settling for just any basically acceptable partner. Thus, she became open to experience, choosing growth moves rather than security moves.

The closing stage of therapy entails acceptance of existential dilemmas and construction of ways to have an authentic life within existential limitations. Insights that have transferred from therapy into life outside the sessions are put into words and evaluated.

May and Yalom (2000) view the process of existential therapy as dissolving **affect blocks.** Affect blocks are places where a client gets emotionally stuck, like roadblocks in the journey of life. Some clients are not even aware of their range of feelings because they have become taken over by anxiety when they allow themselves to feel. A major effort in such cases is to investigate "What do you feel?" For example, if a woman is overwhelmed with guilt because she has not provided her parents with grandchildren, she may be unaware of her own responses to being without offspring. She may actually prefer a child-free life, but she has been unable to admit this threatening feeling into awareness. A related question is "What do you want?" In my example, the therapist might ask the question, "Outside of a child, what do you want?" If the woman's considered answer involves things that require great personal freedom and funds, maybe she does not want to devote herself to motherhood. May and Yalom emphasize that we need to realize that "every yes involves a no"—that our decisions involve assigning priorities and assessing values. That is, each choice has an existential meaning.

R e f l e c t i o n

I've heard that you can understand people's real values if you look at what they do with their extra money and their spare time. Why do you think this might be true? What do you do with extra money and spare time? In other words, what do you choose to do? What do you give up or let go in order to do these things?

Humanistic, Person-Centered Process

The goals of humanist, person-centered therapy are similar to those of existential therapy, reasonably enough. Person-centered therapy aims to produce the *fully functioning person*, someone who accepts herself and her feelings, is self-confident and self-directed, perceives things flexibly, is realistic in goals, behaves with maturity, is open to experience, and accepts others. When Rogers (1961) tried to conceptualize the process of therapy, he rejected the idea of individuals moving from one stable state (distressed) to another stable state (healthy). Instead, he realized that positive change occurs along a continuum from rigidity to flexibility, from stuck to flowing. Rogers hypothesized a continuum of client feelings and perceptions that are represented during the process of therapy:

> This process involves a loosening of feelings. At the lower end of the continuum they are described as remote, unowned, and not now present. They are then described as present objects with some sense of ownership by the individual. Next they are expressed as owned feelings in terms closer to their immediate experiencing. Still further up the scale they are experienced and expressed in the immediate present with a decreasing fear of this process. Also, at this point, even those feelings which have been previously denied to awareness bubble through into awareness, are experienced, and increasingly owned. At the upper end of the continuum, living in the process of experiencing a continually changing flow of feelings becomes characteristic of the individual.
>
> The process involves a change in the manner of experiencing. The continuum begins with a fixity in which the individual is remote from his experiencing and unable to draw upon or symbolize its implicit meaning. Experiencing must be safely in the past before a meaning can be drawn from it and the present is interpreted in terms of these past meanings. From this remoteness in relations to his experiencing, the individual moves toward the recognition of experiencing as a troubling process going on within him. Experiencing gradually becomes a more accepted inner referent to which he can turn for increasingly accurate meanings. Finally he becomes able to live freely and acceptantly in a fluid process of experiencing, using it comfortably as a major reference for his behavior.
>
> The process involves a shift from incongruence to congruence. The continuum runs from a maximum of incongruence which is quite unknown to the individual through stages where there is an increasingly sharp recognition of the contradictions and discrepancies existing within himself to the experiencing of incongruence in the immediate present in a way which dissolves this. At the upper end of the continuum, there would never be more than temporary incongruence between experiencing and awareness since the individual would not need to defend himself against the threatening aspects of his experience. (pp. 156–157)

SMALL GROUP EXERCISE

At another point in *On Becoming a Person*, Rogers (1961, pp. 133–156.) gives examples of the statements a client made at each stage of the process outlined in the earlier excerpt. Look at each example reprinted below and discuss where on the continuum you would place it in terms of feelings, experiencing, or congruence. Don't look for right or wrong answers—just explain why you place the statement where you do. The idea is to learn from what classmates say about the statements.

Example: "Disorganization keeps cropping up in my life." The problem is seen as coming from outside the self. This statement might be a bit past the first level of the continuum because it reflects a sense of present ownership.

1. "I can't ever do anything right—can't ever finish it."
2. "There were so many things I couldn't tell people—nasty things I did. I felt so sneaky and bad."
3. "It always seems a little bit nonsensical to talk about one's self except in times of dire necessity."
4. "My conscious mind tells me I'm worthy. But some place inside I don't believe it. I think I'm a rat—a no-good."
5. "I think inside I'm oversexed, and outside not sexy enough to attract the response I want. . . . I'd like to be the same inside and out."
6. "I can feel myself smiling sweetly the way my mother does, or being gruff and important the way my father does sometimes—slipping into everyone else's personalities but mine."

Throughout existential and person-centered therapy, the relationship between the client and counselor is paramount. The counselor is a role model and a companion in the journey toward self-transformation. As Prochaska and Norcross (1999) note, the therapist serves to compensate for the client's rigid style of thinking. By giving genuine reactions and expressing authentic feelings about what the client says and does, the counselor acts as a "surrogate information processor," demonstrating a "pattern of processing that organizes information using structures, symbols, or schemas that evoke richer, more intense, and more conscious expressions of life" (pp. 143–144).

Customary Techniques of Existential and Humanistic Therapy

Existentialism began as a philosophical position, and philosophies do not require techniques. Accordingly, many existential therapists adapt techniques from other theories while keeping existential issues foremost in work with clients. May and Yalom (2000) wrote that existentialism "deals with the *presuppositions underlying therapy of any kind.* . . . There are very few adequate training courses in this kind of therapy simply because it is not a specific training in technique" (p. 282). In existential/humanistic therapy sessions, **focused listening** is the main technique as the counselor listens for themes in the client's talk that reflect the struggles with meaning and identity underneath the themes.

Confrontation

In reading accounts of existential therapy, I noticed that **confrontation** is another frequently used technique. Yalom (1980) reported a case in which a woman complained about her grown children's disrespect for her opinions and dismissal of her ideas. Yalom, tuning in to his own feelings, found that he reacted negatively to the childish whining quality of her complaints, which led him to not take her seriously. He confronted her with this feeling she engendered in him and suggested that her children might feel the same way. This confrontation helped her become aware that she acted like a child in several areas and thus was partly responsible for others' reactions to her.

May and Yalom (2000) also use confrontation to focus on each client's responsibility for his or her own distress: "When patients say they 'can't' do something, the therapist immediately comments, 'You mean you *won't* do it'" (p. 289). For example, one of my clients constantly complained about every member of her family, yet had a miserable Sunday dinner with them each week, bitterly insisting that she *could not* stop complying with this Sunday demand. On confrontation, it turned out that two other members of the family had quit going long ago; she had to face the fact that she *chose* to go. She eventually made up a plan with the goal of attending Sunday dinners some of the time but not always, combined with strategies to detoxify the most distressing interactions occurring while she was there. She realized she was not helpless even in the face of strong, emotion-laden urges.

R e f l e c t i o n

Do you have any demands (from outside or within yourself) that you feel you *can't* reject? For example, some women of my generation feel that they *can't* go out of the house without makeup on. Other people, like my Sunday-dinner client, think that they *must* comply with customs like sending greeting cards, buying birthday presents, or going to ghastly family reunions. In contrast, some of us feel that we *can't* ask for our family's help in a crisis, *must* stand on our own two feet, and *can't* admit weakness. Choose one or two of your *can't* or *must* situations, and see whether you can make a plan for at least partly relieving yourself of the demand. If you can't think of a plan, ask a friend or classmate to help. Whether or not you take their guidance, it will be an interesting exercise.

As noted earlier, Viktor Frankl's practice of psychotherapy based on existential thought was named **logotherapy.** *Logo* is Greek for "word" or "speech," the basic symbolic system used by humans for communicating meaning. The name Frankl chose suggests a focus on meaning. Along with confrontation,

Frankl's logotherapy made use of techniques that are also common in the practices of other theorists.

Logotherapy Techniques

Frankl used **paradoxical intention** as early as 1939 (Lantz, 1986). A paradox is a seeming contradiction, like "the lonely crowd" or "sounds of silence" or, some would say, "leisure suit." In paradoxical intention, the counselor asks clients to exaggerate a symptom rather than try to suppress it, or to purposely act out whatever they fear. You read about this technique used by Adler, and you will see it as part of behavioral therapies as well. A client who is afraid to go out in crowds, for fear of fainting, might be asked to find a crowd, go into it, and try to faint. An insomniac might be ordered to stay awake all night no matter what. Neither of these clients is likely to be able to achieve what they fear, and this failure to have the feared response helps eliminate the fear or, what is sometimes worse, the anticipatory "fear of fear."

Another technique of logotherapy is **dereflection,** a cousin of Adlerian prescriptions for social service. Many clients come to therapy totally focused on themselves and their inner states. The counselor tries to counter this preoccupation by prescribing situations that encourage the client to focus on something else. That is, she tries to change the client's **hyperreflection** by suggesting a distraction. Dereflection activities might include helping others through volunteer work, taking up a neglected creative or athletic effort, or joining an interest group.

Attitude adjustment is the same thing as *cognitive reframing,* a crucial part of cognitive-behavioral therapy. This technique involves changing the labels we use when thinking about ourselves and others. In the process of changing the words we use to describe things, we change the feelings we have about them. Sometimes the way we phrase our behavior or feelings undermines our opinion of ourselves. Think of my 19-year-old client who thought of herself as a *loser* because she didn't have a steady boyfriend; when she learned to think of herself as *selective* instead, her attitude changed.

Finally, Frankl used a technique that is rarely discussed in psychotherapy training: **appealing.** He discovered that some clients could find relief from distress when he verbally exhorted them to keep at it and try hard. Appealing to the client to do better, pointing out the benefits of solving the problem, and reassuring the client of his or her ability to persevere in improving—these homespun remedies were incorporated into a sophisticated existential framework.

Nondirective Techniques

In contrast to existentialists like Frankl and Yalom, person-centered therapists "tend to avoid evaluation. . . . [They] do not interpret for clients, do not question in a probing manner, and do not reassure or criticize clients" (Raskin & Rogers, 2000, p. 137). The word *nondirective* describes this approach, because it does not *direct* the course or content of therapy. Clients are trusted to select their own therapist, decide on how long therapy should last and how frequent sessions should be, choose the topics discussed, and achieve their own insights. The relationship between client and therapist is one of equality and genuineness that the client has probably not experienced before: It is a new type of relationship, not a repetition of old ones (as presupposed in psychodynamic theory, by transference).

Nondirective techniques create a psychological environment favorable to growth as a person. These techniques include open questions (avoiding yes-or-no questions), reflections of emotion and meaning, paraphrases, background support like "umm-hmm" and "I see," and repetition of key words.

Because of these nondirective techniques, Rogerian therapy is frequently ridiculed for employing formulaic, superficial response patterns that are mere repetitions:

CLIENT: I murdered the Bible salesman yesterday.

THERAPIST: So, I hear you saying that you killed the Bible salesman yesterday. How did that feel?

In reality, reflection of emotion and paraphrase of meaning are skilled and considered responses, designed to encourage the most authentic exchange possible. As Gendlin (1961) explained, "A good client-centered response formulates the *felt, implicit* meaning of the client's present experiencing" (p. 240). Given that there are many responses to a client statement, including silence, experienced therapists choose which response to give. Consider this example:

CLIENT: I guess it's all my fault.

THERAPIST: You take some of the blame on yourself. (adapted from Gendlin, 1962)

The counselor knows from earlier talk and from the emotion displayed in the client's nonverbal language that the client *doesn't* really think it is all his fault. In responding, the counselor reflects not the actual words of the client but their meaning, and also gives the client a way to distribute the blame more realistically.

Moreover, the therapist chooses *which part* of a client's utterance to reflect. Leona Tyler (1969) suggested, "In making this instantaneous decision about what to respond to, one general principle is useful. Whenever the client's remarks have involved two or more persons, try to respond in terms of *his* side of the relationship rather than that of someone else" (p. 39). Tyler gives the example of a client from the military talking about an unreasonable army officer. The counselor could choose to remark upon the officer, "He must have been a very unpleasant person," or to remark upon the client, "You seem to dislike people of that sort intensely." The client-centered remark opens the conversation to understanding the client, instead of leading to more exposition on the officer's bad qualities.

SMALL GROUP EXERCISE

Here are some client statements to which you could respond in many ways. Discuss with your group how reflections of these statements could take several forms. Write down three of your best ideas for counselor's responses. If time permits, read your responses to the class as a whole.

1. "My parents won't let me do anything. My friends all get to do stuff that my parents would hit the ceiling if I did."
2. "Since my husband filed for divorce, my main goal every day is to keep from bursting into tears in public. That's all I can handle."
3. "I just can't concentrate on my schoolwork. I can't pay attention in class. My mind starts to wander."

Self-Disclosure

Self-disclosure refers to a counselor's talk in session about her own thoughts, feelings, and experiences. It is a controversial therapeutic technique, with some training programs banning it completely and others encouraging certain types of disclosure. Because of the *genuineness* condition of existential/humanistic counseling, the therapist is encouraged to self-disclose. But first, you may benefit from a bigger context by reading Tyler's (1969) reasons for *discouraging* self-disclosure:

> It is inadvisable to talk about oneself because it tends to confuse the client about the structure of the situation, blurring one of the distinctions between counseling and conversation, the fact that in counseling the spotlight is focused on one participant, not on both. More important still, it is inadvisable because it may very easily have an effect exactly the opposite of the one intended. Because his [the counselor's] grasp of the client's meaning is incomplete and because his own experience is not comparable with the other person's in all particulars, the recounting of it may give the impression of a *failure* to understand. (p. 40)

In this way, a counselor's talking about his own problems with an adventurous 3-year-old daughter may seem way off-base to a client whose own 3-year-old is setting fires and torturing pets!

Nevertheless, in Rogerian terms, talking about one's self is encouraged in certain contexts. Personal responses to what the client says, for example, are considered signs of genuineness. In many situations, a client's story has made my eyes fill with tears, and I have never felt that I should hide this. Nor have I tried to draw attention to it, which might backfire if a client decided to edit her talk so as not to upset me. Sharing a personal thought might occur when a client says, "I guess it's all my fault," and the therapist responds, "I don't think you believe it's *all* your fault." Seligman (2001) suggests that self-disclosure should (1) serve a therapeutic purpose; (2) be short; (3) fit in smoothly with the thoughts being expressed by the client; (4) focus on the client, not the counselor; (5) provide immediate reactions to client material, not highly charged personal information like a history of sexual abuse; and (6) reflect caring and acceptance of the client.

Seligman (2001) provides good, clear guidelines to follow. However, research does not necessarily support them. Knox, Hess, Petersen, and Hill (1997) analyzed thirteen clients' reports of therapist self-disclosures that the clients themselves found helpful. These clients most often cited their counselors' telling them personal information from the past, not their reactions immediate to the therapeutic relationship at the time. What they found beneficial was their counselors' talk about their own families, leisure activities, or experiences similar to the clients'. The immediate type recommended by Seligman and others was *never* cited as an example of a helpful self-disclosure. The positive consequences of the helpful self-disclosures reported by the clients were insight or a new perspective, improved or equalized therapeutic relationship, and use of the therapist as a role model to make positive changes or increase client self-disclosure.

Group Work

Yalom is renowned as an existential therapist and also as an expert in group psychotherapy. He wrote the major textbook on group therapy in the United States. He perceived the group as a particularly effective treatment from an existential/humanist view. He wrote that group work could "shift the patient's gaze from himself or herself onto others. . . . Therapists may ask patients to reflect on how others feel at the moment; therapists may in a flowing, unstructured manner provide training in empathy for others" (1980, p. 474). For example, Yalom assigns extremely self-absorbed members to introduce new patients to the group and help them talk to the group, a deflection technique.

May and Yalom (2000) list four benefits of group therapy:

- Clients learn how their behavior is viewed by others.
- Clients learn how their behavior makes others feel.
- Clients learn how their behavior creates opinions others have of them.
- Clients learn how their behavior influences their opinion of themselves. (adapted from p. 296)

The existentially oriented group is assisted to be open about the members' here-and-now process and impressions. Statements that would probably never surface in ordinary conversation are freely aired. For example, I co-led a group in which one member told another one she hated him because he reminded her of an old boyfriend; another member complained that he was disgusted by the same guy's articulate way of speaking; yet another member burst into tears, saying that everyone else was too screwed up to pay any attention to him. All three contributions provide openings for insight.

DISCUSSION IDEAS

Consider each of the three group members' statements in terms of the four benefits listed by May and Yalom. What learning could potentially proceed from these statements? If you were a group facilitator, what would you do next, if anything?

Enlistment of Parents and Teachers

Because the humanistic approach is not tied to graduate degrees in psychology, Rogers and his followers broadened the sphere of practitioners of empathy, congruence, and positive regard. Parents learned these principles in Child Relationship Enhancement Family Therapy, during either a six-month group format or a three-month individual-family format. A reduction in child and parent-child problems resulted, as a number of research studies confirmed. Rogers's student and associate Thomas Gordon created a workshop for parents, intended as a preventive measure against mental health problems. The theory behind Gordon's Parent Effectiveness Training (PET) is client-centered and emphasizes the core conditions as well as democratic family organization (Ellinwood & Raskin, 1993). PET now exists in popular workshop, self-help, and counselor training formats.

Gordon also invented a Teacher Effectiveness Training (TET) workshop that strengthens empathy, congruence, positive regard, and democratic structures among child educators. One study involved 600 teachers and 10,000 students from kindergarten to eighth grade. Teachers trained to high levels of TET qualities were compared with teachers who did not offer high levels of these qualities. Students of the high-conditions teachers were found to have better attendance, more gain in academic achievement, fewer disciplinary problems, fewer acts of vandalism, increased intelligence scores in grades K through 5, higher creativity scores, and more spontaneous, higher-level thinking (Ellinwood & Raskin, 1993).

Clearly, all significant figures in children's lives could benefit from enhanced person-oriented skills.

Play Therapy

A student and, later, colleague of Rogers, Virginia Axline, carried his theory into the realm of child psychology. (Rogers himself had worked extensively in child guidance settings, had written his dissertation in child psychology, and had taught psychological assessment of children before deciding to focus on adults in the 1940s.) Axline's 1947 book *Play Therapy*, revised in 1969, is considered a classic in the field. Client-centered (also called *relationship* and *experiential*) play therapy with children is especially appropriate because they may not have the words to discuss their inner lives or the abstract thinking to categorize their range of feelings (Ellinwood & Raskin, 1993). Play is also a perfect fit for Rogers's theory because play is invented by the child, not directed by an adult authority. The make-believe element of play allows children to express feelings and demonstrate events that are not allowed in their ordinary life. Instead of providing a psychologically safe place for open conversation, the play therapist provides a psychologically safe place for open self-expression through dolls, games, building blocks, doll houses, trucks, puppets, and other toys (Semrud-Clikeman, 1995). Through observing the child and interacting with her as she plays, the counselor can determine the child's worries, wishes, desires, fears, and developmental struggles such as individuation, separation, and exploration. I used to play a board game called Danger, Dinosaurs! with my child clients. In this game, a player wants to collect dinosaur bones, which are given as rewards on certain spaces and surrendered on others. There are only so many spots where you can lose dinosaur bones, and so you need to collect only enough to protect you from those. Extras do you no good. However, one of my child clients always devoted himself to collecting *all* the dinosaur bones, though he knew he didn't need them. He even stole mine! From his behavior, I could hypothesize that he operated from a principle of scarcity, never feeling that he had enough. I wondered what deprivation or model of scarcity mentality he was acting out.

After child clients are comfortable with playing in session, the counselor often reflects or summarizes the feelings they are nonverbally expressing. "You want to have extra bones, just in case . . . ?" As in any client-centered therapy, the therapist provides genuineness, empathy, and unconditional positive regard.

Uses of Existential/Humanistic Therapy

Because of their focus on universal human dilemmas and the basics of therapeutic alliance, existentialist and humanist counselors view their systems as applicable to all kinds of problems. Regardless of their theoretical approach, most, if not all, practitioners include meaning and relationships in case conceptualization. But some areas of human distress lend themselves distinctively to the existentialist and humanistic approaches.

Boundary Situations

People on the verge of change need to consider the deeper meaning of the change. When I moved to the South from the Midwest, my home since birth, I had to face the facts that I was placing my career as a writer above my career as a classroom teacher, and that I was giving up my long-time social group for closeness to my husband. Such changes bring one's values to the forefront, and sometimes it is not easy to acknowledge them and integrate them into the self-concept. May and Yalom (2001) define these changes and their attendant concerns as **boundary situations,** "a type of urgent experience that propels the individual into a confrontation with an existential situation" (p. 291).

The ultimate boundary situation is one's own death. Existentialists are experts in the meaning of death, so people who are facing terminal illness and life-threatening disease or injury benefit from existential therapy, which often includes a review of what one's life has meant. The death of parents, spouses, and other people who are close also bring up crises of personal meaning. Yalom and Vinogradov (1988), reporting on four bereavement therapy groups for widows and widowers, found that dwelling on loss, pain, and emotional unburdening took a smaller piece of the time than expected: "Many members struggled with complex questions of growth, identity, and responsibility for the future, questions that have not often been identified in discussions on bereavement groups as being of particular therapeutic import" (pp. 444–445). In other words, spouses' deaths brought up personal existential questions among the living. Lantz (1989) tells the story of a couple he saw in therapy who had abandoned their son when he came out as gay and then later felt guilty when he died of AIDS. The couple, in a dereflection Adler would have approved, gave presentations about their experience to families of gay men. As they explained, "these speeches help us turn a mistake into something meaningful" (p. 292).

Other losses, too, can be turned into occasions for existential revelations, as when people come to counseling due to the loss of a dearly held goal and need to ponder its meaning and grapple with their freedom to change their attitudes and grow in the face of disappointment. Many people in the modern age have lost jobs and careers they had thought were lifetime commitments. Others find retirement from work a boundary situation. Half the people who marry lose their spouses through divorce. Many of us at some point face the realization that we don't have the abilities or resources to fulfill career aspirations or to succeed in the college major or training course we once chose. These are all crises of meaning and identity for which existential therapy is especially appropriate.

R e f l e c t i o n

Have you ever met with a *boundary situation?* If so, can you think about the experience in existential terms? Did it call forth questions of meaning, values, identity, and freedom, for example? If you can't think of a situation of your own, think about a family member's, friend's, or fictional character's.

Chronic Emotional Hunger

Bugental and Bracke (1992) identified "the modern narcissistic patient who manifests few traditional symptoms but experiences a chronic aimlessness, emptiness, and lack of purpose" (p. 29). They believe that the central problem for these clients is an existential one, worsened by a widespread disintegration of community and the overvaluing of individualism and outward tokens of success. Workaholism and shopaholism are surface complaints stemming from a deeper emptiness. "The existential-humanist orientation is particularly suited to offer meaningful help to those who will become entangled in these problems" (p. 29) because it directly addresses the dilemmas inherent in life.

Persistent Disorders

Many problems that have lasted a long time and have taken over the sufferer's life come from a conviction that the self is an object without will (May & Yalom, 2000). I like Opalic's (1989) description of such a takeover as "the thematized existence of neurotic patients" (p. 400), because it captures the lack of variety and richness in the experience of such individuals. Depression, neurotic anxiety, addictions, posttraumatic stress disorders, obsessive-compulsive disorders, and borderline and narcissistic personalities can all be conceptualized as responses to the facts of meaninglessness, freedom (and the accompanying responsibility), isolation, and death. These problems often represent choices of security over growth, no matter how uncomfortable the security is to maintain, and choices of external control—blaming things outside the self instead of taking responsibility. Existentialist therapists bring these choices up for re-appraisal, while humanistic therapists expect that the core issues will arise within the context of the genuine relationship.

Some persistent disorders occur within families rather than within individuals alone. Lantz (1989) used existential family therapy to treat sexual dysfunction, anorexia nervosa, schizophrenia, and food abuse, mainly through dereflection, which, as noted earlier, involves efforts to "redirect family focus away from its narrow and destructive range of concern" (p. 293). In treating an overweight family, for example, Lantz refused to dwell on food, instead asking the family to "reflect upon what they were other than a group of people who shared a weight problem. . . . All members of the family were surprised to notice that as they 'gained meaning' they 'lost weight' and that they were losing weight without trying to lose weight" (p. 296). The family stayed slim at one-, two-, and three-year follow-ups.

DISCUSSION IDEAS

Can you think of any psychological disorders that would *not* be well addressed in existential or humanistic therapy? Explain your reasoning.

Social Activism

Carl Rogers's belief in the goodness of human nature extended to world arenas in ways that few other psychological theories ever have. This is why he eventually called his theory "person-centered" rather than "client-centered": The people served were not always clients. As mentioned earlier, parent training and teacher training systems are based on Rogerian concepts of empathy, genuineness, and unconditional positive regard. Rogers also applied his theory to career counseling, management training, industry, leadership and administration, organizational development, healthcare, and cross-cultural understanding. In addition, he was an activist for social justice and world peace, giving workshops and lectures aimed at solving interracial and international tensions. Shortly before his death in early 1987, Rogers even organized the 1985 Vienna Peace Project, where leaders from thirteen countries met, and in 1986 he organized peace workshops in Moscow.

Case Conceptualization: An Example

Following is a description of existential/humanist therapy by Irvin Yalom. As you read, focus upon how the therapist conceptualizes the client's life in terms of meaning.

THE WORKAHOLIC

I. D. Yalom (1980)

The less the life satisfaction, the greater the death anxiety. This principle is clearly illustrated by one of my patients, Philip, a fifty-three-year-old, highly successful business executive. Philip had always been a severe workaholic; he worked sixty to seventy hours a week, always lugged a briefcase brimming with work home every evening, and during one recent two-year period worked on the east coast and commuted weekends to his home on the west coast. He had little life satisfaction: his work afforded safety not pleasure; he worked not because he wanted to, but because he had to, to assuage anxiety. He hardly knew his wife and children. Years ago his wife had had a brief extramarital affair, and he had never forgiven her—not so much for the actual act, but because the affair and its attendant pain had been a major source of distraction from his work. His wife and children had suffered from the estrangement, and he had never dipped into this potential reservoir of love, life satisfaction, and meaning.

Then a disaster occurred that stripped Philip of all his defenses. Because of severe setbacks in the aerospace industry, his company failed and was absorbed by another corporation. Philip suddenly found himself unemployed and possibly, because of his age and high executive position, unemployable. He developed severe anxiety and at this point sought psychotherapy. At first his anxiety was entirely centered on his work. He ruminated endlessly about his job. Waking regularly at 4 A.M., he lay awake for hours thinking of work: how to break the news to his employees, how best to phase out his department, how to express his anger at the way he had been handled.

Philip could not find a new position and, as his last day of work approached, he became frantic. Gradually in therapy we pried loose his anxiety from the work concerns to which it adhered like barnacles to a pier. It became apparent that Philip had considerable death anxiety. Nightly he was tormented by a dream in which he circled the very edge of a "black pit." Another frightening recurrent dream consisted of his walking on the narrow crest of a steep dune on the beach and losing his balance. He repeatedly awoke from the dream mumbling "I'm not going to make it." (His father was a sailor who drowned before Philip was born.)

Philip had no pressing financial concerns: he had a generous severance settlement, and a recent large inheritance provided considerable security. But the time! How was he going to use the time? Nothing meant very much to Philip, and he sank into despair. Then one night an important incident occurred. He had been unable to go to sleep and at approximately 3:00 A.M. went downstairs to read and drink a cup of tea. He heard a noise at the window, went over to it, and found himself face to face with a huge stocking-masked man. After his startle and the alarm had subsided, after the police had left and the search was called off, Philip's real panic began. A thought occurred to him, a jarring thought, that sent a powerful shudder through his frame, "Something might have happened to Mary and the children." When, during our therapy hour, he described this incident, his reaction, and his thought, I, rather than comfort him, reminded him that something *will* happen to Mary, to the children, and to himself as well.

Philip passed through a period of feeling wobbly and dazed. All of his customary denial structures no longer functioned: his job, his specialness, his climb to glory, his sense of invulnerability. Just as he had faced the masked burglar, he now faced, at first flinchingly and then more steadily, some fundamental facts of life: groundlessness, the inexorable passage of time, and the inevitability of death. This confrontation provided Philip with a sense of urgency, and he worked hard in therapy to reclaim some satisfaction and meaning in his life. We focused especially on intimacy—an important source of life satisfaction that he had never enjoyed.

Philip had invested so much in his belief in specialness that he dreaded facing (and sharing with others) his feelings of helplessness. I urged him to tell all inquirers the truth—that he was out of a job and having trouble finding another—and to monitor his feelings. He shrank away from the task at first but gradually learned that the sharing of vulnerability opened the door to intimacy. At one session I offered to send his resume to a friend of mine, the president of a company in a related field, who might have a position for him. Philip thanked me in a polite, formal manner; but when he went to his car, he "cried like a baby" for the first time in thirty-five years. We talked about that cry a great deal, what it meant, how it felt, and why he could not cry in front of me. As he learned to accept his vulnerability, his sense of communion, at first with me and then with his family, deepened; he achieved an intimacy with others he had never previously attained. His orientation to time changed dramatically: no longer did he see time as an enemy—to be concealed or killed. Now, with day after day of free time, he began to savor time and to luxuriate in it. He also became acquainted with other, long-dormant parts of himself and for the first time in decades allowed some of his creative urges expression in both painting and writing. After eight months of unemployment, Philip obtained a new and challenging position in another city. In our last session he said, "I've gone through hell in the last few months. But, you know, as horrible as this has been, I'm glad I couldn't get a job immediately. I'm thankful I was forced to go through this." What Philip learned was that a life dedicated to the concealment of reality, to the denial of death, restricts experience and will ultimately cave in upon itself. (pp. 208–210) ■ ■

DISCUSSION IDEAS

1. Was it the sixty- to seventy-hour work week that made Philip a *workaholic?* What else do you think caused Yalom to use that label? How do you define *workaholic?* Does everyone who works long hours qualify for the label?

2. When Philip first went to Yalom, what did he *think* he was anxious about? Why did Yalom believe that was not the main source of anxiety?

3. Why was the attempted home invasion the event that threw Philip into a panic? When he talked about the event in therapy, why did Yalom choose not to comfort him?

4. What gave Philip a sense of urgency? How did he use that sense of urgency?

5. For what reason did Yalom encourage Philip to tell the truth about his joblessness?

6. What do you think about the offer to send Philip's resume to a friend? Would you do this kind of favor to a client? Under what circumstances, or none? Explain your reasoning.

7. Why was Philip glad that he couldn't get another job immediately? What did the therapy do for him that wouldn't have happened otherwise? What might have happened if Philip had not sought counseling?

Critiques of Existential and Humanistic Approaches

Like any philosophical stance and the actions that follow from it, existentialism and humanistic therapy have been disparaged.

Biology Blindness

At the time existentialism and humanistic therapy were blossoming, it was modern to think of psychological distress as a matter of thought and emotion, not physiology. With today's advanced research on cell, brain, and endocrine systems, we know that mood disorders and schizophrenia, as well as attention deficit disorder (ADD) and obsessive-compulsive disorder (OCD), have physiological features that can be addressed through interventions in biology, such as Ritalin for ADD, Prozac for OCD, lithium for manic-depressive disorder, and exposure to bright light for certain types of depression. Tendencies toward some mental illnesses are passed along genetically. Biological and environmental influences interact to produce psychological problems. Existentialists and humanists did not concern themselves with the physiological approaches to relief, and some modern practitioners still reject biological explanations and treatments.

Physiological components may have led to one of Rogers and his colleagues' failures, the Mendota schizophrenia study (Truax, 1970). Rogers's team provided client-centered therapy to sixteen schizophrenics. Even though the therapists in the study were chosen for their high levels of the core conditions, the therapy group did not improve significantly more than a control group. This outcome may be explained within Rogers's model, considering the less-discussed conditions for change. Condition 1 is that "two persons are in psychological contact," and Condition 6 is that "the communication to the client of the therapist's empathic understanding and unconditional positive regard is to a minimal degree achieved" (1957, p. 96). Several lines of evidence confirm brain deficits in schizophrenics that interfere with their processing of interactions with others, so in the Mendota study, contact and communication were probably lacking. Rogerian therapy did not turn out to be the treatment of choice for schizophrenia, which is usually controlled with drugs.

Equivocal Research Findings

Research support for the approaches discussed in this chapter has been criticized. The desired outcomes of *self-actualization*, *growth*, and *full functioning* imply processes, not products, and are difficult to quantify—and scientific research demands quantification. There is no controlled research on the effectiveness of existential therapy, and it is not included in combined analyses of outcomes. On the other hand, the variables of empathy, genuineness, and positive regard are often rated in psychotherapy process and outcome research, and they have made a strong showing as contributors to therapeutic change. Rogers's claims that these variables are *necessary and sufficient* have not found consistent research endorsement (Greenberg, Elliott, & Lietaer, 1994), though many researchers conclude that the conditions are *necessary* but not *sufficient* (Stubbs & Bozarth, 1994). However, after studying psychotherapy research spanning more than forty years, Stubbs and Bozarth criticized combinations of studies on the core conditions, saying that such combinations were putting together studies that were too different to be combined, with each study lacking replication in another. Mitchell, Bozarth, and Krauftt (1977) believed that early studies of the core conditions did not include counselors who rated high on levels of the core conditions in the first place. The best support for Rogerian thought comes from common factors research, discussed in Chapter 1.

Questions of Diversity

Theoretical questions about Rogerian therapy have also arisen. Can one positive, genuine relationship correct for all past and present relationships that held onto conditional regard? Do all people really have an actualizing tendency? What happens when the therapist does *not* have respect for the client and is unable to produce unconditional positive regard—are there other therapists or orientations that might work for this client?

Sometimes multicultural psychologists mention certain groups that prefer directive counseling to nondirective, unstructured sessions. These clients want advice and guidance that client-centered counseling does not provide. Vontress, Johnson, and Epp (1999) acknowledged that "culturally different clients may desire an unequal relationship with their counselor, owing to their culture's belief that professionals are wiser and able to provide accurate advice" (p. 41). Nonetheless, Vontress and co-authors insist that professionals must maintain *philosophical equality* with the client, and that "it is detrimental to the human spirit" when the counselor assumes the role of outside expert (p. 42).

Finally, some critics view existential and client-centered therapy as elitist, designed for the highly verbal, cognitively able client who has time and money to spend on self-actualization. From these critics' point of view, such therapeutic approaches have nothing to offer people struggling with real-world problems like poverty and prejudice. Yet Rogers's own engagement with real-world problems is a refutation in itself, demonstrating his belief that humanistic theory could indeed combat widespread social problems. And Frankl certainly knew extreme deprivation, yet he endorsed a stance of inner freedom that can spur people to meaningful action within horrible contexts. The accusation that counseling consists of "contemplating your belly-button" or, as Maslow put it, "high IQ whimpering on a cosmic scale" (1968, p. 16) could be leveled at some practitioners of almost any theoretical orientation.

KEY TERMS

actualizing tendency	flow	nondirective techniques
affect blocks	focused listening	organismic valuing
appealing	freedom	process
attitude adjustment	fully functioning	paradoxical intention
authenticity	person	peak experiences
boundary situations	fusion	person-centered
confrontation	humanism	phenomenological stance
congruence	hyperreflection	positive psychology
death anxiety	incongruence	self-actualization
dereflection	I/Thou relationship	self-disclosure
empathy	isolation	unconditional positive
existential anxiety	locus of evaluation	regard
existential guilt	logotherapy	willing
existentialism	meaninglessness	wishing

Exploring Key Terms

First, each member of your group needs to do some homework: Write an original sentence using each one of the key terms, as it is used in existential/humanist psychology. Change the tense or word ending of the term if necessary. Your sentence should be sensible and the context should reflect the meaning of the word. For example,

NOT
Seymour, I think you have some affect blocks.

BUT, RATHER,
Seymour, I think your affect blocks are preventing you from mourning your gerbil's death.

Meet in your group and pass around all the sentences you have produced. Copy other members' sentences that you think will help you remember the key terms.

LIBRARY, MEDIA, AND INTERNET ACTIVITIES

1. Explore the websites that cover existential and humanistic thought. Three major sites are *www.personcentered.org*, *www.logotherapy.univie.ac.at*, and *www.meaning.ca*. At *www.meaning.ca*, be sure to look at International Network on Personal Meaning and its links. Write a description of something you find interesting on the websites.

2. The journals on existential and humanistic therapy are *The Humanistic Psychologist, International Forum for Logotherapy, Journal of Humanistic Psychology, Review of Existential Psychology and Psychiatry, Journal of Humanistic Education and Development*, and *Person-Centered Review.* Search for these in your library or discover how you can acquire them if your library doesn't carry them. Get one issue of one of the journals and read all the abstracts in the issue (these are the short summaries preceding each article). Write down your impressions of the journal and what kind of material it covers.

3. Follow up on either group therapy (I. D. Yalom) or play therapy (Virginia Axline). Write a short report adding to this chapter's coverage of those techniques.

4. "Carl Rogers and the Person-Centered Approach": In this videotape, Rogers's biographer Howard Kirschenbaum guides us through Rogers's life and work. Many audio and video examples of Rogers counseling clients and working with groups, plus over 100 photographs, illustrate this comprehensive, 60-minute presentation. Go to *www.HowardKirschenbaum.com* for ordering information. Check with your department and library to see whether they own this item.

REFERENCES

Axline, V. M. (1969). *Play therapy* (Rev. ed.). New York: Ballantine Books. (Original work published 1947)

Bachelor, A., & Horvath, A. (1999). The therapeutic relationship. In M. A. Hubble, B. L. Duncan, & S. D. Miller (Eds.), *The heart and soul of change* (pp. 133–178). Washington, DC: American Psychological Association.

Bauman, S., & Walso, M. (1998). Existential theory and mental health counseling: If it were a snake, it would have bitten! *Journal of Mental Health Counseling, 20*(19), 13–27.

Buber, M. (1970). *I and thou* (W. Kaufman, Trans.). New York: Scribner's.

Bugental, J. F. T., & Bracke, P. E. (1992). The future of existential-humanistic psychotherapy. *Psychotherapy, 29*, 28–33.

Crumbaugh, J. C. (1977). The Seeking of Noetic Goals test (SONG): A complementary scale to the Purpose-in-Life test (PIL). *Journal of Clinical Psychology, 33*, 900–907.

Csikszentmihalyi, M. (1990). *Flow: The psychology of optimal experience.* New York: Harper & Row.

Ellinwood, C. G., & Raskin, J. J. (1993). Client-centered/humanistic psychotherapy. In T. R. Kratochwill & R. J. Morris (Eds.), *Handbook of psychotherapy with children and adolescents* (pp. 258–287). Boston: Allyn & Bacon.

Frankl, V. (1984). *Man's search for meaning.* Boston: Washington Square Press. (Original work published 1946)

Gendlin, E. T. (1961). Experiencing: A variable in the process of therapeutic change. *American Journal of Psychotherapy, 15*, 233–245.

Gendlin, E. T. (1962). *Experiencing and the creation of meaning.* New York: Free Press of Glencoe.

Greenberg, L. S., Elliott, R. K., & Lietaier, G. (1994). Research on experiential psychotherapies. In A. E. Bergin & S. L. Garfield (Eds.), *Handbook of psychotherapy and behavior change* (4th ed., pp. 509–539). New York: Wiley.

Guttmann, D. (1966). *Logotherapy for the Helping Professional: Meaningful Social Work.* New York: Springer.

Hergenhahn, B. R. (2001). *An introduction to the history of psychology* (4th ed.). Belmont, CA: Wadsworth.

Hutzell, R. R., & Peterson, T. J. (1985). An MMPI existential vacuum scale for logotherapy research. *The International Forum for Logotherapy, 8*, 97–100.

Knox, S., Hess, S. A., Petersen, D. A., & Hill, C. E. (1997). A qualitative analysis of client perceptions of the effects of helpful therapist self-disclosure in long-term therapy. *Journal of Counseling Psychology, 44*, 274–283.

Laing, R. D. (1969). *The divided self.* New York: Pantheon.

Lantz, J. (1986). Family logotherapy. *Contemporary family therapy, 8*, 124–135.

Lantz, J. (1989). Family logotherapy with an overweight family. *Contemporary family therapy, 11*, 287–297.

Maslow, A. H. (1968). *Toward a psychology of being* (2nd ed.). Princeton, NJ: Van Nostrand.

May, R. (1961). *Existential psychology.* New York: Random House.

May, R. (1969). *Love and will.* New York: Norton.

May, R. (1977). *The meaning of anxiety* (Rev. ed.). New York: Norton. (Original work published 1950)

May, R., & Yalom, I. (2000). Existential psychotherapy. In R. J. Corsini & D. Wedding (Eds.), *Current psychotherapies* (6th ed., pp. 273–302). Itasca, IL: Peacock Publishers.

Mearns, D., & Thorne, B. (2000). *Person-centred therapy today.* London: Sage Publications.

Mitchell, K. M., Bozarth, J. D., & Krauft, C. C. (1977). A reappraisal of the therapeutic effectiveness of accurate empathy, non-possessive warmth, and genuineness. In A. S. Guvman & A. M. Razin (Eds.), *Effective psychotherapy: A handbook of research.* New York: Pergamon.

Opalic, P. (1989). Existential and psychopathological evaluation of group psychotherapy of neurotic and psychotic patients. *International Journal of Group Psychotherapy, 39*, 389–411.

Prochaska, J. O., & Norcross, J. C. (1999). *Systems of psychotherapy* (4th ed.). Pacific Grove, CA: Brooks/Cole.

Raskin, N. J., & Rogers, C. R. (2000). Person-centered therapy. In R. J. Corsini & D. Wedding (Eds.), *Current psychotherapies* (6th ed., pp. 133–167). Itasca, IL: Peacock Publishers.

Rogers, C. R. (1940). The processes of therapy. *Journal of Consulting Psychology, 4,* 161–164.

Rogers, C. R. (1957). The necessary and sufficient conditions of therapeutic personality change. *Journal of Consulting Psychology, 21,* 95–103.

Rogers, C. R. (1961). *On becoming a person.* Boston: Houghton Mifflin.

Rotter, J. B. (1966). Generalized expectancies for internal versus external control of reinforcement. *Psychological Monographs, 80.*

Russell, J. M. (1978). Sartre, therapy, and expanding the concept of responsibility. *American Journal of Psychoanalysis, 38,* 258–269.

Seligman, L. (2001). *Systems, strategies, and skills of counseling and psychotherapy.* Upper Saddle River, NJ: Prentice-Hall.

Seligman, M. E. P., & Csikszentmihalyi, M. (2000). Positive psychology: An introduction. *American Psychologist, 55,* 5–14.

Semrud-Clikeman, M. (1995). *Child and adolescent therapy.* Needham Heights, MA: Allyn & Bacon.

Singh, J., & Tudor, K. (1997). Cultural conditions of therapy. *The Person-Centered Journal, 4,* 32–46.

Smith, M. L., Glass, G. V., & Miller, T. I. (1980). *The benefits of psychotherapy.* Baltimore: Johns Hopkins University Press.

Stephenson, W. U. (1953). *The study of behavior.* Chicago: University of Chicago Press.

Stubbs, J. P., & Bozarth, J. D. (1994). The Dodo Bird revisited: A qualitative study of psychotherapy efficacy research. *Applied & Preventive Psychology, 3,* 109–120.

Triandis, H. C., & Bhawuk, D. P. S. (1997). Culture theory and the meaning of relatedness. In P. Earley & M. Erez, *New perspectives on international industrial/organizational psychology* (pp. 13–52). San Francisco: New Lexington Press.

Truax, C. B. (1966). Reinforcement and nonreinforcement in Rogerian psychotherapy. *Journal of Abnormal Psychology, 71,* 1–9.

Truax, C. B. (1970). Effects of client-centered psychotherapy with schizophrenic patients: Nine years pre-therapy and nine years post-therapy hospitalization. *Journal of Clinical and Consulting Psychology, 35,* 417–422.

Truax, C. B., Wargo, D. G., & Silber, L. D. (1966). Effects of group psychotherapy with high accurate empathy and nonpossessive warmth upon female institutionalized delinquents. *Journal of Abnormal Psychology, 71,* 267–274.

Tyler, L. (1969). *The work of the counselor* (3rd ed.). New York: Meredith Corporation.

Vontress, C. E. (1996). A personal retrospective on cross-cultural counseling. *Journal of Multicultural Counseling and Development, 24,* 156–167.

Vontress, C. E., Johnson, J. A., & Epp, L. R. (1999). *Cross-Cultural Counseling: A Casebook.* Alexandria VA: American Counseling Association.

Yalom, I. D. (1980). *Existential psychotherapy.* New York: Basic Books.

Yalom, I. D., & Vinogradov, S. C. (1988). Bereavement groups: Techniques and themes. *International Journal of Group Psychotherapy, 38,* 419–446.

Gestalt Therapy

A Selection from

The Gestalt Approach, 1973

Fritz Perls

I am convinced that the awareness technique alone can produce valuable therapeutic results. If the therapist were limited in his work only to asking three questions, he would eventually achieve success with all but the most seriously disturbed of his patients. These three questions, which are essentially reformulations of the statement, "Now I am aware," are "What are you doing?" "What do you feel?" "What do you want?" We could increase the number by two, and include these questions: "What do you avoid?" "What do you expect?" These are obviously extensions of the first three. And they would be enough of an armamentarium for the therapist.

All five of these are healthily supportive questions. That is, the patient can only answer them to the degree that his own awareness makes possible. But at the same time, they help him to become more aware. They throw him on his own resources, bring him to a recognition of his own responsibility, ask him to muster his forces and his means of self-support. They give him a sense of self because they are directed to his self.

His verbal answers to them may come from the intellect, but his total response, unless he is completely desensitized, comes from his total person and is an indication of his total personality. Aside from the pat answers which are always readily available to him there will nearly always be some additional reaction—a confusion, a hesitation, a knitting of the brow, a shrug of the shoulder, a suppressed "What a silly question!," a bit of embarrassment, a wish not to be bothered, an "oh, gosh, here he goes again," an eager leaning forward, and so on. Each of these responses is many times more important than the verbal answer. Each one of them is an indication of the self and of the patient's style. At first the patient's behavior may be of more value to the therapist than it is to him. The therapist, having a wider area of awareness, can see the behavior as a function of the total personality. The patient, whose awareness is still limited, may be completely oblivious to anything but his verbal answer. Or, if he is not oblivious, he may be unable to grasp the significance of his style of response. But eventually there will be a click in the patient's awareness, too. This will be the first big step he makes in therapy.

The therapist can help the patient to this self-discovery by acting, as it were, as a magnifying mirror for him. The therapist cannot make discoveries for the patient; he can only facilitate the process in the patient. By his questions he can bring the patient to see his own behavior more clearly and he can help the patient determine for himself what that behavior represents.

And the acute therapist can find plenty of material right under his nose; he needs only to look. Unfortunately, even this is not so easy, for to look and to see requires that the therapist is completely empty and unbiased. Since *contact always occurs on the surface,* it is the surface that the therapist must see. But make no mistake about it, that surface is much broader and more significant than the orthodox therapists will admit. First of all, their preconvictions prevent them from seeing much of it. And second of all, they tend to take it for granted, to talk about it contemptuously as "obvious." This is where they make their mistake. As long as we take anything for granted and dismiss it as obvious we have not the slightest inclination to change nor do we have the tools with which to do it.

But consider for a moment this fact: everything the patient does, obvious or concealed, is an expression of the self. His leaning forward and pushing back, his abortive kicks, his fidgets, his subtleties of enunciation, his split-second hesitations between words, his handwriting, his use of metaphor and language, his use of "it" as opposed to his use of "you" and "I"; all are on the surface, all are obvious, and all are meaningful. These are the only real material the therapist has to work with. His preconvictions will not help the patient at all.

The therapist's questions, then, will be based on his observations and directed towards bringing certain factors within the area of the patient's awareness. He uses the technique of asking questions rather than of making statements so that the burden of recognition and action is placed where it belongs—on the patient. But his questions are actually translations of his observations. Such as: "Are you aware of your speech?" might represent the following observation and might be turned into the following statement: "I am aware that you speak extremely rapidly. I also notice that you are continuously short of breath. It would be beneficial to you to become aware yourself of what you are doing so that we can cope with the excitement you are dissipating in this way." . . .

Of course, all of the therapist's questions are interruptions of some on-going process in the patient. They are intrusions, very often miniature shocks. This leads to an apparently unfair situation. If the therapist has to frustrate the demands of the patient but feels himself free to fire questions, is this not an unfair situation, an authoritarian procedure, completely antithetical to our effort to elevate the therapist from the position of a power figure to a human being? Admittedly, it is not easy to find the way through this inconsistency, but once the therapist has resolved the psychotherapeutic paradox of working with *support* and *frustration* both, his procedures will fall correctly into place.

The therapist is not, of course, the only one who can ask questions. And it is impossible to enumerate the many things the patient can do with this technique. His questions can be intelligent and therapy-supporting. They can be irritating and repetitious. They can be the "what did you says" and the "what do you means" of the semantically blocked. Nor is it always apparent from which area of confusion the patient's questions arise. Sometimes he does not know whether he can trust the therapist, so he will use questions to test him. If he has obsessional doubts, he will ask the same question over and over again.

The majority of questions the patient asks are seductions of the intellect, related to the notion that verbal explanations are a substitute for understanding. As long as such patients are fed with interpretations, especially if they are emotionally blocked, they'll snuggle happily back in the cocoon of their neurosis and stay there, purring peacefully. (pp. 73–77) ■ ■

DISCUSSION IDEAS

1. What does the word *armamentarium* mean? What does this word choice suggest about the therapist-client relationship?

2. Notice that there are no *Why?* questions listed in the first paragraph of the reading. Mentally change all the questions to *Why?* questions. What difference would it make? Do the next two paragraphs throw any light on the absence of *Why?* questions?

3. What are some examples of nonverbal messages? Why does Perls think they are more important than verbal answers? Do you agree?

4. According to this passage, what activities are proper for a therapist? From the impression you formed from the whole reading, what activities would Perls consider improper for a therapist?

5. Who are the "orthodox therapists," do you think? What do they miss, in Perls's view?

6. Explain the clause "verbal explanations are a substitute for understanding." Can you think of an example?

7. What does the last sentence mean? Why are the patients like satisfied cats when they are "fed with interpretations"?

An Introduction to Gestalt Therapy

Do you ever have the feeling that you are so busy with daily life and material goals that you have lost joyfulness, lost the fullness of living, somehow lost yourself? Are you a person who feels poignantly nostalgic for childhood, when you felt more free, natural, and playful than you do now? These are feelings that the Gestalt psychotherapists take seriously, because they indicate the spiritual poverty of much adult existence. A poet of the same era as Gestalt psychotherapy, e. e. cummings, wrote: "pity this busy monster, manunkind,/ not. Progress is a comfortable disease" (1944).

According to Gestalt psychotherapy, people have problems because they are cut off from parts of themselves that they need for wholeness, integration, and balance. They may be alienated from their own feelings, their bodies, or other people. It is human nature to be whole, but life experience teaches us to fragment ourselves because some parts are unacceptable and will be punished. We are taught from an early age to snuff out our spontaneity. For example, by the time he was 2, my well-disciplined nephew would approach a new and interesting stimulus (like a pretty ashtray on a low coffee table), then put his hands behind his back and say to himself out loud, "No!" The requirements of polite and productive society include continual suppression of parts of ourselves, and this sounds familiar to you because the idea is also key in psychodynamic, Jungian, and existential theories, and in the everyday raising of children and curbing of adolescents.

"In a healthy natural existence, our daily life cycle would be an open, flowing process of organismic needs emerging into awareness" (Prochaska & Norcross, 1999, p. 167). How long has it been since you had a day that felt like that—and how would you know? Sometimes awareness is so limited that our days seem like long lists of to-do items, and any moments of pure joy are passed over quickly as nonimportant. Similarly, organismic needs for food, water, rest, exercise, sex, and even deep breaths can be ignored. We don't admit feelings of anger, frustration, sadness, and hate into our awareness because they interfere with our attention to our to-do list. Some people even seem to have had their funny-bones removed. In Gestalt thought, when people are successful at cutting needs and feelings out of awareness automatically, they become rigid, confined, and stuck in unfulfilling habits. These habits can control behavior ("I never wear sweatpants out of the house") and thoughts ("I can't recover from my war experiences").

Gestalt therapy consists of reintegrating split-off parts of the self and the world so that our natural tendency toward equilibrium can guide us. We can think of the way a boat naturally rights itself upon the water, or the way a healthy infant naturally demands what it needs. Gestalt psychotherapists believe that our psyches would work the same way if we allowed them to. Disowned aspects of ourselves do not disappear, but they are expressed in bodily ways and can cause inner conflicts (here you can easily see the Freudian background of the Gestaltists). We feel best when we are *centered* as natural organisms rather than *split* as social beings.

Speaking of Splits: Gestalt Psychology and Gestalt Therapy

Frederick (Fritz) Perls (1893–1970) is the person most identified with Gestalt psychotherapy. Other psychologists such as his wife, Laura Perls, and Paul Goodman participated fully in the energetic, freewheeling process of developing Gestalt therapy and its techniques. Fritz Perls decided to call the new approach by the name **Gestalt** when giving a title to its foundation text, *Gestalt Therapy: Excitement and Growth in the Human Personality* (Perls, Hefferline, & Goodman, 1951). Laura Perls objected to the label *Gestalt* (Clarkson & Mackewn, 1993), probably because she had a graduate degree in Gestalt psychology (Humphrey, 1986).

Why would she object? Laura Perls and others, including Hefferline and most Gestalt psychologists, don't see a direct connection between Gestalt psychology, which has to do with perception and cognition, and Gestalt therapy, which deals with personality, psychopathology, and counseling (Henle, 1978). As Sherrill (1986) put it, "Gestalt therapists see close kinship between the two Gestalt systems; Gestalt psychologists deny any meaningful similarity" (p. 54).

The Gestalt psychologists of Germany in the early 1900s (Wolfgang Kohler, Max Wertheimer, and Kurt Koffka, notably) studied the way that the brain organizes incoming sensory stimuli into Gestalts, which are forms with internal organization and coherence.

Gestaltist Principles of Perception and Cognition

You have probably seen illustrations of the principles the Gestaltists derived. For example, the *principle of proximity* says that when stimuli are close together, they tend to form one perceptual unit:

\\   \\   \\   \\   \\   \\

You are likely to perceive this figure as six sets of paired slashes rather than as twelve slashes.

The *principle of closure* says that when incomplete figures are perceived, the mind usually completes the figure:

/ \
/___\

Here, you are likely to perceive a triangle rather than two rows of typed slashes and underlines.

Another Gestalt phenomenon is the *figure/ground relation,* in which we organize what we see into a shape in the foreground (the figure) and a rather formless background (the ground). Your introduction to psychology textbook probably presented an example of an ambiguous figure/ground, such as a picture that represents either a vase or two human profiles, or the drawing in Figure 7.1, which portrays either a young woman or an old woman, depending on how you look at it. (According to Gestalt psychologists, though, reversible figure/ground relationships are relatively rare. You don't see many unless they are contrived artistically, as the textbook examples are.)

Fritz Perls seized upon these and other ideas from the German Gestalt psychologists and applied them to all kinds of human experience, not just perception. Perls's applications of terms like *Gestalt, closure,* and *figure/ground* were loose, approximate, metaphorical, and imaginative. For example, when Perls discussed our organization of the environment, he said that **figure** emerges based on need or habit and ground recedes, and the **ground** becomes a new figure when the need is met or attention shifts. (So for a thirsty student a drinking fountain stands out in the school hallway, while for a student anxious about an exam grade the bulletin board where marks are posted stands out. In the case of a student who is both thirsty and anxious, it is only after she checks her grade that she notices the drinking fountain and her own thirst.) Basically, Perls used the words *figure* and *ground* to make the distinction between *important* and *unimportant* elements of the environment (Henle, 1978). And he used

FIGURE 7.1   Reversible Figure
and Ground

Gestalt for organized systems of feelings, thoughts, and behaviors, not just visual perceptions.

Perls liked the idea that our perceptions seek *closure* of incomplete figures, and he applied this term more generally to human experience as well. He believed that in the present we seek closure of conflicts and injuries from the past—and that this is a goal of psychotherapy. He also linked the natural process of perception, which creates a whole out of differing pieces, with an **organismic self-regulation,** in which the self searches for wholeness by integrating polarities. We will return to this topic in the next section.

Because of this inexactness in transferring the terminology from one arena to another, Gestalt psychologists wish that Perls had latched onto some other theory for his approach. They are especially annoyed that some of Perls's beliefs are in contradiction with conventional Gestalt psychology yet share the same name. For instance, Perls ridicules science, while the Gestalt psychologists are proud to be scientists. Gestalt psychologists believe that individuals' needs rarely influence the perceptions of figure and ground, while the Gestalt therapists see inner needs as the organizing principle of figure and ground. For such reasons, I have been careful to write "Gestalt psychotherapy" rather than "Gestalt psychology." Throughout the rest of this chapter, I will be talking about Gestaltism in the loose terms of Gestalt psychotherapy.

Essential Concepts in Gestalt Therapy

In the essential concepts of Gestalt therapy, you will perceive its roots in psychodynamic thinking as well as its metaphors based on perceptual processes.

Awareness

In Gestalt therapy, *awareness* is the key to positive growth and personal integration. Gestaltists used the word in a deeper sense than most people usually do: Awareness is "the capacity to be in touch with your own existence, to notice what is happening around or inside you, to connect with the environment, other people and yourself; to know what you are feeling or sensing or thinking; how you are reacting at this very moment" (Clarkson & Mackewn, 1993). In this sense, we are rarely in a state of awareness in our daily lives. This keeps us off balance, and we try bad solutions to problems over and over without noticing their futility. Gestalt psychologists attempt to encourage awareness rather than directly influencing behavior change, on the assumption that behavior change will grow out of fuller awareness.

Polarities

"The most important problems for Gestaltists are conflicts within the individual, such as those between **top-dog** and **under-dog,** or between the person's social self and natural self, or between the disowned parts of the person and the catastrophic expectations that keep the person from expressing polarities that may meet with disapproval or rejection" (Prochaska & Norcross, 1999, p. 177). *Catastrophic expectations* are created when as children we act independently and spontaneously, only to find ourselves severely punished or rejected. We grow up to think that following our impulses is dangerous, to the point where we lose touch with parts of our selves.

   Polarities within each of us include adult versus child, worried versus carefree, responsible versus wild, loving versus hateful, intellectual versus emotional, strong versus weak, generous versus stingy. Sometimes, minority versus mainstream is a polarity within one individual, as with traditional Jamaican versus conventional American or lesbian versus straight. Both polarities need to be integrated into the self-concept. If you are centered, that is, psychologically hovering in the middle between polarities, you will be aware of which side needs attention (or expression) at the moment, and you will maintain **homeostasis,** which is balance or equilibrium. Gestalt therapists believe that we are naturally inclined to *organismic self-regulation:* Our organisms know what will achieve balance. The most prevailing need at the moment will be the figure, and it will fade into the background when it is fulfilled, with another need taking its place as the figure. In this way, we creatively adjust to inner and outer environments: We go with the flow. Living in the here-and-now represents another centered position, being neither stuck in the past nor preoccupied with the future (Perls, 1969a).

The battle between *top-dog* and *under-dog* is Perls's substitute for the superego-id conflict imagined by Freud. The two dogs in our psyches represent warring polarities, animated this way by Perls (1970):

> The top-dog is opposed to another personality, which I call the under-dog. Both have their characteristics and both fight for control. The top-dog is characterized mainly by righteousness. Whether he is right or wrong, he always knows what the under-dog should do. But the top-dog has very few means by which to reinforce his demands. He is really just a bully and tries to get his way by making threats. If you don't do as he says, then you will be punished, or something terrible will happen. The under-dog who receives these orders is not righteous; on the contrary, he is very unsure of himself. He does not fight back or try to control by being a bully or by being aggressive. He fights back with other means. "Tomorrow," "I promise," "Yes, but . . . ," "I do my best." So these two, the top-dog and the under-dog, live a life of mutual frustration and continued attempts to control each other. (p. 21)

The under-dog does not really try to change. This is its power, like that of a un-cooperative toddler. Some people attempt to make others (especially their therapists) act out their top-dog while they play the under-dog, helpless to change. But this just keeps the same pattern alive: Only through being aware of both tendencies can a person make reasonable choices. For example, women who let their top-dog try to enforce strict dieting eventually let their under-dog rebel by overeating, instead of choosing a more tolerable middle-of-the-road approach to dieting. Inability to accept opposites within one's self constitutes psychological distress not only in Gestalt theory but also in many other theories, such as psychodynamic and humanistic.

R e f l e c t i o n

What are some of the polarities you experience within yourself? What types of struggles do your under-dog and top-dog engage in? Some of the polarities Fritz Perls mentions in his autobiography *In and Out the Garbage Pail* (1969b) are promiscuity and loyalty, contempt and enthusiasm, shame and pride, coolness and passion, and laziness and energy.

Contact, Boundaries, and Support

You can be aware only through experience—that is, through first-hand contact with persons and situations. Remembering, explaining, predicting, and analyzing are not the main processes leading to awareness: contact is. **Contact** is awareness of what is going on here-and-now and the flow from moment to moment. We use the same type of contact imagery when we say someone is "out of touch" or "not quite with it" or "not all there," or when I ask you to "stay with me" as I speak to you. Contact between the client and counselor is critical for therapy to succeed, similar to Rogers's accurate empathy and genuineness conditions.

Boundaries are the lines between ourselves and others—lines that both connect us and separate us. Connectedness and separation are polarities inherent in human contact. In the optimal environment, we connect with what is good for us and reject what is harmful. We withdraw to rest and to reflect. In psychological imbalance, we connect with harmful elements and reject elements that would guide us toward homeostasis. We also seek a balance in boundaries of self: With weak ego boundaries we might confuse others' needs with our own, while with rigid ego boundaries we feel alone and alienated.

Balance is possible only with **support,** which is provided by one's self and by the environment, which in turn includes other people. Perls believed that we all possess the self-support we need but may have neglected or rejected it. This is why Perls as a therapist often put people in frustrating situations and left them there, where they could discover their own inner supports. In Gestalt terms, anxiety occurs when we feel that we do not or will not have the support we need. Perls notes that anxiety comes especially from preoccupation with future events that we fear we can't handle.

When our habitual support system is absent, and we have not gained the use of new supports, we reach **impasse,** a deadlock or stalemate. This is the paralyzing spot where movement forward or backward seems impossible. At this point, people are likely to seek psychotherapy. Their organism tells them that they are at a dead end unless something really different happens, and they are motivated to seek new supports. The idea of impasse is striking as I write this book, because recently the World Trade Center in New York was destroyed by terrorists. This devastating event drove many Americans into a state of impasse personally—a psychological place where they became highly aware of the inattentive way they were living their daily lives—and with such awareness, they revised their approach to themselves, their work, their country, and other people.

Interference with Healthy Tendencies

When aspects of inner awareness are shut down or distorted, you are out of touch with at least some of your emotions and needs. In Gestalt terms, these emotions and needs would guide you toward healthy self-regulation if you were able to heed them. The processes that are barriers to healthy awareness can be divided into four types.

Shoulds   You act according to rules that you've learned so well that they seem natural. However, they actually work against your organismic needs. **Shoulds** are tactics of **neurotic self-regulation.** It's reasonable to believe that your kitchen counters should be tidy and clean; it's neurotic to clean the counters so carefully that you are late for the movies. I have a friend whose boyfriend once pinched his hand painfully against the doorframe while moving a sofa for her; she immediately ran to the doorframe to inspect for bloodstains and dents. The idea that her home *should* be flawless took precedence over concern for her boyfriend.

We have more global *shoulds*—such as "I should be perfect" and "I should always put others' needs before my own" and "I should have a positive personality"—that de-center us, blocking the path of organismic self-regulation, which is flexible rather than rigid. Perls pointed out that in automatically being polite and agreeable with other people, we are often "rude to ourselves," disregarding our own interests, concerns, and opinions (Perls, Hefferline, & Goodman, 1951, p. 152).

Contact Boundary Disturbances   These are distortions in perceptions of borders: failure to make accurate contact with self and others as individuals. One type of boundary disturbance occurs when you believe that your thinking and emotions really belong to someone else, or are shared by someone else. Another occurs when there is a conflict between self and self-image. Five types are listed in Table 7.1.

Interruptions—Automatic Self-Regulating Actions   Before you know it, you stop acknowledging an experience or expressing yourself, without even realizing that you stopped or how you stopped. When I was a teenager, the Beatles released a record called the White Album. It was very popular, and it played often at my home and at my workplace. Yet I had an odd feeling about it that I always dismissed. Years later, after its popularity had faded and I heard tunes from it only occasionally, it came to me in a flash: I didn't *like* the Beatles' White Album! That is what the odd feeling was, only I was immersed fully in a culture where not liking the White Album was inconceivable. So I *didn't* conceive of it, until I was less immersed and more in touch with my own tastes.

Disowning and rejecting tendencies toward action make up another category of automatic self-regulation. You may have a good feeling about a fellow student, but you never approach him in the hallway because you have automatically ruled out being so forward with people you don't know. Thus, you deprive yourself of contact without even knowing it. As Perls (1969a) put it, "With full awareness you become aware of this organismic self-regulation, you can let the organism take over without interfering, without interrupting; we can rely on the wisdom of the organism" (pp. 16–17). Self-control frequently brings about the opposite of what we thought we wanted. Rigorous dieting is an example. Severe diet restriction causes the body to lower its metabolism in response to low supplies, slowing down weight loss. It also creates both a sense of deprivation that makes breaking the diet inevitable and a rigidity of thought that makes it hard to recover from a slip-up.

Intrusion of Unfinished Business   Unresolved emotions and issues from the past affect the present. Transference is an example of **unfinished business:** The client repeats his or her past patterns of interaction in the relationship with the therapist. If the client's mother has been intrusively over-helpful, the client

TABLE 7.1
Contact Boundary Disturbances

- **Introjection:** Taking in others' views and values to the point where they seem like your own. For example, children develop a conscience through interjecting their parents' *dos* and *don'ts*. As you mature, you review the opinions of others before integrating them into your own way of thinking, and you may revise the rules of your conscience as well. In introjection that is disturbed, however, you do not allow review and revision but instead embrace someone else's values completely. People who convert to religious and political cults often introject in this unquestioning way. Introjection is one route that delivers the *shoulds* that control us.

- **Projection:** Assigning undesired parts of yourself to others, especially when you feel guilty or angry. If it seems that everyone else is obsessed with material success, for example, you may yourself harbor a guilty wish for wealth. Projecting feelings or motivations onto other people prevents you from seeing them accurately in their own right, thus creating a barrier to contact.

- **Retroflection:** Directing an action or thought toward yourself rather than toward others. For example, you may have a habit of rugged independence that prevents you from making emotional contact with other people. Some people take anger at their circumstances and turn it toward themselves; this may explain the behavior of people who gain relief by cutting themselves. If you usually assuage negative feelings by eating comfort food rather than by asking your friends to comfort you, you may be engaging in retroflection.

- **Deflection:** Turning aside direct contact with another person or yourself. You may have had clients who deflected contact by telling long pointless stories or, conversely, by remaining silent. You sometimes deflect conversation away from a highly charged topic onto a milder one, or deflect attention away from yourself onto another person or topic. Children deflect physical contact when they duck to avoid big smooches, and adults do the same thing more subtly. Like the other strategies we use to control contact boundaries, deflection is not harmful unless used habitually or exclusively.

- **Confluence:** Agreeing in opinion and feeling with someone else to the point where the boundary between you is blurry. This kind of merging usually involves pushing the differences between you out of awareness. You may feel at one with your beloved in the first bloom of romance, and only later see the differences between you. The unhealthy course would be to deny or downplay those differences because you feel a threat to your deep connection. A healthy course is to delight in the differences that keep the relationship interesting.

will act as though the therapist is that way, too. Unfinished business may include feelings like suspicion and fear as well as memories and fantasies. Unresolved resentments and unexpressed emotions compose much unfinished business and need to be addressed in the here-and-now so that they can cease their psychological clamor for attention. For example, many women, seemingly mysteriously, choose male partners who mirror the women's fathers in being abusive, cold, absent, or alcoholic. From a Gestalt point of view, however, there is no mystery, since the daughter's unfinished business with an out-of-contact father will be revisited in other relationships with men until she gets *unstuck*, usually by accepting what is past rather than trying to relive it correctively. Many of Gestalt's techniques aim to complete unfinished business. According to Levitsky and Perls (1970), "Unfinished business is the Gestalt therapy analogue of the perceptual or cognitive incomplete task of Gestalt psychology" (p. 146).

The Therapeutic Process

Clients should realize that they don't really need a psychotherapist but have the inner support they need. They can get in touch with their own immediate being and organismic tendencies toward healthy choices. The more awareness and contact they achieve, the more choices they will have. Greenberg, Rice, and Elliott (1993) describe the *Gestalt contact cycle*: "In this cycle, *awareness* leads to the mobilization of *excitement*. This in turn leads to *action*, oriented toward *contacting* the environment, need satisfaction, and *completion* of the cycle. Thus the person is continually organizing him- or herself to make contact with the environment to meet the need" (p. 39; italics in original).

The Therapeutic Relationship

The person of the therapist is paramount in Gestalt practice, as it is in Rogerian practice. However, Perls disagreed with Rogers about positive regard—he believed that clients should get in-the-moment feedback from counselors, so that they realize how they are viewed by mature others. Thus, Perls would encourage the counselor to act bored, irritated, or impatient if that's the way he or she felt. In flagrant violation of some dearly held therapeutic rules, Perls (1969a) even fell asleep while clients talked. The Gestalt therapist also admits to being mistaken, saying the wrong thing, and using harmful strategies in sessions and in his or her own life. Instead of being a purely positive role model, the counselor is a role model of integrating polarities and remaining centered. In another contrast with the client-centered model, the Gestalt practitioner purposely frustrates clients, refusing to protect them from discomfort and responsibility. Interpretation is also sparse in most Gestalt psychologists' interactions, because clients need to provide their own interpretations instead of accepting expert opinion from the outside. An analysis of taped therapy interviews by Brunink and Schroeder (1979) found that Gestalt therapists behaved significantly differently from psychoanalytically oriented and behavioral therapists: Specifically, the Gestalt counselors "provided more direct guidance, less verbal facilitation, less focus on the client, more self-disclosure, greater initiative, and less emotional support" (p. 572).

Like the therapist's role, the process of Gestalt therapy is hard to pin down, since this approach has a greater range of acceptable practices than any other system (Yontef & Jacobs, 2000). It is practiced both briefly and at length, in settings varying from individual sessions to small groups to dramatic demonstrations in front of large audiences. Individual therapists choose their own styles and are encouraged to be spontaneous and creative. I will summarize two descriptions of process that you might find among followers of Gestalt.

Perls's Peeling the Onion

The process that Perls (1970) observed involves successive removal of **layers of neuroses,** and, by way of illustration, he invoked the image of peeling an onion. This process might occur within one session and then re-occur in subsequent sessions, or it might take place sequentially over the course of many sessions. Each layer represents a different level of contact with the environment, including other people. Growth and actualization come about through awareness, and awareness is possible only through contact (rather than through, say, avoidance or self-centeredness). Perls gave each layer a name, as in the following example:

1. The **phony layer.** This layer is just what it sounds like. People respond to their environment in stereotypical ways, manipulate situations according to habit, and behave inauthentically in social settings. For example, Phil, a college freshman at the phony level, was compelled to declare a marketing major due to his father's influence. Phil agreed that marketing might be a good choice because he had worked in a restaurant during high school and had been truly interested in its operations. At college, Phil put on an air of self-confidence and brightness, and he sought the good opinion of students with wealthy and professional backgrounds.

2. The **phobic layer**. At this level, people feel fearful and helpless, but they keep the feelings hidden. At mid-year, Phil got low grades, but concealed his distress and self-doubt by claiming that the general education classes were Mickey-Mouse and boring. Phil was tormented by the fear that his parents would hit the ceiling if he did not stay in college. However, he spent most of his energy in covering up his troubles, and didn't have much left over for improving his studies.

3. The **impasse layer.** Here, people feel that they are stuck and don't know what the next move should be. This is the point where people often seek help, wanting someone else to take over and tell them what to do. After three semesters of poor grades, Phil dropped into the career counseling center, under the pretense of wanting to choose the best career direction. He also arranged to study with his girlfriend, who was a marketing major herself.

4. The **implosive layer.** It's at this level that the phony identity begins to collapse in upon itself. People feel that they are dead inside, or cut off from their former selves. The career center assessed Phil, and he was advised to seek personal counseling for his depression and anxiety. Meanwhile, through seeing his girlfriend's genuine skill and talent at academic work, Phil realized that he did not have the capacities he had always claimed.

5. The **explosive layer.** The explosive layer involves letting go of the old self. Clinging to an inauthentic version of self takes up a lot of energy, and when that self is finally abandoned, the energy is quickly freed as though in a combustive reaction, which is why the layer is called explosive. After giving up all his pretenses, Phil decided to quit college and attempt to work his way up from the bottom in the restaurant business. With enthusiasm, he returned to the career center to research restaurant chains that were most promising for advancement.

Profile of a Theorist

FRITZ PERLS (1893–1970)

One of Fritz Perls's principal biographers described him as "a bastard and a saint," and by many accounts, it was an apt description. Born in Berlin in 1893, Perls grew up under the shadow of oppressive anti-Semitism. As early as elementary school, he was characterized as a gifted but difficult student, and stories of his rebellion and truancy during his adolescence abound. Theater classes in high school awakened in Perls a gift for keen observation of human behavior and presaged the flare for drama that would mark his style of psychotherapy years later.

Following high school, Perls pursued a degree in medicine. He graduated in 1921 and practiced in Berlin as a neuropsychiatrist. Perls identified socially and philosophically with members of the left-wing intellectual Bauhaus movement, and it was during this time that he had his first experience of psychoanalysis with Karen Horney. Brief though it was, it proved deeply influential and set the tone for his own challenge to orthodox psychoanalysis later.

In 1926 he went to Frankfurt and worked at the Institute for Brain Damaged Soldiers, a position that fostered his growing belief in the importance of treating both mind and body. He met and married Laura Posner, a graduate student of Gestalt psychology with a devout interest in existential philosophy. Her influence on Perls is often debated, and he intermittently credited and denied her contributions to his work.

In 1933, Perls, with his wife and a young daughter, fled Nazi Germany for Amsterdam, which proved almost as dangerous, and the family soon relocated to South Africa. There, the Perlses successfully established themselves as psychoanalysts, and quickly regained financial and professional stability. Perls later embarked on a trip to Vienna with the express purpose of meeting and aligning himself with Freud, the master of psychoanalysis. However, his visit with the declining Freud lasted only a few minutes and Perls left bitterly disappointed. Many mark this event as a turning point in Perls's career, when he broke with traditional analysis, denouncing the detached approach as ineffective and a product of Freud's own inability to tolerate interpersonal interactions. Perls spent the rest of his career exploring and promoting the importance of active and intimate sharing between therapist and client.

Perls's theories began to take shape in his first book, *Ego, Hunger and Aggression*, published in 1947. The book reflects the early convergence of his psychoanalytic roots with Gestalt psychology, existential themes, and theories of holism, among other influences. Over the remaining decades of his life, Perls continued to develop his theory and therapeutic techniques, moving further away from traditional analysis, and incorporating influences from fields as diverse as art, medicine, and Zen Buddhism.

Following World War II, Perls moved to the United States, where he met with both increasing support and harsh criticism for his bohemian and controversial style of therapy. Authenticity and personal responsibility were sacrosanct to Perls, and he was reported to have belittled and exploited those people he perceived as artificial or overly dependent.

One of the central tenets of Gestalt psychotherapy is the integration of polarities, the synthesis of opposing elements within the psyche. Perls's own personality and the theory that grew out of his life experience appear to have been shining examples of the coexistence of polarities within a single man.

Polster's Three Stages

Miriam Polster (1987), a central figure in the development of Gestalt therapy in the United States, described a three-stage process of change. In terms of Perls's model, Polster's begins at the impasse layer.

1. *Discovery.* At this stage, people discover that they are not what they seemed, and that situations are not what they appeared before. Phil, for example, had never admitted to depression or anxiety before the career counselor brought such topics up. Nor had he ever realized that he lacked academic tendencies until he compared himself with his girlfriend, up close. In this discovery, he saw that his problems in school stemmed from the fact that it was not the right environment for him.

2. *Accommodation.* Having scrapped their old identity, people learn what new choices are possible and experiment with new ways of being. When Phil told his girlfriend that he was leaving college, she was not surprised, and it didn't change her feelings for him. She had known before he did that he was not suited for academia. Phil's parents' disappointment was tempered by their perception of a newly hopeful, energetic son. At this stage, he found that he had support he had never previously counted on.

3. *Assimilation.* Finally, people set out to change their environment so that the genuine self can emerge. From several choices, Phil decided on a worksite within driving distance of his old college (and girlfriend). He made it clear to his bosses that his goal was to work his way to the managerial level, and they were glad to help him develop his career.

Techniques of Gestalt Therapy

Whereas existential and person-centered practitioners use a limited number of strategies, Gestalt therapists are unlimited in scope: In a way, they are creative artists. Many of Perls's strategies reflected his participation in theater and his friends' involvement in theater, dance, and movement (Clarkson & Mackewn, 1993). Korb, Gorrell, and Van de Reit (1989) asserted that in Gestalt, "the most powerful interventions are focused in the present, are awareness-oriented rather than discussed, and are based on the understanding that important personal learning is made through a discovery process" (p. 107).

Body Awareness

Gestaltists think that the mind versus body polarity is one of the most misleading. Perls evidently had an uncanny ability to read posture, fidgets, and other body language accurately, and this ability was a key part of his therapy technique. In later life, Perls devoted most of his time to lectures and demonstrations and "astonished his audiences by the amount of personal information he could pick up just by watching how they spoke, sat or walked" (Clarkson & Mackewn, 1993, p. 4). He believed that every emotion has a physiological component. When a client has taught herself to cut off part of her natural self, her body strains toward the cut-off impulses. "The holding back is achieved by tensing muscles which are antagonistic to those which would be involved in expressing the punishable impulse" (Perls, Hefferline, & Goodman, 1951, p. 147). For example, if a therapist notices that her client clenches his jaw habitually, she would suspect that some impulse to speak is being repressed. A curled-in posture could indicate an attempt to protect one's vulnerable areas. Perls noted that there are conscious, rational grounds for suppressing impulses, and these were not his concern. When the holding-back is *not* under the control of awareness, it nonetheless displays itself in bodily and mental ways.

SMALL GROUP EXERCISE

Take a ten-minute break and go with your small group to the closest gathering spot—a vending area, cafeteria, study room, or hallway. Individually, write down your observations about the body language you see among the people there. Include your guesses about how the body language reflects the person's psychological state. Return to your classroom to compare notes with others in your group. Discuss similarities and differences in your observations and your guesses.

The Gestalt line of thinking on repression is very much like Freud's. Freud also saw repression underlying physical and psychological symptoms. However, while Freud believed that recovery of the *content* of repression was curative, Gestaltists believe that awareness of the *process* of repression is the key. Thus, they call attention to the bodily signs they notice and ask the client to work with those. Sometimes this involves giving the body symptom its own voice: "If your clenched jaw could speak, what would it say?" At other times the work involves emphasizing the body symptom until its meaning emerges into awareness: "I notice that you are wringing your hands. Exaggerate your wringing hands. Wring them really hard. Where do you feel the wringing?" and so forth. These tactics are intended to call forth a *safe emergency*, a combination of aroused intensity and the therapist's affirmation and support (Yontef & Jacobs, 2000). In this atmosphere, creative adjustment to the natural self is possible.

People naturally describe many emotions in physical terms, when they call a problem "a headache," or refer to being heavy-hearted or light-hearted, or to dragging their feet or feeling shaky about something. I have described certain events as so boring that they made my elbows hurt. Emotions can often be located in the body, and a Gestalt counselor will often ask the client, "Where do you feel your anger (pitifulness, embarrassment, hope, sadness)?" Exploration of the physical feelings associated with emotions can fine-tune awareness of what the emotions are more effectively than mere discussion *about* them. For example, you can imagine that anger experienced as one's head about to blow up is different from anger experienced as an ache in the stomach. A problem that is a headache is different from a problem that is a pain in the butt.

Reflection

Think of a strong emotion you have had recently or that you remember well. Can you locate where it was located in your body? Does its location clarify the emotion for you in any way?

Experimentation

Experimentation is encouraged in Gestalt therapy—indeed, Perls had a background in drama and liked improvisation. The strategy of experimentation is related to the **paradoxical theory of change** (Beisser, 1970): *Trying* to reach an ideal gets you stuck in the same patterns. You don't get anywhere. So, you should try something new just to see how it feels. Heightened emotions or awareness may result.

A Gestalt counselor may give experimental homework. For example, a client complains that her husband never chats with her when he gets home in the evening. To get him to talk, what tactics has she tried so far? She saves up interesting topics to share with him, for one thing, and she tries to start a conversation when he walks in the door, before he becomes absorbed in something else. In keeping with the paradoxical theory of change, she has persisted in these tactics for years without any success. A Gestalt therapist would advise a reversal—that is, doing the opposite of what she usually does. Since pursuit has not succeeded, she might try retreating. She might make sure that *she* is absorbed in something else, or even briefly out somewhere else, when her husband gets home. But she must do these things pleasantly so that the possibility of conversation stays alive. The experiment could have several enlightening outcomes. First, the husband might eventually pursue conversation himself, and the wife would get what she wanted. Second, she might discover that she enjoys herself *without* the conversation she thought she needed, and thus discover a part of herself that was neglected. Third, the husband might *never* pursue conversation. This alternative highlights an aspect of the Gestalt approach that suggests the client is looking not for a solution or for relief from distress in the experiment but, rather, for some deeper understanding. In this case, the deafening silence heightens an awareness of a reality more disturbing than chat habits in the marriage.

Experiments, then, are designed to clarify experience and to call forth awareness of how experiences are interrupted or regulated. The wife in the example above might be limiting her experience of dissatisfaction in the marriage in order to avoid acknowledging deeper problems. Another experiment Perls liked was turning statements about others into statements about the self, on the premise that we are most hostile to qualities in others that remind us of our denied selves. So he might have encouraged the wife who says, "He never pays any attention to me," to say aloud, "I never pay any attention to me," and to see how that statement feels. Does she feel that she is not worth listening to?

Focusing on the here-and-now and intensifying present experience are facets of yet another Gestalt experiment: "What are you aware of now?" is a common question designed to keep the client in the moment. Instead of providing guidance or interpretation, the counselor is likely to advise the client to "Stay with that" when an emotion or intense observation emerges. In Gestalt terms, the client has not had much practice at "staying with" a strong impression until it comes into meaningful focus. More energy has been spent getting past it or pushing it away. The therapist acts as a supporter and a model of being able to survive experiencing fully. Sometimes we fail to stay with positive emotions as well. We walk out into a perfect sunny morning and allow ourselves to enjoy it only briefly before our attention moves on, or we note our partner's good mood without relishing her joy.

The Gestalt therapist makes use of the client's imagination to make experience vivid. If a patient describes his life as "being alone on a desert," the counselor may suggest, "Imagine you are actually on that desert, right now. What do you experience?" (Yontef & Jacobs, 2000, p. 327). Other imaginative experiments include fantasizing about telling off someone you are angry with, having an ideal day, and walking through a pleasant place.

Role Playing

Role playing is an experiment in which the client or clients take on different perspectives and act them out in session. The goal is to resolve unfinished business and integrate polarities by arousing emotions, discovering needs, and shifting one's point of view. Imaginatively, clients act out aspects of themselves, and perspectives of others, that they usually deflect or suppress. Perls was inspired by many role-playing methods, including the *empty-chair technique* created by J. L. Moreno, who began staging expressionist experimental theater in 1920s Europe. Moreno is considered the founder of psychodrama (Wulf, 1998).

Empty-Chair Technique

The empty-chair technique is the one you see most often in depictions of Gestalt therapy, both fictional and real. It's also a technique frequently borrowed by counselors of other types, probably due to its dramatic effectiveness in helping clients and their therapists grasp an individual's unique dynamics. Two chairs are used, with each one assigned a character, attitude, emotion, or quality. The client moves back and forth between the two chairs, alternately speaking from the perspective of each. If you were a client having trouble with a certain teacher in school, you would take one chair as yourself and the other chair as the teacher. Or, you might act out an inner conflict and let the two sides battle it out. The counselor sustains a here-and-now focus and cheers each chair on by acting as the director. A favorite empty-chair dialog is the one between top-dog and under-dog, described earlier in this chapter. The top-dog sits in a chair and tries to persuade, bully, and threaten the under-dog to be a good person, while the under-dog occupies the other chair and pleads helplessness, using "yes, but" excuses and stubbornness to retain its power not to change.

Leslie Greenberg and colleagues have extensively investigated the empty-chair technique (Clarke & Greenberg, 1986; Greenberg, 1979, 1980, 1983, 1991; Paivio & Greenberg, 1995). Their findings indicate that it facilitated depth of experiencing, integration of polarities, and conflict resolution. For these outcomes, the empty-chair approach held its own or had superior results in comparison with other approaches (empathic reflection of feelings and cognitive-behavioral problem-solving). Greenberg and associates assert that "the softening of the harsh internal critic emerges as a key factor in resolving intrapsychic splits" (p. 143).

SMALL GROUP EXERCISE

Discuss how you would feel if you were asked to do an empty-chair exercise. What would you think? Would you resist or cooperate, or enact a combination of resisting and cooperating? Why? If you were a therapist suggesting an empty-chair exercise, how do you think you could encourage a hesitant client to open up to the idea? Are there any multicultural points of view that you need to consider when using the empty-chair technique?

Dream Work

Role playing is a key feature of Gestalt **dream work.** Perls wrote, "In Gestalt Therapy we don't interpret dreams. We do something much more interesting with them. Instead of analyzing and further cutting up the dream, we want to bring it back to life. . . . We find all we need in the dream, or in the perimeter of the dream, the environment of the dream. The existential difficulty, the missing part of the personality, they are all there" (Perls, 1969a, pp. 68–70).

First, the client presents the dream in detail, in the present tense. Then the dreamer plays the roles of the persons and objects in the dream, sometimes using the empty-chair technique to produce dialogs between different parts of the dream. Each part represents projections or aspects of the dreamer. Dreams that come back repetitively and dreams with emotional intensity make especially good material. Unusual elements and gaps in dreams are investigated as well as common contents. For example, a dream that involved *no* activity might represent a client's stuckness. My friend dreamed about an encounter with a rock star and remarked, "I had not dreamed about a man in years." A cautious, subdued woman, she had peopled her dream with the extreme of a macho showoff—maybe a neglected side of herself?

In Chapter 4, I told you about a time in my life when I was experiencing writer's block and dreamed that I had lost my truck in a parking garage and needed to find it fast. A Gestalt counselor would ask me to *be* the truck and talk from its point of view. I'd say, "I am your truck and I usually take you places with no trouble. You like me and my unusual color, Planet Gold. I can get you somewhere now, but I won't. You put me in this gloomy, dull, concrete place, and now I'm hiding from you." In Gestalt terms, the truck represented the part of me that writes flowingly and easily, an unusual talent (Planet Gold) by which I make my living. Thinking about what the truck complained about, I saw that I was trying to complete a section of my book that was dry, boring— and concrete! I also realized that my writing ability had hidden from me. This was my "existential difficulty." I needed to think of a creative approach to the section, something that would make it come alive for me, in order to get over the block. This is what I did, and the block disappeared. Not only did this dream analysis help me at the time, but it also gave me insight into future writing blocks and how to overcome them. Maybe it will help you, too.

SMALL GROUP EXERCISE

From a Gestalt perspective, explore a dream presented by one of your group members. Use the methods described above for ten or fifteen minutes. Then discuss how well you think the method worked, especially for clarifying the dreamer's situation and awareness. If no one in your group has a dream to present, ask members to pretend that the following dream is their own and to answer the group's questions as if it were their own.

> *I am flying through the air just over the treetops. I can see the ground and the fields and buildings clearly. It is very easy to fly. I realize that I have a tiny airplane grasped tightly in my left hand, and that the plane is providing the power and leading the direction I fly. If I let go, I will drop down to the ground.*

Psychodrama

When role playing is performed by several people in a Gestalt group, it is one of the most impressive therapeutic techniques. Instead of a single client acting out various parts, members of a group are assigned parts representing significant individuals in a directed re-enactment of a past experience. The client whose experience is being dramatized acts as director, along with the therapist, to inform and guide the other characters in their actions and responses. In this way the past is brought into the present (Korb, Gorrell, & Van de Riet, 1989). Often, the character of the client is played by the client, and in this role she experiments with alternative ways of behaving in the situation, while others behave in their assigned characters. For example, a person who is berating herself for being quiet in a family argument might be directed to jump in and speak her piece in a loud voice during the **psychodrama.** Alternatively, group members might portray abstractions, such as the childish side of the actor or an imaginary monster. Such experiments are preferable to listening to a client explain and justify behavior. In Gestalt therapy, *doing it* is always preferable to *talking about it*.

J. L. Moreno, who popularized psychodrama as a therapeutic technique, beginning with children in the parks of Vienna in the 1920s, explained how psychodrama works:

> Aristotle's definition of tragedy itself as an "imitation of action and life" . . . underwent a profound change. Psychodrama defines the drama as an extension of life and action rather than its imitation, but where there is imitation the emphasis is not on what it imitates, but upon the opportunity of recapitulation of unsolved problems within a freer, broader and more flexible social setting. The "extension" is an indispensable requisite to the drama in an expanding world. The "double," the "flying horse" and a "hallucinated devil" are just as real and as much entitled to life space as the real persons acting. Their enactment may arouse the spontaneity of the subjects and may make space for unlived lives and unthought-of action. Within the infinite number of imaginary worlds life itself appears as but one strained variety. The patient-actor is like a refugee who suddenly shows new strength because he has set foot into a freer and broader world. Catharsis is generated by the vision of a new universe and the capability of new growth. (Moreno, 1946/1972, pp. 15–16)

Group Work

Throughout his life as a popular psychologist and especially during his period as a guru in California at the famous Esalen Institute from 1964 to 1969, Perls used group therapy extensively. Perls's version of group was different from most others. Groups were usually short term, often consisting of only one intensive two- to three-hour session. In one pattern, just one person at a time sat in the **hot seat** to work with the therapist. The other group members observed and sometimes participated when called upon by the therapist. However, even this participation was focused on the hot-seat individual. This pattern was really one-to-one therapy in a group setting. Members who were silent benefited from **spectator learning** (identifying with the interaction and being aware of their own inner responses to what went on) (Frew, 1988; Korb, Gorrell, & Van de Riet, 1989; Perls, 1969b). When the group members did participate, they represented a social environment and its feedback to the client and therapist. Frew (1988) described "the absolute logic of practicing Gestalt therapy in groups (in which the individual can experience the interacting 'self' in an environment which can talk back)" (p. 78).

Another pattern, developed at the Gestalt Institute of Cleveland (Frew, 1988), involves the group members as clients more fully, inasmuch as they are encouraged to express feelings of their own relevant to the central interaction or a therapist-directed theme. They each contribute as individuals rather than just as respondents to the hot-seat situation, and they build more of a group identity than would be the case in the hot-seat pattern. Here is a snippet from a session in which Fritz Perls directed a group using a thematic approach:

FRITZ: Now I would like you, each one of you, now to tell the group how you manipulate the world. You can do it by ingratiating yourself, playing crybaby, playing tragedy queen, or whatever.

CLAIRE: I say I'm not good enough.

FRITZ: This is one of the famous tragedy queen plays. If you only depress yourself enough, then the whole world will get depressed: we call them the gloom casters, the crepe hangers, the melancholic people. They start gloom casting; if everybody else is depressed, then they go away.

MARK: I think I manipulate the world by criticism. By criticizing.

FRITZ: By criticizing?

MARK: Right. And presuming that there is a better way to do things. And perhaps my way is the better way. That's what I would probably suggest.

FRITZ: These depressing games play a tremendous part in this, our social context. Not only do we depress ourselves, but many sports, for instance, and many business deals are meant to depress the other person. If I win my tennis game, then you feel depressed. Some people go to such extremes that they are real killers. They have nothing else in mind than to make themselves feel better and superior. The same goes for business deals. The rationale is forgotten as long as I get the better of the customer.

JOHN: I manipulate the world by having accidents.

FRITZ: What's the purpose of that?

JOHN: I let someone else take care of me.

FRITZ: Yes.

JANE: I manipulate the world by always trying to hide what I'm feeling and yet still expecting people to understand. Outside of the smile, I like to imply a threat, possibly a physical violence if I don't get my way.

FRITZ: That is close also to a very famous way of manipulating called blackmail. (Perls & Baumgardner, 1975, pp. 109–110)

In a survey of 251 Gestalt and Gestalt-oriented therapists in the United States (Frew, 1988), 91 percent used groups in their practice at some time, and 98 percent considered the group an effective technique for Gestalt therapy. Few used the hot-seat pattern exclusively, in comparison with 83 percent who used a mixture of individual, interpersonal-dynamic, and whole-group focuses. Only 1 percent ranked *spectator learning* as the most important factor in group therapy. This last finding represents just one way that Gestalt psychotherapy today is different from some of Perls's original techniques.

DISCUSSION IDEAS

1. What was your reaction as you read the transcript from Perls's group? Do you understand how each member's response is an example of manipulation? Is the group different from what you have seen or learned about therapy groups before? Would you like to be a member of a Gestalt therapy group?
2. Have you ever had an insight into yourself or others from watching a counseling session of someone else, or from reading a case study? Discuss examples in class. What do you think of *spectator learning* in group therapy? Do you see any advantages of it?

Language Modification

Gestalt techniques usually include an examination of how clients' use of language reveals their world view and typical methods of avoidance. Clients are encouraged to stay in the here-and-now through the therapist's insistence on using the present tense and the word *I*. For example, if a client says, "My mother was wildly unpredictable," the Gestaltist will ask her to restate the sentence using the word *I* and bringing it into the present. "I am angry about my mother's unpredictability" might be the restatement.

Substituting language of responsibility for language of avoidance is another Gestalt tactic. Here are some substitutions that you might be asked to make if you were a Gestalt client:

- Substitute"I choose not to" for "I can't."
- Substitute "I want to" for "I have to."
- Substitute "I decide not to" for "I'm not able to."

Just think of how you would speak when making such substitutions: "I choose not to understand women (or men)," "I want to drive five children to soccer practice," and "I decided not to attend your party." Similarly, a Gestalt therapist might exhort you to add "and I take responsibility for it" after each statement about yourself: "I am depressed today, and I take responsibility for it." "I handed in my paper late, and I take responsibility for it." "I got an A in statistics, and I take responsibility for it."

Since Gestalt counselors feel comfortable with directiveness, they can ask clients to change their talk, requesting quiet talkers to speak loudly, requiring people to turn questions into statements, encouraging a tentative remark to be expressed boldly, or even ordering boring speakers to act more excited. Clients are encouraged to become aware of their habitual turns of speech, such as the kinds of metaphors they use. I had a client with dissertation-writing problems who expressed himself in sentences like "I might as well get my nose cut now, so I'll propose my topic today," "My committee ganged up on me," and "My adviser beat me up on my first chapter," showing that he saw himself as a victim of violence in the dissertation process.

R e f l e c t i o n

Choose one or more examples of language modification from the section above, and experiment with it over the course of a day. For instance, substitute "I want to . . ." the next time you hear yourself say, "I have to. . . . " Write down examples. What awareness did you gain from the exercise? Write a comment on your experiment.

Creative Process

A good summary of Gestalt techniques focuses on the creative elements they all share. Zinker (1991) lists what creative process offers:

To expand the person's repertoire of behavior.

To create conditions under which the person can see his life as his *own creation*.

To stimulate the person's experiential learning and the evolution of new self concepts from behavioral creations.

To complete unfinished situations and to overcome blockages in the awareness-contact cycle.

To integrate cortical understandings with motoric discoveries.

To discover polarizations which are not in awareness.

To stimulate the integration of conflictual forces in the personality.

To dislodge and reintegrate introjects and to generally place "misplaced" feelings, ideas, and actions where they belong in the personality.

To stimulate circumstances under which the person can feel and act stronger, more competent, more self-supported, more explorative and actively responsible for himself. (p. 74)

Uses of Gestalt Therapy

A consideration of Gestalt therapy's underlying theory predicts the type of client it has most often assisted: people who are too well socialized, rigid, subdued, and inhibited. These clients benefit from working with their polarities and integrating the selfish, wild, sexy, exhibitionist, and free sides of themselves with the surface complaisance they have cultivated so far. Gestaltists also treat anxiety and depression, though, unlike the DSM and most theories, they do not view these problems as categories of mental disorder. Depression, according to Gestalt thinking, is just a sign of unresolved anger and sadness, treatable through unfinished-business techniques. And anxiety is a sign of over-preoccupation with the unforeseeable future and the bad things it possibly holds, relieved by Gestalt emphasis on the here-and-now. Rehearsal for the future is discouraged.

Gendered Lives

Gestalt is one of the few theories that involved strong women in its development from the very beginning (publicly, that is; women have contributed to most famous psychological theories, even Freudianism, but rarely received credit until recently). The inclusion of women in theorizing may have led to Gestalt's success with problems that are associated with conventional womanhood (Sharf, 2000). Social demands for politeness, unselfishness, submissiveness, pleasantness, and compliance are more strongly felt by women: As just one example, women are often told to smile by strangers, while for men this is an unheard-of request. More deeply, women are expected to sacrifice their self-interests for their children more than men are, and women's identities are more wrapped up in their children and spouses than men's are. Women physically take care of aging parents, even their husbands' parents. They suffer keenly when children grow up and when marriages fail. These conditions create women who have denied their own leanings so often that they need awareness exercises even to identify their own desires, separate from the desires of others. They are at increased risk of low self-esteem, ineffectuality, and depression (Enns, 1987). Enns suggests a feminist version of Gestalt therapy, including "(a) creating self-definitions and owning personal power, (b) developing awareness of unexpressed anger and using it constructively, and (c) expanding personal options by incorporating behavioral alternatives that have been previously unconsidered" (p. 93).

Men also suffer from restricted sex roles and the splitting-off that fulfilling sex roles entails. Even today, a man who decides to raise children while his partner works for a paycheck is widely considered less than a man, no matter how wonderful a parent he is and no matter how little skill he has at paid pursuits. Historically, men have felt pressured to make major decisions, drive in heavy traffic, advance in income level, and be handymen, as well as to interrupt their lives and put themselves in terrible danger serving in the military. The strain of stringent standards of being a man can cause gender-role conflict and "increases in depression, anxiety, anger, substance abuse, loneliness, and other interpersonal problems" (Blazina, 2002, p. 24). These gendered polarities harm men's contact with other people and the environment, especially in the form of "a fragmented and unintegrated perspective of the world of relationships, that of our partners, and ourselves. This often includes an inability to move beyond splitting the world and significant others into artificial dichotomies of gratifying or ungratifying" (p. 27). Obviously, Gestalt therapy's focus on integration is appropriate for such problems.

Couples and Families

Many of the problems experienced by couples are within the realm of Gestalt theory, since such intimate relationships are often vexed by contact boundary disturbances, especially when complicated by sex-role demands and social expectations, as heterosexual marriage is. Some of the boundary problems Gestalt techniques investigate in couples are these:

- *Introjection.* June has been with Steve since they were in high school, and now that she's 40 years old, she automatically agrees with his opinion on everything from world politics to loud plaids. This agreement isn't just to keep the peace: June has taken on Steve's values herself.

- *Projection.* Whenever Ann is quiet and pensive, Dan treats her as though she is depressed, because that's what it means when *he* is quiet and pensive. This causes problems: Ann doesn't like to be treated like a depressed person when she's merely thinking.

- *Retroflection.* Jana chides herself for not being able to live up to Loren's fastidious demands around the house. She may be avoiding the truth that she is angry not at herself but at Loren, for being so fussy.

- *Deflection.* One or both partners may avoid touchy subjects between them by deflecting attention to something else. Many couples use their children as an outside focus that helps them remain unified (at least on one level). It may not be a problem until the children rebel or grow up.

- *Confluence.* In a close relationship, it's a virtue to feel the other partner's joys and pains. However, each person needs to maintain some separation from the other's emotional state. For example, Ken was unable to help Mary when her parents died because he was so devastated by her sadness. Similarly, the partners of depressed individuals experience difficulty in maintaining their own joys in life.

A Gestalt therapy perspective on the family "focuses on the configural patterns that structure the interactions among family members and greatly characterize the family as a unit. Such configural patterns form social Gestalten" (Lawe & Smith, 1986). In therapy, once family members have identified the patterns that govern their interactions (often driven by the contact boundary problems exemplified above), they experiment with changes in the patterns, first in therapy sessions and then at home. For example, an overbearing father might experiment with letting everyone else in the family speak before he does. You will see this therapy process again in the chapter on family systems theory.

Traumatized Clients

Almost any psychologist acknowledges that the source of current emotional problems can be past traumas, even from the distant past. Although Gestalt psychotherapists treat traumatized clients, they refuse to *explain* current problems by past traumas. Indeed, if past traumas did explain current problems well, then everyone who had experienced the same trauma would have the same current problem—and this is not true. Some people who have witnessed the horrors of war do not suffer from posttraumatic stress disorder, and some who have been abused as children, raped, injured, or imprisoned eventually regain their pretrauma level of mental health. Gestalt theory would place past trauma that is still active in the category of unfinished business. The goal of therapy is not to forget the trauma but to integrate it into a complete current self, usually not by talking *about* it but by re-experiencing it.

Holman and Silver (1998) have studied incest survivors, Vietnam veterans, and firestorm survivors, and their research findings support the Gestalt perspective: People "focused on a distressing and seemingly unresolvable past" (p. 1159) are significantly more psychologically disturbed than others with the same experiences behind them. Similarly, people able to weave the past into an integrated life story are able to live with it. Other ways of being stuck in the past are to negate or deny negative experiences, through suppression, repression, or motivated forgetting. Gestalt techniques designed to make contact with split-off aspects of the self are used in these situations.

Physical trauma, too, has psychological effects that respond to Gestalt therapy. In a study that related Gestalt principles to the psychological struggles of disabled people, Livneh and Sherwood (1991) found that the discordant poles of experience were victim versus oppressor, healthy versus sick, independent versus dependent, coping versus succumbing, and disabled versus intact. Disability disrupts homeostasis, and people with disabilities are faced with restoring equilibrium to their lives. Livneh and Sherwood suggested techniques such as role play (including empty-wheelchair), self-awareness exercises, and exaggerations to help clients come to terms with their losses.

Early, repetitive trauma in relationships with parents often underlies personality disorders, which are usually considered quite difficult to treat. Many people with borderline personality disorder, for example, had parents who failed to nurture them sufficiently, resulting in the suppressed development of their natural selves during childhood (for example, they persisted in seeking parental attention when they ordinarily would be branching out into the world). They grow up into people who have chronically troubled relationships with other people, continually seek the perfect person and continually are disappointed, and paradoxically fear and desire closeness. Greenberg (1989) explains how Gestalt therapy can address borderline features. **Splitting** occurs when a client can only see others (including the therapist) as all good or all bad, and obviously this is a polarity in Gestalt terms. **Awareness** of one's own feelings and preferences is lacking in the borderline, who needs to learn to feel and want without reference to someone else. Finally, borderline clients are often full of rage and terrified that they will let it loose and never get it back under control again. The setting of Gestalt sessions allows **experimentation** with expressing strong feelings in an atmosphere where they will have no awful repercussions.

Psychosomatic Complaints

Since Gestaltists reject the idea of a clear mind/body split, they view symptoms of psychopathology as appearing in emotion, thought, behavior, and body. Their investigation of posture, gesture, and other nonverbal features reflects this idea. Illnesses, too, are part of a client's psychological makeup. As Perls (1973) put it, "We describe a psychosomatic event as one in which the gross physical disturbances are more impressive than the ones that occur on a mental or emotional level" (p. 55). He viewed headaches, for example, as "excuses for withdrawal in thousands of cases in daily life" (p. 56), when an uninhibited person would find inner support for withdrawing in a direct fashion. Cohn (1970) provides an account of curing a 9-year-old's constant severe stomachaches using techniques of Gestalt therapy. She encouraged awareness of body and feeling by placing her hand on the girl's stomach and asking questions like "Where and how does it hurt?" "How does my hand feel?" "Is the pain usually the same, or does it get worse at times?" and "What does the pain say?"

Poor Candidates for Gestalt Practice

Gestalt therapy assists people who are limited in their enjoyment of life and out of touch with their spontaneous impulses. But what about people who love life, behave directly on impulse, and trample everyone else around them with enthusiasm? According to Shepherd (1970), such people may use Gestalt excuses for continuing to exploit others and recklessly seeking pleasure. Delinquents, sociopaths, and clients with poorly developed empathy do not need to feel more free. A Fritz-Perlsian therapist would be hard-pressed to encourage the integration of such a client's Inner Adult. Note, however, that Laura Perls and other Gestalt theorists emphasized interpersonal sensitivity and responsibility much more than Fritz did.

DISCUSSION IDEAS

One of the problems Gestalt therapists target is perfectionism. Think of some examples of perfectionist behavior. Imagining yourself as a Gestalt therapist, how would you conceptualize a client with these behaviors? In other words, what terms would you use in attempting to understand the problem? What Gestalt techniques would you consider trying? Picturing a specific perfectionist person you know will help you in this exercise.

🐾 Case Conceptualization: Two Examples

The following case conceptualizations will give you an idea of how widely Gestalt treatment can range. As you read, try to get an image of both the clients and the therapists in your mind's eye.

GESTALT THERAPY FOR EATING DISORDERS

Karen Angermann (1998)

The client, Nela, is referred by her husband. Nela eats only rice and fruit, exercises obsessively, and isolates herself from their social life. As the therapist collects information he learns Nela's "symptoms" keep her from interacting with her spouse's colleagues who all have "beautiful, pleasant wives and happy children" and [have] resulted in the loss of [her] job. These "symptoms" also keep her husband from working overtime as much as he would like, so they can have all the things they desire. Her mother is an alcoholic (on-and-off the wagon) and her father (deceased) was a workaholic. Her mother-in-law is pressuring the couple to have children "before she dies." She is 30 years old, but looks like a teenager. Nela has a younger brother, whom she was responsible for while her mother lay in drunken stupors and her father was at work. The therapist observes: Nela barely makes eye contact; her speaking voice is shallow; she answers questions as if she expects someone to correct her; her hands are tightly clasped in her lap; she appears to have every muscle tensed.

SOURCE: Excerpt from Karen Angermann (1998). "Gestalt Therapy for Eating Disorders," *Gestalt Journal*, 21, 38–45.

Such observation allows a picture, or pattern, to emerge about the client, her family, her relationships, her peer groups, her style of communicating, and the way she carries or experiences her body. If the therapist works with third-party providers, she would have to "label" the problem (i.e., give a diagnosis) and establish the methods of interventions for working with the client.

Rules and Games of Gestalt Therapy

Gestaltists are not "stuffy" people; they refer to their therapeutic techniques as rules and games. In addition to the flexibility offered by the established techniques for individual and group therapy, therapists are limited only by their own creativity in applying other interventions (which, by the way, must adhere to the theoretical underpinning of GT [Gestalt Therapy]). Below is an illustration of GT rules and games for treating eating disorders. One caveat: these techniques must be approached cautiously and with respect for the theory which guides them—haphazard application (e.g., without supervision) is ill advised.

The Rules

1. The here and now, the immediacy of moment-to-moment experience is the most potent principle in therapy. Even when the material for therapy comes from the past, it is examined, to be understood as it affects the present. The woman in the previous scenario may describe how she has played the role of caretaker of others (mother, brother). This past experience affects her "here and now experience" in that she now wants someone to take care of her.

2. The principle of "I and thou" emphasizes that communication is an interaction between sender and receiver (Levitsky and Perls, 1970). The eating disorder client does not communicate her needs. When she speaks, she does not direct herself in the direction of a receiver. This perpetuates feelings of isolation and being misunderstood. The therapist states, "To whom are you speaking" to raise awareness about the lack of direction in her self-expression. This brings awareness to how she has been avoiding contact with others.

3. Awareness in language is further emphasized by distinguishing between "I and it language." The semantic difference brings about awareness of responsibility and involvement (Levitsky and Perls, 1970). The eating disorder client refers to her body as "it" not "mine"; she refers to parts of her body by "it" or "that," not by the names of body parts. The therapist wants to bring awareness to the "it" by having the client name the body part (e.g., "my stomach feels . . ."). Additionally, this rule is applied to the expression of *should* and *have to*, e.g., "I have to exercise three hours every day. . . ." Of course the client does not have to do this! The therapist facilitates the client's awareness of choice.

4. The awareness continuum is applied in all therapeutic interventions. Awareness moves the client away from trying to answer "why" and toward "what" is experienced and "how" it is experienced. It is used to assist the clients in distinguishing between reality in their environment and the confabulations

in their heads. For eating disorder clients these dichotomies lie in how they see themselves and how they believe others see them (physically), what they think of themselves (ugly, bad, worthless), and what they assume others think of them. There is usually a stark difference between these perceptions and realities.

5. Clients are encouraged to make statements, rather than ask questions. In asking questions, the client wants information fed to her—information or answers which she already possesses, but may be too lazy or afraid to uncover for herself. The therapist asks the client to change her questions to statements. [The client's question] "How do I manage to get so wrapped-up in what others think of me?" becomes the client's statement "I am so wrapped up in what others think of me. . . ."

The Games

Gestalt games, or interventions, are abundant. In working with clients with eating disorders these interventions can serve to (a) bring awareness to how they use the eating disorder to cope with or avoid stress in their lives; (b) bring awareness to their outer world, moving food and exercise from the foreground to the background; (c) help [clients] explore the parts of [themselves that they project onto] others; (d) bring awareness to their values; (e) explore new ways of making contact and dealing with confluence, retroflection and introjections; (f) [help] clients recognize boundary violations and establish healthy boundaries; (g) [deal] with splits; (h) [use] experiments, such as art therapy, to draw out all facets of the self.

Eating disorders serve an adaptive function for clients by either helping them cope with or avoid stressors in the environment. Gestalt therapists want to uncover what adaptive function the eating disorder serves and how the client uses the eating disorder to avoid responsibility, thus maturation. Going back to Nela's case, her eating disorder symptoms may be the only way she can express her needs and defend against feelings of loneliness and inadequacy. Suppose she equates denial of her needs with the fact that she is not important, not worthy—messages from her parents which she internalized as a child. She has taken this internalization to the extreme that she no longer needs food. She is not even worthy of it. To Nela, "it is too frightening to need anyone or any thing." First, the therapist has Nela take responsibility for this statement by saying "I am too frightened. . . . " This directs awareness to what she is feeling. From this point a therapist can help Nela confront her fear by having her play a game of dialogue. Nela would be asked to dialogue with her "unworthy self." She plays both roles, the worthy self and the unworthy self, in order to confront the denied part of herself.

In another session Nela becomes aware of her anger toward her father for not taking care of her when her mother was drunk. At the same time, she feels guilty for never saying good-bye to him when he was dying in the hospital. This unfinished business can be addressed using the two-chair technique: Nela sits in one chair and faces a second, empty one where her father is imagined sitting. Nela could express her angry feelings as if she were talking with her father. She could also ask him to understand why she didn't say good-bye. This brings closure to the unfinished business, reducing, if not eliminating, its effect on Nela's present situation. . . .

Eating disorder clients deny many parts of who they are. Often these parts are projected onto other people. Playing the projection can address hidden elements of the self. Nela's case can be used as an example. Nela thinks her sister-in-law is very responsible because she is a full-time mom. Her perception of herself is that she is irresponsible, a failure because she did not protect her brother from the mother's violent outbursts. Her projection of herself as a responsible person is placed on her sister-in-law. Nela is then instructed to role-play a responsible and irresponsible person. This brings about awareness of her conflicting perceptions of herself. . . .

The manner in which our hypothetical client Nela isolates herself is an example of retroflection. She believes she cannot depend on others, so she avoids them through self-isolation. She depends on her bathroom scale to provide stability. Her self-starvation is an expression of her anger against others which she acts out on herself. A few experiential methods for dealing with retroflection with eating disorder clients are teaching meditation or yoga, self-massage, and discovering other nurturing activities the clients might enjoy, such as bubble-baths or artistic endeavors. Finally, therapists must help clients become aware of introjections learned from family, from culture (in this case, media images) and from peers. Perhaps Nela has interjected the expectations of what a good daughter should be and of what a good wife ought to be doing and not doing. The eating disorder provides a way for her to avoid dealing with these introjections: Good daughters take care of their parents and good wives have jobs, are thin, make babies and take care of the home. She has frozen her physical and emotional development so that she cannot be responsible for others and cannot work. Nela's anger at trying to be the daughter and wife she believes she should be, instead of the person she really is, is unleashed in the eating disorder. . .

Termination

There is no definitive point for termination in Gestalt therapy, The client, as much as possible, is responsible for the progress of therapy, and the therapist is the guide through the process. Primarily, it is the client's responsibility to decide to continue or to terminate therapy. Clients can use awareness of the therapeutic goals to evaluate therapy. I would add that when dealing with eating disorder clients, Gestaltists would have to be more active in determining the appropriateness of termination of therapy. It may be appropriate to bring the client to awareness of feelings behind the desire to terminate, especially when it appears premature. Therapists communicate nurturance and encourage clients to take the risk of continuing therapy so they might then leave therapy engaged in the ever-evolving process of self-actualization. (pp. 38–45)   ■ ■

GROSS EXAGGERATION WITH A SCHIZOPHRENIC PATIENT

Henry T. Close (1970)

Gross exaggeration has been used by therapists of many persuasions in communicating with their severely disturbed patients. However, this exaggeration has been used in the service of communication and has not been commented on as a specific technique in and of itself, with its own theoretical rationale. Here I would like to present an example of gross exaggeration, and suggest some theoretical points of view that would support this kind of intervention.

The patient discussed here is a twenty-four-year-old male who had dropped out of several colleges, finally suffering a severe breakdown shortly after being drafted into the army. He had recently been driving his parents to distraction by his incessant rambling and incoherent communications, which were full of bizarre sexual symbolism. Two incidents will serve to introduce him: His first appointment with me was with his parents for the evaluation interview. I asked them, "What brings you here?" The patient volunteered, "We got this letter that said to be here at 8:30." On another occasion, he and his parents walked into the office for a family interview, and he opened the conversation by saying, "Mamma told me not to say anything to open the conversation today."

After two months of outpatient therapy, the patient was hospitalized. I had seen him daily for two months preceding the following interchange, which occurred during a session in his room.

The patient reported feeling that he was a nothing and had to bend over backward to avoid offending people. He said that he was keeping his shirts in his drawer instead of hanging them up in the closet because the rattling of the coat hangers might disturb the patients in the other rooms.

T.: [*With exaggerated affect and gestures*] I certainly agree with you. I can't imagine anything worse than your disturbing the tranquility of the ward by rattling your coat hangers. After all, what right do *you* have to make all the racket?

P.: I can hear M- when he rattles his coat hangers in his room.

T.: That is different! M- is *somebody.* He has a right to make noise. You do not! You certainly don't think that you are as good as *he* is, do you? It would be terrible for *you* to make that kind of noise. You will just have to keep your shirts in the drawer.

P.: But even the drawer makes some noise when you open it and close it.

T.: By golly, you're right. I'd forgotten about that. I guess the only thing for you to do is pile your shirts over there on the floor—but don't unwrap them—the crumpling of the paper would make *way* too much noise!

P.: That's right! I remember once I unwrapped a big package, and instead of crumpling up that big piece of paper, I laid it under the bed. I did right, didn't I?

T.: You sure did. That was absolutely right. The only thing you should have done differently is to have covered it with a blanket, lest a mosquito land on it.

P.: [*Warm, spontaneous laughter.*]

T.: Look, I'll tell you one way you might be able to get your shirts hung up. If you will go out to the TV room and turn the TV up full blast, then you could dash madly back to your room before anybody turned it down, and the TV would drown out the rattling of the hangers. Or, even better than that, turn up the stereo and the TV, and make this coincide with R-'s singing [a constant nuisance on the ward], *then* dash madly back to your room. I'll bet you could get your shirts hung up before all the chaos outside subsided. No one at all would hear the coat hangers.

P.: [*Smiling warmly, starts to make some comment.*]

T.: Wait a minute. I've got another idea. If you really wanted to do this right, you could set off the *fire* alarm—that would get the staff all upset, as well as the patients, and you would have plenty of time to hang up your shirts.

P.: [*Laughs warmly.*]

T.: An even better way than that would be to turn up the stereo and the TV, get R- to start singing, and then *start* a fire in the sitting room. That would *really* cause a racket, and while everybody was running around wildly, screaming and hollering, you could be in here hanging up your shirts in complete serenity.

The patient appeared to enjoy this interaction very much. Following the interview, staff members commented that he seemed to be a bit more assertive with other people, and a few days later it was noticed that his shirts were hanging in the closet. The rationale for this kind of gross exaggeration can be made from several theoretical frameworks.

Gestalt therapy would view the patient as playing the fearful "good boy" dominated by the catastrophic expectations and *shoulds* propounded by the tyrannical top-dog. Instead of asserting himself appropriately and directing his aggression toward the outside, he directs it against himself, punishing himself to a ridiculous extent. The therapist then assumes the role of the patient's top-dog and makes explicit the internalized conversation. The patient can then come to a centering, with the extremes of self-effacement and external manipulation having been explored.

The "double-bind" theory of Bateson, Haley, and Jackson would suggest that in the past, when the patient has tried to assert himself, he has been placed in a position where he cannot win. The therapist places the patient in another double-bind, whose significant instructions go: (1) Display no aggression; make no noise (with coat hangers). (2) Display much aggression; make much noise (setting fire to the lobby). (3) Do not take any of this literally; do not obey me. (4) Recognize that all of this is sarcasm. The exaggeration of the therapist makes it impossible for the patient to avoid recognizing this as an impossible message, which can be responded to with pleasure and humor rather than anxiety.

Finally, regardless of other reasons, the use of gross exaggeration is fun and can be an opportunity for warm interaction and enjoyment between patient and therapist. (pp. 194–196) ■ ■

DISCUSSION IDEAS

The cases you have just read involved Gestalt treatment for an eating disorder and for symptoms of schizophrenia. The following questions will help you analyze the cases for yourself.

1. How are nonverbal communications understood and used in each case?
2. List the Gestalt concepts used by each therapist in understanding the client.
3. List the Gestalt techniques used by each therapist. What is the goal of each of these techniques?
4. Name some differences between the two case conceptualizations and treatments. How is each one tailored to the specific client and problem?
5. If you read these cases with all references to *Gestalt* removed, would you know anyway that they were examples of Gestalt therapy? Why or why not?
6. Discuss how psychodynamic, Adlerian, existential, and humanist therapists might work with one of these clients. What similarities might you see among all conceptualizations and treatments?
7. Were there any elements of the case conceptualizations or treatments that you would not endorse? If so, explain why.

Critiques of Gestalt Therapy

Gestalt therapy ignites enthusiasm in both its supporters and detractors. Consider some of the detracting points of view.

Perls's Pervasive Personality

Many of the harshest criticisms of Gestalt psychotherapy are aimed at Fritz Perls himself. Perls was flamboyantly narcissistic and loved to shock people. He also relished an audience; in particular, he loved to have a cultish group of admirers, which he gathered at Esalen in the 1960s. He violated some of our deeply held taboos—for example, falling asleep in sessions and having sex with clients, two ends on a spectrum of inappropriate behaviors.

You need to realize that Perls's personality is not Gestalt psychotherapy. Though some followers imitate Perls's outrageous style, many do not, and even many of his contemporaries acted more unselfishly and thoughtfully. Laura Perls always took a stance of greater sensitivity to others than Fritz did. Still, the therapy is marred by practitioners who adopt its techniques and a Fritz-Perlsian style without theory or follow-through.

Individualism and Cultural Limits

As Perls taught it and demonstrated it, Gestalt therapy was notably individualistic, in contrast with cooperative or collectivist. Many critics see selfishness and cruelty in this individualism. Perls wrote and promoted the Gestalt Prayer in the 1960s, which was widely quoted, printed on posters popular in hippie emporiums of the time, and actually used in marriage ceremonies:

> I do my thing and you do your thing.
> I am not in this world to live up to your expectations
> And you are not in this world to live up to mine,
> You are you and I am I,
> If by chance we find each other, it's beautiful.
> If not, it can't be helped.

In each line, you can find a denial of human interrelatedness—you have to wonder how long the marriages lasted that took this formula seriously. More than a decade ago, Saner (1989) noted that "Fritz Perls' notorious Gestalt prayer is a statement of the world reflection of his personal attitude towards life and of his American years in particular" (p. 59); like him, many people find Gestalt's individualism bound to the culture of affluent White American males and thus irrelevant to the lives of most people on the planet. As Shepherd (1970) puts it, "Relationships may too often be viewed as projections and as clearly secondary in importance to internal happenings, and the marked influence of family and other external pressures and difficulties may be ignored. The emphasis on the patient himself as being solely in possession of the key to his own destiny and happiness can distort the realities of everyday existence" (p. 238).

In some Gestalt practices, this stance makes the theory inadequate for dealing with clients who value interrelatedness over individuality. However, in another mode of practicing, the same viewpoint can be helpful. A Gestalt counselor dedicated to having the client be the source of interpretations and perceptions is less likely to inflict his or her own cultural values. And a focus on integrating polarities can assist clients who feel split between the demands of two cultures, as so many of our citizens are today. In one case, for example, a Mexican family encouraged their daughter to enter college with a helping-profession goal, and she never identified her unhappiness at school until her career counselor brought to her attention the fact that her skills and interest inventories all pointed to a math profession. In the same way, the few people from my working-class city who went to college had to balance their professional-class aspirations with the skeptical attitude (or total mystification) of their families at home. "How long can you *stay* in college, anyway?" the father of a Ph.D. candidate once asked.

Anti-Intellectualism

A strong streak of anti-intellectualism (also alive and well in American culture) runs through Perls's writing. "I object to any explanatoriness as being a means of intellectualizing and preventing understanding," Perls wrote in his auto-biography, *In and Out the Garbage Pail* (1969b, n.p.). Intellectualizing, in Perls's conception, was *always* a defense mechanism designed to avoid experiencing the truth. In most psychological theories, by contrast, intellectualization has this function only in certain circumstances. Spurning intellectuality, Perls often produced prose like "The intellect is the whore of intelligence. It's a drag on your life" (1969a, p. 71). Such sentences are certainly beyond rational parsing. Statements and actions insulting to academics alienate many psychologists from Gestaltism. Most of us treasure rationality and the scientific method just as much as emotions and sensuality. Clients from backgrounds that prize the intellect, such as traditional Jewish culture, will not respond well to an anti-intellectual approach.

Philosophical Sloppiness

In the introduction to this chapter, I explained how Gestalt psychologists hate to be confused with Gestalt psychotherapists. In feeling that some pieces of their theory were cannibalized by Gestalt psychotherapy and other important elements discarded, the Gestalt psychologists are joined by Freudians, Adlerians, existentialists, and Zen Buddhists. Many theorists perceive Gestalt as having cobbled together a theory to justify a set of practices; this cobbling is a *pragmatic* approach. As Saner (1989) points out, however, "The pragmatic approach of combining several different theories into a new theoretical body of thought without original research represents a possible pitfall. The pragmatic synthesizers generated exciting new insights but succumbed also to blind spots due to their own psychological pre-dispositions and preferences" (Saner, 1989, p. 61).

This potluck nature of Gestalt psychotherapy probably explains the small number of professionals who espouse it as their major theory. When Prochaska and Norcross (1999) reviewed surveys of over 1,000 psychologists, psychiatrists, counselors, and social workers from several representative studies, they found that only 1–2 percent named Gestalt as their primary affinity. The same review revealed that 27–53 percent of the practitioners identified themselves as eclectic (mixed), while a different survey found that among eclecticists, 23 percent listed Gestalt as among their top four approaches (Sharf, 2000). Therefore, Gestalt is much more often used as part of a mixed therapeutic approach than by itself. In fact, Gestalt *techniques* are what you will see most often practiced, taught, and discussed—not the theory of Gestalt therapy.

KEY TERMS

awareness	impasse	projection
confluence	introjection	psychodrama
contact	layers of neuroses:	retroflection
deflection	phony, phobic,	role playing
disowning	impasse, implosive,	shoulds
dream work	explosive	spectator learning
experimentation	neurotic self-regulation	splitting
figure	organismic self-	support
Gestalt	regulation	top-dog
ground	paradoxical theory of	under-dog
homeostasis	change	unfinished business
hot seat	polarities	

Exploring Key Terms

Individually, take the role of a Gestalt psychotherapist, and write a case conceptualization of a character or couple on television or film. (Think of Homer and Marge Simpson, James Bond, Jerry Seinfeld, or a soap opera couple.) Also write a plan for what techniques you will use to treat your client(s). Use at least fifteen of the key terms accurately and in a meaningful context.

In your small group, exchange your writings and discuss them. Make improvements so that the meanings of the key terms are clear and distinct. Mark key terms that were not used by anyone in the group and discuss their meanings. Copy your writings for the whole class or distribute them electronically so everyone can use them in studying.

LIBRARY, MEDIA, AND INTERNET ACTIVITIES

1. Surf websites devoted to Gestalt psychotherapy:

www.Gestalt.org provides articles, interviews with major figures in Gestalt, photographs of Esalen and Perls, radio shows made from Esalen in the '60s, lists of reading material, and so on.

www.Gestaltassociates.com will give you a view of how you can get advanced training in Gestalt therapy.

www.aagt.org is the website of the Association for Advancement of Gestalt Therapy. It includes a section called "About Gestalt Therapy," which summarizes major topics you studied in this chapter.

www.enabling.org/ia/Gestalt provides links to Gestalt associations and institutes worldwide.

2. *Gestalt Therapy Verbatim* and *In and Out the Garbage Pail* (both published in 1969) are books that give you a sense of Perls's voice and style. *Verbatim* includes many transcripts of actual sessions with Perls. *In and Out* lets you follow Perls's train of thought, both in prose and in his drawings and poems. Read twenty-five to fifty pages of one of these books and report your impressions.

3. Choose a Gestalt technique (such as psychodrama) or theoretical term (such as awareness) that interests you. Using *Psychological Abstracts* or a psychological science database like *PsycInfo,* find five journal articles on this technique or term. Periodicals devoted to Gestalt theory include *The Gestalt Journal, Gestalt Review, Gestalt! (an ejournal), British Gestalt Journal,* and *Australian Gestalt Journal.* Write a summary that pulls together three of the five articles.

4. Appendix B of Fagan and Shepherd's *Gestalt Therapy Now* (published in 1970, but still easily found in libraries) lists many audiotapes and films of Gestalt therapy sessions, workshops, and demonstrations. A 1969 movie directed by Paul Mazursky, *Bob & Carol & Ted & Alice,* poked fun at trendy Gestalt group therapy. Consult with your librarian about how you could find these items today. If possible, listen to or view a sample.

REFERENCES

Angermann, K. (1998). Gestalt therapy for eating disorders: An illustration. *Gestalt Journal, 21,* 19–47.

Beisser, A. (1970). The paradoxical theory of change. In J. Fagan & I. L. Shepherd (Eds.), *Gestalt therapy now* (pp. 77–80). New York: Harper & Row.

Blazina, C. (2002). The fragile masculine self model: Implications for clinical use. *Texas Psychologist, 52*(3), 24–27.

Brunink, S. A., & Schroeder, H. E. (1979). Verbal therapeutic behavior of expert psychoanalytically oriented, Gestalt, and behavior therapists. *Journal of Consulting and Clinical Psychology, 47,* 567–574.

Clarke, K. M., & Greenberg, L. S. (1986). Differential effects of the Gestalt two-chair intervention and problem solving in resolving decisional conflict. *Journal of Counseling Psychology, 33,* 11–15.

Clarkson, P., & Mackewn, J. (1993). *Fritz Perls.* London: Sage.

Close, H. T. (1970). Gross exaggeration with a schizophrenic patient. In J. Fagan & I. L. Shepherd (Eds.), *Gestalt therapy now* (pp. 194–196). New York: Harper & Row.

Cohn, R. C. (1970). A child with a stomachache: Fusion of psychoanalytic concepts and Gestalt techniques. In J. Fagan & I. L. Shepherd (Eds.), *Gestalt therapy now* (pp. 197–203). New York: Harper & Row.

Cummings, E. E. (1972). *Complete poems 1913–1962.* San Diego: Harcourt Brace Jovanovich.

Enns, C. Z. (1987). Gestalt therapy and feminist therapy: A proposed integration. *Journal of Counseling and Development, 66,* 93–95.

Fagan, J., & Shepherd, I. L. (1970). *Gestalt therapy now.* New York: Harper & Row.

Frew, J. (1988). The practice of Gestalt therapy in groups. *Gestalt Journal, 11,* 77–96.

Greenberg, E. (1989). Healing the borderline. *Gestalt Journal, 12,* 11–56.

Greenberg, L. S. (1979). Resolving splits: Use of the two-chair technique. *Psychotherapy: Theory, Research, and Practice, 16,* 316–324.

Greenberg, L. S. (1980). The intensive analysis of recurring events from the practice of Gestalt therapy. *Psychotherapy: Theory, Research, and Practice, 17,* 143–152.

Greenberg, L. S. (1983). Toward a task analysis of conflict resolution in Gestalt therapy. *Psychotherapy: Theory, Research, and Practice, 20,* 190–201.

Greenberg, L. S. (1991). Research in the process of change. *Psychotherapy Research, 1,* 3–16.

Greenberg., L. S., Rice, L. N., & Elliott, R. (1993). *Facilitating emotional change: The moment-by-moment process.* New York: Guilford.

Henle, M. (1978). Gestalt psychology and Gestalt therapy. *Journal of the History of the Behavioral Sciences, 14,* 23–32.

Holman, E. A., & Silver, R. C. (1998). Getting "stuck" in the past: Temporal orientation and coping with trauma. *Journal of Personality and Social Psychology, 74,* 1146–1163.

Humphrey, K. (1986). Laura Perls: A biographical sketch. *Gestalt Journal, 10,* 5–11.

Korb, M. P., Gorrell, J., & Van de Riet, V. (1989). *Gestalt therapy: Practice and theory* (2nd ed.). Boston: Allyn and Bacon.

Lawe, C. F., & Smith, E. W. (1986). Gestalt processes and family therapy. *Individual psychology, 42,* 537–544.

Levitsky, A., & Perls, F. S. (1970). The rules and games of therapy. In J. Fagan & I. L. Shepherd (Eds.), *Gestalt therapy now* (pp. 140–149). New York: Harper & Row.

Livneh, H., & Sherwood, A. (1991). Application of personality theories and counseling strategies to clients with physical disabilities. *Journal of Counseling and Development, 69,* 525–538.

Moreno, J. L. (1972). *Psychodrama* (4th ed.). Beacon, NY: Beacon House. (Original work published 1946)

Paivio, S. C., & Greenberg, L. S. (1995). Resolving "unfinished business": Efficacy of experiential therapy using empty-chair dialogue. *Journal of Consulting and Clinical Psychology, 63,* 419–425.

Perls, F. (1947). *Ego, hunger and aggression.* London: Allen & Unwin.

Perls, F. (1969a). *Gestalt therapy verbatim.* Lafayette, CA: Real People Press.

Perls, F. (1969b). *In and out the garbage pail.* Lafayette, CA: Real People Press.

Perls, F. (1970). Four lectures. In J. Fagan & I. L. Shepherd (Eds.), *Gestalt therapy now* (pp. 14–38). New York: Harper & Row.

Perls, F. (1973). *The Gestalt approach and eyewitness to therapy.* Palo Alto, CA: Science & Behavior Books.

Perls, F., & Baumgardner, P. (1975). *Gifts from Lake Cowichan and Legacy from Fritz.* Palo Alto, CA: Science and Behavior Books.

Perls, F., Hefferline, R. F., & Goodman, P. (1951). *Gestalt therapy: Excitement and growth in the human personality.* New York: Julian Press.

Polster, M. (1987). Gestalt therapy: Evolution and application. In J. K. Zeig (Ed.), *The evolution of psychotherapy* (pp. 312–325). New York: Brunner/Mazel.

Prochaska, J. O., & Norcross, J. C. (1999). *Systems of psychotherapy: A transtheoretical analysis* (4th ed.). Pacific Grove, CA: Brooks/Cole.

Saner, R. (1989). Cultural bias of Gestalt therapy. *Gestalt Journal, 12,* 161–171.

Sharf, R. S. (2000). *Theories of psychotherapy and counseling* (2nd ed.). Belmont, CA: Brooks/Cole.

Shepherd, I. L. (1970). Limitations and cautions in the Gestalt approach. In J. Fagan & I. L. Shepherd (Eds.), *Gestalt therapy now* (pp. 234–238). New York: Harper & Row.

Sherrill, R. E. (1986). Gestalt therapy and Gestalt psychology. *Gestalt Journal, 9,* 53–66.

Wulf, R. (1998). The historical roots of Gestalt therapy. *Gestalt Journal, 21,* 81–93.

Yontef, G., & Jacobs, L. (2000). Gestalt therapy. In R. J. Corsini & D. Wedding, (Eds.), *Current psychotherapies* (6th ed., pp. 303–339). Itasca, IL: F. E. Peacock Publishers.

Zinker, J. (1991). Creative process in Gestalt therapy. *Gestalt Journal, 14,* 71–88.

CHAPTER **8**

Behavioral Therapies

A Selection from

"How to Discover What You Have to Say—
A Talk to Students," 1981

B. F. Skinner

My title will serve as an outline. It begins with "How to," and this is a "How to" talk. It is about a problem we all face, and the solution I propose is an example about verbal self-management, using my *Verbal Behavior* (1957) as the basis of a technology. At issue is how we can manage our own verbal behavior more effectively.

Verbal behavior begins almost always in spoken forms. Even when we write, we usually speak first, either overtly or covertly. What goes down on paper is then a kind of self-dictation. I am concerned here only with written behavior and even so with only a special kind, the kind of writing at the heart of a paper, a thesis, or a book in a field such as the analysis of behavior. What such writing is "about" is hard to say—indeed, that is just the problem. Certain complex circumstances call for verbal action. You have a sheet of paper and a pen; what happens next? How do you arrive at the best possible account?

I argue that thinking is simply behaving, and it may not be too misleading to say that verbal responses do not express ideas but are the ideas themselves. They are what "occur to us" as we consider a set of circumstances.

It is hard to give a "how to" talk without posing as an authority. I hasten to say that I know that I could write better than I do, but I also know that I could write worse. Over the years I believe I have analyzed my verbal behavior to my advantage. What distresses me is that I should have done so so late. Possibly some of what I have learned may help you at an earlier age.

The next word in my title is "discover." If it suggests that verbal behavior lurks inside us waiting to be uncovered, it is a bad term. We do not really "search our memory" for forgotten names. Verbal behavior, like all behavior, is not inside the speaker or writer before it appears. True, I have argued that most behavior is *emitted* rather than elicited as in a reflex, but we also say that light is emitted from a hot filament, although it was not *in* the filament in the form of light.

A first step is to put yourself in the best possible condition for behaving verbally. La Mettrie thought he had supporting evidence for his contention that man was a machine in the fact that he could not think clearly when he was ill. (Freud on the other hand said that he could write only when experiencing a certain discomfort.) Certainly many writers have testified to the importance of diet, exercise, and rest. Descartes, one of the heroes of psychology, said that he slept ten hours every night and "never employed more than a few hours a year at those thoughts which engage the understanding. . . . I have consecrated all the rest of my life to relaxation and rest." Good physical condition is relevant to all kinds of effective behavior but particularly to that subtle form we call verbal.

Imagine that you are to play a piano concerto tomorrow night with a symphony orchestra. What will you do between now and then? You will get to bed early for a good night's rest. Tomorrow morning you may practice a little but not too much. During the day you will eat lightly, take a nap, and in other ways try to put yourself in the best possible condition for your performance in the evening.

Thinking effectively about a complex set of circumstances is more demanding than playing a piano, yet how often do your prepare yourself to do so in a similar way? Too often you sit down to think after everything else has been done. You are encouraged to do so by the cognitive metaphor of thinking as the expression of ideas. The ideas are there; the writer is simply a reporter.

So much for the condition of your body. Equally important are the conditions in which the behavior occurs. A convenient place is important. It should have all the facilities needed for the execution of writing: pens, typewriters, recorders, files, books, a comfortable desk and chair. It should be a pleasant place and smell good. Your clothing should be comfortable. Since the place is to take control of a particular kind of behavior, you should do nothing else there at any time.

It is helpful to write always at the same time of day. Scheduled obligations often raise problems, but an hour or two can almost always be found in the early morning—when the telephone never rings and no one knocks at the door. And it is important that you write something, regardless of quantity, every day. As the Romans put it, *Nulla dies sine linea*—No day without a line. (They were speaking of lines drawn by artists, but the rule applies as well to the writer.)

As a result of all this, the setting almost automatically evokes verbal behavior. No warmup is needed. A circadian rhythm develops which is extremely powerful. At a certain time every day, you will be highly disposed to engage in serious verbal behavior. You will find evidence of this when traveling to other time zones, when a strong tendency to engage in serious verbal behavior appears at the usual time, though it is now a different time by the clock.

It may be a mistake to try to do too much at first. Such a situation only slowly acquires control. It is enough to begin with short sessions, perhaps 15 minutes a day. And do not look for instant quality. Stendhal once remarked, "If when I was young I had been willing to talk about wanting to be a writer, some sensible person might have said to me: 'Write for two hours every day, genius or not.' That would have saved ten years of my life, stupidly wasted in waiting to become a genius."

Verbal behavior may occur to you at other times of day, and it is important to put it down in lasting form. A notebook or a pocket recorder is a kind of portable study. Something you see, hear, or read sets off something relevant, and you must catch it on the wing. Jotting down a brief reminder to develop the point later is seldom enough, because the conditions under which it occurred to you are the best conditions for writing a further account. A longer note written at the time will often develop into something that would be lost if the writing were postponed.

When you construct the best possible conditions for the production of verbal behavior and have provided for catching occasional verbal responses on the wing, you are often *surprised* by what turns up. There is no way in which you can see all of your verbal behavior before you emit it.

I am not talking about how to *find* something to say. The easiest way to do that is to collect experiences, as by moving about in the world and by reading and listening to what others say. A college education is largely a process of collecting in that sense. And so, of course, is exploration, research, and a full exposure to daily life.

Many famous writers have worked mostly under aversive pressure. Balzac wrote only when he needed money, Dostoevski only in return for advances he had received. Aversive control may keep you at work, but what you write will be traceable to other variables if it is any good. Moreover, it is under such conditions that writers report that writing is hell, and if you write primarily to avoid the consequences of not writing, you may find it hard to resist other forms of escape—stopping to get a cup of coffee, needlessly rereading something already written, sharpening pencils, calling it a day.

There may be an aversive element in maintaining the schedule which builds a circadian rhythm. It is not always easy to get up at five o'clock in the morning and start writing. Even though you make the space in which you work so attractive that it reinforces your behavior in going to it, some aversive control may be needed. But other variables must take over if anything worthwhile is written. Positive reinforcement may be as irresistible as negative, but it is more likely to lead you to say what you have to say effectively.

Some kind of record of the number of words or pages you write may act as a reinforcing consequence. For years, an electric clock on my desk ran only when the light was on, and I added a point to a cumulative record whenever the clock completed twelve hours. The slope of the curve showed me how much time I was spending each day. A simple calculation reinforces that reinforcer. Suppose you are at your desk two hours a day and produce on the average 50 words per hour. That is not much, but it is about 35,000 words a year, and a book every two or three years—which I myself have found reinforcing enough.

Other immediate consequences are more effective in discovering what you have to say. Saying something for the first time that surprises you, clearing up a confusing point, enjoying what you have written as you read it over—these are the things which, in the long run, are most likely to produce verbal behavior which is your own. The best reason for liking what you have written is that it says what *you* have to say. (pp. 1–5). ■ ■

DISCUSSION IDEAS

1. What did you know about B. F. Skinner before you read the passage above? For example, what do you know about his work in psychology? Did anything about the passage from his talk surprise you? Did anything fit in with what you already knew about Skinner?

2. When you talk about someone's behavior, what do you usually mean? "I didn't like my boyfriend's behavior at my family reunion," for instance— what does the speaker probably mean? Is the idea of speech and writing as *verbal behavior* unusual to you?

3. Explain the example of the filament and the light. How is it a metaphor for verbal behavior? That is, in the comparison, what is the filament and what is the light?

4. What is a circadian rhythm? Why is it important to establish such a rhythm for writing?

5. Do you recognize the psychologists and writers referred to by name in Skinner's talk? What do you think the references to these people show about B. F. Skinner?

6. What is aversive control? Why is it not a very good motivator for writing?

7. What conditions for writing are under your control, according to Skinner? Do you already practice some of Skinner's recommendations? How are the conditions for writing fiction, poetry, or personal letters different from those for writing school papers or work-related reports?

8. Think of some other tasks and duties that Skinner's advice applies to. How do you control the conditions under which you engage in these activities? For example, do you set a schedule or use rewards and consequences?

An Introduction to Behavioral Therapy

Are people who avoid writing mentally ill? Are procrastinators abnormal? Of course not! But they can still use the kind of help that Skinner describes in the excerpt above. They can learn to perform writing tasks more skillfully, easily, and comfortably. Behavioral therapy (also called behavior therapy) applies to life's demands in a broad way because it is based on **learning theory.**

Learning Theory

Sometimes what we learn serves us well, but at other times we learn things that hold us back from our best performance and our most fulfilling relationships. For example, in my work with blocked writers, I've found that somewhere they learned that each sentence should be perfected before they move on to the next one. This misleads them in several ways. For one thing, they lose track of what they were trying to say while they decide whether to use a comma or not. Besides that, their progress is so slow that they are plagued with worry about ever finishing, at the same time as they are trying to write, so their energies are divided between worrying and writing. If they can *un-learn* this stop-and-fix behavior, they can become more productive and better writers.

In short, there's a *behavior* that needs to be changed—and in behavioral therapy, that is the focus. It's based on learning theory, not personality theory or psychopathology theory. Maladaptive and adaptive behaviors are learned the same way, through reward and punishment (and related processes). The same teacher who rewarded perfect punctuation may have ignored or punished creative thoughts. A paper marked up in red to indicate errors teaches a young writer to focus on correctness. I see adult writers who have learned this lesson so well that they are paralyzed until they're sure that every sentence is free of errors.

Notice that I said "somewhere they learned that each sentence should be perfected." When I act as a behavior therapist, where and when and why they learned this is not the main issue. If I were acting as a psychodynamic therapist, I'd investigate the family roots of this internal demand for perfection. (In fact, all the severely blocked writers I have met bring up their demanding fathers.) But for a behaviorist, delving into history is a means to an end, not an end in itself. The historical antecedents can be helpful in understanding what keeps the problematic behavior going currently, today. Yet we don't always need to know the origins of a problem in order to change it. Systematically changing the consequences of a behavior can alter it, and learning a substitute behavior can replace it.

The rules of behavior apply to

- improving an already good life (becoming more productive at work, supporting your children's interests, enjoying sex more),
- getting rid of a bothersome habit (procrastinating, biting your nails, overeating), and
- short-circuiting serious problems (urges to steal, throwing tantrums, alcoholism, phobias).

In this chapter, I will ask you to apply behavioral change principles to a habit or problem of your own. You'll find that you have been applying these principles to your own and others' lives for a long time. Perhaps you've promised yourself a treat like a snack or a session of e-mailing after you've studied a certain amount. Or if you've cared for children, you may have used Time Out to interrupt and control bad behavior. In both of these cases, you controlled what *followed* a behavior. Skinner suggested controlling what *precedes* a behavior, like creating a comfy setting for writing and carrying a notebook all the time. Finally, you have probably chosen to hang around people who succeed in meeting goals like yours; for instance, being in a social group with good study habits enhances your own academic behavior. This social component of behavior control is called *modeling*, because you look at other people as models to imitate. Notice again that regulating the preceding, following, and social contexts of behavior can occur without an analysis of the history behind why you act in certain ways.

DISCUSSION IDEAS

Think of other behavioral control examples from everyday life. If you are an athlete or musician, you use the principles of controlling what precedes and follows practice. If you are a parent, you manipulate rewards and punishments to influence your children's behavior. We all imitate other people who seem to be carrying off some task we wish to master.

Behavior, Emotion, and Cognition

Actions, feelings, and thoughts are all interrelated. Being depressed is certainly a feeling, but it involves negative thinking and a lack of energy for action. On the brighter side, love is an emotion tied to positive thinking and boundless energy. The interaction of behavior, emotion, and cognition presents a problem for theorists like me who want to distinguish between behavioral therapy (Chapter 8, which you are reading now) and cognitive-behavioral therapy (Chapter 9). The dividing line isn't really clear; for that matter, most behaviorist practitioners use cognitive psychology. I have collected into Chapter 8 theories and techniques that come into play when the client's main complaint is a behavior or set of behaviors that needs to be changed, while for Chapter 9 I have collected theories and techniques that focus on more global complaints involving combinations of emotions, thoughts, and behaviors. So, a couple who comes to therapy saying that they argue too much and don't have enough sex would be a Chapter 8 couple, while a couple who comes in saying that the love and joy has gone out of their lives would be a Chapter 9 couple.

Essential Concepts in Behavioral Therapy

The fundamental terminology of behavioral therapy will be familiar to you if you've studied educational psychology. You will recognize most of the concepts from everyday life experiences like raising children and training pets.

Classical Conditioning

At the dawn of the twentieth century, the physiologist Ivan Pavlov in Russia first described **classical conditioning.** In his work with the digestive processes of dogs, Pavlov discovered that a light caused dogs to salivate if the light had repeatedly indicated they were about to be fed. Even when no food was presented, eventually the light brought about the same response as food did.

Pavlov's work was parallel to that of John B. Watson, an American psychologist who is called the father of behaviorism. Watson believed that our history of learning, not genetics or instinct, makes us what we are—a radical position for the time. He also believed that psychologists could discover what stimuli predict what responses in individuals, with **stimulus** meaning an outer or inner condition, and **response** meaning anything a person did. Watson eventually became wildly successful in the advertising business by applying these principles.

He realized that people buy a product not only because of its performance but also because of the other stimuli associated with it, and so he manipulated the images connected to each brand name.

In Pavlov's laboratory, it became clear that the stimulus-response pattern could be changed once established. A bell could become associated with feeding and eventually call forth salivation in dogs, but when the bell kept ringing with no presentation of food, it stopped calling forth salivation. This process is called **extinction.** The response is extinguished; it disappears. My friend Mark was raising three small children on public aid, and he felt bad when they begged to stop for fast food whenever they saw the golden arches. He simply could no longer afford to treat them. However, he said that after about three months of his driving right on by, the children stopped their begging for fast food completely. That is, when the stimulus of the golden arches no longer meant the possibility of treats, the response of begging underwent *extinction.*

Unfortunately, extinction sometimes happens to positive behaviors. Behavioral principles don't work according to values automatically, so the parents who are glad to leave their child alone while she plays quietly by herself may accidentally be extinguishing such activity by ignoring it (withdrawing attention, contact, and praise). This is why child psychology specialists Christophersen and Mortweet (2001) advise parents to express their love and approval with brief, frequent nonverbal physical contact whenever the child is doing something right: one to two seconds at least fifty times a day.

R e f l e c t i o n

Think about Watson's assertion that we buy products based on images associated with them, not on their relative performance. Peruse magazine or television advertisements and list what images are associated with products to make them attractive. Sometimes the images are not even relevant or realistic: A popular wine commercial on television these days associates wine drinking with slenderness and athletic skill.

Operant Conditioning

In the early twentieth century in the United States, psychologist Edward Thorndike (1911) investigated how behavior is changed by what comes after it, a process called **operant conditioning** or *instrumental conditioning.* (A *stimulus* comes before a behavior, while a *reinforcer* comes after it.) Thorndike experimented with cats, who were rewarded with escape and a fish treat (*reinforcers*) when they learned to open their cage doors. Each time a cat made an escape, the next escape trick was learned more quickly. With these and other animal experiments, Thorndike developed two laws of learning. One, the **law of exercise,** says that the more often a connection between a behavior and its consequence is made, the stronger the connection becomes (and, conversely, with disuse the connection becomes weaker). The **law of effect** says that if a connection is followed by a "satisfying state of affairs" it will be strengthened (and, conversely, if it is followed by an "annoying state of affairs" it will be weakened). So, the more often Mark stopped when his children whined and begged, the stronger the connection became between seeing the fast-food sign, begging, and the satisfying state of getting treats.

Beginning in the 1930s, B. F. Skinner followed in Thorndike's footsteps with animal research on operant conditioning. Skinner eventually applied learning principles to the behavior of humans, in addition to that of animals, as you saw in the opening passage of this chapter. (Thorndike also went on to apply the psychology of learning to humans and made many suggestions for changing the educational system.) However, Skinner avoided referring to inner states like "satisfying" and "annoying" because they were not observable. He used the word **reinforcement** to apply to anything that changed the frequency of a response. So *reinforcers* increase the likelihood of a response, and *punishments* decrease the likelihood of a response. Among reinforcers, moreover, there are *positive reinforcers* such as treats, money, and praise and *negative reinforcers* such as relief from pain or distress. Notice that both types of reinforcement make behavior *more likely*. Thus, for example, you may wear your new sunglasses because you get relief from glare in your eyes (**negative reinforcement**), because you get compliments on them (**positive reinforcement**), and because you fear early wrinkles (**punishment** for *not* wearing them).

Skinner focused on reinforcement as a learning tool, since punishment involves many negative by-products unless it is given under extremely restrictive conditions, which I will outline later on. A key concept of reinforcement theory is **contingency,** which means that a reinforcement must occur after a certain, identifiable response, not just any response. In other words, the reinforcement is contingent upon the behavior. Reward alone does not work—this is the principle behind giving salespeople commissions. If each salesperson got the same paycheck no matter what, you can imagine that some would not work very hard. (Others would—because reinforcers other than pay motivated them.) As a busy student, you can understand contingency well. If you are taking four classes, and you are guaranteed an A in one of them, and your study time is limited, you're most likely to study for the other courses, where your grade is dependent, or *contingent*, upon your studying.

According to Skinner (1974), how much you repeat a behavior depends on more than just the nature of the reinforcer. It depends on the **schedule of reinforcement.** If you are rewarded every single time you perform a particular behavior, you will probably learn it fast. On the other hand, as soon as rewards stop coming, you will cut back on the behavior. The behavior will be extinguished through lack of reward. If Skinner's pigeons got a food pellet every time they pecked a bar, they stopped pecking soon after the pellets stopped coming. Most of us don't learn through continuous reinforcement, though. We learn through intermittent reinforcement—sometimes we get the reward, and sometimes we don't. So, before Mark completely stopped visiting fast-food joints, sometimes his children got rewarded and sometimes they didn't. Therefore, it took many, many unfruitful sightings of the golden arches before the children disconnected the stimulus from the possibility of treats. Behavior created by intermittent reinforcement is more difficult to extinguish than that created by continuous reinforcement. This principle is what keeps people gambling even though they lose much more often than they win. Much foolish or useless behavior that mysteriously continues has probably been intermittently reinforced. If you once had a boyfriend or girlfriend too long, and now wonder why you kept the relationship going, consider whether you were getting intermittent reinforcement.

In the 1950s, John Dollard and Neil Miller (1950) continued learning theory explorations of human behavior. They were interested in extending psychoanalytic theory by investigating neuroses as products of experience (not only of instincts). If neuroses come from experience, they must follow laws of learning (Patterson, 1980). Like Skinner, Dollard and Miller perceived that cues evoke responses, and responses are strengthened under certain conditions. Furthermore, they studied **counterconditioning,** in which the cue-response relation is reversed. For example, enough pleasant experiences (or lack of unpleasant ones) after a cue can make you change your previously negative response to the cue. While training as a psychologist, I was happy to get a practicum assignment in the rehabilitation unit at a big hospital; however, the first day I went to work there, I began to sweat and feel queasy on the elevator. My previous experience in a hospital had involved the extended and useless treatment of a family member on the cancer ward, and the smells and sights of the second hospital brought my earlier feelings back strongly. I was afraid I would not be able to continue my practicum because I felt so terrible, but I persisted. On the fourth day of work, I strolled into the hospital without a single bad reaction. The counterconditioning provided by my absorbing practicum work and my humorous boss had completely overcome my old responses.

DISCUSSION IDEAS

Your experience in school provides you with examples of learning theory in practice, for both the better and the worse. Did you ever experience counterconditioning by being turned on to a subject you previously disliked, or being turned off to a subject you previously liked? Describe how this happened. Also think about what kinds of positive and negative reinforcers are given to grade school children. Do you remember your responses to the reinforcements and punishments from grade school? Exchange some stories that demonstrate how learning theory works.

Profile of a Theorist

B. F. SKINNER (1904–1986)

Burrhus Frederick Skinner has often been hailed as one of the most influential psychologists of the twentieth century. He was born in 1904 in the small Pennsylvania railroad town of Susquehanna, where his parents and grandparents had lived for two generations. Fred, as he was called by those who knew him, was the older of two sons. In his youth, he was known to be intellectually astute and not one to shrink from challenging teachers and authorities with whom he differed. By the time he graduated from high school, he had developed a strong desire to write as well as a knack for creating and building gadgets and small machines. This skill for building foreshadowed his breakthrough inventions in the field of experimental psychology.

Following graduation from high school, Fred left home in search of greater intellectual challenge and freedom from the restrictions of the tight-knit community of Susquehanna. He attended Hamilton College in Clinton, New York, but soon found the qualities that made him an exception at home were commonplace in this small liberal arts school.

While Fred was visiting home in the spring of 1923, his younger brother Edward died suddenly, leaving Fred to fill the considerable void created by his absence. Fred had often been characterized as the more independent and emotionally autonomous of the two brothers, and after Edward's death, he felt the need to draw closer to his parents and assume a more active role within the family.

Fred went on to complete his degree at Hamilton, during which time he crossed paths with several prominent writers, including Ezra Pound and Robert Frost. His literary ambition grew, and though he returned home following graduation to be closer to his family, he postponed getting a job and convinced his father to support him while he pursued a career in writing. After a year of abysmal frustration, Fred concluded he had nothing to say and turned instead to a related field: the study of human behavior.

As a young graduate student at Harvard, Fred exhibited a propensity for objective observation that coincided nicely with the burgeoning work of behaviorists such as John Watson and Clark Hull. He used his inventive skills to create new and unique devices to measure units of behavior in laboratory animals with unprecedented success. Fred completed his Ph.D. in 1931 and stayed on at Harvard for an additional five and a half years to continue his laboratory research through a combination of grants and fellowships.

In 1936, Fred left Harvard and assumed a teaching and research position at the University of Michigan, despite the fact that little of his work had prepared him to teach within the world of mainstream psychology. Nonetheless, these were fruitful years for Skinner. He married Yvonne Blue, had two daughters, and published his first book, *The Behavior of Organisms*. In addition, and as a result of his foray into fatherhood, it was during this time that he created his notorious "baby tender," an apparatus for streamlining baby care in the form of an enclosed crib with a window and a continuous supply of fresh warm air. The invention engendered both praise and condemnation and contributed to the characterization (by some) of Skinner's particular brand of psychology as clinical and mechanistic. Other inventions created by Skinner were much less controversial and led to significant advances in researchers' ability to observe and record behaviors and responses without influencing or altering the variables being observed.

Though his laboratory experiments focused on the behaviors of rats, pigeons, and the occasional lobster, Skinner spent much of his later career applying his theories to human development. In the summer of 1945, he wrote *Walden Two*, the story of a utopian society where individuals were deliberately shaped through operant learning and reinforcement. Skinner went on to apply his principles to classroom learning, devising machines and teaching techniques that employed immediate reinforcement and accommodated a range of abilities within a single classroom. While his ideas about the crucial importance of abandoning "mentalist" theories of psychology in favor of behaviorism were never fully embraced by mainstream social scientists, he continued to write compelling treatises on the nature of learning and development. His work spawned useful therapeutic and learning interventions, such as *behavior modification*, that continue to rest at the core of treatment strategies used in mental health and learning environments worldwide. Skinner was managing a full and productive work schedule as a writer and lecturer until the time of his death from leukemia in 1986.

Generalization and Discrimination

We are classically conditioned not only to exact stimuli but also to stimuli that remind us in some way of the original one(s). I once had a cockatiel who sat on my shoulder when I got ready for work in the morning, except that he would fly off to sit on the shower curtain rod when I picked up my hairspray bottle. I had accidentally hit the bird with a shot of the smelly stuff often enough that he had learned an avoidance response when he saw it coming. Then I started noticing that he flew off my shoulder at different times—such as when I picked up the ketchup bottle at the table, or the round kitchen cleanser can. Though I'd never squirted him with ketchup or cleanser, the shape of the containers was enough to scare him off. This phenomenon is called **generalization**, because the response is *generalized* to all similar stimuli. Another example from the bird world is the fact that many imported parrots fear men in hats and gloves, because they were captured in the wild by men dressed that way. Similarly, humans often fear other humans who remind them of bad experiences, such as women who act like intrusive mothers and men who act like abusive fathers.

In the process of learning, we often start out with generalized responses and then fine-tune them as we see the results of our behavior. This stimulus **discrimination** can be seen in children's language development. For example, toddlers who have begun to use the *-ed* ending for past tense often say "getted" instead of "got" and "goed" instead of "went"; they have generalized the *-ed* ending even to words that have irregular past tenses. But parents, teachers, and other people tend to correct children and provide the standard past tenses when they make these errors, so the children learn to *discriminate* between the correct and incorrect uses of the *-ed* ending. Even if no one corrected their language, toddlers would eventually learn most irregular past tenses through imitating other people's talk, or *modeling*. In similar ways, we learn how to discriminate appropriate behaviors according to our surroundings; for example, we hug friends when we are happy, but we don't hug professors (or most therapists) when we are happy. Stimulus discrimination works *against* behavior therapy when people learn something in one setting but can't generalize it to another setting. For instance, this happens when drug abusers are able to use self-control in hospital settings but go back to their old impulsiveness when they return home.

Anxiety and Avoidance

Joseph Wolpe, a South African psychiatrist, studied treatments for anxiety in the 1950s, looking at alternatives to traditional psychodynamic approaches. Using a counterconditioning basis, he developed treatments that replaced anxiety responses to cues with relaxation and assertiveness. If threatening cues were paired with nonanxious responses, the anxiety response would be overcome, in a process Wolpe called **reciprocal inhibition.** The anxiety is *inhibited* by a *reciprocal* (contradictory) response, under the reasoning that anxiety can't coexist with relaxation or assertiveness. These responses serve to reduce or minimize anxiety. According to Wolpe (1990), anxiety is the causal agent in all neurotic reactions. It is your nervous system's response to threat, based on classical conditioning. Phobics avoid certain stimuli like dirt or heights; schizophrenics avoid contact with people; hypochondriacs avoid disease. Avoidance itself has the powerful consequence of anxiety reduction. Checking things, for instance, is a common behavior among obsessive-compulsive people. They may return to their homes several times each morning to make sure the coffeepot, iron, and stove are all turned off. The problem is that this checking is reinforced every time by a feeling of relief. If the stove *was* left on, the relief at going back reinforces checking. If it *wasn't* left on, relief from worrying about it reinforces checking.

In keeping with stimulus generalization, we learn to experience anxiety in the context where it was first found. A child rejected by peers for games at recess comes to hate not only the game of Red Rover but the playground and classroom, too. Even as an adult, this person may dislike the smell of chalk, organized games, and work situations that require choosing teams. He may also become anxious when merely thinking of any of these stimuli and learn to avoid even imagining them, in a process called **avoidance repression** (Wilson, 2000). He might be one of those people who claim that they remember nothing from grade school, or he might prefer to not be around when others are reminiscing about their school years.

Social Learning

Mary Cover Jones, under John Watson's supervision in 1924, is known for the first experimental use of *modeling* in the removal of anxiety. The researchers worked with a child named Peter who had many objects of fear including white rats, rabbits, and fur coats. Jones had Peter observe other children playing happily with rabbits; these children served as models and showed that there was nothing to fear from bunnies. Jones later added *counterconditioning* to the systematic program, and Peter was freed from most of his fears. Modeling—watching others perform a feared act comfortably—is still a major technique of behavior therapy, used not only in eliminating phobias but in assertiveness training and social skills improvement. In everyday life, parents often use an older sibling's behavior as a model for younger children: "Look at Clara! She likes to keep her room clean and nice."

Modeling is also a major force in the natural learning process. Albert Bandura (1986) described **social learning theory,** which adds the influence of thought processes to stimulus-response-reinforcement theory. He emphasized, for example, that to learn something, it helps

- if you are paying attention,
- if you are able to remember it,
- if you have some motivation to learn it,
- if you believe you are capable of learning it, and
- if you have some reason to believe you will benefit from learning it.

Notice that these are not strictly observable behaviors. They mostly seem to take place within an individual. A strict behaviorist would not allow for these inner factors, but most modern behavior therapists believe in their importance. From a social learning point of view, successful modeling also involves other inner factors, such as whether you admire the person who serves as a model and whether you perceive her as similar to you. Social learning theory holds true not only for learning specific skills like driving a car and baking bread but also for learning complex, unstated rules. Bandura (1974) noted that people change "their judgmental orientations, conceptual schemes, linguistic styles, information-processing strategies, as well as other forms of cognitive functioning" (p. 864) based on observing other people.

R e f l e c t i o n

Think of something that you were supposed to learn at some point, but didn't. Among the inner factors of learning listed above, can you see one or more that were weak or lacking in this experience? My own example is that I never learned how many days are in each month of the year, something that most people know. I never paid much attention to the monthly day count, never had a big motivation to know it, and, since I always have a calendar, I see no real benefit to learning it. Therefore, even though others have told me several nifty ways to remember it, I don't. (On the other hand, I know my VISA card numbers by heart!)

Active Style

Behavioral therapy is distinguished by its active style—clients not only talk, but *do* things. Clients are active all the way from the beginning of the process, when they assist the therapist in identifying what behavior they want to change and why. In order to pursue behavior change, they need to be educated about learning theory, including the essential concepts I have described here. And they help plan the treatment, accepting and rejecting ideas concerning how the treatment will be executed. For example, a client hoping to integrate physical fitness into her life will participate in designing a plan that takes into account her other activities and her preferences.

The client usually carries the plan into the natural environment, acting outside of the therapy session. Often the majority of the work is done without the counselor present. Homework is a common feature of behavioral therapy. If you were trying to change your eating habits, you would do things like keep records of what you eat, note down details of situations that increase your eating, fill out assessments of your risky eating settings, and do research on substitutions of healthy for unhealthy food. Spiegler and Guevremont (1998, p. 491) point out that if every hour in therapy sessions is followed up with four hours of homework, the total amount of therapy for twenty weekly one-hour sessions is eighty hours, not twenty.

More than other therapeutic approaches, behavioral therapy enlists nonprofessional helpers from the natural environment. For example, in one exercise program, a woman's husband tabulated her jogging points (awarded for distance and speed), and then agreed to take her out to her choice of social activity for every so many points earned (Watson & Tharp, 1997). Sometimes others in the client's family are requested to *stop* certain punishing or reinforcing behaviors, such as nagging or offering a stiff drink at the end of the day. Bosses and coworkers cooperate in some behavioral management plans—for example, allowing a client to go smoke at mandated intervals during a gradual reduction program.

The focus on behavior and involvement of natural helpers make behavior therapy appealing multiculturally. Individuals from some cultures dislike the

confessional nature of many talk therapies, and the practical emphasis of behavior therapy is more acceptable. Culturally, some people inherit a strong
value on self-discipline (from certain Chinese and Jewish backgrounds, for example), and this value can be well exercised in behavioral techniques. Finally,
involvement of the extended family is most effective when the family is traditionally a source of help, support, and intervention, as it is in most ethnic
minority American cultures.

Due to its specific goals as well as its active style, with hours outside of sessions well used, behavior therapy is often the basis of *brief therapy*, with an upper
limit of twenty-five sessions (Koss & Schiang, 1994). Many clients expect and
prefer short-term treatment, and cost-benefit considerations make it attractive to
managed healthcare organizations. Even when a brief therapy's orientation is
psychodynamic or transpersonal (as described in Chapter 12), several characteristics of the treatment are likely to be behavioral.

Scientific Approach and Research Support

By its very nature, behavioral therapy takes a scientific approach. The results are
observable, testable, countable, measurable: How many cigarettes did the client
smoke? Did the client make the telephone calls she planned, or not? These are
different questions than, Is the client happier? Has the client achieved closure for
old, unfinished business?

When selecting case studies for a collection, editors Wedding and Corsini
(1989) described themselves as "overloaded with excellent articles. Behavior
modification outstrips all other systems in the quantity of cases reported, and
we were forced to make some very hard decisions" (p. 112). Because behavioral
approaches use careful measurement and assessment techniques, and because
they clearly define the treatments, they can be well described in writing. The
results can be reported in numbers and analyzed statistically and graphed.
These scientific advantages have led to the **manualization** of many behavioral
treatments. That is, a step-by-step approach can be written down and used by
other therapists, counselors, and clients themselves. Examples of step-by-step
treatments for twelve common disorders can be found in David Barlow's (1993)
Clinical Handbook of Psychological Disorders. The strong points of manual-based
treatments are that they facilitate the training of therapists and other helpers,
increase the spread of effective treatments among clinicians, and help counselors and clinics assert their effectiveness in using scientifically evaluated
methods and having understandable outcome statistics to show for it (Wilson,
1998, p. 372).

Behavioral methods dominate the list of empirically supported treatments
(Nathan & Gorman, 1998; see also Chapter 1 for a discussion). The research
support for behavioral treatments grows so fast that two books are devoted
to the subject each year: *Progress in Behavior Modification* and *Annual Review of
Behavior Therapy*. If they are not in your college library, you can track them
down through the National Medical Library at *http://gateway.nml.nih.gov*.

> ### *R e f l e c t i o n*
>
> Think of a time when you tried to change your behavior: dieting, quitting
> smoking or some other habit, getting up or going to bed at different
> times, exercising more regularly, studying harder. What tactics did you
> use to try to change? If you were successful, list three reasons for your
> success. If you were partly successful or failed, list three reasons for
> your lack of success.
>
> Jot down any connections you can make between your efforts to change,
> their effectiveness, and the essential concepts of behavior therapy.

The Therapeutic Process

The course of behavioral therapy follows identifiable stages. Sometimes the
process loops back to earlier stages as it progresses.

The Therapeutic Relationship

I mentioned high activity level as an essential concept of behavior therapy, and
this feature extends to the counselor. The behavioral therapist is not neutral or
detached, even when he or she is following a manual for treatment. The therapist must gain the client's trust and must present the treatment as credible, or
the client will not cooperate with the many efforts she will be asked to make
outside the session. An encouraging and hopeful atmosphere is a necessity
when you are asking people to do difficult things—not just to talk about their
problems for an hour a week! In a study of ninety-four clients with various
problems, clients who received behavioral therapy rated their counselors
higher on accurate empathy, self-congruence, and interpersonal contact than
did clients who received psychoanalytical insight-oriented therapy (Sloane,
Staples, Cristol, Yorkston, & Whipple, 1975). Some readers found this outcome
surprising, because the behaviorists' emphasis on the observable and the measurable is sometimes equated with a cold, mechanical approach.

The counselor in behavior therapy acts as a collaborator in identifying
goals and planning treatments with the client. Clients' input is crucial, because
no one will follow a plan that they feel is forced upon them, as long as they are
free to quit. However, the relationship is not equal because the counselor has
more knowledge of learning theory, can think of various ways to reach the
same goal, and is an expert in looking at a plan and seeing loopholes. When I
was a counselor for blocked student writers, I was always wary of plans like
"I'll get a lot done this summer at Cape Cod" or "I'll clear up that Incomplete
over spring break." I knew that such plans needed strong reinforcers and detailed time management, or they would get blown away by the beach breezes.

Goals and Targets

In the cases above, I might say, "So, what exactly do you need to do to clear up that Incomplete?" or "Let's make a list of just what you want to get done at Cape Cod." Behavior therapists are famous for insisting on clear goals that can be evaluated for completion. We need to know what behaviors are targeted for change. If a blocked writer tends to procrastinate by distracting himself with other activities, he may need to target beach-going as a behavior to eliminate. If he has trouble writing because he has trouble being alone, he needs to increase his tolerance for isolation. If he has both problems, or more, we need to decide which one to target first and most strongly. Early in the therapy process, counselors and clients think about what goals and behaviors are desired, what the advantages and disadvantages of the goals are, and whether they are achievable in the time frame available. For example, when I convened a group of blocked dissertation writers, their common overall goal was to finish the paper—but we also had to target intermediate goals for our five-week program. Each person had to identify some progress point that was measurable and could conceivably be achieved in five weeks.

Sometimes goals are slippery. You may think that you want to stop fighting with your girlfriend, but upon analysis you see that you would like to take steps toward getting out of the relationship entirely. You might say that you want to get a job, but what you really want is for your parents to stop nagging you about it. Selecting appropriate goals often blurs into the next part of the process: assessing the situation.

R e f l e c t i o n

Think of something you would like to change about yourself. You will consider this change in the light of behavior therapy throughout exercises in this chapter, so choose something you don't mind discussing with your classmates. What would your goal be in changing this behavior? See whether you can describe specific behaviors that you would like to stop, adjust, or develop. How will you know when you achieve your goal? Think small when you are just starting out. If time permits, enlist the help of your small group in deciding on goals and targets. To inspire you, here is a list of topics that have been addressed by behavior therapy:

smoking cigarettes	nail biting
procrastinating	pursuing a hobby
interrupting others	being pessimistic
eating too much or too little	shyness
watching too much television	self-centeredness
exercising	bad moods
drinking too much	spending too much money

being a bully	unreasonable prejudice
throwing fits of anger	time management
social withdrawal	child or pet management
study habits	not listening
work habits	daydreaming
making conversation	jumping to conclusions
phobias	making excuses

Assessments

Figuring out exactly what is going on constitutes assessment, and it occurs throughout behavior modification. One important set of assessments takes place at the beginning, when the client or clients describe their problems. This most likely begins with the client's self-report, followed up by questions. As counselors, we need to discover what specifically the client means by his or her general descriptions. We see people who say, "I'm depressed," while what they mean covers a wide range of emotions, especially since in everyday life we use the word "depressed" to describe anything from feeling regret over breaking a souvenir from Paris to stifling a murderous rage with a quart of vodka. Once we have some behavior attached to a complaint, we collect information such as

- when the behavior occurs,
- how frequently it occurs,
- what usually comes before and after the behavior,
- what the client thinks and feels during the behavior, and
- what the client has already tried in order to solve the problem.

According to Prochaska and Norcross (1999), most behavior problems fall into the categories of excess, deficit, and inappropriateness. Problems of **excess** involve doing too much of something, such as eating or sleeping or working too much. Problems of **deficit** involve not doing enough of something, like when a student avoids speaking up in class or a job hunter freezes during interviews. Problems of **inappropriateness** involve doing something that is considered normal but doing it in situations or at ages that your culture finds strange. For example, when a 9-year-old girl behaves seductively toward adult men, we therapists see a red flag. Some problems encompass all three categories: When we see a 9-year-old who sleeps until noon, barely eats, and acts seductively toward adult men, we are seriously concerned.

In our investigation, we keep in mind that some stimulus has occasioned the behavior, and something follows it that reinforces it (or has reinforced it in the past). The problem doesn't usually happen in all situations. For example, one client might steal from work but not from his children's piggybanks; another might tug her hair when she is bored but not otherwise. Times when the problem does *not* happen can tell you a lot about what stimulus *is* cueing it. In thinking about reinforcement, ask what maintains the behavior, within the person or the situation or both. Remember that the compulsive checker achieves relief every time he checks. And the seductive 9-year-old might enjoy her feeling of power over men. It's quite possible that she's had positive feedback for such behavior, in that adults sometimes think flirtatiousness is cute in little girls. She may have actually received treats and privileges from acting this way.

Lazarus and Lazarus (2000) describe situations in which the stimulus-response-reinforcement process has maintained abusive relationships. In this and many other cases, the abuser benefits from his or her behavior:

> *Sally's husband was often abusive. One morning, over breakfast, Hank began yelling at her because she was on the phone instead of keeping him company. Later, after Hank went to work, Sally picked up his shirts from the laundry, ran some other errands for him, and decided to cook his favorite dish for dinner.*
>
> Sally, alas, believed that if she could only create an ideal loving home atmosphere, her husband's abusiveness would stop. [Without realizing it], she was in fact *rewarding* her husband's negative behavior. In response to his outbursts, Hank found his chores done for him and he was served his favorite dinner. Why would he change his treatment of his wife when she responds so positively?
>
> The events that follow an action will weaken or strengthen the likelihood it will occur again. If Sally is nice to Hank when he treats her badly, [he learns] to continue being abusive. By putting up with Hank's abusive behavior, Sally gives him the message that it's okay to treat her that way. If she showed him instead that she was willing to be especially kind and helpful *only when he was considerate and loving,* a positive pattern might be more likely to develop.
>
> Tommy believed that kindness would overcome unkindness. He sent flowers to his wife whenever she flared up at him, hoping this gesture would put her in a good mood. Instead, it only encouraged her to flare up at him even more. (p. 62)

DISCUSSION IDEAS

Think of examples in which an unwanted behavior is unintentionally reinforced. For example, are there any ways that bad study habits are reinforced in your life? Are there ways that you reward your partner, friends, or family for acting in ways you don't actually like? Discuss how this state of affairs comes about.

Also recall the behavior you want to change (named in the *Reflection* box above). How is this behavior reinforced?

You won't collect information merely through interviewing, however. You're more likely to get a complete picture when you use several different ways of collecting data. Here are some of the ways behaviorists assess the situation.

- *Imaginative re-run.*   The client remembers a specific episode and tries to relive it in imagination, describing events and feelings. It's helpful if he can recall the thoughts that occurred to him in the process so that you can see how he was interpreting the episode.

- *Role playing.*   If the problem occurs interpersonally, have the client construct a scene in which you play the other party and act out a sample situation. For example, for a student who doesn't participate in class, you could act as the professor.

- *Physiological recording.*   For some problems, bodily measurements are meaningful. Weight, blood pressure, cholesterol count, cotinine levels (for smoking treatments), and blood alcohol levels are examples. Some conditions will prompt you to ask your client to visit a physician; for example, lethargy and weight gain can be symptoms of thyroid deficiency, while they are also signs of depression.

- *Observations.*   It can be instructive to see the client behave in an actual environment. Children's behavior on the schoolyard or in the classroom is often charted by trained observers watching for incidents of aggression, social rejection, sexualized play, and so forth. When I studied writer's block, I videotaped my participants' computer monitors as they wrote a short essay.

- *Record-keeping.*   Almost always, the client needs to keep records related to the problem: Examples include calorie counts; exercise logs; tallies of cigarettes, drinks, or social contacts; diaries of conflicts; and ratings of urges, cravings, and moods. These should be collected *before* the treatment begins, so that you have a **baseline** for comparison later. Otherwise, how will you know whether the treatment is working?

- *Inventories and questionnaires.*   Several printed (and, now, computerized) methods of collecting information are used by behaviorists. These are constructed to discover more about problem behaviors, including getting more specific information about what precedes and follows these behaviors. A sample of one such instrument follows.

THE EATING SELF-EFFICACY SCALE

Drs. Shirley Glynn and Audrey Ruderman (1986) developed a questionnaire to measure a person's perceived self-efficacy in coping with a variety of tempting eating situations. This gives you a fine-grained analysis of the different situations in which a person has to learn to control his or her eating. Use of the scale allows a person who wants to develop greater self-control over eating to see that there are a number of causes of overeating and to realize which situations are easiest or most difficult to deal with.

Instructions: For each item, rate the likelihood that you would have difficulty controlling your overeating in that situation. Use this scale:

1	2	3	4	5	6	7
no difficulty controlling eating			moderate difficulty			most difficulty controlling eating

How difficult is it to control your overeating . . .

1. after work or school
2. when you feel restless
3. around holiday time
4. when you feel upset
5. when you feel tense
6. with friends
7. when you are preparing food
8. when you feel irritable
9. as part of a social occasion dealing with food (at a restaurant or dinner party)
10. with family members
11. when you feel annoyed
12. when you feel angry
13. when you are angry at yourself
14. when you feel depressed
15. when you feel impatient
16. when you want to sit back and enjoy some food
17. after an argument
18. when you feel frustrated
19. when tempting food is in front of you
20. when you want to cheer up
21. when there is a lot of food available to you (refrigerator is full)
22. when you feel overly sensitive
23. when you feel nervous
24. when you feel hungry
25. when you feel anxious or worried (reprinted in Watson & Tharp, 1997, p. 52)

Behavior rating forms can be filled out by people other than the client so that you can combine and compare information from different sources or more reliable sources. Parents and teachers often complete rating forms for children's behavior, such as the Conners Rating Scale, for hyperactivity (Conners, 1969); the Child Behavior Checklist (CBC), for problems including social withdrawal, attention problems, and aggression (Achenbach, 1991); and the Behavior Assessment System for Children (BASC), to identify dimensions of conduct and behavior problems (Reynolds & Kamphaus, 1998). These scales have the advantage of being accompanied by manuals that provide *norms,* or average scores for people in various contexts. You can find out where your client stands in relation to a bigger population. When you plan to use an inventory or questionnaire, try to find one that is standardized in this way by looking up the behavior or problem you wish to measure at the Buros Institute for Mental Measurements (*www.unl.edu/buros*).

Reactivity

If you've ever kept track of everything you eat, each cigarette you smoke, every drink you take, or every time you bite your nails, you have already realized that just keeping track makes you behave differently. You might decide not to have a fourth cookie just because you don't want to write down that you had four cookies instead of three. This phenomenon is called **reactivity of measurement,** and it occurs often in behavioral treatment. In a study on treatment of obesity, self-recording daily weight and daily caloric intake was as effective as the combination of behavioral therapy *and* self-recording, with both treatments' benefits maintained at three-month follow-up (Romanczyk, 1974).

More subtle forms of reactivity also exist. For example, when a child is aware of being watched and of a parent writing something down, the child may increase or decrease a behavior, even one unrelated to the record-keeping. When you are trying to establish a baseline, be sure to inquire about the recorder's perceptions of reactivity. Getting information in several different ways also helps you arrive at an accurate baseline, since some measures and reporters are more reactive than others.

Evaluating Reinforcements

Before starting on a treatment plan, your client should help you identify reinforcements that will make daily efforts appealing. Obviously the same reinforcers won't reward all people: I would work hard to earn an afternoon of reading psychology journals, while other people would consider that afternoon a punishment. If a client is not able to think of rewards, you can use the Pleasant Events Schedule (Lewinsohn & MacPhillamy, 1971), which lists 320 possibilities, from "listening to the sounds of nature" to "criticizing someone." Besides reflecting individual tastes, the reinforcer should relate logically to the treatment goal if possible. For example, transferring money to a fund for new clothes may be a good reinforcer for calorie restriction. (Clearly, food rewards are inappropriate here.) And for a teenager who breaks curfew, reinforcement for meeting curfew could logically consist of gradually later curfew times in exchange for each week of promptness, up to a negotiated hour.

Ideally, the goal state itself becomes the reward for behavior management. We hope that the joy of being able to play piano eventually rewards the hours of drudgery involved in practice, and we expect children to become self-motivated over time in efforts like playing instruments, studying, and contributing to family harmony. As Bandura (1974) described it, humans have "a capacity for self-direction. They do things that give rise to self-satisfaction and self-worth, and they refrain from behaving in ways that evoke self-punishment" (p. 861). Bandura also pointed out that we surround ourselves with people who share similar standards, and thus we gain social reinforcement for our efforts.

There is evidence that giving rewards completely unrelated to the task may undermine interest in the rewarded task (Condry, 1977). It may also lower the quality of the performance. You can see this in everyday life: The pre-teen you hire to mow your lawn is never going to do as good a job on your yard as the landscaping enthusiast next door does on his own. And the pre-teen hireling will never volunteer to mow your lawn for the sheer pleasure of it. The same is true for sex: In spite of what the movies might suggest, prostitutes rarely volunteer for a recreational roll in the hay. When I was a child, my parents presented me with math and phonics workbooks as treats, and I saw them as pleasurable in themselves, while children who were rewarded for doing math and phonics avoided the subjects in their spare time. Today's parents witness a similar pattern when their children devote considerable time to mastering complex computer games but refuse to exert themselves otherwise (even for reward). Because of circumstances like these, you need to choose a reward that doesn't devalue doing the task for its own sake.

R e f l e c t i o n

For the behavior you want to change, make a list of reinforcers. Think about immediate rewards, such as pleasurable activities, and incremental ones, such as setting money aside for relevant treats. What are some of the self-satisfaction rewards you expect to enjoy? What self-punishments will you avoid by changing the behavior? What intrinsic benefits will come from meeting your goals? Most behavior therapists recommend writing out the benefits and keeping the list handy to help you resist temptation.

Psychoeducation

In behavioral treatment, the psychologist acts as an educator about the principles of behavior management. Clients are not always aware of their responsiveness to cues or of the reinforcements they are giving or receiving. In the Lazarus and Lazarus (2000) example, the exploited spouses probably didn't realize that they were rewarding the behavior they disliked. I found that blocked writers frequently did not even try to analyze what settings and conditions were conducive to their *good* writing sessions, even though this type of analysis can lead to immediate improvement. Finally, parents who ignore their well-behaved children may be shocked to find that they are on the road to extinguishing an enviable situation.

I often say that every couple in their first pregnancy should be offered a videotape on the nature of reinforcement schedules. Many problems with child management could be avoided through education about how behavior is maintained and extinguished. For example, if a parent or caretaker *never* responds to a temper tantrum with sustained attention or with giving in to a demand (such as staying up later or wanting a treat), the tantrums will cease. Certainly, the child will throw *more* tantrums at first because he is still waiting for that intermittent reinforcement, but this **response burst** won't last in the face of continuous lack of response.

Clients may not have accurate factual information relevant to their problems, in which case the therapist must provide it. Even basic facts about calories consumed and calories expended may have been forgotten by someone with a weight problem. Similarly, nutrition facts are not widely understood, and misinformation is widespread. One father I know refused to let his grade-school daughter eat any refined sugar, and he forbade her to go to friends' birthday parties because he knew she would eat sweets there. A better understanding of dietary sugar—and of the importance of children's peer groups—would have been helpful to his daughter. Similarly, obsessive-compulsive clients with dirt phobias often overestimate the dangerousness of germs and can benefit from realistic appraisals of pathogen risk.

DISCUSSION IDEAS

A young mother, Jessica, carries candy with her everywhere and hands it to her 2-year-old when he gets rowdy, to get him to calm down. What is she teaching him? What effects might you expect from this practice? If you were Jessica's counselor, what principles of behavior management would you teach her?

Application of Techniques

With a basic understanding of the client's goals, what behavior needs to change, and what the client will find reinforcing, treatment can begin. If the client has several problems, targeting one or two behaviors is critical. It could be that successful work on those will result in **transfer of training;** that is, the improvements will spread out to untargeted areas. For instance, if a person with lots of problems on the job focuses first on building better relationships with co-workers, she may find that their good will relieves some of the other difficulties. She may also use some of her relationship-building skills outside of work and discover that outside friendships help her put job hassles into perspective.

Therapist and client decide on a plan of action together. In determining what techniques to propose, the therapist takes into account empirically supported treatments for the client's particular problem, the principles of learning theory, the examples set by other clinical practice, and her own judgment. Usually, the techniques involve stimulus control, planned reinforcement of desired behaviors, self-regulation, fear reduction methods, modeling, or aversion therapy—individually or in a combination of two or three. These are all discussed in the next section of the chapter. Keep in mind, however, that from this course alone you are not prepared to manage some of the complex behavior modification programs and will need to seek more education and supervised practice. There are opportunities for training throughout life, such as workshops and seminars offered in cities across the country by the National Association of Cognitive-Behavioral Therapists (find them at *www.nacbt.org*).

Remember that though your treatment plan focuses on behavior, there are cognitive elements to consider. The client, for one thing, needs to accept the rationale for what you plan, and she needs to believe that it will work. She must commit herself to trying the plan. Often, client and therapist write up a contract in which they commit themselves to a course of action and a method of evaluation. (This document can include a statement of the client's informed consent to treatment, too.) The client can also commit herself publicly; in fact, smoking cessation rates are higher among people who publicly announce that they're quitting than among those who do not. In addition, she can recruit others in her life to help. Spouses and best friends are frequently called upon, though the effects on the relationship need to be considered first. You don't want the treatment to become an arena for an already existing battle.

In some behavior change programs, the therapist-client partnership I describe does not exist. For example, children whose lives are affected by parent effectiveness training, or who are being behaviorally treated for conduct problems or attention deficits, do not have a major say in planning. Behavior programs are used to alter the lives of retarded, chronically mentally ill, and incarcerated people who are unable to fully consent; they are also used to change the nature of school and work for normal people, without their express endorsement. Behavior managers must consider the ethics of these situations and use the ethical principles of the helping professions in making decisions (see Chapter 3 for a discussion).

Feedback, Measurement, and Reevaluation

Throughout treatment, the client and therapist evaluate its progress. Clients usually keep records of behavior (and sometimes thoughts and emotions) every day. They also keep track of rewards they earn and, perhaps, comments on how effective or challenging the program feels subjectively. Sometimes very simple records are kept. For example, a man who wants to have seven or fewer drinks per week carries an index card with *S, M, T, W, Th, F, S* lines in his wallet and tallies his seven drinks as he has them, then refuses all further drinks till the next Sunday. Believe it or not, this system can work. In part, it raises awareness of the consequence of having too many drinks at once—namely, a period of several days with no drinks at all. If the man accepts a drink over his seven maximum, he writes on that day's line the situation in which he had the extra drink and his mood or thoughts when he took it. This helps the therapist and client not only identify the contingencies that encourage him to overdrink, but also plan how to avoid or short-circuit them.

In this case, limiting the drinking was its own reward. When other rewards are used, they, too, need to be recorded and evaluated. You can always refine a plan that is not working well. For example, in my dissertation writers' group, we planned a system in which each person contracted to work for forty-five minutes followed by fifteen minutes of a pleasant activity before returning to writing for forty-five minutes, during each one of the long work sessions they scheduled for the week. At our next group session, however, not a single person had stopped the pleasant activity after fifteen minutes, and only one had returned to writing at all that day. Obviously, there was something wrong with the reward system. One man's pleasant activity was playing with his dog, and one woman's activity was e-mailing with friends. These were examples of rewards that didn't have clear enough stopping points built in, and the fifteen minutes went by without notice. As a group, we made up a list of rewards that really would take around fifteen minutes, such as listening to *three* songs on the radio or CD, watching *five* scenes of a taped soap opera episode, and replying to *one* friend's e-mail. We also decided that the group members needed to set their kitchen timers to ring after fifteen minutes. The new system of rewards worked.

Rewards also need revision when they are just not rewarding enough. For example, setting aside money for future clothes shopping didn't work for a client who had over fifty pounds to lose before she could fit into the clothes she liked (entailing ten to twelve months on a reasonable diet). That reward was too distant to be satisfying in the short run. Saving the money for a weekly massage was a better plan, especially since the length of the massage she could afford was directly tied to how well she had followed her diet and exercise program. The masseuse gave her positive feedback on her progress every week, adding another meaningful reinforcer.

Termination, Maintenance, and Relapse Prevention

Termination in behavior therapy is different from most other terminations of treatment. The therapist and client can usually agree on whether a behavioral goal is reached, because it has been clearly defined. Did the client quit smoking? Has he limited his drinks to seven a week for ten weeks? Did she lose fifty pounds? Is the writer producing an average of twenty pages a week and taking them to his graduate adviser? Is the child disrupting the classroom 50 percent fewer times a day or wetting the bed only one night a week? Sometimes everyone is satisfied with these goals and ready to begin the termination stage, and sometimes new goals and plans are instituted with new evaluation periods.

There are cognitive elements associated not just with treatment planning but with termination as well (Stuart, 1980). Clients need to recognize and have personal interpretations of how they have changed. They need to conceptualize the effects of continuing with desired behaviors so that they are motivated. So, if I lose fifty pounds during behavior therapy, I need to visualize myself as thin for a lifetime, including the health, beauty, and financial benefits I will enjoy permanently.

Therapists and clients also need to discuss how to maintain the improvements achieved, because there is some evidence that otherwise newly developed behaviors will deteriorate or not transfer to new conditions of life. It could be that a client needs to maintain monitoring practices indefinitely. Plans for solidifying the support systems offered in everyday life are made at termination. For example, friends, spouses, and family members can be enlisted for the long run. And clients should possess information about support groups that will help maintain their improvements, such as Weight Watchers, Rational Recovery, and Parents Without Partners. In most cases, you can help clients develop a bibliography of self-help and inspirational readings relevant to their situation. Most important, clients need a plan for what to do in case of a relapse. This always involves being able to think of the failure as temporary and resolvable.

To avoid setbacks, clients are encouraged to list their high-risk situations as well as their ideas about how to deal with them. Watson and Tharp (1997) list four extremely common risky scenes: "(1) Being emotionally upset, (2) Social settings in which you are tempted, (3) Drinking, and (4) Unexpectedly encountering the to-be-avoided objects" (p. 289). All clients should have clear, specific ideas about how they intend to behave in these four scenes. Furthermore, most life changes have costs as well as benefits. A former hard drinker who has regulated his habit has probably also lost a big part of his social group, and so has a teenager who has given up delinquency. Such losses require a compensating reorganization of lifestyle on a long-term basis. Hiss, Foa, and Kozak (1994) designed a relapse prevention program that integrated the concepts discussed in this section. In comparison with a treated group who did not receive the program, the treated group with added relapse prevention showed significantly fewer returns of symptoms at a six-month follow-up.

Finally, many termination plans include schedules of booster sessions, in which the client checks back in with the therapist to discuss maintenance and progress. Revamping of self-regulation programs can occur in these sessions, and the client can recommit to the new behavior. Many religious people are familiar with functions of this type in weekly organized worship services.

R e f l e c t i o n

If you are able to get rid of the behavior you have targeted, what do you think will be your risky situations for relapse in the future? What plans would help you deal with these situations?

Customary Techniques and Uses of Behavior Therapy

Reading this chapter, you already have a good idea of what techniques are used in behavior therapy. The following categorization will elaborate on what you know and exemplify many of the applications of these techniques.

Contingency Management

Contingencies can operate at two times: before a behavior and after it. Many behavioral treatments consist of manipulating the situation that precedes a behavior and the situation that follows it. Four examples of frequently used contingency management systems are described below.

Stimulus Control

Analyzing and manipulating preceding contingencies is called **stimulus control.** Skinner's recommendations about creating a comfortable site for writing and making sure you are in a good physical state before writing are examples. In behavioral treatment for insomnia, clients are encouraged to control sleep-related stimuli by using the bed only for sleeping, regularizing bedtimes, darkening the room, and avoiding certain foods and excitement before bed. Individual clients are helped to identify conditions that encourage desirable behavior and to create these conditions; for example, writers need to note the conditions under which they are most productive, and then reproduce them. We also need to avoid doing things that seem to sabotage our efforts: I, for one, avoid leaving the house or reading fiction before I start writing in the morning (or I may not recover from the distraction). For more stimulus control, before I stop work for the night I look over my outline for the next day and put the materials I will need on my desk or on the floor nearby. In these ways, I have set the scene most conducive to my writing success.

Psychophysiological methods address control over the mind-body connection: Sometimes a bodily event or feeling is the instigator of psychological distress. The stimulus to be controlled is the bodily state, and **biofeedback** is the method. Through messages (feedback) given by measuring devices such as blood pressure cuffs, people can learn to operantly condition the responses of their nervous systems, by way of pathways that are not yet clear (Wickramsekera, Davies, & Davies, 1996). Once able to influence heart rate, blood pressure, temperature of hands and feet, sweat gland activity, and brain electrical activity, clients can learn to relax at a basic physical level. Biofeedback is used for anxiety, headaches, irritable bowel syndrome, panic, performance fears, and other problems that challenge the line between mind and body.

Shaping

A gradual approach to behavior management is exemplified by **shaping.** When the behavior that is desired doesn't occur naturally, there is no opportunity to reward it. So we reward behaviors that come closer and closer to the desired goal, in a process of **successive approximations.** A toddler who strews her toys all over the floor must at some time, by accident, end up with most of them in a heap. Employing shaping, the mother and father praise the child, making remarks like "You have all your toys together on this side of the room. Great! It looks so nice," and so on. The child learns to corral the toys on one side of the room, and eventually puts some of them on shelves, at which point the parents start praising the shelf action. Over many successive approximations, with praise for behavior more and more close to the ideal, the child puts most toys away without nagging. Language development is a process that most parents naturally shape through praise. Early babbling is met with lavish delight, and increasingly intelligible speech is rewarded as the child becomes proficient.

Differential Reinforcement and Response Withdrawal

Responses and rewards can be used to ensure that certain behaviors become more frequent while others fade away (become extinct). In **differential reinforcement,** rewards are delivered when the client is *not* performing an undesirable behavior. A teenager who attempts to control calorie intake by throwing up food can contract to reward herself at the end of every day in which she does *not* throw up. Kazdin (1994) gives examples from institutions in which patients reduced self-injuries and even seizures through being rewarded for problem-free intervals.

Another way to look at this technique is that responses are *withdrawn* when undesirable behaviors occur. Time Out is a familiar **response withdrawal** technique used effectively with children. When children misbehave, the attention and excitement they create are often rewarding in themselves and perpetuate misbehavior, whereas Time Out in a quiet, out-of-the-way place removes this type of reward. The absence of human interaction and distraction also allows the child to calm down mentally and physiologically.

Token Economies

The more closely in time a reward or punishment follows a behavior, the more effective it is as a reinforcer. But sometimes desirable and appropriate reinforcers are simply not feasible directly following a rewardable behavior. In such cases, **token economies** can substitute symbols of reinforcers, such as poker chips or points, and these are earned or lost according to clearly defined behaviors. "The main function of tokens and points is to bridge the delay between the time you perform the desired behavior and the time you can receive the reinforcer" (Watson & Tharp, 1997, p. 222). The variety of rewards available in a token economy allows for changes in personal preferences at different times. Here are some examples from Christophersen's Home Chip System for child behavior management (Christophersen & Mortweet, 2001; adapted from pp. 226–227):

Behaviors That Earn Chips

Making bed	+2
Picking up clothes in bedroom	+2
Getting dressed on time	+2
Sharing with brother	+4
Taking verbal feedback without arguing	+4
Doing homework (per 15 minutes)	+8

Privileges and Their Value

Watching television	5 chips/½ hour
Snacks	5 per snack
Going to friend's	10 chips

Behaviors That Lose Chips

Talking back	−2
Coming downstairs after bedtime	−2
Interrupting	−4
Stalling (not responding to request within 5 seconds)	−4

You can see why this system is called an *economy*.

SMALL GROUP EXERCISE

Individually, work on designing a token economy that would improve your living situation—apartment house, family home, dormitory, or neighborhood. Focus on a specific, limited improvement. Bring your design to your small group and exchange among yourselves. Discuss and revise the economies together. Choose one that you consider a good example, prepare it, and distribute it to the class as a whole, on paper or electronically.

Punishment as an Aversive Method

Aversive means *unpleasant and punishing,* and punishment is one of the most widely used forms of behavior control. Spanking, starving, beating, imprisoning, fining, torturing, and shocking are clearly examples. Socially aversive techniques include incurring the disapproval of people you care about, getting a bad reputation, being embarrassed, losing face, getting bad grades, being scolded, and being rejected. Social sanctions (punishments) work only on those people who care about the reactions of others.

Punishment is not often used in scientific treatment of bad behavior because it can have many negative side effects. Children who are physically punished usually adopt the strategy personally and are physically abusive themselves, even into adulthood. Repeatedly punished people can become so fearful and timid that they can't function effectively in everyday life, where we need to assert ourselves, and they may miss out on the pleasures of life by choosing safety over openness to experience. Individuals who are aversively controlled can also become generally angry and hateful, with a permanent chip on both shoulders.

Furthermore, punishment has lasting benefits only under strict conditions. Many research studies have concurred on these conditions:

- Punishment must be immediate, so that the person knows exactly what they are being punished for.

- It must be intense enough that the person cannot think the bad behavior was worth it.

- It needs to be meaningful to the offender—for example, fining a millionaire ten dollars is not felt as punishment.

- It should be delivered early in the course of the behavior so that the behavior does not gain a pattern of reaping benefits or being ignored.

- It should be consistently applied across all situations so that the offender does not experience intermittent reinforcement for bad behavior (which, as you know, makes extinction difficult). For example, you probably let your parking meter run out in car lots where you know ticketing is inconsistent—you are willing to take the chance. In lots that have reputations for strict ticketing and towing, most of the meters are fed.

- The punisher needs to retain a calm manner so that the source of the punishment does not appear to be his or her anger rather than the offender's behavior.

- Punishment should be accompanied by reinforcement of alternative, adaptive behaviors. (Adapted from Prochaska & Norcross, 1999)

Bandura (1986) identified other elements that make punishment effective. For instance, combining negative consequences with a reasoned explanation of why the behavior is unacceptable produces more future self-restraint than punishment alone. Self-restraint, of course, is the best outcome since it doesn't require extensive outside surveillance efforts. In addition, punishment that relates directly to the harmfulness of the transgression is more corrective than unrelated punishment. Bandura gives examples of arranging for arsonists to work in hospital burn units and for drunk drivers to assist on physical rehabilitation wards.

DISCUSSION IDEAS

Consider the following transgressions in terms of the facilitative conditions for punishment described above.

1. An 18-year-old gets pulled over for speeding and an open beer can is found in the car.
2. Your steady boyfriend or girlfriend dates someone else behind your back while you are gone for the summer.
3. An 8-year-old shoplifts a candy bar.
4. A college student displays terrible table manners.

In your community or social group, what are the usual consequences of these behaviors? Do they violate the conditions for effective punishment? What conditions do they meet?

What course of punishment would you design for each transgression if you followed the guidelines for effective punishment?

Aversion Therapy

Although, overall, positive reinforcement of good behavior is more effective and less risky than punishment of bad behavior, some people still submit themselves to **aversion therapy,** especially to break habits they deplore in themselves. One stop-smoking method involves having the client smoke cigarettes as fast as she can until she is about to vomit. This episode is repeated until cigarette stimuli are so firmly connected with nausea that the client has no desire to smoke. Aversive treatments for alcoholism also exist (Sandler & Steele, 1991). These establish a pairing of liquor (and liquor-related cues) with nausea or electric shock to achieve a conditioned distaste for drinking. One common treatment, use of the drug Anabuse, involves aversive **response cost.** A person takes Anabuse every day with no effects unless he or she drinks alcohol, in which case severe nausea, shortness of breath, and swelling occur, often requiring hospitalization. This aversion approach differs from conditioning treatments, because most clients never do drink while on Anabuse. The awareness of the price that will inevitably be paid for drinking is enough to deter the action. These forms of aversive behavior modification are usually practiced as last resorts, and are considered when the undesirable behavior is clearly dangerous. For example, shock therapy is used in institutions to decrease head-banging and self-mutilation among mentally retarded children. The use of shock, nausea, and reactive drugs for behavior management is a specialty area; if you practice ordinary clinical counseling or social work, you will refer clients to specialists for aversion treatments of this nature.

Fear Reduction Methods

If you think of the things that make you anxious, you can see how anxiety is related to fear, and perhaps understand why Wolpe (1990) believed that anxiety was the basis of most neuroses. If I have test anxiety, it means that I fear taking tests, due to something in my learning history. My friend Anita is anxious when she thinks she may be the center of attention, which prevents her from making presentations that would advance her career. This anxiety also causes her to avoid talking much at social gatherings, and therefore she rarely makes new friends outside of work. If she wants to, she can go to a behavioral therapist for help and get rid of the anxiety. Fear reduction is one of the most solidly proven uses of behavior therapy (Barlow, 1993; Emmelkamp, 1994).

Systematic Desensitization

Earlier, I told you about my practicum experience in the hospital, and how my anxiety reactions to the setting abated in just a few days. This is an example of **desensitization.** Through repeated exposure to the feared stimuli, with no bad consequences and good new experiences, I lost my learned association of hospital sights and smells with pain and hopelessness. Desensitization is necessary all the time in everyday life. If we thought about all the dangers involved, we would never drive our cars anywhere. When I first moved to a big city, the images of violence and squalor on the morning news disturbed me on and off throughout the day; now that I've lived here for over a year, I go about my business without a thought of the horrors around me.

Anxiety has a physiological basis, as you know if you have given a performance and felt your heart race and your palms sweat. Relaxation, which also has a physiological basis, is a competing emotion, and according to the principle of counterconditioning, anxiety and relaxation cannot co-exist for long. The trick is to make relaxation win out. The *systematic* part of **systematic desensitization** involves a careful sequencing of anxiety and relaxation to ensure that anxiety loses. The technique was developed by Joseph Wolpe (1958); remember, he saw anxiety as avoidance-based and worked to help patients reduce avoidance. Take a look at how Foa and Kozak (1986) conceptualize the process:

> Fear is evoked by information that activates an existing fear structure containing propositions about stimuli, responses, and their meaning. Changes in such a structure, we have proposed, require the integration of information that is incompatible with some elements of the fear structure. (p. 27)

The "existing fear structure" is what your history has taught you about a situation. This structure kicks in when you perceive similar conditions. For example, one hospital smells pretty much like another one and brings out the same responses (stimulus generalization). But when you have new experiences under similar stimulus conditions, with new nonthreatening information coming in, the old fear structure loses its sting. I had interesting work on the rehab unit and a boss who amused me every day: These constituted the new information that extinguished the old anxiety responses to hospitals. If I had carefully and consistently avoided hospital work, however, I would still have the old responses. This is probably the basis for folk wisdom about "getting back on the horse" after falling off.

When you use systematic desensitization in therapy, you work with the client to prepare in two ways:

- The client learns deep muscle relaxation. A **progressive relaxation** technique codified more than seventy years ago (Jacobson, 1938/1929) still prevails. It instructs clients to tense and relax various skeletal muscle groups until they are able to create deep states of relaxation.

- With the therapist's help, the client draws up a list of anxiety-causing events and organizes these events according to how anxiety-producing they are. Spiegler and Guevremont (1998) give an example concerning a client who was anxious about dating. From most to least, the **anxiety hierarchy** looked like this:

10. Initially greeting date
 9. Saying goodnight
 8. Being on the date
 7. Driving to pick up date
 6. Getting ready to go on date
 5. Calling someone for date
 4. Asking for potential date's telephone number
 3. Talking to potential date in class
 2. Meeting an attractive member of the opposite sex
 1. Thinking about going on date next weekend (p. 207)

When the client has learned to relax at will, he is led through imagining the anxiety-evoking events, from the least to the most anxiety promoting, all the while practicing relaxation. When the client is able to imagine "thinking about going on date next weekend" without any anxiety, he moves on to "meeting an attractive member of the opposite sex" and on up the hierarchy. When completed, the client will be able to date in the real world with little or no anxiety.

This technique is called **imaginal** because the events are images in the client's mind. A similar desensitization technique can operate **in vivo,** or in real life. A friend with agoraphobia (fear of going out in public) went to a behavior therapist and produced a hierarchy that began with walking out onto the porch to check the mail and ended with going to the shopping mall. The therapist came to his house and accompanied him out onto the porch repeatedly, slowly hanging back until my friend could go out onto the porch while she stayed inside the front door, and then instructing him to go out on the porch while she was not present. They practiced each step of the anxiety hierarchy, ending up at the shopping mall. This *in vivo* procedure is called **exposure and response prevention,** because the client is exposed to a feared situation and then prevented from performing a fearful response (in my friend's case, fleeing back into the house immediately). The therapist's comforting and supporting presence acts as the competing relaxation response. Exposure and response prevention is usually successful for obsessive-compulsive behaviors such as hand-washing and checking.

Flooding and Implosion

Flooding is based on the same thinking as desensitization: Avoidance of exposure to a feared situation has been reinforced by the relief of not facing it. The situation is not necessarily fearful in itself but, rather, calls forth "fear structures" in the client. Flooding assumes that with prolonged or repeated exposure to the situation, with no actual aversive consequences, anxiety cannot be sustained. Fear and avoidance of the situation will be reduced or extinguished. Wolpe (1990) gives an example from his own practice:

> [Dr. E., a dentist, suffered from two disabling neurotic fears]: an inability to give dental injections because of a fear of the patient dying in the chair, and an extravagant fear of ridicule. Since attempts to desensitize Dr. E. to these were making painfully slow progress, I decided to try flooding. Under light hypnosis he was asked to imagine giving a patient a mandibular block, then, withdrawing the syringe, standing back and seeing the patient slump forward, dead. Dr. E. became profoundly disturbed, sweating, weeping, and wringing his hands. After a minute or so, noticing that the reaction was growing weaker, I terminated the scene and told him to relax. Two or three minutes later, the same sequence evoked a similar, but weaker reaction. The sequence was given three more times, at the last of which no further reaction was observed. Dr. E. said that he felt he had been through a wringer—exhausted, but at ease. At the next session, the fear of ridicule was introduced. Dr. E. imagined that he was walking down the middle of a brilliantly lighted ballroom with people on both sides pointing their fingers at him and laughing derisively. At the fifth flooding session, it was clear that nothing remained to be treated. Four years later, at an interview, Dr. E. stated that his recovery had been fully maintained. The same was true 23 years later. (p. 223)

Dr. E.'s treatment was imaginal, but flooding is also done *in vivo*—for example, involving periods of sitting in a room with harmless spiders or other objects of unreasonable fear also present. It is expected that in a flooding experience, anxiety increases at first, reaches a plateau, and then decreases steadily (Foa & Kozak, 1986). My friend Laurie designed a self-flooding treatment she used whenever a man broke up with her. She'd turn off her phone, line up continuous heartbreaking romantic music on the stereo, get some hard liquor, lie down on the couch, and cry pitifully until bored. She said, "Why not get all that stuff over with in one night rather than dragging it out for weeks in little pieces?"

Implosive therapy involves flooding techniques in which the choice of aversive situation has a conventional aspect. According to implosive therapists, some situations are feared not because of an identifiable negative event with the stimulus in the client's past, but because the situation calls forth inner stimuli associated with sex and aggression, including Oedipal themes, death wish impulses, fear of castration, sexual guilt, violent fantasies, and penis envy (Stampfl, 1970). Hogan (1968) presents a case of implosion for snake phobia in which the therapist narrates a snake attack with clearly phallic imagery, closing with the client tearing the snake apart bare-handed and eating it in raw chunks, only to have it reproduce in her stomach and gnaw her from within. Implosive therapists report that the emotional release caused by thoroughly frightening imaginal exposure, with no adverse consequences in reality, exhausts the affect of the situation and leaves the client relieved.

Flooding and implosion are elements in treatments of choice for posttraumatic stress disorder (PTSD), a collection of long-lasting symptoms stemming from extreme trauma such as rape, natural disasters, and wartime horrors (Foa & Meadows, 1997).

Assertiveness Training

Relaxation is a good counterconditioner for anxiety about objects and situations that are difficult or damaging to avoid, such as riding in elevators, going out in public, and visiting the dentist. The situations remain the same after therapy, only the client doesn't find them as distressing. But some anxiety-producing situations *can* be changed by the client's activity, especially interpersonal situations. In these situations, *assertiveness* rather than relaxation acts as a counterconditioner to anxiety. "Actively expressing admiration, irritation, and appropriate anger can inhibit anxieties over rejection, embarrassment, and possible failure" (Prochaska & Norcross, 1999, p. 281). Here are some occasions that call for assertiveness:

A friend asks you to do a favor that will be a big burden for you.

Your dinner guests keep staying long after you are ready to go to bed.

At a restaurant, your food is served cold when it should be hot.

You feel a surge of affection for your best friend.

Your doctor ends the appointment before you've asked all your questions.

You hold an opinion different from everyone else's in the room, while everyone acts as though you agree with them.

Your adult daughter housesits while you are on vacation and buys $300 worth of clothes on your credit card.

What would you do in these cases? Chances are, in some cases you would *assert* yourself by expressing your feelings, in other cases you would feel uncomfortable asserting yourself but do it anyway, and in still others you would not assert yourself at all. Some of you might even respond aggressively in some cases, such as yelling at the waitress, writing a nasty note to your daughter, or saying something sarcastic to your friend. Most people vary between situations in their level of assertiveness. I rarely object to someone else's choice of restaurant even when I am not happy with it; but I always insist on having time to myself for exercising, no matter who might feel insulted or neglected.

Be sure to think about a client's cultural status in terms of the level and context of assertiveness. Many Asian-American women wish to shake off the deference that keeps them from asserting themselves in the Western world, while others see it as essential to their femininity. People who work under White male authority, such as women and minorities, must learn very sophisticated modes of assertiveness to avoid being labeled pushy or considered threatening.

R e f l e c t i o n

In what situations do you feel perfectly confident asserting yourself? Do you have more trouble expressing negative or positive feelings? Can you think of a situation in which you wish you had asserted yourself more? Why did you choose not to at the time?

When a person's work life, social life, or leisure time is impaired because he or she is not assertive enough, behavior therapy can help. In particular, **assertiveness training** (also called assertion training) helps clients learn social skills they need to express themselves appropriately—that is, neither submissively or aggressively. It assists them in untangling themselves from overdependent and exploitive relationships.

Assertiveness training often proceeds by role playing with a therapist or in therapy groups and getting feedback on one's behavior. Suggestions on how to phrase a strong feeling and how to persist in the face of discouragement come from other members of the group or the therapist, and the practice sessions serve as desensitizers. As in other desensitization procedures, a client often works through a hierarchy of assertive behaviors, from the most difficult to the least, in a certain area. For example, a woman who has trouble refusing to spend extra time with her boyfriend might specify "Telling my boyfriend I need to be home by midnight on Saturday night" as the easiest task and "Telling my boyfriend I want to go out with my girlfriends on Saturday night" as the hardest.

A cognitive component of assertiveness therapy is crucial, though it is *behavior* that must ultimately be changed. Frequently we hold beliefs that make us unassertive, and these need to be challenged. In the best-selling self-help assertiveness book *When I Say No, I Feel Guilty* (Smith, 1975), the reader is encouraged to adopt a "Bill of Assertive Rights," including "You have the right to judge your own behavior, thoughts, and emotions, and to take the responsibility for their initiation and consequences upon yourself" and "You have the right to change your mind." Assertiveness training is used in combination with other treatments for depression, eating disorders, agoraphobia, obsessive-compulsive disorders, and sexual problems (Bergin & Garfield, 1994), because these problems often include a component of conflict avoidance.

Modeling

Behavioral therapy frequently draws upon the strong effects of watching others behave, both positive and negative (Bandura, 1986). **Modeling** works in several ways in everyday life, and behaviorists make use of all these ways systematically in therapy. Children look to their parents as models of behavior, as the parents are well aware—sometimes disconcertingly so. My friend Pam was aghast to overhear her 5-year-old, acting as the mother in a playing-house game, screeching at the top of her lungs, "You kids shut up! Mommy's meditating!" We purposely model skills for others when we teach activities such as doing long division, making bread, and hitting a golf ball. We also get our ideas about what is fun, what is frightening, what is socially acceptable, and what is punishable by watching how others behave. That is why we attempt to act happy and excited about our child's first day of school, rather than expressing our doubts or fears.

Counselors use live models, sometimes themselves, in teaching skills (like assertiveness) and reducing fears. For example, Ost, Stridh, and Wolf (1998) devised a group treatment for spider phobia in which the therapist approaches and handles spiders, assists a group member in doing the same with her spiders while the others watch, and then instructs all the members to approach and handle their spiders with the assistance of other members and the therapist. In this way, clients at lower levels of anxiety can act as models for more anxious clients. This is called **participant modeling.** When live models are not possible, symbolic models may be used, such as characters in films, cartoons, and books. Children going through parents' divorces are given books that portray how child characters cope with the situation. We use symbolic models with adults, too, when we recommend novels or films with characters who cope with a problem similar to the client's. Joshua and DiMenna's (2000) *Read Two Books and Let's Talk Next Week: Using Bibliotherapy in Clinical Practice* is a good source.

In **covert modeling,** the model exists within the client's imagination and is called upon when the client chooses how to behave. The therapist helps the client develop an imaginative character who is braver, more assertive, less fearful, or saner, who can act as a reference point when the client is under stress. Sometimes clients choose people they know as *covert models* of desirable behavior; for example, Jan admires Brian's ability to stand up for himself under pressure, and she asks herself what Brian would do when she is put in that kind of spot.

More rarely, behavior therapy makes use of **negative, contrast,** or **stressful modeling.** For example, a therapist might describe or act out a situation in which the character is so self-effacing and submissive that she gets brutally taken advantage of, in order to spur a client's assertiveness in reaction to the model (Rosenthal & Steffek, 1991). In our communities, ticketed dangerous drivers are often required to watch films showing characters experiencing the consequences of reckless or drunken driving, such as undergoing a field sobriety test on the street in front of observers, getting put into a cop car, being fingerprinted and having mug shots taken, and so on. These negative models can be effective when the client makes an emotional identification with them.

Self-Management Methods

When I was working in an anxiety clinic a few years ago, I had a case load that included several clients who avoided action that was crucial for their future goals, such as making appointments with their academic advisers, filling out the paperwork to change their majors, or telling their in-laws that they were not going to have babies anytime soon. And me? I knew I had to go get my wisdom teeth pulled: I'd been warned three times over the past few years, but kept putting it off. One day I woke up asking myself, "What would my clients think if they knew that *I* won't even go to the dentist?" So I picked up the phone book and called, using some form of backwards *modeling* from client to therapist.

I have always had to coerce myself to make dentist appointments. When I moved to a new town and had to go to a dentist, I used behavioral principles to make the behavior more likely. First, I told my husband during our morning coffee that I was going to choose a dentist and make an appointment that same day (*public commitment*). Then, once I had a list of the dentists on my insurance plan, I looked at all the addresses and chose a few that were closest to home, since a long drive to and from the dentist's office would discourage me from going (*stimulus control*). Among the nearby dentists was one whose office was in the same strip mall as a great bakery and across the street from a big bookstore. I chose this dentist, figuring that I'd go to the bakery and bookstore after each dental appointment (*positive reinforcement*). And I could try to make all my appointments on Fridays, when that bakery makes the best challah in town. Even though I am fully aware of the long-term benefits of dentistry, I built in favorable *immediate consequences*, which are more compelling than delayed consequences.

In this process, I was practicing **self-management,** in that I was applying behavioral strategies to my own plans. Because behavioral interventions are easy to understand, many of them are offered for use without the help of a therapist. Self-help books like *Mastery of Your Anxiety and Worry* (Craske, Barlow, & O'Leary, 1992) and *Feeling Good: The New Mood Therapy* (Burns, 1999) take ordinary people through the steps of behavioral treatment. Even while reading this chapter, you may have consciously applied some of the principles in your own life.

Sometimes a goal of therapy is to achieve self-management, so that the therapy sessions are no longer needed. This type of approach is often very brief, including as few as one to five sessions. Hospital nurses, counselors, and psychologists advise patients in how to comply with medical directions, control pain, cope with dietary restrictions, and stick to exercise programs. People who have suffered heart attacks, for example, always undergo a course of behavioral therapy that helps them maintain heart-healthy lifestyles. And students first attending college are offered brief orientation courses or study skills workshops that give them tips for developing good habits at school. These are behavioral interventions with self-management goals.

Though some of us are able to learn self-management skills on our own, many people benefit from having a counselor guide them at first. The fact that we are responsible for almost all of our own behavior is scary, so the belief that we are capable of controlling our situations and actions must be instilled in order for behavior therapy to work (Kanfer & Gaelick-Buys, 1991). Behavioral therapists are careful to discourage being seen as miracle workers because that just fosters the dependency they are trying to eliminate. A conviction of self-efficacy (that is, the capability to organize one's behavior and perform adequately) is the best guarantee of ongoing ability "to manage ever changing circumstances, most of which contain ambiguous, unpredictable, and often stressful elements" (Bandura, 1986, p. 391) and may be the best predictor of happiness (Day & Rottinghaus, 2004).

Reflection

Develop a written plan for self-management of the behavior you would like to change or take more control over. Look at each technique discussed above and consider whether you can apply it to your desired change.

Group Work

I have referred to several situations in which behavioral treatments are applied to more than one client at a time: assertiveness training groups, support groups, workshops, and couples therapy. This practice is so common that group work can be considered a technique of behavioral therapy. Group members act as cotherapists by providing emotional support, wisdom from their own experience, role-playing cooperation, and straightforward feedback on each other's behavior from a nonexpert's perspective (Rose & LeCroy, 1991). In a group that shares a shocking or extreme behavior, such as self-mutilation or shoplifting, a person feels free to talk about the problem without negative judgment. Other groups, in contrast, ask for less individual self-disclosure while providing psychoeducation on behavior management, such as parent effectiveness classes and life simplification seminars. Behavioral training is often designed for specific groups that deal with specific situations, such as police officers who respond to family crisis calls (Bard, 1972).

The behaviorist approach lends itself to couples therapy because changes in high-frequency negative events can begin immediately. While altering small behavioral units may seem like putting a Band-Aid on a gunshot wound, "these changes seem to be the essential means of preparing the way for tackling the larger issues in marriage" (Stuart, 1980, p. 57). Each partner's willingness to make a change in the way he or she acts toward the other in everyday life, right away, builds a basis for trust, "a necessary antecedent for more venture-some investments" (p. 58). Reviewing research on behavioral marital therapy, Hahlweg, Baucom, and Markman (1998) concluded that with behavioral therapy, the chance of marital improvement rises from around 30 percent (with no treatment) to about 70 percent—a meaningful increase. When compared to other approaches, improvement in behavioral couples therapy was about the same, but at three- to nine-month follow-up, the behavioral approach showed better stability of change.

Case Conceptualization: An Example

The following case study demonstrates a behavior change program that you are capable of performing or assisting a client with at this point. Note, however, that you would need to study more detailed descriptions and practice under supervision in order to be qualified for the more intense behavioral modification programs, such as treatment for obsessive-compulsive disorder (rather than a specific obsessive habit or two), elaborate token systems, or aversion therapy.

CHANGING THE COACH

Tom Ciborowski and "Adele" (1997)

Adele wrote, "All my life I've had a problem with yelling. It began when I was a little kid trying to speak to my father. He has poor hearing and tends to speak too loudly, and as a result everyone in my family talks too loudly. And we have the tendency to yell when we're frustrated/stressed. In February I was made head coach of the fifth and sixth grade girls' basketball team at the school where I volunteer. The first thing that came to my mind was how my high school coach used to yell at us, and how it brought our spirits down. So, this and my experience with my loud family led me to choose as my project *controlling my yelling.*"

"My goal is to eliminate yelling at my players. I have to remember that some of my young girls don't even know how to dribble or shoot. Not only are they inexperienced, many . . . lack self-confidence. If I can keep my frustration and yelling under control, it will be easier for me to increase my players' motivation and confidence. If I yell they won't learn as much and will disrespect me. I am definitely willing to change whatever I have to change to get my yelling under control."

Adele kept a daily record of her stress level during basketball practice, which she rated from 1 to 10."1 didn't put a zero on the graph because there's never a day when I'm totally stress free." She noted reasons why she felt stressed. "I had a lot of studying to do, many papers to write, and my midterms were coming up soon." And, "The girls were just cutting up, and no one seemed to be listening to me."

After each team practice she also wrote a diary entry about her interactions with the girls. Here is her entry from February 10. "Today was frustrating for all of us. We worked on shooting. I got mad at them because they weren't trying hard enough and giving up. I told them if they didn't want to learn to go and sit down on the side. Many of them told me, 'I can't do it,' or 'I can't reach the basket.' I yelled and told them if they weren't willing to try, why even stay on the team? I told them I didn't want to coach those who didn't want to learn, and that I didn't want to waste my time. I totally lost my cool, got a migraine, and completely lost my appetite. Stress level was 10."

Adele's diary entry one week later: "Played a game with my girls. We had fun and they learned to block out and play defense. I didn't stress out as much as I did the past week. They listened to me more than usual today. Maybe I should think of more games to play. I didn't yell at them today. We had a team talk to see if there were any problems, and my girls complimented me on being an understanding coach!"

These are two of the shorter entries in Adele's daily log. For every practice or game day for 2 months she made a diary entry. Whenever something went wrong, she tried to figure out what its antecedents were, and what she could do to change her behavior. In her report she also presented a graph of her daily stress level for the 2-month period. See the Pre-Plan stage, at the left, in Figure 8.1.

Adele's First Plan for Change

Following our advice, Adele continued observing and recording her own behavior. She was then in position to design an effective plan.

She wrote, "By then I knew what triggered my yelling. It was a combination of different variables. One was being a student. Another was that my mind was always racing around the clock trying to figure out plays/strategies for my players, in addition to trying to comprehend all my school work. Also, my players sometimes didn't listen to me when I was trying to explain things. My ill health, migraines, and not eating right added fuel to my fires. But the most stressful variable was feeling stressed, plus having awful referees. All these set off my yelling. Some days at practice were good, but some were awful, and before I thought of my plan I yelled at them until they almost wanted to quit."

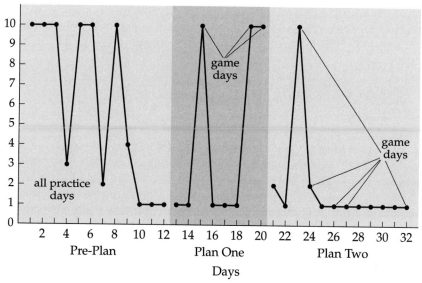

FIGURE 8.1   Adele's Stress Level

Adele has a good grasp of both the long-term and short-term antecedents to her yelling. Now what change strategy would she design?

"I finally thought of a plan to keep myself from yelling. It had five steps:

1. Be aware of my stress and frustration when my girls aren't listening to me.
2. To show my disappointment with them without yelling, ask them calmly to go shoot free throws. Then I will go to the other basket and shoot ten free throws myself before I coach them again;
3. While shooting my free throws, I will think of the consequences of yelling at them—I'll lose their respect if I yell too much—and of the problems and inexperience my girls are faced with;
4. Before each free throw, do relaxation exercises to relieve my tension;
5. After my free throws, go back to coaching."

Adele's plan allows her to "take a break" before things get out of hand, and to substitute relaxation for yelling. She also reminds herself of the unwanted consequences of yelling.

"This plan worked just fine. My girls were shocked that I didn't yell at them during practice, except when they played around too much. My stress level would start to go up, but when I became aware that it was accumulating, and I was about to yell, I just went off to the side and told the team captain to run the drills while I cooled off.

"I had one big downfall in my plan. I forgot that I couldn't shoot free throws during games. Boy, did I yell a lot during the first games. I yelled at the referees because they called horribly, and I yelled at my girls because they weren't concentrating and working together. I yelled and yelled and couldn't stop myself from yelling. My girls were afraid to talk to me because I was so angry."

Adele's setback is absolutely typical: something unanticipated comes up, and the plan has to be changed.

Adele's Second Plan for Change

She wrote, "I was finally able to think of another plan to follow while we had games. If I did start yelling, one of my girls would tug on my shirt and tell me I was starting to yell. That reminded me. Of course, it didn't always work because my girls were afraid to tell me or I was just too angry to calm down. But the times I did follow this plan I calmed down and was a more effective coach. It was funny: Sometimes the girls had to tug on my shirt so hard it pulled me down into my chair. They began making a game out of it, and said it was like pulling on a horse's harness. Also, after the games, I played a game with them, and then bought them all ice creams. More and more I got my yelling under control, and I got better at relaxing. On the practice days I continued my plan as I had before, shooting free throws and relaxing."

Adele's records showed that in the period before her first plan she yelled at her players on one third of the practice days. She yelled on 4 of the 8 days during her first plan—50%—but after beginning the second plan, she yelled only 1 out of 12 days—12.5%. She wrote, "This doesn't mean I didn't start to feel stressed during games. I did. But I was able to bring it under control."

She reduced her stress as well. Look at Figure 8.1. You can see that by the end of her program she significantly reduced her stress level.

Adele concludes, "All of my players, the athletic director, and the players' parents complimented me on my coaching. They never expected my girls to become better players or winners. My girls were second to last during the regular season, but in the post-season tournament we surprised everyone and took third place overall. I was happy about my girls' performance, and they were happy to be winners. In my heart, they were champions all along. And, I was asked to be coach again next year." (Adapted from Watson &Tharp [1997], pp. 26–29) ■ ■

DISCUSSION IDEAS

1. What assessments did Adele perform before planning the change treatment? What else could she have done?

2. What was Adele's overall problem? What was the target behavior? What was the history of Adele's problem? Was this history important in treatment planning?

3. What is the value of Adele's written analysis of benefits and reasons for her change?

4. List the techniques Adele used in her plans, along with the behavioral terms for these techniques.

5. Why did Adele need to alter her self-management program? What did she add to the treatment?

6. Do you think that Adele's behavior change will transfer to other areas of her life? What will she have to do to ensure this transfer?

7. If someone from one of the other theoretical stances you have studied encountered Adele as a client, how might treatment be different?

———————————————————

Critiques of Behavior Therapy

Behavior therapy has been widely criticized, and its adherents have countered each criticism with an argument of their own. I will summarize four common topics in this debate.

Dubious Ethics of Social Control

Behavior modification, an earlier label for behavior therapy, gained a negative image from imaginative portrayals in widely read books such as George Orwell's *1984* (1949), Aldous Huxley's *Brave New World* (1932), and Anthony Burgess's *A Clockwork Orange* (1962; made into a film by Stanley Kubrick in 1971). These works portrayed massive social control of individual behavior. At the expense of spirituality, moral choice, and human dignity, citizens were behaviorally conditioned into passivity and conformity. (In contrast, B. F. Skinner believed that behavioral conditioning could be applied in the service of a happy, productive society, and described such a world in his one novel, *Walden Two* [1948].)

Some critics still view behaviorist techniques as ethically dangerous: Who, they ask, chooses the goals—the individual or a social system that benefits from conformity? Attempts to change homosexual orientation through conditioning, to make frustrated housewives happy about their circumstances, and to curb the rebelliousness of youth serve as real-life examples. Certainly, institutional control of prison inmates, mental patients, and students is frequently done for the benefit of the people in authority.

Advocates of behavior therapy insist that most clients are never treated against their will. Because of the collaborative nature of behavior therapy, clients identify what behaviors they wish to change and what techniques they will put into practice. In fact, when clients sign an informed consent document, what they are consenting to is probably much clearer in behavioral treatment than in other forms of psychotherapy. The collaborative nature of the approach also protects against the imposition of mainstream cultural standards on unwilling clients. While behavioral therapy has a distinctly American independence-and-control ethos, whom to be independent from and what to control are matters left up to the individual client. Research outcomes of behavior therapy in the United States demonstrate effectiveness with clients regardless of race or ethnic background (Paniagua, 1994).

Behavioral methods performed upon people unable to give consent, such as the chronically mentally ill or other institutionalized people, are still problematic. We can hope that helping professions' codes of ethics prevail in decision making, and we can actively promote ethical use of all psychological change techniques. Spiegler and Guevremont (1998) assert that after successful treatment, clients actually have more options than before since they are not stuck in rigid, self-defeating patterns. An extreme example is offered by Lovaas (1987), who reported on the outcome of intensive behavioral treatment for young autistic children. After over two years of treatment, 47 percent of the children in the experimental group achieved normal intellectual and educational functioning, while only 2 percent of the control group children did so. This outcome is extremely impressive considering that autism entails severe psychological handicaps, emotional hardships for families, and the high costs of lifetime institutionalization.

Limitations of Standardized Treatment

The manualization of behavioral treatments has come under criticism (see Strupp & Anderson, 1997). Psychologists fear that therapy will become a matter of following mechanical directions, taking away the sophisticated artistry and skill inherent in the helping professions. They also worry that less educated people will take over their jobs for less money. The lack of flexibility in performing manualized treatment is often cited as a problem that puts both therapists and clients into pigeonholes.

On the other hand, behavioral theorists today realize that the common factors of successful therapy, such as the therapeutic alliance and belief in the treatment, still account for a large portion of client improvement. When these factors are added to therapist competence in a proven effective treatment, the result is better than common factors alone produce. And as far as flexibility in treatment is concerned, Wilson (1998) argues that there is no evidence that counselors from *other* orientations flexibly alter their approach when they encounter a lack of progress with a client. In short, we appear to stick to our favored courses— behaviorist or otherwise.

Superficial Approach

Whose problems are limited to fear of spiders? Not many, say some doubters. Behavioral therapy changes superficial and small things, and does not address long-standing, deep-seated psychopathology. Fixing a fear of women by assigning a charted goal of speaking to so many women each day addresses the symptom, not the heart of the matter. Enhanced insight, more awareness, higher quality of life, and general happiness are more meaningful pursuits.

The behavioral point of view on this issue is that behavior, thought, emotion, and environment are all interrelated and affect each other. A change in behavior *does* address other realms of a person's life. For instance, when obsessive-compulsive clients were successfully treated with *either* drug therapy or behavioral therapy, both treatments showed the same effects on the brain, seen by positron emission tomography (PET) scans (Baxter et al., 1992). Besides, behavioral change is observable and has results people trust, unlike psychoanalysis. Abstractions like happiness and insight are not accessible to manipulation, the way behavior is.

Biased Reports of Research

Though reviews of research show the superiority of behavioral treatments over others, the true state of affairs is not represented. Behavioral studies fit into the tradition of scientific inquiry, in that their operations are clearly defined and their outcomes can be translated into numbers. Treatments that don't fit the tradition in this way are left out of reviews and meta-analyses: Studies of alternative treatments usually consist of case studies and small-sample clinical accounts, which don't hold up under statistical scrutiny even though they might be just as valid. Also, some process-focused systems are philosophically opposed to statistical analysis of outcomes, and nonscientific accounts of process are short-changed in outcome literature.

From the behavioral stance, these criticisms are not of interest. Clients who want behavior change and its harvests benefit from the behaviorists' commitment to scientific method and empirical accountability. Unlike practitioners of other orientations, behaviorists want to know when their theories don't work out clinically, so that they can change them, resulting in continual improvement of the services they provide.

KEY TERMS

anxiety hierarchy
assertiveness training
aversion therapy
avoidance repression
baseline
biofeedback
classical conditioning
contingency
contrast modeling
counterconditioning
covert modeling
deficit
desensitization

differential
   reinforcement
discrimination
excess
exposure and response
   prevention
extinction
flooding
generalization
imaginal
implosive therapy
inappropriateness
in vivo

law of effect
law of exercise
learning theory
manualization
modeling
negative
   reinforcement
negative modeling
operant conditioning
participant modeling
positive reinforcement
progressive relaxation
punishment

reactivity of
   measurement
reciprocal inhibition
reinforcement
response
response burst
response cost
response withdrawal

schedule of
   reinforcement
self-management
shaping
social learning theory
stimulus
stimulus control
stressful modeling

successive
   approximation
systematic
   desensitization
token economies
transfer of training

Exploring Key Terms

Individually, write a description of a problem that could be changed. You can choose from several sources:

1. a problem that you have (maybe the one you have written a Reflection about);

2. a problem that you have seen in your work (with a client, patient, or student, for example);

3. a problem that you perceive in a person you know well; or

4. a problem in a group such as a specific family, couple, household, circle of friends, or workplace.

After you write the description, create a behavioral assessment and intervention plan, using twenty of the key terms listed above.

Bring your paper to your small group and exchange it with those of other members. Refine the intervention plans as a group to make sure all the key terms are used precisely and appropriately, and offer suggestions for terms that could be added to each case. Make a list of the terms in the list that are not used in any of the papers and discuss the definitions of those. If possible, distribute copies of your cases to the class as study aids.

LIBRARY, MEDIA, AND INTERNET ACTIVITIES

1. Here are the titles of some of the major journals in behavioral psychology.

Behavior Modification
The Behavior Therapist
Behavior Therapy
Behavior Research and Therapy
Behavioural Interventions
Child and Family Behavior
   Therapy
Clinical Behavior Therapy
   Review

Corrective and Social Psychiatry and
   Journal of Behavior Technology
   Methods and Therapy

Journal of Applied Behavior Analysis

Journal of Behavioral Assessment
   and Psychopathology

Revista Mexicana de Analisis de la
   Conducta (Mexican Journal of
   Behavior Analysis)

Find out which of these journals your library carries, and list their call numbers and locations. Look at the table of contents of a recent issue of one of them. Write down your impressions of the type of articles the journal publishes.

2. The homepage of the Buros Institute of Mental Measurements is *http://www.unl.edu/buros/*. This site gives basic information on psychological assessment measures. Look up the site, and use the Descriptors button to find tests related to Behavior Modification, Behavior Problems, and Behavior Analysis. Follow up on tests that are relevant to your clinical or educational interests. List the measures you find and write a paragraph of description for each one.

3. For sources on bibliotherapy, look up "bibliotherapy" as a topic under Books on *http://www.amazon.com*. Find books that would be useful to you in your area of counseling. In the library or at a bookstore, survey one of these books and write a description of it.

4. Use "token economies" as a search term in *http://www.google.com*. Surf the sources that interest you and write a report of your findings.

5. Go to a bookstore and find out where the self-help books are shelved (usually, these are near the Psychology and Health sections). Choose a self-help book and identify behavioral strategies that are encouraged in its chapters. Write an evaluation of how well presented you think the strategies are in the self-help book.

6. Here are the titles and descriptions of some video recordings of B. F. Skinner discussing behaviorism. Locate and watch one of the videos and write a summary and evaluation. If possible, round up a nonpsychologist to view with you and include his or her reactions in your evaluation.

B. F. Skinner on Counseling.   This video explores the relationship between counselor and client, the role of therapist as environmental engineer, choice of values, and the role of moral struggle and personal responsibility in behavior change. OCLC 22404306.

Business, Behavior, and the Bottom Line.   Skinner discusses theories concerning behavior modification, including scheduling, shaping, and positive reinforcement, as they are used in education, business, and industry. OCLC 5549825.

Dr. B. F. Skinner Interviewed by Richard I. Evans (part of a series titled *Notable Contributors to the Psychology of Personality*).   Skinner evaluates Freudian theory and views on motivation, operant conditioning, schedules of reinforcement, punishment, and teaching machines. He also discusses World War II, the American educational system, and the application of operant conditioning in society at large. OCLC 29523798.

Token Economy: Behaviorism Applied.   Skinner outlines treatment for mentally ill, criminal, and retarded individuals, demonstrating the application of theories in a mental health facility. OCLC 20816173 and 15042554.

REFERENCES

Achenbach, T. M. (1991). *Manual for the child behavior checklist: 4–18 and 1991 profile.* Burlington: University of Vermont, Department of Psychiatry.

Bandura, A. (1974). Behavior theory and the models of man. *American Psychologist, 29,* 859–869.

Bandura, A. (1986). *Social foundations of thought and action.* Englewood Cliffs, NJ: Prentice-Hall.

Bard, M. (1972). Training police as specialists in family crisis intervention. In C. J. Sager & H. S. Kaplan (Eds.), *Progress in group and family therapy* (pp. 879–924). New York: Brunner/Mazel.

Barlow, D. H. (1993). *Clinical handbook of psychological disorders* (2nd ed.). New York: Guilford.

Baxter, L. R., Schwartz, J. M., Bergman, K. S., Szuba, M. P., Guze, B. H., Mazziotta, J. C., Alazraki, A., Selin, C. E., Ferng, H. K., Munford, P., & Phelps, M. E. (1992). Caudate glucose metabolic rate changes with both drug and behavior therapy for obsessive-compulsive disorder. *Archives of General Psychiatry, 49,* 681–690.

Bergin, A. E., & Garfield, S. L. (1994). *Handbook of psychotherapy and behavior change* (4th ed.). New York: Wiley.

Burns, D. D. (1999). *Feeling good: The new mood therapy* (Rev. ed.). Wholecare.

Christophersen, E. R., & Mortweet, S. L. (2001). *Treatments that work with children.* Washington, DC: APA.

Condry, J. (1977). Enemies of exploration: Self-initiated versus other-initiated learning. *Journal of Personality and Social Psychology, 35,* 459–477.

Conners, C. K. (1969). A teacher rating scale for use in drug studies with children. *American Journal of Psychiatry, 126,* 884–888.

Craske, M. G., Barlow, D. H., & O'Leary, T. (1992). *Mastery of your anxiety and worry.* Albany, NY: Graywind Publications.

Day, S. X., & Rottinghaus, P. (2004). The healthy personality. In B. Walsh (Ed.), *Counseling psychology and optimal human functioning* (pp. 1–25). Mahwah, NJ: Lawrence Erlbaum Associates.

Dollard, J., & Miller, N. E. (1950). *Personality and psychotherapy.* New York: McGraw-Hill.

Emmelkamp, P. M. G. (1994). Behavior therapy with adults. In A. E. Bergin & S. L. Garfield (Eds.), *Handbook of psychotherapy and behavior change* (4th ed., pp. 379–427). New York: Wiley.

Foa, E. A., & Kozak, M. J. (1986). Emotional processing of fear: Exposure to corrective information. *Psychological Bulletin, 99,* 20–35.

Foa, E. B., & Meadows, E. A. (1997). Psychosocial treatments for post-traumatic stress disorder: A critical review. *Annual Review of Psychology, 48,* 449–480.

Glynn, S. M., & Ruderman, A. (1986). The development and validation of an Eating Self-Efficacy Scale. *Cognitive Therapy and Research, 10,* 403–420.

Hahlweg, K., Baucom, D. H., & Markman, H. (1998). Recent advances in therapy and prevention. In I. R. H. Falloon (Ed.), *Handbook of behavioral family therapy* (pp. 413–448). New York: Guilford.

Hiss, H., Foa, E. B., & Kozak, M. J. (1994). Relapse prevention program for treatment of obsessive-compulsive disorder. *Journal of Consulting and Clinical Psychology, 62,* 801–808.

Hogan, R. A. (1968). The implosive technique. *Behavior Research and Therapy, 6,* 423–431.

Jacobson, E. (1938). *Progressive relaxation.* Chicago: University of Chicago Press. (Original work published in 1929.)

Joshua, J. M., & DiMenna, D. (2000). *Read two books and let's talk next week: Using bibliotherapy in clinical practice.* New York: Wiley.

Kanfer, F. H., & Gaelick-Buys, L. (1991). Self-management methods. In F. H. Kanfer & A. P. Goldstein (Eds.), *Helping people change: A textbook of methods* (4th ed., pp. 305–360). New York: Pergamon.

Kazdin, A. E. (1994). *Behavior modification in applied settings* (5th ed.). Pacific Grove, CA: Brooks/Cole.

Koss, M. P., & Shiang, J. (1994). Research on brief psychotherapy. In A. E. Bergin & S. L. Garfield (Eds.), *Handbook of psychotherapy and behavior change* (4th ed., pp. 664–700). New York: Wiley.

Lazarus, A. A., & Lazarus, C. N. (2000). *The 60-second shrink: 101 strategies for staying sane in a crazy world*. Atascadero, CA: Impact Publishers.

Lewinsohn, P. M., & MacPhillamy, D. J. (1971). *Pleasant events schedule*. (Available from Peter M. Lewinsohn, Department of Psychology, Straub Hall, University of Oregon, Eugene, OR 97411.)

Lovaas, O. I. (1987). Behavioral treatment and normal educational and intellectual functioning in young autistic children. *Journal of Consulting and Clinical Psychology, 55*, 3–9.

Nathan, P. E., & Gorman, J. M. (Eds.). (1998). *A guide to treatments that work*. New York: Oxford University Press.

Ost, L., Stridh, B., Wolf, M. (1998). A clinical study of spider phobia: Prediction of outcome after self-help and therapist-directed treatments. *Behavior Research and Therapy, 36*, 17–35.

Paniagua, F. A. (1994). *Assessing and treating culturally diverse clients: A practical guide*. London: Sage.

Patterson, C. H. (1980). *Theories of counseling and psychotherapy* (3rd ed.). New York: Harper & Row.

Prochaska, J. O., & Norcross, J. C. (1999). *Systems of psychotherapy: A transtheoretical analysis* (4th ed). Pacific Grove, CA: Brooks/Cole.

Reynolds, C. R., & Kamphaus, R. W. (1998). *BASC: Behavior Assessment System for Children: Manual including preschool norms for ages 2–6 through 3–11*. Circle Pines, MN: American Guidance Service.

Romanczyk, R. G. (1974). Self-monitoring in the treatment of obesity: Parameters of reactivity. *Behavior Therapy, 5*, 531–540.

Rose, S. D., & LeCroy, C. W. (1991). Group methods. In F. H. Kanfer & A. P. Goldstein (Eds.), *Helping people change: A textbook of methods* (4th ed., pp. 422–453). New York: Pergamon.

Rosenthal, T. L, & Steffek, B. D. (1991). Modeling methods. In F. H. Kanfer & A. P. Goldstein (Eds.), *Helping people change: A textbook of methods* (4th ed., pp. 70–121). New York: Pergamon.

Sandler, J., & Steele, H. V. (1991). Aversion methods. In F. H. Kanfer & A. P. Goldstein (Eds.), *Helping people change: A textbook of methods* (4th ed., pp. 202–247). New York: Pergamon.

Skinner, B. F. (1957). *Verbal behavior*. Acton, MA: Copley Publishing Group.

Skinner, B. F. (1974). *About behaviorism*. New York: Vintage.

Skinner, B. F. (1981). How to discover what you have to say—a talk to students. *Behavior Analyst, 4*, 1–7.

Sloane, R. B., Staples, F. R., Cristol, A. H., Yorkston, N. J., Whipple, K. (1975). *Psychotherapy versus behavior therapy*. Cambridge, MA: Harvard University Press.

Smith, M. J. (1975). *When I say no, I feel guilty*. New York: Bantam Books.

Spiegler, M. D., & Guevremont, D. C. (1998). *Contemporary behavior therapy* (3rd ed.). Pacific Grove, CA: Brooks/Cole.

Stampfl, T. G. (1970). Implosive therapy: An emphasis on covert stimulation. In D. J. Leavis (Ed.), *Learning approaches to therapeutic behavior change* (pp. 182–204). Chicago: Aldine Press.

Strupp, H. H., & Anderson, T. (1997). On the limitations of therapy manuals. *Clinical Psychology: Science and Practice, 4*, 76–82.

Stuart, R. B. (1969). Token reinforcement in marital treatment. *Advances in Behavior Therapy: Proceedings of the conference* (pp. 221–230). New York: Academic Press.

Stuart, R. B. (1980). *Helping couples change: A social learning approach to marital therapy*. New York: Guilford Press.

Thorndike, E. L. (1911). *Animal intelligence*. New York: Macmillan.

Watson, D. L., & Tharp, R. G. (1997). *Self-directed behavior: Self-modification for personal adjustment* (7th ed.). Pacific Grove, CA: Brooks/Cole.

Wedding, D., & Corsini, R. J. (1989). *Case studies in psychotherapy.* Chicago: F. E. Peacock Publishers.

Wickramasekera, I., Davies, T. E., & Davies, S. M. (1996). Applied psychophysiology: A bridge between the biomedical model and the biopsychosocial model in family medicine. *Professional Psychology: Research and Practice, 27,* 221–233.

Wilson, G. T. (1998). Manual-based treatment and clinical practice. *Clinical Psychology, 5,* 363–375.

Wilson, G. T. (2000). Behavior therapy. In Corsini, R. J., & Wedding, D. (Eds.), *Current psychotherapies* (6th ed., pp. 205–240). Itasca IL: F. E. Peacock Publishers.

Wolpe, J. (1958). *Psychotherapy by reciprocal inhibition.* Stanford, CA: Stanford University Press.

Wolpe, J. (1990). *The practice of behavior therapy* (4th ed.). New York: Pergamon.

CHAPTER **9**

Cognitive-Behavioral Therapies

A Selection from
Love Is Never Enough, 1988

Aaron T. Beck

Sybil and Max were happily married for several years, during which time Sybil worked and Max went to medical school. After their children were born, Sybil gave up her position as a teacher and dedicated herself to the children and her husband. Max, a promising medical researcher, was away from home a good deal, although he considered himself a devoted husband and parent. A critical event in their marriage occurred when Max called Sybil from a distant city where he was attending a medical convention:

MAX: [*Sybil will be glad I'm getting on so well, meeting a lot of people, learning a lot.* Note: Italics represent Max and Sybil's inner thoughts.] I'm having a great time. How are you?

SYBIL: [*He's having a great time while I have two sick kids on my hands.*] Joan and Freddie are sick.

MAX: [*Oh no, she's going to lay something on me.*] What's the matter with them?

SYBIL: [*Will he respond? Show a sense of responsibility?*] They have chicken pox. They're running a fever.

MAX: [*Chicken pox is usually not serious. She's exaggerating the problem.*] You don't have to worry. They'll be all right.

SYBIL: [*Why doesn't he offer to come home?*] All right.

MAX: [*I hope she's reassured.*] I'll call tomorrow.

SYBIL: [*He's never around when I need him.*] You do that! [sarcastically]

Max and Sybil see the same situation in completely different ways, and so evaluate each other's actions—and each other—totally differently. This difference in perspective is typical of distressed marriages and often leads to more serious problems.

Max does not view the children's illness as serious enough to warrant his immediate attention. He knows that if Sybil really *needed* him, he would "come running," but in his own mind he glosses over the fact that Sybil seems deeply concerned. He believes that Sybil is overreacting and tries to reassure her that everything will be all right. In any event, he doesn't want to be controlled by her "worrisomeness."

Sybil, on the other hand, views Max as derelict in his duties. He "gets a free ride" while she is left with all the family responsibilities. The following list summarizes the differences in their attitudes:

Sybil's Attitude	*Max's Attitude*
1. Max should offer to come home.	1. Since Sybil doesn't really need me, there's no reason to make the offer.
2. I should not have to ask him.	2. I'm not a mind reader: If she needs me at home, she should say so.
3. He should know I need him. He can make this sacrifice for me.	3. She's overreacting. She can handle the situation without my having to make a sacrifice.
4. He's selfish and irresponsible. He places his advancement before everything else.	4. She's demanding and controlling. She's jealous of my career. She can't stand to have me enjoy myself.

In their dealings with others, both Sybil and Max are considered very nice. Socially they appear to be a happy couple, yet they have reached a serious impasse in their marriage, as their conversation reveals. Much of their exchange—the most important part—is unspoken: Sybil wants Max to *offer* to come home, and Max avoids making such an offer. Because of these unspoken thoughts, they both start to attribute negative qualities to each other. Max becomes selfish and irresponsible in Sybil's eyes; Sybil becomes demanding and jealous to Max.

On further analysis, there are deeper currents in the interaction. Although Sybil is, indeed, worried about the children, she does not feel completely helpless. What she really wants is a sign from Max that he really cares about what she is going through and that he is responsible enough to be willing to pitch in. She recognizes that it would be a sacrifice for Max to come home, and she wouldn't even consider the possibility if it weren't important to her. But she wants—and expects—him to make such an offer. His willingness to make the sacrifice would show that he cared, was responsible, and made the family his top priority. If he should make such an offer, then she might let him off the hook and tell him to stay. In this context, his not offering to come home is a *negative symbol* that he doesn't care and is irresponsible.

Max, on the other hand, sees the family problem in purely practical terms. He is oblivious to the symbolic meaning of his not offering to come home. His only thought is that an immediate return is unnecessary because Sybil is capable of managing without him. Since he thinks only of the practical considerations and not of the symbolic meanings to Sybil—her worries about the children and her wish for him to be present—he alienates her. . . .

If we tried to judge the conflict between Max and Sybil impartially, it might be difficult to render an absolute decision: Should Max come home, or at least offer to? Is Sybil right in expecting such an action? A simple verdict would be that neither is totally right or totally wrong. But such a verdict would miss the real conflict, which is broader and more complex than simply whether Max returns home. The real issues in their minds are: *"Will Sybil support me at work?"* and *"Will Max support me at home?"*

When we overlook the more abstract issues in marital conflict, we may be misled into thinking of overly simple solutions to the problems. The concrete question of Max's coming home is of significance largely because it represents a broader principle: what Max does or does not do when Sybil wants his support has *symbolic meaning.*

The broader principles that marital partners subscribe to, but are often not aware of, have been described as "virtues." These virtues have to do with fairness, caring, consideration, responsibility, respect, and the like. Thus, a single, concrete action stands for a broad, abstract principle. In Sybil's mind, if Max offers to come home, then it means that he *cares,* is considerate, responsible, and fair; if he does not make the offer, it means that he doesn't care, is inconsiderate, irresponsible, and unfair. For Sybil the choice is cut-and-dried. (pp. 69–74) ■ ■

DISCUSSION IDEAS

1. Reread the first two sentences. How is this background important to your understanding of the situation between Sybil and Max?

2. Why is Max's making the offer to come home more important than actually coming home?

3. What are some of Max's unexpressed fears? What are some of Sybil's unexpressed fears?

4. What are the two people aware of during the conversation? What issues are not in their awareness?

5. Can you think of a dialog with someone that went this way in your own life—in which there were unstated symbolic meanings?

6. Give other examples of "single, concrete actions" that stand for "broad, abstract principles" in your relationships or in our society.

7. Would you like to read more of the book *Love Is Never Enough*? Do you know other people who would benefit from the book, from what you can tell so far? Why do you think it holds its own on mass-market bookstore shelves after more than fifteen years in print?

Introduction to Cognitive-Behavioral Theory

In Sybil and Max's conversation, the words they spoke (their verbal behaviors) were barely notable—an ordinary exchange between partners, on an everyday topic, in plain language. It was what each partner *thought* that made the conversation "a critical incident in their marriage," according to Beck. How many times have you heard comments like these?

- "You got me all wrong! I didn't mean that you have fat thighs!"
- "I told him I enjoyed his company, but he took it the wrong way."
- "All I said was, Isn't that your fourth beer?"

Clearly, our words do not always communicate what we intended, or they communicate *more* than we intended—or at least more than we wanted brought out in the open. When Susan says to Patrick, "Isn't that your fourth beer?" it would be hard *not* to read-in a message.

Making a meaning out of a behavior is something done inside our heads, something not observable. In the last chapter, we saw examples of therapy focused on measurable, observable stimuli and responses; in this chapter, we consider therapy that focuses on the element of the *meanings* behind stimuli and responses. As I mentioned, even behavioral therapies today integrate cognitive components. Cognitions include inner processes like interpretations (as in the examples above), wishes, plans, motivations, fantasies, problem-solving, hopes, expectations, reasoning, attention, imagery, judgments, doubts, and daydreams. We say, "I told myself that I had better do such-and-such" and "I argued with myself over that," showing that we experience something like inner speech, which is not observable but still drives our actions. Significant to our goals as counselors, inner consolidation and understanding of learning are necessary to make behavior change stick around and transfer to the new situations life hands us. We have to "get it."

One of my friends was facing his third prison term, for running hot guns between Chicago and St. Louis. "But I haven't touched any drugs!" he said in disbelief: His previous stretch was for dealing drugs. And before he got sent up that time, he was quite stunned, because he had totally given up armed robbery, his first offense. He didn't "get it"! We told him that if he had to learn to obey the law crime by crime, he was going to spend most of his life in jail. He had to grasp the bigger principle. This grasp is what cognitivists see lacking in strict behaviorism.

Essential Concepts

Albert Bandura went beyond straight stimulus-response learning theory when he investigated the effects of what we expect, how competent we feel, who we see as models, and what we observe vicariously—none of which are behaviors. The field of cognitive psychology blossomed in the 1960s with Ulrich Neisser's *Cognitive Psychology* (1967), which presented research on "all the processes by which . . . sensory input is transformed, reduced, elaborated, stored, recovered, and used" (p. 4), emphasizing the ways we process information (sensory input) in a stage between stimulus and outward response. All seven of the cognitive-behavioral systems I introduce in this chapter share the **mediational position** (Dobson & Block, 1988), which is "that cognitive activity mediates the responses the individual has to his or her environment, and to some extent dictates the degree of adjustment or maladjustment of the individual" (p. 29).

Cognitive psychologists study how people choose, remember, and see principles behind incoming information. This is an individual process, even though it follows certain laws. For example, if your whole class went to a bookstore, you would not all run through it like rats through a maze toward the same cheese. Each person would choose which section of the store to go to: Some would visit the cookbooks, some the computer section, some the poetry shelves, some the coffee shop—and some would go wherever their friends went. You would also have differing affective (emotional) interpretations of the experience: Interest, excitement, resentment, boredom, impatience, envy, and pleasure would all be in the mix. Even an individual's behavior would not be consistent from one bookstore trip to the next. If you were writing a paper in a psychology class this week, you might hit the psychology collection even though usually you would head for the CDs. The state of your body, too, might determine what you did: If you had a headache or forgot your reading glasses, you might go have a latté in a situation where otherwise you would browse. This illustrates how human behavior is more complex than most animals' behavior, and understanding humans requires investigating their inner workings.

Two pioneers of the cognitive-behavioral approach, Albert Ellis and Aaron Beck, came from backgrounds in traditional psychoanalysis. In the 1950s, both independently theorized that most psychological distress stemmed from faulty or damaging mental processing of experience, rather than from "esoteric themes such as castration anxiety or psychosexual fixations" (Beck, 1991, p. 369). They also questioned the constraints of psychoanalytic therapy: With his hallmark bluntness, Ellis thought, "Why, when I seemed to know perfectly well what was troubling a patient, did I have to wait passively, perhaps for a few weeks, perhaps for months, until he, by his own interpretive initiative, showed that he was fully 'ready' to accept my own insight? Why, when patients bitterly struggled to continue to associate freely, and ended up by saying only a few words in an entire session, was it improper for me to help them with several pointed questions or remarks?" (Ellis, 1962, p. 7).

Connections Among Behavior, Emotion, and Cognition

When I see my niece *cop an attitude,* I mean that

- she is acting a certain way, like rolling her eyes and shrugging her shoulders;
- she is feeling frustrated, irritated, bored, or defensive;
- she is thinking that I and other conspiring adults are unbelievably stupid.

Thus, an *attitude* involves behavior, emotion, and thought all rolled into one. The intimate connections among these three modes are basic concerns of cognitive psychology. In changing the name of his main theory from Social Learning Theory to Social Cognitive Theory, Albert Bandura focused on how "the human mind is generative, creative, proactive, reflective, not just reactive" (2001, p. 4). You might say that psychodynamic theories put emotion (especially conflict) first, and behavioral theories put actions first, while cognitive theories put thinking first.

Moreover, cognitive theories put faith in the power of thinking to override emotional and behavioral impulses. We all know this power: Just think of standing in a long, crowded grocery store line with the person behind you continually bumping his cart into your backside. You develop a hefty irritation and decide to turn around and tell the clod off—but when you turn, you see that this person is trying to balance on two crutches and keep his full cart under control. Suddenly, your irritation dampens, and your plan to complain disappears. A thought, a realization, has changed your feelings and behavior.

But you can also think of instances in which emotion drives thought. I can decide to buy my friend the first-class plane ticket she wants because I can afford it, she is a good friend, and flying coach has always been a particular complaint of hers. However, I made up all these good reasons motivated by the emotional fact that I fear conflict with her and want to avoid an argument or hurt feelings. The notion that emotion and thought are neurophysiologically and psychologically separate is questionable (R. Lazarus, 1984), and the matter of whether one mode always has primacy over the other is debatable, but these questions and debates are not central to performing therapy.

Aaron Beck, one of the fathers of cognitive therapy, wrote that early in his career as a psychoanalyst, he noticed the connections among behavior, emotion, and cognition: "I was struck by how ascertaining the idiosyncratic or special meanings people attached to events helped to explain what might otherwise have represented quite inexplicable affective and behavioral reactions" (1991, p. 369). A Filipina classmate of mine once told me that where she came from, offering a guest just a sandwich or chips would be a clear insult, because serving several cooked dishes was expected, even when the guest was not invited for a meal. Imagine how many American hosts might end up mystified by their Filipino guests' reactions, totally unaware that there was a "special meaning" attached to a little snack.

Phenomenological Approach

Very much like existential and Adlerian approaches, cognitive therapies focus on subjective meaning. In the example above, being offered a variety of cooked foods when visiting has a subjective meaning (good will and respect) for some Filipinos, but not for many Americans. In the same vein, my Icelandic classmate said that it would be rude for a guest not to ask questions about the photographs displayed in a host's home, while I would never take this as a sign of rudeness. Our culture, and the various subcultures we belong to, provide interpretations of information from the physical and social environment. These interpretations make up our **phenomenological** existence.

It's always interesting to encounter a social group with a different world view from our own. Being an academic, I usually live among people who, whether or not they like it or admit it, characteristically take note of whether another person is intelligent or not. A few years ago, I took pottery classes at a studio where advanced students of ceramics usually worked, and I had a glimpse of a whole different way of noticing—these potters spoke of other people in terms of whether they could work with porcelain, whether they had good color sense in glazing, how thin the walls of their thrown pots were, and so on. Whether another person was smart or dumb simply didn't enter into their view of him. My cleverness and knowledge of Shakespeare meant nothing, whereas my lumpy short pots branded me in this environment. I was telling my remedial English students about this experience, and they laughed and said, "Now you know how *we* feel in *here!*"

Private experience provides us with interpretations of incoming information. We have personal ways of processing events, on a more individual level than our cultural and subcultural tendencies. A person who grew up in a home governed by sudden rages may, as an adult, feel touchy about signs of conflict that someone else might not even notice. The tranquil rural farm scenes of Illinois gave my mother shortness of breath and a panicky feeling, since she remembered being trapped "in the middle of nowhere" on a failing farm during her childhood. Those same scenes produce peaceful, nostalgic feelings in other people. Such individual response tendencies become part of our personalities, or what George Kelly called our set of **personal constructs** (see Chapter 2). These are our characteristic ways of viewing the world around us: what catches our attention, what we think is important, what we remember for a long time, what touches us emotionally, and so on.

DISCUSSION IDEAS

Recall the example of my mother's panic at scenes that most people find relaxing; can you think of any idiosyncratic responses of your own? Or do you have friends and relatives who display unusual reactions to incoming information? Do you know the learning history behind any of these responses?

Automaticity

Aaron Beck's early inklings about the role of cognition in psychology came when he was treating clients from a traditional psychoanalytic stance. Beck (1991) summarized the experience:

> At one point I observed to my surprise that my patients experienced specific types of thoughts of which they were only dimly aware and that they did not

report during their free associations. In fact, unless they were directed to focus their attention on these thoughts, they were not likely to be very aware of them. Although these thoughts seemed to be on the periphery of the patients' stream of consciousness, they appeared to play an important role in the psychic life of these patients. . . . These thoughts (cognitions) tended to arise quickly and automatically, as though by reflex; they were not subject to volition or conscious control and seemed perfectly plausible to the individual. They were frequently followed by an unpleasant affect (in the case of the depressed patients) that the patients were very much aware of, even though they were unaware of, or barely aware of, the preceding automatic thoughts.

When I directed the patients to focus their attention on these "automatic thoughts," they began to report a string of them, particularly in response to a cognitive probe, "What are you thinking right now?" Connecting these thoughts brought out certain negative themes such as deprivation, disease, or defeat. Grouped together they fell into the category of a negative view of the present, past, and future experiences. Later, in working with more severely depressed patients, I noted that these types of thoughts were no longer peripheral but occupied a dominant position in consciousness and were repetitive. (p. 368)

Beck was identifying a level of thought that occurs beyond voluntary thoughts, which are usually quite accessible. At the level beyond voluntary, **automaticity** was operating; in other words, the thoughts spontaneously occurred without beckoning. We have automaticity in our behavior, too, as you know from your habits when driving a car, cooking in your familiar kitchen, and going through other daily routines. We even call it "being on automatic pilot," when we accidentally drive toward work on our day off, or feel for the clutch in a rented automatic-transmission car. Similarly, our minds have an automatic pilot that steer us in habitual directions without much attention. Remember that in Max and Sybil's case, both partners were operating from principles of which they were not consciously aware. These principles usually come with an emotional component and seem believable to the person who holds them.

Many psychological disorders involve a systematic bias in processing information such as social and environmental cues. That is, automatic thoughts control the person's response to the outside world. A cognitive profile of several psychological disorders is shown in Table 9.1.

According to cognitivist belief, conscious control can be applied to systematic biases, overcoming maladaptive responses to people and situations.

DISCUSSION IDEAS

The list of systematic biases in Table 9.1 is sketchy. See whether you can further explain the relationships between the biases in column two and the disorders in column one. For example, why do deficiencies in problem-solving dispose a person toward suicidal behavior?

TABLE 9.1
Systematic Biases in Processing Information

Disorder	Bias
Depression	Negative view of self, experience, and future
Hypomania	Inflated view of self and future
Anxiety disorder	Sense of physical or psychological danger
Panic disorder	Catastrophic interpretation of bodily/mental experiences
Phobia	Sense of danger in specific, avoidable situations
Paranoid state	Attribution of bias to others
Hysteria	Concept of motor or sensory abnormality
Obsession	Repeated warnings or doubts about safety
Compulsion	Rituals to ward off perceived threat
Suicidal behavior	Hopelessness and deficiencies in problem-solving
Anorexia nervosa	Fear of being fat
Hypochondriasis	Attribution of serious medical disorder

SOURCE: Beck and Weishaar (2000), p. 251.

Behavioral Merger

Lack of success in treating depression by behavioral means led therapists to consider the cognitive concepts set forth by Albert Ellis and Aaron Beck (Rachman, 1997). While radical behavioral psychologists, like B. F. Skinner, have usually been at odds with cognitive psychologists, behavioral and cognitive *therapists* have been in sympathy. Behavior therapists quickly saw the necessity of integrating cognitive elements such as trust, hope, self-efficacy, modeling, and consolidation of learning into their treatments (see Chapter 8). However, they still saw behavior change as the main point, whereas cognitive therapists see behavioral exercises as *methods* for producing change. Behavioral methods such as self-monitoring, diaries, hierarchies of tasks, bibliotherapy, operant conditioning, stimulus control, systematic desensitization, relaxation, modeling, enlistment of significant others, and exposure are all commonly used in cognitive treatments. In cognitive approaches, you will see homework assignments and real-world experiments that are not distinct from behaviorists' interventions. Behavioral methods are used for assessment (such as obtaining baseline data), testing old ways of thinking, and putting new insights into action. Cognitive therapy adds verbal methods such as question-and-answer dialog, logical reasoning, and disputation. Because most modern cognitive approaches integrate the two, as a group they are called *cognitive-behavioral*, as reflected in this chapter's title.

Couples therapist R. B. Stuart (1980) views cognitive and behavioral interventions contributing to different stages of therapy. Each intervention supports the improvements achieved by the other: "(1) Cognitive change to potentiate new action. (2) Behavior change to potentiate new experience. (3) Cognitive change to potentiate the repeat of the desired actions by conceptualizing their effects" (p. 49).

Reverence for scientific method and empirical proof is also shared by behavioral and cognitive therapists. Belief in clearly defined goals, reliable record-keeping, treatment integrity, and measurement of progress and outcomes (Rachman, 1997) has resulted in published research that holds water for most of the scientific community. This stance also allows practitioners to test their hypotheses and to alter their approaches based on evidence, making cognitive-behavioral therapy (CBT) an evolving field.

Problem-Solving

Many cognitive-behavioral therapies can be seen as **problem-solving** enhancements, if we define *problem* as a situation or set of situations "which, by virtue of their novel aspects, complexities, ambiguities, or conflicting stimulus demands, present circumstances that involve the failure of 'automatic' effective action" (D'Zurilla & Goldfried, 1971). A person with pervasively biased cognitions, like those listed in Table 9.1, creates automatic responses in the face of stress—responses that are not conducive to effective action. Furthermore, psychological distress decreases a person's ability to concentrate, recall, and reason (Beck, Rush, Shaw, & Emery, 1979), all of which are needed to define a problem and think up a variety of potentially effective responses to choose from. A strictly behavioral therapy assists a person in learning to perform an effective response when presented with a certain situation, whereas a cognitive component seeks to prepare the person to deal with day-to-day problems in general (D'Zurilla & Goldfried, 1971). One of the first efforts the therapist makes is to help the client see problems as normal, natural parts of life, most of which are manageable.

The Therapeutic Process

Cognitive-behavioral treatment takes several forms, as described in the next few sections. Commonalities exist in the essential concepts as well as in the process of treatment.

The Therapist's Role

Cognitive-behavioral therapy is a persuasive methodology, in that the therapist works to convince the client that his or her way of viewing the world is not the only one or, for that matter, the most correct one. The role of the therapist is one of teacher or guide, a catalyst through which educational and corrective experiences come about. The counselor must have the qualities important to any helping professional, such as being trustworthy and inspiring confidence.

In cognitive-behavioral treatment particularly, counselors verbally challenge the client's systems of belief. Thus, they must possess sharp reasoning themselves and a good rhetorical ability to present their arguments. If you are a person known for your powers of persuasion, you are well suited for the verbal aspect of CBT. Further intellectual expertise is needed in inferring the schemas from which clients are working and in devising dialogs and experiments to disconfirm biases.

Cognitive-behavioral therapists do not present themselves as a blank slate, since transference is not important therapeutically. Instead, modeling has a place in the relationship, and often the therapists admit their own imperfections, beliefs, and values, so that clients can observe that a person does not have to be super-human to deal effectively with life's challenges.

Goals of Therapy

A successful course of therapy can be gauged by the client's development of a new way of thinking, substituted for an old way that has not been working well. For example, as I suggested above, perceiving problems as normal and manageable is a huge change for many clients. They have previously automatically thought, "I can't stand this," "This is awful," "I will never get over this," or something else equally helpless and extreme. Seligman (1992) has elaborated on the theme of **learned helplessness,** a dismal pattern of thought developed through repeated past experiences in which pain was inescapable.

The successful client becomes his or her own therapist, able to continue using cognitive reality-testing and thought control long after sessions have ended.

Initial Interviews

In the first stage of the process, the therapist works to establish rapport and trust with the client. The informational interview begins to socialize clients into the style of cognitive treatment by eliciting discussion about how they typically see the world, themselves, and other people. Clients who give general labels to their problems are encouraged to provide specific examples. In the first session, the therapist is likely to educate the client about self-monitoring and ask him or her to record thoughts, feelings, or interactions between sessions. They also go through a sample of the recording technique together.

Early in the process, the therapist and client come up with a list of problems they will address, along with some ideas about which ones hold highest priority. The therapist's aim is to produce some initial symptom relief right away, in order to build trust in the treatment and hope for its success. Usually, some specific behavioral advice can improve a small aspect of the client's life. Let me give you an example. In my work with troubled writers, I discovered a way that helped them deal with intrusive thoughts while writing. They needed to keep scratch paper close at hand while writing at their desk and then, when a distracting thought occurred, to write a key word describing the thought on a scrap of paper, put it immediately into a desk drawer, and say to themselves, "That takes care of that for now." This simple trick (a thought-stopping technique) usually allowed them to return to their writing, and when the same thought tried to intrude, they would think, "I took care of that already," and carry on. This is the type of small improvement that gives a client early faith in cognitive techniques.

The Middle Stage

In the central sessions of therapy, each session balances thought and behavior topics. The therapist and client rationally investigate the client's patterns of belief, often using three questions to go over a specific situation that occurred in the time between sessions (Beck & Weishaar, 2000):

- What is the evidence for this belief?
- How else can you interpret the situation?
- If it is true, what are the implications?

During this middle stage, the client does homework assignments that are designed to reveal automatic thoughts and the assumptions that generate them. For example, Max and Sybil, from the opening story in this chapter, would first delve into the unspoken meanings behind their utterances in the phone conversation. Then they would discuss the principles from which they were working: Max is unsure that Sybil will support his work, and Sybil is unsure that Max will support her at home. There is an emotional distrust of each other underlying the incident. They then examine the evidence for and against distrusting each other and proceed through the questions. This process is labeled **guided discovery** because the therapist serves as a guide.

The Last Sessions

Cognitive-behavioral therapy tends to be brief, from one to twenty-five sessions. As the clients become self-guiding in the reality-testing techniques, they refine their ability to identify cognitions and analyze them logically. Counselors often taper off the timing of sessions, making them less and less frequent. Clients may leave individual therapy and enter CBT groups, where they serve partly as co-therapists for others. Like behavioral therapy, cognitive approaches include relapse management training in the termination phase and may offer booster sessions every few months. When the clients' major goals are met and they have mastered the techniques of cognitive analysis, they are able to become their own guides.

Sample Cognitive-Behavioral Treatment for Childhood Anxiety

Sixteen sessions of a cognitive-behavioral treatment plan for childhood anxiety are summarized in Table 9.2. Though you may not recognize all the interventions, you can see how the process is mapped out in steps that build upon each other.

TABLE 9.2
A Cognitive-Behavioral Treatment Plan for Childhood Anxiety

	Purpose	Sample Items
Session 1	Build rapport Provide information about treatment Gather information about child's anxieties	Personal facts game Introduction to feelings Learn about homework tasks
Session 2	Review treatment goals Identify different types of feelings; normalize fear/anxiety Begin to construct hierarchy of anxiety-provoking situations	Match faces with feelings Feelings role play Calm, nervous situation cards
Session 3	Distinguish anxiety from other feelings Introduce and identify somatic feelings related to anxiety Introduce "freeze frame" for when child is too anxious to continue with tasks	Questions about anxiety-provoking situations for self and others Modeling and role playing of situations *F* = Feeling frightened?
Session 4	Review identifying somatic responses to anxiety Introduce tense versus relaxed Introduce relaxation training	Robot vs. rag doll example Discussion of tension and anxiety Progressive muscle relaxation (three muscle groups) through modeling and practice
Session 5	Review relaxation training Introduce thoughts–response connection; self-talk	Role play specific scenarios from child's anxiety hierarchy Cartoons with empty thought bubbles *E* = Expecting bad things to happen?
Session 6	Review anxious self-talk Review relaxation training Introduce active coping strategy—how to change the situation	Make reminder cards of strategies learned so far (recognition, self-talk, attitudes, and actions) Model steps; have child problem solve *A* = Attitudes and actions that will help?
Session 7	Review relaxation training Introduce concept of self-evaluation and reinforcement	Make card for results and rewards Feelings barometer to rate performance List preferred rewards *R* = Results and rewards?

TABLE 9.2 (continued)

	Purpose	Sample Items
Session 8	Introduce FEAR (Feelings, Expectations, Actions, Reward) acronym Apply skills to low-anxiety situations Practice all skills learned in previous sessions	Have child make own FEAR card Role play and practice various anxiety-provoking situations; imaginal and in vivo
Session 9	Practice FEAR plan with imaginal and in vivo scenarios	Modeling of FEAR to cope with scenario Practice using situation cards of low anxiety arousal created by child
Session 10	Continue practicing skills applied to low level imaginal and in vivo situations	Cartoon strips with empty bubbles Modeling and role play Practice with low-anxiety situation cards
Session 11	Practice skills for imaginal and in vivo scenarios that produce moderate anxiety	Modeling and role play Use imaginal, in office, and first out of office exposure
Session 12	Practice skills for in vivo scenarios that produce moderate anxiety	Role play situation Arrange for child to be transported to anxiety-provoking location Modeling coping skills; practice of skills
Session 13	Practice skills for imaginal scenarios that produce high anxiety	Develop cartoon story of situation and coping strategies Role play situation and coping
Session 14	Practice skills for in vivo scenarios that produce high anxiety	Arrange for high-anxiety situation out of office Practice skills Offer relaxation exercises when needed
Session 15	Continue practicing skills for in vivo scenarios that produce high anxiety	Same as Session 14; develop "commercial" to teach others about anxiety and coping
Session 16	Review and summarize training program Make plans with parents for maintenance and generalization Bring closure to therapeutic relationship	Tape child's commercial Give certificate of achievement Arrange for final session in 1 week

Source: Christophersen & Mortweet (2001), pp. 70–71.

Identify systematic desensitization techniques (Chapter 8) in the CBT program for child anxiety presented in Table 9.2. List the other techniques in the program, and give examples of their possible uses in other types of cases.

Varieties of Cognitive-Behavioral Treatments and Their Uses

Beck and Ellis began a movement that now encompasses many schools of treatment. In this section, I will summarize Beck's **Cognitive Therapy,** Ellis's **Rational-Emotive Behavior Therapy,** and five other significant forms of cognitive-behavioral treatment.

Albert Ellis's Rational-Emotive Behavior Therapy

"If the Martians ever come down to visit us and they are reasonably sane, they will probably die laughing at our self-inflicted nuttiness!" (Ellis, 1987, p. 367). Albert Ellis's treatment was originally called Rational Therapy (around 1955); then it was labeled Rational-Emotive Therapy (RET); and finally, in the early '90s, it became known as Rational-Emotive Behavior Therapy (REBT), tracing the course of Ellis's incorporations through the years.

Profile of a Theorist

ALBERT ELLIS (1913–)

Accounts of Albert Ellis's life are similar to his style of psychotherapy, packed with examples of proactive problem-solving and decisive action. Ellis was born on September 27, 1913, in Pittsburgh, Pennsylvania. When he was 4, his family moved to the Bronx in New York City. Critical of both parents, Ellis described himself as a semi-orphan who essentially raised himself. His father traveled and had little to do with his children when he was home. After the couple divorced in 1924, Ellis's father lived nearby but saw the children even less. According to Ellis, his mother spent more time playing mahjong and socializing with friends than parenting, leaving the young Ellis to fend for himself and, frequently, for his siblings as well.

In addition to neglectful parents, Ellis faced significant health problems as a child. Hospitalized eight times between the ages of 5 and 8 for kidney disease, he was forbidden to participate in sports or active play and, perhaps as a result, was a shy and fearful youth. Yet he credited these events with motivating him to become a "stubborn and pronounced problem-solver." Like Adler, whose influence is apparent in Ellis's theory of behavior and change, he believed his ability to overcome adversity in childhood was an example of how one's perception of a problem shapes its outcome. Refusing to be miserable, he took pride in his independence and his ability to understand others, choosing to turn competence into confidence.

Though his first ambition was to become a writer, Ellis experienced little success and, consistent with his pragmatic approach to life, obtained degrees in accounting and business. He continued to write while working and developed expertise on the subjects of sex, love, and marriage. While providing informal help to friends, he discovered a proclivity for counseling and decided to enroll in the graduate program in clinical psychology at Teachers College, Columbia University. He received his doctorate in 1947.

The success of his own style of couples counseling along with a dissatisfaction with Freudian theory kept Ellis from feeling at home in the traditional psychoanalytic world. Though sexuality played a central role in his writing and his work with clients, Ellis found Freud's theories of sexual development to be rigid and his form of therapy ineffectual. He identified more with neoanalytic thinkers, such as Adler, Horney, and Sullivan, sharing with them a belief that cognition and perception were critical to human behavior.

By the 1950s, Ellis was forging new therapeutic territory, confronting clients' *irrational beliefs* and incorporating directive techniques to problem-solving. Ellis radicalized the passive role of the analyst, choosing to engage with clients actively by challenging them to *discipline* their thinking. As noted earlier, he named this type of counseling Rational-Emotive Therapy and later modified it to include a behavioral component (Rational-Emotive Behavior Therapy).

This cognitive-behavioral approach did not win Ellis much support in academic circles initially, but his clinical success attracted national attention. He founded the Institute for Rational-Emotive Therapy in the early '60s, and training and therapy centers affiliated with the New York institute spread across the country and to several countries overseas. Ellis is well known for his irreverence and his almost belligerent style of working with clients. However, those who know the man and his work contend that he "exudes humanism" and should be credited with bringing a style of therapy to the average client that is both more pragmatic and more effective than traditional analysis.

The Nature of Unhappiness   Albert Ellis started from a belief that human beings have inherent rationality, but are also burdened with strong inborn tendencies to think irrationally and create states of poor mental health within themselves. Western civilization inculcates some senseless and superstitious ideas, and on top of that, "because of their upbringing and their genetic tendencies, some people are significantly more prone than are others to think, emote [feel], and behave self-defeatingly" (1987, p. 373). Ellis did not believe in the psychological separateness of thought and emotion.

Because thinking is usually verbal, what we say to ourselves determines our emotions and behavior. This is why self-damaging behaviors persist in spite of being punished or at least not rewarded, whereas a straight conditioning theory would expect them to be extinguished. Repeating the same illogical statements to ourselves perpetuates disordered behavior and emotion. Did you ever know someone who seems constantly to choose relationships in which he is rejected? Why does he keep doing that? He probably says to himself each time, "See, I *am* a loser. No one will ever want a long-term relationship with me." Therefore, his thought that he is a loser *is* rewarded, because he seems to be right. Unless he learns to combat that thought, and substitute a more rational one like "I haven't found the right way to choose relationships yet," he is in trouble.

The therapist assists in such a learning process. Reorganizing a client's thinking and the way he sees and interprets outward events is the goal. Therefore, clients must first identify what self-verbalizations are driving their emotions and behavior. Then they need to replace those with logical self-talk that serves their human needs more effectively. The REBT therapist is an expert in this identification and change process, partly because she has heard it all before. Indeed, most harmful self-talk can be boiled down to several basic themes, as listed in the next section.

Eleven Irrational Beliefs   From 1954 through 1962, Ellis developed his rational approach to therapy, publishing a series of articles and finally a book, *Reason and Emotion in Psychotherapy* (1962). In this book he set forth a list of eleven **irrational beliefs** that lead to unhappiness and neurosis. This list and various forms of it appear in hundreds of articles, chapters, books, and audiotapes, as well as on handouts disseminated at workshops and schools of counseling.

1. *It is essential that a person be loved or approved by virtually everyone in the community.*   This is an unobtainable goal, and the person who strives for it becomes less self-directing, more insecure, and less genuine.

2. *A person must be perfectly competent, adequate, and achieving to be considered worthwhile.*   This perfectionist attitude leads to psychosomatic illness, a sense of inferiority, and a constant fear of failure that undermines the courage to learn (because mistakes are inevitable).

3. *Some people are bad, wicked, or villainous and therefore should be blamed and punished.*   Wrong or immoral acts are the result of stupidity, ignorance, or emotional disturbance. All people are fallible and make mistakes. Rational people do not blame themselves or others but attempt to correct their own behavior and stop misdeeds by others. Blame and punishment do not result in less stupidity, more intelligence, or a better emotional state.

4. *It is a terrible catastrophe when things are not as a person wants them to be.*   The rational person realizes that frustration is unavoidable. He or she avoids exaggerating unpleasant situations and works at improving them if possible or accepts them if they can't be improved. Unpleasant situations may be disturbing, but they are not terrible or catastrophic unless a person defines them as such.

5. *Unhappiness is caused by outside circumstances, and a person has no control over it.* Outside forces and events, while they can be physically assaulting, usually are psychological in nature. People disturb themselves by telling themselves how horrible it is when someone is unkind, rejecting, annoying, and so on. The person's own reactions to the mistreatment are under his or her control because he can change his definitions of and attitudes toward the events.

6. *Dangerous or fearsome things are cause for great concern, and their possibility must be continually dwelt upon.* Worry and anxiety do not prevent dangerous events and may make them worse. The concern may prevent a person from taking effective action before, during, or after the event. A person who is rational recognizes that potential dangers are not as catastrophic as he or she fears.

7. *It is easier to avoid certain difficulties and self-responsibilities than to face them.* Actually, avoiding a task is often harder and more painful than performing it and leads to later problems and dissatisfactions, including loss of self-confidence. A challenging, responsible, problem-solving life is an enjoyable life.

8. *A person should be dependent on others and should have someone stronger on whom to rely.* Maximizing dependency leads to loss of independence, individualism, and self-expression. The person who is rational strives for independence and responsibility but does not refuse to seek or accept help when necessary.

9. *Past experiences and events are the determinants of present behavior; the influence of the past cannot be eradicated.* Rationally, what was once necessary behavior in certain circumstances may not be necessary at present; past solutions to problems may not be relevant in the present. The presumed influence of the past may be used as an excuse for avoiding changing behavior. The present can be changed by analyzing past influences, questioning those acquired beliefs that are harmful, and forcing [oneself] to act differently in the present.

10. *A person should be quite upset over other people's problems and disturbances.* The person who is rational determines whether the behavior of others warrants becoming disturbed and, if so, then attempts to do something that will help the other person to change. If nothing can be done, the person accepts it and makes the best of it.

11. *There is always a right or perfect solution to every problem, and it must be found or the results will be catastrophic.* The insistence on finding a perfect solution leads to anxiety or panic, since it doesn't exist. Perfectionism results in poorer solutions than are actually possible. The rational person considers various possible solutions and chooses the best or most feasible one, even though it is flawed. (Adapted from Ellis, 1962)

A counselor following REBT treatment is not interested in DSM diagnoses, because his or her diagnosis is made by identifying which of the irrational beliefs the client holds most dearly, and are doing the most damage.

R e f l e c t i o n

On a note card, write key words from each of the eleven irrational beliefs so that you can remember what they are. Carry this note card for a few days and refer to it when you become anxious, worried, depressed, impatient, hurt, frustrated, or fearful. Which of the beliefs could be operating? Can you identify your favorite knee-jerk irrational thoughts? (My classmates and I enjoyed playing this game, and we usually agreed with each person's choice of his or her top irrational beliefs.)

Techniques   Ellis is known for being directive and confrontational with his clients. He sees little purpose in fulfilling clients' need to be loved, since he believes that "I absolutely need to be loved" is another irrational belief. And Ellis disagreed with the practice of letting clients dwell on their pasts—he called it "indulgence therapy." Therefore, an REBT session looks different from other counseling sessions. The therapist may be actively arguing with the client and calling his or her beliefs ridiculous. Though many REBT practitioners are gentler than Ellis, they are always more active and talkative participants in the therapeutic dyad than other types of counselors. Humor is a hallmark of REBT: When encouraged to do so, people can often see the funny side of their exaggerated, childlike beliefs.

REBT uses an alphabet mnemonic, **A B C D E F,** to teach clients the basic system. It starts with A, B, C:

A—Activating event: An episode of new information or interaction coming in from outside, or a thought coming from within. *Sera's husband brings his after-dinner cigar out on the balcony, and she sees that it is huge.*

B—Belief: The often spontaneous, often irrational perception or thought within the client's mind in response to A. *Sera thinks, "Nick knows that I want to watch our favorite television series together in fifteen minutes, and that cigar will take all night to finish! He hates to smoke just half, and he will never come in on time to watch our show. He is so inconsiderate, I just can't stand it. He always does things like this to ruin our time together."*

C—Consequence: Emotional and behavioral outcomes arising from B. *Sera leaves the balcony without talking to Nick and starts banging pans around in the kitchen, doing the clean-up they usually do together and feeling victimized and ignored.*

Part of what Sera needs to realize, and what an REBT therapist would insist that she see, is that C didn't follow directly from A. It came through a very powerful B, one that had nothing to do with Freud even though a cigar was involved. Sera responded in the rigid, demanding, and absolute mode that

REBT labels as childlike. This mode frequently embraces words and phrases like *must, should, ought to, have to,* and *got to.* The C can even become an Activating Event in itself and start another cycle. For instance, Sera can think, *Nick is purposely ignoring me* (A), then *Nick doesn't love me any more* (B), then *I should not have to be so miserable in this marriage, and Nick ought to feel bad about the whole thing* (C).

The D, E, F part of the mnemonic follows through what will happen due to therapy:

D—Disputing intervention: The therapist (and later, the client herself) asks questions about the B that came between A and C. Does Nick *know* what time it is? Does he want to smoke that particular whole cigar? Does he do considerate things, ever? Could there be another reason for his choice of cigar, other than to ruin her evening? How bad could it really be if they missed watching part of their show together? Isn't it true that she *can* stand an incident like this, even if he is ignoring her?

E—Effective new philosophy: The client learns to substitute more adaptive thoughts in place of the beliefs that often involve unrealistic and overgeneralized attributions (such as "He is so inconsiderate, I just can't stand it"— neither clause is true). New thoughts for Sera might be "Nick usually enjoys our time together," and "He will probably notice soon that his cigar is going to edge into our time," and "If he smokes through the time for our show, I'll just start watching without him and he can catch up when he comes in." All of these new thoughts would lead to the next step.

F—Feelings (new): Sera's new trains of thought lead to more effective and rational behavior, like being affectionate toward Nick, leaving him alone, and watching the program herself. She might even simply go ask him if he plans to smoke that whole cigar!

SMALL GROUP EXERCISE

Using the Sera and Nick story as a model, develop another A-B-C story that shows how B (not A) creates C. Then, taking the role of an REBT therapist, discuss how you would lead the client through a D-E-F sequence.

Besides questioning and reasoning, REBT counselors prescribe behavioral exercises to combat irrational beliefs. An extremely self-conscious person might be assigned to wear a silly outfit to work or burst into song in a public place, in order to see that most bystanders are only mildly interested if they even notice at all. Clients also receive reading and listening assignments from the many REBT books, articles, worksheets, and audiotapes available at bookstores and through the Albert Ellis Institute in New York City (*http://www.rebt.org*).

Reflection

Frequently, the source of humor in a story is a character's rigidity or irrationality. Think of television comedies or films that focus on an irrational character's flaws. For example, on *Friends*, Monica's uptightness and her perfectionism create funny situations. Do you think it's true that we find funniest the flaws that we ourselves share to some extent? Are your favorite humorous stories based on some of your own qualities?

In spite of Ellis's somewhat harsh view of human cognition and his sense of the ridiculousness of many human pursuits, he insists, "I am really an optimist about mental health. I have written hundreds of articles, chapters, and books and have recorded scores of cassettes on how people have enormous power to think about their thinking, to use rationality and the scientific method, and to radically control and change their emotional destiny—providing they really work at doing so. . . . I believe that, along with their powerful self-defeating and self-destructive tendencies, humans also have great self-changing and self-actualizing powers" (1987, p. 374).

Aaron Beck's Cognitive Therapy

Beck and Ellis, in the same country and during the same period, arrived at surprisingly similar conclusions about the role of cognition in clinical psychological problems, and the teachability of new, adaptive cognitions. However, Beck's work has attracted more attention among psychologists, partly because his writing is more scholarly and partly because his early efforts were toward treating depression, which had remained beyond behavioral treatment so far (Rachman, 1997). I myself have drawn from Beck's writing several times in the introduction to this chapter.

Errors in Information Processing   Parallel to Ellis's irrational beliefs, Beck created a list of faults in information processing. These are flaws in perception and interpretation that maintain negative beliefs even when evidence is scant or absent.

1. **Arbitrary inference:** Drawing a specific conclusion in the absence of supporting evidence or in the presence of contrary evidence. For instance, a client might say that he's lazy, even though he's never missed a deadline and is widely known for his energetic productiveness.

2. **Selective abstraction:** Focusing on a detail taken out of context, ignoring other meaningful features of the situation, and labeling the whole experience

on the basis of this fragment. Sera, in my earlier example, focused on Nick's choice of after-dinner cigar, out of a whole set of circumstances that suggested the couple would be following their normal pattern for the evening.

3. **Overgeneralization:** Drawing a general rule or conclusion on the basis of one or more isolated incidents and applying the concept across the board to related and unrelated situations. Sera decided that Nick was inconsiderate (a general conclusion) based on his choice of after-dinner cigar (an isolated incident). Then, she decided he was not going to help in the cleaning-up, based on his inconsiderateness (applying the concept to another situation).

4. **Magnification** and **minimization:** Errors in evaluating the significance or magnitude of an event. These errors are so gross that they distort the event. For example, if your Uncle Ned got drunk and foolish at your reception, you would be *magnifying* to say that your whole wedding was ruined. If your fiancé drunkenly addressed you by the wrong name as you said your vows, you'd be *minimizing* to say that everything went perfectly.

5. **Personalization:** A tendency to relate external events to yourself when there is no basis for making such a connection. Some people take bad weather as a personal insult, or think that their vehicle attracts heavy traffic, or perceive long waiting lines as assaults.

6. **Absolutist dichotomous thinking:** Placing all experiences in one of two opposite categories: flawless or defective, immaculate or filthy, saint or sinner. You read about this type of thinking among *splitters* in psychodynamic theory. Often, a client describes himself or herself using a negative and extreme category. (Adapted from Beck, Rush, Shaw, & Emery, 1979, p. 14)

Beck thinks that we all operate from our own **core schemas,** which are systems of beliefs that are related in a network. Our schemas give us consistent ways of looking at situations: As suggested earlier, Kelly (Chapter 2) would call the same things *personal constructs.* These schemas develop from past experiences such as our upbringing and particular traumas, and Beck remains closer to the psychodynamic tradition than Ellis does. We may have a negative *core schema* that usually lies dormant but becomes activated by some outer or inner situation that resembles its psychodynamic source. For example, I am hypersensitive to signs of violence, and I recently broke out into hives when my partner was swearing furiously at a stubborn electrical repair. Though his rage was not in the slightest related to me, my body responded as though I were in danger.

In cognitive therapy (CT), a relapse prevention stage at the end of therapy identifies early maladaptive schemas, emphasizing developmental patterns and long-term interpersonal difficulties that may signify dangerous relapse situations (Young, Beck, & Weinberger, 1993). An important distinction between approaches is that, unlike Ellis, Beck does not apply the same set of irrational beliefs to all disorders. Rather, Beck has identified core schemas that underpin specific clinical problems. Several of these take the form of the information-processing biases shown in Table 9.1.

The Cognitive Triad   Beck's close observation of the symptoms and basic beliefs of depressed people generated the most theoretically coherent and empirically supported treatments for depression (Hollon & Beck, 1994). As noted in Chapter 1, empirically supported treatments (ESTs) are therapies that have been validated in controlled research experiments. In Beck's model, depressed people are plagued by a **cognitive triad** of beliefs:

1. They see the *self* as "defective, inadequate, diseased, and deprived" (Beck, Rush, Shaw, & Emery, 1979, p. 11).

2. They interpret *experience* as negative, even when evidence exists for a neutral or positive interpretation instead, or a mixed viewpoint. They see life making outrageous demands and placing impossible obstacles in their paths, and everyday tasks appear extremely difficult and taxing.

3. They see the *future* as continuing in this grim fashion and expect failure to be inevitable.

The Beck Depression Inventory (BDI; Beck, 1987) is a twenty-one-item scale that is widely used as a research and clinical assessment tool. Each item inquires into a particular aspect of depression, including elements of the cognitive triad and seven bodily symptoms (such as appetite and sleep changes).

Reflection

If possible, find a copy of the BDI. Your professor might bring one to class, and there's one in the appendix of Beck, Rush, Shaw, and Emery (1987), in other books in your school library, and in self-help books at the store. Take the inventory for yourself. The higher the overall score, the more depression is indicated. Cutoffs for mild depression have been set at 10 to 13 points (Lezak, 1995). Describe your reaction as you took the inventory. Put yourself in a client's place—what might the client think of it? What could you do as a counselor to prepare a client to take the BDI comfortably and accurately?

The Process of Cognitive Therapy   Like REBT, CT seeks to identify, challenge, and change dysfunctional thought patterns. Beck's emphasis is on **collaborative empiricism,** in which client and therapist treat automatic thoughts as hypotheses that can be tested out in behavioral experiments and be subjected to logical scrutiny. A questioning technique called **Socratic dialog** is used in the verbal collaboration, in which the therapist asks a series of questions that elicit exceptions and counterarguments to challenge the client's original assertions about self, experience, and the future. Thus CT clients are not directly indoctrinated into a philosophical system, as they are in REBT, but, rather, are led to become their own truth-seekers. The goal of a CT counselor is that "in response to traumatic situations, the average person will still maintain interest in and realistically appraise other non-traumatic aspects of his life" (Beck, Rush, Shaw, & Emery, 1979, p. 16), instead of allowing extreme, absolute, and negative interpretations to dominate all areas of living.

Meichenbaum's Stress Inoculation Training

Donald Meichenbaum was trained as a behaviorist, and this background is clear in the interventions he has formulated. In his early work with hospitalized schizophrenics in the 1960s, he noticed that patients who had undergone an operant conditioning treatment imitated the experimenters' instructions, telling themselves to "give healthy talk; be coherent and relevant," even when they were not being conditioned (Patterson, 1980). Under stress, they were using self-instruction to control their behavior, and this realization led Meichenbaum to a lifetime of research on how explicitly training people to talk to themselves could lead to changes in thought, emotion, and behavior. He based some of his thinking on the developmental research of Vygotsky and Luria, who analyzed the development of self-direction in children. These Soviet psychologists thought that children progressed from following parental instructions to following internalized verbal commands (Dobson & Block, 1988). Meichenbaum found success in training hyperactive children to be less impulsive through talking to themselves (Meichenbaum & Goodman, 1971) and continued to refine his ideas about why people fail at coping with stressful events.

Stress inoculation training (SIT) is now a generic cognitive-behavioral program used for many different problems involving **stress** (a perception that life's demands have exceeded one's abilities to cope), whether by overcoming, reducing, or tolerating inner and outer burdens (Meichenbaum, 1985). Stress comes in many forms, including

- an acute, time-limited variety, such as preparing for surgery, medical examinations, or major evaluation such as licensure exams.

- a sequence originated by a specific event (death, divorce, job loss, disaster) that triggers a series of stressors (loss of status, job-seeking, fear); posttraumatic stress disorder (PTSD) is an example.

- repeated, intermittent exposures to stressors such as student examinations, competitions, or physical disorders like headaches.

- continual, chronic stressors such as an ongoing medical or psychiatric illness, prolonged family discord, or occupational dangers and strains. (Adapted from Meichenbaum, 1993)

To address this variety, SIT has been designed as "a flexible, individually-tailored, multifaceted form of cognitive-behavioral therapy" (Meichenbaum, 1996, p. 4).

The label identifies a medical analogy, in which inoculations of a weak form of a disease protect a person against exposure to severe cases. In the central phase of treatment, clients are exposed to a graded hierarchy of fears and taught to apply problem-solving tactics while being supported and guided by the therapist. Thus, they become inoculated against future stressors.

Three Phases of Intervention Three overlapping phases enhance clients' coping skills (Meichenbaum, 1996).

1. During the *conceptualization phase*, the collaborative relationship between client and counselor is established. Clients are educated about what stress is, the role of their self-talk in dealing with stress, and how they may accidentally add to stress levels themselves. They are encouraged to look at threats and frustrations as problems to be solved or to be faced with adaptive strategies. Interviews, self-monitoring, paper-and-pencil tests, and reading materials are used to help clients conceptualize their specific stressors and responses. They gather information about their fears, identify situations that bring stress, and consider strategies different from the ones they usually practice. Hope for successful intervention is instilled.

2. The second phase consists of *skills acquisition and rehearsal*. Coping skills training is tailored to the client's problems and may include "emotional self-regulation, self-soothing and acceptance, relaxation training, self-instructional training, cognitive restructuring, problem-solving, interpersonal communication skills training, attention diversion procedures, using social support systems, and fostering meaning-related activities" (1996, p. 4). By means of a graded hierarchy of stressful situations, skills are practiced in the clinical setting and then rehearsed in vivo.

3. The final phase provides opportunities for *application and follow-through*. Clients use their coping skills in increasingly difficult situations. As they become proficient, learning may be cemented through their teaching the skills to other people. High-risk situations and warning signs are identified in a relapse prevention component. A sense of responsibility for improvement and for future behavior is encouraged.

Wide Range of Applications Because of SIT's generality, it has been used in a large number of settings, for many problem populations (Meichenbaum, 1993). In cases involving psychological strain in anticipation of medical procedures, SIT has been successfully used to alleviate the fears of surgical patients, parents of pediatric leukemia patients, and chemotherapy recipients. Psychiatric patients making readjustments to life outside the hospital have benefited from SIT practice on the high-risk situations they will meet. A multifaceted treatment for PTSD victims and their significant others has had encouraging results. SIT can be packaged as an educational program in self-control rather than as a form of psychotherapy, eliminating the drawback of stigma among people like combat veterans and athletes. And highly stressed occupational groups such as disaster relief workers, police officers, and probation officers are often trained by fellow workers in the same field, with a psychologist as an SIT consultant.

An admirable feature of the SIT philosophy is that not only individuals need to change but also environments such as institutions, families, and businesses. Some situations are more stressful than they need to be, and clients are encouraged to consider changes in the source of the stressor as well as in themselves. SIT programs have been developed to help schools ease the transition for mature returning college students and to assist businesses in preparing workers for the stresses of overseas placement.

SMALL GROUP EXERCISE

Choose one of the stressful situations below, and brainstorm about stress inoculation procedures that could be used to help the person deal with the situation.

- A 7-year-old needs to have her tonsils removed.
- A college student's grandfather dies.
- A Korean-American woman is exhorted to find a husband because her younger sister is ready to marry, and the oldest daughter must marry first.
- A high school sophomore's social group begins drinking beer every weekend.
- A college sophomore wants to change her major to a subject her parents have discouraged.

Present your ideas to the class as a whole.

Glasser's Reality Therapy

If Carl Rogers's approach reminds us of the perfect daddy we never had, William Glasser's approach reminds us of the smart, tough drill sergeant we never had. From Glasser's point of view, how the world treats us is a reflection of how well we are doing psychologically: Reality is the test. He explained his terminology in *Reality Therapy: A New Approach to Psychiatry* (1965):

> All patients have a common characteristic: they all deny the reality of the world around them. . . . Whether it is a partial denial or the total blotting out of all reality of the chronic backward patient in the state hospital, the denial of some or all of reality is common to all patients. Therapy will be successful when they are able to give up denying the world and recognize that reality not only exists but that they must fulfill their needs within its framework. (p. 6).

Glasser's focus on the demands of external reality makes reality therapy a natural choice for clients who are acting-out or delinquent, and the approach is most frequently used in schools and other settings that focus on behavior control. Often, reality therapy clients are in trouble with society—in jail, in mental hospitals, on probation, in halfway houses or foster homes, or unemployed. They are frequently "addicts, child abusers, psychotics, criminals, school failures, sex deviants, and the many others who do not come for counseling voluntarily" (Glasser, 1992). The techniques of the treatment accommodate short, irregular, emergency contacts between the counselor and client if necessary, and the language of the treatment is that of common-sense advice. Dr. Phil, the popular television psychologist, is an example of a reality therapist. His down-to-earth, humorous, "How's *that* workin' out for ya?" style appeals to people, even when he is challenging the effectiveness of the behavior they cling to.

Assigning blame to external events such as abusive upbringing or bad company is discouraged as excuse-making. "Expending time and energy to discuss the reasons that underlie ineffective behavior serves only to reinforce clients' belief that they are only minimally capable of making changes" (Wubbolding, 1996, pp. 8–9). Similarly, emotions are not highlighted: Feelings are discussed "in connection with the actions involved, but as infrequently as possible in isolation" (pp. 9–12). When Glasser consults with schools, parents, and institutions, he encourages them to avoid blame and recrimination but to emphasize the **natural consequences** of a person's actions. For example, grounding a teenager for staying out past curfew is a punishment; however, if the teenager has to complete chores at home or school at the usual times no matter how tired he is from staying out late, that is a *natural consequence*. This emphasis helps people understand the effect their behavior has in reality, rather than in an artificial reward and punishment system.

Control Theory, Choice Theory, and Human Behavior Reality therapy is not based on control theory, but **control theory**—also known as *cybernetics*—does provide a possible explanation of how it works, and Glasser (1981) uses metaphors and terms from control theory to explain his approach. Cybernetics, the understanding of self-regulating systems, applies to physics, engineering, mathematics, economics, and medicine, as well as to human systems like bureaucracies, governments, schools, and businesses. The same principles also serve as models for human functioning (Carver & Scheier, 1982). Our behaviors can be seen as adjustments that we make when there is a discrepancy between a desired state (a reference value, in cybernetic terms) and a present condition. Let me give you an example on the physical level. Each citizen of Houston has a desired state in the form of an ideal temperature. If we are to stay in this desired state, we need to wear as close to nothing as we can get by with for outdoors, while carrying a long sleeved shirt and a sweater for interiors, which are air conditioned from cool to meat-locker level. So we go through the day taking clothes on and off, adjusting for the discrepancy between our environment and our reference value.

In the psychological arena, too, the process of self-regulation involves setting desired states for ourselves, observing our actions, and evaluating the actions by comparing their outcomes with the desired states (Carver & Scheier, 1982). We make attempts to match the reference value with the present state. Neurotic or maladaptive behavior comes from flaws in these matching attempts. First, we may not see how to get to the desired state: "[M]any people want to be 'fulfilled,' or 'likable,' or 'successful' but have no idea what actions will move them in the direction of those superordinate goals. Indeed, they often do not know where to begin in *determining* what concrete steps will provide such superordinate discrepancy reduction" (p. 125). Second, if we have continually failed at reaching desired states, we expect future failure and refuse to exert sustained effort toward our higher goals. Third, we may have developed faulty ideas about what will get us from a present state to a desired state. (For example, throwing lavish parties does not get you a devoted circle of friends, and a series of heists doesn't gain you financial security.) On top of these difficulties, throw in the facts that our desired states sometimes change and that external conditions are always tossing in unexpected twists, and it's no wonder so many people go off track.

Because the term *control theory* applies to so many different systems, in the 1990s Glasser started using **choice theory** to describe self-regulatory behavior in human beings.

Needs and Responsibility   According to Glasser, we all share a set of universal needs, which are needs for survival, belonging, power or achievement, freedom or independence, and fun. From these needs, we devise a personal vision of what we want, images of what will satisfy our needs. Behavior consists of the choices we make in trying to get this satisfaction. In reality therapy, the concept of individual choice and responsibility is critical (Glasser, 1998). We choose our thoughts, emotions, and behaviors, and these choices make up the quality of our lives. The goal of reality therapy is to help people make better choices and have more control over their lives, within the constraints of the outside world (reality).

The WDEP System   The reality therapist makes use of a cluster of interventions that make sense given the basic concepts of control theory, needs, and choice. The acronym for the four modes of intervention is WDEP, for Wants, Direction and Doing, Evaluation, and Planning.

- *Wants*   A client's understanding of his wants is a major step in reality therapy. Friendly, fair-minded questioning by the counselor helps clarify what the client wants from himself, family, friends, job, co-workers, teachers, bosses, children, society in general, and counseling.

- *Direction and Doing*   Dr. Phil's classic question "How's *that* workin' out for ya?" addresses the topic of direction: Where is a client's behavior taking her? Is it toward one of her wants, or away? A reality counselor uses **time projection** questions such as "If you continue in the same way, where will you be in five years? One year? Where will your family be? How will you look at this situation in one year?" and so on. The therapist encourages vivid and specific details in the answers, which will help the client see consequences.

- *Evaluation*   Clients' evaluations of themselves are "the cornerstone of reality therapy" (Wubbolding, 1996, pp. 9–13). In this intervention, they look at their behavior in terms of its impact on other people and on their own satisfaction. They also are asked to state how their behavior is evaluated by external rules, such as whether it is against the law, against company policy, against school rules, or against probation requirements. Furthermore, they evaluate their actions based on unwritten norms of acceptability. Whether their wants are realistic, appropriate, and worthwhile, and whether getting what they want is worth what they must do to get it, are questions of evaluation.

- *Planning*   The client's thorough evaluation should lead to formulation of a plan for action. Reality therapists encourage a plan that is simple, realistic, measurable, immediate, involved, committed, continuous, and within the client's powers (not dependent on other people's efforts).

The Reality Therapist   Like all counselors, reality therapists need to express empathy, congruence, and positive regard. But the nature of reality therapy also demands some specialized qualities (Wubbolding & Brickell, 1998), such as a good measure of energy, since therapists using this approach often work with reluctant clients and in settings outside a comfortable office. Active confrontation is frequently used, so the counselors must be able to convey a caring attitude while being challenging. They need a positive but not naive view of human nature because their practice requires realistic balancing of complex forces. They need hope and an ability to reframe: "For the reality therapist, a lazy person has great potential, a resistant person has deep convictions, and a manipulative person is creative" (p. 48). And, finally, they must have the cultural sensitivity and competence to understand that "reality" is not the same for all clients (Wubbolding et al., 1998).

Reality therapy makes use of imaginative techniques for getting through to difficult clients, so the ability to think creatively is paramount. Paradoxical intent, metaphors, and parallel tales draw upon the counselor's creative resources. The counselor most frequently has two entities to serve—the client and the agency that wants the client to change (e.g., legal authorities, teachers, parents)—so tact and flexibility are required, as well as a firm grounding in the ethical decisions involved. Though reality therapy uses the language of everyday life, its practice is sophisticated. The William Glasser Institute (*www.wglasserinst.com*) awards certificates after an eighteen-month training process.

Lazarus's Multimodal Therapy

> A fundamental premise of the multimodal approach is that patients are troubled by at least several specific problems that may require a wide range of specific treatments. Another basic assumption is that durability of results is a function of the effort expended by patient and therapist across seven dimensions of personality—behavior, affect, sensation, imagery, cognition, interpersonal relationships, and biological factors. (Lazarus, 1985, p. 1)

The abbreviation for these dimensions, critical to multimodal therapy, is BASIC-ID. "D" stands for the whole biological dimension instead of "B," so the acronym is memorable as BASIC I. D. (as in "basic identity"). According to Lazarus and his many followers, to know how a behavior influences and is influenced by the other six dimensions is to understand the principles of a personality. Few problems have a single cause or a single cure. Multimodal therapy is characterized by **technical eclecticism,** meaning that it borrows techniques from many sources without subscribing to the associated theories. For example, the empty-chair dialog could be used without belief in the Gestalt idea of closure. Theoretically, multimodal therapy is rooted in social cognitive theory (Bandura, 2001).

R e f l e c t i o n

Choose a typical behavior of your own (you can even choose a positive one this time). List the letters BASIC-ID down the left side of a page, and write the behavior after B. After each of the other letters, write down how the *behavior* affects and is affected by each dimension: *affect* (emotion), *sensation* (your five senses, including physical pleasure and pain), *imagery* (pictures in your mind or fantasies, dreams, memories), *cognition* (attitudes, values, opinions, ideas), *interpersonal relationships*, and *drugs/biology* (all drugs, health problems, illnesses).

One of the advantages of multimodal practice is its inclusion of a large, systematic base of assessment on which to build a treatment plan. Each client then stands out as an individual rather than as a diagnosis. Three anorectic teenagers might be given very different treatments, depending on their BASIC-ID profiles. This quality makes Lazarus's plan applicable across cultures and subcultures, because significant differences among people are accommodated in the BASIC-ID assessment. For each client, the counselor constructs a **Modality Profile.** Here is Lazarus's (1985) illustration of the Modality Profile of a 32-year-old woman with a diagnosis of alcohol dependence.

MODALITY PROFILE: A SYSTEMATIC ASSESSMENT

Behavior	Excessive drinking	Aversive imagery
	Avoids confronting most people	Assertiveness training
	Negative self-statements	Positive self-talk assignments
	Always drinks excessively when alone at home at night	Develop social outlets
	Screams at her children	Instruction in parenting skills
Affect	Holds back anger (except with her children)	Assertiveness training
		Anger expression exercises
	Anxiety reactions	Self-hypnosis and/or positive imagery
	Depression	Increase range of positive reinforcement
Sensation	Butterflies in stomach	Abdominal breathing exercises
	Tension headaches	Relaxation or biofeedback
Imagery	Vivid pictures of parents fighting	Desensitization
	Being locked in bedroom as a child	Images of escape and/or release of anger
Cognition	Irrational self-talk about low self-worth	Cognitive disputation
	Numerous regrets	Reduction of categorical imperatives (shoulds, oughts, musts, etc.)
Interpersonal relationships	Ambivalent responses to husband and children	Possible family therapy and specific training in use of positive reinforcement
		Support group to control alcohol abuse— Alcoholics Anonymous
	Secretive and suspicious	Self-disclosure training
Drugs/biology	Reliance on alcohol to alleviate depression, anxiety, tension	Possible use of disulfiram and antidepressant medication

In this profile, you can see several interrelated problems that a conventional alcohol assessment might not uncover.

Multimodal assessment has a multicultural advantage because it takes a holistic approach including social, cultural, and interpersonal aspects; it can include both directive and nondirective methods; and it considers each client as unique, "with a combination of qualities and characteristics, with a different story to tell" (Palmer, 2000, p. 33). Levels of acculturation, as well as pockets of acceptance and rejection of cultural background, will come through in a culturally sensitive BASIC-ID profile.

Multimodal Process   In the initial interview, the counselor educates the client about the multimodal method, establishes rapport, and investigates presenting problems. An important question is "Who or what appears to be maintaining the problems?" Clients usually take home a twelve-page Multimodal Life History Questionnaire (Lazarus, 1981). If possible, following instruction in how it works, they fill out the first two columns of their Modality Profile themselves. Then they compare their own with the one the counselor completes. Together, the client and counselor look at the profile and discuss priorities and treatments.

The client also rates, from 1 to 10 (low to high), their tendencies on each of the seven dimensions, producing a **structural profile.** For example, the rating for *behavior* is based on these questions: "How active are you? How much of a 'doer' are you? Do you like to keep busy?" and the rating for *interpersonal relationships* is based on these: "How much of a 'social being' are you? How important are other people to you? Do you gravitate to people? Do you desire intimacy with others?" The Multimodal Life History Questionnaire, Modality Profile, and structural ratings allow the client and counselor to discuss many aspects of the client's life and personality, not just the problem areas.

The therapist chooses an array of treatments to pursue over the course of counseling, as you can see from the sample Modality Profile. Most of the interventions are cognitive-behavioral, which is why I included the system in this chapter. Therefore, a multimodal therapist needs to be competent in many techniques and to have resources available for others (such as a physician referral system, a directory of support groups, and a bibliography of self-help materials). In treatment of minor depression in an adult, Lazarus (1992) combined "assertiveness training, a 'sensate focus' on enjoyable events, coping imagery, time projection, cognitive disputation, role-playing, densensitization, family therapy, and biological prophylaxis [medication]" (pp. 56–57). This approach also lends itself to a concerted effort by a variety of therapists (Lazarus, 2000).

Bridging and Tracking   In therapeutic sessions, the counselor addresses the client on her own terms first; in other words, he focuses initially on the modalities she has rated strongly in her structural profile, and uses these as a basis to reach other dimensions he considers important. For example, if a client has rated *imagery* highly, the counselor may ask about a dream she found memorable and then use aspects of the dream to bring up discussions about interpersonal relationships, which she has rated low on her structural profile. This process is called **bridging,** because it builds a bridge between a preferred modality and a less familiar one.

Tracking involves paying attention to the order in which different modalities usually take precedence for each client. For example, a client may first present an intellectual interpretation of a situation (*cognition*), which leads to *sensations* like muscle tension and shortness of breath, which, in turn, are followed by emotions (*affect*) such as wanting to escape or avoid. This C-S-A pattern would call for a treatment sequence in the same order—for example, disputation of the interpretations first, relaxation training second, and covert desensitization or guided imagery third.

Strengths of Multimodal Treatment   In conceptualizing multimodal theory, Lazarus emphasized breadth of therapy over depth, pointing out that clients equipped with several different tools are likely to find a useful tool among them when a new problem situation arises (Lazarus, 1996). Lazarus also was keeping in mind the need for brief, intensive therapies that nonetheless had some staying power and transfer of learning.

Long-standing, pervasive, and complex behavior patterns are difficult to change, and one advantage of combining techniques is that one of them may produce an initial improvement in some small area, instilling hope and confidence (Kazdin, 1994). Furthermore, separate but co-occurring behaviors may respond better to different interventions than to the application of the same strategy to all. A teenager's alcohol use, for example, may respond to contingency management techniques, while her pot smoking is better controlled through relaxation training. Multicomponent interventions also address the many ways that a problem behavior can continue and be maintained. Eliminating aggressive behavior in children, Kazdin (1994) suggests, requires multiple interventions such as reinforcements and punishment for the child, parent education on discipline techniques, and social skills training for the child, who is likely to have poor peer relations.

While it may seem that multimodal therapists are throwing together a hodgepodge of techniques, remember that they are following a unified theory rooted in the BASIC-ID system of understanding human behavior.

Linehan's Dialectical Behavior Therapy

Like multimodal theory, dialectical behavior therapy (DBT) assumes a basic interrelatedness of clients' behavioral, emotional, and cognitive worlds (Linehan, 1993). Unlike Lazarus's approach, DBT was designed for a particular type of client: people diagnosed with borderline personality disorder (BPD). Nowadays DBT is also used experimentally for drug abuse, eating disorders (Telch, Agras, & Linehan, 2001), PTSD, and antisocial personality disorders, but the primary focus and the validating research have been on borderline clients, the majority of whom are women.

The term *dialectical* describes the interaction of two conflicting forces. In DBT, the **dialectics** are between

- the need for the client to accept herself and also to change,
- the client's getting what she needs and losing it if she becomes more competent, and
- the client's maintaining the validity of her experience while learning to interpret it differently (Linehan, 1993).

Dialectics imply change, and clients learn to become comfortable with change in themselves, others, and the environment.

Effective treatment for BPD was seriously needed because the disorder is life-threatening and has repercussions for the sufferers' acquaintances, co-workers, workplaces, and society in general. The DSM-IV-TR criteria describe a pattern beginning by early adulthood and including unstable and intense interpersonal relationships, unstable sense of self, self-damaging impulsivity (in sex, spending, substance abuse, and the like), recurring suicidal or self-mutilating behavior (like cutting and burning oneself), intense and unstable moods, chronic feelings of emptiness, difficulty controlling anger, transient paranoia or dissociation under stress, and frantic efforts to avoid abandonment (American Psychiatric Association, 2000). Dialectical behavior therapy is an all-out effort by a team of therapists, in group and individual work, to apply a broad array of cognitive and behavioral techniques to the problem of BPD, which is often considered the least treatable psychological diagnosis. Borderline clients need a combination of insight, support, social skills, and problem-solving skills that are difficult to juggle amidst their self-injuries, shifts of feeling about their therapists, and fear of change (thus, interference with their own therapy).

Treatment Tied to Emotional Regulation   According to Linehan (1993) and colleagues, the source of such severe pathology is biosocial—that is, an unfortunate biological vulnerability to intense emotions, combined with an upbringing that rejected or punished such emotions. "An invalidating family is problematic because people in it respond to the communication of preferences, thoughts, and emotions with nonattuned responses—specifically, with either nonresponsiveness or more extreme consequences than more sensitive, validating environments" (1993, p. 3). When you studied object relations theory in Chapter 4, you saw the same kind of thinking about responsive and unresponsive environments in childhood.

DBT usually requires a year's commitment from both counselors and clients, in which clients attend one-hour weekly individual sessions and two-hour weekly skills training and problem-solving groups, with daily homework assignments ("Dialectic Behavior Therapy," 2002). The treatment is clearly structured and guided by a manual (Linehan, 1993). Each common problem of the borderline client receives attention, as shown in the handout on maintaining interpersonal relationships reproduced in Figure 9.1. A steady, supportive, collaborative therapeutic alliance, though difficult to achieve, is critical to the success of DBT: Such an alliance is not only necessary for the interventions to work, but it also provides the validating relationship previously absent from the client's life. Counselors take special training in DBT, usually at workshops for teams. A schedule of training programs can be found, for example, at *http:// www.behavioraltech.com*, which is the website for the Behavioral Technology Transfer Group.

Mindfulness   Linehan introduced new concepts into standard cognitive-behavioral therapy, including the Zen practice of mindfulness. Coming from eastern spiritual traditions, mindfulness attends to an acceptance of things that can't easily be changed, without denying them or lashing out uselessly ("Acceptance and Change," 2002; Hahn, 1975). Mindfulness exercises validate the existence of negative emotions, which is crucial for clients who have been told that they just need to "change their attitudes" (Linehan, 1993). They also reduce vulnerability to these emotions by putting them into perspective and suggesting ways to tolerate them. Figure 9.2 is an example of a distress tolerance handout that focuses on teaching distraction. Notice that the client is never told that the negative emotions are not legitimate or real—just that she can distract herself from them. Other distress tolerance handouts focus on self-soothing, improving the moment, and listing the pros and cons of tolerating the disturbance.

R e f l e c t i o n

Review the handout reproduced in Figure 9.2. Which (if any) of the suggestions do you use when you are emotionally upset? What other tactics do you find helpful in distress tolerance? How might you teach these tactics to others?

Effectiveness of DBT   Since the publication of DBT treatment manuals in 1993, the effectiveness of this approach has been studied in comparison to treatment-as-usual, treatment by experts in borderline personality disorder, usual inpatient treatments, and skills training groups alone (Koerner & Linehan, 2000). The findings indicate that DBT has produced superior outcomes in reducing undesired behavior (such as suicide attempts), retaining clients in treatment, or reducing days of hospitalization, or all three. Other studies have found DBT effective in treatment of not only borderline personality disorder but also parasuicide (such as cutting), substance abuse, and binge eating (Telch, Agras, & Linehan, 2001).

Guidelines for Relationship Effectiveness: Keeping the Relationship

A way to remember these skills is to remember the word **"GIVE" (DEAR MAN, GIVE):**

*G*ENTLE

*I*NTERESTED

*V*ALIDATE

*E*ASY MANNER

Gentle	Be COURTEOUS and temperate in your approach.
No attacks	No verbal or physical attacks. No hitting, clenching fists. Express anger directly.
No threats	No "manipulative" statements, no hidden threats. No "I'll kill myself if you. . . ." Tolerate a no to requests. Stay in the discussion even if it gets painful. Exit gracefully.
No judging	No moralizing. No "If you were a good person, you would. . . ." No " You should. . . ," "You shouldn't. . . ."
Interested	Listen and be interested in the other person.
	LISTEN to the other person's point of view, opinion, reasons for saying no, or reasons for making a request of you. Don't interrupt, talk over, etc. Be sensitive to the person's desire to have the discussion at a later time. Be patient.
Validate	Validate or ACKNOWLEDGE the other person's feelings, wants, difficulties, and opinions about the situation. Be nonjudgmental out loud: "I can understand how you feel, but. . . "; "I realize this is hard for you, but. . . ." Listen to the other person.
Easy manner	Use a little humor. SMILE. Ease the person along. Be light-hearted. Wheedle. Use a "soft sell" over a "hard sell." Be political.

SOURCE: Linehan (1993).

FIGURE 9.1   Interpersonal Effectiveness Handout

DISTRACTING

A useful way to remember these skills is the phrase "Wise Mind **ACCEPTS.**"

With **A**ctivities:
Engage in exercise or hobbies; do cleaning; go to events; call or visit a friend; play computer games; go walking; work; play sports; go out to a meal; have decaf coffee or tea; go fishing; chop wood; do gardening; play pinball.

With **C**ontributing:
Contribute to someone; do volunteer work; give something to someone else; make something nice for someone else; do a surprising, thoughtful thing.

With **C**omparisons:
Compare yourself to people coping the same as you or less well than you. Compare yourself to those less fortunate than you. Watch soap operas; read about disasters, others' suffering.

With opposite **E**motions:
Read emotional books or stories, old letters; go to emotional movies; listen to emotional music. *Be sure the event creates different emotions.* Ideas: scary movies, joke books, comedies, funny records, religious music, marching songs, "I Am Woman" (Helen Reddy); going to a store and reading funny greeting cards.

With **P**ushing away:
Push the situation away by leaving it for a while. Leave the situation mentally. Build an imaginary wall between yourself and the situation. Or push the situation away by blocking it in your mind. Censor ruminating. Refuse to think about the painful aspects of the situation. Put the pain on a shelf. Box it up and put it away for a while.

With other **T**houghts:
Count to 10; count colors in a painting or tree, windows, anything; work puzzles; watch TV; read.

With intense other **S**ensations:
Hold ice in hand; squeeze a rubber ball very hard; stand under a very hard and hot shower; listen to very loud music; sex; put rubber band on wrist, pull out, and let go.

SOURCE: Linehan (1993).

FIGURE 9.2   **Distress Tolerance Handout**

Shapiro's Eye Movement Desensitization and Reprocessing

Eye movement desensitization and reprocessing (EMDR) was developed in the 1990s by Francine Shapiro (1995) to help people who had undergone trauma, especially those with symptoms of posttraumatic stress syndrome (PTSD), including flashbacks to traumatic events, nightmares, intrusive thoughts of the episode(s), avoidance of related stimuli, numbing of normal emotionality, exaggerated startle responses, and interpersonal difficulties. EMDR came along in an era when it was evident that Vietnam combat veterans with PTSD were not getting better with age, and when the traumas of rape and childhood sexual abuse were open topics. The treatment is clearly cognitive-behavioral in that it combines systematic desensitization and substitution of positive thought patterns for negative ones.

As explained by Shapiro, these behavioral and cognitive approaches are not at the heart of EMDR, which works through a neurophysiological reprocessing of disturbing events assisted by rapid, rhythmic back-and-forth eye movements. These eye movements unblock the distressing experiences from a neurologically trapped state and release them, allowing an inherent physiological tendency toward mental health to flow naturally.

EMDR Process Therapy progresses in stages, beginning with determination of a baseline of dysfunction and one or more target memories. After that, the client is educated about EMDR procedures and trained in self-soothing and relaxation. Then, the client re-experiences a chosen target memory and the associated disturbing scene, in which the client immerses herself as she watches the therapist's hand moving rapidly back and forth fifteen to thirty times, 12 to 14 inches from the client's face. (In the latest forms of EMDR, eye movements can be replaced by musical tones, flashes of light, or finger taps on alternate sides of the client.) The client then rests, reports on feelings, images, thoughts, and distress level, and the therapist chooses target material for the next set of eye movements. A potential positive thought about the memory, such as "I did the best anyone could" or "I was able to survive," is gradually introduced into the eye movement periods.

If the client and therapist become blocked at the disturbing-scene phase of the treatment, the therapist assists by guiding the rest-period discussions to encourage new perspectives. This intervention, called the **cognitive interweave,** invites a thinking approach to mitigate the strong feeling approach. At the end of a session, which typically lasts 90 to 120 minutes, the client is returned to a state of comfort through guided imagery and relaxation. Between sessions, the client is encouraged to keep a log of memories, dreams, thoughts, and situations that are distressing. She is also reminded to do relaxation exercises. Each EMDR session follows the same pattern.

The EMDR Controversy EMDR and its originator were widely criticized throughout the 1990s. Psychologists were shocked that a newcomer to the field boldly was pronouncing relief from PTSD and similar disorders in short order (often after only three sessions) ("EMDR," 2002). In the scientific community, the aggressive promotion of a treatment that hadn't been cautiously evaluated in controlled experiments was considered suspicious. Many people also viewed as suspicious the quick copyright of the trademark "EMDR" by Shapiro and her establishment of training for licensure in the technique. Trainees are not allowed to distribute detailed EMDR techniques or to train other people, unless they become certified by Shapiro's EMDR Institute. This could be a protection against poorly trained EMDR practitioners, but it has a side effect in research: The people who deliver the treatment in research studies are already financially and intellectually invested in its effectiveness.

Yet, much research has been performed comparing EMDR with no treatment, exposure treatments, conventional CBT, nonspecific treatments (such as relaxation), EMDR without the eye movements (EM), and so forth. The latest meta-analysis of thirty-four experimental studies (Davidson & Parker, 2001) found that EMDR was more effective than no treatment and nonspecific treatments and, in terms of outcome, was equal in effectiveness to other exposure treatments (in vivo, imaginal, cognitive-behavioral). EMDR without the EM was just as effective as with them, which calls into doubt the neurophysiological basis that Shapiro espouses for the rhythmic stimulation component.

Some critics see EMDR as riddled with "scientific weaknesses" and "contradictory to typical practices of behavior therapists, for whom acceptance of an intervention has, in the past, been contingent on its validation. EMDR should not be an exception to this most cardinal rule" (Acierno, Hersen, Van Hasselt, Tremont, & Meuser, 1994, p. 297). Other critics of the research appear to view the EMDR controversy as a normal reaction to a splashy new treatment—as a debate that will be resolved, in time, through more careful research (Lohr, Kleinknecht, Tolin, & Barrett, 1995). Meanwhile, an APA task force on empirically supported procedures has listed EMDR as a "probably efficacious" treatment for civilian PTSD (Prochaska & Norcross, 1999). By the time you are reading this textbook, EMDR may be as quaint as the Mashed Potato or as classic as the waltz.

Case Conceptualization: An Example

Therapist Edwin R. Gerler employed the multimodal framework to identify the full range of his client Marshall's problems and to choose treatment tactics (Gerler, 1985). In his opening remarks on the case, Lazarus notes that "a 'push-button' panacea approach was avoided; some clinicians might have concluded that the client was depressed and therefore in need of antidepressant medication. . . . This case shows that a unitary approach would have led to incomplete treatment" (p. 139). Marshall was a 40-year-old, single, sixth-grade teacher. Treatment began with the construction of his Multimodal Profile of problems.

MARSHALL'S MULTIMODAL PROFILE

Behavior	He could not organize his time for work. He had trouble sleeping. He ate and drank too much. He sometimes did not get out of bed on weekends.
Affect	He felt angry about his being ineffectual. He felt guilty about his lack of caring for the children he taught. He felt restless and wanted to do something other than teaching. He feared that he might be fired.
Sensation	He craved sensory stimulation from producing and consuming artistic products such as music and poetry.
Imagery	He was preoccupied with artistic imagery and was unable to concentrate on the everyday duties of his teaching job.
Cognition	He had irrational thoughts about how he would be fired from his job if he did not concentrate more energy on his work. These thoughts distracted him from doing what he needed to improve his teaching and from getting the help he needed to improve. He had trouble disciplining his thinking.
Interpersonal relationships	His relations with children in the classroom were often tense.
Drugs/biology	He gained weight as a result of excessive eating and drinking. He had increasing difficulty maintaining a regular exercise program. He experienced fitful sleep.

Procedures Used to Resolve Marshall's Concerns

Behavior and Physiology   Marshall's apparent ineffectiveness as a teacher was rooted, in part, to behavioral and physical problems. His overeating and occasional excessive drinking contributed to his gaining weight and inability to sleep. The weight gain and inability to sleep, in turn, reduced Marshall's willingness and ability to exercise regularly and thus reduced his energy for teaching. It is noteworthy that just a year or so before seeking help Marshall had been an avid runner, averaging 40–50 miles of running each week. During his third session with me, he explained that his running had diminished to under 10 miles each week and that a medical examination had uncovered no physical problems to account for the lack of energy for and dedication to running.

To begin to alleviate Marshall's overeating and excessive drinking I asked Marshall to monitor his eating and drinking patterns. Self-monitoring has sometimes been used successfully to change behaviors of this kind. McFall (1970), for instance, noted the effects of self-monitoring on smoking behavior. Marshall seemed faithfully to record the times of his eating and drinking, but the procedure did not reduce Marshall's excesses. The record did, however, provide better information about the extent of his poor habits.

As an alternative method to self-monitoring, Marshall and I worked out a behavior contract that designated specific times and places for Marshall to eat and drink. One facet of the agreement was that Marshall could eat food and drink alcoholic beverages at only one place in his home, namely, at the kitchen table. He had previously found many other places at home to eat and drink, particularly in his recreation room while watching television.

The behavior contract paid off. He organized his eating and drinking to the extent that he no longer had snack foods and alcoholic drinks available to him during late-night television watching. His sleep improved. Further counseling about sleep problems also convinced Marshall that he needed less sleep than he had once thought. He tried going to bed about 1½ hours later than normal, which resulted in his being tired and in his usually getting to sleep within 15 minutes of going to bed. On his own he decided not to stay in bed if he was unable to get to sleep quickly. His new approach was to leave bed, read or watch television for about 30 minutes, and then return to bed. This change initiated by Marshall added to quality sleep.

The benefits of better sleep and reduced eating and drinking increased Marshall's energy somewhat, and he was able to exercise more regularly. His running improved, but instead of concerning himself about mileage, Marshall settled on running 20–30 minutes for 5 days each week. He was thus less compulsive about increasing his weekly mileage and seemed more energetic. Coincidentally, he reported feeling much less tired while teaching during the last hour or so of the school day. In summary, improved physical habits had personal benefits for Marshall which also undoubtedly had positive effects on the children with whom he worked in the classroom.

Affect, Interpersonal Relations, and Cognition   Marshall seemed to suffer at times from a kind of "delusion of uniqueness" (Sullivan, 1947) in regard to his feelings about teaching; that is, he talked almost as though no one else in teaching felt as guilty, angry, and restless about professional inadequacies as he did. To ease this situation I arranged for him to join a teacher effectiveness group wherein teachers discussed not only their work in the classroom but also their feelings about the work. I knew the leader to be group-centered and an empathic listener. I also knew that the group consisted mainly of teachers who had expressed feelings of "teacher burnout" and that the group would provide a better than average chance for Marshall to overcome his apparent feelings of being alone with his problems.

Somewhat reluctantly, Marshall agreed to join the group. He commented while agreeing to join that he really did not need "another meeting in his life." He stayed with the group for only three sessions, remarking that the people in the group simply wanted "to shoot the breeze for a couple of hours" and that he did not have the time for such a group. We discussed his feelings about the group and finally decided not to pursue membership in a counseling group.

What seemed to help Marshall more than anything else in dealing with his feelings about teaching was our discussion of irrational thinking. I recommended that he read Chapter 3, "Irrational Ideas Which Cause and Sustain Emotional Disturbances," from *Reason and Emotion in Psychotherapy* (Ellis, 1962). He especially benefited from our discussing the following irrational ideas explained in the Ellis book:

- The idea that one should be thoroughly competent, adequate, and achieving in all possible respects if one is to consider oneself worthwhile. (p. 63)
- The idea that it is awful and catastrophic when things are not the way one would very much like them to be. (p. 69)
- The idea that if something is or may be dangerous or fearsome one should be terribly concerned about it and should keep dwelling on the possibility of its occurring. (p. 75)

The latter idea, in particular, intrigued Marshall. He disclosed during our discussions that he secretly feared being fired for not "teaching energetically." The notion that dwelling on this possibility would do nothing but increase the chances of its occurring made sense to Marshall. After much consideration of irrational thinking, his fear seemed to diminish, as evidenced by his more relaxed demeanor. Some of the children in his classroom, incidentally, commented to him about the easing of tension in the classroom.

Sensation and Imagery   Marshall was consumed with a desire to experience artistic sensations and images. He was distracted from his everyday work in the classroom by listening to music and, most especially, by trying to write poetry. After several counseling sessions, we agreed that his interest in poetry was positive. (In fact, he showed some promise as a poet, having had poetry published in several respected publications.) We agreed further that writing poetry would be of little benefit to him if writing it caused him to feel guilty about incompetent teaching and caused him to fear losing his livelihood in teaching.

I recommended that he set a time limit (perhaps 2 to 3 hours a day) wherein he would write poetry exclusively. I also recommended that he think of ways to share some of his own enjoyment of artistic imagery and sensation with the children in his classroom. Thereafter, he set aside about 30 minutes near the end of each school day for himself and his students to engage in artistic, creative expression. At times, the students showed him their work, and he disclosed some of his as well. He reported, however, that the time became mostly a private time for everyone in the classroom.

Conclusion

Marshall's concerns centered on his inadequacies as a teacher. The concerns grew from many parts of his life and hence needed to be treated from a multimodal perspective. As a counselor/consultant, I used the multimodal approach to alleviate some of his personal concerns and in so doing to increase his effectiveness in the classroom.   ■ ■

DISCUSSION IDEAS

1. Why does Lazarus suggest that Marshall's unimodal diagnosis would be depression? Do you think this is true?

2. List the interventions involved in Gerler's treatment of Marshall. Label each one as either mainly cognitive or mainly behavioral.

3. Which interventions did not work out as planned? What did the counselor do when they failed?

4. What did Marshall do on his own during treatment? Would you expect this from a client? Why or why not?

5. Why did changing the measurement of running from miles to minutes per day help Marshall's exercise program?

6. Do you think that the multimodal treatment was preferable to antidepressant treatment? Explain your answer. Would the two treatments have equivalent results, in your opinion?

7. How did Gerler and Marshall know the therapy was working? What evidence did they have? What other forms of evidence could be collected in this case?

Critiques of Cognitive-Behavioral Therapies

Cognitive-behavioral approaches have inspired lively argument, and I will summarize several criticisms and counter-arguments here.

Prescriptive Model

You probably noticed that all the cognitive-behavioral treatments presented here are more directive than others you have studied. They are more structured, have measurable results, and are designed for time-limited interventions. Most are manualized so that counselors everywhere can follow the same treatment plan. Critics wonder whether this amount of prescriptiveness is optimal. Is direct teaching the best way for therapy to progress? Or is it the case, as Patterson (1980) suggests, that "[l]asting changes in personality and behavior may be achieved better by the slower process in which individuals work through their problems in their own way and at their own pace" (p. 92)?

I agree that a slower self-discovery process should occur; but I would argue that in directive treatment there is nothing that precludes such a process and, indeed, many things that enhance it. The changes in world view that are accelerated in cognitive-behavioral therapies are bound to engender a world that reacts differently to a client. For example, a more assertive client finds a less frustrating and disappointing world around her, which reflects her back in different ways than before and slowly changes her after therapy is over.

Cultural Concerns

An overview of cognitive-behavioral treatments certainly impresses us with their negative view of dependency and their emphasis on rationality, two values associated with Western thought and not necessarily with other philosophies. Most such treatments, however, build in client participation at the goal-setting stage, so that the client's cultural or subcultural values will not be violated. An exception occurs in some applications of Glasser's reality therapy, in which the counselor *is* the express agent of mainstream culture.

Unfinished Business

Lack of attention to early experiences and unfinished business from the past characterizes most cognitive-behavioral treatments, say some critics. And this, they insist, is a neglect of psychologically important matters: "Are we to believe that such traumatic events as being beaten by one's mother, molested by one's father, bereaved of both parents, rejected by peers, and ridiculed by teachers are less significant in producing emotional disturbances in children than are the beliefs children possess about these events?" (Prochaska & Norcross, 1999, p. 349). A present-oriented treatment places too much responsibility on the individual, in a stance that could place blame on the victim rather than on the victimizers. It also may ignore or downplay the reality of terrible conditions in the outside world that affect the client and all of us. There really are things out there to be upset about, and people who have gained individual peace by ignoring them are not ideal citizens.

Brainwashing

With its emphasis on changing minds and its de-emphasis on emotional ventilation, cognitive-behavioral therapy seems too much like a superficial word game to some people. Beck's approach seems as simplistic as "the power of positive thinking," and Ellis's irrational-belief indoctrination appears akin to brainwashing. Patterson (1980) notes that the techniques of brainwashing—persuasion, suggestions, and repetition—are the same as Ellis's, and may have their effect in the same way, especially when the "indoctrinator genuinely and sincerely believes in what he or she is indoctrinating and is concerned about the subject's accepting it" (p. 93). This criticism may be one that relies heavily on the association of theory with Ellis's style, which is notoriously disputative, challenging, insistent, and directive. Other cognitive-behavioral counselors convey a gentler, more collaborative style.

Evolution

Like behavioral therapy, cognitive-behavioral therapy has shown a commitment to empirical evaluation and revision, as well as an openness to integrating other points of view in its ongoing development (for example, the therapeutic alliance is now given more attention than in previous decades). These are strengths that are compatible with scientific evolution, and also with today's drive toward short-term treatments with provable effects. Ultimately, the potential for translation to computer-assisted forms gives this form of treatment another edge in the twenty-first century (Hester & Delaney, 1997).

KEY TERMS

A B C D E F system
absolutistic dichotomous
    thinking
arbitrary inference
automaticity
bridging
choice theory
cognitive interweave
Cognitive Therapy
cognitive triad
collaborative empiricism
control theory
core schemas
dialectics
guided discovery
irrational beliefs
learned helplessness

magnification and minimization
mediational position
Modality Profile
natural consequences
overgeneralization
personal constructs
personalization
phenomenological
problem-solving
Rational-Emotive Behavior Therapy
selective abstraction
Socratic dialog
stress
structural profile
technical eclecticism
time projection
tracking

Exploring Key Terms

First, each individual needs to sort the alphabetized key-term list above. Write seven headings to label the seven cognitive-behavioral treatments discussed in the chapter (those identified with Ellis, Beck, Meichenbaum, Glasser, Lazarus, Linehan, and Shapiro) and an eighth heading, General. Write each key term below the heading it most closely belongs to, and write terms that could be used in all cognitive-behavioral theories under General. A term can fit under both a specific heading and the General category.

After you have sorted, compare your lists with those made by others in your group. Discuss discrepancies until you can agree on a common version of the sorting. Have each member of the group take one or two headings and explain out loud, briefly, all the terms in the category. Help each other come up with clear definitions.

LIBRARY, MEDIA, AND INTERNET ACTIVITIES

1. Cognitive-behavioral therapy is used for a wide array of problems. Using a psychology literature database like PsychInfo, find five articles in psychology journals that you think would be helpful to yourself or to a therapist in a field of interest to you. Read the article abstracts and write a paragraph explaining why you think they would be helpful, and then list the citations. Some ideas for topics: substance abuse, depression, generalized anxiety, obsessive thinking, agoraphobia, PTSD, grief, eating disorders, obesity, narcissism, borderline personality disorder, schizophrenia, chronic pain, school problems, delinquency, bullying, shyness, learning disabilities.

2. Here are some websites focusing on cognitive-behavioral therapy. Investigate these sites and write a report about what information you can find on them.

www.rebt.org
www.CognitiveTherapyNYC.com
http://iacp.asu.edu
http://www.padesky.com
www.beckinstitute.org
www.wglasserinst.com

3. Visit a large bookstore and look through the self-help books and self-help articles in popular magazines. Choose one source and explain how cognitive-behavioral principles are used in the advice it gives.

4. Of the seven cognitive-behavioral treatment programs discussed in this chapter, choose one to investigate further by looking up a book on it. Read the introduction, first chapter, and one other chapter and write a review of the book for the use of other counselors.

5. Using a name as the *subject* key word in a library search, find biographical information on one of these cognitive-behavioral pioneers: Albert Ellis, William Glasser, Arnold Lazarus, Donald Meichenbaum, and Francine Shapiro. Write a page on how the person's biography relates to the theory he or she developed.

6. William Glasser has written several books on how his theory applies to personal freedom, positive addictions, quality schools, and counseling situations. Find one that is related to your practice or work setting and read the introduction, first chapter, and one other chapter. Write an evaluation indicating whether the book would be useful to you or others in the field.

REFERENCES

"Acceptance and change in psychotherapy." (2002). *Clinician's Research Digest, 20*(7), 5.

Acierno, R., Hersen, M., Van Hasselt, V. B., & Tremont, G. (1994). Review of the validation and dissemination of eye-movement desensitization and reprocessing: A scientific and ethical dilemma. *Clinical Psychology Review, 14*, 287–299.

American Psychiatric Association. (2000). *Diagnostic and statistical manual of mental disorders* (4th ed., text revision). Washington, DC: Author.

Bandura, A. (2001). Social cognitive theory: An agentic perspective. *Annual Review of Psychology, 52*, 1–26.

Beck, A. T. (1987). *Beck Depression Inventory.* San Antonio, TX: The Psychological Corporation.

Beck, A. T. (1988). *Love is never enough.* New York: Harper Perennial.

Beck, A. T. (1991). Cognitive therapy: A 30-year perspective. *American Psychologist, 46*, 368–375.

Beck, A. T., Rush, A. J., Shaw, B. F, & Emery, G. (1979). *Cognitive therapy of depression.* New York: Guilford.

Beck, A. T., & Weishaar, M. E. (2000). Cognitive therapy. In R. J. Corsini & D. Wedding, *Current psychotherapies* (6th ed., pp. 241–171). Itasca, IL: F. E. Peacock.

Carver, C. S., & Scheier, M. F. (1982). Control theory: A useful conceptual framework for personality-social, clinical, and health psychology. *Psychological Bulletin, 92*, 111–135.

Christophersen, E. R., & Mortweet, S. L. (2001). *Treatments that work with children: Empirically supported strategies for managing childhood problems.* Washington, DC: APA.

Davidson, P. R., & Parker, K. C. (2001). Eye movement desensitization and reprocessing (EMDR): A meta-analysis. *Journal of Consulting and Clinical Psychology, 69*, 305–316.

"Dialectical behavior therapy." (2002). *Harvard Mental Health Letter, 19*(2), 1–3.

Dobson, K. S., & Block, L. (1988). Historical and philosophical bases of the cognitive-behavioral therapies. In K. S. Dobson (Ed.), *Handbook of cognitive-behavioral therapies* (pp. 3–35). New York: Guilford.

D'Zurilla, T. J., & Goldfried, M. R. (1971). Problem solving and behavior modification. *Journal of Abnormal Psychology, 78*, 107–126.

Ellis, A. (1962). *Reason and emotion in psychotherapy.* New York: Lyle Stuart.

Ellis, A. (1987). The impossibility of achieving consistently good mental health. *American Psychologist, 42*, 364–375.

"EMDR." *Harvard Mental Health Letter, 18*(8), 4–5.

Gerler, E. R. (1985). A multimodal approach for the counselor/consultant: A case study. In A. A. Lazarus (Ed.), *Casebook of multimodal therapy* (pp. 139–146). New York: Guilford.

Glasser, W. (1965). *Reality therapy: A new approach to psychiatry.* New York: Harper & Row.

Glasser, W. (1981). *Stations of the mind.* New York: Harper & Row.

Glasser, W. (1992). Reality therapy. In J. K. Zeig (Ed.), *The evolution of psychotherapy: The second conference* (pp. 270–277). New York: Brunner/Mazel.

Glasser, W. (1998). *Choice theory.* New York: HarperCollins.

Hahn, T. N. (1975). *The miracle of mindfulness.* Boston: Beacon.

Hester, R. K., & Delaney, H. D. (1997). Behavioral self-control program for Windows: Results of a controlled clinical trial. *Journal of Consulting and Clinical Psychology, 65,* 686–693.

Hollon, S. D., & Beck, A. T. (1994). Cognitive and cognitive-behavioral therapies. In A. E. Bergin & A. L. Garfield (Eds.), *Handbook of psychotherapy and behavior change* (4th ed., pp. 428–466). New York: Wiley.

Kazdin, A. E. (1994). *Behavior modification in applied settings* (5th ed.). Pacific Grove, CA: Brooks/Cole.

Koerner, K., & Linehan, M. M. (2000). Research on dialectical behavior therapy for patients with borderline personality disorder. *Psychiatric Clinics of North America, 23,* 151–167.

Lazarus, A. A. (1981). *The practice of multimodal therapy.* New York: McGraw-Hill.

Lazarus, A. A. (1985). A brief overview of multimodal therapy. In A. A. Lazarus (Ed.), *Casebook of multimodal therapy* (pp. 1–16). New York: Guilford.

Lazarus, A. A. (1992). The multimodal approach to the treatment of minor depression. *American Journal of Psychotherapy, 46,* 50–57.

Lazarus, A. A. (1996). Some reflections after 40 years of trying to be an effective psychotherapist. *Psychotherapy, 33,* 142–145.

Lazarus, A. A. (2000). Multimodal therapy. In R. J. Corsini & D. Wedding (Eds.), *Current psychotherapies* (6th ed., pp. 340–374). Itasca, IL: F. E. Peacock.

Lazarus, R. (1984). On the primacy of cognition. *American Psychologist, 39,* 124–129.

Lezak, M. D. (1995). *Neuropsychological assessment* (3rd ed.). New York: Oxford University Press.

Linehan, M. M. (1993). *Skills training manual for treating borderline personality disorder.* New York: Guilford.

Lohr, J. M., Kleinknecht, R. A., Tolin, D. F., & Barrett, R. H. (1995). The empirical status of the clinical application of eye movement desensitization and reprocessing. *Journal of Behavior Therapy and Experimental Psychiatry, 26,* 285–302.

McFall, R. M. (1970). Effects of self-monitoring on normal smoking behavior. *Journal of Consulting and Clinical Psychology, 35,* 135–142.

Meichenbaum, D. (1985). *Stress inoculation training.* Elmsford, NY: Pergamon.

Meichenbaum, D. (1993). Stress inoculation training: A 20-year update. In P. M. Lehrer & R. L. Woolfolk (Eds.), *Principles and practice of stress management* (2nd ed., pp. 373–406). New York: Guilford.

Meichenbaum, D. (1996). Stress inoculation training for coping with stressors. *The Clinical Psychologist, 49,* 4–7.

Meichenbaum, D. H., & Goodman, J. (1971). Training impulsive children to talk to themselves. *Journal of Abnormal Psychology, 77,* 115–126.

Neisser, U. (1967). *Cognitive psychology.* New York: Appleton-Century-Croft.

Palmer, S. (2000). Developing an individual therapeutic programme suitable for use by counselling psychologists in a multicultural society: A multimodal perspective. *Counselling Psychology Review, 15,* 32–50.

Patterson, C. H. (1980). *Theories of counseling and psychotherapy* (3rd ed.). New York: Harper & Row.

Prochaska, J. O., & Norcross, J. C. (1999). *Systems of psychotherapy: A transtheoretical analysis* (4th ed.). Pacific Grove, CA: Brooks/Cole.

Rachman, S. (1997). The evolution of cognitive behaviour therapy. In D. M. Clark & C. G. Fairburn (Eds.), *The science and practice of cognitive behaviour therapy* (pp. 1–26). Oxford: Oxford University Press.

Seligman, M. E. P. (1992). *Helplessness: On depression, development, and death.* New York: Freeman.

Shapiro, F. (1995). *Eye movement desensitization and reprocessing.* New York: Guilford.

Stuart, R. B. (1980). *Helping couples change.* New York: Guilford.

Sullivan, H. S. (1947). *Conceptions of modern psychiatry.* Washington, DC: William Alanson White Psychiatric Foundation.

Telch, C. F., Agras, W. S., & Linehan, M. M. (2001). Dialectical behavior therapy for binge eating disorders. *Journal of Consulting and Clinical Psychology, 69,* 1061–1065.

Wubbolding, R. E. (1996). Reality therapy: Theoretic underpinnings and implementation in practice. *Directions in Mental Health Counseling, 6*(9), 1-17.

Wubbolding, R. E., & Brickell, J. (1998). Qualities of the reality therapist. *International Journal of Reality Therapy, 17*(2), 47–49.

Wubbolding, R. E., Al-Rashidi, B., Brickell, J., Kakitani, M, Kim, R. I., & Lennon, B., et al. (1998). Multicultural awareness: Implications for reality therapy and choice theory. *International Journal of Reality Therapy, 17*(2), 4–6.

Young, J. E., Beck, A. T., & Weinberger, A. (1993). Depression. In D. H. Barlow (Ed.), *Clinical Handbook of Psychological Disorders* (2nd ed., pp. 240–277). New York: Guilford.

CHAPTER 10

Systemic Approaches: Family Therapy

A Selection from
"Stories of Psychotherapy," 1992

Cloe Madanes

I was always puzzled by how seemingly powerful and competent adults could be such helpless and incompetent parents. And I was even more interested in how little children, apparently helpless, could be powerful helpers in the family. I noticed that although the family appears to be a traditional hierarchical organization, with parents in charge of the children, it rarely is truly organized in this way. How often does a parent side with a child to help the other parent? How many children help their parents' marriage stay together? How many children succeed in separating their parents? These and many similar questions led me to think that perhaps, as a therapist, to organize a family in a hierarchical model was not necessarily the best idea.

I developed new strategies that violate the model of the traditional family hierarchy and that perhaps are part of a new model of the family as a network. The communication style in this new model is lateral, diagonal, and from the bottom up. A network is like a fishnet, where the nodes are all linked together in a three-dimensional structure. . . . [Madanes gave nine case examples in this paper; three of them are reprinted here.]

Case Five

Special techniques must be used when a small child presents a problem. As a teacher of psychiatric residents, I was indignant when I heard that the staff of the Department of Child Psychiatry had been trying to hospitalize a five-year-old boy for temper tantrums. Fortunately, the stepfather refused to allow the hospitalization and I was asked to supervise the therapy.

When the mother, son, and younger sister came to the first session, the therapist asked the boy to dramatize his temper tantrums. He puffed up his chest, flexed his arms, made an ugly face, and said, "I'm the Incredible Hulk," as he hit the furniture and screamed. He then showed the therapist how he also could be Frankenstein's monster.

After commenting on how bright and imaginative he was, the therapist asked the boy to pretend to be the Incredible Hulk and Frankenstein's monster again and then the mother to hug and kiss him. Next, the mother was asked to pretend to have a tantrum herself and the boy was to hug and kiss *her*. They were asked to do this at home every day and to end their performance with milk and cookies.

After one session, the boy's tantrums disappeared. The mother and son had helped each other in playful, affectionate ways, without punitive intrusions from outside agents. The tantrums had turned into play in which mother and child could express their love and reassure each other.

Case Six

Another approach is to organize children to take turns in unusual ways. Tommy, a 21-year-old man, was depressed, delinquent, and drug abusing. He said he was the "life ruiner" of the family, and that his brother and sister were perfect.

The therapist suggested that it was not fair that there should be only one "life ruiner" in the family. If the brother and sister were willing to take turns, Tommy only would be the life ruiner one week out of three, so he would have two weeks out of three to do something else—get a job, study, have some fun. The brother and sister agreed, although the parents protested that it would be better not to have a life ruiner at all. When the older brother had his turn at being the life ruiner, he decided it was time to move out of the parents' house. The parents were upset and old conflicts between the father and this son resurfaced. It became clear that Tommy had been drawing the father's anger to himself, distracting the father from his deep resentment toward his intellectual, sensitive older son, who looked down on the father's blue-collar job. As the father and older brother resolved their old conflicts, Tommy did not have to be the life ruiner any more. He found a job and a girlfriend and moved on with his life.

Case Seven

One of the middle children in a family often called our institute because she was concerned that her mother might become depressed when the daughter left home to be married. The mother was a widow, a recovering alcoholic who had been overwhelmed by the death of her husband, which had left her with ten children ranging in age from 14 to 30. In the sessions, it was clear that the mother was central to all of their lives, and that no matter how much she gave of herself, it was never enough. The therapist organized the family so that each child was a helper to another child and a helpee of someone else. These helper-helpee relationships between the children were assigned irrespective of age, so that, for example, the youngest child ended up being the helper of the oldest. The idea was that the children should take turns at turning to each other for assistance and only ask the mother for help as a last resort. Encouraged by the children's competence and by their love for one another, the mother was able to focus on her own needs, and even developed the courage to introduce the children to a man whom she was considering marrying. (pp. 42–44) ▪ ▪

DISCUSSION IDEAS

1. What point of view on human nature do you think Madanes holds? What clues to her beliefs did you find in the passage above?

2. What would a strict behaviorist do for the mother and child in Case Five? Would the behaviorist treatment work equally well, do you think? Even if both treatments stopped the tantrums, what other effects would be different?

3. What function did Tommy's "life ruining" serve in the family in Case Six? Have you ever seen a case in which one child does all the misbehaving? What function did it serve for other members of the family?

4. What would probably happen to Tommy as an individual client in the counseling setting with which you are familiar?

5. Why did the mother in Case Seven hesitate to introduce her suitor to her children? What gave her the courage to introduce him?

6. How did each case demonstrate Madanes's point that the family is a network and not a hierarchy?

7. Do you find the cases believable? What other details would you like to know?

8. In the same paper as the above passage, Madanes said, "Too many people become lost in menial and sordid details of everyday life and behave as though the family were a factory that, at the end of the day, has to produce clean dishes. The family provides refuge from the hardships of society" (p. 46). Do you agree? If so, can you think of an example?

Introduction to Family Systems Theory

A recruiter for college football sat next to me on a long plane trip once, and being a vocational psychologist, of course I quizzed him about his job. He talked about studying videotapes of the prospective player's games, interviewing the player himself, interviewing his high school coach, and scrutinizing the statistics of his play. "Best of all," he said, "is when I can get myself invited to the kid's house for dinner and see the whole family together in their own home."

"You can tell something about how he'll do on the football team from that?" I asked.

"You can tell everything," the recruiter said.

Think for a minute about why he said that. What could someone tell about *you* from visiting your family for dinner?

The football recruiter told me that every recruit represented a big investment and a gamble for the university, and many of the make-or-break qualities of the player weren't shown on the field or in individual interviews. The student athlete needs the maturity to balance study and athletics, the self-control to resist the worst temptations of college social life, and the ability to cooperate with peers and authorities, for example. He doesn't need to be brilliant intellectually, but he does need to have a good head on his shoulders and realistic expectations. Whether and how his family will support his college pursuits, and how his leaving will change the family scene, affect the player's ability to focus on his goals. Clues about all of these things, as you will see in this chapter, can be gathered from a sample of his behavior in his most fundamental social group: his family.

I don't know when college football recruiters began using family assessment, but they may have had the jump on the Western mental health establishment. When family therapy blossomed in the 1950s, it came from many different sources at once. Alfred Adler in the 1920s perceived the family system as active in the individual's psychology, as did many therapists from a psychoanalytic background. With his child guidance clinics in Vienna and clinics started in the United States by his student Rudolf Dreikurs, Adler was one of the first psychologists actually to treat the family as an interacting group. Meanwhile, the social work movement at the turn of the century integrated what we now call family therapy in its practice of making home visits to troubled families. Investigations into how schizophrenia comes about led Gregory Bateson and Murray Bowen to perceive that parental patterns of communication could affect a child in ways that make him or her unable to decode or produce ordinary conversation and emotional expression. Getting to these insights required that they observe interactions among the mother, father, normal siblings, and schizophrenic patients. Bowen eventually decided that these interaction patterns could explain not only the psychology of severely disturbed patients but the psychology of all of us, on a continuum from ordinary to psychotic (Bateson, Jackson, Haley, & Weakland; Bowen, 1976).

Common Sense and Culture

Family dynamics, of course, have been related to individual psychology in common-sense thinking for centuries before being a focus of professional psychologists. In the multiethnic neighborhood where I grew up, a family situation was always invoked to explain a person's success, failure, criminality, social skill, temperament, personal habits, and choice of mate. A review of models of helping in seven non-Western countries (Barbados, Koria, Nigeria, Pakistan, Singapore, Sudan, and Zambia) revealed a pervasive assumption that "the family plays the most significant role in the resolution of mental health problems. An underlying notion seems to be that the whole family shares the problem and suffers with the individual, and it is the family that will help the disturbed individual" (Lago & Thompson, 1996). Traditional healers such as shamans, medicine men, clergy, Sufis, curanderos, and hakeem involve family and community in their cures. Damaged social relations and feelings like envy, anger, and loneliness are sources of mental and spiritual distress (often seen as the same thing).

Integration of Therapeutic Viewpoints

Marriage and family therapy in the United States came from several distinct sources over the first part of the twentieth century; by the century's end, separate schools of thought began to blend (Gurman & Kniskern, 1992), and this trend has continued. It is now difficult to set aside one theoretical stance (for example, that the family is a psychological unit) or one technique (for example, graphic ways of depicting family relationships) as belonging to only one type of family therapy. Furthermore, when various types of couple and family treatments are compared in studies of outcome, all the approaches achieve similar success rates even though their theories diverge (Baucom, Shoham, Mueser, Daiuot, & Stickle, 1998; Edwards & Steinglass, 1995; Shadish, Ragsdale, Glaser, & Montgomery, 1995). Many of the boundaries between formerly competing viewpoints have loosened. For these reasons, I choose an integrated presentation in this chapter. To clarify separate viewpoints, I include a table that will help you see the difference in emphases among five traditional categories of family systems thought (Table 10.1). Being able to identify the hallmarks of separate approaches will assist you in reading research reports and in taking standard examinations on the topic of family therapy.

Family therapy has grown in practice since the 1950s and is expected to grow further. It has become more professionalized, in that training is more standard across various programs (Gurman & Kniskern, 1992), and credentials are increasingly necessary and significant. Part of the reason for growth is that researchers have provided evidence that family therapy is effective. In a meta-analysis of seventy-one studies that compared marriage and family therapy (MFT) to no treatment, Shadish, Ragsdale, Glaser, and Montgomery (1995) found that MFT clients did significantly better than similar clients who were not treated. Clients who received MFT had a 67 percent success rate, while untreated clients had a 37 percent success rate—an effectiveness larger than you usually see in medical, surgical, and pharmaceutical outcome studies. Across various studies, these better odds held for child conduct disorders, family relationship problems, communication/problem-solving difficulties, phobias, schizophrenic symptoms, and global psychiatric symptoms. In addition, family therapy appears to be less expensive than traditional individual treatments, and cost effectiveness is a major concern in the current climate.

Profile of a Theorist

MURRAY BOWEN (1913–1990)

Murray Bowen is perhaps best known for his comprehensive theoretical approach to family therapy. Like many of his predecessors and contemporaries, Bowen came to psychology through psychiatry and medicine, specifically as a specialist in the area of childhood schizophrenia. As the psychoanalytic movement gained momentum in the early decades of the twentieth century, concomitant developments in systems theory were piquing the interest of a number of social scientists. In the 1940s, Bowen was among the first to blend the two fields when he moved from the format of individual psychoanalysis to treating multiple members of a family simultaneously.

Born and raised in Waverly, Tennessee, Bowen was the oldest child of a large, close-knit family. After graduating from medical school, he served five years in the military and then began his medical career in psychiatry. Relying on his psychoanalytic training, Bowen pioneered efforts to apply psychodynamic

TABLE 10.1
Categories of Family Theories

Orientation	Emphasis/Dominant Theory	Terminology	Names
Systemic	Multigenerational patterns/Social learning, especially modeling	Differentiation and fusion Triangulation Genograms Chronic anxiety Family projection process	Murray Bowen M. McGoldrick James Framo Peggy Papp
Structural	Family's set of demands and rules (often unstated)/Organizational theory	Disengagement and enmeshment Boundaries Subsystems Coalitions	Salvador Minuchin B. Montalvo M. P. Nichols
Strategic	Quickly outwitting resistance to change/Communication theory and cognitive-behaviorism	Circular causality Power and control Directives Paradoxes Reframing Miracle question	Jay Haley Cloe Madanes Paul Watzlawick Steve deShazer
Experiential	Emotional deadness/Existentialism and humanism	Congruent communication Awareness Alienation Growth experiences Gestalt techniques	Carl Whitaker Virginia Satir Leslie Greenberg Susan Johnson
Narrative	Dominant stories that shape families/Phenomenology	Externalizing Reflecting team Therapeutic letters Unique outcomes Meaning of problem	Michael White David Epston Tom Andersen Harlene Anderson Harold Goolishian

principles to the treatment of severe emotional problems. He believed that the core tenets of Freudian theory could be used to understand a host of mental disorders, including schizophrenia. Bowen consistently pointed to two fundamental concepts—namely, that emotional illness develops in relationship to others, and that healing treatment takes place in the context of a therapeutic relationship.

With these basic concepts as a foundation, Bowen began developing his theory by focusing on relationship patterns between mothers and schizophrenic children at the Menninger Clinic in Topeka, Kansas. From there, he moved to the National Institute of Mental Health (NIMH) in 1954, where he was the first director of the newly formed Family Division. He began by treating members of a family separately, but soon found that approach to be counterproductive. When he decided to treat the entire family as a single unit, Bowen solidified his place as a major founder of family therapy. Along with a panel of others, he launched a program of research that served to raise awareness of his model for treatment to the national level.

In 1959, Bowen moved to Georgetown University, where he hoped to further his research; however, the department chairman who hired him died shortly after his arrival and Bowen lost the support he needed to keep his project going. Nevertheless, he continued working on his theory, and during his thirty-one years at Georgetown he developed what is now recognized as one of the most comprehensive theoretical approaches to family therapy. His constructs of triangulation, multigenerational transmission, and differentiation of self are widely acknowledged as important contributions to the field of family therapy. Of the major schools of thought taught today, Bowen's theory is generally hailed as the most representative of the psychodynamic approaches. Bowen continued refining his theory late into his career until he died in 1990, following a lengthy illness.

Essential Concepts

Systems theorists agree on several fundamental ideas.

The Family as a System

This chapter and the next one examine people in the context of the **systems** they belong to—the networks of human relationships that closely affect their psychological life. For many people, the most important system is the family, whether that is defined as a couple, a **nuclear family** (father, mother, and children), or an **extended family** (grandparents, parents, children, and other relatives). Some people's families include members who are not related by blood or law, such as very long-term friends, same-sex partners, and neighbors who function like sisters, brothers, uncles, parents, or offspring.

The people in a family are related to each other in a complex, meaningful way. The family system has been compared to a machine, whose functioning is a composite of the functioning of all of its parts; to natural systems like ecology and the biological body; and to other human organizations like corporations and workforces. All these are good comparisons because they capture the manner in which the family system is both fluid and stable. External conditions, inputs, and events create change in the system, but its way of dealing with them shows stability, a tendency toward **homeostasis.** That is, maintenance of the status quo is reinforced, and deviation from family norms is punished. Subtly or overtly, the status quo is supported, and this has both positive and negative consequences (Sayger & Horne, 2000). The family system has **boundaries** that separate it from other systems even though it interacts with them. Furthermore, changes in any part of the system affect other parts and might reverberate through the whole system, in a process of **circular causality.** The death of a parent is an extreme instance, in which the economic, emotional, philosophical, and social structure is thrown off balance. Often a change in one member of a family or one aspect of family life has unexpected effects on the system. An example that I've seen recently in popular media is loss of income, which, surprisingly, can improve the quality of family life when material success has unbalanced the other joys of life.

That's How We Do Things Around Here: Stable Family Styles

Some of the shared, stable aspects of a family system are obvious. For example, in my neighborhood some families had religious art and shrines in their living rooms, and some did not. Some ate dinner around a table every evening, with all members required to be there, while some had no organized dinner, with members flying through catching a bite to eat on their way out of the house for some other activity. Many families enforced a period of peace and quiet when the father came home from the factory, when the mother would serve him a big piece of pie and he would be left alone to read the paper or watch television. Many families had no father, and children got an hour or two of independence between their school day and the time their mother came home from work. Several families had two or more patterns that alternated depending on a parent's drinking, insanity, unemployment, or periods in jail.

    As children, we only glimpse the way other people live, and so our own family's ways seem normative to us. We are used to our own family's use of space, sense of time, customs, gender roles, and sets of assumptions about the outside world (whether it is threatening or welcoming, for instance). The more interaction your family has with the outside world (that is, the more **permeable** the family boundary is), the more different ways of doing things and looking at things are available; and, ordinarily, as you get older, your family changes to accommodate changes in the individuals within it. One common example occurs during adolescence, when customs such as a family dinnertime often change to accommodate the child's activities outside the home (such as sports, clubs, and teenaged socializing). Reiss (1981) points out that the usage of space in a home reflects changes in the family's system. For instance, when my brother entered high school, my parents had his bedroom remodeled with a spacious built-in desk and bookshelves, and when my father retired, he set up another room as a home office. Both of these changes reflected changes in the roles our menfolk played, and both symbolized what we respected and valued in their activities.

These are surface features of the family system. Other features are subtler; they may be hard to see from within, yet are deep-seated and persistent. The levels of emotional distance, privacy, or intimacy between members seem natural to them but may seem odd to people from other types of families. Family communication style is an example. I come from a family of "announcers": When we leave a room or setting, we say, "I'll be right back," or "I'll try to find that videotape now," or (very commonly), "I've got to get back to work." I'm now married into a family of "non-announcers": One minute they're sitting at the blackjack table with you and the next minute they've picked up their chips and left, only to return later, all without a word. I notice that the whole family, regardless of age and sex, is like this, and it took me a while to shrug off their mysterious comings and goings. In my family, these would be cause for speculation and concern.

Researchers studying family systems measure such features as use of time and space, planning and punctuality, and level of synchronization (e.g., Reiss, 1981). They have found significant family differences in amount of activity; in some families, for example, members tended to move from room to room an average of eleven times per hour, while in others, members did so an average of fifty-four times an hour. Rate and amount of speech within families are steady, with some family groups speaking slowly and rarely and others quickly and often. What topics are okay to bring up with which family members, and when and where, are settled into patterns. Even the amount of impulse control is frequently mutual: The walls of my friend April's house bore dents from her husband and sons' habit of punching them for emphasis. As a system, a family has a hierarchy, with some members having more power and control than others. In an old-fashioned patriarchal family, the father has the last word on any decision, to an extent that would be unacceptable to most of today's American families. Parents usually hold more power than children, though some families organize around children's desires more than others do. Power and control are allocated to different members of the family in various ways. An example you may have noticed through comparing with your friends is how much your parents' and grandparents' wishes are heeded concerning choice of college major and career. Like most family processes, this one follows spoken or unspoken **rules** that may involve much more than the student and parents themselves. My student Ana was able to choose her major, psychology, because she is the third daughter, and both her older sisters had already become physicians. Otherwise, her Korean parents would not have allowed Ana to take up a major they consider frivolous, with such a blurry career future.

SMALL GROUP EXERCISE

Compare and contrast the families of the people in your small group, focusing on one of the following recurring situations: weekday dinners, television watching, bedtimes, allowances, housework, coordination of schedules, religious practices. Each group member in turn should answer a specific question, such as "Who cooks dinner?" "Who decides what to watch on television?" or "When do children stop having pre-set bedtimes?" Discuss the circumstances under which these usual practices are changed or ignored, if at all.

What assumptions about the family and the outside world were expressed by your customs? Did each of you know a family that dealt with the matter quite differently?

Subsystems and Boundaries

Within the family, some parts form **coalitions** and **subsystems** with their own power, rules, and relationships to other individuals and subsystems. The mother and father form the parental and spousal subsystem, and the children have their own sibling subsystem, often affected by their birth order and sex. These two subsystems are fairly stable. The baby of the family is still the baby even when he is a 40-year-old taxi driver, while the oldest child gets to claim greater wisdom than the rest of the siblings throughout life. A sibling who has been sick or problematic often gets cast in that role forever. Some subsets of children are emotionally closer than others; when distant in age, the oldest and the youngest may never be close. On the other hand, in families like my mother's, the oldest sibling took charge of all the children, and always had a parental relationship to the younger ones. Other subsystems form for temporary reasons, such as two daughters ganging up to request their own bedrooms.

One basic subsystem is the **triangle,** a system of three members in which two are distressed by conflict, deficit, or alienation in their relationship, and a third member is brought in to stabilize their togetherness or to provide escape from the tension of the twosome. "Having a baby to save the marriage" is a common, and commonly disastrous, example. Both parents' focusing on one child's accomplishments or problems is another. You will often see a married person become close with his or her own parent in a period of couple distress or boredom.

A couple can also *triangle in* a counselor, speaking to each other through the counselor when communication between them has broken down. Other outsiders who get triangled in by distressed couples include illicit lovers, police, and social service agencies. Sometimes the triangle does its job, stabilizing all the relationships within it in a relieving way. At other times it serves to conceal a remaining problem or even makes it worse. A triangle that lasts a long time becomes rigid and often does not have the flexibility needed to adapt to changes from the outside or from one of its members.

The Family System as Historical

"Certain basic patterns between the father, mother, and children are replicas of the past generations and will be repeated in the generations to follow" (Bowen, 1976, p. 78). Each nuclear family doesn't make up its own ways of thinking, interpreting, and behaving. We are strongly influenced by our family history, going back to our grandparents' generations and even earlier ancestors. A newly formed couple usually looks to their parents' example when setting up their life together, trying to imitate the strong aspects and avoid the negatives. Much of the modeling after one's parents and grandparents is not conscious, though, but comes through what Murray Bowen (1978) calls a **multigenerational transmission process.** In Bowen's intergenerational model, patterns of relating within the family are passed down, as are many other assumptions about family and world. So, when both partners of a heterosexual couple were raised in families with strong, clear gender roles, they are most likely to enact gender roles in their marriage without thinking about it, or even when trying to resist them. Many women who act outside the gender roles much of the time are still more concerned with social planning, housekeeping, and childcare arrangements than their husbands are. They would find it difficult to give up these automatic feminine-role preoccupations.

Orientations to past, present, and future, attitudes toward money, a sense of what is fair, viewpoints on work and leisure, ideas about family duty—all of these are multigenerational. Marrying someone very much like or very much unlike your opposite-sex parent is a response to family history. Raising children in the same way you were raised, as well as striving for the opposite, are both reactions to the past that might be either conscious or outside of your awareness. A family's emotional reactions to one member's behavior are predictable from history: One family might consider a daughter's decision to drop out of college a legitimate personal choice, while another might consider it a serious betrayal of family expectations or a major family failure. Some children grow up with frequent references to historical family figures like Uncle Joe the story-teller, Grandmother Aguila the adventurous settler, and Great-Grandfather Ames the wise judge, and family stories serve as moral tales that teach what is admired, abhorred, and expected by the clan.

Each partner's cultural history contributes to the family system: "Every family's background is multicultural. All marriages are to a degree cultural intermarriages. . . . Understanding the various strands of a family's cultural heritage is essential to understanding its members' lives and the development of the particular individual as well" (McGoldrick & Giordano, 1996, p. 6).

SMALL GROUP EXERCISE

According to McGoldrick and Giordano (1996), "Ethnicity remains a major form of group identification and a major determinant of our family patterns and belief systems." Do members of your small group agree with this statement? To what degree? As an aid to discussing the issue, look at how McGoldrick and Giordano describe ethnic traits in the following passage.

> Certain common ethnic traits have been described as typical for families of one or another group. For example, Jewish families are often seen as valuing

education, success, family connections, encouragement of children, democratic principles, verbal expression, shared suffering, and having a propensity
to guilt and a love for eating. Anglos have been characterized as generally
emphasizing control, personal responsibility, independence, individuality,
stoicism, keeping up appearances, and moderation in everything. By contrast,
Italian American families are generally described as valuing the family more
than the individual; considering food a major source of emotional as well as
physical nourishment; and having strong traditional male-female roles, with
loyalty flowing through personal relationships. African Americans are often
described as favoring an informal kinship network and spiritual values.
Their strength to survive is a powerful resource, and they tend to have more
flexibility in family roles than many other groups. In Hispanic cultures,
family togetherness and respect, especially for elders, are valued concepts.
People are appreciated more for their character than for merely their vocational success. They may also hold on to traditional notions of a woman's role
as the virgin and the sacrificial sainted mother, who tolerates her husband's
adventures and absence with forbearance. Chinese families stress harmony
and interdependence in relationships, respect for one's place in the line of
generations, ancestor worship, saving face, and food as an emotional and
spiritual expression. For Asian Indians, purity, sacrifice, passivity, and a
spiritual orientation are core values, and death is seen as just one more
phase in the life cycle that includes many rebirths. (p. 10)

Do you know families who fit any of these ethnic trait descriptions? Do you
know families who do not fit the description of their ethnic traits? In your
own family, how does your ethnic background affect values and beliefs,
if at all?

Variation in Historical Focus

Among family therapists, you find a range of how fully counselors explore
family history. Although all seem to agree that history is a driving force in the
present, they do not agree on whether understanding it is necessary for positive change. Therapists who have an object relations approach to families (e.g.,
Scharff & Scharff, 1991) see parents re-enacting disturbed relationships with
people from their own pasts (a psychodynamic point of view, discussed in
Chapter 4), to the detriment of their family. Consider, for example, a woman
whose father frequently became overwhelmed with his large family and left
town for weeks at a time. Eventually, she carried into her own family a terrible
fear of being abandoned and would go into strange, tearful rages whenever her
husband or adolescent children were minutes late or slightly remiss in calling
home. A psychodynamic therapist would consider this case ripe for insight-
oriented reflection and resolution of the past. A cognitive-behavioral family
therapist would not investigate the past more thoroughly but, rather, would encourage present changes in the woman's inaccurate judgments and the emotions stemming from them. This therapist would think that the woman's past

was influential but that emotionally processing it was not especially helpful: If a problem is still current, it must be reinforced by present circumstances (though its source may be in the past) (Haley, 1972).

Family Life Cycle

The family experiences predictable events or periods over the course of time, such as the birth of the first child, children's leaving home, the death of grand-parents, children's marriages, and retirement. At age 40 to 50, adults in the United States generally revise relationships with their parents, becoming adult equals or even allowing the younger generation more power over the older. Each of these events in the **family life cycle** affects the whole system, and a family counselor can help clients prepare for predictable change by asking how they imagine they will deal with it and helping them rehearse in advance, in a stress inoculation process (see Chapter 9). For example, a well-documented fact is that marriage quality plummets dramatically on the birth of the first child, especially for wives (Shapiro, Gottman, & Carrere, 2000). However, research reveals certain relationship qualities that weaken or prevent this effect, such as having a strong marital friendship and a feeling of control in life, and these qualities could be enhanced in family counseling for couples. Sometimes cultural customs build in extended-family preparation for expectable life changes; for example, the Bar Mitzvah and Bat Mitzvah among Jews mark the end of childhood, and several Native American tribes hold elaborate ceremonies of transition to womanhood. (See *www.peabody.harvard.edu/exhibitions.html* to read about the Apache Changing Woman ritual.)

Other family crises are frequent but usually not predicted. Chronic illness, accidental death, divorce, job loss, early pregnancy, incarceration, workplace up-heavals, and victimization by crime create wide-ranging ripples in the system. Discontinuous changes, in particular, disrupt long-held family patterns. Roles change noticeably: For example, when my friend Liz's father lost his high-paying sales position, both teenaged children had to take jobs for the first time in their lives and to leap into more mature roles within the family. More often than you may realize, disruption and role shifts offer an opportunity to improve the family pattern rather than degrade it. Such an improvement frequently eventuates when a son or daughter comes out as gay or lesbian, and the family finds itself enriched by adaptation to the situation (Sanders & Kroll, 2000).

Strangers at Home: Geographical Changes

Immigration disrupts the family multigenerationally. A family that was once extended to include uncles, aunts, grandparents, cousins, and second-cousins-once-removed is transformed into a parents-and-children group in a new culture. If the family gets to move to an ethnic neighborhood in the new country, assim-ilation occurs more slowly but family patterns are more stable (McGoldrick &

he reminds me of Dad. But he *isn't* Dad, and I shouldn't act like he is." In making this separation between emotion and reason, Dave would be *differentiating*.

In contrast, *fusion* refers to emotions and thought being tangled up together: "People with the greatest fusion between feeling and thinking function the poorest. They inherit a high percentage of life's problems. Those with the most ability to distinguish between feeling and thinking, or who have the most differentiation of self, have the most flexibility and adaptability in coping with life stresses, and the most freedom from problems of all kinds. Other people fall between the two extremes, both in the interplay between feeling and thinking and in their life adjustments" (Bowen, 1976, p. 59). The characters on soap operas exemplify people who are dominated by their emotional systems: They fit Bowen's description of people with fusion as "less flexible, less adaptable, and more emotionally dependent on those about them. They are easily stressed into dysfunction, and it is difficult for them to recover from dysfunction" (p. 65). I realized while watching my soap this morning that the *whole plot* would disappear if the characters were able to reasonably reflect on their emotional reactions. Shawn walked in to see her father with his arms around an ex-girlfriend—and if she had stopped for a moment and considered some reasonable explanation for the scene she witnessed, much dramatic storm and stress would've been avoided. The genre depends on people leaping to emotionally distressing conclusions on the tiniest shred of evidence, and then basing their behavior on their emotional conclusions.

In Bowen's view, we all have **pseudo-selves,** identities that we create to conform and promote harmony, and pseudo-selves follow beliefs and principles because they are held by a group, not because they are part of a reasonable system composed by the individual. College students who say that they are completely different at home than at school are talking about a pseudo-self in one setting or the other (or both). Pseudo-selves are a by-product of fusion, since the pseudo-self identity has an emotional basis. The less differentiation within oneself, the less differentiation one has from other family members, because the emotions of other family members can easily control behavior. This is the mechanism of *fusion*, and it's sometimes confusing because the term refers to both fusion within one person (no division between thought and feeling) and fusion between two people (no division between the other person's feelings and one's own).

Broadening the term's usage even further, families as a whole possess a level of differentiation or fusion. Fused families seek the security of one-ness, and the more the outside environment threatens them, the more they cling to security operations, becoming **closed systems.** People tend to marry others at the same level of differentiation (high or low) in a *multigenerational transmission process.* (You may recall this term from my earlier discussion.) In short, traits are carried from generation to generation. A newly married couple in which both partners are low in differentiation will establish a family system lower in differentiation than their own original families and pass this pattern down. Bowen (1966) believed that eventually schizophrenic children would be produced in this manner. (Schizophrenics are often unable to tell the difference between messages from within them and from outside, and they are not able to evaluate other people's statements rationally; Bowen saw such features as extreme cases of fusion.)

R e f l e c t i o n

Reread the description of *pseudo-self.* What settings or situations bring out a pseudo-self in you? How do you know? Is this pseudo-self one that you'd like to change, or are you satisfied with it?

Being able to let reason organize your actions is only one side of the coin. Emotional reactions, if not given their due, sabotage the fullness of experience. **Experiential** family theorists like Virginia Satir and Carl Whitaker emphasize the destruction wrought by **emotional deadness,** which is shown by a lack of spontaneity and expressiveness in the family. Such families are notable for interpersonal distance and politeness. They strike you as cautiously sidestepping emotional situations. To them, such situations would be stressors that the family system cannot accommodate, even though they come from within. Even lively families may have areas of emotional deadness—as when all members conspire to cover up a family secret, or to suppress mutual grief over a death. Marital dissatisfaction, from an experiential point of view, stems from alienation and emotional deprivation (Johnson, 1986).

SMALL GROUP EXERCISE

Bring to class examples of comic strips and Sunday funnies that feature families as regular characters. Choose one of these comic families and analyze its interactions in terms of family systems psychology.

The Nature of Positive Change

Every psychotherapist, from whatever school derived, strives to teach the primary patient and his environment to "relate better"—that is, to be less easily offended, turned off, sulky, depressed, or unproductive; to learn self-confidence, even under stress; to stand up to formerly unconquerable obstacles and overcome them; to achieve a better understanding of inner conflicts and one's goals and purposes in life. This means that patients and families are encouraged and persuaded to gain a new perspective on life and environment, no matter how non-directive the therapeutic techniques applied are. (Laqueur, 1976, p. 414)

Adler focused on the subjective, socially constructed patterns of living called "lifestyle," and helped people to correct faulty goals, convictions, and assumptions within a given lifestyle that restricted personal behavior and impeded individual development. His approach to working with couples emphasized cooperation and equality between the sexes, an essential foundation for building a life together. (Bitter, Christensen, Hawes, & Nicoll, 1998, pp. 95–96)

These two quotations nicely summarize the nature of positive change from a family systems perspective: better relationships, self-confidence, self-understanding, new perspectives, and individual development within a framework of cooperation and fairness. A healthy family balances each member's separateness with collective togetherness and possesses the flexibility to shift this balance according to stress, family life cycle changes, and information flowing in from outside the system.

Change in family systems can occur on two different levels, or somewhere in between. A **first-order change** attempts to relieve the anxiety occurring in the system but doesn't alter the organization of the system itself. For example, the therapist who suggested that Sharon's blended family cease piano lessons and practice was endorsing a first-order change. All the members, individually and collectively, would still have the same problems to solve, but the household would shake off being stuck on piano lessons as the unworkable solution. A **second-order change** in that family might be strengthening the sibling subsystem, which was almost nonexistent when the parents went to counseling. A coalition and support system between the two girls would alter the structure of the family. Another second-order change might come from Mike's working on his own unfinished business with *his* **family of origin,** since he came into Sharon's family with some unrealistic hopes and dreams transferred from his own childhood onto the daughters.

In this process, Mike would feel and experience what was previously locked up as inconsistent with his story of the big happy musical family. If he were able to have a heightened emotional experience of the pressure and tension that came from his tightly closed family system, he would gain a new perspective on what he wanted for his step-daughters. He might question the script he was directing for the new family. Families "come to therapy with these scripts tightly written. Their problem is that their scripts do not help them function in a way that *they* find useful" (Cecchin, 1987, p. 411). In social constructivist terms, "an acceptable outcome would be the identification or generation of alternative stories that enable them to perform new meanings, bringing with them desired possibilities— new meanings that persons will experience as more helpful, satisfying, and open-ended" (White & Epston, 1990).

Therapist as System Member

The therapist becomes part of a system, herself plus the family in treatment, no matter whether she maintains an outsider's stance (as in psychoeducational therapy) or throws herself into the fray (as in experiential therapy) (Nichols & Schwartz, 2001). What family therapists have in common is the introduction of themselves as something new into the system: "The successful introduction of a significant other person into an anxious or disturbed relationship system has the capacity to modify relationships within the system" (Bowen, 1976, p. 47). Under some theories, the counselor tries to pare her involvement down into that of a mere perturber of the system, allowing the system to come up with a response (Cecchin, 1987). In individual therapy, we often talk about entering the client's world and seeing it from his or her perspective. But the family therapist has to enter several worlds simultaneously, as well as a world shared by all the individuals, which probably differs from any one person's version.

Most counselors take on a role, a style of interacting with the family. Ferber and Ranz (1972) labeled four such roles for family therapists:

1. The *mediator.*   This person negotiates a contract between management and labor (usually, parents and children) that both can live with, and that allows the fruits of both their investments in the system.

2. The *diplomat.*   This counselor translates among the languages and the worlds represented by family members so that they can understand each other and get along without war. (Bowen [1976] names a similar role: the psychopolitician.)

3. The *director* or *co-author.*   This person asks the family to recreate their drama and then plunges in to help rewrite the script with a more satisfactory ending. In this role, the counselor assumes that the family needs an outsider to guide it somewhere new.

4. The *Lone Ranger*   Ferber and Ranz's analogy deserves reprinting here: "We see the family as a ship on a long voyage. The therapists fly in by helicopter, somewhere in mid-voyage, conduct an inspection of some or much of the ship, peruse the charts of the waters ahead, the plans for the navigation, and the ship's log. They suggest some changes in the course of the voyage, perhaps fix some machinery gone awry, often clarify the relationships amongst the crew members, and attempt some small changes in their relationships. Then they board their helicopter, usually leaving a wireless address, and fly off while the ship continues on its way." (pp. 359–360)

Murray Bowen (1976) has been criticized for his arm's-length stance of **neutrality** in family therapy, his desire to remain objective and refuse to become triangled in to the family's problems. Though this sounds too distant a role to some people, neutrality doesn't mean that the therapist is cold and aloof; instead, the therapist takes a stance of **curiosity** (Cecchin, 1987). Based on the idea that each system's patterns make sense within it, we are curious about "how ideas, behaviors, and events participate in creating and maintaining the integrity of the system" (p. 408). From a framework of curiosity rather than social control or expert instruction, the therapist may "perturb the system" (p. 408) in such a way that it will find its own way to reorganization.

On the other hand, experiential therapists (for example, Virginia Satir and Carl Whitaker) thrive on personal involvement with family members and self-disclosure, allowing themselves to show their own anger and other emotions during the session. Experiential therapists admit that they themselves get something out of each counseling encounter, and grow from joining each family system. Other therapists are masters at manipulating family patterns by giving advice, directives, and assignments, clearly placing themselves in the role of seasoned coaches for the family team.

Family therapy has more often included pairs or teams of therapists than individual therapy has. Sometimes a male and female therapist team up to reproduce a couple subsystem, perhaps modeling ways of handling conflict and decision making. Having counselors who don't always agree, in any sex combination, may open the family to the idea of multiple legitimate ways of interpreting a situation. A creative use of multiple counselors appears in Andersen's (1987) **reflecting team,** a technique popularized by narrative therapists. A team of two or three people behind a one-way screen observes a therapist's interview with family members. Once or twice during the interview, the setting switches to light up the team members discussing the interview, while the therapist and family watch. The therapist then asks the family to comment on what the team said. This way, the family sees that there are different versions of the same world even among therapists, and ideally the family creates an alternate version of their own that includes new modes of relating to each other.

The Process of Family Therapy

Like most processes that draw from many sources, family therapy processes vary from treatment to treatment. However, the beginning-middle-end sequence resembles that of other types of counseling, only more people are involved in both client and counselor roles. A counselor, after interviewing a whole nuclear family, may choose which members need to come in for future sessions. For instance, Mike and Sharon's counselor asked just the parental subsystem to attend. This is a common request, because interventions at the couple level are frequently seen as powerful treatments at the individual and family levels at the same time (Johnson, 1986). The counselor may also ask for drop-ins by relatives or others who function in the family system, yet are not part of the presenting family—especially grandparents, aunts, and uncles. Very young children are frequently left out of the regular sessions, or are observed in a therapy playroom. Reluctant family members are encouraged to come to a trial session, and they are given special attention in attempts to entice them to return.

Family therapists are famous for sharing their work, so observers, trainees, and co-counselors are invited into the room or to observe through a one-way mirror. Many sessions are also videotaped for purposes of education, training, and clients' review. Family sessions are so full of activity that any momentary, single point of view will miss part of the rich interaction. Even if you videotaped your own family at the dinner table, you would find facial expressions, side communications, and body language on the tape that you missed the first time.

The Initial Stage

In the initial stage, which may range from one to six sessions, the counselor's job is to engage the family members in the therapy process and begin to develop ideas about how the family system works. The counselor's entry into the family is called **joining,** like joining a club with its own rules and language. The counselor attempts to **accommodate** or follow along with the style, language, and emotional tone that already exist in the family. For example, some families are jokey, in which case the therapist makes use of humor, and some families are slow in pace, a pattern the therapist would follow by leaving conversational space open and speaking slowly herself. Joining is an indication of respect for the family and their choice to let an outsider into the system.

Meanwhile, the counselor attends to clues about the system. In what order do the family members enter the room? How and where do they choose to seat themselves? How does each person respond to welcoming comments?

Besides observing, the counselor collects information verbally by asking questions, starting discussions, or asking the family to interact on some task (drawing, putting together a puzzle). He or she finds out what the family has done so far to solve their difficulty. This part of the process includes *assessment*, which continues in the middle stage as well. I will give you five formats for assessment endorsed by various systems theorists.

Dattilio's Cognitions   Dattilio (1994, pp. 322, 323) proposes exploration of patterns of cognition (thought, focus, explanation) that affect "virtually every aspect of family life." The categories of cognition for each family member are these:

1. Selective attention (which individual is noticed)
2. Attributions (how individuals explain why any given event occurs)
3. Expectancies (what individuals predict will occur in the short-, middle- or long-term future)
4. Assumptions (individuals' perceptions about how the world works)
5. Standards (how individuals think the world should be).

This exploration is rarely done through direct questioning; instead, the counselor encourages a group discussion and infers cognitive patterns from what people say and do.

Andersen's Family Process   Some first-session questions suggested by Andersen (1987) are these: "Who was the person who first had the idea to come here?" "Who did this person consult first? Who second?" "Who was most pleased by the idea? Who was the most reserved?" "If the person who first presented the idea had not done so, would another person have done it?" "Which of you talked the most together about the meeting beforehand?" "When you woke up this morning, who most looked forward to coming here?" "What did you hope to achieve from this meeting?" (p. 418).

Goldenbergs's Treatment Planning   Family therapists Irene and Herbert Goldenberg (2000, p. 392) address the following questions in an attempt to determine the direction of treatment as they watch the family interact:

1. Is treatment for the entire family needed?
2. Who are the appropriate family members with whom to work?

3. What underlying interactive patterns fuel the family disturbance and lead to symptoms in one or more of its members?

4. What specific interventions will most effectively help this family?

Haley's Problem Solution Haley (1987) divides the initial interview into four stages:

1. Social Stage: Introductions, each member's name, major activities and interests. Establish rapport.

2. Problem Stage: Each family member's definition of the problem.

3. Interaction Stage: Therapist identifies family structure by observing repetitive interactions among family members.

4. Contract Stage: Therapist establishes exactly what, according to each family member, would constitute resolution of the family's problems.

The following small group exercise gives you a chance to put Haley's system into action.

SMALL GROUP EXERCISE

This exercise was created by Banyard and Fernald (2002), making use of Haley's plan for first-session assessment. You need a volunteer family counselor (maybe your instructor) and four volunteers to be the Jones family in this role play, the instructions for which are listed in Table 10.2. The rest of the class observes and discusses the questions in Table 10.3 after the role play. The role play should take just twenty to thirty minutes, so the counselor needs to divide the time among the four stages, allowing five to seven minutes per stage.

Dreikurs's Child Goals Child misbehavior is almost always of interest when a family is troubled. Alfred Adler's student and colleague Rudolf Dreikurs (1950) believed that children would disclose the **goals** of their bad behavior if interviewed properly. Parents and children are asked to describe a specific problem event, and the event is investigated in a way that suggests the goal to the child. Here's an example from Bitter and colleagues (1998):

> "Dad tells me that the two of you had a big fight in the car on the way over here today. Any idea why you were fighting?"
>
> The counselor neither accepts nor rejects the children's response, but acknowledges it, saying, "That's a possibility. I have another idea; would you like to hear it?"
>
> "Could it be that you were fighting just to keep Dad busy with you?" (Attention Getting: Goal 1)

TABLE 10.2
Instructions Given to Volunteers Who Will Role-Play Family Members

1. *No talking or planning.* Do not speak with one another until you re-enter the classroom.

2. *The Jones family.* When you re-enter the classroom as a member of the Jones family, seat yourself in the chairs of Dr. —'s "office." The family should include two parents and two children. The first family member to speak selects whatever family position he or she wishes—for example, father or oldest daughter. The family member speaking second selects another family position, and so forth until all four members of the family have presented themselves. The last two family members to speak must make certain that the family includes two parents and two children.

3. *Family problem and structure.* The Jones family should have one or more family problems that bring them to therapy. Also, the family should include (a) a disengaged (peripheral) parent, who is removed, isolated, and aloof from other family members; (b) an overinvolved (enmeshed) parent, who is overly concerned and preoccupied with other family member's lives, thereby making it difficult for them to lead autonomous, independent lives; and (c) a scapegoated child, regarded by family members as "the problem" but whose behavior actually is a symptom of the family's difficulties or perhaps the parent's underlying unresolved marital struggles. The fourth family member contributes to the family structure in whatever manner he or she wishes.

4. *Spontaneity.* To the best of your ability, be spontaneous. Play as fully as you can whatever family position and character type (e.g., blamer, hysteric, clown, pessimist, martyr, peace maker, overactive child, substance abuser) you select, and allow the family struggle/dance to evolve however it happens. Enjoy being a member of the Jones family.

Source: Banyard & Fernald (2002).

TABLE 10.3
Questions Provided to Class for the Family Therapy Demonstration

1. *Interview stages.* The interview you are about to observe has four stages (social, problem, interaction, contract). Can you identify each of the stages?

2. *Definitions of the problem.* What are the various family members' definitions of the problem? Are some of their definitions one-person definitions? Are there any multi-person definitions?

3. *Structure and roles.* What is the structure of the Jones family? Do Mr. and Mrs. Jones work together as parents? Are they a unified executive team? Does the Jones family include a coalition, two family members conspiring against a third family member? And does the Jones family have a problem child serving as scapegoat?

4. *Family functioning.* Is the Jones family functional, dysfunctional, or some combination of both?

5. *Family dance.* Does the Jones family engage in a family dance, a predictable family interactional pattern that occurs frequently, especially when the family is under stress?

Source: Banyard & Fernald (2002).

"Could it be that you fight in order to show Dad that you are the boss and no one
   can make you stop?" (Power Struggle: Goal 2)

Could it be that you fight in order to get even with Dad?" (Revenge: Goal 3)

Given the nature of fighting, it is next to impossible for it to be a demonstration of
inadequacy or an assumed disability (Withdrawal: Goal 4) but when such a goal
is suspected, it can be disclosed with "Could it be that you would like to be left
alone?" (pp. 109–110)

When the correct guess is given, children will give a "recognition reflex," a
facial expression that says, "You're right." Dreikurs (1950) believed his four proposed goals were nonconscious in children. Bitter (1991) explained three more,
usually conscious, goals of misbehavior in children: "getting" (taking candy
from a store), "self-elevation" (tattling), and "avoidance" (not doing homework). These, too, are recognized by children when suggested as goals by the
therapist. Dreikurs asserted that telling a child *why* she behaves in a certain
way can be very helpful to her, and can be done by anyone who works with
children (not just trained counselors). The focus is on the current purpose of the
behavior, not the life history that led to it. Other ways of achieving the goal can
then be discussed.

The Middle Stage

The intervention stage grows out of the hypotheses formed by the counselor in
the initial sessions, and those hypotheses are usually consistent with the theory
(or theories) of family systems that the counselor holds. For example, some
therapists delve into the past much more than others do, according to whether
they emphasize solutions that lie in re-experiencing and re-interpreting the
past, or in changing thought and behavior in the present. In Sharon and Mike's
case, an experiential therapist would ask Mike to get into the ignored needs and
neglected aspects of his self stemming from a childhood in a performing family. A more behaviorist counselor would continue to focus on advice such as
halting the daughters' piano lessons, and finding other concrete ways for Mike
to join the family without seeming like a bossy intruder.

In this stage, the family must realize that they *as a group* are the client, no
matter whom the family projection process has named as the problem member.
Most family counselors share their ideas about what is going on and what they
are doing with the family, just as the Lone Ranger therapists did with the
navigational crew in the analogy above. Some interventions, though, are assignments that will reveal the family to itself in different lights, without any
pre-explanation.

Throughout the middle stage, the counselor re-evaluates her hypotheses
and designs interventions to test them as true or false. Take the case of June,
discussed earlier: If the counselor discovers from June's life history that she has
never before chosen an emotionally unavailable man, the counselor would have
to question an object relations hypothesis having to do with June's father.

As the family works through the middle stage, they usually do homework to supplement sessions. Most counselors make sure the family achieves noticeable success with initial recommendations (Bitter, 1998): The earlier suggestion about piano relief, for example, was a recommendation sure to ease some family tensions right away. With increased confidence, the family can develop more openness and depth, become more flexible, and perceive more alternatives to their established ways.

The Closing Stage

Most families don't want to stay in counseling indefinitely, in good part because of the scheduling difficulties it involves. Some clients wish to terminate sessions when first-order changes are satisfactory—that is, when the anxiety in the system has been eased, even though it's still the same system. If it was not an anxiety-provoking system to start with, this makes a lot of sense. At any rate, the family controls the length of therapy: "The family determines its priorities in much the same way that it determines how often to see a personal physician, a banker, or any other sort of consultant" (Papero, 1995, p. 29). In this consulting model, the family can decide to leave the door open to return for future crises.

In the termination phase of treatment, clients solidify the gains they have made, such as improved problem-solving techniques, stronger internal support systems, less fear of threats from the outside world, and more equanimity about change (inner and outer). They may watch videotapes from early sessions to identify old patterns that have changed, or reminisce about treatment in other ways. They brainstorm about how they will identify slippage into their old patterns and what to do if they see it. Many family therapists choose to terminate by a gradual dropping off in frequency, and some even plan to see a family twice a year without a designated ending. I personally like the bi-yearly plan because it accepts that the family is a living organism, not a closed chapter.

Customary Techniques of Family Therapy

Although in the past, certain techniques could be clearly matched with theories, this is no longer the case. The categories of family systems thought have blended together, particularly in sharing some common techniques. In this section, I divide these into history-taking techniques, hypothesis-building techniques, and interventions for change. You will see that sometimes one technique can be used to serve any of these three purposes.

History-Taking Techniques

With the exception of brief, solution-focused therapies, counselors like to gather three generations of family history. This would cover you, your parents, and your grandparents. Histories are often portrayed in graphic, visual, and concrete

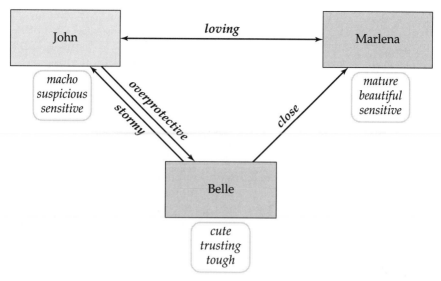

FIGURE 10.1   Belle's Family Map

forms. One technique (Bitter, 1988) is to draw a map of the family and ask a member to use three adjectives to label each person, including herself. She then provides one adjective to describe the relationship between each pair of family members. Such a **family map** produced by Belle, daughter of John and Marlena, might look like the diagram in Figure 10.1.

In narrative form, you can see that Marlena is a mature, beautiful, sensitive woman who enjoys mutual closeness with her daughter and mutual love with her husband, John. According to Satir, each description tells something about the describer's self-worth and need for survival. In this example, then, Belle might describe her father as *macho* because his traditional maleness influenced her, whereas his wife Marlena might describe him as *strong* if she had drawn her own family map, because this quality was one that she depended on. Belle's description of herself as *tough* seems to invite our thoughts about her response to having two *sensitive* parents. The maps and exchange of maps among family members give rise to discussions about similar and different views of what each member contributes to the others' self-worth and survival.

A fancier, more detailed graphic account is presented in a **genogram,** which reflects as many generations as can be accounted for, and uses special symbols to indicate relationships, patterns of functioning (such as repeated early marriages, addictions, or high achievements), and critical life events (McGoldrick, Gerson, & Shellenberger, 1999). For example, a jagged path between people indicates a conflictual relationship, three parallel lines between them indicates **enmeshment** (too much closeness), two parallel lines indicate closeness, and a pair of lines across the path indicate **disengagement** (too much distance) or emotional cutoff (physical or psychological running away). You can find detailed examples and instructions for constructing genograms on the Internet at *http://www.genogram.freeservers.com* and by typing in "genograms" as a key term on your search engine. McGoldrick, Gerson, and Shellenberger's (1999) book, *Genograms: Assessment and Intervention,* contains fascinating examples from families of public figures like Sigmund Freud, Bill Clinton, and Jackie Kennedy.

Using simpler, individual timelines is often sufficient for counseling purposes. Each family member is asked to draw a long line from birth to the present and to fill in significant events and periods in his or her life. This is a technique sometimes employed in individual therapy to help the counselor understand how clients see their life story. In family therapy, similarities and discrepancies among members' lines provide valuable clues about the family system. For example, if children mark a grandmother's death on their lines and neither parent marks it, something odd is going on about the loss. Similarly, family secrets can emerge, as in a family where only one teenager notes the period of a sibling's time in drug rehab on her timeline. Two members' timelines matching almost exactly and mismatching with the rest of the family's implies a strong, closed subsystem.

R e f l e c t i o n

Construct a family map or timeline for yourself. Enlist a family member to create one for him- or herself without looking at yours. Write down what you learned from this activity. What might a counselor think from looking at the two drawings?

DISCUSSION IDEAS

Look at Belle's family map again. If Belle were your client, what would you follow up on to understand her family system? For example, what do the words she uses to describe her parents suggest about Belle herself? What types of descriptors are missing?

Hypothesis-Building Techniques

Obviously, history-taking techniques turn into family assessment techniques as they are reviewed by the therapist and clients. As families discuss their history, the counselor can observe how the members interact, who seems to have power at various junctures, what topics are hot and cold, what level of conflict is tolerable, and many other features that help build theories about how the family system operates. Since **chronic anxiety** is a theme that drives many families to seek help (Bowen, 1966), the counselor keeps track of what topics and interactions seem to produce anxiety, taking into account not only the content of people's reactions but also their body language, withdrawal, agitation, and methods of staving off worry. When a family doesn't know or doesn't want to discuss their history, information can be gleaned from each member's description of "a typical day" in the family (Bitter et al., 1998), followed by the discussion the subject elicits.

Nonverbal techniques can appeal to tongue-tied adults and children. In the immensely popular **Family Drawing Technique,** the examinee is asked to draw a picture of the whole family. Sometimes the counselor includes a request for a picture showing the family doing something together, in which case it is called a *Kinetic Family Drawing* (Oster & Gould, 1987). After the drawing, the client is asked to identify the family members if they are not already named on the picture. Figure 10.2 shows a Kinetic Family Drawing made by Jane, age 15, who was chronically depressed, abused drugs, and skipped school (Oster & Gould, 1987, p. 51).

DISCUSSION IDEAS

How would you describe Jane's family in words? As a therapist, what hypotheses might you develop from looking at her drawing? How could you test your hypotheses?

Family sculpting, originated by Virginia Satir, is a dramatic version of the Family Drawing Technique in which a member silently arranges the others (and herself) in a meaningful scene and directs a pantomime of the scene. For example, a wife was asked to dramatize the scene of "our family after dinner." She placed her husband in his lazy-boy and asked him to doze off, told the two teenaged sons to rush out of the kitchen and turn on the TV, and placed the preteen daughter in the kitchen helping to clean up, telling her to treat every object she touched as though she were furious at it, never to look at the mother as she worked, and to persist in trying to leave the kitchen with her mother dragging her back in. The individual family members had not perceived how abandoned and misused the mother felt at these times before she directed the silent drama. The counselor was led to hypothesize that, for one thing, the family was weak in understanding their emotional effects on each other and that, for another, gender roles were endorsed (whether or not the individuals would approve). Both of these hypotheses are ripe for further exploration. In another family sculpting exercise, a family member is asked to position other members in such a way as to reflect the emotional dynamics between family members.

Such techniques probably remind you of Gestalt therapy; in fact, they are derived directly from Gestalt methods. Family therapists also use other forms

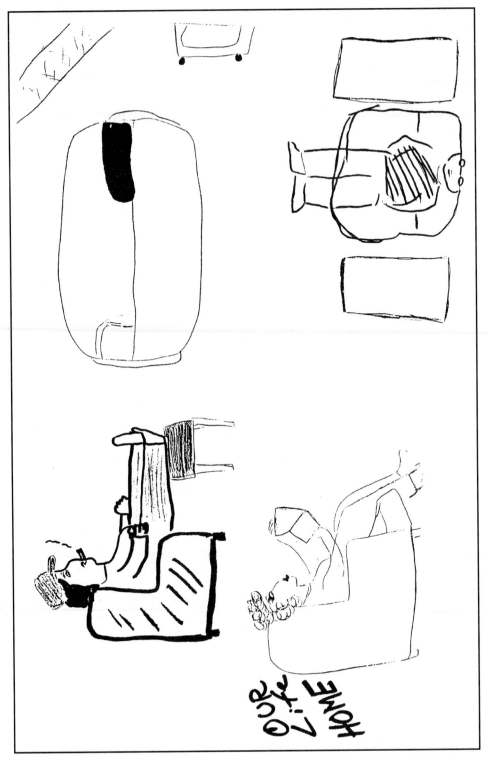

FIGURE 10.2   Jane's Kinetic Family Drawing

feelings are not given attention in everyday life (p. 212). "The goal of therapy is not to get rid of feelings but to help clients become aware of their meaning and to become more responsive to the action tendencies toward which feelings prompt them. . . . The goal is to increase clients' awareness of emotion so that it is available as orienting information to help them deal with the environment" (Greenberg & Safran, 1989, p. 21). Each individual's awareness of other family members' primary emotions can increase empathy and alter behavior toward them.

The emphasis on emotion and felt experience may seem to contradict Bowen's elevation of intellectual functioning under stress, through *differentiation*. However, Bowen (1976) made clear that intellectual function should not be confused with **intellectualization,** verbal defenses against emotion. Intellectualization is the way emotionally trapped people "explain away their plight" (p. 67): They use intellect in the service of emotion. For example, a wife with an abusive husband could use *intellectualization* to excuse his bad behavior as an outgrowth of a sad childhood, and remain in the abusive marriage. This is different from the freedom to use calm reasoning in decision making.

6. *Externalization:* **Externalization** is the most well-known technique of narrative therapy. It involves using language that separates the problem from the personal identity of the clients, implying that there are parts of the person that are uncontaminated by the symptom (O'Hanlon, 1994). Problems are personified, so that Anorexia, Crappy Attitude, and Depression are seen as enemies of the person and the family—enemies that can be conquered and have been resisted in the past.

7. *Writing letters:* Most people cherish more than one letter that has meant a lot to them. Narrative therapists make use of this talismanic quality of **letters.** Here is an excerpt from a letter that narrative therapist David Epston wrote to a client:

> I take it that telling me, a virtual stranger, your life story, which turned out to be a history of exploitations, frees you to some extent from it. To tell a story about your life turns it into a history, one that can be left behind, and makes it easier for you to create a future of your own design. [Also,] your story needs to be documented so it isn't lost to you and is in a form available to others whom you might choose to inspire. They will come to understand, as I have, how you were, over time, strengthened by your adverse circumstances. Everyone's attempts to weaken you by turning you into a slave, paradoxically strengthened your resolve to be your own person. This, of course, is not to imply that you haven't paid dearly for this and haven't suffered. You almost accepted your family's attitude towards you and this accounted for the doormat lifestyle that you lived for some time. (O'Hanlon, 1994, p. 20)

Such a letter from a significant person helps the client to cognitively restructure his or her life story. As indicated in the excerpt, clients who benefit from narrative therapy are encouraged to write letters, make tapes, and consult with other similar people, extending a helping hand themselves. Having an audience for the new story helps cement reorganization of identity, including a sense of social usefulness.

8. *Person-to-person relationships:*   While generally family counselors want the group to realize its complex interdependence, sometimes the best tactic is to strengthen communication and understanding between each pair of people within the system. Given the nature of subsystems and coalitions, in most families there are some pairs that are more cued in to each other than others: Two sisters might know more about each other than their brother; a mother and daughter might talk about topics where the father never treads. The external world also can restrict contact between people who live together daily. I recently saw a case in which the parents realized they knew hardly anything about their young children's unique personalities until they all participated in a six-week TV fast. Family counselors sometimes prescribe one-to-one communication between pairs, allowing no talking about others and no talk about impersonal issues, to improve the flow of information in the system as a whole. Pairs are encouraged to press for **congruent communication,** in which a person's body language and facial expression are in tune with her verbal content. Contrasts between verbal and nonverbal messages (incongruent communication) disable understanding between people, since they must constantly guess at the true message.

9. *Psychoeducation:*   When a family undergoes a major upheaval, such as one member's first psychotic episode, brief crisis-oriented treatment is desirable for the whole system. In such cases, education about stress management, problem-solving, and relapse prevention can be empathetically provided by a family counselor (Fadden, 1998). Families of patients in a head-injury rehabilitation unit, for instance, are grateful for counselors who can give them information about what to expect and the best courses of action when the patient comes home different from before. These families are understandably focused on the patient's survival and may not have considered the repercussions in terms of family dynamics.

Behavioral Exercises   Four categories of common behavioral interventions are described in the following sections.

1. *Paradoxical intention:*   With its roots in Adlerian psychology, like so many therapeutic notions, **paradoxical intention** is a staple of family therapy. The counselor may instruct a family member to repeat a symptom instead of resisting it. Madanes's Case Five demonstrates paradoxical intent. The child is requested to have a temper tantrum every day, and the mother is instructed to pretend to have one, too. Since both prove themselves able to control tantrum-like behavior, they can no longer claim that they are at its mercy. Similarly, adolescents often respond to the Winner's Bet, in which the therapist bets that they cannot keep misbehaving continuously over a sustained period. They find it impossible to be as bad as they think they are.

2. *Marking boundaries:* Upsetting the subsystems and coalitions in the family changes the flow of communication and therefore provokes change in the system. The goal is often a shift in power relations, which Haley (1972) viewed as central to family dynamics. In Madanes's Case Seven, the therapist created new subsystems in which children were paired to help each other, relieving the mother of great responsibility. When two family members are enmeshed in too much interdependence, a counselor may request that they disengage for a time—for example, refraining from private conversations for a week. A couple subsystem may be strengthened by an order to go away from the family for a weekend together, not to discuss the family during this time, and not to tell the family about the weekend when they return.

3. *Behavioral and cognitive-behavioral methods:* The techniques discussed in Chapters 8 and 9 can also be employed in treating families. Home token economies, for instance, may be instituted to modify children's behavior for the benefit of everyone. Principles of contingency management, reinforcement, and shaping assist the family disrupted by disorganized and unsynchronized activity; for example, all members might agree on a time of day when everyone is required to check in with the rest. And in counterconditioning, conflictual families are instructed to do things that produce competing affect, such as playing an amusing game for two hours. Many families use this technique spontaneously, such as when a bickering mother and daughter decide to do something they both enjoy together, like shopping or going on a bike trip. These behaviorist techniques are accompanied by cognitive changes, as the family discusses how they interpret their new experiences with the counselor.

4. *Directives and assignments:* In Madanes's Case Six, the brothers and sister were ordered to take turns at being the family's "life ruiner" for a week at a time, and when Tommy was not the sole life ruiner any more, old conflicts arose that had been masked by his role. Family therapists are famous for thinking up unusual directives and assignments to shake up the system. Some of their directives exaggerate the problem to absurdity in order to provoke reactions. For example, if a father and son are enmeshed in a subsystem that excludes the mother, they might be told that they *cannot* include her in any activity or conversation. She would be told that she should remove herself from any situations where they might experience closeness with her, and that she should seek emotional closeness with some other family member instead. Such a plan assumes that the men will *not* be satisfied with the arrangement, and perhaps that the mother can stop beating her heart against a wall trying to get the men to satisfy her need for closeness.

DeShazer (1988) and others claim to have achieved good results from the simple directive "Do something different." For example, a child's bedwetting was cured by rearranging his bedroom so that the view from the bed was completely different. If what you are doing is not effective, something different is certainly called for.

Uses for Family Therapy

Almost every difficulty that seems individual really affects the family as a whole, and the more you study family systems the more you believe family treatment is appropriate for everything. Bowen (1976) did family therapy with individuals at times, as paradoxical as that may sound. He believed that if one member of a family becomes better differentiated and de-triangulated, the entire system can change even if the other individuals never enter the office. Individual therapists include analyses of family systems in their work to various extents; for example, financial counselors inquire into family patterns of spending, saving, and discussing money. The family system is also of great consequence when you assess a client's cultural background.

You will see family therapy, including couples therapy, sought when something extreme has happened or is about to happen, usually involving the world outside the system. Families with children and adolescents threatened with expulsion from school, couples on the brink of divorce over in-law problems, systems wrenched out of shape by sudden unemployment or illness, blended families whose blend is oil and water, and parents who may lose custody of their children due to neglect, abuse, or divorce, are common customers. If these sound like the territory of social work, it's because the family systems tradition began with social workers' home visitations.

A death in the family brings the extended system together and also provides a stage for old, old conflicts. Paul (1986) suggests that family work with grief is preferable to individual work because individual relief "may actually deaden the relational possibilities for the client in his or her family" (p. 16). The emotions and conflicts surrounding grief are better not confined and excluded from the family. Similarly, the individual anorexic is rarely cured without family involvement; most theories about the etiology of anorexia are family-based. Minuchin (1970) claimed an 80 percent cure rate for anorexia using structural family therapy.

The modern American family life cycle frequently includes a gender crisis: A woman yearns to be more than a wife and mother at some point, throwing the complex dependencies and subtle (or not-so-subtle) role agreements out of kilter. Other women find themselves without a comfortable role when children grow up and leave home, and these children, in turn, are affected by the feeling that they abandoned their mothers. Offspring frequently do not live up to their culture's expectations, by being gay or lesbian, choosing to be child-free, or selecting careers unusual for their sex or class background. Some family therapists deal specifically with these problems, examining "gender-role concepts in order to liberate clients from artificial and unnecessary limitations" (Gale & Long, 1996, p. 11).

For adult individual disorders such as alcoholism, couples and family therapy helps when used as part of a multicomponent package. The home interpersonal environment that inadvertently enhances or maintains symptoms can be changed to a context that encourages healthy behavior and helps an individual cope (Baucom, Shoham, Mueser, Daiuto, Stickle, 1998). Edwards and Steinglass (1995) found that nonalcoholic spouses involved in treatment switched their focus from partners' drinking to making changes in the relationship and in their own lives. When spouses, families, and social networks were included in the process, treatment resulted in less drinking, higher employment, lower rates of institutionalization, and less marital separation (Edwards & Steinglass, 1995). Dropout rates were lower than the 50 to 70 percent rate for outpatient alcoholism treatment.

In cases involving schizophrenia, obsessive-compulsive disorder, and agoraphobia, family members improve the patient's chances by understanding their role as a source of stress and protection against stress. Family coping skills training improves the prognosis for schizophrenia and other disorders, with less relapse and rehospitalization. In the anxiety clinic where I worked, we recruited family members as surrogate therapists who assisted in providing exposure experiences for obsessive-compulsive, panicked, and socially anxious clients.

Laqueur (1976) described multiple family therapy, in which many families join to help each other. This practice has Adlerian predecessors, of course. In multiple family therapy, there are two clients: the family-in-focus and the audience. The audience and focus family benefit from identification with each other, modeling behavior, and acting as co-therapists with reactions and questions. In this process, the counselor is able to see the family in relationship with an outside system, which otherwise she knows about only through their report. Multiple family therapy also "allows the suprasystem, the outside world, society, to enter into the therapeutic relationship" (p. 409).

Many family theorists are concerned with much bigger systems than the blood-related family. Papero (1995) summarized Murray Bowen's views in this way: "The same processes operate in society that operate in the family. Anxiety, which Bowen believed to be fueled by increasing population and dwindling resources, moves through society in waves. Groups of people respond to increases in anxiety with greater difficulty in thinking and with more automatic responses. Fads and panics come to determine social behavior during periods of heightened anxiety, and the more thoughtful segments are hard-pressed to maintain their own beliefs and principles in the face of such pressure" (p. 18).

DISCUSSION IDEAS

What do you think of the application of systems theory to society? What social behavior have you observed during periods of heightened anxiety? Other than increasing population and dwindling resources, which were in the foreground in the 1950s, what conditions today create increases in anxiety in our society? Do you think family systems theory has any practical application to social problems?

Case Conceptualization: An Example

"THE DAUGHTER WHO SAID NO"

Peggy Papp (1983/1989)

Peggy Papp is a creative clinician who integrates several family therapy approaches in her work. Here are the opening stages of one family's treatment.

Step 1: Gathering Information

The information I obtained from the first session is here summarized since information gathering tends to make tedious reading. Rachel, 23, requested therapy for herself, and her sisters, Clare, 31, and Sandy, 26; her mother agreed to participate in therapy, but her father emphatically refused. Having been pushed into various kinds of therapy by his wife for the last five years, he told Rachel in no uncertain terms she would have to solve her problem herself.

I agreed to see the family without him, believing I could involve him later. Some therapists will not see the family unless everyone is present for the first session. Since my way of dealing with resistance is indirect rather than direct, my decisions are based on an evaluation of each case. In this situation it seemed important to go along with father's resistance since it was obviously a reaction to his wife's pressure. Also, the intensity of his feelings was a good indication he could be involved at a later date.

Only mother and Rachel appeared for the first interview as Sandy was in the hospital having her first baby, and Clare refused to come after a fight with Rachel.

Rachel appeared frail and flat-chested, but animated, with huge dark eyes and a thin face. She was exceptionally articulate, expressing herself in colorful language and sometimes adding a comic delivery. Her mother, a large, handsome, robust woman with short, white hair, stylishly cut, possessed the style and flair of a seasoned actress. With the exuberance of Lady Bountiful she embraced family therapy, saying she "believed" family members should help one another and she would do anything to help Rachel. She tempered each criticism of her with "there's really nothing wrong with you, you're a wonderful child but—."

Rachel had begun dieting four years ago during her second year at college. Since that time she had slowly but steadily lost weight until she finally weighed 89 pounds. She had not menstruated for a year and a half. During the last three years she had made several attempts to leave home but failed, each time feeling depressed, isolated, lonely, and coming back home. She now had an interim job as a secretary but was dissatisfied with it. Although living at home, she was talking about moving into an apartment of her own.

The primary concern of Rachel and her mother was not her weight loss or her diet, but the psychological implications, which they saw in terms of Rachel's intrapsychic problems. Rachel's previous individual therapy of one year had focused on the classical individual symptoms of anorexia—high expectations, overachievement, perfectionistic attitudes, obsessions, and control over the body—but had not connected these in any way with the family system.

The mother was interested in our helping Rachel with her high expectations of herself, describing her as being "obsessively and rigidly perfectionistic." She also stated Rachel had been a rebellious child all her life. "I have been worried about Rachel since she learned to say no. It has been no and no and no and no and no and no and no ever since then. She has not wanted to adopt any of our standards, and I question her judgment." She gave as an example of this Rachel's not wanting to join B'nai B'rith or date Jewish boys, and her tendency to pick a boy up off the street and make a date with him. Rachel accused her mother of match making. "I feel like it's mating season. I'm in heat and it's time to find a male for me quick before I'm not eligible any more. I don't enjoy that." Mother then mentioned drugs and Rachel admitted she had experimented in college with pot, speed, LSD, and mescaline and ended with, "I don't regret anything."

Mother had kept everything away from father over the years to protect Rachel and to avoid a conflict. When asked what he would have done had he known about these things, she stated, "I don't know. I wasn't going to give him a chance! The girls have accused me of being manipulative and maybe I am but I have to be." She spoke of the many disagreements between her and her husband, describing a long-standing conflict because of her closeness with her parents.

At the end of the session, after consultation with the team, I told Rachel and her mother we felt we did not have enough information at this point to make any suggestions and would like to delay our comments until we had met with other members of the family. Rachel agreed to try and get Clare to come to the next session but Sandy was still recuperating from the birth of her baby.

In the following session, Clare, a thin, attractive woman, fashionably dressed, was more than happy to give her impressions of Rachel and other family members. She described Rachel as being "very difficult" and her family as being one in which it was difficult to become independent, as her mother was controlling and "throws guilt around a lot." Both she and Rachel had rebelled against her mother's control, but Sandy "is the model daughter, model sister, model grandchild and, now having had a baby, will be the model mother. She never displeases anyone. She is the buffer, the peacemaker."

Both Rachel and Clare spoke of their being afraid of their father when they were growing up. He was very conservative and strict about dates, two-piece bathing suits, boy friends, hours, and so on. The mother, more lenient, took this opportunity to say that she was also afraid of his wrath and stated pathetically, "Thank God he never hit me." She compared him unfavorably with her own father and started to cry. "I tried very hard to get my family to help me, and my father would talk to my husband in a gentle manner and say how precious a wife is, how nothing really was as precious as a wife, and really she's the only one who is most important in life. But my husband would become antagonistic toward such conversations." She went into individual therapy at the recommendation of her doctor when she developed stomach trouble, and her doctor put pressure on her husband to go with her. Both blamed him for her physical problems.

Rachel and Clare defended their father and accused their mother of being overly close to her family and rubbing the father's nose in it. Rachel then spoke of her father and her as being the "underdogs in the family. We're ostracized by the rest of them." Rachel had given me the first clue as to how she fit into the power struggle between her parents: She identified with the father's underdog position. I now wanted to know the function of this identification: how it was used in the on-going day-to-day battle between the parents and how the sisters responded to it. The following dialogue was included to demonstrate how these questions were explored.

PEGGY [Peggy is the therapist]: So you feel you're the bad guy and your father is the bad guy in the family. In what way do you feel you can bring comfort to your father?

RACHEL: Because I can understand his viewpoint.

CLARE: If there are two bad guys, then you both share the burden?

RACHEL: There's company.

PEGGY: How do you go about giving him company?

RACHEL: We have a lot of common interests, we both like cars and nature and the Bronx Zoo, and we have a good time. We go across the country together.

PEGGY: What do you think his life would be like if you weren't around?

RACHEL: I don't know—I guess he'd survive.

PEGGY: Do you think he'd be lonely?

RACHEL: Maybe, sometimes—I'm nice company for him.

PEGGY: Then who would there be around to really understand him?

RACHEL: (*Long pause.*) I don't know.

PEGGY: You don't think your mother could understand him?

RACHEL: She will never ever. I shouldn't say that, but as far as I can see, it'll be a very tough thing for my mother to ever understand how my father feels about her family. She will never ever see how he feels about her.

MOTHER: But who do I think of when I want somebody to make nice to me? I go right back to the womb. On Tuesday I spent the day with my mom and dad and it was a good day. It was a hard day. I took them shopping. They're very old.

PEGGY: Do you feel they're the only ones who nurture you?

MOTHER: (*Nodding.*) Who really take care of me. I don't want anyone here to feel bad, but Sandy also takes care of me.

RACHEL: But you demand too much. You're very hard to give to when you demand.

PEGGY: Let's see, then. When you feel ganged up on by Rachel and your husband, you then go for nurturing to your parents. And who does your husband go to?

MOTHER: There's always been a young man in his life who treats him like God. Now it's Roy.

PEGGY: You're saying that he always finds someone who is like a son to him?

MOTHER: Yes, Roy is like a son.

PEGGY: Was he disappointed he didn't have a son?

MOTHER: (*Whispers.*) Very.

PEGGY: You whispered that "very." You don't want the girls to hear that?

MOTHER: (*Emphatically.*) Very displeased that he didn't have a son.

PEGGY: Do you think they don't know that?

RACHEL: I'm daddy's son.

PEGGY: In what way have you been his son?

RACHEL: Just—my interest in things which aren't typically feminine. I'm not scared of bugs, little things like that. Cars. Daddy asked me to cook hamburgers on the barbecue pit because I can handle it. (She *imitates* a boy.)

PEGGY: What's that like for you to be his son?

RACHEL: I kinda like it. (She *laughs* and acts like a boy again.) I don't mind, but I don't think he thinks of me as a boy.

PEGGY: Do you think of yourself as a boy?

RACHEL: No. I was saying that I felt so independent on this move. It always bugs me to depend on people.

PEGGY: What do you think it's going to be like for him, your moving out?

RACHEL: I think it's going to be all right for him. Already they're talking about switching homes with me.

PEGGY: Do you think he's going to miss you?

RACHEL: Maybe. He said he was going to miss some things but not others.

PEGGY: Well, do you think your mother's going to be able to take care of his loneliness?

RACHEL: Not unless she starts to look at him from a more objective point of view.

PEGGY: Do you think you can teach her?

RACHEL: I try, I really try. Then she accuses me of ganging up on her.

CLARE: (*Defending mother.*) Daddy's not nice all the time, either.

Step 2: Connecting the Symptom with the Family System

After this exchange, the therapist left the session to have a consultation with the group. We formed a hypothesis based on answering the following questions:

What function does the symptom serve in the system? We speculated that Rachel was starving herself in order to remain a son to her father and fill up the emptiness in his life that she perceived was left by her mother. By not eating, she kept herself looking like a boy, prevented herself from maturing into womanhood, and implicitly promised to remain the guardian of her parents' marriage. The symptom served to keep her at home where she could continue to serve as her father's ally in his battle with her mother and to give her mother a reason for remaining close to her family. By identifying with her father as the underdog in the family, she formed a coalition with him in the service of fighting against her mother's control. The symptom also served the function of freeing the other sisters to establish independent lives outside the family, since Rachel had accepted the responsibility of mediating the parents' marriage.

How does the family function to stabilize the symptom? When Mother and Father became involved in a power struggle that they could not resolve, Mother moved closer to her parents and compared Father unfavorably to her own father. Father retaliated by siding with Rachel against his wife, and Rachel joined him to get back at her mother. She became involved in masculine activities to please her father, knowing he felt alienated in a family of women. She cannot give up the symptom as long as she believes she is needed to be a son to him. The power struggle between mother and Rachel has taken many forms over the years, including Rachel's taking drugs, quitting jobs, leaving school, dating non-Jewish boys, and disassociating herself from the family's religious beliefs, as well as her present symptom of self-starvation.

What is the central theme around which the problem is organized? The central theme in this family seems to be control—who is going to control the beliefs and values of the others. This is a conventional family that places high value on conformity, respectability, achievement, duty, and family loyalty. Mother is less concerned about some of Rachel's other activities than she is about her not accepting the tenets of the Jewish faith. She complains that her husband rejects her father's value of a wife as being something "precious."

Since we have not yet seen father and Sandy, we are unable at this point to obtain a complete picture of the way each individual operates to maintain control around these central issues.

What will be the consequences of change? If Rachel stopped being a son to her father, she would have to abandon him to what she perceives to be an unloving wife, and she would also be robbed of her major weapon against mother. If she left home, mother and father would have to face their conflicts alone and would probably create a triangle involving Sandy or Clare. Mother might move even closer to her own parents and father closer to his surrogate son, Roy. This would widen the breach between the parents. If father agreed to come for therapy in order to try and resolve these issues, he would lose a major battle with his wife regarding the value of therapy.

Rachel would have to confront the outside world and its relationships rather than centering her life on the family. This would mean her taking responsibility for becoming an adult woman sexually, professionally, and socially.

What is the therapeutic dilemma? The family must decide between Rachel continuing to be symptomatic or facing the above consequences. (pp. 195–201) ■ ■

DISCUSSION IDEAS

1. What different definitions of the problem are there in this family? Is Rachel scapegoated, do you think? What other problems can you see in the family, outside of Rachel's?

2. Analyze the parents' relationship in terms of subsystem boundaries.

3. Are there instances of triangulation you can identify? What function does the third party in the triangle serve in each instance?

4. Is the grandparents' generation involved in the problem? How?

5. What is the nature of the alliance between Father and Rachel? How is the coalition related to the information in paragraph 1?

6. Are traditional gender roles involved in this family system? How?

7. In your small group, brainstorm some hypotheses about this family, some ideas about how to test the hypotheses, and a few ideas for interventions if your hypotheses seem correct upon testing. Give a five-minute presentation to the rest of the class, and compare and contrast your ideas with others'.

8. Read the rest of the story in the Papp case study. The References list for this chapter includes both the reprinted and original sources.

Critiques of Family Systems Counseling

The effectiveness of family therapy has been supported in several applications (Alexander, Holtzworth-Munroe, & Jameson, 1994; Baucom et al., 1998), and most of the theory is accepted as sound. Nevertheless, you should be aware of the criticisms that have been leveled at the practice of family systems therapy.

Intrusiveness

Minuchin (1992) tells a story of showing a videotape of his work to German professionals in the early 1970s. This videotape captures a session in which a family with an anorexic girl was directed to have lunch in the session so that Minuchin could experience the dynamics of eating in that family. In Germany, the audience recoiled and called Minuchin a Nazi: "A land whose psyche had been occupied by Nazism was supersensitive to the implications of power" (p. 7). The family, especially in European and U.S. culture, is a private entity, and some people see home visits and intense questioning as suspicious intrusions. This is especially true when the intervention is mandated or suggested by the legal system, as in child placement investigations or abuse evaluations.

Another example of intrusiveness occurs when therapy emphasizes second-order change in the family even though short-term advice and concrete help would be more appropriate. A family systems counselor may see an overhaul when only a tuneup is needed (Nichols & Schwartz, 2001). This broad view may engender the neglect of an individual family member while fiddling with the system as a whole. The individual in family therapy never gets the full-time attention and support that a private client does.

Sexism

Many counselors-in-training, upon viewing tapes of early family therapists, see the counselor as clearly siding with Dad. In attempts to establish clear lines of power and responsibility, theorists in the 1950s who saw gender roles as natural put the father at the head of the table, wearing the pants (Luepnitz, 1988). When a family system was out of balance, "Mothers often took the weight of the 'unbalancing,' while fathers were more gently handled. I heard mothers being cajoled to 'stay out,' 'back off,' 'clam up,' and even 'grow up,' while fathers were congratulated for their 'common sense'" (Luepnitz, 1988, p. 13). Today's family systems theorists are more flexible, realizing that there are many highly functioning families with power shared regardless of gender role. Along with assigning power to men, the old guard of psychopathology theory minimized the father's role in explaining children's problems and usually blamed the mother. One striking example is the early theory of the schizophrenogenic mother, which, though no longer considered valid, is still held by many (Fadden, 1998). This theory held that the mother's conflicting demands and emotional blackmail created schizophrenia in her child, but it made no such claim about the father's contribution to the problem.

Traditional Western male values have dominated some family systems thought. Examples include Bowen's elevation of autonomy, being-for-self, and intellectual focus (masculine virtues) versus seeking love and approval, being-for-others, and relatedness (feminine virtues that sound a lot like *fusion*). On the other hand, Virginia Satir during the same period insisted on the value of human interdependence and sensitivity, and gave credit to the emotional side of experience. Carl Whitaker, as well, took great joy in upsetting traditional domestic arrangements and values.

Training of Therapists

Many standard academic programs in psychology don't train therapists in skills necessary to work with families (Fadden, 1998). Yet, research shows that training and supervision are key: Studies have found that where clinicians didn't have specialized training, the outcome of family therapy was not good, but where they were trained and closely supervised, family treatment was especially successful. Treatment integrity (whether or not principles of family therapy were actually followed) and therapist competencies were correlated with outcome.

If academic psychologists do get training in family theory, the training is often post-graduation or outside their program. Many acclaimed family therapists have degrees in social work, medicine, or another helping field, supplemented by workshops, training, and supervised practice. If you wish for more training in family counseling, visit the website for the American Association for Marriage and Family Therapy (*http://www.aamft.org*), where you will find conferences, workshops, events, and training programs announced.

Long-Term Results

Whether the results of family therapy are maintained in the long run is still not clear. One study found a 30 percent relapse rate following behavioral therapy for couples after two years; another 38 percent of those couples divorced during a four-year follow-up period (Baucom et al., 1998). For alcohol problems, treatment gains seem to dissipate after one year (Edwards & Steinglass, 1995) for both family and individual treatment. However, few of the programs studied included intensive aftercare (maintenance and relapse prevention) plans, which probably would improve success rates at follow-up. Like most psychological interventions involving mostly talk, family therapy suffers from a lack of well-designed outcome research.

KEY TERMS

accommodate

boundaries

chronic anxiety

circular causality

circular questioning

closed systems

coalitions

cognitive restructuring

congruent communication

curiosity

differentiation

disengagement

emotional cutoff

emotional deadness

enmeshment

experiential

extended family	neutrality
externalization	nuclear family
Family Drawing Technique	paradoxical intention
family life cycle	parentification
family map	parts party
family of origin	permeable
family projection process	primary emotion
family sculpting	problem-determined system
first-order change	pseudo-selves
fusion	reflecting team
genogram	reframing
goals	reprocessing
homeostasis	rules
identified patient	scapegoat
impermeable	second-order change
intellectualization	social constructivist
joining	subsystems
letters	symptom functionality
Miracle Question	systemic
multigenerational transmission	systems
process	triangle
narrative	unique outcome questions

Exploring Key Terms

Individually, choose a group of five to seven key terms that are related. Write a two- or three-sentence passage using these terms in ways that clarify their definitions, preferably describing a family situation. If necessary, change the words' form to fit your context. Bring your passages to your small group for revision: Does each passage remind you clearly of what the terms mean? Is the use of each term completely accurate? Are the spelling and punctuation of each passage correct? After revision, distribute your group's passages to the whole class, on paper or electronically. Check off terms on the list above to see which ones are not covered in your collection of passages, and write definitions for those.

LIBRARY, MEDIA, AND INTERNET ACTIVITIES

1. Surf the website for the American Association of Marriage and Family Therapy at *http://www.aamft.org*. There you can find a Video Catalog that lists forty-two videotapes of live, unedited sessions by famous family therapists, called the Master Series. See whether your department or library owns any of these or will order them. Just reading the descriptions is educational. Also look at the Resources for Practitioners to see what is available to you as a counselor.

The APA divisions to look for are *37* (Child, Youth, and Family Services) and *43* (Division of Family Therapy). These are linked to *http://www.apa.org/divisions*. List four or five elements of these websites that you might find useful in your practice.

2. Here are the names of the major journals in family therapy:

American Journal of Family Therapy

The Family Journal: Counseling and Therapy for Couples and Families

Contemporary Family Therapy

Family Process

Family Therapy

Journal of Family Psychotherapy

Journal of Feminist Family Therapy

Journal of Marital and Family Therapy

Journal of Systemic Therapies

Psychotherapy Networker (formerly *Family Therapy Networker*), a magazine

Find the journals that are available to you in the library or on the Internet. Read two articles of interest to you and prepare a five-minute summary of one of them to present in class.

3. Virginia Satir Teaching Tapes are available from Golden Triad Films, Inc., 3312 Broadway, Kansas City, MO 64111. Again, talk with the school or department librarian about whether they can be borrowed or ordered.

4. Construct a genogram of your own family or another one you know well. You can find instructions at *http://www.genogram.freeservers.com* or by looking under the key word "genogram" on your search engine. Many books and articles on family systems also include instructions.

5. Deborah Anna Luepnitz's book *The Family Interpreted* provides a feminist critique of eight approaches to family therapy. Read a chapter and summarize the critique.

6. Following is a list by Hesley and Hesley (2001) of films that are useful in addressing family issues. Watch one of them (or choose one you know well) and write a brief synopsis, noting several of its main psychological lessons as well as what kind of clients might benefit from watching the film and discussing it. List additional movies you think would be useful to discuss with a family.

Parent-Child Relationships: *A Bronx Tale, The Great Santini, To Kill a Mockingbird, Life Is Beautiful, Ma Vie en Rose, Mask, The Miracle Worker, October Sky, Ordinary People, The Other Sister, Parenthood, Searching for Bobby Fischer*

Single Parents: *The Accidental Tourist, As Good as It Gets, Erin Brockovich, Kolya, Mrs. Doubtfire, Places in the Heart, Tender Mercies, To Kill a Mockingbird, Ulee's Gold*

Blended Families/Step-Parenting: *Fly Away Home, Stepmom, Tender Mercies, Unstrung Heroes*

Sibling Relationships: *Eating, Hannah and Her Sisters, Marvin's Room, The Myth of Fingerprints, Ordinary People, Soul Food, A Thousand Acres*

Family Conflict: *Before and After, The Brothers McMullen, Dancer, Texas—Pop. 81, Eating, Hannah and Her Sisters, Home for the Holidays, Like Water for Chocolate, Long Day's Journey into Night, Marvin's Room, Matilda, The Myth of Fingerprints, On Golden Pond, Ordinary People, Stuart Saves His Family, Terms of Endearment, A Thousand Acres, American Beauty*

Adoption and Custody: *The Good Mother, Losing Isaiah*

Letting Go: *Breaking Away, Dancer, Texas—Pop. 81, Father of the Bride, Little Women, A River Runs Through It*

REFERENCES

Adler, A. (1925/1968). *The practice and theory of individual psychology.* Totowa, NJ: Littlefield, Adams.

Alexander, J. F., Holtzworth-Munroe, A., & Jameson, P. (1994). The process and outcome of marital and family therapy: Research review and evaluation. In A. E. Bergin & S. L. Garfield (Eds.), *Handbook of psychotherapy and behavior change* (4th ed.) (pp. 595–630). New York: Wiley.

Anderson, H., Goolishian, H. A., & Windermand, L. (1986). Problem-determined systems: Towards transformation in family therapy. *Journal of Strategic and Systemic Therapies, 5,* 1–13.

Andersen, T. (1987). The reflecting team: Dialogue and meta-dialogue in clinical work. *Family Process, 26,* 415–428.

Banyard, V. L., & Fernald, P. S. (2002). Simulated family therapy: A classroom demonstration. *Teaching of Psychology, 29,* 223–226.

Bateson, G., Jackson, D. D., Haley, J., & Weakland, J. (1956). Toward a theory of schizophrenia. *Behavioral Science, 1,* 251–264.

Baucom, D. H., Shoham, V., Mueser, K. T., Daiuto, A. D., & Stickle, T. R. (1998). Empirically supported couple and family interventions for marital distress and adult mental health problems. *Journal of Consulting and Clinical Psychology, 66,* 53–88.

Beck, A. T., & Weishaar, M. E. (2000). Cognitive therapy. In R. J. Corsini & D. Wedding (Eds.), *Current psychotherapies* (6th ed., pp. 241–171). Itasca, IL: F. E. Peacock.

Bitter, J. R. (1988). Family mapping and family constellation: Satir in Adlerian context. *Individual Psychology, 44,* 106–111.

Bitter, J. R. (1991). Conscious motivations: An enhancement to Dreikurs' goals of children's misbehavior. *Individual Psychology, 47,* 210–221.

Bitter, J. R., Christensen, O. C., Hawes, C., & Nicoll, W. G. (1998). Adlerian brief therapy with individuals, couples, and families. *Directions in Clinical and Counseling Psychology, 8,* 95–112.

Bowen, M. (1966). The use of family theory in clinical practice. *Comprehensive Psychiatry, 7,* 345–374.

Bowen, M. (1976). Theory in the practice of psychotherapy. In P. J. Guerin (Ed.)., *Family therapy: Theory and practice* (pp. 42–90). New York: Gardner.

Bowen, M. (1978). *Family therapy in clinical practice.* Northvale, NJ: Aronson.

Cecchin, G. (1987). Hypothesizing, circularity, and neutrality revisited: An invitation to curiosity. *Family Process, 26,* 405–413.

Dattilio, F. M. (1994). Families in crisis. In F. M. Dattilio & A. Freeman (Eds.), *Cognitive-behavioral strategies in crisis intervention* (pp. 316–338). New York: Guilford.

DeShazer, S. (1991). *Clues: Investigating solutions in brief therapy.* New York: Norton.

Dreikurs, R. (1950). The immediate purpose of children's misbehavior, its recognition and correction. *Internationale Zeitschrift feur Individual Psychologic, 19,* 70–87.

Edwards, M. E., & Steinglass, P. (1995). Family therapy treatment outcomes for alcoholism. *Journal of Marital and Family Therapy, 21,* 475–509.

Fadden, G. (1998). Research update: Psychoeducational family interventions. *Journal of Family Therapy, 20,* 293–309.

Ferber, A., & Ranz, J. (1972). How to succeed in family therapy: Set reachable goals—give workable tasks. In C. J. Sager & H. S. Kaplan (Eds.), *Progress in group and family therapy* (pp. 346–375). New York: Brunner/Mazel.

Framo, J. L. (1972). Symptoms from a family transactional viewpoint. In C. J. Sager & H. S. Kaplan (Eds.), *Progress in group and family therapy* (pp. 271–308). New York: Brunner/Mazel.

Fuligni, A. J. (2002). Family obligations and acculturative stress in Chinese American adolescents. *Child Development, 73,* 302–314.

Gale, J. E., & Long, J. K. (1996). Theoretical foundations of family therapy. In F. P. Piercy, D. H. Sprenkle, J. L. Wetchler, et al. (Eds.), *Family therapy sourcebook* (2nd ed., pp. 1–24). New York: Guilford.

Goldenberg, I., & Goldenberg, H. (2000). Family therapy. In R. J. Corsini and D. Wedding (Eds.), *Current psychotherapies* (6th ed., pp. 375–406). Itasca, IL: Peacock Publishers.

Greenberg, L. S., & Johnson, S. M. (1986). Affect in marital therapy. *Journal of Marital and Family Therapy, 12,* 1–10.

Greenberg, L. S., & Safran, J. D. (1989). Emotion in psychotherapy. *American Psychologist, 44,* 19–29.

Gurman, A. S., & Kniskern, D. P. (1992). The future of marital and family therapy. *Psychotherapy, 29,* 65–71.

Haley, J. (1972). Family therapy. In C. J. Sager & H. S. Kaplan (Eds.), *Progress in group and family therapy* (pp. 261–270). New York: Brunner/Mazel.

Haley, J. (1987). *Problem solving therapy.* San Francisco: Jossey-Bass.

Hesley, J. W., & Hesley, J. G. (2001). *Rent two films and let's talk in the morning: Using popular movies in psychotherapy* (2nd ed.). New York: Wiley.

Johnson, S. (1986). Bonds or bargains: Relationship paradigms and their significance for marital therapy. *Journal of Marital and Family Therapy, 12,* 259–267.

Johnson, S. M., & Greenberg, L. S. (1985). Emotionally focused couples therapy: An outcome study. *Journal of Marital and Family Therapy, 11,* 313–317.

Johnson, S. M., & Greenberg, L. S. (1987). Integration in marital therapy: Issues and progress. *Journal of Integrative and Eclectic psychotherapy, 6,* 205–215.

Lago, C., & Thompson, J. (1996). *Race, culture, and counselling.* Buckingham, England: Open University Press.

Laqueur, H. P. (1976). Multiple family therapy. In P. J. Guerin (Ed.)., *Family therapy: Theory and practice* (pp. 405–416). New York: Gardner.

Luepnitz, D. A. (1988). *The family interpreted: Feminist theory in clinical practice.* New York: Basic Books, 1988.

Madanes, C. (1992). Stories of psychotherapy. In J. K. Zeig (Ed.), *The evolution of psychotherapy: The second conference* (pp. 39–50). New York: Brunner/Mazel.

McGoldrick, M., Gerson, R., & Shellenberger, S. (1999). *Genograms: Assessment and intervention* (2nd ed.). New York: Norton.

McGoldrick, M., & Giordano, J. (1996). Overview: Ethnicity and family therapy. In M. McGoldrick, J. K. Pearce, & J. Giordano (Eds.), *Ethnicity and family therapy* (pp. 1–27). New York: Guilford.

Minuchin, S. (1974). *Families and family therapy*. Cambridge, MA: Harvard University Press.

Minuchin, S. (1992). The restoried history of family therapy. In J. K. Zeig (Ed.), *The evolution of psychotherapy: The second conference* (pp. 3–10). New York: Brunner/Mazel.

Nichols, M. P., & Schwartz, R. C. (2001). *Family therapy: Concepts and methods* (5th ed.). Boston: Allyn & Bacon.

O'Hanlon, B. (1994). The third wave: The promise of narrative. *Psychotherapy Networker, 18,* 18–29.

Oster, G. D., & Gould, P. (1987). *Using drawings in assessment and therapy*. New York: Brunner/Mazel.

Papero, D. V. (1995). Bowen family systems and marriage. In A. S. Gurman & N. S. Jacobson (Eds.), *Clinical handbook of couple therapy* (pp. 11–30). New York: Guilford.

Papp, P. (1989). The daughter who said no. In D. Wedding & R. J. Corsini (Eds.), *Case studies in psychotherapy* (pp. 195–224). Itasca, IL: F. E. Peacock. (Reprinted from P. Papp, *The process of change*, pp. 67–120, New York: Guilford, 1983.)

Paul, N. (1986). The paradoxical nature of the grief experience. *Contemporary Family Therapy, 8,* 5–19.

Reiss, D. (1981). *The family's construction of reality*. Cambridge, MA: Harvard University Press.

Sanders, G. L., & Kroll, I. T. (2000). Generating stories of resilience: Helping gay and lesbian youth and their families. *Journal of Marital and Family Therapy, 26,* 433–442.

Sayger, T. V., & Horne, A. M. (2000). Common elements in family therapy theory and strategies. In A. M. Horne (Ed.), *Family counseling and therapy* (pp. 41–61). Itasca, IL: Peacock Publishers.

Scharff, D. E., & Scharff, J. S. (1987). *Object relations family therapy*. Northvale, NJ: Jason Aronson.

Shadish, W. R., Ragsdale, K., Glaser, R. R., & Montgomery, L. M. (1995). The efficacy and effectiveness of marital and family therapy: A perspective from meta-analysis. *Journal of Marital and Family Therapy, 21,* 345–360.

Shapiro, A. F., Gottman, J. M., & Carrere, S. (2000). The baby and the marriage: Identifying factors that buffer against decline in marital satisfaction after the first baby arrives. *Journal of Family Psychology, 14,* 59–70.

Watzlawick, P., Weakland, J. H., & Fisch, R. (1974). *Change: Principles of problem formation and problem resolution*. New York: W. W. Norton.

White, M., & Epston, D. (1990). *Narrative means to therapeutic ends*. New York: Norton.

CHAPTER 11

Systemic Approaches: Culture and Gender Bases

A Selection from

The Mismeasure of Woman, 1992

Carol Tavris

The power to name and diagnose—as Thomas Hobbes said, the power to make definitions—is the ultimate authority. Labels and diagnoses, as we've seen in the case of "PMS," have tremendous capacity both to liberate and to oppress. They reassure the worried that their problems are identifiable and probably treatable; but they create worries in people who didn't think they had a problem, let alone one that needed treatment. Most of all, the definitions that people choose to explain their personalities and their lives lead to different courses of action. A woman who thinks she has a chronic disease may be persuaded to enlist in unending group therapy; a woman who thinks she has a personality disorder may begin a lengthy course of analytic treatment; a woman who thinks she needs a better job may be persuaded to enroll in school. People must be careful about the labels they choose to apply to their problems, because definitions have consequences.

Self-defeating Personality Disorder and codependency are the latest incarnations of an old American game that we might call "Name What's Wrong With Women." Every few years a wave of best-selling books sweeps over the land, purporting to explain to women the origins of their unhappiness. In many of the self-help versions of these books, the author begins by describing how she herself suffered from the disorder in question, and, through persistence, effort, or revelation, found the cure.

Thus, in the 1950s, women's problem was said to be their inherent masochism, an idea that derived from Freud's theory that female psychology includes an unconscious need for, and pleasure in, suffering. Wrong, said Martina Horner in the late 1960s. The problem is women's fear of success; the cure is to understand and then overcome their internal barriers to achievement. Wrong, said Marabel Morgan, Phyllis Schlafly, and other religious conservatives in the 1970s. The problem is that women *want* success, when they should be spending their energies being obedient to God and husband; the cure is to strive to become "The Total Woman," "The Fulfilled Woman," or "The Positive Woman." Wrong, said Colette Dowling in 1981. The problem is that women have a "Cinderella Complex—a hidden fear of independence"; they must struggle against their desires to be rescued by Prince Charming. Wrong, said a spate of writers in the early 1980s. The problem is that women "say yes when they mean no," and "when they say no, they feel guilty"; the cure is assertiveness training. Wrong, said Robin Norwood in 1985. The problem is that women love too much. Wrong, said a flurry of books in rebuttal. It's not that women love too much but that they love the wrong men—men who are immature, angry, abusive, chauvinistic, and cold. Wrong, said Melody Beattie in 1987; the poor guys aren't to blame, because they are sick. Women love too much because they are codependent—addicted to addicts, addicted to bad relationships.

Long ago in *The Feminine Mystique,* Betty Friedan wrote of "the problem that has no name"—the vague emptiness and desolation that plagued many women in the postwar era. But in fact the problem has gone by far too many names. The symptoms that all of these books attempt to treat are invariably the same: low self-esteem, passivity, depression, dependency on others, an exaggerated sense of responsibility to other people, a belief that it is important to be good and to please others, and an apparent inability to break out of bad relationships. I do not doubt that many women are unhappy, and I do not doubt that these descriptions apply to many women—and to a goodly number of men. But it is time to ask why these psychological diagnoses of women's alleged inner flaws, which keep returning like swallows to Capistrano, year after year, fail to deliver on their promises. And it is time to ask why the explanations we make of female problems differ in kind and function from those we make of male problems.

Thus, the problems that are more characteristic of men than women—such as drug abuse, narcissism, rape, and other forms of violence—are rarely related to an inherent male psychology the way women's behavior is. When men have problems, it's because of their upbringing, personality, or environment; when women have problems, it's because of something in their very psyche. When men have problems, society tends to look outward for explanations; when women have problems, society looks inward.

For example, psychologist Silvia Canetto has compared attitudes toward people who attempt suicide (typically women) with those toward people who abuse drugs (typically men). Both of these actions, says Canetto, are "gambles with death"; both actions can be lethal although the individual may not intend them to be. Suicide attempters and drug abusers share feelings of depression and hopelessness. Yet mental-health experts tend to regard suicide attempts as a sign of a woman's psychological inadequacy, reports Canetto, whereas they regard drug abuse as "caused by circumstances beyond the person's control, such as a biological predisposition."

Likewise, people speculate endlessly about the inner motives that keep battered wives from leaving their husbands. Are these women masochistic? Do they believe they deserve abuse? Are they codependent, unwittingly collaborating in the abuse against them? Whatever the answer, the problem is construed as the battered wives, not the battering husbands. But when experts ponder the reasons that some husbands abuse their wives, they rarely ask comparable questions: Are these men sadistic? Do they believe they deserve to abuse others? Rather, their explanations focus on the pressures the men are under, their own abuse as children, or the wife's provocations. Male violence is not considered a problem that is inherent in male psychology; but the female recipients of male violence are responsible because they "provoked" it or "tolerated" it or "enabled it" or are "masochistic"—problems presumed to be inherent in female psychology. A man who gets into a fight with a stranger and hits him may spur an observer to ask: "Why is this guy so aggressive and hostile?" But if the same man goes home and hits his wife, the same observer is likely to wonder: "Why does she stay with him?" Of course, almost everyone knows people who are, often or on occasion, self-defeating, sadistic, dependent, martyrish, or who otherwise behave in annoying and exasperating ways. And I do not deny that therapy can be helpful for such individuals. But the question is: Do they have *problems,* or are they sick? Further, as the examples of Self-defeating Personality Disorder and codependency illustrate, many of the problems associated with women today can be considered signs of mental illness only in comparison to a male standard of what is healthy and normal. (pp. 173–176)   ■ ■

DISCUSSION IDEAS

1. Tavris's discussion of premenstrual syndrome (PMS) occurs elsewhere in the book *The Mismeasure of Woman.* From what you know of PMS, how does it have the "capacity both to liberate and to oppress"? What do jokes about PMS suggest about women and mental health?

2. What labels have been (or could be) applied to you? (For example, are you an egghead, a workaholic, a sorority gal, a weirdo?) What consequences could these labels have?

3. As Tavris lists in paragraph 3, several explanations have been offered for women's problems. Have you heard of any of these theories or books, and if so, what do you recall about them? What do the explanations have in common?

4. What difference does it make whether you look inward or outward for explanations of problems?

5. Reread the example developed in the last paragraph about batterers and abused wives. Is Tavris's point of view consistent with your experience?

6. The DSM-IV-TR reports that, among personality disorders, antisocial, paranoid, schizoid, schizotypal, narcissistic, and obsessive-compulsive personality disorders are more commonly diagnosed in men, while borderline, histrionic, and dependent disorders are more commonly diagnosed in women. Major depressive episodes, major depressive disorder, dysthymic disorder, panic disorder, agoraphobia, phobias, and social phobia are also more commonly diagnosed in women than in men. As far as you can tell, what would Tavris say about this pattern? If you know DSM diagnosis, what do *you* think about this pattern?

Introduction to Culture- and Gender-Based Approaches

As children, my brother and I planned a wonderful future together as garbagemen and often acted out our fantasy in play, trading off who got to drive the truck and who got to stand on the back and whistle. I knew all along that for our fantasy to come true, I had to grow up to be a man, and I suspected this might be a sticking point. Years later, I was surprised when my friend Laurie mentioned going through the same thought process when she and her two brothers would play an adventure-heroes fantasy: The first thing she had to do in this game was to turn into a boy.

We never played a game in which our brothers needed fantasy sex changes.

Who could say that two people are psychologically the same when one child believed that she had to be fundamentally altered in order to drive a truck or be a hero, and the other could go into the pursuit just as he was? And furthermore, he imagined no worthwhile pursuit that required such a fundamental alteration of *him*.

Look again at the content of our childhood games, and you can see the strong influence of our little worlds, our cultures. Both Laurie's family and mine were crawling up toward middle-class. Laurie's brothers took their roles from comic books of the time, and my brother and I took ours from what we saw on our city street. Laurie lived in the country and probably never witnessed the joyful life of garbage collection, and we were not allowed adventure comics in our home. It was only through other kids' fantasies that those stories leaked into our play life. All of our ideas about ourselves and what was fun, important, and possible came filtered through the accidents of birth.

The power of these accidents of birth—what race, gender, class, culture, and subculture a person belongs to—has been newly acknowledged in modern psychotherapy theory in the past forty years or so. The freedoms and constraints of our life situations determine so much of our psychological make-up that many mental health professionals focus on these conditions in helping others understand themselves, their strengths, and their dilemmas.

R e f l e c t i o n

Think about your favorite fantasies as a child. How were they related to your accidents of birth—your race, gender, class, culture, and subculture? Can you think of a friend who had childhood fantasies different from your own, with differences you can trace back to accidents of birth?

Why Do Group Differences Matter?

"It's a small world," we say, and "People are the same all over." The Golden Rule prescribes that we treat others as we would like to be treated. Sayings like these reflect the commonality among human beings, a commonality that is huge. Our most basic needs, such as sustenance, safety, belonging, communication, meaning, and power, are probably shared. Personality across the globe is mixed from the same fundamental ingredients: extroversion, openness to experience, agreeableness, conscientiousness, and neuroticism, and their opposites (McCrae & Costa, 1997; Paunonen, Jackson, Trzebinski, & Forsterling, 1992). We all look at the world of human activity as divided up into the same categories: social, enterprising, artistic, systematic, realistic (hands-on), and intellectual (Day & Rounds, 1998). And we all face a common fate, death.

On the other hand, how we express these common needs, personality traits, and perceptions, how we put them in order of priority in our lives, and how free we are to follow whatever inner compass our genes provide us are all matters depending on context. Many people believe that in Western cultures like ours, individual independence is glorified and rewarded, while in Asian cultures like the Japanese, belongingness and conventionality are glorified and rewarded. Then, even within Western culture, there is evidence that men seek independence more actively and women seek belongingness more actively (for example, Gilligan, 1982). So while rugged independence is considered a virtue by culture as a whole, women have a subculture that doesn't court the virtue very enthusiastically. Other subcultures in the Western world also elevate belongingness over independence, even while making their way in a mainstream that treasures independence more highly. Just the variability in our values of independence and belongingness shows that each person exists in a web of demands, some of which are common human demands, some of which are dictated by the mainstream culture where they live, some of which are determined by the subcultures to which they belong, and some of which may spring from unique personal attributes. (However, keep in mind that people don't announce that they want to be a utility-rate-structure analyst, a lap-dancer, or a Buddhist monk if they have never heard of such a thing, no matter how well their genetic and personality make-up suits the job.)

Do Differences Imply Different Pictures of Psychological Health and Illness?

Existentialists like Irvin Yalom (Chapter 6) view all of us as struggling with matters of meaninglessness, mortality, responsibility, and freedom. I agree with this conceptualization, so the question is, Are individual and group distinctions merely colorful overlays on these basic struggles, or do they really make a difference in psychological terms?

I think that they do make a difference to us as mental health professionals.

A core group of mental health disorders are diagnosed worldwide (Comas-Diaz, 1996): schizophrenia, bipolar disorder (that is, depression with at least one manic episode), major depression, and the anxiety disorders involving phobias, panic, and obsessive-compulsive disorder. Exactly how these disorders are acted out, how they develop over time, how they are treated, and whether they improve, are matters heavily influenced by culture (including the cultures of gender and class). For example:

- Among depressed children, boys are more likely to openly misbehave (**externalize**) while girls are more likely to withdraw (**internalize**). The same difference seems to occur in depressed adult men and women (Cochran & Rabinowitz, 2003).

- In Asian cultures, anxiety often takes the form of bodily aches and pains (Tanaka-Matsumi & Higginbotham, 1996), whereas an anxious European might experience constant worry instead.

- Low-income clients are more likely to receive brief, drug-centered therapy than their middle- or upper-class counterparts (Lott, 2002), who are more likely to receive longer, insight-oriented therapy from higher-status professionals.

- While academically conducive behaviors and attitudes tend to be the same for White and Black lower-class, high-achieving students, these behaviors and attitudes are associated with introjective depression in Black but not White adolescents (Arroyo & Zigler, 1995).

- Many studies show consistently low use of mental health services by African Americans, Asian Americans, and Hispanics, although these groups report levels of psychological distress similar to those of others in this country (Lee & Ramirez, 2000).

As counselors, we benefit from being aware of the variety of cultural tugs that operate on each client. Consider two similar clients who complain of feeling helpless and dependent: The male client has not only this feeling but a layer of shame about it since it is unmasculine, while the female client's shame is faint or nonexistent on this issue. A third similar person might be a female from a culture that endorses women's helplessness and dependence as desirable, and she might not become a client at all, despite having the same feelings.

Sex is the most meaningful information we have about ourselves and others. It's what Bem (1981) called a "cognitively available schema," something basic to our identities, the first question we ask about a newborn baby, always on our list of self-descriptors. (Among adult Americans, our work is also always on this list.) Fagot and Leinbach (1989) discerned that "society suffuses the gender distinction with affect, making gender what is perhaps the most salient parameter of social categorization" (p. 663). When psychology researcher Diane Halpern (1985) tried to write scenes *not* associated with femaleness or maleness (so that she could manipulate the sex of the characters experimentally), she found the task unexpectedly taxing. "The difficulty in selecting plausible activities that are devoid of sex-role assumptions demonstrated the pervasiveness of these assumptions" (p. 366). People in Internet chat who refuse to identify their sex are met with widespread irritation, and people who misidentify their sex on the Web are met with fury.

Gender is soaked with meaning, both cognitive and emotional. Thus, the client's experience of being a woman or a man is relevant to every therapist's case conceptualization. Though many writers use the words *sex* and *gender* interchangeably, strictly speaking, *sex* is the biological category (male or female), while *gender* is the socially created image belonging to one of those categories. So, for example, we have women who don't strike us as particularly feminine and men who do, and women who fit the image of masculinity better than some men do. Gender is masculinity and femininity, and the inner experience of those qualities.

Cultural background is an essential part of identity and behavior. People who belong to mainstream, privileged groups are less likely to be aware of this than others. I thought I knew the ropes of looking for an apartment in my college town—until I looked for an apartment with a Black male roommate. Only then did a whole other dimension of the enterprise appear, revealing an ugly side of my community. Differences that are easily seen or heard, such as a person's skin color, accent, nonstandard English, advanced age, disability, or funny clothes, make people respond distinctively and often prejudicially in everyday life. How we see ourselves mirrored every day has a large psychological effect, so others' knee-jerk responses to us as stupid, incompetent, insentient, invisible, or inferior affect how we view ourselves, including the ways we protect and repair ourselves from such responses.

Many of the counselor's tasks involve concepts of "what is normal, socially acceptable, and valued, and of what facilitates the individual's integration into roles considered personally and socially meaningful" (Dumas, Rollock, Prinz, Hops, & Blechman, 1999). Our own and our clients' gender and cultural background affect these concepts intimately. However, there are common features that define a core of healthy functioning, regardless of one's background or current setting (Day & Rottinghaus, 2003):

- accurate understanding of social expectations;
- reasonable assessments of our own interests, capabilities, and limitations;
- good control over our own behavior;
- cognitive and behavioral flexibility;
- energy; and
- hope for the future.

Inconsistencies in Clinical Judgment

One reason that gender and culture matter is that they can influence mental health diagnosis and treatment (Comas-Diaz, 1996) in several complex ways. For example, White boys are more likely to inappropriately receive learning disability diagnoses than other boys and girls are, middle-class clients are more likely to be considered neurotic than those of a lower social class, and Black lower-class clients are more likely to be classified as alcoholics than middle- or upper-class Blacks or any Whites (Lopez, 1989). Lopez reviewed research on biases according to sex, race, social class, age, mental retardation, and ethnicity. He looked at biases that exhibited themselves in **overpathologizing** (perceiving greater disturbance in one group than in another), **minimizing** (judging symptoms as normal in some groups and not in others), **overdiagnosis** (finding one diagnosis appropriate as a function of the client's group membership), and **underdiagnosis** (judging a disorder less likely to occur in particular groups). The most consistent evidence of bias was for the mentally retarded, whose symptoms were underdiagnosed or minimized. The second most consistently biased judgments were made on the basis of social class, with the lower social class overpathologized. There was also a consistent bias in judgments of Black and White patients. Evidence for consistent bias according to gender was not found. This finding means that clinicians were not driven by prejudice across the board when treating women or men. However, there are specific symptoms and disorders that seem to invite gender bias; for example, women with problems of social withdrawal, depression, emotionality, and unassertiveness were judged as less disturbed than men with the same symptoms.

While bias is usually taken to mean that two groups are being evaluated differently, Lopez (1989) pointed out another type of bias—one that occurs when groups are treated the same despite the presence of differences that the mental health professional should take into account. Specifically, clinicians may neglect to consider cultural differences, developmental norms for children and the elderly, gender differences, sexual orientation differences, and differences due to conditions like mental retardation and hearing impairment.

Essential Concepts: Psychological Effects of Culture and Gender

We stumble into this world already branded by states that affect our psychological development.

Role Expectations and Stereotyping

We expect ourselves and others to conform to inner images we've developed from family teaching and example, media presentations of different types of people, personal experience, religious teachings, and institutional customs. These images are **stereotypes**. Stereotypes of femininity include, on the positive side, kindness, softness, interpersonal skill, politeness, attention to detail, sensitivity to beauty, nurturance, and orderliness; and, on the negative side, neuroticism, hysteria, weakness, slyness, manipulativeness, dependency, bitchiness, and lack of reason.

Stereotypes of masculinity also include both positive and negative qualities. Brannon and David (1976) summarize four main images that guide perceptions of men:

- No sissy stuff: The stigma of all stereotyped feminine characteristics and qualities, including openness and vulnerability,
- The big wheel: Success, status, and the need to be looked up to,
- The sturdy oak: A manly air of toughness, confidence, and self-reliance,
- Give 'em hell: The aura of aggression, violence, and daring. (p. 12)

Obviously, living up to the positive expectations, and living with the negative ones, is quite a chore for both sexes—one that takes its toll psychologically. Women are more likely than men to attempt suicide, experience depression and anxiety, lose their sex drive, feel chronically fatigued (Silverstein, 2002), and have unexplained aches and pains. Men misbehave more in grade school, have more learning disabilities, get suspended from school twice as often, are nine times more likely to be hyperactive, are less likely to attend college and graduate school, are four times more likely to be victims of homicide, and are five times more likely to kill themselves (Pollack & Levant, 1998).

Prejudgments about individuals from any group can fall far from the mark, partly because each of us is a member of several different groups. Scott Russell Sanders (1987), in his essay, "The Men We Carry in Our Minds," ponders how class, race, and sex are confounded:

> I was slow to understand the deep grievances of women. This was because, as a boy, I had envied them. Before college, the only people I had known who were interested in art or music or literature, the only ones who read books, the only ones who ever seemed to enjoy a sense of ease and grace were the mothers and daughters. Like the menfolk, they fretted about money, they scrimped and made-do. But when the pay stopped coming in, they were not the ones who had failed. Nor did they have to go to war, and that seemed to me a blessed fact. By comparison with the narrow, ironclad days of fathers, there was an expansiveness, I thought, in the days of mothers. They went to see neighbors, to shop in town, to run errands at school, at the library, at church. No doubt, had I looked harder at their lives, I would have envied them less. It was not my fate to become a woman, so it was easier for me to see the graces. Few of them held jobs outside the home, and those who did filled thankless roles as clerks and waitresses. I didn't see, then, what a prison a house could be, since houses seemed to me brighter, handsomer places than any factory. I did not realize—because such things were never spoken of— how often women suffered from men's bullying. I did learn about the wretchedness of abandoned wives, single mothers, widows; but I also learned about the wretchedness of lone men. Even then I could see how exhausting it was for a mother to cater all day to the needs of young children. But if I had been asked, as a boy, to choose between tending a baby and tending a machine, I think I would have chosen the baby. (Having now tended both, I know I would choose the baby.)
>
> So I was baffled when the women at college accused me and my sex of having cornered the world's pleasures. I think something like my bafflement has been

felt by other boys (and by girls as well) who grew up in dirt-poor farm country, in mining country, in black ghettos, in Hispanic barrios, in the shadows of factories, in Third World nations—any place where the fate of men is as grim and bleak as the fate of women. Toilers and warriors. I realize now how ancient these identities are, how deep the tug they exert on men, the undertow of a thousand generations. The miseries I saw, as a boy, in the lives of nearly all men I continue to see in the lives of many—the body-breaking toil, the tedium, the call to be tough, the humiliating powerlessness, the battle for a living and for territory.

When the women I met at college thought about the joys and privileges of men, they did not carry in their minds the sort of men I had known in my childhood. They thought of their fathers, who were bankers, physicians, architects, stockbrokers, the big wheels of the big cities. These fathers rode the train to work or drove cars that cost more than any of my childhood houses. They were attended from morning to night by female helpers, wives and nurses and secretaries. They were never laid off, never short of cash at the month's end, never lined up for welfare. The fathers made decisions that mattered. They ran the world.

The daughters of such men wanted to share in this power, this glory. So did I. They yearned for a say over their future, for jobs worthy of their abilities, for the right to live at peace, unmolested, whole. Yes, I thought, yes yes. The difference between me and these daughters was that they saw me, because of my sex, as destined from birth to become like their fathers, and therefore as an enemy to their desires. But I knew better. I wasn't an enemy, in fact or in feeling. I was an ally. If I had known, then, how to tell them so, would they have believed me? Would they now? (pp. 111–117)

DISCUSSION IDEAS

1. What was Sanders's life before college like? What evidence do you have for your speculation?

2. What did Sanders *not* see about the lives of women? What did he see about the lives of men?

3. What was the difference between the college women and the women Sanders knew growing up? Why did the college women see Sanders as the enemy?

4. What do you think are the answers to the two questions Sanders asks at the end of this passage?

"Human beings love to divide the world and its inhabitants into pairs of opposites," wrote Carol Tavris (1992, p. 90). We often have **mirror-image stereotypes:** opposite notions of two groups simultaneously (if men are warlike, women must be peaceful). Ideas of men and women as opposites are present in ancient Eastern and Western philosophy, in psychodynamic and Jungian theory, in theories that label men **instrumental** and women **expressive,** and in feminist versions of men's **rationality** as opposed to women's **relationality.** Wherever there is a visible difference, this tendency toward thinking in opposites appears. However, thinking like this makes differences seem permanent and stable, which limits the amount of potential improvement there can be in relationships and social policies. The mirror-image stereotype also suggests that there is a nice symmetry going on, obscuring real-life inequalities between the opposites. (When an exam score is questionable, who is going to argue for and receive a higher grade, an active person or a passive one? So, are the two qualities complementary and equal?)

R e f l e c t i o n

Have you noticed any other examples of mirror-image stereotyping? For example, is a group you belong to often described in contrast to some other group? Think about the way people talk about Republicans and Democrats, Greeks and independents, rich and poor. Do the mirror-image stereotypes distort reality in harmless or dangerous ways?

The language we use makes opposites where perhaps there are other kinds of difference as well. For example, the stereotype holds that men are independent and women dependent. If we reach outside the stereotype, though, we can see that many men completely depend on women to do their housework, shopping, social planning, wardrobe management, scheduling, health monitoring, spelling, and punctuation, as well as their business with God; many women single-handedly maintain complex households, social networks, educational plans, patterns of consumption, and several men. The words *independent* and *dependent* fail to describe the real situation.

Many researchers have devoted themselves to untangling essential male-female differences from stereotypes. They "dispute that male-female differences are as universal, as dramatic, or as enduring as has been asserted" (Hare-Mustin & Maracek, 1988, p. 456), and found the sources of difference in society and culture rather than in biology. Though popular culture focuses on sex differences in emotion (consider, for example, Gray's [1992] *Men Are from Mars, Women Are from Venus* approach), scientific research fails to find an innate difference in the ways men and women process, understand, express, and feel emotion (Wester, Vogel, Pressly, & Heesacker, 2002). Differences in emotion are observed only when individuals are responding to pressure to present themselves normatively (that is, when the situation seems to demand masculine or feminine responses). Counselors must not confuse these situational pressures with biological sex: "If a culture arranges the experiences of its children and adults so that gender will be associated with differential expectations, opportunities, and consequences, it is those arrangements that we must study to understand their outcomes for behavior" (Lott, 1996, p. 155).

If we explain differences among groups as results of infant-mother dynamics and cultural background, we downplay economic conditions, social role conditioning, and historical change—that is, we seek to explain differences instead of to explain domination (Hare-Mustin & Maracek, 1988). And domination of power and resources may account for obvious differences among groups most efficiently.

Role Strain and Conflict

Most of us play more than one role and are happy for the variety; however, there are psychological stresses involved in the juggling act. One of them, **role strain,** comes from hanging onto too many roles and finding their demands taxing. The professional woman who also wants to be a perfect homemaker and mother watches each day disappear in a stream of routine duties, many of them taken for granted. Feelings of inadequacy, resentment, and loss of her old self emerge. Many children and teenagers these days feel overextended by pressure to excel in academic and extracurricular areas, to the point where some attend a lesson, practice, or rehearsal every evening of the week, never getting a chance to lie down on the grass and look up through the flowering dogwood tree.

In **role conflict,** the demands of the roles we play are not in harmony. For example, ambitious people must work overtime on their way to fulfilling professional, financial, or artistic goals, while their roles in the family demand that they be home regularly and frequently, and pay some degree of attention while there (especially if they are women). People who are immersed in their vocations may feel guilty for neglecting other people in their lives and for ignoring their own needs outside of work. They may also escape the complex demands of interpersonal intimacies through involvement with work and the more well-defined social relationships there.

Modern American men encounter many situations in which they are expected to act outside of sex-typed behavior; for example, fathers are expected to raise children, and male psychologists are expected to be empathetic and nurturant. But as Wester and Vogel (2002) point out: "Although most men are able to adapt to such demands, unfortunately some men experience conflict and confusion regarding the differences between these expected behaviors and their socialized male role. They are unsure about how to balance what they see as being masculine with the behaviors their current situation requires, and they feel ashamed of their seeming inability to cope with such changes" (p. 370).

One study reported in the *New York Times* found that 83 percent of working mothers and 72 percent of working fathers experience "conflict between their job demands and their desire to spend more time with their families" (Allen, Herst, Bruck, & Sutton, 2000, p. 278). Another finding from the same study determined that 40 percent of employed parents report work-family conflict at least some of the time. Allen and colleagues also reviewed multiple studies of work-family conflict and summarized its associations with intentions to leave jobs, unwillingness to go above and beyond the call of duty for the work organization, lowered life satisfaction, depression among women with children, alcohol abuse, job burnout, and work-related stress.

SMALL GROUP EXERCISE

Think about what role strains and role conflicts you have experienced, or are now experiencing. Does your job as a student require trade-offs in other areas of your life? Do you feel pressured? Does anyone else in your life wish you had fewer roles? If you have escaped role strains and conflicts, speculate about why.

Newly Americanized children experience role conflict between their immigrant parents' expectations and their own desires, as you can see in this passage by Jade Snow Wong, daughter of Chinese immigrants:

> By the time I was graduating from high school, my parents had done their best to produce an intelligent, obedient daughter, who would know more than the average Chinatown girl and should do better than average at a conventional job, her earnings brought home in repayment for their years of child support. Then, they hoped, she would marry a nice Chinese boy and make him a good wife, as well as an above-average mother for his children. Chinese custom used to decree that families should "introduce" chosen partners to each other's children. The groom's family should pay handsomely to the bride's family for rearing a well-bred daughter. They should also pay all the bills for a glorious wedding banquet for several hundred guests. Their daughter belonged to the groom's family and must henceforth seek permission from all persons in his home before returning to her parents for a visit.
>
> But having been set upon a new path, I did not oblige my parents with the expected conventional ending. At fifteen, I had moved away from home to work for room and board and a salary of twenty dollars per month. Having found that I could subsist independently, I thought it regrettable to terminate my education. Upon graduating from high school at the age of sixteen, I asked my parents to assist me in college expenses. I pleaded with my father, for his years of encouraging me to be above mediocrity in both Chinese and American studies had made me wish for some undefined but brighter future.
>
> My father was briefly adamant. He must conserve his resources for my oldest brother's medical training. Though I desired to continue on an above-average course, his material means were insufficient to support that ambition. He added that if I had the talent, I could provide for my own college education. When he had spoken, no discussion was expected. After this edict, no daughter questioned. (from "A Chinese Evolution," 1971, p. 121)

How many generations will experience such clear-cut splits between two cultural traditions? It is possible that within the next two generations, people will be thinking of themselves as world citizens due to television and computers, which "penetrate local experience and allow access to information and persons in many other places" (Arnett, 2002, p. 778). This **globalization** process can be seen in youth cultures in places like India, Japan, and Africa, which share more with each other (and U.S. youth culture) than with the old local cultures of their own countries. And, as Arnett points out, "[t]he values of the global culture are based on individualism, free market economics, and democracy and include freedom of choice, individual rights, openness to change, and tolerance of differences" (2002, p. 779). The world's youth, except where governments prevent citizens from communicating with the rest of the globe, will probably develop a **complex hybrid identity** that won't be geographically determined. The traditional hierarchy of placing men over women is being overturned worldwide.

DISCUSSION IDEAS

To what extent do people in your classroom possess "complex hybrid identities"? For example, do you switch codes of politeness or conversation according to the cultural setting you are in, without feeling that such switching is inauthentic? What problems do you think globalization of identity might entail?

Prejudice, Trauma, and Violence

A visibly different group whose members are geographically a minority manifests behavior that stems not just from cultural differences but from experiencing a **minority status.** "A continuing history of discrimination has necessitated— and still does—important behavioral adaptations for survival, mutual support, self-esteem, achievement, choice, and hope" (Dumas et al., 1999). For example, minority teenagers often form peer networks with anti-academic biases that reflect the negative school experience of many of their members. This anti-academic bias is not present in the original culture, but has become identified with the culture because of minority status (Dumas et al., 1999). Thus, for example, an academically ambitious Black teenager might be enthusiastically supported at home, yet find himself in conflict with his peer-group culture. This is a tough problem for an adolescent. Minority status may also create social habits of caution, mistrust, reticence, and secretiveness that stem from being in the minority, not from the original culture. These habits are products of repeated prejudicial treatment.

Thoughtless **prejudice** affects women, minorities, and the aged in many ways. For example, gay men who lost intimate partners to untimely deaths suffered from a lack of sympathy based on other people's failure to recognize their deep relationship, including support-group members and employers (O'Brien, Forrest, & Austin, 2002). The same employers would go out of their way to show support for a heterosexual man whose wife had died. Even when a visibly different person is from a privileged class, he or she is not protected from bias, from within and without. Chicana psychologist Melba Vasquez (2001) provides this example:

> Several years ago, I worked with a young Chicano undergraduate, referred by his distraught mother. She thought that she had protected him from prejudice by raising him in an upper middle class neighborhood and by sending him to private schools. The wall of protection from prejudice by avoiding identity with the Chicano population was shattered when a professor accused him of cheating on an exam. His mother intervened with the professor, insisting that the professor provide another examination. The student did extremely well on it. As it turned out, a White student had cheated by copying from the Chicano student, and the professor assumed the Chicano student must have done the cheating. In psychotherapy, the Chicano student acknowledged that when he saw other Mexican American students, he assumed that he was "better than them." The attempts to avoid identification with his cultural group and his detachment from "them" had resulted in his erroneous belief that he had to do this to be and feel competent and successful. However, society (in this case, in the form of the biased professor) did not allow the detachment. Psychotherapy consisted of "reworking" his negatively internalized stereotypes and "reformulating" his identification with his heritage, partly by engaging in a variety of ethnic and cultural activities. As he "opened his eyes," he was delighted to find talent and creativity and to enjoy feelings of comfort among other Chicanos. Although his therapy was short-term, he seemed launched in his determination to change his images of this part of his identity. (p. 121)

The student in this example was grappling with his inner sense of what it means to be Chicano, his **racial identity.** Racial identity has been studied by psychologists as a series of stages or statuses characterized by attitudes toward one's own race and attitudes toward other races, with appreciation of multiculturalism as the most advanced category (Helms, 1990).

Judging other groups as lesser beings creates an acceptance of violence toward them, as we see in domestic violence and hate crimes. Battered wives display psychological problems as well as physical harm, and people chosen as victims of violence due to their color or sexual orientation also carry at least a double burden of harm, as do sexually abused children. The more economically dependent on their husbands women are, the more likely they are to experience physical abuse (Riger, 2000). Yet financial independence does not protect women from violence: Women who are separated are victims of violence thirty times more often than married women. Many women experience rape or sexual assault sometime in life. Feeling that you live under threat of violence, whether you escape it or not, is limiting and draining. Moreover, many victims never take action against their attackers, "silenced by shame, fear of blame, confusion over what is acceptable male sexual behavior, loyalty to their victimizers, or fear of reprisals" (Maracek, 2001, p. 313).

Men are expected to accept violent games as pastimes and, ultimately, to go to war. Even now, many men suffer from posttraumatic stress disorder (PTSD) due to the violence they witnessed or participated in during the Vietnam war. Men who hang back from aggressive sports and war are widely ridiculed in mainstream culture and may consider themselves less manly than others, an image that often results in psychological defense tactics that bolster masculine identity at the price of emotional well-being (Blazina, 2001).

R e f l e c t i o n

What was the most recent personal experience that made you aware of the stereotypes of (or prejudice against) people of your race, religion, or gender? How often do you have such an experience? Can you explain the frequency or infrequency?

Profile of a Theorist

MELBA VASQUEZ

Melba Vasquez has been described as a pioneer in the field of ethnic minority and multicultural psychology. The list of awards and citations for her contributions to the field in the areas of multiculturalism and social justice is long, and the roots of her work extend deep into her own history. Melba grew up in a small central Texas town in the 1950s. The first of seven siblings born to parents of Mexican American heritage, she lived her early life surrounded by a large extended family. Vasquez attended both public and parochial schools during her childhood, and credits each with shaping her view of her place in the world and subsequently influencing choices she has made, both professionally and personally.

When reflecting on the factors that have affected her world view and career, Vasquez applies the concepts of multicultural psychology she and others have worked to advance. She acknowledges her supportive family, her exposure to a private school education, and her many mentors as privileges and *unearned advantages* not afforded to all. Yet she also recognizes the impact of the *unearned disadvantages* and oppression of being a Hispanic female in a White-dominated culture. Her parents were politically active in their local community and modeled for Melba the value of activism. At a young age, she learned to believe that "proactive involvement was the way to direct the pain and anger of disenfranchisement" (2001, p. 65). Messages endorsing the importance of family, education, and social activism combined to propel Melba toward a career in education and, ultimately, counseling psychology. Likewise, experiences of discrimination, degradation, and objectification inspired her to pursue work that could effect lasting change. She entered Southwest Texas State University in 1969 and received her bachelor's degree and teaching certification in 1972. During her undergraduate career, Melba was encouraged by various mentors and professors to pursue a graduate degree.

While working on her master's in counselor education, Melba taught middle school before returning to the University of Texas to complete a doctorate in counseling psychology. Encouraged once again by supportive mentors, she assumed an active role in professional organizations and worked with other Hispanic psychologists to found the National Hispanic Psychological Association in the late 1970s. During her work in college counseling centers following her graduation, she continued to develop her interest in multicultural issues. Along the way, she also became a proponent and author on the subject of ethics in psychotherapy and counseling and has published numerous articles and book chapters. In addition, she coauthored the oft-noted *Ethics in Psychotherapy and Counseling* with Ken Pope, Ph.D., and has served on multiple APA Ethics Committees and the APA Board of Social and Ethical Responsibility.

Melba credits Affirmative Action with enabling her to become the successful psychologist, author, and proponent of multicultural counseling and ethics that she is today. The controversy over fairness and equality is not an issue she avoids. Instead, she points to the fact that psychological knowledge can and should inform the debate over Affirmative Action. Through her writings and work on professional ethics, she encourages careful consideration of policies that can make or break the promotion of social justice. Leading by example, she links mentoring and social activism to the betterment of the field. She is currently in private practice in Austin, Texas, but her public work continues.

Economic Status

For many groups, minority status overlaps with poverty, crime, limited educational opportunities, and poor health due to low socioeconomic status. Certainly, women as a group are poorer than men as a group, around the world. They have fewer of the top jobs (holding only 35 percent of these in 1998) and many more of the low-prestige, poorly paid service jobs such as being nursing-home aides, file clerks, and housekeepers (holding 83 to 93 percent of these in 1998) (Sharf, 2002). Even in our field, the helping professions, the bulk of the hands-on work is done by women, while the higher-paid, high-status careers belong mostly to men. Women also do most of the unpaid work of the world, such as raising children, maintaining a household, acting as volunteers, and caring for the sick and elderly. The Framingham Heart Study measured high levels of stress and stress-related heart disease "among workers who had more than one person making work demands on them and little control over the pacing of their own work" (Ferree, 1987)—a description that fits most working mothers' situation.

The wages of women are between two-thirds and one-half of White men's in the United States, depending on the women's racial/geographic background (women of Mexican origin earn 49 percent of a White man's earnings; African American women, 60 percent; White women, 71 percent). Minority men also earn less than White men (Mexican Americans, 57 percent; and African Americans, 74 percent) (Sharf, 2002).

Counselors who are aware of gender and cultural issues in understanding human beings emphasize financial independence or security. Though wealth doesn't buy happiness, an income that can't pay for the necessities of life invites physical danger, poor health, victimization, truancy, downward mobility, family separation, and, for many people, shame. Lott (2002) surveyed the literature on people's beliefs and concluded that poor people tend to be regarded as "lesser in values, character, motivation, and potential" (p. 107), especially in the eyes of the nonpoor. Counselors working with the poor should develop contacts in social service agencies that can help clients who are doubly or triply burdened by poverty on top of other problems.

The American Psychological Association acknowledges the responsibilities of counselors to improve our awareness of the psychological effects of poverty, and encourages us to participate in efforts to improve material conditions. The APA document *Resolution on Poverty and Economic Status*, adopted in 2000, outlines the organization's stance on these matters, and you can read it at *www.apa. org/pi/urban/povres.html.*

DISCUSSION IDEAS

Social science experiments have definitively discovered that certain ingredients ensure group hostility (R. Brown, 1986):

1. ethnocentrism (setting a higher value on the assets and traits of your group than on those of other groups);

2. stereotyping (believing that groups have quite distinct character profiles); and

3. unfair distribution of scarce resources.

Discuss examples of intergroup hostility that you have seen yourself, and ascertain whether the three ingredients were present. Can these ingredients explain hostility between boys and girls and men and women? Neighborhood gangs? Neighborhood ethnic groups? High school cliques? (Remember that scarce resources can take many forms, not just money—grades, trophies, prizes, attention, praise, opportunity, advancement, and status are resources, too.)

As a counselor, how might you see group hostility affecting your individual clients?

The Process of Therapy

Therapists who have gendered or cultural points of view might follow almost any of the other counseling processes described in this textbook. The difference is a focus on the social, historical, and environmental situation of clients from distinguishable groups such as women, Blacks, Korean-Americans, gay men, or Native Americans. An underlying process is the discovery that "the personal is political"—that private life is not really private, but determined by a bigger social context. For example, an alcoholic Native American client served by a culturally oriented counselor might receive conventional cognitive-behavioral treatment, with the addition of conversation about alcoholism among Native Americans and its historical, situational, and biological roots. This counselor would also be aware of specific problems faced by a traditional Native American attempting to give up drinking and would address these directly. At another level, the counselor would draw relevant Native American beliefs and world views into the process of exploring the individual's problem, and discuss with the client what native treatment systems could be enlisted. At a very intense level of cultural orientation, some counselors would encourage the client to take political action to change the situations that promote alcoholism among Native Americans.

Gender-oriented therapy, too, can be visualized along a continuum like the one in the example above. At one end is **nonsexist therapy,** in which counselors avoid value-laden differential descriptions of men and women, assume that gender-role loosening is desirable, reject the idea of innate sex differences, and view legal, economic, and cultural inequalities between men and women as a source of personal pathology. They avoid investing themselves with unnecessary power and authority over women in particular, who need to become their own heroes, experts, and protectors (Enns, 1997). At a more intense level is **feminist therapy,** which is like nonsexist therapy, but with a deep rejection (not just criticism) of traditional culture and power structures as suspect male creations. Feminist therapy calls for a total recasting of social relations; active political involvement is an ingredient of the healing process, for both clients and counselors (Augsburger, 1986). Some feminist therapists do not see male clients at all, and some radical feminist counselors work completely outside the conventional mental health system, even discarding the accepted credential procedures of the field (formal education, supervised practice, and licensure) (Wyckoff, 1977). Many professional and lay therapists, all along this continuum, avoid diagnostic labels and prefer social constructivist approaches to understanding women's dilemmas (L. Brown, 1986).

Therapist Role and Training

Diversity training is now a part of almost all programs in the helping professions, and it is a guiding principle in American Psychological Association accreditation and practice documents (APA, 1978, 1993). However, the issue of whether required training such as multicultural curricula really alleviates prejudice is largely unstudied, and when the effects of this training are evaluated, the results are not encouraging (Rudman, Ashmore, & Gary, 2001). Some evidence exists of a **backlash effect,** in which participants become even more prejudiced against identifiably diverse groups. The type of multicultural education that compares features of various groups (for example, Hispanic families are closer than Euro-American families) may encourage stereotyping and not take into account individual clients' endorsement or rejection of their cultural heritage.

Probably the best methods to avoid incorrect judgments about clients based on their group membership are those that help us identify and reduce biases in reasoning about the causes of people's behavior and feelings (e.g., Turk, Salovey, & Prentice, 1998). Arnoult and Anderson (1998), for example, suggest that clinicians make lists of questions to assess the adequacy of their reasoning, such as

- "Have I examined the problem from several perspectives?"
- "Have I given careful thought to the direction of causality?" (For instance, does a child misbehave because of parents' lack of affection, or do the parents lack affection because of the child's persistent misbehavior?)
- "Have I considered the possibility of regression effects?" (Regression effects refer to the tendency of any extreme state to change to a more normal one, no matter what else occurs; for example, severe depression usually lifts no matter what the therapist does.)
- "Have I given equal attention to each alternative cause?" (If you have decided that the client's cultural background is an active ingredient in his presenting problem, consider reasons that have nothing to do with cultural background.) (Adapted from p. 226)

Research supports the common-sense idea that forming firm intentions and plans not to judge people in stereotypical ways really does inhibit the automatic habits associated with stereotypical beliefs and prejudicial feelings (Gollwitzer, 1999). Experimental participants were able to suppress automatic gender stereotypes, negative evaluations of the homeless, and judgments of the elderly by consciously planning to eliminate these biased thoughts when the occasion came up. This is excellent news for counselors who wish to derail their automatic thoughts about diverse groups.

An Ethnographic Perspective

Ethnography is the description of culture, and an ethnographic perspective seeks to comprehend the viewpoint of people inside the culture. O'Connor (1995) presents guidelines for applying an ethnographic attitude to health care.

- What can I learn from this patient or from members of this group of people about the way individuals and the group define the world, order their concerns, understand right behavior, assess circumstances, define health and illness, establish goals for life and for treatment of illness, etc.?

- How can I incorporate the concerns and perspectives of this patient or patient population into the ways in which I structure and deliver health care: shaping of procedures and protocols, office hours, scheduling, waiting room arrangement, furnishings, uses of space, forms of address and conversation, uses of time, inclusion of ethnically significant or valued foods in dietary plans, treatment planning and decisions, etc.?

- What can I modify in my own thinking and behavior to facilitate establishment of relationships of trust and mutual respect (e.g., understanding provider education and patient education as two sides of the same coin; understanding that two views of a health problem and its appropriate solutions may have to be taken into account; understanding that patients' goals are at least as important as providers' goals in formulating a plan for care)?

- How can I negotiate treatment and prevention plans that are acceptable both to me and to my patients, even if we have different beliefs about why things are important or how they work (remembering that negotiation means both sides will probably have to compromise)?

- How can I establish a working partnership in which both points of view contribute to outcomes at all levels (including, e.g., design as well as delivery of health-care services, design and operation of health care facilities, institutional and broader health policy change and implementation)? (pp. 222–223)

SMALL GROUP EXERCISE

Divide into five discussion groups, with each group taking one of the ethnographic guidelines as a topic. Brainstorm about your group's topic, including explanation of the idea, examples of when the idea might be important to counseling practices, and specific details of how the topic might be applied. For example, what office hours and scheduling practices would be best for a specific type of client you see or plan to see? If you implemented the optimum hours, what changes would be necessary in the design and operation of your office, clinic, or school?

Gender Inquiry

Philpot, Brooks, Lusterman, and Nutt (1997) wrote, "[P]eople seldom have the opportunity to sort out how they learned to be a boy or girl, a female or male adolescent, and later, a man or woman" (p. 217). Yet this is probably the most meaningful category we join in life. In the exploration of gender in therapy, the authors suggest a **gender inquiry,** "an array of questions that we hope will stimulate conversation about gender and its role in people's lives and relationships. There is no right way to use this inquiry, and each situation will suggest where to place the focus" (p. 219). The inquiry is organized by developmental stages, and I will excerpt a few interesting questions from the complete version.

- *Childhood.*   Do you remember anything that your parents did that strengthened your sense of being a boy (girl)? What was it? Were there things that you were forbidden to do when you were little because your mother or father didn't think that girls (boys) should do that sort of thing? Were there things that you were specifically encouraged to do because of your gender?

- *Puberty.*   What did you learn about how you were expected to act with boys or girls, and from whom? Did you get different messages from different sources? How did this affect you? Did you sometimes wish you could have remained a child rather than entering puberty? Why?

- *High school years.*   Moving from middle school or junior high school to senior high school is often a stressful time. What special challenges did this transition pose for you as a young woman (man)? Did you feel that, as a member of your sex, there were particular expectations about same-gender friendships, participation in sports, personal appearance, competitiveness, and career choice?

- *College or early work experience.*   Tell me something about your early work experience. Do you think that your gender had anything to do with the kinds of jobs that were available to you? Were there things you might have liked to try that seemed off-limits because you were male or female? Did you sense any difference in the way men and women in general were valued in your work situation? [In the context of college:] Do you think gender had any effect on your choice of courses or college major? What sort of social relations did you develop in college toward members of your own gender? Toward the other gender? What were the qualities you most sought in a possible mate at that time? Have your ideas remained pretty much the same? If not, how have they changed?

- *Adulthood.*   How would you compare your role as a woman (man) with how your mother (father) acted? Do you think that there are issues in any of your male-female relationships that are hard to talk about with one another? Do you sometimes feel that there is no way to explain something to another person because a man (woman) won't understand what you are feeling or trying to explain? Have changing ideas about the roles of men and women over the last few decades had an impact on your relationship? Could you describe the impact?

SMALL GROUP EXERCISE

Divide into six small groups. Five of the groups should each take one developmental stage from the gender inquiry above and discuss how they would answer the questions as clients. You should also reflect on how the counselor can guide the questions and further discussion of them so that the client is comfortable talking. Add relevant questions to the inquiry. The sixth group will discuss how the gender inquiry could be altered to make up a cultural inquiry, which investigates how and what clients learn about being members of their ethnic or subculture group. If time permits, each group should report to the class as a whole on one or two useful insights from the discussion.

_____

Consciousness Raising

"Consciousness raising is the name given to the feminist practice of examining one's personal experience in the light of sexism; i.e., that theory which explains women's subordinate position in society as a result of a cultural decision to confer direct power on men and only indirect power on women" (Gornick, 1972, p. 802). In many feminist approaches to therapy, **consciousness raising** is an important feature, emphasizing that "the personal is political" and alleviating the isolation that many women feel. As in many therapeutic processes, **normalization,** or the idea that you are not alone in your difficulty, is powerful. Consciousness raising is "the intensely felt realization that what had always been taken for symptoms of personal unhappiness or dissatisfaction or frustration was so powerfully and so consistently duplicated among women that perhaps these symptoms could just as well be ascribed to *cultural* causes as to psychological ones" (Gornick, 1972, p. 804).

Consciousness raising could also be a feature of culturally sensitive approaches to therapy. To what extent is the client's complaint explained by position in society and culture of origin rather than by individual psychopathology?

Individual Choice

Integral to the process of culture- and gender-based therapy are questions of individual choice. In this sense, I see existential and humanist approaches as being especially in tune with the orientations in this chapter. Even when a client views her or his own problems in a big context of social demands and political power, she or he still has to decide what to accept, what to adjust to, what to rise above, what to resist, and what to change. For a gay man, struggling for acceptance while living in his small Midwestern home town may be a psychologically debilitating choice, no matter how noble the cause. As I always say, some people need therapy, and some people need a suitcase. Many other choices, less drastic than relocation, must be made with awareness of the gender and cultural messages they carry. In one of my graduate programs, all the male professors were called "Dr. so-and-so," while the two female professors were called by their first names, Anna and Carmen. The women had clearly decided that the egalitarianism they upheld by having graduate students call them by their first names was more important than the equality of status implied if they were called "Dr.," as their male peers were. (I'm not at all sure I would make the same choice.)

Problem Solving

When a personal difficulty is considered in light of its context, and choices must be made, good problem-solving skills are critical. A gender- or culture-based approach needs to include psychoeducational processes that assist clients in articulating their goals, seeing all their options, evaluating each option thoroughly, choosing a course of action, and assessing the results in terms of the original goals.

Customary Techniques of Therapy

Many characteristics of gender- and culture-aware counseling reflect its democratic, egalitarian ideals.

Shared Power

In her guidelines for an ethnographic perspective, O'Connor (1995) emphasized a two-directional flow between professional and client—a mutual responsibility that also characterizes nonsexist and feminist therapies (Maracek, 2001). Though psychotherapy cannot be a relationship among equals, since someone is being paid to provide expertise, how to ensure **shared power** has been a matter of debate. Feminist therapists usually involve clients in decisions such as how often to meet, what goals to pursue, and even where to meet and how much the fee should be. They also pride themselves on clearly explaining what techniques they are using and why. As you have read, other schools of therapy share these collaborative methods, such as Rogerian and behavioral treatments.

Strict rules against therapist **self-disclosure** are often questioned and violated by feminist counselors. Because of the mutuality they value, these therapists usually will share a bit about themselves, especially when they have struggled with the same problems as the client (Maracek, 2001). Revealing your own background can make cultural differences from your client explicit, and open up discussion of how these differences might affect your relationship. Similarities that are not obvious can also be brought into the discussion; for example, I was raised mainly among Italian- and Mexican-Americans, although I don't look like either group.

Consciousness-Raising Groups

The setting for the process of consciousness raising is often a group of four to ten people. In fact, consciousness raising is best done in a group whose members can share the diversity of their experiences and discover a core of similarity among their lives. Though consciousness-raising groups are an invention of the 1960s and '70s women's movement, today's self-help and support groups are their offspring and include groups organized around common problems, sexual orientation, racial and ethnic identification, and interests. A distinguishing feature of these groups is that they can be led by a professional, conducted by a designated group member, or thrive without a leader at all following a feminist model of power-sharing.

Social Action

One of Alfred Adler's enduring legacies is the curative value of turning one's concerns outward in constructive action (see Chapter 5). For feminist therapists, acting to right the unequal system of power in law, economics, religion, and social customs is a move toward psychological health. A client might be invited to join a **social action** group, attend a rally supporting people similar to herself or less fortunate, work on a political campaign, or seek to educate herself about a global or local problem. Counselors themselves have put energy into change on a larger level as part of their responsibility to their clients, some of them believing that "limiting one's practice to counseling individuals was tantamount to treating the symptom and ignoring the disease" (Enns, 1997, p. 206). This technique stands in contrast to many therapies that maintain a separation between an individual's private sphere and the public arena.

DISCUSSION IDEAS

What do you think about social action as part of healthy psychology? Do you participate in activities that contribute to the larger society? If so, do they also contribute to your mental health? How? Would you encourage a client to take part in social action as an addition to her or his therapy—for example, by communicating your approval of an African-American student's plan to join the Black Students Association on campus?

Use of Native Healers

Professionally provided mental health care is only one recourse for most people in psychological distress, and most cultures and subcultures include other help systems for people in need of help. For example, it is very common in the United States and elsewhere to use prayer in grappling with emotional distress, aside from seeing a counselor. It's also common for people to consult a nutritionist or naturopath, investigating what foods (or their avoidance) might contribute to a better sense of well-being.

When you work with someone from a strong ethnic culture, their treatment choices may include **native healers** specific to the culture, such as shamans, medicine men, priests, yogis, sufis, astrologers, elders, and herbalists or rootworkers (Lee & Armstrong, 1995). It is important to you as a counselor to know what other systems of care are being called upon (O'Connor, 1995). Your help may have been sought neither "as the first resort nor as the final effort" (p. 27), and other systems may be acting on different aspects of the problem. Common concepts of alternative healing systems are views emphasizing harmony and balance, the importance of pertinent *energies*, and supernatural, spiritual, or metaphysical dimensions of distress. Getting the whole picture of the therapeutic efforts combined in a client's system of mental health care is part of being respectful of other cultures and responsible in your own practice. The American Psychological Association (1993) emphasizes this responsibility in its *Guidelines for Providers of Psychological Services to Ethnic, Linguistic, and Culturally Diverse Populations.*

If all goes well, your treatment will effectively dovetail with other healing efforts. However, you may find, as I once did, that the client's system is internally contradictory and confusing. A schizophrenic client saw me for counseling and visited a psychiatrist to manage her drug therapy; she also consulted a telephone faith healer and a local naturopath. Both the faith healer and the naturopath encouraged her to give up her psychotropic drugs, while I and the psychiatrist saw them as critical to her safety and independence. Although we could endorse the naturopath's nutritional advice at least, we both felt that the faith healer, who took our client's credit card number and charged by the telephone minute, was a charlatan. Our client saw us all as equally authoritative.

Crisis Centers

Rape crisis and domestic violence centers sprang up in the 1970s, usually created by community-based feminist organizations. They saw that traditional legal and medical approaches to rape and battering victims often viewed women as responsible for their own victimization, and frequently dealt with victims in dismissive, insensitive, or simply clumsy ways. The crisis centers provided a context outside the conventional, male-dominated system, a context "in which women are believed, supported, and receive direct help for working through the aftermath of sexual violence" (Enns, 1997, p. 177). Feminist counselors frequently volunteer their expertise at crisis centers, providing direct services and training crisis counselors. The techniques of crisis work are different from psychotherapy because of the brevity of contact between counselor and client. Many feminist therapists make sure they are trained for brief crisis management situations.

Uses for Gendered and Cultural Approaches

Many clinicians would say that gendered and cultural approaches should be part of every counseling process. In this section, I will focus on some situations where considerations of gender and culture dominate the treatment.

Preadolescent Gender Intensification

During preadolescence, pressures to conform to sex stereotypes increase, including the association of femininity with sociability and submissiveness, and masculinity with autonomy and aggression. Girls experience a significant decrease in self-worth, magnified self-consciousness, and less confidence in their schoolwork even if their grades are high (Bosacki, 2000). Many sociologists and psychologists think of this developmental period as a turning point for girls, when their powers move under a cloud that sometimes never lifts. Feminist counselors are particularly equipped to intervene at this point to provide role models and psychoeducation on girls' equal potentials, and to help them navigate the confusing social landscape.

Affirmative Psychotherapy for Gays, Lesbians, and Bisexuals

Gay, lesbian, and bisexual clients and couples come to counseling for many of the same problems that heterosexuals present. However, there is nearly always an extra layer of challenge and usually pain for people with minority sexual orientations, almost all of whom report negative experiences directly related to prejudice. "The less severe end of the spectrum of such experiences includes verbal harassment and social rejection; the extreme end includes discrimination and violent crimes. For some, a rejecting home environment provides no refuge from a hostile society" (Haldeman, 2001, p. 796). Add to the usual pressures from parents a pressure to be someone quite different from what you basically and elementally *are*, and you can imagine one of the situations that brings gay and lesbian clients to counseling. A therapist with a gendered approach to understanding the context of human behavior can offer well-rounded affirmation, where another counselor might focus on conflicts within the client and neglect the contribution from outside.

Emotional Self-Awareness for Men

Though the limitations on women's traditional roles are obvious, it may be that male **gender-role socialization** is actually more rigid. For example, when you think about early childhood, girls can play with trucks *and* dolls and are considered cute in their denim overalls *and* their party dresses, while boys who play with dolls and like party dresses are greeted with major concern by adults. Girls in grade school are praised for excellence in math (formerly a boy's arena), while boys who show early acute sensitivity to poetry (girls' purview) probably do not find the same enthusiastic approval. Boys and men are "continually given mixed messages about violence, sexuality, alcohol, and emotional sensitivity" (Brooks & Good, 2001, p. 15), which eventually take their toll by impairing close, relaxed, noncompetitive, nonexploitive emotional connections with women or other men, at least in comparison with most women's ease in such connections.

Many theorists and psychotherapists (represented in collections like Brooks & Good, 2001; Levant & Pollack, 1995; Pollack & Levant, 1998;) have focused on the psychology of men through a gender-aware lens. They pay special attention to the treatment of problems associated with male roles and expectations: violence, shame, alcoholism and substance abuse, posttraumatic stress disorder, impulsiveness, risk-taking, loneliness, relationship dysfunction, and the consequences of cutting off aspects of the self.

Family Therapy

In 1994, McGoldrick noted that a nuclear family with an employed father and homemaker mother represented only 6 percent of the U.S. population (cited in Norsworthy, 2000). Thus, images of the supposedly perfect nuclear family are considerably at odds with most people's experience, especially in terms of the expectations of each sex. "From a feminist theoretical framework, how the power structure within the family operates is critical in understanding overall family functioning and the well-being, or lack thereof, of individual members" (p. 521). Whose needs are attended to and whose are ignored, who gets to make demands on others and who does not, and which members are allowed what rights are questions of power and usefully viewed with gender awareness. Feminist family therapists look at how larger systems operate in actual practice in the family, in contrast to earlier family systems theorists who acknowledged such operations but didn't examine them as closely or, in many cases, critique them. While the family is often presented as a self-sufficient unit, in reality it draws on cultural and social structures and can be threatened by the same structures. For example, the school system can perform socializing duties once considered the job of parents; it can also intervene legally when neglect or abuse of children is suspected. Feminists critique the model of normalcy as patriarchal, while many family therapists have encouraged the father to act as the natural head of the family. A gender-oriented family therapist will devote more attention to forces outside the family, to gender-role acceptance and rejection, to equalizing power relationships between the sexes, and to developing the capacity in all members to listen to one another.

🐾 Case Conceptualization: An Example

THE "GIVING" THERAPIST AND THE FEMALE PATIENT

Helen Goldhor Lerner (1988)

Dr. T. was home on the last lap of a three-month maternity leave when she received a telephone call from Ms. S., a 25-year-old woman in long-term, psychoanalytically oriented therapy. Ms. S., who had been hospitalized the year before for an immobilizing depression, began the call by recognizing that Dr. T. was not due back for another week; nevertheless, she (Ms. S.) was "cracking up" and in need of an emergency appointment. The crisis, as she described it, involved her father, who was visiting for three weeks and purportedly driving her crazy by criticizing her homemaking and offering endless unsolicited advice about parenting. Ms. S. appeared to be upset, but functioning well.

Dr. T., who was nursing her baby at the time of the call and was struggling with loyalty conflicts of her own regarding work and family, wanted to say, "I appreciate that you're having a hard time, but we'll talk about it next week at our scheduled appointment." Instead, she agreed to meet with Ms. S. the following day. During the session, Ms. S. complained about her situation but showed no genuine motivation to change or challenge the status quo with her father. Dr. T. noted this and explored the patient's reactions in response to both requesting and receiving the additional hour. Ms. S. discussed her feelings of discomfort as well as her "gratitude" for the additional time, and dutifully explored the many meanings that the additional session had for her. At the same time, she remained stuck and resistant to making use of Dr. T.'s help.

A central theme in Ms. S.'s treatment concerned her reluctance to set limits with her father to protect her relationship with her husband and daughter from what she viewed as her father's intrusive, patronizing attitudes and behaviors. Earlier psychodynamic exploration had revealed that Ms. S. feared that her firmness and clarity on such issues would devastate her father and result in his feeling intolerably excluded by the patient and her new family. This fear, at first unconscious, resulted in part from a projection of her accumulated rage stemming from her long-standing pattern of silent submission to her father's perceived needs. It was also an externalization of her own separation anxiety. . . . Her fear of "hurting" her father and her resistance to change were also rooted in the realities of the family system; there was evidence that any move on Ms. S.'s part to assume a more differentiated stance or to clarify her primary commitment to her new family was followed by her father's depression and withdrawal, and the subsequent reinstatement of the old pattern by Ms. S.

In helping Ms. S. to struggle with her dilemma. Dr. T. had made any number of accurate and well-timed interpretations. The implicit message from Dr. T. to the patient might be summarized as follows: It is all right for you to clarify your priorities, your preferences, and your primary commitment to your new family, even if your father, in response, becomes depressed or angry. Your relationship with your father is very important, but it is not your job to protect him from depression by sacrificing your own development. And yet, a nontherapeutic double bind was invoked by Dr. T.'s own guilt and anxiety about clarifying treatment boundaries that "excluded" the patient. In the example just discussed and in many others, Dr. T. was reluctant to refuse the patient's requests for extra sessions or evening phone calls, although she would attempt to explore the meaning of such requests. When Ms. S. tested her further by failing to comply with an agreed-upon plan for paying off her large outstanding balance, Dr. T. made this a continuing topic of therapeutic exploration but did not take a clear position regarding her continuing the work in the face of Ms. S.'s failure to make her agreed-upon payments.

Viewed from one perspective, Dr. T. was failing Ms. S.'s unconscious tests regarding the degree of separateness, self-assertion, and limit-setting that was permissible in the patient's life. In addition, granting Ms. S.'s requests for a "special" hour or phone call implicitly communicated that Dr. T. neither expected nor encouraged Ms. S. to use her own competence to manage her life between scheduled appointments. Dr. T.'s anxiety about the patient's relapsing into another immobilizing depression paralleled and subtly encouraged the patient's sense of responsibility and overconcern for her "fragile" father, who she unconsciously believed needed protection from the realities of her adult life. It also paralleled the father's protective and overconcerned stance with Ms. S., his little girl whose potential competence and maturity he feared recognizing.

A turning point in the treatment occurred when Dr. T. was able to use supervision to shift her therapeutic stance and warmly but firmly hold fast to the agreed-upon boundaries of therapy. For example, when Ms. S. called her at home at 7:00 in the morning to cancel her afternoon appointment for that day. Dr. T. told her during the following session, "When you call me to cancel a session, I would like you to do so during working hours." When the patient argued that she could not pay her bill because she was too depressed to seek employment, Dr. T. responded. "I appreciate that you are feeling depressed, but it is necessary that you find a way to meet your payments in order for your therapy to continue." In regard to telephone calls, she told Ms. S., "I've been thinking about our work together, and from now on I prefer that you do not call me at home. I think our work belongs here, in our scheduled sessions. I find I am most able to be helpful in this way."

Dr. T. was able to firmly clarify limits and boundaries without lengthy explanations (which would have implicitly conveyed discomfort or guilt) and without negatively interpreting the motives for the patient's requests. That is, Dr. T.'s comments and interventions in no way suggested that Ms. S.'s requests were reflective of excessive dependency, demandingness, or other pathological underpinnings. Equally as important, Dr. T. was able to calmly and empathically "sit still" through the patient's displays of hurt, withdrawal, and anger while maintaining the therapeutic boundaries. What followed was Ms. S.'s own slow but steady moves toward assuming a more differentiated stance in her own life. She more clearly defined her own thoughts and feelings on important issues, even when this brought anger and disapproval from significant others. She began to take less responsibility for others' feelings and more responsibility for ensuring the quality and direction of her own life. When her moves toward greater autonomy and independence predictably evoked strong resistance in others, she did react with a moderately severe depressive episode. However, when Dr. T. maintained a calm, nonreactive position and continued to keep the work within the boundaries of the two scheduled weekly hours (despite the patient's requests for additional sessions), Ms. S. rather quickly worked through her depression and continued to move ahead.

Dr. T.'s initial difficulty maintaining treatment parameters and clarifying appropriate limits had multiple sources. First, she had an exaggerated sense of guilt about the negative impact of her pregnancy and leave of absence on her patients (complicated by her own conflicted wish to be rid of professional responsibilities entirely), and she responded with attempts to be all-giving and available. Second, Dr. T.'s own sibling position as a youngest child, combined with her gender and sex-role socialization, contributed to her considerable discomfort with exercising authority. Adding to this problem was the absence of a clear theoretical framework that would allow her to question her giving stance. Throughout her training, Dr. T. (who was one of the two women in her training program) had been praised by teachers and supervisors for her "maternal," intuitive, and caring capacities, as if these traditionally feminine qualities were sufficient to facilitate change and could not be exercised to excess. Finally, Dr. T. . . . easily became anxious about her female patient's perceived vulnerabilities and failed to recognize that even the most severely disturbed individuals need a therapist who can model appropriate self-seeking and self-assertive behaviors, maintain treatment boundaries, and resist assuming an anxious, over-responsible and overfunctioning position. (pp. 130–134) ▪ ▪

DISCUSSION IDEAS

1. How is this case description different from the others you have read?
2. What professional and ethical decisions did Dr. T. face?
3. What features of family systems theory can you identify in this case conceptualization?
4. What elements in Dr. T.'s culture affected her treatment of Ms. S.? What elements in Ms. S.'s culture affected her behavior?
5. Explain the parallel between Dr. T.'s worry about the client and the client's worry about her father.
6. How did role modeling function in the treatment of this client?
7. Does this case resonate with you personally? Do you think you have been overprotective of a client or student, to his or her actual detriment? Have you seen or heard of cases like this?
8. Is there a member of your own family or extended family that everyone else protects? How? Do you think that your family's cultural background explains any patterns of protectiveness you can see?

Critiques of Gendered and Cultural Approaches

Gendered and cultural emphases in counseling have their detractors. I will summarize some of the major opposing points of view, as well as the relevant counterarguments.

Redundancy with Other Approaches

As you read this chapter, you may have felt déjà vu. The overlap between gender- and culture-aware theories and other theories that endorse phenomenology, social construction of experience, and contextual influences on individual psychology is striking. For example, Adlerian psychology looks much like the theory explained in this chapter. However, you have seen that in spite of Adler's sensitivity to context, he was still blinded by social expectations about the right and natural roles of women and men (e.g., normal women desire motherhood, normal men are heterosexual). Adler's example points up how a keen questioning of widely accepted normative judgments about groups is critical for understanding individuals.

Treatment formats in gendered and culture-based therapies also overlap greatly with other theoretical bases. Providing illustrations of gender-based psychotherapy with men, Brooks and Good (2001) include psychoanalytic models as well as cognitive, interpersonal, psychoeducational, family systems, and existential treatments. I emphasize that gendered and cultural approaches involve matters of focus and awareness more than treatment mode, though I have pointed out some processes and techniques that are particularly well suited to the focus.

Encouragement of Victimology

I have written here about how women and minorities of various kinds are victimized. Feeling safe from unequal treatment, prejudice, and violence is reserved for a specific slice of the American apple pie. However, awareness of being a victim or potential victim isn't a life sentence of doormat status, nor is it a license to float on a raft of self-pity and expect special favors. Some conservative commentators criticize gendered and cultural explanations of individuals' problems as "cults of victimhood." They see women and minorities as requesting special privileges because of historical mistreatment. When individuals wish to excuse their bad behavior through their own victimization (past and present), they irritate and exasperate the rest of us.

Remember that it is extremely healing when a client realizes that her suffering is not self-made, that there is an explanation for it outside herself, in society and culture. Victims of childhood sexual abuse provide abundant examples. Gender- and culture-based therapies make use of these explanations as elements in self-understanding and action, not as a stopping place. The word **empowerment** comes up again and again, obviously the opposite of **victimhood**. Empowerment entails developing and discovering competence and self-direction in as many spheres of life as possible, not giving up helplessly or exploiting one's victimized status.

Moral Conflicts

Those of us who endorse a multicultural perspective, and attempt a nonjudgmental point of view on **value systems** unlike our own, eventually experience moral conflicts because our own value systems come into play, and we believe that they are right. If we didn't value human equality, respect for the freedom and dignity of all, and relief from human misery, we wouldn't be interested in multiculturalism in the first place (Fowers & Richardson, 1996). But what do we do when asked to accept cultural practices that don't share those values, which seem so natural to us? For example, racism, sexism, heterosexism, and ethnocentricity are ingrained in more cultures than not, and are expressed in practices such as ethnic cleansing, female circumcision, female infanticide, persecution of gays and lesbians, and tossing troublesome wives into the fire. Negy (2000) fears that multicultural educational materials too often present "defensive and romanticized cultural characterizations" (p. 442). How can therapists "challenge and subvert" practices they see as crippling and oppressive without being "psychological colonialists" (Kliman, 1994)? Luckily, such cultures include their own dissidents with whom we can fairly side. Moreover, with globalization will come shared values of "freedom of choice, individual rights, openness to change, and tolerance of differences" (Arnett, 2002, p. 779)—partly because these are the expressed values of the countries that energize television and computer proliferation, and partly because these values are needed to unify people across cultural and national boundaries.

R e f l e c t i o n

I once counseled a student who would not leave her family home to go to graduate school, even though I and her other professors strongly believed she would enjoy great success with an advanced degree. The student felt that her duty to her depressed parents, who depended on her to hold the family together emotionally, was more important than her own professional advancement. Have you ever had a values conflict with a client or someone whom you were trying to help, or advise? What were your thoughts when dealing with your values conflict? Do you think you dealt with it well? What alternatives did you think of when dealing with it?

KEY TERMS

backlash effect	internalize	rationality
complex hybrid identity	minimizing	relationality
consciousness-raising	minority status	role conflict
empowerment	mirror-image	role strain
expressive	stereotypes	self-disclosure
externalize	native healers	shared power
feminist therapy	nonsexist therapy	social action
gender inquiry	normalization	stereotypes
gender-role	overdiagnosis	underdiagnosis
socialization	overpathologizing	value systems
globalization	prejudice	victimhood
instrumental	racial identity	

Exploring Key Terms

Have your small group choose a film from the following list to view individually or together if you can schedule it. All these films involve gendered and cultural topics. (More films are listed in Chapter 3.) After you have all watched the movie and taken notes, get together and write a report in which you use terms and concepts from gendered and cultural psychological approaches to interpret the events and characters in the movie. Use as many terms as apply. In your reviews, discuss how this film might be used in psychotherapy, and with what kind of clients. Present the reviews in class, or if time precludes this, distribute copies of them to everyone. The reports will help everyone study the terms in a meaningful context.

Love! Valor! Compassion! (1996)

The Banger Sisters (2002)

Beloved (1998)

The Joy Luck Club (1993)

Saturday Night Fever (1977)

City Slickers (1991)

Kissing Jessica Stein (2002)

Mask (1988)

Monsters Ball (2002)

Cocoon (1985)

The Breakfast Club (1985)

Breaking Away (1979)

In the Heat of the Night (1967)

LIBRARY, MEDIA, AND INTERNET ACTIVITIES

1. The American Counseling Association (ACA) has published its Cross-Cultural Competencies and Objectives on its website, *www.counseling.org*. Relevant divisions of the ACA are the Association for Multicultural Counseling and Development, the Association for Gay, Lesbian, and Bisexual Issues in Counseling, and Counselors for Social Justice. These can also be found through the general ACA website.

2. If you go to *www.lib.uci.edu/rrsc/asiamer.html*, you'll find the website for Asian American Studies Resources, an extensive collection of Asian study sites, constructed by the University of California at Irvine Library. It includes bibliographies, magazines, audiovisual materials, research programs, movement groups, gay Asian resources, and more. Another useful website, *www.pbs.org/blackpress*, covers the history of Black journalism and its current state, with biographies of major Black journalists. And at *www.nytimes.com/library/national/race*, a series of in-depth articles from the *New York Times* is reprinted, covering various features of race relations in the United States. Investigate these websites, and use search engines to find the URLs for other sites that will be valuable to a counselor interested in cultural influences on individual psychology.

3. Find the website developed by J. M. O'Neil on masculinity.

4. Several American Psychological Association divisions concentrate on matters of gender and culture. Survey three or four from the list below, all accessible through *www.apa.org/divisions.*

Division 9: Society for the Psychological Study of Social Issues

Division 17: Counseling Psychology

Division 35: Psychology of Women

Division 44: Society for the Psychological Study of Lesbian, Gay, and Bisexual Issues

Division 51: Society for the Psychological Study of Ethnic Minority Issues

Division 52: International Psychology

REFERENCES

Allen, T. D., Herst, D. E. L., Bruck, C. S., & Sutton, M. (2000). Consequences associated with work-to-family conflict: A review and agenda for future research. *Journal of Occupational Health Psychology, 5,* 278–308.

American Psychological Association, Task Force on Sex Bias and Sex-Role Stereotyping in Psychotherapeutic Practice. (1978). Guidelines for therapy with women. *American Psychologist, 33,* 1122–1123.

American Psychological Association. (1993). Guidelines for providers of psychological services to ethnic, linguistic, and culturally diverse populations. *American Psychologist, 48,* 45–48.

Arnett, J. J. (2002). The psychology of globalization. *American Psychologist, 57,* 774–783.

Arnoult, L. H., & Anderson, C. A. (1998). Identifying and reducing causal reasoning biases in clinical practice. In D. C. Turk & P. Salovey (Eds.), *Reasoning, inference, and judgment in clinical psychology* (pp. 209–232). New York: Free Press.

Arroyo, C. G., & Zigler, E. (1995). Racial identity, academic achievement, and the psychological well-being of economically disadvantaged adolescents. *Journal of Personality and Social Psychology, 69,* 903–914.

Augsburger, D. W. (1986). *Pastoral counseling across cultures.* Philadelphia: Westminster Press.

Bem, S. L. (1981). Gender schema theory: A cognitive account of sex-typing. *Psychological Review, 88,* 354–364.

Blazina, C. (2001). The fragile masculine self model: Implications for clinical use. *Texas Psychologist, 52*(3), 24–27.

Bosacki, S. L. (2000). Theory of mind and self-concept in preadolescents. *Journal of Educational Psychology, 92,* 709–717.

Brannon, R., & David, D. S. (1976). The male sex role: Our culture's blueprint of manhood, and what it's done for us lately. In D. S. David & R. Brannon (Eds.), *The forty-nine percent majority* (pp. 1–45). Reading, MA: Addison-Wesley.

Brooks, G. R., & Good, G. E. (Eds.). (2001). *The new handbook of psychotherapy and counseling with men.* San Francisco: Jossey-Bass.

Brown, L. S. (1986). Gender-role analysis: A neglected component of psychological assessment. *Psychotherapy: Theory, Research, and Practice, 23,* 243–248.

Brown, R. (1986). *Social psychology* (2nd ed.). New York: Free Press.

Cochran, S. V., & Rabinowitz, F. E. (2003). Gender-sensitive recommendations for assessment and treatment of depression in men. *Professional Psychology: Research and Practice, 34,* 132–140.

Comas-Diaz, L. (1996). Cultural considerations in diagnosis. In F. W. Kaslow (Ed.), *Handbook of relational diagnosis and dysfunctional family patterns* (pp. 152–170). New York: Wiley.

Day, S. X., & Rottinghaus, P. (2003). The healthy personality. In B. Walsh (Ed.), *Counseling psychology and optimal human functioning* (pp. 1–25). Mahwah, NJ: Lawrence Erlbaum Associates.

Day, S. X., & Rounds, J. (1998). Universality of vocational interest structure among racial and ethnic minorities. *American Psychologist, 53,* 728–736.

Dumas, J. E., Rollock, D., Prinz, R. J., Hops, H., & Blechman, E. A. (1999). Cultural sensitivity: Problems and solutions in applied and preventive intervention. *Applied and Preventive Psychology, 8,* 175–196.

Enns, C. Z. (1997). *Feminist theories and feminist psychotherapies.* New York: Haworth Press.

Fagot, B. L., & Leinbach, M. D. (1989). The young child's gender schema: Environmental input, internal organization. *Child Development, 60,* 663–672.

Ferree, M. M. (1987). She works hard for a living: Gender and class on the job. In B. B. Hess & M. M. Ferree (Eds.), *Analyzing gender: A handbook of social science research* (pp. 322–347). Newbury Park, CA: Sage Publications.

Fowers, B. J., & Richardson, F. C. (2002). Why is multiculturalism good? *American Psychologist, 51,* 609–621.

Gilligan, C. (1982). *In a different voice.* Cambridge, MA: Harvard University Press.

Gollwitzer, P. M. (1999). Implementation intentions: Strong effects of simple plans. *American Psychologist, 54,* 493–503.

Gornick, V. (1972). Consciousness. In C. J. Sager & H. S. Kaplan, *Progress in group and family therapy* (pp. 801–818). New York: Brunner/Mazel.

Gray, J. (1992). *Men are from Mars, women are from Venus.* New York: Harper Collins.

Haldeman, D. C. (2001). Psychotherapy with gay and bisexual men. In G. R. Brooks & G. E. Good (Eds.), *The new handbook of psychotherapy and counseling with men* (Vol. 2, pp. 796–815). San Francisco: Jossey-Bass.

Halpern, D. F. (1985). The influence of sex-role stereotypes on prose recall. *Sex Roles, 12,* 363–375.

Hare-Mustin, R. T., & Marecek, J. (1988). The meaning of difference: Gender theory, post-modernism, and psychology. *American Psychologist, 43,* 455–464.

Helms, J. E. (Ed.). (1990). *Black and White racial identity: Theory, research and practice.* Westport, CT: Greenwood Press.

Kliman, J. (1994). The interweaving of gender, class, and race in family therapy. In M. P. Mirkin (Ed.), *Women in context* (pp. 25–47). New York: Guilford.

Krugman, S. (1998). Men's shame and trauma in therapy. In W. S. Pollack & R. F. Levant (Eds.), *New psychotherapy for men* (pp. 167–190). New York: Wiley.

Lee, C. C., & Armstrong, K. L. (1995). Indigenous models of mental health intervention. In J. G. Ponterotto, J. M. Cases, L. A. Suzuki, & C. M. Alexander (Eds.), *Handbook of multicultural counseling* (pp. 441–456). Thousand Oaks, CA: Sage.

Lee. R. M., & Ramirez, M. (2000). The history, current status, and future of multicultural psychotherapy. In I. Cuaellar & A. Paniagua (Eds.), *Handbook of multicultural mental health* (pp. 279–309). San Diego, CA: Academic Press.

Lerner, H. G. (1988). *Women in therapy.* Harper & Row, 1988.

Levant, R. F., & Pollack, W. S. (Eds.) (1995). *A new psychology of men.* New York: Basic Books.

Lopez, S. R. (1989). Patient variable biases in clinical judgment: Conceptual overview and methodological considerations. *Psychological Bulletin, 106,* 184–203.

Lott, B. (1996). Politics or science? The question of gender sameness/difference. *American Psychologist, 51,* 155–156.

Lott, B. (2002). Cognitive and behavioral distancing from the poor. *American Psychologist, 57,* 100–110.

Maracek, J. (2001). Bringing feminist issues to therapy. In B. D. Slife, R. N. Williams, & S. H. Barlow (Eds.), *Critical issues in psychotherapy* (pp. 305–319). Thousand Oaks, CA: Sage.

McCrae, R. R., & Costa, P. T. (1997). Personality trait structure as a human universal. *American Psychologist, 52,* 509–516.

Negy, C. (2000). Limitations of the multicultural approach to psychotherapy with diverse clients. In I. Cuaellar & A. Paniagua (Eds.), *Handbook of multicultural mental health* (pp. 439–453). San Diego, CA: Academic Press.

Norsworthy, K. L. (2000). Feminist family therapy. In A. M. Horne (Ed.), *Family counseling and therapy* (3rd ed., pp. 515–538). Itasca, IL: F. E. Peacock.

O'Brien, J. M., Forrest, L. M., & Austin, A. E. (2002). Death of a partner: Perspectives of heterosexual and gay men. *Journal of Health Psychology, 7,* 317–328.

O'Connor, B. B. (1995). *Healing traditions: Alternative medicine and the health professions.* Philadelphia: University of Pennsylvania Press.

Paunonen, S. V., Jackson, D. N., Trzebinski, J., & Forsterling, F. (1992). Personality structure across cultures: A multimethod evaluation. *Journal of Personality and Social Psychology, 62,* 447–456.

Philpot, C. L., Brooks, G. R., Lusterman, D., & Nutt, R. L. (1997). *Bridging separate worlds.* Washington, DC: American Psychological Association.

Pollack, W. S., & Levant, R. F. (1998). *New psychotherapy for men.* New York: Wiley.

Riger, S. (2000). *Transforming psychology.* New York: Oxford University Press.

Rudman, L. A., Ashmore, R. D., & Gary, M. L. (2001). "Unlearning" automatic biases: The malleability of implicit prejudice and stereotype. *Journal of Personality and Social Psychology, 81,* 856–868.

Sanders, S. R. (1987). The men we carry in our minds. In S. R. Sanders, *The paradise of bombs* (pp. 111–117). Boston: Beacon Press.

Sharf, R. S. (2002). *Applying career development theory to counseling* (3rd ed.). Pacific Grove, CA: Brooks/Cole.

Silverstein, B. (2002). Gender differences in the prevalence of somatic versus pure depression: A replication. *American Journal of Psychiatry, 159,* 1051–1052.

Tanaka-Matsumi, J., & Higginbotham, H. N. (1996). Behavioral approaches to counseling across cultures. In P. B. Pederson, J. G. Draguns, W. J. Lonner, & J. E. Trimble (Eds.), *Counseling across cultures* (4th ed., pp. 266–292). Thousand Oaks, CA: Sage.

Tavris, C. (1992). *The mismeasure of woman.* New York: Simon & Schuster.

Turk, D. C., Salovey, P., & Prentice, D. A. (1998). Psychotherapy: An information-processing perspective. In D. C. Turk & P. Salovey (Eds.), *Reasoning, inference, and judgment in clinical psychology* (pp. 1–14). New York: Free Press.

Vasquez, M. (2001). Advancing the study of Chicana/o psychology. *Counseling Psychologist, 29,* 118–127.

Vasquez, M. J. T. (2001). Reflections on unearned advantages, unearned disadvantages, and empowering experiences. In J. Ponterotto, J. M. Casas, L. A. Suzuki, & C. M. Alexander (Eds.), *Handbook of multicultural counseling* (2nd ed., pp. 64–74). Thousand Oaks, CA: Sage.

Wester, S. R., & Vogel, D. L. (2002). Working with the masculine mystique: Male gender role conflict, counseling self-efficacy, and the training of male psychologists. *Professional Psychology: Research and Practice, 33,* 370–376.

Wester, S. R., Vogel, D. L., Pressly, P. K., & Heesacker, M. (2002). Sex differences in emotion: A critical review of the literature and implications for counseling psychology. *The Counseling Psychologist, 30,* 630–652.

Wong, J. S. (1971). A Chinese evolution. In T. C. Wheeler (Ed.), *The immigrant experience* (pp. 121–124). New York: Doubleday.

Wycoff, H. (1977). *Solving women's problems through awareness, action, and contact.* New York: Grove Press.

CHAPTER **12**
Transpersonal Development

🦋 A Selection from

Going to Pieces Without Falling Apart, 1998

Mark Epstein

Psychotherapy has long been aware of the defensive nature of much of our day-to-day thinking and has striven to find ways of undermining its tenacious hold over our minds. Once Freud figured out that the purpose of so much of our thinking is to isolate us from the flow of gratifying experience, he began to see this dynamic in many of his friends and patients. Much of the liberating promise of early psychoanalysis stemmed from its attempts to cure this isolating tendency of the human mind. But scattered within Freud's writings we find references to his frustrations in actually effecting the kinds of changes he was reaching for. He thought deeply about the reasons for the self-imposed isolation of the thinking mind but had difficulty translating his insights into a method of change. While his insights were revelatory, he did not have the method of the Buddha within his grasp.

In a short, masterful, and little discussed paper written in 1915 called "On Transience," Freud reached for a fearless mental posture that unknowingly paralleled that of the Buddha while at the same time offering a parable about the limitations of his analytic method. Recounting a summer walk that he took through a "smiling countryside" with a "taciturn" friend and a "young but already famous poet," Freud described how his friends were unable to smile back at the beauty that surrounded them. They could admire the sights, he observed, but they could not feel. They were locked into their own minds, unwilling or unable to surrender to the beauty surrounding them. Like Kelly [one of Epstein's patients] on her first retreat, but without her self-awareness, they were unconsciously guarding themselves against engagement with something that might disappoint them.

"The proneness to decay of all that is beautiful and perfect can, as we know, give rise to two different impulses in the mind," wrote Freud at the beginning of this essay. "The one leads to the aching despondency felt by the young poet, while the other leads to rebellion against the fact asserted." Either we get depressed when confronted with impermanence, suggested Freud, or we devalue what we see and push it away. Just as Freud described these two possible reactions, so did the Buddha. He called them attachment and aversion, although Freud's terms of "aching despondency" and "rebellion against the facts" would have done just as well.

Only by cultivating a mind that does neither, taught the Buddha, can transience become enlightening. This is, in fact, the heart of the Buddha's teaching: that it is possible to cultivate a mind that neither clings nor rejects, and that in so doing we can alter the way in which we experience both time and our selves.

Like the Buddha, Freud did not want to yield to either of the two alternatives of attachment or aversion. He was seeking a third option but had trouble finding the words to describe what it could be. Like a Japanese Zen master whose full attention is focused on the sound of the crickets or the taste of a strawberry, Freud sought to return his friends to a more intimate and immediate experience of the moment.

"It was incomprehensible, I declared, that the thought of the transience of beauty should interfere with our joy in it. . . . A flower that blossoms only for a single night does not seem to us on that account less lovely." Yet Freud's exhortations did not move his friends. He was unable to open their senses to the beauty surrounding them. Their hearts remained closed, their minds stubbornly disconnected from their bodies, their avoidance of transience overshadowing their sights, smells, and perceptions.

Why, asked Freud, do we prevent the flow in moments such as these? Why do we hold ourselves back from contact? Why do we hold ourselves so aloof? His friends' disengagement on their summer walk obviously had all kinds of reverberations. Would they not hold themselves back from love just as they were holding themselves back from nature?

In Freud's discussion of his two friends' hard-heartedness, he had the realization that they were trying to fend off an inevitable mourning. In their obsessional way, they were isolating themselves and refusing to be touched. His description is powerful because it mirrors our refusal to embrace the transience of all that is important to us, including our own selves. To one degree or another, we are all, like his friends, in a state of abbreviated, or interrupted, mourning. Acutely aware of our own transience, we alternate between an aching despondency and a rebellion against the facts. We cling to our loved ones, or remove ourselves from them, rather than loving them in all of their vulnerability. In so doing we distance ourselves from a grief that is an inevitable component of affection. Using our best obsessional defenses to keep this mourning at bay, we pay a price in how isolated and cut off we can feel. (pp. 61–64) ■ ■

DISCUSSION IDEAS

1. What is the criticism, suggested by Freud and Epstein, of *thinking?* Why would thinking need to be cured?

2. Why were Freud's friends unable to feel the beauty of the countryside?

3. What are the two possible responses to beauty and perfection? What labels did the Buddha give these reactions? How are these reactions different from full, focused attention?

4. Epstein writes about Freud's friends: "Their hearts remained closed, their minds stubbornly disconnected from their bodies." What relationship between the mind and the body is suggested here?

5. Can you give an example of distancing yourself from an experience in order to protect yourself from "inevitable mourning"? Can you give an example from a person you know or a character in fiction or film?

6. How about feeling "isolated and cut off"? Most of us feel this way at least once in a while. For example, the phenomenon of being "lonely in a crowd" is common. What do you do when you feel this way?

Introduction to Transpersonal Approaches

In the passage above and your discussion of it, you pondered cases in which people are trapped inside themselves, personally responding so strongly that they could not enjoy nature's pleasures. **Transpersonal psychology** is just what it sounds like—an approach to the self beyond the ego and the individual personality. It includes "those deeper or higher aspects of human experience that transcend the ordinary and the average" (Wilber, 1996, xviii). Western psychology has usually focused on strengthening the ego, acting in concert with one's authentic personality, and self-actualization of the individual. But most of the world's population believes that there is a level of consciousness beyond the individual, and that ordinary people have access to a spiritual domain that transcends bodily limitations. Eastern philosophies like Buddhism, Hinduism, and Sufism are practiced by millions of people in over 100 countries. Meditation and yoga, and practices related to these, are "the most widespread and popular of all current psychotherapies" (Walsh, 2000). William James, Carl Jung, Erik Erikson, and Abraham Maslow all concurred that there exists a state of awareness beyond the ego-centered norm. The position that put Jung outside of traditional Freudian psychodynamics (see Chapter 4) was his belief in the unconscious as a reservoir of symbolic wisdom from the history of human experience (Goud, 2001), not an intrapsychic battleground. And Maslow was the founder of Western *transpersonal psychology*, calling it the fourth force of psychology, with the first three forces being behaviorist, psychoanalytic, and humanistic approaches. Transpersonal psychologists share with many other theorists the idea that there is an inborn drive toward positive growth in each of us; the difference is that transpersonal approaches take that growth into a further spiritual realm.

Essential Concepts of Transpersonal Approaches

Belief in an unusually broad psychological range of experience is fundamental to transpersonal approaches.

Focus on Spiritual Experience

Throughout transpersonal therapy, the counselor focuses on spiritual experience instead of individual pathology. The theory is that wider aspects of humankind, life, psyche, and the world have healing properties of their own. Self-transcendence is a natural motive for humans. We can see evidence of this in the way that almost everyone has a feeling for nature and an instinct to seek nature as a restorative setting. Other drives may be substitutes for the ego-transcendence, a need that is possibly as great as the needs for safety, power, and social contact. "We may need the good, the true, and the beautiful if we are to thrive; we may need to express kindness, care, and compassion if we are to live fully" (Walsh, 2000, p. 420). While Western approaches to psychotherapy develop many methods for reducing negative emotions, many methods of enhancing the positive emotions are theoretically underdeveloped and underused in practice. Students of counseling, usually well versed in cognitive and behavioral systems, often see themselves "searching for more holistic and expansive ideas about the human psyche that better fit the totality of their own experiences and those of their clients" (Russell-Chapin & Rybak, 1996, p. 171).

Maslow (1976) was particularly interested in **peak experiences,** which are moments of deep inspiration, spiritual intensification, wonder, and ecstasy set clearly apart from ordinary life. These provide us with glimpses of **transcendental reality.** Though enraptured peak experiences are rare, milder forms of such episodes occur in most people's lives.

A Higher Reality

Eastern approaches are based on a belief that a higher reality binds together all phenomena. In contrast, traditional Western psychology elevates the autonomy of each person and a clear sense of boundaries between self and others and physical settings. Meditation and yoga, two techniques I will describe in this chapter, encourage awareness of a connection among all forms of life. Furthermore, there is an inherent unity in this connection: Everything fits together into One when you achieve the proper perspective. The interdependent-network idea of systems psychology (Chapter 10) comes closer to Eastern thought than individual psychologies do.

Realms Beyond Ego

Through transcendence, peak experiences, higher awareness, meditative insight, energy flow, and processes like these, we can return to the greater Self or Oneness. Western psychology usually stops at the stage of the mature, well-defended ego; in Asian thought, the next stage is transcendence of that ego into a larger **Self** (capitalized to differentiate the term from the ego-defined individual self). This requires a shift of consciousness that is powerful and positive. Self-preoccupation, self-attachment, and self-passion are traps that create psychological uneasiness. Waking consciousness is suspect, limited, superficial, underdeveloped, and undercontrolled. Our minds are usually clouded with thoughts, images, and fantasies that distort reality. "The result is said to be an encompassing, illusory distortion of experience that remains unrecognized until we subject our perceptual-cognitive processes to direct, rigorous scrutiny, as in meditation" (Walsh, 2000, p. 417). In Western terminology, these distortions might be called neuroses, psychoses, disturbed object relations, stuckness, splitting, irrational beliefs, and automatic thoughts. Table 12.1 summarizes a different point of view.

Enlightenment is waking from the dream of life. Transpersonal counselors believe that the mind can be trained in compassion, insight, and joy. Wilber (1993a) suggests that transpersonal experience may be truly cross-cultural, not

TABLE 12.1
The Four Noble Truths

Disease	Bad states of mind
Aetiology (source of disease)	Craving, attachment, aversion/avoidance, selfishness
Prognosis	A cure is possible, but not easy
Remedy	Ethics, moral discipline Pure mind, tranquil absorption Wisdom: seeing through false pretenses; practicing generosity, loving words, good will, compassion

SOURCE: Adapted from Brazier (1995), p. 19.

constrained by the controlling beliefs and language of any single culture: "A diamond will cut a piece of glass, no matter what words we use for 'diamond,' 'cut,' and 'glass'—and a soul can experience God, no matter what words we use for 'soul,' 'experience,' and 'God'" (p. 25).

SMALL GROUP EXERCISE

Each member should take some time to think about the three remedies listed in Table 12.1: ethics, pure mind, and wisdom. Try to think of a person you know who exemplifies one of these remedies. Describe this person to your group. Are there any fictional characters who come to mind as examples?

If you had to choose among the three remedies you would pursue, which one would it be? Why? Did you choose something that is already a strength of yours, or something that would address a current weakness?

Think of a client, student, or someone you have tried to help lately. How might these remedies apply to that person's situation?

Emphasis on Change

While many Western personality theories seek to identify our stable traits and habits, the Eastern point of view is that we are at any moment a shifting collection of impressions, thoughts, images, and emotions constantly in flux. Change, not stability, is the theme. "The self-concept and its boundaries are then increasingly recognized as constructed rather than given, fluid rather than rigid, and capable of considerable expansion" (Walsh, 2000, p. 418). This point of view is attractive to us as helping professionals, because it suggests that there are no hopeless cases, not even violent criminals and sociopaths.

In terms of developmental levels and stages, there is a deeper wisdom past what we usually call maturity in adults. Allport (1955) asserted that a mark of positively advancing maturity was "the extent of one's feeling of self-involvement in abstract ideals" (p. 45). Maslow suggested that beyond physiological needs, security and dependency needs, and belonging and self-esteem needs, there exist **being-needs,** including needs for "creativity, beauty, simplicity, connection, meaning, service, advancement of knowledge, and society's improvement" (Battista, 1996a). Pre-ego infancy is followed by a coherent sense of self and setting (ego strength), and then transpersonal growth lies beyond. The developmental point of view refutes a common misconception, which is that spiritual growth is an *alternative* to ego strength. In actuality, ego strength is valued in Eastern wisdom; it is deemed necessary for further growth toward enlightenment.

Altered States of Consciousness

Altered states of consciousness are sought as part of healthy human growth. Many people experience transient states of altered awareness—near death; with rituals, fasting, and drugs; in nature; amidst great beauty; during sex; in childbirth (Walsh, 2000). While many Westerners think of these states as hallucinations or neurological side effects, transpersonal thinkers see them as glimpses into another reality, more true in many ways than everyday consciousness.

The Process of Therapy

The process of transpersonal growth has been described metaphorically as "transforming of a caterpillar into a butterfly; awakening from a dream to reality; moving from captivity to liberation; going from darkness to light; being purified by inner fire; going from fragmentation to wholeness; journeying to a place of vision and power; returning to the source; and dying and being reborn" (Fadiman & Frager, 2002, p. 454). Other descriptions of the process include awakening from a trance, freeing self from illusions, purifying the mind, unfolding potentials, uncovering true identity, and being enlightened (Walsh, 2000).

Slow, Cumulative Practice

Most practices that lead to ego transcendence are done on a daily basis, starting with the simplest tasks and working up to more demanding levels over time. Higher levels are more demanding and intense. Like any skill, these practices are initially not very rewarding and may be frustrating, so a person has to start with commitment and with belief that the system will eventually help. This part of the process is not too different from anything that you ask your client to do outside of sessions, such as daily monitoring or homework. However, many clients may view meditative or yoga exercises as too weird and unrelated to their real-life problems. Since you will probably be using Eastern practices in a treatment that integrates several approaches, you can present them as ways to make other interventions more effective, using metaphors such as a seed falling on fertilized soil. These practices are often relaxing, and most people accept relaxation as a valid psychological tool.

Healing of Dichotomies

Growth is the healing of a series of **dichotomies** within the individual—persona and shadow, mind and body, organism and environment. Many of the theories you have studied in this textbook acknowledge the psychological dangers of exaggerating polarities like dependence and freedom, male and female, and active and passive. In Eastern thought, these polarities are just part of language, which is not the same as reality. True consciousness sees the unity of things that are apparently opposite in our language and everyday thinking.

Another form of healing is **disidentification,** in which a person learns that emotions and thoughts are not as compelling as they may seem. Like language, they are connected to reality but don't control it. In disidentification, you learn to say to yourself, "This is my emotion, but *I* am not my emotion. This is my thought, but *I* am not my thought." In such a manner, you can stop struggling against your emotions or thoughts and refuse to let them define you completely. Disidentification is very important to approaches like Linehan's therapy for borderline clients who habitually are overwhelmed by emotional storms (see Chapter 9).

Finally, the transpersonal process seeks to balance movement and stillness. Effort, investigation, and ecstasy are part of the process, but achievement- and excitement-oriented Westerners also need to treasure concentration, calm, and equanimity.

Reflection

Think of the last time you experienced a strong negative or uncomfortable emotion. What if you had said to yourself, "This is my emotion, but *I* am not my emotion"? Do you think it would have made a difference? Do you think you would be able to benefit from disidentification practice?

Stabilization

Transpersonal theorists often think of therapeutic process along developmental lines. In a troubled person, some positive press toward health has been blocked, even though this positive movement is our natural tendency. The blockage usually involves negative habits of mind that distort perceptions and trap people inside their individual selves. Walsh (2000) summarizes the levels as starting with the recognition of mental disarray and lack of discipline, and ending (for some practitioners) with stabilization—in which "altered states become altered traits, peak experiences merge into plateau experiences, and temporary transpersonal experiences stabilize into enduring transpersonal stages of development" (p. 428).

The Therapeutic Relationship

Describing the role of the therapist in transpersonal counseling, Walsh and Vaughan (1993, p. 154) quote from Eastern philosophy:

> To straighten the crooked
> You must first do a harder thing—
> Straighten yourself.

If you intend to use meditation, yoga, and even exercise in treating clients, you should be a practitioner yourself. It's widely agreed that being able to speak from experience helps you persuade clients that these practices are worthwhile. Furthermore, the essence of the practices is much more experiential than verbal, so your understanding is incomplete if you just read about it.

Meditation and yoga are usually undertaken under the supervision of a teacher. You can find instruction almost anywhere in the United States, even in small towns. The functions of an instructor or guide include providing suggestions to make your efforts more effective, to deal with distractions, to sustain your motivation, and to provide support and interpretation for the feelings that surface as you go along (Fontana, 1999). You will serve these functions for your clients, and you may want them to add the assistance of a class given in the community. You will also serve as a traditional counselor, in that you will discuss the client's insights and experiences as they relate to her or his presenting problems.

Many people learn meditation and yoga on their own, working with the guidance of self-help books. I found that there is a huge array of these, and it took me an hour at the bookstore to choose one that seemed right for my understanding and preferences in style. Though some purists may say that you cannot learn from a book, thousands of people have benefited from doing so. Of course, reading the book is not enough; as I noted earlier, it is only a supplement to the actual practice. Reading, by itself, would be ineffective, just as reading about dieting will not make you lose weight. Self-regulation and self-control are so critical to these pursuits that people who are able to go it alone seem quite capable of being their own gurus (spiritual guides).

Meditation, yoga, and exercise practices can be taught to groups in a few sessions and are cost-effective—two advantages over conventional psychological interventions. Because of these advantages, the Eastern ways may take on more prominence in the Western world for preventive as well as curative purposes, which they already serve in most of the world.

Customary Techniques of Transpersonal Therapy

In 1910, William James wrote: "The faculty of voluntarily bringing back a wandering attention over and over again is the very root of judgment, character, and will." Read that statement again. It's a broad, extreme claim. In one of the early levels of meditation, you realize that your control over your **attention** is not well developed at all. Indeed, Eastern techniques are used to develop the discipline of attention. Like a muscle, **concentration** strengthens with use, and these techniques are essentially exercise routines from expert personal trainers.

SMALL GROUP EXERCISE

Discuss your own experiences of "wandering attention." Under what circumstances does it usually happen to each of you? Are the conditions more often outer (something in the setting) or inner (something within yourself)? For example, when my parents were dying, I found it difficult to pay attention to some activities that usually engaged me fully, such as conversations with my colleagues. However, my worries left my mind when I was teaching a class.

How would your life improve if you had good control over your attention? If you know anyone with an attention deficit, tell your group how the condition affects this person's life.

Meditation

"Zen Buddhism is based on the practice of meditation as a means of directly experiencing the principles and truths of Buddhism—that is, the experience of 'enlightenment'" (Fadiman & Frager, 2002, p. 502). Each of us is capable of a direct, personal understanding of Truth. Buddhism comprises many different schools, which emphasize different aspects of enlightenment. Two major ones are *sayana*, emphasizing compassion, and *Theraveda*, emphasizing self-discipline. Many people think of Buddhism as other-worldly and supernatural. But as you can tell from these emphases, that is far from the truth. How you behave in everyday life is extremely important in major schools of Buddhism. Notice in Table 12.1 that almost all of the remedies for human unease are practices performed in the everyday world. As such, they link Eastern thought with Western, such as Adler's prescriptions for altruistic service and Erikson's idea of generativity (i.e., conveying a legacy to others, as a strength of mature age). Our behavior has an effect on the world and ourselves: **Karma** is the psychological residue left by past behavior. The consequences of our thoughts and action are the aspects of our individual selves that go on forever. (In Buddhist spiritual thought, there are no immortal souls.) In Eastern systems, daily life and activity should be brought into harmony with ideals, and meditative awareness into all daily activities.

Dr. Herbert Benson (1975) of Harvard Medical School and the Mind Body Institute in Cambridge developed a technique for evoking the **relaxation response,** a variant of meditation that can be tailored to a client's beliefs and preferences. The relaxation response can be practiced through traditional meditation, prayer, progressive muscle relaxation, jogging, swimming, Lamaze breathing, yoga, tai chi, and even knitting and crocheting. Benson's program includes repetition, during these activities, of a personally meaningful word or phrase, awareness of breath, and focused attention. The program has been successfully applied to chronic pain, anxiety, depression, anger, insomnia, PMS, headaches, and work and school performance.

In meditation, people learn to control their attention, concentrate fully, reject distraction, and perceive clearly. The experienced meditator can reduce harmful thoughts and increase positive ones, and is able to stop thoughts at will (Walsh, 2000). Because the mind takes on the qualities of whatever it attends, meditators are encouraged to attend to people who are kind, generous, and wise, and to images that are peaceful and natural. When you look at meditation and yoga books at the store, you will find none that are purely print: Beautiful images interpenetrate the written passages. Meditators can also use *disidentification,* a form of controlled attention that I discussed earlier. Through disidentification, they are able to observe their emotions from a calm distance: "As the student becomes more aware of emotional reactions to various situations, the emotions tend to lose their hold" (Fadiman & Frager, 2002, p. 523). Furthermore, "when we recognize our own suffering, or dissatisfaction, the Buddha in us will look at it, discover what has brought it about, and prescribe a course of action that can transform it into peace, joy, and liberation" (Fadiman & Frager, p. 503). In this sense, each client has a self-adjusting mechanism that will act as his or her inner counselor when meditative awareness is achieved. Mental unease is the product of **delusions** (false pretenses), **craving** (attachment to positive stimuli), and **aversion** (avoidance of negative stimuli) intensified out of control. But this out-of-controlness is a transient state that can give way under the power of disidentification. People can accept the world as it is without experiencing disappointment or anger. In a process very much like cognitive reframing, "the problem doesn't change, but one's attitude toward it and the way one copes with it do" (p. 507).

Think about an example from our own professional world. My friend Paula counsels victims of domestic abuse all day. Around five years into her career, she began to view men on the street, and even men she knew, as dangerous and controlling. She was not able to accept dates because she was afraid of men, given what she heard about over and over at work. When Paula meditated on this problem, she took the feeling of fear as an object and observed it. The images that appeared to her revealed what she attended to, which was the violence of men, and showed that she rarely attended to men who were not scary or weird. Her next assignments to herself were to meditate as vividly as possible upon men she knew, and male fictional characters, who were gentle and peaceful. This practice influenced her daily life by adjusting for the unbalanced view her work had created. While the problem of male violence did not change, it became different to Paula.

Breathing

"Learning to pay attention to the breath is the beginning of meditation. It is a means of noticing that we are alive, calming ourselves and returning to the here and now" (Brazier, 1995, p. 67). David Fontana, a well-known meditation teacher, explains the connection between mental control and breathing in the following passage.

"CONCENTRATION AND BREATHING"

Owing to its fundamental importance to meditation, we need now to go more deeply into what is meant by concentration and how it is achieved. By concentration we do not mean the fierce, browbeating intense mental effort that was sometimes demanded of us when mastering lessons at school. In meditation, concentration is far more subtle. The mind rests lightly, but pleasantly and clearly, upon the point of focus. When it strays, it is gently brought back to this point of focus, without irritation or frustration. Negative responses such as irritation and frustration only discourage the mind from reminding us when our attention wanders in the future. After all, why should the mind remind us when all it gets for its pains is our anger? Instead, we should feel gratitude toward the mind for its help. Beginners often say that the mind becomes bored when concentrating on only one thing. Just so—and this is precisely why it wanders off, like a child with a short attention span who is constantly seeking something new.

But as concentration develops, this boredom passes and is replaced by a realization of what can be described as the qualitative experience of life itself. Although we experience what it is to be alive at each waking moment from the day we are born, how often do we pause in order to contemplate what this wonderful experience of life actually is? How often do we stop being distracted by mental chatter and by the world that is outside our heads, and abide instead in the pure experience of just being? Sometimes called *content-less awareness* or *suchness*, this experience of pure being is a taste of the mental state from which all our other mental states arise, a brief glimpse of the very ground of our own nature.

For regular meditation practice, the breath is typically used as the point upon which to remain focussed while our chattering minds are busy trying to distract us. Even when [we are] using various other techniques . . . , it is usual to spend the first few minutes of each session watching the breath, and allowing the mind to become peaceful and still. Use of the breath for this purpose has many advantages. For example, the breath is always with us, so that we can turn to it not only during our meditation sessions but whenever we wish to calm ourselves during the day. In addition, the breath follows a gentle rhythm of inhalation and exhalation, which in itself helps to bring a state of peaceful awareness—and if we notice that the breath is shallow or unnecessarily rapid, the very act of deepening it and slowing it down helps to relax and centre ourselves. Above all, concentration upon the breath brings us into direct contact with the moment-by-moment process upon which our very lives depend. The breath has always been linked in the great traditions with the spirit—the invisible, indwelling essence that symbolizes the non-material nature of our true self. (1999, pp. 58–59)

Attention to breathing is an easy technique, widely applicable in many settings and with many clients. Pam Hoggins, a child and family therapist in Denver, uses breathing techniques with troubled children: "When I teach kids deep breathing, I present it as a way to 'clean out the hurt [or anger, or bad thoughts]. In through the nose, out through the mouth, and concentrate on feeling the bad things flow away.' I think just practicing the routine helps them get centered and calmed down, and a little magical thinking helps everyone from time to time. I have used the technique with my own kids and grandchildren for years, for everything from upset feelings to dentist-office trauma to childbirth, and it has always helped" (personal communication, October 2002).

Breathing exercises are basic to both meditation and yoga. Think about it: Breathing is necessary to bodily and mental functioning, and the breath is a constant interchange between inner and outer worlds. A meditation exercise offered by Zen master Nhat Hanh (quoted in Brazier, 1995, p. 106) exemplifies the purpose behind conscious breathing:

Breathing in, I calm my body.
Breathing out, I smile.
Breathing in, I dwell in the present moment.
Breathing out, I know it is a wonderful moment.

R e f l e c t i o n

Try the following technique from yoga for meditative deep breathing. It's called *north-south breathing*. Have paper and pencil ready to use when you're done.

1. Close your eyes, or focus your vision on a candle flame.
2. Block off the right nostril with your thumb. Inhale deeply and slowly through the left nostril.
3. Now let go of the right nostril and block off the left nostril with your thumb. Breathe slowly out through the right nostril.
4. As you breathe in and out, visualize the air you breathe as a cleansing breeze, energy, or light.

5. For the next breath, reverse the order: Breathe in through the right nostril and out through the left.
6. Repeat the process twelve times.

As soon as you are done, focus on the paper and write about your experience. Describe how you felt during the north-south breathing. Did you get a glimpse of why it might be useful psychologically?

Yoga

Yoga comes from the Hindu spiritual tradition. Its basic aim is to strengthen innate positive subconscious tendencies that will defeat negative tendencies. This is done through a regimen of prescribed exercises that combine physical and mental directives. The regimen releases, purifies, and strengthens **vital energy,** thereby uniting the physical world and consciousness.

Most of the yoga practiced in the United States is **hatha-yoga,** which emphasizes cultivating the body, the vehicle of vital energies (**pranas**), in order to facilitate advanced meditation and higher states of consciousness. A series of postures known as **asanas** are performed daily; these postures limber the body, exercise the spine, stimulate nerves and organs, manipulate blood flow, vary pressure on body parts, and increase breathing capacity. Different postures are combined and sequenced to ensure balanced stimulation of the whole body. The asana you have seen depicted most often is the lotus posture or *sukhasana,* a crossed-leg seated pose with hands on knees, palms up, index fingers and thumbs touching. Strengthening and mobilizing vital energy leads to reformation of the psyche. The asanas are components of a system that also includes healthy diet, breathing exercises, and mental concentration.

Below is another example of an asana: the mountain pose, or *tadasana.*

MOUNTAIN/TADASANA

Mountain pose is the foundation for all of the standing postures and improves posture, groundedness, stability, and confidence.

1. From a standing position, bring the feet hip width apart, parallel; lift up the toes, spread them wide and place them back on the floor. Feel your weight evenly balanced through the bottom of each foot, not leaning forward or back.
2. Pull up the knee caps, squeeze the thighs and tuck the tailbone under. The legs are straight, but the knees are not locked back.
3. Inhale and lift out of the waist, pressing the crown of the head up toward the ceiling, feeling the spine long and straight.

4. Exhale and drop the shoulders down and back. Gently press the chest/sternum toward the front of the room.
5. Reach the fingers down toward the floor to lengthen the arms. Inhale the arms up, turning the palms at shoulder height, bringing the arms into a raised H position.
6. Exhale; relax the shoulders down from the ears while still reaching the crown and fingers up.
7. Breathe and hold for 4–8 breaths.
8. To release, exhale the arms down to your sides or bring the palms together in front of your chest.

Source: Timothy Burgin & yogaclass.com (2000).

Raja-yoga is the branch concerned with mental control, which appears similar to Buddhist meditation and other forms of meditation. The breath is a focus of concentration in early yoga practice, and later you learn to concentrate on a single thought. As Fadiman and Frager (2002) point out, "The path of Yoga is basically the process of turning the consciousness away from the activities of the external world back to the source of consciousness—the Self" (p. 487). In both the Hindu and Buddhist systems, over-concern with external settings, situations, and reactions to them is a barrier to deeper awareness. Mental calm is achieved through meditation practice, holding the body motionless in asanas, and periods of discipline such as fasting and silence.

The philosophy of yoga includes **karma-yoga,** the idea that our actions have inner as well as outer effects, that good actions transform us into good people. Acting unselfishly, following ethical principles, and taking worldly responsibilities seriously are ideals to balance with spiritual discipline. Such a philosophy is completely consonant with many other religious points of view, such as Christianity and Judaism.

Below is a sample of instructions from *www.yogabasics.com,* a website where you can find much more about asanas, principles, and meditation.

YOGIC MEDITATION

Sit in a comfortable position, either cross-legged on the floor or in a chair. Sit up tall with the spine straight, the shoulders relaxed and the chest open. Rest the hands on the knees with the palms facing up. Lightly touch the index finger to the thumb. Relax the face, jaw, and belly. Let the tongue rest on the roof of the mouth, just behind the front teeth. Allow the eyes to lightly close.

Breathe slowly, smoothly and deeply in and out through the nose. Let the inhale start in the belly and then rise gently up into the chest. As the breath slows and deepens, let go of any thoughts or distractions and allow the mind to focus on the breath. Feel the breath as it moves in and out of the body, feeling it move through the nose, throat, windpipe and lungs. Feel the body as it rises and falls with each breath. Bring as much of your awareness and attention to your body and breath as possible with each moment. As the thoughts return to the mind, let them go, and return the focus back to the body and breath.

Practice this meditation for 10–20 minutes. To end, gently let the eyes blink open, inhale the palms together in front of the heart, exhale and gently bow. Take a moment or two before moving on with the rest of your day. (copyright 2001–2002 Timothy Burgin & yogaclass.com)

Source: Timothy Burgin & yogaclass.com (2000).

Profile of a Theorist

TIMOTHY LEARY (1920–1996)

Timothy Leary was born in 1920 in Massachusetts to Irish Catholic parents from dramatically different backgrounds. He described his mother's family as traditional and "suspicious of all things joyous" while he claimed his father's family to be "sexy, fun-loving, and self-oriented." Though his family promoted his education in traditional settings, he also received a strong message to challenge convention and think for himself. His father left the family when Timothy was an adolescent, but rather than harboring resentment toward him, Timothy often cited his father's courage in finding his own way.

Timothy was accepted to West Point, but was disciplined for his role in an alcohol-related incident during his first year. As punishment, the Honor Committee dictated that he be ignored by his peers. The social isolation took a toll on Leary, and he left West Point, but not before negotiating his own exoneration, foreshadowing a pattern that would play out again in later years.

Following expulsion from the University of Alabama, Leary lost his deferment from military service and was sent to basic training. Because the military needed psychologists, Timothy was able to finish his degree in the service.

In 1944, Timothy married and moved to Berkeley, California, where he completed his doctorate in psychology. By the mid-1950s, he was teaching and serving as the director of Psychological Research for the Kaiser Foundation. Publication of his book *Interpersonal Diagnosis of Personality* established him as a primary figure in the development of interpersonal theory, along with Harry Stack Sullivan and George Herbert Mead. Leary's work lent empirical support to the fundamental tenets of the theory, most notably the principle of *circumplex structure*, which posits that variables that measure interpersonal relations can be arranged around a circle in two-dimensional space. His model encouraged practical application of interpersonal theory in both academic and clinical settings.

Leary's theory of *existential transaction* represented a departure from traditional therapy by suggesting that the relationship between patient and therapist should be an egalitarian exchange of information. In 1960, the director of the Harvard Center for Personality Research was impressed by Leary's new way of conceptualizing therapy and convinced him to teach at Harvard. While on vacation in Cuernavaca, Leary had his first experience with psychedelic substances and subsequently began a program of research with graduate students to explore the effects and therapeutic potential of LSD on the human brain. Encouraged by positive findings, Leary conducted another study on prison inmates and achieved even more remarkable results. However, due to the growing concern over illicit drug use, LSD was made illegal and Leary's experiments came to an abrupt halt. Lacking the necessary support from Harvard, Leary left the university to pursue his studies with private funding. The controversy over his use and promotion of LSD grew exponentially and he was eventually arrested on drug charges. Following a dramatic escape from prison in 1970, Leary sought asylum in Switzerland but was ultimately extradited to the United States and sent back to prison until 1976.

During the last two decades of the twentieth century, Leary's interests turned to the information revolution, which he believed represented as radical a break from conventional thinking as psychedelic drugs had in the 1960s. Throughout his eventful life, Leary consistently billed himself as a philosopher and scientist whose aim was to "enliven the human spirit and raise the level of social consciousness." Though many have criticized his methods, his empirical studies and bold challenges to conventional approaches continue to inform the field of psychotherapy. Leary died of prostate cancer in 1996.

Psychedelic Drugs

Spirit travels—also known as soul flights or soul journeys—have been used by shamans (spiritual healers) to enhance sensitivity to intuitive wisdom, probably for over 3,000 years (Walsh, 1996). After training and preparation, the shaman or the followers, or both, ingest naturally occurring psychoactive substances that send them into altered states of consciousness. In these states, assisted by rituals such as drumming, dancing, and chanting, visions arrive that allow the participants to receive supernatural guidance and insight. The drugs are used only for healing and sacred purposes (Walsh, 2000).

In the United States, psychedelic therapy in the 1950s and 1960s (until its criminalization) made use of the ego-dissolving experience as an adjunct to structured therapy (Bravo & Grob, 1996). Harvard psychologists Timothy Leary and Ram Dass (Richard Alpert) led research programs to investigate the effects of psychedelic drugs such as psilocybin and LSD (lysergic acid). Their experiences quickly led them to abhor conventional academic structures, and the feeling was mutual. Each of them continued mystical pursuits outside of established Western institutions. Ram Dass has published a series of widely read, influential books including *Be Here Now* (1971) and the recent *Still Here: Embracing Aging, Changing, and Dying* (2001).

In a report of seventeen years of clinical research on LSD and its therapeutic use, Stanislav Grof (1993) concluded that "LSD appeared to be a powerful catalyst of the mental processes activating unconscious material from various deep levels of the personality" (p. 96). This partly accounted for his observation of huge differences in individual responses to the drug. However, a common response was "a temporary or enduring feeling that the individual has achieved a global, nonrational, and transrational understanding of the basic . . . problems that beset existence" (p. 105), which describes spiritual or mystical experiences deriving from religion, meditation, indigenous healing practices, and rites of passage. A famous experiment took place at Harvard in 1962, when Walter Pahnke and colleagues gave twenty graduate students either psilocybin or a placebo before Good Friday chapel services. The psilocybin group's reports fit a typology of mystical experience to a significantly greater extent than the placebo group's. Most notably, twenty-five years later the psilocybin subjects still felt that the 1962 experience had genuinely mystical elements and was uniquely valuable to their spiritual lives (Bravo & Grob, 1996).

Experimentation with psychedelics left the laboratory and became associated with wild, rebellious youth in the 1960s and 1970s. The possession of psychedelics was outlawed in 1966; illicit distribution continued with the usual drawbacks of criminal drug dealing, such as pollution of the substances, misrepresentation, and the involvement of dealers not motivated by spiritual goals. Today, shamanic drug use in its spiritual healing form is employed in Siberia and Latin America (Walsh, 1996).

Mindfulness

Mindfulness is an aspect of meditation and yoga, but I want you to consider it separately because it is something of value to you and your clients whether you embrace transpersonal approaches or not. Mindfulness can add joy to your life on an everyday basis, which is psychologically good for all of us.

Once when I was waiting for a friend in a hotel lobby, I looked over the newsstand. On the cover of a popular women's magazine, "The Secret of Happiness" was emblazoned as a preview of an article inside. This just tickled me greatly, to think that the secret of happiness was available in a slick magazine at the Dallas Hyatt while people were fasting and trekking across Tibet to find it. I had to buy the magazine and discover the secret. It was there. The article described the knack of living in the moment, without letting preoccupations about the past, or plans and worries about the future, cloud the enjoyment of little pleasures in the immediate present. I looked around the lobby with its beautiful decor, felt the comfort of my plush chair, noticed the subtle lighting and soft music, admired the fashionable clothes of passers-by. Giving up my irritation that my friend was late and my nervousness about a paper I would be giving in the morning, I was happy.

Happiness rarely occurs in huge, lengthy, unadulterated chunks. For the most part it comes in moments that pass by quickly and will go unnoticed without the practice of **mindfulness**—full involvement in the experience of the here-and-now. Linehan (see Chapter 9) uses mindfulness practices to help clients with borderline personality disorder soothe themselves. Enjoying the newness and novelty of each moment of experience often involves heightened sensory awareness. For a long time, I joked that ironing was my meditation form, but I'm not sure that's a joke. I immerse myself in the warmth coming up from the board, the fresh smell of clean clothes, the gentle hiss of the steam, and put thoughts of what comes before and after the moment out of my mind.

Mindfulness can also be practiced through immersion in the emotions of the moment, without a need for acting on them or suppressing them. A psychotherapist explains the value of emotional mindfulness:

> The most basic fear experienced by people coming to see me for therapy is of being overwhelmed by the force of their own emotions if they relax the grip of their egos. They fear that if they give up control, they will lose control, that their unconscious will, if given a chance, rise up and inundate them. In some way, this reflects the classic view of the unconscious as a seething cauldron of demonic forces that have to be tamed by the light of reason and analysis. While respecting the power and complexity of the Freudian unconscious, my Buddhist understanding has made me suspicious of my patients' fears. It is my experience that emotions, no matter how powerful, are not overwhelming if given room to breathe. Contained within the vastness of awareness, our emotions have the power to connect us with each other rather than driving us apart. Mindfulness can serve as a vehicle for desensitizing ourselves to our fears of our own feelings, breaking down the self-imposed barriers that keep us at a distance, not just from each other, but from ourselves. (Epstein, 1998, p. 111)

Physical Exercise

You may not immediately think of exercise in a category with meditation and yoga, but most regular exercisers will see the similarity immediately. The use of exercise to maximize psychological health is well documented in personal narratives, case studies, and research reports (Burbank & Riebe, 2002; Chung & Baird, 1999). Eastern philosophies reject the strict division between the mind and body, and the relation between improved quality of life and physical fitness is inarguable, markedly among older adults (Riebe, Burbank, & Garber, 2002). Cardiovascular and respiratory fitness, strength, flexibility, and balance, as well as relief of depression, improved general outlook, and sharper cognitive function are goals of exercise training (Burbank, Padula, & Hirsch, 2002) that fit well with the yogic ideal. In empirical studies, no controlled study has *ever* found exercise ineffective as a primary or added treatment for mild to moderate depression, and it is four to five times more cost effective than traditional treatments (Tkachuk & Martin, 1999). Exercise may have its effect partly through the pathway of an alteration in cognitive processes, "a fresh perspective that combines the linear and the intuitive" (Hays, 1995, p. 34). This description also fits a perspective that comes about with meditation.

Interest in the holistic view of mind/body interactions is evident in behavioral health fields today, as well as in the general population. The idea that patients with certain personality characteristics and frames of mind (for example, optimistic versus pessimistic) respond better or worse to medical treatment was an early precursor to today's investigations into similar connections. In the expanded holistic view of healing, biochemical changes correspond to psychological changes (Buffone, 1984) and cause-effect relations between the two are interwoven. Psychological theories for the positive effects of exercise include improvements in self-mastery, ability to distance from negative thoughts and emotions, and immersion in pleasant activities (that is, attending to the positive) (Tkachuk & Martin, 1999).

Furthermore, descriptions of altered states of consciousness from long-term exercisers and meditators are remarkably similar, as you can tell from the following account by a runner (quoted in Sachs, 1984):

> This occurred in the midst of the APA 1977 San Francisco convention—got up early one morning and caught a bus to Golden Gate Park and began what I'd expected to be a fairly typical, 6 mi. run. I ran from the main gate of the park a couple of miles to the "end" of the park and turned around to return. As I was running back, I suddenly became aware of the environment in an unusual way—the sun and shade and trees and grass and sky were becoming part of me, or better yet—me part of them. My awareness and sensitivity took a quantum leap into a place I'd never been before.
>
> The next sensation was one that I hope to have again because it was incredible. There was an incredibly strong sense that my whole life was leading up to that very moment—all the anguish, all the joy, all the work—everything—had been pointing me toward being there, at that time, running. About the time that I grasped the past and present, the future began unfolding—no specifics but a sense of flow, a sense of me in time and space that went beyond that moment into a future. It was both awesome and comfortable, reassuring.
>
> I kept running the whole time and found myself deviating from a straight path to run to a tree that seemed to reach out to me. There were squirrels and rabbits and birds everywhere, and they also seemed tuned in to me in a way I'd never experienced before. There must be a word for that but I don't know what it is.
>
> The final piece of this that I remember acutely is that my mother was there. She was just there. A strong sense of her presence. I knew she knew what I was doing and experienced it with me. I don't often think about my mother any more—she died in 1956.
>
> As I reached the top of the park, I jogged into a Japanese garden, sat on a rock and wept uncontrollably. As I wept, all the strong sensations began fading and I returned to "normal." I started to run back to the bus stop and, filled with

unbelievable energy, I couldn't stop running and ran all the way back to the hotel at Union Square. (pp. 279–280)

Peak experiences like the one described may be uncommon when clients practice meditation, yoga, or exercise for psychological benefits, which usually involve less strenuous efforts.

Encouraging physical exercise as an adjunct to therapy can sound reasonable to most clients, and your skills in behavior management equip you to help with maintenance of an exercise plan. Additionally, including exercise as part of treatment makes it very clear that the clients are expected to participate actively in their therapy (Buffone, 1984). Some clients, particularly adolescents, discount the power of mere talk and may respond better to an organized exercise program than to traditional verbal counseling. The same could be said of senior citizens who believe that psychology is hocus-pocus or that it is embarrassing to see a counselor.

Constructive Living

The Japanese therapeutic systems, Morita and Naikan, constitute the **constructive living** approaches. These therapies came to the United States after World War II. As their name suggests, constructive living systems are active programs of personal development, and practitioners usually do not call them therapies. The guide is a teacher, and the person who seeks help is a student.

Morita Therapy   **Morita therapy** was designed for a certain type of Japanese client who suffered from *shinkeishitsu-sho*, a disorder that in old Western terms would be referred to as *neurasthenia*, characterized by worry, nervousness, fears, psychosomatic pain, perfectionism, and self-criticism (Ishiyama, 1988). The theory of Morita, developed from both Western and Eastern sources, is that crippling self-preoccupation can be replaced with preoccupation with purposes and behavior toward those purposes (Reynolds, 1976). Clients are taught to experience their neurotic symptoms and, instead of struggling with them, to accept them and keep proceeding toward goals anyway by performing small life tasks, eventually moving on to larger ones. In residential Morita therapy, clients live an extremely structured life of bedrest, boredom, and work, punctuated by journal writing, reading teacher feedback on the journal, group discussion, and graduated task assignments. Their daily lives are stripped down to bare necessities and then built up with more activities, and their appreciation for small accomplishments and amusements blossoms. Morita techniques are also applied in nonresidential talk therapy settings, with similar structured activities and attention to purposeful action. In the cognitive-behavioral tradition, Moritists believe that "our behavior remains within our control no matter what we are feeling, so it is in the realm of behavior that we can effectively take responsibility and bring about improvements in our lives. And what we do may indirectly affect what we feel" (Reynolds, 1989). The following excerpts from a personal account of a Morita student capture an American's experience of the approach:

Over the next few weeks I became more active, more organized, more detailed and more thorough. Being more conscious of details, I improved the quality of my work. I became more productive because I didn't wait to feel like doing something before I did it. It wasn't that I didn't want to be busy or do excellent work before, not at all; it is just that I didn't know how to sustain my best efforts because my emotions were interfering. . . . Morita guidance helped teach me to keep my eye on the ball, to observe what was in front of me and to remember my purpose. It helped me to play ball whether I felt like it or not. Normally, I sat on the sidelines if I felt nervous or frightened and waited until I felt better before I joined in. . . .

I have always procrastinated. Always. I waited until I felt I could do my best before I attempted anything important. Unfortunately, I rarely felt "ready" according to my own standards; so I literally spent more time preparing to do than doing. Now I keep doing and worry less about feeling ready. As a result, procrastination and indecision have lessened. Now I don't sit down and think about what I should do. If I am having a problem making a decision, I busy myself with some other task while trying to decide. . . .

One night, years ago, I had a dream which disturbed and haunted me for a long time. In the dream a man I loved was yelling at me in disgust. He shouted, "You know what your problem is? You don't know the pleasure of taking pains." As I awoke I heard him repeating this phrase. I felt hollow, aching, diminished. Later, as I clipped along slip-shod in life, I would hear his voice in the distance, "You don't know the pleasure of taking pains." Years later I am beginning to deal with the content of that dream.

Where I used to lash out, now I labor. The loud clamoring of my emotions has reformed into a music of feeling and doing with intricate harmony, delicate and faint like an echo, yet as real and palpable as my heartbeat.

The Morita lifeway supports not only the taking of pains, but also the treasures and pleasures in the taking of those pains. The feelings of patience and gratitude while doing furnish hopeful energy for the next venture. I understand that I am in the process of reducing character defects and expanding attributes, a process of refinement. Yet I can accept myself as I am, as I go along. I am becoming responsive to the outside and responsible to the inside. When I review my day's activities I can smile instead of agonizing over what I did or didn't do. On some days action, thought and feeling link together like a ceaseless prayer. I can finally envision a way of re-vision. (Reynolds, 1989, pp. 89–93)

Naikan Therapy   Developed by lay priest and businessman Ishin Yashimoto, **Naikan therapy** is based on the practices of a sect of Buddhist monks, but shares with Catholicism the central, daily practice of examination of the conscience. The theory is that excessive self-concern and thoughtlessness for others are the roots of neurosis. A shift of focus toward righting the social balance through selfless action relieves symptoms (Reynolds, 1981).

In Japan, Naikan training is done in residence at a one-week retreat. Clients—called *Naikanshas*—are assigned a bare cubicle, too small to lie down in, and are instructed to think over their lives with family members, close friends, and associates one at a time, from the early past to the recent present (Reynolds, 1989). The meditation begins with the mother or primary caretaker.

The Naikansha answers three specific questions about each person, within an assigned period (for example, in preschool years):

1. What did that person do for me?
2. What did I do for that person in return?
3. What trouble and inconvenience did I cause that person?

The client is forbidden to think about the other person's flaws or failings, focusing on his or her own behavior instead. In the retreat model, an instructor comes by every two hours or so, from 5 A.M. till 9 P.M., to hear the Naikansha's reflections, to assist with concentration if necessary, and to give the next assignment of person and period. The instructor does not counsel, confront, or evaluate. In nonretreat models of Naikan therapy, clients use diaries maintained at home and brought to the therapist's office for comment, tape-record their meditations, or produce evidence of their reflections in some other way (Reynolds, 1981). After intensive Naikan training, clients are encouraged to practice the reflection at least twice daily, with the evening session focused on answering the three questions in terms of that day.

The theory underpinning Naikan is that as children we begin to use other people for our own satisfaction without appreciating them or repaying them for their contributions to our lives. Naikan meditation helps us realize that in spite of our taking people for granted, hurting them, and exploiting them, we have been loved and cared for. "An existential relief follows from squarely facing one's self at one's worst" (Reynolds, 1981, p. 546). Part of the relief stems from not having to keep up a mask or delude ourselves about what we have done. The natural outgrowth of this experience is gratitude and the desire to be of service to others. Much like narrative approaches to therapy, a new life story is constructed, a story that affects us differently than our old version did.

The Japanese have applied Naikan to people with relationship impairments, psychosomatic complaints, addictions, neuroses, and criminal behavior. It has also been implemented in prisons, schools, and businesses as a character-building course.

Uses for Transpersonal Techniques

In the following discussions, I will emphasize that transpersonal techniques are not focused on pathological symptoms, but instead on enhancing innate positive tendencies.

Existential Conditions

Most people who take up meditation and yoga do so on their own, outside of the mental health system. Usually, they are engaged in struggles with existential issues of mortality, responsibility, choice, and meaning. They may have found that goals such as money, sex, prestige, and power create unsatisfying searches for more of the same, without the expected feelings of wholeness and fulfillment. Conversely, they may have failed at accumulating worldly success and seek some other sense of worthiness. Eastern philosophy would label either path (through worldly success or failure) as derailed, doomed to suffer by alienation from natural goals: transcendence, selfless service, and cultivation of wisdom.

Counselors often assist people in reflection on life's meaning when the awareness of death looms large. Some of the Eastern-style questions that can be answered in therapeutic dialogue are these: "What would you regret if you died today?" "What do you leave behind (that is, what is your *karma*)?" "From your point of view as a dying person, what is truly important?"

Mortality is not the only condition of old age addressed by transpersonal psychology. In a famous experiment (Alexander, Langer, Newman, Chandler, & Davis, 1989), seventy-three nursing-home residents were randomly assigned to three-month programs of meditation, mindfulness training, relaxation, and no treatment. After the three months, the meditation and mindfulness groups showed significant improvement on blood pressure, associate learning (connecting word pairs meaningfully), word fluency, and internal locus of control (feelings of effectiveness), while the relaxation and no-treatment groups declined on those measures. The meditation and mindfulness groups also rated themselves as better able to cope, less old, and less impatient, while the other two groups felt less able to cope and older. Researchers were surprised to find that three years after the experiment, 100 percent of the meditators and 87.5 percent of the mindfulness group were still alive, in comparison with 65 percent of the relaxation group, 75 percent of the no-treatment group, and 62.5 percent of the other nursing home residents. Brammer (1984) includes body approaches and altered consciousness as promising counseling interventions for older adults.

Stress Reduction

As you know from your own experience, extreme stress doesn't improve your character or your performance. Stress has negative effects on both physical and mental health and puts people at higher risk for alcohol and drug abuse, interpersonal relationship problems, depression, anxiety, and suicide. Concerned about the high levels of stress inherent in medical training and careers, researchers Shapiro, Schwartz, and Bonner (1998) designed a study in which medical students were randomly assigned to an eight-week course in mindfulness meditation (which included daily practice) versus a no-course, wait-list treatment. In the meditation group, the researchers found reductions in depression and anxiety and increases in overall empathy levels and spiritual awareness. The findings suggest that the meditation worked by reducing overall anxiety levels, which led to the other benefits. The improved empathy levels were of particular interest to these researchers, who were aware that medical school tends to diminish "the humanistic qualities fundamental to optimal patient care" (p. 582). In short, medical doctors who practice mindfulness are likely to treat their patients more humanely than others do.

A long-lasting reduction in the stress hormone *cortisol* is a boon to mental and physical well-being. McKinney and colleagues (McKinney, Antoni, Kumar, Tims, & McCabe, 1997) produced significant decreases in depression, fatigue, total mood disturbance, and cortisol levels among healthy adults who participated in six biweekly sessions of guided imagery and music. These sessions used classical music and therapist support to enhance mindfulness of inner experiences. Similar sessions were used to enhance self-soothing in women with bulimia nervosa, who are considered lacking in the capacity to maintain a calm state, especially when alone (Esplen, Gallop, & Garfinkel, 1999). Compared to a bulimic control group who did self-monitoring exercises, the bulimics in the guided-imagery group not only significantly reduced bingeing and vomiting but also improved psychological functioning.

The heightened sense of well-being that results from stress reduction (Walsh, 2000) could have wide-ranging effects on addictive craving, binge eating (e.g., Kristeller & Hallett, 1999), anorexia, borderline personality traits, obsessive-compulsive habits, and most other psychological problems.

Professional Improvement for Helpers

Even though counselors are usually well equipped with empathy and insight, meditation could enhance these skills (as it did for the medical students). Also prized by helping professionals is the ability to focus and concentrate on the client's presentation, rather than being perceptually clouded by ego interference. As psychiatrist Mark Epstein (1998) wrote,

> One of the powerful consequences of my introductory experiences with the spiritual traditions of the East was that I became much less afraid of being with another person without being in control of the situation, a useful capacity in my role as a psychotherapist. And meditation further encouraged a trust that was difficult for me to find elsewhere, a trust in surrendering to the moment, to an emotional experience, no matter how threatening. (p. 90)

Finally, therapists' secondary trauma or burnout, caused by continual exposure to sadness and disorder, can be relieved through transpersonal techniques.

Relief of Physical Disorders

The psychological component of many physical disorders is inarguable: High blood pressure, cholesterol, coronary artery disease, asthma, diabetes, Crohn's disease, fibromyalgia, PMS, migraine, and chronic pain are examples. Relaxation and stress reduction can alleviate some of these disorders; for others, compliance with a helpful treatment regimen (for example, exercise and medication) depends on optimism and organized thinking. In a five-year study Orme-Johnson (1987) looked at hospital admission rates for serious illness in 2,000 meditators, versus a matched sample of nonmeditators, and found 87 percent less hospitalization among the meditators, with larger differences between older meditators and nonmeditators.

Eastern practices complement Western medicine, giving it a psychological boost. For example, patients undergoing phototherapy for psoriasis were randomly assigned to guided-meditation or no-meditation groups, with the meditation conducted by audiotape during sessions in light booths (Kabat-Zinn et al., 1998). The patients who meditated showed an accelerated rate of skin clearing, improving at a rate 60 to 70 percent faster than that of the no-tape group. The meditators also showed reduced distress and increased well-being on psychological tests. These results accrue importance when you realize that the increased rate of healing means a lower number of phototherapy sessions, which in turn means a possible reduction in the risk of skin cancers as well as a reduced cost of treatment.

Maximizing Counseling Benefits

Despite the multiple-session design of Western-style therapies, the most frequent number of actual visits to an outpatient psychotherapist or counselor is *one*, and the next most frequent number is *two*. Yet Western therapies work over long periods of time—one common definition of *brief* therapy is twenty-four sessions. Therefore, most clients don't stay in therapy long enough to receive the benefits. In contrast, the experience-based teaching of many Eastern approaches, which depend on a few simple principles (breathing, mindfulness, attention to what needs to be done, gratitude exercises), are likely to bring about some immediate relief after one or two sessions. Reynolds (1989) suggests, first, that these approaches would at least provide some service to one-shot clients and, second, that the immediate relief might convince enheartened clients to return. In a survey of therapies in which meditation plays a central role, Snaith (1998) identified the advantages as abbreviated therapist time, increases in clients' feelings of self-efficacy, and clients' realization that they played the major role in their own improvement.

※ Case Conceptualization: An Example

In his exploration of Eastern thought, Mark Epstein (1998) sought out Ram Dass, the famous guru of altered consciousness, and later applied what he learned to his work as a psychiatrist. In this case conceptualization Epstein shows how meditation illuminated therapy.

BREATHING AND CONTROL

Ram Dass [gave] me an opportunity, however briefly, to touch the ground of my being, to break a path through my self to the realm behind personal identity and the unconscious. Love did not depend on how together I felt, nor was it something that I had to *do*. It was the more natural state, one that I had to learn how to permit.

Buddhism has developed a variety of means of driving this lesson home, some involving the interpersonal approach that Ram Dass demonstrated for me and some involving meditation practice, which is really practice in restoring the balance between doing and being. One reason for the growing appeal of Buddhism to psychotherapists is because of its success in teaching people how to reconnect with this vital and neglected capacity of the self.

A patient of mine, a successful professional in city government in her early fifties, described her struggles with meditation at her first retreat in terms that clearly reflect this paradigm. While the meditation instructions were simply to *watch* her breath, Kate spent most of the first few days trying hard to *regulate* it. Her breathing should be relaxed, she thought. It should be deep and rhythmical. She should be able to feel every bit of it. Watching the breath became a project, and Kate attacked it with all of the gusto that she regularly applied to difficult problems at work. As she listened to the meditation instructions, however, Kate began to realize that this was not the approach that was being counseled. She saw that her striving led only to a feeling of frustration and failure, but as she tried to change her mode of relating, she began to notice a pain in her abdomen that felt like the constraint of an iron band around her waist. The pain intensified as she approached the end of each exhalation; she began to be aware of a fear as she exhaled, of something like being alone in the vastness of a great desert.

With ample time to explore the ins and outs of this phenomenon, Kate made some breakthroughs. A great caretaker in her intimate relationships, but afraid to let herself be vulnerable, Kate recognized that her approach to the breath was analogous to her approach to her lovers. As long as she could make a project out of them she was fine. But underneath this was a fear that if she was not always doing something, she would be "dropped." If she stayed in control, she did not have to face these fears, but if she were to give it up, she would have to face the horrifying mix of her dependent feelings and her presumptions of her lover's unreliability. She was afraid, she realized, of "falling apart completely."

Kate was comfortable, she began to see, in the realm of manipulation, where doing and being done to are the key modes of relating. But, as the iron band in her abdomen continually reminded her, she was steeling herself against any alternative. Her breath could not be a source of comfort, nor even an object of meditation, unless she first confronted how much she feared annihilation. She needed that iron band to prevent any sudden descent into the abyss.

When we talked all this over after the retreat, Kate smiled ruefully and told me, with some shame, how her mother used to instruct her in her breathing when she was young, teaching her the "right" way to do it. Kate's memory shows that she internalized her mother's inability to let go, which could be seen in her own inability to relax into her breathing in meditation. This need to be in control reflected a basic lack of trust in herself that was very similar to what I had carried into my meeting with Ram Dass.

As my encounter with Ram Dass made clear to me, meditation did not have to be the only venue for Kate's kind of breakthrough. It could also come in the context of a therapeutic relationship in which the need of the ego to maintain control is successfully relinquished. There is nothing about psychotherapy, per se, that could not foster this kind of realization, except that, for many in our culture (both therapists and patients), it is an entirely alien concept. Just as we are taught that doing is preferable to being, so are we reared to think of separateness as the key to our growth and of connection as something that is rooted in childhood. (pp. 80–82) ■ ■

DISCUSSION IDEAS

1. What might be some of the differences between *doing* love and *permitting* it? Can you think of a story or film that deals with these differences?

2. Why do you think "the balance between doing and being" is a "vital and neglected capacity of the self"? Do you ever have times when you see yourself as *doing* rather than *being?* What are these times like?

3. What was Kate's problem with breathing at the retreat? How did the problem express itself in thoughts, physical feelings, and emotions?

4. How did the breathing problem serve to reveal Kate's relationships in a new light?

5. Why does Epstein mention the "ample time to explore the ins and outs" at the retreat?

6. Do you, or does someone you know, hate to be "out of control"? Do you know why?

7. Do you agree that we are "reared to think of separateness as the key to our growth and of connection as something that is rooted in childhood"? Can you think of an example of this indoctrination?

Critiques of Transpersonal Approaches

Criticisms of transpersonal psychology are often based on incomplete understanding of its principles. In the following sections, some misconceptions are clarified.

Religion, Not Psychology

It's true that there are religious underpinnings to transpersonal practices. Buddhism is a religion, though not in the sense we usually understand the term, since it is not dogmatic, nor does it refer to a God. Because it is a way of life, a community, a body of literature, a description of civilization, and a healing tradition, it falls into many different categories. In our field of helping professions, we focus on the healing tradition. Since both psychology and religion draw from philosophical bases, they are destined to overlap in many ways. For example, humanistic psychology with its emphasis on empathy and uncritical positive regard overlaps a great deal with the dogma of Western Christianity. Furthermore, *most* psychological experiences can be thought of as religious or mystical—demons, possession, evil, crises of faith, ecstasy, loss of life direction, and so on.

The potential danger of the overlap between psychology and religion lies in encouraging clients to give up their existing beliefs about morality, worship, afterlife, and rules of conduct. Many people do not want their religious practices questioned by their counselors, and most do not come to therapy wanting to convert. Some religions discourage their members from seeking help from counselors outside the faith. However, the transpersonal experiences that come from practices like meditation and yoga are encompassing enough to fit into a variety of conventional religious frameworks without creating upset. In general, counselors need awareness of clients' religious viewpoints so that they can avoid insult and make use of the strengths inherent in each one. For example, a prayer-oriented client already knows a lot about meditation and chanting.

Excuse for Breaks with Reality

Eastern psychotherapy has been besieged with alternative explanations for altered states of consciousness: Transpersonal experiences represent infantile helplessness, meditation is self-induced catatonia, mystical experience is neurotic regression to union with the breast, transpersonal ideas are examples of irrational thinking. Such criticism is a reasonable outgrowth of many psychologists' experience with the ego dissolution involved in psychotic and borderline states, a dissolution certainly different from ego transcendence. However, education about the developmental theory behind transpersonal psychology should appease the critics who take this stance.

Far from being endorsements of irresponsibility, Asian therapies are the second most researched of all therapies, behind only behavior therapies (Walsh, 2000). The mistaken idea that Eastern philosophy ignores worldly things, and encourages apathy and inaction, also stems from lack of education concerning the selfless service aspect of this approach.

Transpersonal Excuses

The misuse of spiritual ideas and practices to support psychological problems is as common as the misuse of political ideology for personal pathological ends. For example, a practitioner of Hinduism, Buddhism, or Christianity may refuse to express anger or assert herself, maintaining a depressive stance that prolongs psychological suffering rather than transforming it (Battista, 1996b). Battista also identifies individuals who practice "offensive spirituality" or "narcissistic spirituality, in which a person asserts that he or she is spiritually evolved, hence entitled to special rights and privileges that others should recognize and support" (p. 259). Cult leaders David Koresh and Jim Jones are examples of people who used spiritual claims to justify misuse of authority. Misuses of spirituality have led some critics to confuse transpersonal philosophy with narcissistic self-absorption. In truth, however, the focus of these practices is on overcoming attachment and preoccupation with the self. To therapists and clients interested in cultivating an awareness of offensive spirituality, Battista suggests reading the satires of mystical defense mechanisms in S. I. Moon's (1988) *The Life and Teachings of Tofu Roshi* and J. Nichols's (1981) *The Nirvana Blues*.

Inadequacy for Some Disorders

Transpersonal practices offer little help for psychoses and severe neuroses. In fact, psychologically healthy clients (sometimes called the "worried well") benefit most. Contemplative disciplines require an already sturdy ego (Perez-De-Albeniz & Holmes, 2000; Wilber, 1993b). Remember that transpersonal experience is a developmental level *beyond* ego coherence, not a substitute for it. This is why conventional therapeutic tactics are not rejected but, in fact, embraced by counselors with transpersonal viewpoints. Meditation, yoga, and exercise most often serve as components of multimodal, eclectic, or integrative treatments.

KEY TERMS

altered states of
   consciousness
asanas
attention
aversion
being-needs
concentration
constructive living
craving

delusions
dichotomies
disidentification
hatha-yoga
karma
karma-yoga
mindfulness
Morita therapy
Naikan therapy

peak experiences
pranas
raja-yoga
relaxation response
Self
transcendental reality
transpersonal
   psychology
vital energy

Exploring Key Terms

Bring your notes from studying other theories to a group meeting. In a discussion, relate each of the above terms to a concept from another chapter, pointing out either similarity, dissimilarity, or both. When all members agree on a relationship, write it down. Distribute on paper or electronically for the rest of the class.

LIBRARY, MEDIA, AND INTERNET ACTIVITIES

1. Journals most relevant to this chapter are the following:

Journal of Humanistic Psychology,

Journal of Transpersonal Psychology,

ReVision: A Journal of Consciousness and Transformation,

Journal of Consciousness Studies,

International Bulletin of Morita Therapy, and

Common Boundary.

Locate the journals that your library carries, and ask the librarian how you might find the others. Search social science databases using key terms for a disorder of interest to you (for example, "eating disorders," "depression," "school delinquency") combined with key terms from transpersonal psychology. Make a list of five sources that involve transpersonal approaches to the disorder you chose.

2. Here is a list of websites that offer further education about topics in transpersonal psychology. Review three of them, and write a one-page description of the types of information available on each. Make your page helpful to other students doing research in the area.

www.umassmed.edu (University of Massachusetts stress reduction site)

www.maslow.com

www.healthemotions.org

www.ageless.com/yoga.htm

www.yogabasics.com

www.dharma.org (center for Buddhist studies)

www.tm.org (transcendental meditation)

http://vlib.org/Religion

3. Visit a large bookstore, and look under Eastern Philosophy, Self-Help, Psychology, and Health for materials on transpersonal psychology. If you wanted to take up one of the practices described in this chapter, what book would you choose? Why?

4. Look further into physical exercise as an adjunct to psychotherapy. Make a bibliography of ten sources you could use in writing a paper on this topic.

5. If you are interested in the "Tune in, turn on, drop out" era, look up the works of Ram Dass, available in books and on audiotapes. What websites are current on Ram Dass's life and times?

6. The Japanese therapies of Morita and Naikan are still in their early years in the United States. Search for library sources and websites that could update your knowledge about these approaches in the Western world.

REFERENCES

Alexander, C. N., Langer, E. J., Newman, R. I., Chandler, H. M., & Davies, J. L. (1989). Transcendental meditation, mindfulness, and longevity: An experimental study with the elderly. *Journal of Personality and Social Psychology, 57*, 950–964.

Allport, G. W. (1955). *Becoming: Basic considerations for a psychology of personality.* New Haven: Yale University Press.

Battista, J. R. (1996a). Abraham Maslow and Roberto Assagioli: Pioneers of transpersonal psychology. In B. W. Scotton, A. B. Chinen, & J. R. Battista (Eds.), *Textbook of transpersonal psychiatry and psychology* (pp. 52–61). New York: Basic Books.

Battista, J. R. (1996b). Offensive spirituality and spiritual defenses. In B. W. Scotton, A. B. Chinen, & J. R. Battista (Eds.), *Textbook of transpersonal psychiatry and psychology* (pp. 250–260). New York: Basic Books.

Benson, H., Greenword, M. M., & Klemchuk, H. (1975). The relaxation response: Psychophysiologic aspects and clinical applications. *International Journal of Psychiatry in Medicine, 6*, 87–98.

Brammer, L. M. (1984). Counseling theory and the older adult. *Counseling Psychologist, 12*, 29–37.

Bravo, G., & Grob, C. (1996). Psychedelic psychotherapy. In B. W. Scotton, A. B. Chinen, & J. R. Battista (Eds.), *Textbook of transpersonal psychiatry and psychology* (pp. 335–343). New York: Basic Books.

Brazier, D. B. (1995). *Zen therapy.* New York: Wiley.

Buffone, G. W. (1984). Future directions: The potential for exercise as therapy. In M. L. Sachs & G. W. Buffone (Eds.), *Running as therapy: An integrated approach* (pp. 215–225). Lincoln: University of Nebraska Press.

Burbank, P. M., Padula, C. A., & Hirsch, M. A. (2002). Applying the transtheoretical model: Challenges with older adults across the health/illness continuum. In P. M. Burbank & D. Riebe (Eds.), *Promoting exercise and behavior change in older adults* (pp. 209–234). New York: Springer.

Burbank, P. M., & Riebe, D. (Eds.). (2002). *Promoting exercise and behavior change in older adults.* New York: Springer.

Chung, B., & Baird, K. (1999). Physical exercise as a counseling intervention. *Journal of Mental Health Counseling, 21*, 124–136.

Epstein, M. (1998). *Going to pieces without falling apart.* New York: Broadway Books.

Esplen, M. J., Gallop, R., & Garfinkel, P. E. (1999). Using guided imagery to enhance self-soothing in women with bulimia nervosa. *Bulletin of the Menninger Clinic, 63*, 174–191.

Fadiman, J., & Frager, R. (2002). *Personality and personal growth* (5th ed.). Upper Saddle River, NJ: Prentice-Hall.

Fontana, D. (1999). *Learn to meditate: A practical guide to self-discovery and fulfillment.* San Francisco: Chronicle Books.

Goud, N. H. (2001). The symbolic identity technique. *Journal of Humanistic Counseling, Education, and Development, 40*, 114–122.

Grof, C., & Grof, S. (1993). Addiction as a spiritual emergency. In R. Walsh & F. Vaughan (Eds.), *Paths beyond ego: The transpersonal vision* (pp. 144–146). New York: Penguin Putnam.

Grof, S. (1993). Realms of the human unconscious: Observations from LSD research. In R. Walsh & F. Vaughan (Eds.), *Paths beyond ego: The transpersonal vision* (pp. 95–106). New York: Penguin Putnam.

Hays, K. F. (1995). Putting sport psychology into (your) practice. *Professional Psychology: Research and Practice, 26*, 33–40.

Ishiyama, F. I. (1988). Current status of Morita therapy research: An overview of research methods, instruments, and results. *International Bulletin of Morita Therapy, 1*(2), 58–83.

Kabat-Zinn, J., Wheeler, E., Light, T., Skillings, A., Scharf, M. J., Cropley, T. G., et al. (1998). Influence of a mindfulness meditation-based stress reduction intervention on rates of skin clearing in patients with moderate to severe psoriasis undergoing phototherapy (UVB) and photochemotherapy (PUVA). *Psychosomatic Medicine, 60,* 625–632.

Kristeller, J. L., & Hallett, C. B. (1999). An exploratory study of a meditation-based intervention for binge eating disorder. *Journal of Health Psychology, 4,* 357–363.

Leary, T. (1957). *Interpersonal Diagnosis of Personality.* Hoboken, NJ: Wiley.

Maslow, A. H. (1976). *Farther reaches of human nature.* New York: Viking.

McKinney, C. H., Antoni, M. H., Kumar, M., Tims, F. C., & McCabe, P. M. (1997). Effects of guided imagery and music (GIM) therapy on mood and cortisol in healthy adults. *Health Psychology, 16,* 390–400.

Moon, S. I. (1988). *The life and teachings of Tofu Roshi.* Boston: Shambhala Publications.

Nichols, J. (1981). *The nirvana blues.* New York: Ballantine Books.

Orme-Johnson, D. W. (1987). Transcendental Meditation and reduced health care utilization. *Psychosomatic Medicine, 49,* 493–507.

Perez-De-Albeniz, A., & Holmes, J. (2000). Meditation: Concepts, effects, and uses in therapy. *International Journal of Psychotherapy, 5,* 49–68.

Ram Dass (1971). *Be here now.* New York: Crown Publishers.

Ram Dass (2001). *Still here: Embracing aging, changing, and dying.* New York: Riverhead Books.

Reynolds, D. K. (1976). *Morita psychotherapy.* Berkeley: University of California Press.

Reynolds, D. K. (1981). Naikan psychotherapy. In R. J. Corsini (Ed.), *Handbook of innovative psychotherapies* (pp. 544–553). New York: Wiley.

Reynolds, D. K. (1989). *Flowing bridges, quiet waters: Japanese psychotherapies, Morita and Naikan.* Albany: State University of New York Press.

Riebe, D., Burbank, P. M., & Garber, C. E. (2002). Setting the stage for active older adults. In P. M. Burbank & D. Riebe (Eds.), *Promoting exercise and behavior change in older adults* (pp. 1–28). New York: Springer.

Russell-Chapin, L. A., & Rybak, C. J. (1996). The art of teaching Jungian analysis. *Journal of Humanistic Education and Development, 34,* 171–182.

Sachs, M. L. (1984). The runner's high. In M. L. Sachs & G. W. Buffone (Eds.), *Running as therapy: An integrated approach* (pp. 273–287). Lincoln: University of Nebraska Press.

Shapiro, S. L., Schwartz, G. E., & Bonner, G. (1998). Effects of mindfulness-based stress reduction on medical and premedical students. *Journal of Behavioral Medicine, 21,* 581–599.

Snaith, P. (1998). Meditation and psychotherapy. *British Journal of Psychiatry, 173,* 193–195.

Tkachuk, G. A., & Martin, G. L. (1999). Exercise therapy for patients with psychiatric disorders: Research and clinical implications. *Professional Psychology: Research and Practice, 30,* 275–282.

Walsh, R. (1996). Shamanism and healing. In B. W. Scotton, A. B. Chinen, & J. R. Battista (Eds.), *Textbook of transpersonal psychiatry and psychology* (pp. 96–103). New York: Basic Books.

Walsh, R. (2000). Asian psychotherapies. In R. J. Corsini & D. Wedding (Eds.), *Current psychotherapies* (6th ed., pp. 407–444). Itasca, IL: Peacock Publishing.

Walsh, R., & Vaughan, F. (Eds.). (1993). *Paths beyond ego: The transpersonal vision.* New York: Penguin Putnam.

Wilber, K. (1993a). Paths beyond ego in the coming decades. In R. Walsh & F. Vaughan (Eds.), *Paths beyond ego: The transpersonal vision* (pp. 256–266). New York: Penguin Putnam.

Wilber, K. (1993b). The spectrum of pathologies. In R. Walsh & F. Vaughan (Eds.), *Paths beyond ego: The transpersonal vision* (pp. 148–152). New York: Penguin Putnam.

Wilber, K. (1996). Foreword. In B. W. Scotton, A. B. Chinen, & J. R. Battista (Eds.), *Textbook of transpersonal psychiatry and psychology* (pp. xvii–xx). New York: Basic Books.

CHAPTER **13**

Integrative Innovation: The Example of Cognitive-Interpersonal Therapy

❧ A Selection from

The Interpersonal Theory of Psychiatry, 1953

Harry Stack Sullivan

My work has shown me very clearly that, while early experience does a great many things—as I have been trying to suggest thus far—the development of capacity for interpersonal relations is by no means a matter which is completed at some point, say, in the juvenile era. Very far from it. And even preadolescence, which is a very, very important phase of personality development, is not the last phase. . . .

I have suggested that an important aspect of the preadolescent phase is that, practically for the first time, there is consensual validation of personal worth. Now it is true that some children are fortunate, indeed; through the influences to which they have been subjected in the home and school, they are about as sure as they can be that they are worthwhile in certain respects. But very many people arrive in preadolescence in the sad state which an adult would describe as "getting away with murder." In other words, they have had to develop such remarkable capacities for deceiving and misleading others that they never had a chance to discover what they were really good for. But in this intimate interchange in preadolescence—some preadolescents even have mutual daydreams, spend hours and hours carrying on a sort of spontaneous mythology in which both participate—in this new necessity for thinking of the other fellow as right and for being thought of as right by the other fellow, much of this uncertainty as to the real worth of the personality, and many self-deceptive skills at deceiving others which exist in the juvenile era, may be rectified by the improving communication of the chums and, to a much lesser extent but nonetheless valuably, by confirmatory relations in the collaboration developed in the gang. . . .

We might next look at a few of the warped juveniles who can receive very marked beneficial effect from the maturation of this need for intimacy and from preadolescent socialization, who can at this stage literally be put on the right road to a fairly adequate personality development. For example, there are egocentric people, who go from childhood through the juvenile era and still retain literally unlimited expectations of attention and services to themselves. Some of these people you know as those who sulk when something doesn't suit them; some of them are people who have tantrums under certain circumstances. If the families of these juveniles are so influential that the more adult members of the school community hesitate to "break" the juveniles of these undesirable "habits," then about the last chance they have of favorable change is based on their need for getting along with a chum in preadolescence. As juveniles, they have been classified quite uniformly by other juveniles as thoroughly bad sports; there is a distinct tendency for other juveniles to avoid them, to ostracize them, in spite of some necessity for accommodating to them which is imposed by the influence of the family. It is quite possible that in preadolescence such a person will establish his chumship with some other ex-juvenile who is more or less on the fringe of ostracism, and who had been in the out-group of the juvenile society. That looks as if it wouldn't be too good; and in some instances it is not so good, as I will note later. But it is very much better than what was going on before. Not infrequently people of this kind go through the comparatively brief period of preadolescence and come out very much less inclined to expect unlimited services from others, very much nearer the ideal of a good sport who can "take it," and who doesn't require very special treatment. In other words, two unfortunate juveniles thrown together by their unfortunate social status as juveniles may, under the influence of this growing need for intimacy, actually do each other a great deal of good. And as they show some improvement they will become less objectionable to the prevailing preadolescent society and may actually get to be quite well esteemed in the gang. But the risk is that these bad sports, these self-centered or egocentric juveniles, now formed into two-groups may carry their resentment and misery from the ostracism they have suffered to the length of seeking out and identifying themselves with the most antisocial leadership which can be found.

However, the notion that preadolescence readily consolidates a criminal, antisocial career is the most shocking kind of nonsense, which overlooks almost all instances which happen to be negative. It happens that there is more literature on antisocial gangs than there is on the vastly favorable aspect of preadolescent society. I believe that a study of preadolescent society in the very worst neighborhoods would reveal tendencies other than those leading toward becoming minor criminals. And in some very bad neighborhoods, while there are gangs which are antisocial, there are also gangs which are very much less antisocial, if not actually constituting a constructive element in the neighborhood. (pp. 249–252)   ▪ ▪

DISCUSSION IDEAS

1. Even if you didn't have the copyright date, how would you know that Sullivan was writing in a different era? What would be different if he were writing on the same subject today?

2. In paragraph one, what theory about "early experience" is Sullivan denying? In his eyes, when does personality development end?

3. What is the "consensual validation" of preadolescent society? How can it have a positive influence on the child? Do you remember your best friend and group of friends from ages 9 to 12? Did they have a positive influence on your character?

4. How can spoiled, self-centered children benefit from preadolescent socialization? Why did relationships within their families fail to provide these benefits?

5. In general, how do interpersonal relationships with peers correct some of the flaws of children? How about adults? Do you have any peer relationships that have helped correct your flaws?

6. What prevailing idea about preadolescent groups, or "gangs" as Sullivan labels them, is nonsense? Do you agree that most preadolescent gangs have a "vastly favorable aspect"?

7. According to Sullivan, how are antisocial gangs formed? Does this make sense to you, when you think about the violence among teenagers?

_____

Introduction to Integrative Approaches

Harry Stack Sullivan's interpersonal theory serves as an underpinning for many modern approaches: Sullivan influenced Erik Erikson and Carl Rogers in their humanist points of view, the interpersonal process approach of Edward Teyber (1992), family systems thinkers like Murray Bowen (who was trained under Sullivan), and the group therapy method developed by Irvin Yalom (1995). Yalom wrote that "his [Sullivan's] work has so pervaded contemporary psychotherapeutic thought that his original writings seem overly familiar or obvious" (p. 19). Therefore, Sullivan serves as a good starting point to discuss theories that are integrated into other theories. A recent merging of interpersonal and cognitive approaches (cognitive-interpersonal therapy) will be the main example of integrative theory in this chapter, though there are many mergers to choose from.

Since the late 1970s, people in our field have explored "various ways to cross school boundaries, integrate theories and techniques from two or more approaches, or suggest factors that the different therapies have in common" (Arkowitz, 1992). You've surely noticed as you read the chapters in this textbook that theorists incorporate ideas and practices from earlier approaches as they introduce new points of view. Look at just a couple of examples: At one time, cognitivists (like Albert Ellis) and behaviorists (like B. F. Skinner) came from opposing camps. Behaviorists believed that mental processes were side effects of overt actions, and that therapy's rightful target was action. Cognitivists believed that mental processes drove behavior, and that the rightful target for therapeutic interventions was the client's habitual thinking pattern. Now, however, those two targets are rarely addressed separately, because practitioners became aware that thoughts and behavior interact. Cognitive-behavioral theory developed, and the therapy based on that theory is the most empirically supported so far.

In a similar process, almost all therapies integrate an awareness that childhood experience is a determinant of adult personality, a Freudian viewpoint, but most modern theories reject the idea that our personalities are biologically driven and set by the age of 6. Alfred Adler (Chapter 5) transformed Freudian theory by emphasizing the social roots of personality over the biological. Harry Stack Sullivan highlighted adolescence as a growth period for personality, and Erikson did the same for old age.

A long-lasting, sturdy integration of nondirective (Rogerian), psychodynamic, and behavioristic practices forms Robert Carkhuff's Human Technology (HT), which developed in the late 1960s (Aspy, Aspy, Russel, & Wedel, 2000). Carkhuff's model of stages of counseling and the skills that are used at each stage is the foundation of counselor training across the United States. This shows that at a very basic level, the field of counseling has endorsed integrative approaches for over thirty years. Recently, Constantine (2001) found that counselors with proven ability to conceptualize a culturally diverse client's case also had an eclectic-integrative theoretical orientation. Such an orientation may be necessary to think from multiple relevant points of view.

Historically, the most outstanding work in integrative psychology is the synthesis of psychoanalytic (basically, Freudian) and behavioral approaches. Psychoanalytic concepts such as repression have been explained in terms of reward and punishment, for instance. Paul Wachtel's (1977) ground-breaking book *Psychoanalysis and Behavior Therapy: Toward an Integration* marked a major step forward in the field of integrative psychology. Wachtel took the psychoanalytically based theories of Sullivan and others, which emphasized interpersonal dynamics (more than Freud's intrapsychic conflicts), and showed how they could logically inform behavior therapy and its active real-world interventions (instead of couch-bound treatments like analysis of transference). *Cognitive-interpersonal therapy*, the example of integration I present in this chapter, is an extension of Wachtel's integrationist thrust.

The Shift Toward Integration

Since the 1970s, fewer and fewer theoretical advocates have claimed that they have a one-size-fits-all treatment. Positive growth in practice and research areas combined to create the current shift toward **eclecticism,** employment of elements from a variety of sources.

A Nod to Reality

Various surveys of practitioners since the 1960s have found a large percentage endorsing eclecticism as their choice of approach. Though what this large number of people mean by *eclecticism* is unclear, it is certain that they do not practice a pure form of therapy, with techniques and strategies driven by only one theoretical position. In addition, the more years of experience clinicians have, the less they identify with a single approach (Miller, Duncan, & Hubble, 2002). Therefore, it is most realistic to consider integrationism as an acceptable movement. Recently, a panel of sixty-two distinguished mental health professionals, with an average of thirty years of clinical experience, ranked thirty-eight types of psychotherapy by the extent they expected them to be employed over the next decade (Norcross, Hedges, & Prochaska, 2002). Among these, technical eclecticism and theoretical integration were deemed to be the fifth and sixth most likely to grow. The first four types ranked were cognitive-behavioral, multicultural, cognitive, and interpersonal therapies, all of which have integrationist tendencies. As noted, cognitive-interpersonal therapy is the example of an integrationist treatment I will explore in this chapter.

An increasing number of integrationist therapies have been proven effective for specific client problems. One of the most common and effective integrations mixes psychosocial treatment with prescribed medication like Ritalin, Prozac, or lithium. Another effective combination is the treatment of a client in individual sessions as well as in group or family sessions, typical in programs aimed against domestic violence. Often, clients are encouraged to attend targeted psychoeducational and support groups (like Rational Recovery, Parent Effectiveness Training, Transcendental Meditation, or Weight Watchers) completely outside the therapist's control, meanwhile continuing individual therapy. With a greater range of proven theories and techniques to choose from, a counselor would be negligent to reject some of them on purist theoretical grounds.

Tailoring Treatment to Client, Culture, Therapist, and Stage of Change

Most experts today think that successful counseling depends on a tailoring process, taking into account several features of the client, therapist, and setting. Part of this openness comes from exposure: Different professionals who deal with a specific problem are influenced by each other as they work. Eating disorders, obsessive-compulsive disorder, substance abuse, and depression are often dealt with by teams of professionals in clinics devoted individually to just those problems. In the anxiety clinic where I worked, psychiatrists prescribed medication, a team of cognitive-behavioral trainees designed and attended exposure exercises, and individual therapists provided talk sessions, many of which focused on emotional support. Meeting and discussing cases with the other workers in the clinic bred respect for what various approaches had to offer. Integrated approaches to obesity involve behavioral eating management, exercise therapy, psychoeducation, pharmacological treatment, social influence programs, genetic analysis, and relapse prevention training (Perri, 1998), demonstrating that "a complex *interaction* of physiological, psychological, and environmental variables appears responsible for the poor maintenance of weight loss. Moreover, the relative contributions of the biological, behavioral, and situational factors likely vary from person to person" (p. 528; italics in original). Panic disorder is another example: Though once it was considered biologically caused and treated biochemically, now there are behavioral and cognitive explanations as well, and interventions that address all the potential causes of panic are the most efficacious in getting rid of it (Acierno, Hersen, & Van Hasselt, 1993).

Awareness that cultural background is a meaningful client and therapist feature has also moved integration forward. For example, Atkinson, Thompson, and Grant (1993) developed a model for deciding on the role a therapist should play, based not on a theory of personality but on a theory of cultural interaction. They suggest that the role depends on three factors:

- *The client's level of acculturation,* which is how much the person and his family have adopted the values and customs of the mainstream culture.

- *The locus of problem etiology,* which can be internal (phobias, for example) or external (role conflict, for example). Oppressive external situations like job discrimination and harassment cause psychological difficulties for minorities and women, and the counselor addresses them differently than internally caused problems.

- *Goals of helping,* which are problem prevention and problem remediation.

This **three-dimensional model** gives rise to interesting cultural research: Using the three dimensions in combination, Asian American students (1) rated the counselor role of "facilitator of indigenous support systems" as highly helpful when clients' acculturation was low, their problem internal, and the goal preventive; (2) rated the counselor role of "consultant" as highly helpful when clients' acculturation was high, their problem external, and the goal preventive; and (3) gave the lowest mean ratings for helpfulness across the board to the roles of advocate, adviser, psychotherapist, and facilitator of indigenous healing methods (Atkinson, Kim, & Caldwell, 1998). This kind of investigation invites us to compare what *we* think will help with what the *client* thinks will help. We shouldn't assume a perfect match.

Other individual differences in clients and therapists are also given room in integrative approaches to counseling. For instance, different levels of tolerance for ambiguity and uncertainty predispose clients toward different types of therapeutic collaboration (Bordin, 1979). Sources of ambiguity can be unclearly defined tasks ("Think about how you respond to pressure"), wide latitude offered by the task ("Practice more assertive behavior"), or the anonymity of the therapist, and these can be either liberating or distressing depending on the client's personality. In addition, the issue of whether clients expect the therapist to be similar to them, or to complement them in personality, will affect the working alliance. Finally, clients prefer counseling procedures that are consistent with their individual world views: People who prefer rational, logical, analytic interpretation of experience in general will prefer cognitive approaches, while people who highly value and trust their emotional responses to the world will prefer constructivist approaches (Lyddon, 1989). Fulfilling client expectations and preferences is no small matter in counseling, since this fulfillment enhances cooperation, persistence, and hope.

R e f l e c t i o n

Think of what you would (or do) prefer in a counselor: ambiguous versus clear-cut, similar to you or contrasting with you in personality, logical versus emotional, or somewhere in between on those scales. Can you explain why you have the preferences you do? How do your preferences relate to the theories of counseling you like best?

Current interest in therapy as a *process* (rather than a repeated treatment) also contributes to integrative efforts. Change involves stages and turning points that are recognized by experienced counselors. Different approaches may be appropriate at different stages: "Each task or stage has its own goals, strategies, and change processes" (Johnson & Greenberg, 1987). For example, in the beginning a counselor may use Rogerian conditions to build the working alliance; then, in an action phase, she may choose behavioral interventions such as contracting and contingency management; then, when behavioral changes begin to reward themselves, she may focus on insight into the emotional aspects that contributed to the problem originally, using Gestalt techniques.

DISCUSSION IDEAS

Discuss what each of the following *helper roles* means to you (these are the roles identified by Atkinson and colleagues in their research). Which roles do you prefer someone to perform when you seek help for a problem? In what ways do your cultural background and your personality influence your preference?

Adviser	*Counselor*
Advocate	*Facilitator of Indigenous Support*
Change Agent	*Facilitator of Indigenous Healing*
Consultant	*Psychotherapist*

Effects of Research on Theory

As I suggested above, research on what works with what problem has compelled practitioners to use or recommend techniques outside their accustomed theoretical realm. Empirical investigations—such as random assignment of clients to different treatments, outcome analysis of various therapies, and studies to identify the *effective ingredient* of a therapy through experimental manipulation—became much more common in the last half of the twentieth century. Many historians in the field think that a review by Hans Eysenck (1952) kicked off this surge of research: Eysenck concluded from looking at twenty-four outcome studies that people without psychotherapy did just as well as people with it, a claim that challenged the psychology establishment to prove its worth.

Since the 1970s, many empirical studies compared outcomes of different therapies and found them equally effective. (For example, the 250-patient National Institute of Mental Health Treatment of Depression Collaborative Research Program [Elkin et al., 1989] revealed no differences among interpersonal therapy, cognitive-behavioral therapy, and drug treatment for depression.) The question that followed was inevitable: "How could therapies differing dramatically in their assumptions about human personality, psychopathology, and change result in common outcomes?" (Prochaska & DiClemente, 2002). Many people believe that the key lies not in the differences but in the similarities—that is, in the *common factors* that create positive change. One major example is the relationship between a client and helper, the **therapeutic alliance.** A series of studies found that that expert therapists agreed, to a surprising extent, on the ideal therapeutic relationship—no matter what school of thought they espoused. One such study, involving samples of six theoretical orientations, focused on clients' emotional expression and therapists' response to them. The researchers concluded: "It is notable that, in our study, the therapeutic process follows a similar pattern, regardless of theoretical orientations, depending on whether the therapist-client relationship is poor or well established" (Iwakabe, Rogan, & Stalikas, 2000, p. 396). Frank and Frank's (1991) *Persuasion and Healing* elaborates on the theme that all therapies are influencing processes and can be analyzed in terms of persuasion rather than theoretical stripe.

Three Types of Integrative Approach

Multi-perspective approaches take one of three main directions (Arkowitz, 1992): theoretical integration, technical eclecticism, and common factors orientation.

Theoretical Integration   An integrated conceptual framework blends elements of two or more established theoretical approaches into a unified point of view. This blend involves more than adding extra ingredients to an existing approach, like putting pecans into your chocolate chip cookie recipe. Wachtel (1977), in introducing his radical fusion of psychoanalytical and behavioral approaches, explained the blend this way:

> I am not advocating that behavior therapists adopt a little psychoanalysis or psychoanalysts use a little behavior therapy. My hope is, rather, that in trying to develop a frame of reference that encompasses the observations (and the directions for observation) that have accrued from both traditions, a newer, more complete and integrated approach will be achieved. One fruit of such an integration would be, I hope, the development of more effective ways to do psychotherapy. And we can anticipate that a sounder understanding of the development and maintenance of personality will also have implications for preventing personality disorders and for efforts at social change (p. 6).

A **theoretical integration** approach aspires to be an improvement upon *both* or *all* of the separate approaches that serve as its basis. It is therefore a complex endeavor and rarer than the other two forms of integration. In fact, some arguments claim that no true theoretical integration has yet been achieved (e.g., Lazarus, 1996).

Technical Eclecticism   Most experienced therapists use a collection of techniques that work well together, without a well-defined theoretical synthesis of two or more approaches. Often a single theoretical approach underlies case conceptualization, while practices are borrowed from other theories when they function well. For example, Laura Rice (1988) argued that a firmly Rogerian therapist, emphasizing the qualities of empathy, unconditional positive regard, and genuineness, might borrow from psychoanalysis the strategy of exploring transference (the client's way of responding to the therapist), because it is an example of how the client responds to other people in his world. Yet for a different client—one who has expressed, for instance, a desire to change a long-term habit—the same Rogerian therapist might borrow self-change suggestions from cognitive-behavioral approaches. Both of these borrowings can be done in a way that is consistent with the underlying, client-centered philosophy. You can see how the preferred theory stays the same, but the techniques are eclectic—hence the name **technical eclecticism.**

This is a very practical approach. Eclectic therapists ask the famous question posed by Gordon Paul: "What treatment, by whom, is most effective for this individual with that specific problem, under which set of circumstances, and how does it come about?" (Paul, 1967, p. 109). The focus is on studying what techniques have proven effective for whom, so putting research findings into action is foremost: What has worked best for certain problems, among clients with certain characteristics? Because of its reliance on research, eclecticism is a thoughtful approach, too. It's not a hodgepodge of techniques that appeal to you at the moment, like putting both chocolate chips and Italian sausage into a recipe because both ingredients are delicious. Arnold Lazarus (1989) makes this point forcefully:

> Haphazard, idiosyncratic eclecticism, wherein clinicians and theorists incorporate various ideas and methods on the basis of subjective appeal, should not be bracketed with systematic eclecticism which is based on years of painstaking research and clinical work. Unsystematic eclecticism is practised by therapists who require neither a coherent rationale nor empirical validation for the methods they employ. . . . But systematic prescriptive (technical) eclectics do not simply choose "whatever feels right." They base their endeavours on data from the threefold impact of patient qualities, clinical skills, and specific techniques. (p. 249).

The multimodal approach of Arnold Lazarus (see Chapter 9) illustrates technical eclecticism. Lazarus presents a structure within which to assess and intervene in various areas of human functioning: behavior, affect, sensation, imagery, cognition, interpersonal relationships, and biology. The basis for this approach is primarily social learning theory. The *why* of the treatment is not an emphasis, and when cognitive-behavioral techniques fail to produce the desired effects, treatments from other disciplines are enlisted (Lazarus, 1996).

Technical eclecticism takes into account that techniques may succeed for reasons other than those explained in the theories usually attached to them. For example, a neurosis might be cured by a close relationship with a Freudian therapist, rather than through insight, no matter how the therapist explains the cure. Lazarus believed that we know so little about how theory, technique, and outcome are truly connected that attempts at synthesis (as in *theoretical integration*) are premature. He thought that "integrationists, even when discussing strategies, tend to converse at a level of meaningless abstraction" instead of stating "precisely what they do, and don't do, to and with their clients at specific choice points" (1989, p. 253).

Beutler and Clarkin's **Systematic Treatment Selection (STS)** is a research-based, technically eclectic system that does guide us at "choice points" (Beutler, Alomohamed, Moleiro, & Romanelli, 2002). By studying the empirical evidence concerning more than thirty client and thirty treatment variables, the STS creators devised eighteen treatment principles and guidelines based on the combinations of these variables. These principles and guidelines can be used as a checklist when you are considering integrating two or more approaches. If your eclectic mixture stays consistent with these basic ideas, it is likely to be a solid approach.

1. The likelihood of improvement is enhanced by clients' social support level and weakened by their level of impairment in everyday functioning.

2. Prognosis is worse for patients with chronic and complex problems and worse for clients who are not in much distress. Good social support improves the outlook for clients with chronic and complex problems.

3. Psychoactive medication works best among clients with high functional impairment and complex, chronic problems.

4. The likelihood and amount of improvement among clients with complex, chronic problems are enhanced by multiperson therapy.

5. For functionally impaired clients, the more intense the treatment, the more benefits.

6. Risk is reduced by careful assessment of risk situations in the course of collecting information for the client's diagnosis and history.

7. Risk is reduced and client cooperation is increased when the treatment involves the family.

8. When the client has realistic information about the length, effectiveness, roles, and activities of treatment, risk is lessened and retention is optimized.

9. Risk is reduced if the clinician routinely questions clients about suicidal feelings and intentions.

10. Ethical and legal principles suggest that documentation and consultation are advisable.

11. Therapeutic change is greatest when the therapist is skillful and provides trust, acceptance, and respect for the client, and does so in an environment that both supports taking chances and provides safety.

12. Therapeutic change is most likely when the procedures do not evoke client resistance.

13. Therapeutic change is most likely when the client is exposed to targets of behavioral and emotional avoidance.

14. Therapeutic change is greatest when a client experiences emotional arousal, in a safe setting, until problem responses diminish or extinguish.

15. Therapeutic change is most likely if the initial focus of change is building new skills and altering disruptive symptoms.

16. When the client externalizes, skill building and symptom removal techniques work best; when the client internalizes, insight- and relationship-focused procedures work best.

17. When the client is open to suggestion, directiveness of intervention is effective; when the client is resistant to suggestion, paradoxical interventions or symptom exaggeration is preferable.

18. The likelihood of therapeutic change is greatest when the client's level of emotional stress is moderate, being neither excessively high nor excessively low. (Adapted from pp. 262–263)

Notice that Beutler and Clarkin's STS provides plentiful direction on practical matters and no elaboration of underlying theory. This is typical of a technically eclectic approach and consistent with the goals delineated by a founder of the integrationist school, Marvin Goldfried (1980). Goldfried believed that meaningful commonalities among the therapeutic camps would be found at the level of *clinical strategies*, "principles that guide our efforts during the course of therapy" (p. 994).

SMALL GROUP EXERCISE

1. Lazarus strongly objects to combining techniques just because they appeal to you. With your small group, brainstorm about techniques that are appealing separately but should not be practiced in combined form with the same client or group. Be sure you can explain why the techniques should not be integrated. Explain your best example to the class as a whole. To help get started, think of techniques that help a client break a bad habit or overcome an unreasonable fear. How might two techniques work against each other?

2. Choose one of the Systematic Treatment Selection principles and tell your group how it applies to an attempt at positive change in your own experience (either professional or personal). The attempt may have been an example of successful application of this principle, or an example of an unsuccessful outcome that could be explained by violation of this principle.

Common Factors Orientation The third integrative approach is based on a core of healing elements shared across theories and techniques, "factors most strongly associated with positive therapeutic outcome" (Arkowitz, 1992, p. 275).

These include corrective emotional experience, warmth, empathy, unconditional positive regard, hope, trust, persuasion, challenging misperceptions, changing schemas, restoring morale, providing new experiences, and giving accurate feedback. Theory-specific techniques seem to account for little of the outcome variance in psychotherapy (see Chapter 1), so the multivariate and interactive relationships among common factors are central.

Prochaska's **transtheoretical therapy** is an example of a **common factors orientation** (*trans* in this case meaning "across," so "across theories"), though the creators identify their own theoretical constructs as stages of change, levels of change, and processes of change (Prochaska & DiClemente, 2002). Stages are precontemplation, contemplation, preparation, action, maintenance, and termination—a common course in which change unfolds. Levels are symptoms, maladaptive cognitions, current interpersonal conflicts, family/systems conflicts, and intrapersonal conflicts: Therapists must decide where on this hierarchy the cause of the problem lies, and where to target efforts to solve it. Change processes are consciousness-raising, dramatic relief, self-liberation, counter-conditioning, reinforcement management, stimulus control, self-reevaluation, environmental reevaluation, and the helping relationship: This is an eclectic set of outward or inner activities that people do when they change.

At the Dayton Institute for Family Therapy, psychotherapists Miller, Duncan, and Hubble (2002) undertook a five-year "Impossible Cases Project" to investigate curative factors in difficult therapy cases. They found that "the therapeutic relationship was far more important in terms of outcome than any particular technique or intervention. More important was the finding that the probability of a successful outcome in even the most challenging cases could be improved by simply accommodating treatment to the *client's* perceptions of the presenting complaint, its causes and potential solutions, and ideas and experiences with the change process in general" (p. 187). The client himself comes prepared with a theory of change that suggests what combination of models and theories will work best.

DISCUSSION IDEAS

1. As a counselor, how could you go about discovering a client's ideas about therapeutic change? Look at the list of client perceptions in the quotation from Miller, Duncan, and Hubble. Formulate methods whereby you could explore these client perceptions in an interview.

2. Client characteristics other than the client's own theory of change contribute to therapy outcome. Bordin (1979) provides an example: "I find evidence that the vividness with which a patient is able to recapture experiences and to create fantasied ones is a requirement for successful treatment" (p. 257). Given what you now know about counseling, why do you think Bordin found these abilities necessary?

Cognitive-Interpersonal Therapy as an Integrative Approach

Wachtel's (1977) ideal of integration was an evolving framework, in which new elements can enter and old ones can exit as practice and research illuminate each other. Cognitive-interpersonal counseling is an example. Interpersonal theory, as Sullivan explained it in the 1940s and Klerman and Weissman (Klerman, Weissman, Rounsaville, & Chevron, 1984) realized it in the 1970s, had already integrated aspects of Freudian psychology, such as the critical role of anxiety and defense mechanisms in human behavior, and the roots of adult personality in early experience. Later, Safran (1990a, 1990b) incorporated elements of cognitive theory to create a new model that addresses psychopathology as an interdependent system of interpersonal behaviors, beliefs, feelings, and biology. What cognitive-interpersonal therapy adds to interpersonal theory is a systematic way of uncovering the dysfunctional thoughts about self and relationships that contribute to psychological distress. In the next several sections, I will explain cognitive-interpersonal therapy and highlight its integrative aspects.

Essential Concepts of Cognitive-Interpersonal Counseling

As you might guess from its title, cognitive-interpersonal counseling focuses on the mental processes we apply to our relationships with others.

Self-System

Harry Stack Sullivan (1953) used the term **self-system** to mean something like the personality, only with an emphasis on our concepts of who we are and how we operate in relation to other people. The self-system comes about from early experience with other people, and it evolves and changes through experience with others. Most of us have a wide but quite recognizable repertoire of ways we relate to others. People who know us well can accurately observe when we are "not acting like ourselves." When such an observation is made, we can almost always accept it as fact and explain it. In the same vein, people who don't know us very well may give us perfectly fine gifts that we don't use or like, saying that they are "just not *me*."

Cognitivists call our individual repertoires **self-schemas.** These are cognitive structures based on early experiences, mostly those of satisfaction, security, and anxiety. These early experiences imbue us with inclinations toward certain patterns of thought and behavior, which we then maintain through current attitudes, preferences, avoidances, and habits. For example, a withdrawn person chooses solitary hobbies, which maintain her self-schema. A hostile person creates a mean world around himself.

Reflection

Think about your own self-system. Can you give an example of being told that you "were not acting like yourself" in some situation? Were you able to identify and explain what you did that was uncharacteristic?

Security Operations

Security operations are psychological and interpersonal strategies that serve self-esteem and preserve our self-systems. An interpersonal point of view says that a sense of *security* comes from habitually predicting an experience of relatedness to others, and *anxiety* comes from habitually predicting an unraveling of personal relatedness. In infancy, our survival depends on relatedness to other people, and attachment theorists like Bowlby (1973) believe that the roots of **anxiety** lie in an early perception that relatedness might be disrupted or withdrawn. Our caregiver might not appear with food when we need it, or might provide the food in a manner that is not reassuring. As adults, we still are attuned to possible threats to relatedness and still get anxious when we feel them in the air. Sometimes, we respond to the threat without consciously registering it (and, therefore, without being able to rationally judge whether it is a real threat).

Examples of security operations are attending to self-presentation strategies such as looking attractive and speaking intelligently, diverting a conversation from anxiety-provoking subjects, and screening out anxiety-provoking elements of the interaction, or automatically discounting them. This screening-out process often occurs outside of awareness, and you have witnessed one form of it in people whom you would call "insensitive." I once had a colleague who would continue talking in the face of clear signals that another person wanted out of the conversation; one of my most polite co-workers even turned her back on him and started typing while he talked, a desperate tactic that still didn't get the message through to him.

H. S. Sullivan (1953), the first psychologist to insist that interpersonal (not *intra*personal) dynamics were primary in our personalities, called screening-out **selective inattention,** and deemed it "the classic means by which we do not profit from experience which falls within the areas of our particular handicap. We don't *have* the experience from which we might profit—that is, although it occurs, we never notice what it must mean; in fact we never notice that a good deal of it has occurred at all" (p. 319). My endlessly talking colleague managed, in this way, never to notice what it was about him that made people flee when he appeared in the hallways.

Interpersonal Schemas

During one *Star Trek* episode, the android character Data attempts a romantic relationship with a human woman, which naturally doesn't work out. When his girlfriend finally breaks up with him, Data says, "May I assume we are no longer a couple? Then I will delete the relevant programming." And he goes back to business as usual. For humans, deleting the relevant programming in interpersonal relationships is not this easy. Our progamming consists of the **interpersonal schema** we have developed over years and years. Data's "boyfriend program" was put together through a few hours of studying boyfriend behavior in books and song lyrics, and it was purely cognitive (since Data has no emotional life). Among us humans, the interpersonal schema integrates cognitive and emotional perspectives in "a generic representation of self-other interactions" (Safran, 1990b, p. 107) with a goal of maintaining relatedness. Unfortunately, some interpersonal schemas push this goal farther away rather than approaching it.

Cognitive-Interpersonal Cycles

Interpersonal schemas bring about and are maintained by **cognitive-interpersonal cycles.** As Arkowitz (1992) puts it, "Our past experiences skew our present environment and often lead us to create the very conditions that perpetuate our problems in a kind of vicious circle. For example, the people we choose and the relationships we form may confirm the dysfunctional views that we carry forward from our past and that are at the heart of many of our problems" (p. 269). You probably know an individual or two who are criticized for choosing romantic partners who abuse them, over and over. Though they may insist that they are not consciously choosing such mates, it is no accident. Something in the nature of an abusive relationship confirms their interpersonal schema.

We may all agree that people invoke old, worn-out ways of relating to others (which may once have been functional). But these ways now make them miserable. Learning theory would tell us that with enough feedback, we'd change our habits of relating, just as pigeons learn to peck the right button and rats learn to run the right tunnels in a maze. We would all choose plans, strategies, and behaviors that would make interpersonal connection available, reliable, and satisfying. So, how is persistence of bad habits explained by cognitive-interpersonal theory? Safran (1990b) provides an answer: "The central postulate of an integrative cognitive-interpersonal perspective is that a person's maladaptive interactional patterns persist because they are based upon working models of interpersonal relationships that are consistently confirmed by the interpersonal consequences of his or her own behavior" (p. 97). That is, the person's behavior influences the environment and shapes other's behavior back to him, in a *cognitive-interpersonal cycle*. Most often, the maladapted person is locked in a rigid, narrow, and extreme repertoire of engaging other people, and has the same type of expectations about how they will engage back. Here is Safran's example, which clarifies the situation well:

> As a result of important developmental experiences, a young man comes to view the maintenance of interpersonal relatedness as contingent upon his being intelligent. When he feels anxious in interpersonal situations, he attempts to reduce this anxiety by speaking in an intelligent fashion. This communication style, however, is viewed by others as unnecessarily pedantic, and distances them. In this situation the very operations that are employed to reduce the man's anxiety by increasing his sense of potential interpersonal relatedness have the impact of distancing other people from him. The more anxious he becomes, the more likely he is to engage in the very operations that are interpersonally problematic for him. (p. 98)

An important idea is that we draw certain behavior from others, which is what makes the interaction a cycle. So, a woman who once got in the habit of acting helpless will continue to relate to others as a helpless person, and others are likely to react helpfully but never to take her very seriously as a competent adult. Unless they're psychologists, they'll never react to her helplessness by acting sure that she can take care of herself, so she will never get that kind of feedback. Furthermore, repeated contact will draw impatient or avoidant reactions from others since they don't always want to help, especially since they don't ask for help in return. Why would they, when they consider their acquaintance incompetent?

The same type of cycle can happen to someone who always appears controlled and competent. Thinking that they retain interpersonal contact by never needing support, they rarely see it offered, and they conclude that people are unhelpful and self-sufficiency is crucial. Safran (1990a) points out that patterns like these don't show up as easy-to-see cognitive distortions or obvious interpersonal deficits. Only repeated instances, and lack of variation from a few interaction patterns, bring the combined cognitive and interpersonal problems to the foreground.

The cognitive elements that need uncovering in the preceding three examples are these:

"People will like me only if they are convinced of my high intelligence."

"People will abandon me if I seem competent."

"People will reject me if I show any weaknesses."

In the examples, you can see that cycles based on these cognitions have the opposite of the desired effect: The persons are disliked, abandoned, and rejected. These cycles thus reinforce themselves by creating more anxiety and redoubled efforts in the wrong direction.

SMALL GROUP EXERCISE

In your small group, come up with another example of a habitual inter-personal pattern that could elicit certain types of behavior from others. If a person never varied from this pattern, what could he or she conclude about other people? Have you ever seen an example of a rigid cognitive-interpersonal cycle?

R e f l e c t i o n

Think about cognitive-interpersonal cycles in your own behavior. Do you draw certain types of behavior from other people? For example, my friend Sue is so exuberant and bouncy that people around her seem to come alive and become more interesting than they usually are. Do you have an effect like this? Some other consistent effect?

Profile of a Theorist

ERIC BERNE

Eric Berne was born on May 10, 1910, in Montreal, Canada. His parents immigrated to Canada from Poland and Russia, and both graduated from McGill University there. Berne's father was a physician who died of tuberculosis at age 38, leaving his mother to raise Eric and his sister while working as an editor and writer. Like his father, Berne received an M.D. from McGill University in Canada, and like his mother, he had a talent for writing and published a humorous article in the journal *Human Fertility*. Berne eventually popularized the ideas of interpersonal psychology in books that readers from all backgrounds enjoyed.

In 1936, Berne began a psychiatric residency at Yale University's School of Medicine. While working in New York City and establishing a private practice in Connecticut, he became an American citizen. He married his first wife in 1940 and began training as a psychoanalyst at the New York Psychoanalytic Institute before joining the Army Medical Corps in 1943.

After being discharged from the service and now divorced, Berne moved to Carmel, California, where he resumed his psychoanalytic training under Eric Erikson and wrote his first book, *The Mind in Action*. Capitalizing on work he'd begun while in the army, Berne became a leading group therapist at several hospitals in the area and continued writing journal articles, some of which challenged orthodox Freudian thinking. He moved further away from mainstream psychoanalysis following the rejection of his application for membership to the San Francisco Psychoanalytic Institute. Though some claim the rejection was devastating to Berne, others credit the event with catalyzing the birth of his new psychotherapeutic approach.

Transactional Analysis (TA), as it came to be called, represented a re-conceptualization of Freud's ego states and included an emphasis on the usefulness of group therapy. Berne related ego states to Parent, Adult, and Child roles, which corresponded roughly to Freud's superego, ego, and id. In addition, TA explored the importance of those states in shaping social interactions, communication strategies, and relationships. *Games People Play*, the title of Berne's highly successful book published in 1964, is a direct reference to the TA concept that people behave according to personal *scripts* and consequently participate in transactions, or *games*, that are driven by those scripts. His writing, combined with theory that was not beyond a layperson's understanding, solidified the popularity of TA in a growing field of approaches to psychotherapy.

As with some other well-known figures in psychology, Berne was reported to display discrepancies between his professional and private personas. Charming and confident with professional peers, he reportedly anguished over his three failed marriages and his own inability to sustain a loving relationship. Those closest to him sometimes described him as cruel and demanding, and one biographer wrote that Berne intentionally wrapped himself in a cloak of mystery. He maintained a vigorous schedule between writing and speaking until his death from a heart attack at age 60. Supporters of TA continued to promote its use, as evidenced by the popularity of Thomas Harris's (1969) *I'm O.K., You're O.K.*, based on Berne's work.

Integrative Aspects of Theory and Treatment

Bandura (1986) predated the cognitive-interpersonal principle with his concept of **triadic reciprocity:** Behavior, cognitive, and other intrapersonal factors interact with environment as determinants of each other. Interpersonal theory (Klerman, Weissman, Rounsaville, & Chevron, 1984) focuses on one part of the environment in this formula—namely, other people.

Both specific cognitive techniques and the therapeutic relationship have repeatedly been supported as mechanisms of change. In cognitive-interpersonal therapy, the therapeutic relationship is intertwined with cognitive technique. Any action in the relationship is a cognitive intervention, in that it supports or refutes the client's interpersonal schematic beliefs (Safran, 1990b).

DISCUSSION IDEAS

Reread the Sullivan excerpt at the beginning of this chapter. Discuss Sullivan's ideas about preadolescent peer groups again, this time using the essential concepts of cognitive-interpersonal theory.

The Process of Cognitive-Interpersonal Therapy

For enduring change to occur, basic interpersonal schemas that predispose a person to repeated problems must be changed. A strictly behavioral intervention could provide some relief, but the person would be prone to relapse because core cognitive structures would remain intact (Safran, 1990b), whereas cognitive-interpersonal treatment encourages more global change—an expansion of the self (Muran, Samstag, Ventur, Segal, & Winston, 2001).

Interpersonal Markers

The therapist assessing a client looks for clues in the client's interpersonal style during the session. These clues are called **interpersonal markers** and can include ways of gazing, the manner of holding one's body, the timing of one's replies to others, tics and gestures, tone of voice, and of course the content of what one says. The therapist takes note of these markers and, unlike friends and acquaintances, brings them up as a topic of discussion. So, after a counselor notices several times that the client tends to be long-winded and boring, she might say: "I noticed that when you told a story just now, you put in a lot of extra details that aren't really related to the main point. What was going through your mind when you chose to add those details?"

The client is much more likely to know what was going through his mind at this point, because the experience is fresh, than he would know when generally discussing his problem. Exploring the situation with the therapist, he says that he enjoys being the center of attention, thinks that he is an amusing story-teller, and probably tries to keep the floor for as long as he can, once he gets it. This client does draw attention from his audience, but he also creates problems in that he often receives irritable and frustrated attention because mutual conversation cannot go on. In this way, others draw away from him, and his solution is to try to retain contact through talking longer—exactly the wrong tactic. His counselor may be the only person in his life who would point this out directly.

Therapy as Laboratory

In cognitive-interpersonal process, therapy is similar to a laboratory in which client and counselor seek explanations for what goes on between the two of them and between the client and other people in his or her life. In an early stage, the client and counselor may construct an **interpersonal inventory** (Klerman, Weissman, Rounsaville, & Chevron, 1984), a review of current relationships in the client's life. This inventory includes the following topics about each important person:

- frequency of contact with client, activities shared, and so on;
- expectations of each party in the relationship, with some idea of whether expectations are fulfilled;

- satisfactory and unsatisfactory aspects of the relationship, including specific, detailed examples; and
- how the client would like to change the relationship, either through change on his or her own part or on the part of the other person. (Adapted from p. 87)

Client and counselor look at this inventory as data for their analysis of interpersonal cycles and schemas.

Collaborative inquiry, much like laboratory work, also occurs when the client and counselor use the here-and-now therapeutic relationship to bring into awareness the client's enactments of patterns. They challenge the thoughts and fears behind the habitual patterns and set up experimental tests of old and new interpersonal schemas (Muran et al., 2001).

Therapist's Participation

Though transference (how the client relates to the counselor and others) is important in cognitive-interpersonal therapy, it is dealt with differently than in traditional psychodynamic treatment. The clinician is more active and affirming in the cognitive-interpersonal mode, more like a Rogerian in tone. The transference relationship reflects the client's general and often dysfunctional modes of interacting with other people (Rice, 1988). In the therapeutic relationship, it is hoped that positive experiences will be internalized and take root in the interpersonal schema of the client. The hope is that change will be aided through intervention into processes that are currently maintaining the difficulty.

"Analysis of communications between patient and therapist," Frank and Frank argue, "is equivalent to study of a stress-producing interpersonal communication system, and internalized reference groups in both patient and therapist affect what transpires in therapy" (p. 187). A grasp of the mutuality of communication is indeed important, and counselors in this mode need the ability to observe themselves and identify their own feelings clearly (Safran & McMain, 1992). The counselor has to realize that she may be wrong in some of her identifications of interpersonal markers. Her reaction to the client's style may reflect her own problem, not his! (For example, the counselor who thought her client's stories boring might be having a personal reaction to his stories' contents, if the subjects are of no interest to her or make her anxious.) In short, the cognitive-interpersonal therapist must be sensitive to both sides of the interaction and ready to recognize his or her own interpersonal schemas. The truth of the matter has to come about through **collaboration** with the client. However, interpersonal theorists believe that the more intense and rigid the client's interaction style is, the more likely it is that the therapist's reactions to the client will be similar to other people's reactions (Safran, 1990b).

Integrative Aspects of Process

The working relationship between the cognitive-interpersonal therapist and the client has similarities to other therapeutic alliances, with some alterations. The counselor shares feelings with the client to provide feedback on the client's impact on others (Bordin, 1979), which creates a different bond than discussing cognitive distortions, as Albert Ellis would in Rational-Emotive Therapy. Psychoanalysts and behavior therapists also take major executive roles, in contrast with client-centered and interpersonal therapists, but the strong educational aspect of cognitive-interpersonal treatment resembles cognitive and behaviorist models. A critical breakthrough for cognitive-interpersonal integration was rejecting the traditional "tendency to view a good therapeutic alliance as a prerequisite for the change process, rather than as an intrinsic part of it" (Safran & McMain, 1992).

Customary Techniques of Cognitive-Interpersonal Therapy

In cognitive-interpersonal therapy, the counselor uses himself as a person in a relationship to the client, in order to clarify how the client connects (or fails to connect) with others.

Metacommunication (Reflecting on Interaction)

Many people, clients included, are unaware of the effect they have on others. As I mentioned before, we all tend to screen out anxiety-provoking stimuli, so accurate feedback may never get through in normal circumstances. This calls to mind a friend of mine who always speaks in exaggerated terms of how bad an experience she has had—her move to a new state was more trouble than anyone else's, her work load is more burdensome, her childbirth was more painful. Though all of us in her social group joke around behind her back about her tendency to have *the absolute worst* of anything, no one has ever mentioned this pattern to her. Luckily, she has many other interaction patterns that are positive and attractive, so this one pattern doesn't get in the way of satisfactory human relatedness.

Therapy is a special setting in which the counselor is free to **metacommunicate**—that is, communicate about communication. The counselor *tells* the client what feelings she is having in response to what the client says and does. This helps the client identify interpersonal patterns that need to be changed. For example, the counselor whose client told boring stories explicitly pointed out that they had irrelevant details, while the client's friends would not do so. As the client and counselor investigate the attention-seeking that makes the client draw a story out to deadening length, the client himself can see how he is achieving the opposite of his goal. This kind of realization comes about through **decentering,** which is looking at one's self from the outside.

Discontinuation of Complementary Responding

Patients and therapists mutually reinforce each other's expectations (Frank & Frank, 1991). According to Leary (1957) and Kiesler (1982), human interactions can be mapped out on an **interpersonal circle,** which predicts what behavior will draw what response. For example, hostility will draw hostility, friendliness will draw friendliness, and submissive behavior will draw advice and leadership from others. Dominant behavior elicits respect if it is also friendly, but it elicits distrust if it is also hostile. The behavior and the elicited response are called **complementary:** "To be fruitful, therapeutic interaction must not complement too exactly the client's interpersonal style, or else that style—and the problems associated with it—will be reinforced. Such reinforcement occurs, for example, when a dependent (friendly-submissive) client is provided with too much support (friendly dominance) or when a hostile client too successfully engages the therapist in battle" (Andrews, 1989, p. 808).

The therapist is able to identify what responses are pulled forth by the client and collaboratively to assess whether the eliciting behaviors are interpersonal markers relevant to the client's problem. For example, does the client's slow manner of speech irritate everyone, or just me? If both I and the client see the slow manner as generally irritating, the strategy is then a matter of carefully avoiding that pulled-for response (irritation) and providing an unexpected one instead. This puts the client in a new situation and requires a new type of response back. Part of the cognitive-interpersonal analysis is that the client doesn't have a large enough repertoire of interaction styles. The therapist's **discontinuation of complementary responding** forces the client into something new. Our everyday rules of politeness forbid open commentary on someone else's interpersonal style, so even a counselor's honest remark about style is an unexpected form of responding.

One of my clients at a counseling center was a Ph.D. candidate in her early 60s, returning to school after a long period focused on marriage and children. Because she had been married since youth, she had never found herself an apartment and moved in, on her own steam. This had been the husband's duty, but now that she was divorced, the client had to do it for herself and presented herself as paralyzed by anxiety about it. She had moved into a boardinghouse temporarily. Though smart and dynamic, she had a scattered, frazzled, helpless demeanor interpersonally, which pulled from me a surge of sisterly helpfulness. (In fact, during our metacommunication it turned out that this client *did* have a big sister who usually bailed her out of these situations.) I had to fight against my instincts and respond to her as though she were completely capable of tackling worldly tasks, rejecting my urge to hold her hand through the process. Thus, we had a lot of exchanges like this:

CLAUDIA: But what about heat and water? Don't I have to get utilities hooked up somehow?

COUNSELOR: Oh, yes, of course, right away.

CLAUDIA: But I don't know how . . . I've never done it . . . I guess I'd have to call . . . but who?

COUNSELOR: [painful silence]

CLAUDIA: I suppose it's in the phone book somewhere. . . . [long pause] I could look in the yellow pages . . . but I have classes all day and they're probably not open at night. . . .

COUNSELOR: [biting tongue]

CLAUDIA: I don't have class till 10 tomorrow. . . . I could try to call before that . . . it doesn't really fit my morning routine. . . .

COUNSELOR: Well, this is just a one-shot thing. You can get it done in the morning, I'm sure.

Claudia's feedback to me at termination a couple of months later was revealing. When asked what part of our work she found most helpful, she said, "Oh, that's easy: You never acted like I was a crazy lady." From an interpersonal point of view, I refused to respond to her crazy-lady behavior and chose to respond to her as a grown-up graduate student, and she was able to act like one.

Experiential Disconfirmation

As in the dialogue above, a cognitive-interpersonal counselor who discontinues an expected interactional pattern acts to *disconfirm* problematic interpersonal schemas. Thus, for example, I broke out of this pattern:

Claudia acts helpless . . . [leading to] . . . Sympathy and help

and substituted this one:

Claudia acts helpless . . . [leading to] . . . Confidence in client ability.

In short, Claudia's belief that she was incompetent was disconfirmed by her experience, both with me and with the utility companies.

Cognitive-interpersonal counselors may give homework assignments whose goal is **experiential disconfirmation.** Claudia's success at getting utilities hooked up by herself worked this way. Similarly, a person whose basic communication is a complaint might agree to try eliminating complaints at work for a week, to see whether his negative style was really necessary to connect with other people.

Integrative Aspects of Technique

You have probably recognized in the cognitive-interpersonal approach some techniques that come straight from cognitive therapy, aimed at disconfirming harmful beliefs. These include reality-testing, processing schema-inconsistent information, and collaborative empiricism (see Chapter 9). Clients are given homework assignments that could just as well come from behavioral strategies, such as experimenting with new approaches to other people. And drawing links among the current situation, other situations outside the session, and early experiences is much like psychodynamic treatment. All of these techniques are practiced with a focus on the interpersonal world. The unification of thought, emotion, and behavior interventions with a defined theoretical focus makes the cognitive-interpersonal approach integrative.

Uses for Cognitive-Interpersonal Techniques

When a counselor perceives problems arising from a client's habitual ways of relating to others, the techniques of cognitive-interpersonal therapy are applicable.

Depression and Related Problems

The precursor to cognitive-interpersonal counseling, *interpersonal therapy* (IPT), was originally designed as a short-term, empirically based treatment for clinical depression (Klerman, Weissman, Rounsaville, & Chevron, 1984). The theory is that depression has its roots in long-term problems in interpersonal relatedness, usually concentrated in one of four areas: grief, interpersonal disputes, role transitions, and interpersonal deficits (loneliness and social isolation). The brief IPT treatment focuses on one or two of these areas, follows a clear manual, and lends itself to combination with psychopharmacology. It has demonstrated efficacy as a therapy for depression (American Psychiatric Association, 2000).

Supporting the inclusion of interpersonal theory in a broader arena, IPT has been adapted for adolescent family and school problems, complicated pregnancy and postpartum depression, dysthymic disorder, bipolar disorder, difficulties faced by elderly medical patients (Hollon, Thase, & Markowitz, 2002), substance abuse, marital problems, and eating disorders (Fairburn, 1997). A shorter, lower-level intervention has been designed for use in medical settings, in six 15- to 20-minute sessions designed to help patients deal with stress. This form, called interpersonal counseling (IPC; Weissman, Markowitz, & Klerman, 2000), can be performed by trained health-care professionals.

Personality Disorders and Difficult Therapeutic Alliances

People with personality disorders are known for narrow and extreme interpersonal styles, which reflect cognitive distortions of who they must be and difficulties in emotional processing (of both their own and others' feelings) (Safran & McMain, 1992). They are also notoriously hard to help in counseling since these habits run counter to the establishment of a good working alliance. Cognitive-interpersonal therapy, instead of trying to work around the interpersonal weirdness, makes use of it in the here-and-now relationship. This is a promising area of exploration.

The same approach could also be extended to other clients, such as those who are not necessarily personality-disordered but resistant to forming therapeutic alliances. The first case conceptualization for this chapter provides an example.

Interpersonal Handicaps

Many people come to counseling because they feel lonely and isolated. Their work or school functioning may be adequate, but they characteristically hold jobs and degrees below their true capacities due to inability to use personal friendships, kind feelings, and positive first impressions to their advantage. They look around and see that other people have deep, lasting friendships, and they realize that somehow they've missed the relationship train. Cognitive-interpersonal treatment is well equipped to help these people, in that the counselor can hold up a mirror and help explore what they are doing to create distance instead of warmth in others (Marcotte & Safran, 2002).

🌿 Case Conceptualization: An Example

SELF-FULFILLING PROPHECY, MALADAPTIVE BEHAVIOR, AND PSYCHOTHERAPY

Robert C. Carson (1982)

Several years ago the author received a telephone call from a never-married woman in her late twenties with whom he had had a brief previous acquaintance; in rather direct fashion she requested that he take her on as a psychotherapy client. There appeared to be no emergency, and he felt compelled owing to a heavy schedule to suggest referral to another therapist. The woman declined, but phoned again approximately a year later with the same request. Again, and for the same reason, he attempted to divert the client to another therapist, but she was adamant and requested to be put on his "waiting list." Intrigued, and admittedly somewhat flattered, he thereupon relented and psychotherapy commenced.

One of the peculiarities of the author's therapeutic style is to address questions explicitly and immediately as they arise, and the first question here, obviously, was, "Why me?" The client unabashedly responded with two comments: (1) she thought he would be in some way especially likely to be of help to her, and (2) he reminded her of her father. Only over the course of the subsequent year was he able to gain a full appreciation of how unpropitious a beginning this was.

The client immediately adopted an extremely hostile and suspicious attitude, refused virtually all therapeutic suggestions, and was generally uncooperative and abrasive. She repeatedly gave vent to her perception of the therapist as vain, arrogant, power-driven, Machiavellian, manipulative, and incapable of normal human sensitivities to others' suffering. Every gesture of warmth on the part of the therapist was interpreted as merely additional evidence of the above attributes. In short, it seemed that she was doing everything possible to provoke an exasperated unilateral termination of the relationship. She might have succeeded in doing so, had the therapist not learned long before *not* to do in therapy precisely those things he felt most impelled to do. Instead, he implacably but calmly insisted on a thorough examination of the evidential bases of the characteristics assigned to him, and repeatedly asserted his willingness to be put to *fair* tests, having *explicit* criteria, concerning his personal attitudes and commitments.

This client had had a marked affectional attachment to her father, whom she idealized. As is often the case, however, the father was quite unprepared to handle his daughter's maturation into a physically adult female, and he reacted with strong signals of rejection to any "femininity" she displayed; his almost phobic reaction to female sexuality was voiced crudely and often. On the other hand, he demanded that his daughter be "successful" in the conventional terms of education and the attainment of professional status, a demand the client interpreted as being wholly narcissistically motivated, and which she therefore deviously managed not to fulfill, although giving the appearance of (and in some sense "honestly") trying. He uniformly rebuffed her attempts to become acceptable on any other grounds.

The client's only other important relationship with a male had occurred several years prior to her therapy and involved a young man who also reminded her of her father. While the relationship had begun somewhat idyllically, it ended in the client's being rather cruelly exploited and rejected. She had remained celibate since, and indeed had developed a style of dealing with men that was virtually certain to drive them away in the first minutes of an encounter. She was also lonely and miserable much of the time.

Even with such a brief recounting the reader will probably have little difficulty in reconstructing this young woman's perceptions and beliefs about the characteristics of men, and of what she might reasonably expect from them. In a word, she regarded them as exclusively concerned with the satisfaction of their own needs and as contemptuous and exploitative toward women, particularly but not exclusively in their sexual aspect; in fact, concerning the latter, she had largely bought into her father's definition that a sexual woman must necessarily be a "c—t." Somewhat paradoxically— given her father's pronounced overt aversion to sexuality—she regarded nearly all other men as wishing to convert her to that status. After the affair mentioned above, she relentlessly deprived herself of any opportunity to disprove this hypothesis.

My main point in recounting this vignette, in fact, is to illustrate how the client had organized her life in such a manner as to be virtually certain to fail to disconfirm the principal hypotheses guiding it, and indeed to run a considerable risk of having certain of them actively and positively supported by empirical events. Many men in her acquaintance *were* driven to excessive displays of "macho" and self-aggrandizing behaviors in the face of her withering, unremitting, and obviously conveyed contempt of them, dismissing her as unworthy of the serious attention she secretly craved; others indicated in varying ways that they would be willing to put up with her only as long as it would take to satisfy themselves sexually. Not surprisingly, she brought the same attitudes into her therapy, although, as has already been implied, she somehow intuitively sensed that it might come out differently. After a very long time, in fact, the client came to see the relationship with the therapist as the most honest and rewarding she had ever experienced, and therapy proceeded to a very satisfactory conclusion—the first such outcome this client had ever enjoyed with a male person.

"Might come out differently" is the operative phrase here, because, as already noted, the test of the therapist was a severe one. In fact, at a midway point in therapy, the client explicitly expressed her intention *not* to be influenced by therapy because such an eventuality would indicate, among other things, that: (1) the therapist would be entitled to a "feather in his cap"; (2) he would thereby win a victory in the "obvious" battle of wills between them; and (3) he would gloat unmercifully at the successful conclusion of this alleged contest. She gave no quarter on the point that a successful conclusion might enhance the satisfaction of the therapist out of concern for her and her future happiness. The latter was to come much later, and then at first only grudgingly; but it did come, more or less concurrently with the gradual emergence of the client from the personal hell she had been living. (pp. 64–66) ■ ■

DISCUSSION IDEAS

1. Why did Carson think the beginning of therapy was unpropitious? What might be your reaction as a counselor in this situation?

2. How did Carson respond to the client's hostile accusations? Why did he refrain from terminating?

3. What early experiences of the client were relevant to her current interpersonal relationships?

4. How did the client rebel against her father's demands for her success? Have you ever seen a case of such rebellion?

5. What would have disproved the client's hypothesis about men? Why did she not have disproving experiences with men? How might *selective inattention* be operating?

6. How would you describe the client's interpersonal schema? How did she enact this with the therapist? What did she think Carson's motives were?

7. What was the role of hope in this case?

8. Consider the client from a different theoretical viewpoint. For example, how would a Rogerian therapist conceptualize the case? What might a behaviorist do first? A feminist therapist? What Gestalt techniques might be useful? How important is behavior in this case? How important is cognition?

Critiques of Integrative Innovations

Many criticisms of integrative psychotherapy stem from its very complexity, which is unavoidable.

Syncretism

Integrationists rush to point out that on the shallow end of eclecticism lurks the **syncretic,** the counselor who has a grab-bag of techniques but no organized thought behind their use. All three categories of integration—theoretical integration, technical eclecticism, and common factors orientation—involve thinking through how and why different principles might work together.

This thought process, necessary to legitimate integration, means that you must know more about each theory of counseling than most people do. You also need to be aware of whether techniques are proven to be effective, because there is no reason to add an unsupported strategy to your treatment. Therefore, integrative practice lends itself to the taste of counselors who enjoy wide reading on psychological topics and relish continuing education.

Difficulties of Research

A problem integrative psychotherapy faces scientifically is the difficulty of generation and testing of hypotheses from new points of view. Given that counseling research often involves pitting one therapy against another in outcome studies, even deciding which blend to compare with which is troublesome—and, in any case, is there such a thing as a *pure* example of a certain blend? As Gottlieb and Cooper (2002) note, "This type of research is very hard to conduct, particularly because there is a high level of complexity in approaches, creating significant obstacles to developing a common research strategy" (p. 560).

Defining the Scope of Practice

"After all, without a specific therapeutic orientation, how would we know what journals to subscribe to or which conventions to attend?" (Goldfried, 1980, p. 996). In asking this question, Goldfried was making light of the identity crisis of integrative therapists. Lack of a firm identity, as far as therapeutic stance is concerned, comes with the integrative approach; you also risk being considered unlearned, wishy-washy, or syncretic. Defining one's **scope of practice** is more difficult with integrative therapy because of the variability that is built into it. Yet, it is important ethically to offer only those treatments you are competent to deliver.

In addition, the information you give your client at the outset about what is to be done in treatment will not be cut-and-dried. You could express yourself so vaguely that the client still has no idea what to expect, or you could express yourself so specifically that the client is completely confused by the array of possibilities. It is difficult to say what particular treatments your client will benefit from until therapy has moved along and you have identified the client's patterns. Yet our ethical standards of informed consent require that we let the client know what to expect.

Discovering Other Integrative Possibilities

1. Only one example of an integrative approach was included in this chapter, but there are many others. Look up the journals related to this subject—*Journal of Integrative and Eclectic Psychotherapy* and *Journal of Psychotherapy Integration*—and list five more integrative approaches, each with at least one sentence of description. Some integrations that you may discover in the journals are these:

   humanistic and behavioral

   object relations and self psychology

   person-centered and psychodynamic

   reality therapy and Adlerian

   existentialist and cognitive

   Gestalt and behavior

   family systems and other approaches

2. If you go to *www.cyberpsych.org/sepi*, you'll find the website for the Society for the Exploration of Psychotherapy Integration, founded in 1983 by Marvin Goldfried, Paul Wachtel, and other psychologists interested in psychotherapy integration. Investigate this website and look for events and topics in the field this current year.

3. You may be interested in other integrations that include interpersonal psychotherapy, or want to know more about interpersonal psychotherapy by itself. If so, you can go to *www.interpersonalpsychotherapy.org*, the website address for the International Society for Interpersonal Psychotherapy, formed in May 2000. Another active website is that of the Society for Interpersonal Theory and Research, at *www.vcu.edu/sitar*.

Comprehensive Review: Creating a Theories Chart

Each theoretical approach makes fundamental assumptions about human nature, psychopathology, psychotherapy, and change. A clear understanding of each one separately will help you decide on integrative and eclectic blends that make sense. Now that you have studied many orientations, you will benefit from a summary overview that invites comparison and contrast. In the small group exercise that follows, you will make up a chart of theories and basic features of each. Various sources will provide you with such charts already filled out, but I strongly believe that you will learn more by creating the entries yourselves. This exercise may take up more than one class period, or you may have to work outside class. The charts you produce will be helpful in reviewing for national and state professional examinations, and in preparing for job interviews.

SMALL GROUP EXERCISE

Divide these orientations among the small groups in your class: Psychoanalytical/Psychodynamic, Adlerian, Existential, Humanistic, Gestalt, Behavioral, Cognitive-Behavioral, Family Systems, Gender and Culture Systems, Transpersonal, and Cognitive-Interpersonal. Each group will prepare a *Theories Chart* with the orientations reading across rows and the features reading across columns, as shown in Table 13.1.

Before your small group work, try filling in one of the rows or columns as a class, using the blackboard or overhead projector. Your instructor will help steer you in the right direction.

As you work on your entries, these questions will help you think about each orientation:

1. What important information about the client is necessary in each approach?
2. How important is insight?
3. How important is emotion?
4. How important is history (cultural, family, and personal)?

After you have had practice as a whole class, return to work on your small group's assigned orientations. When your group has finished its chart, collect copies of charts from all other groups. In your group, revise the other charts to your liking. Enlist your instructor's help to make sure your charts are accurate.

Questions to Ask Yourself

When I was studying the Morita psychotherapy method (Chapter 12), I found myself very attracted to it. On plenty of occasions, I thought, "Of course! That's just right!" Sitting on the balcony pondering my endorsement, I realized that the Morita method reflects the way that I conduct (or try to conduct)

TABLE 13.1
Theories Chart

Orientation	Idea of healthy personality	Sources of problems	Curative elements of counseling	Therapeutic relationship	Techniques	Terms	Important names	Varieties and variations
[family systems]								
[Gestalt]								

my own life. I consider myself an extremely emotional person, and I always attend to my emotions as "news from the front," but I call on my rational capacities to determine the course of my day and how I overtly react to other people. I've gotten through many of the hard times in life by putting one foot in front of the other or, in Morita terms, "doing what needs to be done." I've seen so much damage inflicted by uncontrolled emotionality that I steer in the other direction.

Take some time to look over the table of contents of this book and remember your responses to the various psychotherapies. Did you have an experience like mine, in which you had a strong positive feeling about a certain approach? You may have looked at things quite differently from the way I do; for example, if you've witnessed more damage done by overcontrolled, suppressed emotionality, you probably felt more "Of course!" responses to approaches that emphasize awareness of emotions and expressive techniques.

Your personality and outlook on life are important factors when you choose a theoretical approach as your own. This is a good time to review your responses to George Kelly's *personal constructs* in Chapter 2. In your training, you will have opportunities to practice several different approaches. When I was in training, I provided individual therapy under an object-relations oriented supervisor and then under a cognitivist and was able to see, close up, the different approaches put into action. I have worked in a cognitive-behavioral anxiety clinic, on a rehab ward where the approach was behavioral/psychoeducational, in a hospital where my work concerned family systems, and in a community mental health clinic whose director was firmly Rogerian. (I've also worked at sites where the approach was to get through the day without incurring either effort or injury.) You will no doubt find that when you have practiced several approaches, the ones that appeal to you will be clear. However, using techniques that you are uncomfortable with is part of your education, and you may discover that working past your discomfort is valuable. When my supervisor first suggested that I use role playing with a client, I demurred, saying that I never went in for that sort of thing. He insisted, and I found that the role plays the client and I did were the best techniques in the whole treatment. You will be most successful at the therapies that suit your way of thinking and personality style, but the range of treatments from which you select will also evolve as you develop.

SMALL GROUP EXERCISE

Each member of the group should take a few moments to write down the approach he or she is most attracted to and least attracted to. Discuss your preferences and doubts, presenting possible reasons for your likes and dislikes.

🌀 Case Conceptualization: Technical Eclecticism Practice

Following is a case description developed by psychotherapist Jana Reddin Long. The client, Stephen, has seen his school counselor a few times, and she has referred him to you, a counselor in the community.

- Your task at this point is to develop a case conceptualization based on one of the theories you have studied. Use your Theories Chart to help you get started. Remember that you are not required to use a cognitive-interpersonal basis for this exercise, but can make use of everything you know.

- Then decide what you will explore in your first interview with Stephen, and write an outline of the interview and your goals for that session.

- Imagining that your case conceptualization still seems sound after the first interview, map out the techniques you intend to use in Stephen's treatment. Be sure that you can explain why each technique will help, how it relates to the general theory you are using as a basis, and why the techniques work together.

- If relevant, connect your techniques to stages of therapy. (Will they be used all together or in a logical sequence?) Assume you will have about twenty sessions.

- I am encouraging you to take a technically eclectic approach here. Feel free to borrow techniques from the whole array you have learned, if you can justify them. I am not asking you for theoretical integration, since that is a lifetime project.

THE DISPLACED TEENAGER

Jana Reddin Long

Stephen first sought help from his school counselor, Rhiannon, after a few weeks of school had past. He is new at the high school, not only because he is in ninth grade, but also because he has recently moved to town to live with his mother and step-father. He describes this past summer as "total chaos." He has lived with his father and step-mother his whole life in a small town where everyone knew everyone else. But, this summer his mother began asking questions about his father every time he would visit her. She noticed that his clothes were a little too worn, that his shoes were too small. When she would ask him about the types of activities he was involved in at home, he never had much to say since he usually stayed inside the house. He had tried to keep his mother from finding out that his father and step-mother didn't have any money to pay for new clothes or fun activities. It's not like he expected new clothes or wanted to go out with friends anyway. The more his mother asked questions, the more uncertain Stephen was about how to respond. How do you tell your mother that your father doesn't have the money to take care of you because he gambles it away each weekend? And, besides, if his mother found out, then what would she do? She eventually found out when she bombarded Stephen with questions and he blurted out the situation before he knew what he was doing. She was stunned, but immediately told him he wouldn't be living with his father anymore. She was right. One week later he had completely moved to live with his mother and step-father, and two half-siblings. A new family, new town, new school—all in such a short time.

Stephen sought help from Rhiannon, the school counselor, because he feels so miserable. He has so many mixed-up feelings that he has a hard time knowing what he feels at all. And, he hates being at a new school that's so much bigger than his school at home. He's been to see Rhiannon a couple of times. At first, he was uncertain of how much to tell her, and how she would respond. But, so far he's been pleasantly surprised. She seems genuinely interested in him. He actually looks forward to their next session.

"It's been about a month now. I mean, a month since you've been in school. Am I right?" Rhiannon begins the session.

"Yeah, I guess it has been about a month. It's only been about six weeks since I've been living here."

"A lot of changes in such a short period of time. What kind of changes have you experienced?" questions Rhiannon.

"God, what hasn't changed? Everything! I left my parents, my home, my room, my friends. Now I'm at a big school, new town, no friends, new house, new parents. Everything has changed."

"Your whole world has changed. It sounds like it changed overnight," offers Rhiannon.

"Yeah, and it all happened without me." Stephen states in a disgusted tone.

"Without you?"

"No one asked me what I wanted. No one prepared me that all these changes would be happening soon. They just happened," explains Stephen.

"You felt completely out of control."

"I WAS completely out of control!"

"You didn't have any power, any choice." Rhiannon paraphrases Stephen's perspective of the situation.

"Exactly! One minute everything was fine. Then, all of a sudden everything was out of control. If I hadn't opened my big mouth!" Stephen looks down at the floor shaking his head.

"It sounds like you blame yourself for some of the situation."

"I guess. Sometimes I think it's all my fault. If I hadn't told Mom about Dad, then everything would still be the same. I wouldn't be here."

"You blame yourself for telling your mother about your father's behavior?"

"I opened my big mouth. I ratted him out! Mom didn't have to know about Dad's gambling. It's none of her business. She kept asking questions and asking questions all of the time. I didn't know how to answer them. I didn't know what to say. And she wouldn't back down. She just kept asking. Finally, I just broke, I guess. I told her that we didn't have any money at home because Dad lost it all gambling."

"Your mom just kept asking so many questions that you finally told her what was happening," Rhiannon summarizes what she hears Stephen saying.

"I didn't mean to. I promise! I didn't mean to tell on him, to get him in trouble. I really didn't mean to. You believe me, don't you?" asks Stephen.

"You sound afraid. You sound afraid that I will believe you meant to get your father in trouble."

"I just don't want you to think I did it on purpose."

"I probably would have done the same thing in your situation. It sounds like you felt a lot of pressure from your mom."

"Yeah, I did. Do you think my dad knows that I didn't mean to rat on him?"

"You are afraid that your dad will think you did it on purpose?"

"I'm scared he won't talk to me now."

"You're afraid that he won't talk to you. I wonder if you are afraid that he won't love you as much as he used to love you."

"If I thought someone had ratted me out, I wouldn't want to have anything to do with them."

"You're afraid he won't want to be a part of your life."

"Yeah. What if things are never the same again?"

"How were things with your dad before all of this happened?" asks Rhiannon.

"He was usually pretty cool. I mean, he never really bothered me much. We would watch sports together a lot."

"It sounds like you've had some fun times with your dad. How was your relationship with your dad?"

"OK, I guess. I mean, I would get in trouble for regular stuff. You know, cleaning my room and all that. But, he helped me with my homework sometimes. We went to the race track together."

"I wonder if there are aspects to your relationship with your father that you don't like."

"I don't know. I love him. He's my dad." Stephen pauses.

"Go on," coaxes Rhiannon.

"It's just that . . . I wonder why he did it. Why would he gamble so much? I mean, even if he could have just not gambled so much, we would have been fine. We would have had the money to pay our bills."

"You love your dad, but it sounds like you are angry at him too. Sometimes we feel lots of emotions all together—love, anger, disappointment, guilt."

"Yeah, it's hard to know what I'm feeling. I just keep thinking, if he loved me and wanted me to live with him, then why didn't he just stop gambling? Why can't I be as important to him?"

"You feel hurt?" Rhiannon reflects.

"Hurt? I guess. I miss him, but I'm mad at him too. Yeah. I guess I feel hurt."

"How does that feel for you?" Rhiannon explores.

"Hurt, sad, angry. It feels so confusing. It feels so heavy. I feel like I'm carrying around a big rock," describes Stephen. "It's so confusing. I just feel confused. I don't know what I feel, what I want, what's going to happen."

"You have so many feelings and your situation seems uncertain. It sounds like you have lots of unanswered questions. Confused seems like a pretty normal response. I think I would feel confused too." Rhiannon offers reassurance.   ■ ■

Theory, Research, and Your Future

In this textbook, I intended to provide you with a lively overview of the major theories of psychotherapy and the techniques that flow from the theories. You are now ready to follow your own inclinations about what to study in more depth, what kinds of orientations will attract you to a work site, and who will be the optimal supervisors in your training. I encourage you to look back over this book once a year or so and reconsider your approaches, because as you mature professionally, different ideas will appeal to you. Future review of the text will also help you prepare for state and national certification examinations. I have attempted to include most of the theory and technique material that appears on such exams.

I also encourage you to stay in touch with psychological research, even though your days will be full of other concerns. Take a working vacation and attend conferences of organizations like the American Association for Marriage and Family Therapy (*www.aamft.org*), the American Counseling Association (*www.counseling.org*), the National Institute for the Teaching of Psychology (*www.nitop.org*), and the American Psychological Association (*www.apa.org*). Find out through your social sciences librarian which are the major scholarly journals in your particular area of interest (or track down the journal titles listed in this textbook), and subscribe to at least one. Keep switching your yearly subscription until you find one that you like to read.

My favorites for keeping up with the field are periodicals that summarize several major research areas every month: the *Harvard Mental Health Letter* and *Clinician's Research Digest*. By reading these short (six- to eight-page) publications, you can get the gist of research efforts across many areas of psychology. These provide the references for looking up complete articles when they are relevant to your interests. Less scholarly but more fun, *Psychotherapy Networker* is a magazine appealing to practitioners in all areas of counseling, and it can be found on popular newsstands.

Finally, I suggest a leisurely browse through the Psychology and Self-Help sections of a big bookstore once a month or so. You will find out what other psychologists are thinking about and what your clients may be reading or hearing about on television. Given your background in theories of counseling, you will be able to evaluate the pop psychology of the moment and to speak about it intelligently when people ask your opinion.

And they will.

KEY TERMS

anxiety
cognitive-interpersonal cycles
collaboration
common factors orientation
complementary
decentering
discontinuation of complementary
  responding
eclecticism
experiential disconfirmation
interpersonal circle
interpersonal inventory
interpersonal markers
interpersonal schema

metacommunicate
scope of practice
security operations
selective inattention
self-schemas
self-system
syncretic
Systematic Treatment Selection (STS)
technical eclecticism
theoretical integration
therapeutic alliance
three-dimensional model
transtheoretical therapy
triadic reciprocity

Exploring Key Terms

In your small group, choose six terms from the list above and create a matching exercise. Instead of using plain definitions to match the terms with, try to make up examples or quotations (from client or therapist) that illustrate the terms. Place the six terms in one column and scramble the matching illustrations in the other column. Exchange exercises with all other small groups, match the columns, and return the exercises to their creators for scoring. Discuss the exercises in class as a whole. Distribute correct versions of the exercises, electronically or on paper, to everyone.

REFERENCES

Acierno, R. E., Hersen, M., & Van Hasselt, V. B. (1993). Interventions for panic disorder: A critical review of the literature. *Clinical Psychology Review, 13,* 561–587.

American Psychiatric Association. (2000). Practice guidelines for the treatment of patients with major depressive disorder (revision). *American Journal of Psychiatry, 157,* supplement 4.

Andrews, J. D. W. (1989). Integrating visions of reality: Interpersonal diagnosis and the existential vision. *American Psychologist, 44,* 803–817.

Arkowitz, H. (1992). Integrative theories of therapy. In D. K. Freedheim (Ed.), *History of psychotherapy: A century of change* (pp. 261–303). Washington, DC: American Psychological Association.

Aspy, D. N., Aspy, C. B., Russel, G., & Wedel, M. (2000). Carkhuff's human technology: A verification and extension of Kelly's (1997) suggestion to integrate the humanistic and technical components of counseling. *Journal of Counseling and Development, 78,* 29–37.

Atkinson, D. R., Kim, B. S. K., & Caldwell, R. (1998). Ratings of helper roles by multicultural psychologists and Asian American students: Initial support for the three-dimensional model of multicultural counseling. *Journal of Counseling Psychology, 45,* 414–423.

Atkinson, D. R., Thompson, C., & Grant, S. (1993). A three-dimensional model for counseling racial/ethnic minorities. *The Counseling Psychologist, 21,* 257–277.

Bandura, A. (1986). *Social foundations of thought and action: A social cognitive theory.* Englewood Cliffs, NJ: Prentice-Hall.

Berne, E. (1947). *The mind in action.* New York: Simon & Schuster.

Berne, E. (1964). *Games people play.* New York: Grove Press.

Beutler, L. E., Alomohamed, S., Moleiro, C., & Romanelli, R. (2002). Systematic treatment selection and prescriptive therapy. In F. W. Kaslow & J. Lebow (Eds.), *Comprehensive handbook of psychotherapy. Vol. 4: Integrative/Eclectic* (pp. 185–212). New York: Wiley.

Bordin, E. S. (1979). The generalizability of the psychoanalytic concept of the working alliance. *Psychotherapy: Theory, Research, and Practice, 16,* 252–260.

Bowlby, J. (1973). *Attachment and loss. Volume II: Separation: Anxiety and anger.* New York: Basic Books.

Carson, R. C. (1982). Self-fulfilling prophecy, maladaptive behavior, and psychotherapy. In J. C. Anchin & D. J. Kiesler (Eds.), *Handbook of interpersonal psychotherapy* (pp. 64–77). New York: Pergamon Press.

Constantine, M. (2001). Multicultural training, theoretical orientation, empathy, and multicultural case conceptualization ability in counselors. *Journal of Mental Health Counseling, 23,* 357–372.

Elkin, I., Shea, T., Watkins, J. T., Imber, S. D., Sotsky, S. M., Collins, J. F., et al. (1989). National Institute of Mental Health Treatment of Depression Collaborative Research Program: General effectiveness of treatments. *Archives of General Psychiatry, 46,* 971–982.

Eysenck, H. J. (1952). The effects of psychotherapy: An evaluation. *Journal of Consulting Psychology, 16,* 319–324.

Fairburn, C. G. (1997). Interpersonal psychotherapy for bulimia nervosa. In D. M. Garner & P. E. Garfinkel (Eds.), *Handbook of treatment for eating disorders* (2nd ed., pp. 278–294). New York: Guilford.

Frank, J. D., & Frank, J. B. (1991). *Persuasion and healing: A comparative study of psychotherapy.* Baltimore: Johns Hopkins University Press.

Goldfried, M. R. (1980). Toward the delineation of therapeutic change principles. *American Psychologist, 35,* 991–999.

Gottlieb, M. C., & Cooper, C. C. (2002). Ethical and risk management issues in integrative therapy. In F. W. Kaslow & J. Lebow (Eds.), *Comprehensive handbook of psychotherapy. Vol. 4: Integrative/Eclectic* (pp. 557–568). New York: Wiley.

Harris, T. (1969). *I'm O.K., you're O.K.* New York: Harper & Row.

Hollon, S. D., Thase, M. E., & Markowitz, J. C. (2002). Treatment and prevention of depression. *Psychological Science in the Public Interest, 3,* 39–77.

Iwakabe, S., Rogan, K., & Stalikas, A. (2000). The relationship between client emotional expressions, therapist interventions, and the working alliance: An exploration of eight emotional expression events. *Journal of Psychotherapy Integration, 10,* 375–401.

Johnson, S. M., & Greenberg, L. S. (1987). Integration in marital therapy. *International Journal of Eclectic Psychotherapy, 6,* 202–215.

Kiesler, D. J. (1982). Interpersonal theory for personality and psychotherapy. In J. C. Anchon & D. J. Kiesler (Eds.), *Handbook of interpersonal psychotherapy* (pp. 3–24). New York: Pergamon.

Klerman, G. L., Weissman, M. M., Rounsaville, B. J., & Chevron, E. S. (1984). *Interpersonal psychotherapy of depression.* New York: Basic Books.

Lazarus, A. A. (1989). Why I am an eclectic (not an integrationist). *British Journal of Guidance and counselling, 17,* 248–258.

Lazarus, A. A. (1996). The utility and futility of combining treatments in psychotherapy. *Clinical Psychology: Science and Practice, 3,* 59–68.

Leary, T. (1957). *Interpersonal diagnosis of personality.* New York: Ronald Press.

Lyddon, W. J. (1989). Personal epistemology and preference for counseling. *Journal of Counseling Psychology, 36,* 423–429.

Marcotte, D., & Safran, J. D. (2002). Cognitive-interpersonal psychotherapy. In F. W. Kaslow & J. Lebow (Eds.), *Comprehensive handbook of psychotherapy. Vol. 4: Integrative/Eclectic* (pp. 273–293). New York: Wiley.

Miller, S. D., Duncan, B. L., Hubble, M. A. (2002). Client-directed, outcome-informed clinical work. In F. W. Kaslow & J. Lebow (Eds.), *Comprehensive handbook of psychotherapy. Vol. 4: Integrative/Eclectic* (pp. 185–212). New York: Wiley.

Muran, J. C., Smastag, L. W., Ventur, E. D., Segal, Z. V., & Winston, A. (2001). A cognitive-interpersonal case study of a self. *Journal of Clinical Psychology, 57,* 307–330.

Norcross, J. C., Hedges, M., and Prochaska, J. O. (2002). The face of 2010: A Delphi poll on the future of psychotherapy. *Professional Psychology: Research and Practice, 33,* 316–322.

Paul, G. L. (1966). *Insight versus densensitization in psychotherapy.* Stanford: Stanford University Press, 1966.

Paul, G. L. (1967). Strategy of outcome research in psychotherapy. *Journal of Consulting Psychology, 31,* 109–118.

Perri, M. G. (1998). The maintenance of treatment effects in the long-term management of obesity. *Clinical Psychology: Science and Practice, 5,* 526–543.

Prochaska, J. O., & DiClemente, C. C. (2002). Transtheoretical therapy. In F. W. Kaslow & J. Lebow (Eds.), *Comprehensive handbook of psychotherapy. Vol. 4: Integrative/Eclectic* (pp. 165–183). New York: Wiley.

Rice, L. N. (1988). Integration and the client-centered relationship. *Journal of Integrative and Eclectic Psychotherapy, 7,* 291–302.

Safran, J. D. (1990a). Towards a refinement of cognitive therapy in light of interpersonal theory: I. Theory. *Clinical Psychology Review, 10,* 87–105.

Safran, J. D. (1990b). Towards a refinement of cognitive therapy in light of interpersonal theory: II. Practice. *Clinical Psychology Review, 10,* 107–121.

Safran, J. D., & McMain, S. (1992). A cognitive-interpersonal approach to the treatment of personality disorders. *Journal of Cognitive Psychotherapy, 6,* 59–68.

Sullivan, H. S. (1953). *The interpersonal theory of psychiatry.* New York: W. W. Norton.

Teyber, E. (1992). *Interpersonal process in psychotherapy* (2nd ed.). Pacific Grove, CA: Brooks Cole.

Wachtel, P. L. (1977). *Psychoanalysis and behavior therapy: Toward an integration.* New York: Basic Books.

Weissman, M. M., Markowitz, J., & Klerman, G. L. (2000). *Comprehensive guide to interpersonal psychotherapy.* New York: Basic Books.

Yalom, I. D. (1995). *The theory and practice of group psychotherapy.* New York: Basic Books.

Credits

Chapter 4

p. 103: From D. W. Winnicott, "String: A Technique of Communication," from *The Journal of Child Psychology and Psychiatry,* Vol. 1, pp. 49–52, 1960. Reprinted with permission of Blackwell Publishing

Chapter 5

p. 115: "The Application of Adlerian Psychology with Asian-American Clients," by J. M. Carlson and J. D. Carlson, from the *Journal of Individual Psychology,* 56:2, pp. 214–225. Copyright © 2000 by the University of Texas Press. All rights reserved. **p. 139:** Excerpt from Matt Carlson and J. D. Carlson, "The Case of Jin," from *Journal of Individual Psychology,* 56, 2000, 214–225.

Chapter 6

p. 147: From *On Becoming a Person* by Carl Rogers. Copyright © 1961, and renewed 1989 by Carl R. Rogers. Reprinted by permission of Houghton Mifflin Company. All rights reserved. **p. 185:** Copyright © 1980 by the Yalom Family Trust. Reprinted by permission of Basic Books, a member of Perseus Book, L.L.C.

Chapter 7

p. 194: Reprinted by permission of Science and Behavior Books, Inc. **p. 226:** From H. T. Close, "Gross Exaggeration with a Schizophrenic Patient," in *Gestalt Therapy Now* by J. Fagan & I. L. Shepherd (eds.). Copyright © Science and Behavior Books, Inc. Used with permission.

Chapter 8

p. 235: Reprinted with the permission of The Association for Behavior Analysis. **pp. 254/275:** From *Self-Directed Behavior, Self-Modification for Personal Adjustment,* Seventh Edition, by Watson/Tharp. Copyright © 1997. Reprinted with permission of Wordsworth, a division of Thomson Learning. www.thomsonrights.com. Fax 800-730-2215.

Chapter 9

p. 288: From *Love Is Never Enough* by Aaron T. Beck. Copyright © 1988 by Aaron T. Beck, M.D. Reprinted by permission of HarperCollins Publishers, Inc., and Arthur Pine Associates, Inc. **p. 300:** Table, "Treatments That Work With Children," from E. R. Christopherson & S. L. Mortweet, *Treatments That Work with Children: Empirically Supported Strategies for Managing Childhood Problems* (Washington, D.C.: APA, 2001), pp. 70–71; adapted from *Cognitive-Behavioral Therapy for Anxious Children Manual* (2nd ed.) and *Coping Cat* (Ardmore, PA: Workbook Publishing, Inc., 1993). **p. 318:** Reprinted by permission of Guilford Press. **p. 323:** Reprinted by permission of Guilford Press. **p. 327:** Reprinted by permission of Guilford Press.

Chapter 10

p. 338: Copyright © 1992. From C. Madanes, "Stories of Psychotherapy," in J. K. Zeig (ed.), *The Evolution of Psychotherapy: The Second Conference.* Reproduced by permission of Routledge/Taylor & Francis, Inc. **p. 362:** Two tables from Banyard, V. L. and Fernald, P. S. "Simulated Family Therapy: A Classroom Demonstration," in *Teaching of Psychology,* 29, 2002, pp. 223–226. **p. 368:** Copyright © 1987. From *Using Drawings in Assessment and Therapy* by G. D. Oster and P. Gould. Reproduced by permission of Routledge/Taylor & Francis Books, Inc. **p. 376:** Reprinted by permission of Guilford Press.

Chapter 11

p. 390: Reprinted with the permission of Simon & Schuster Adult Publishing Group, from *The Mismeasure of Woman* by Carol Tavris. Copyright © 1992 by Carol Tavris. **p. 398:** "The Men We

Name Index

Subject Index

Absolutist dichotomous thinking, 309
Abstinence, in Freudian psychoanalysis, 93, 95
Abuse, stimulus-response-reinforcement
    process and, 253. *See also* Child abuse;
    Sexual abuse
ACA. *See* American Counseling Association
Accommodation
    by family therapist, 360
    in Gestalt therapy, 208
Acculturation, 64, 141, 319, 466, 467
Active style, of behavioral therapy, 248–249
Actualizing tendency, 151, 189. *See also* Self-actualization
ADD. *See* Attention deficit disorder
Addictions, 184
Adler, Alfred, 115–143, 155, 156, 160, 164, 172,
    177, 303, 341, 356–357, 361, 369, 414, 421,
    437, 464
Adlerian psychology, 115–143, 293, 421
    concepts in, 118–125
    critiques of, 142–143
Adlerian therapy
    basic mistakes and, 126–127
    case conceptualization in, 139–141
    family systems and, 372, 375
    features of, 127–132
    process of, 125–126
    techniques in, 132–137, 177
    uses of, 137–139
Adolescent angst, 162
Adventure-based therapy, 138–139, 143
Advertising, behavioral principles in, 241
Advice-giving, by therapist, 127
Affect blocks, 173
Affirmative Action, 406
Agoraphobia, 268–269, 272, 375
Agreeableness, 394
Albert Ellis Institute, 307
Alcohol dependence and alcoholism, 139,
    260, 266, 317–319, 327, 375–376, 383,
    397, 408, 417
Altered states of consciousness, 434, 447,
    456
Altruism, 110
American Association for Marriage and
    Family Therapy, 383, 497
American College of Physicians, 45
American Counseling Association (ACA),
    44, 46, 48, 55, 497
American Psychiatric Association, 32, 35,
    101, 102, 321, 485

American Psychological Association (APA),
    15, 17, 44–46, 55, 60, 61, 326, 407, 408,
    415, 497
Anabuse, 266
Analytical psychology, 89
Anima and animus, 89
Annual Review of Behavior Therapy, 249
Anonymity, in Freudian psychoanalysis,
    93–94, 95, 100
Anorexia nervosa, 35, 184, 374, 452
Anti-intellectualism, 230
Antisocial personality disorders, 320
Anxiety disorders, 34–36, 139, 394
Anxiety hierarchy, 268
Anxiety
    attachment theory and, 475
    behavioral therapy and, 246, 247, 267–269,
        273
    biofeedback and, 263
    in childhood, 299–302
    cognitive-interpersonal cycles and, 477
    cultural factors in, 395
    depression vs., 37
    ego psychology and, 94
    existential/humanistic therapy and, 160,
        161–162, 173, 185–186, 187
    family therapy and, 366–367, 375
    Freudian view of, 74, 75, 78, 100, 110, 118,
        161, 162, 163
    genetics and, 142
    Gestalt therapy and, 202, 218
    integrative approach to, 466
    meditation and, 451
    object relations psychology and, 100–101,
        103
    participant modeling and, 272
    as perception of threat, 161–162
    REBT and, 305
APA. *See* American Psychological
    Association
Apache Changing Woman ritual, 350
Appealing, as logotherapy technique, 177
Arbitrary inference, 308
Archetypes, 89, 90
Asanas, 441, 442
"As-if" technique, 133–134
Assertiveness training, 270–272, 273, 274
Assessment(s)
    in behavioral therapy, 252–256
    in family therapy, 360–363, 369
    See also Psychological tests

511

Curiosity, in family therapy, 358
Cutting (parasuicide), 322
Cybernetics, 314

"Daughter Who Said No, The" (Papp), 376–381
DBT. *See* Dialectical behavior therapy
Death, 152, 158–159, 160, 171, 172, 183, 184, 394
Death anxiety, 159, 185, 186
Death transcendence, 162
Decentering, 482
Decoding, 96
Defense mechanisms, 78, 80, 81(table), 82–83, 94, 101
Deficit, problems of, 252
Deflection, 204(table), 219–220
Delusions, disidentification and, 438
Denial, 78, 79, 81(table)
Dependencies, client's, 28
Depression, 16, 25, 37, 240, 254, 295, 394, 466
    Adlerian psychology and, 122, 134, 135, 136, 142
    assertiveness training and, 272
    cognitive-behavioral therapy and, 296, 310, 326
    cultural factors in, 395
    existential/humanistic psychology and, 153, 156, 170, 184
    Freudian view of, 78
    Gestalt therapy and, 218, 219
    interpersonal therapy and, 485
    light-exposure therapy and, 188
    meditation and, 451
    mindfulness and, 452
Dereflection, 177, 180, 183, 184
Desensitization, 267, 269, 271, 320
Determinism, 77
Diagnosis
    biases in, 396–397
    vs. case conceptualization, 24
    DSM and, 32–37, 56, 85, 108, 142, 171, 218, 305
    existential/humanist view of, 171
    See also Case analysis
Diagnostic and Statistical Manual of Mental Disorders (DSM), 32–37, 56, 85, 108, 142, 171, 218, 305
    axes of, 32–34, 35
    criticisms of, 36–37
Dialectical behavior therapy (DBT), 320–322
Diaries, 296
Dichotomies, healing of, 435
Dieting, 201, 202. *See also* Weight loss
Differential reinforcement, 263
Differentiation, 343(table), 344, 354–355, 371
Discipline Without Tears (Dreikurs & Cassel), 138

Discouragement, psychopathology and, 125
Discovery, in Gestalt therapy, 208, 209
Discrimination, stimulus, 245–246
Disengagement, in family system, 343(table), 365
Disidentification, 435, 438
Disowning, 203
"Displaced Teenager, The" (Long), 494–497
Displacement, 81(table), 94
Distraction, from negative emotions, 322, 324(fig.)
Distress tolerance (handout), 322, 324(fig.)
Diversity training, 408–409
Divorce, 183, 272, 383
Dodo Bird verdict, 17
Domestic violence, 404, 415
Double-bind theory, 227
Dreams, interpretation and analysis of, 7, 76, 90, 97, 98–99, 130, 136
Dream work, in Gestalt therapy, 213–214
Drinking, limiting, 260
Drives, 77, 83, 90, 94, 117, 151
Drug abuse and addiction, 139, 320
Drug therapies, 16, 395
DSM. *See Diagnostic and Statistical Manual of Mental Disorders*
DSM-IV Casebook (Spitzer et al.), 34
DSM-IV Made Easy: The Clinician's Guide to Diagnosis (Morrison), 36
DSM-IV-TR, 32, 33, 34, 35, 101, 102, 321, 392
Dual relationships, avoiding, 52–54
Dysthymic disorder, 485

Early childhood recollections, 129–130, 140–141
Eating disorders, 139, 222–225, 272, 320, 466, 485
Eating Self-Efficacy Scale, 254–255
Eclecticism, 317, 457, 465, 469–472, 494–497, 489, 494
Education stage, 89
Educational psychology, 240
Edwards Personal Preference Schedule (EPPS), 56
Effect, law of, 242
Ego, 74, 78, 80, 82, 86, 90, 162, 479
Ego and the Mechanisms of Defense, The (A. Freud), 80
Ego boundaries, 202
Ego, Hunger and Aggression (Perls), 208
Ego ideal, 87
Ego psychology, 72, 79, 80–82, 88, 108
    defense mechanisms and, 80, 81(table), 82–83, 94
    dreams and, 99
    goals of psychotherapy in, 82
Ego strength, 82, 86, 434